*No Place for Russia*

WOODROW WILSON CENTER SERIES

## WOODROW WILSON CENTER SERIES

The Woodrow Wilson International Center for Scholars was chartered by the U.S. Congress in 1968 as the living memorial to the nation's twenty-eighth president. It serves as the country's key nonpartisan policy forum, tackling global challenges through independent research and open dialogue. Bridging the worlds of academia and public policy, the Center's diverse programmatic activity informs actionable ideas for Congress, the administration, and the broader policy community.

The Woodrow Wilson Book Series shares in the Center's mission by publishing outstanding scholarly and public-policy-related books for a global readership. Written by the Center's expert staff and international network of scholars, our books shed light on a wide range of topics, including U.S. foreign and domestic policy, security, the environment, energy, and area studies.

Please visit us online at www.wilsoncenter.org.

# No Place for Russia

## European Security Institutions Since 1989

William H. Hill

COLUMBIA UNIVERSITY PRESS

NEW YORK

Columbia University Press
*Publishers Since 1893*
New York   Chichester, West Sussex
cup.columbia.edu
Copyright © 2018 Columbia University Press

Cataloging-in-Publication Data is available from the Library of Congress.

ISBN 978-0-231-70458-8 (cloth)
ISBN 978-0-231-80142-3 (e-book)

Cover design: Guerrilla Design
Cover image: © Alain Jocard/GettyImages

# CONTENTS

# PREFACE AND ACKNOWLEDGMENTS

This volume began more than fifteen years ago as a study of the relationship between NATO and the Organization for Security and Cooperation in Europe (OSCE), with a fellowship with the Eastern European Program at the Woodrow Wilson International Center for Scholars. I was able to pursue this project further, after a stint as head of the OSCE Mission to Moldova, during a 2001–2 term as a Public Policy Scholar at the Wilson Center, funded by a grant from the US Institute of Peace. I somewhat unexpectedly served a second, longer term as head of the OSCE Mission to Moldova from 2003 to 2006. This experience diverted my attention somewhat, and eventually led to a book on the Moldova-Transdniestria conflict and Russia's relations with its former Soviet neighbors in the "near abroad"—*Russia, the Near Abroad, and the West: Lessons from the Moldova-Transdniestria Conflict*—published by the Woodrow Wilson Center Press and Johns Hopkins University Press in 2012.

In writing this volume, I returned to my original project of describing and analyzing Europe's security institutions and post–Cold War security order. However, by that time the European Union had clearly become a much more important security actor, a fact that had been imprinted on my consciousness through extensive work with the EU as an OSCE official during the 2000s.

With the support of a sabbatical during 2014–15 from the National War College and the generosity of the Kennan Institute of the Woodrow Wilson Center in hosting me during this time as a Public Policy Scholar, I was able to put the finishing touches on the research for this book and do the bulk of the writing.

I am indebted to many individuals and institutions for assistance, advice, and enlightenment during the work that went into the research, preparation, and writing of this volume. My mentor in the foreign service, the late Ambassador Warren Zimmermann, introduced me to the Conference on Security and Cooperation in Europe as his executive assistant with the US Delegation to the Vienna Follow-Up Meeting in 1986, which began an ongoing association with the CSCE/OSCE that has lasted thirty years and counting. The late Ambassador Robert Frowick, who served as Zimmermann's deputy at the Vienna meeting and had also served at NATO Headquarters, first introduced me to the intricate interrelationships of these European security institutions. The late Ambassador Samuel Wise—a retired foreign service officer and chief of staff of the US Congress's Commission on Security and Cooperation in Europe, or Helsinki Commission, and Zimmermann's other deputy at the Vienna meeting—gave me a thorough education and grounding in the history, unwritten traditions, procedures, and practices of the Helsinki Process. Along with Sam, Helsinki Commission staff members—such as Lynn Davidson, Bob Hand, Ron McNamara, Orest Deychiakiwski, John Finerty, and Kyle Parker— have been friends, colleagues, and examples of the significant, constructive role the OSCE could play in US foreign policy and European security.

There are too many colleagues and friends to enumerate from the US Department of State, US Department of Defense, and National Security Council staff, and from numerous European foreign and defense ministries and legislatures, all of whom helped me to understand how NATO, the EU, and the OSCE work, and the diverse national strategic cultures that interact in the development of European and Euro-Atlantic institutions. Many of these colleagues from North America and Europe were kind enough to discuss with me and share their insights and understanding of specific institutions, issues, or events I have described and analyzed in this book. My debts to specific individuals for understanding particular issues or events are reflected in the notes. However, it is difficult to overemphasize the contribution of these numerous unnamed colleagues to the development of my own practitioner's understanding of international relations and security institutions.

Washington provides a particularly rich environment of academic and institutional experts on the major national and institutional actors in Euro-Atlantic security affairs, and I have benefited immensely from working with many of these experts since my return to the United States from Moldova in August 2006. For their careful reading and comments on the manuscript, I am especially grateful and deeply indebted to my Foreign Service colleague from Moscow and Washington, Wayne Merry; to one of my successors at the OSCE Mission to Moldova, Philip Remler; to my Foreign Service colleague from Washington, Moscow, Brussels, and Vienna, Paul Fritch; and to my friend, Terry Hopmann, of the Paul H. Nitze School of Advanced International Studies at Johns Hopkins University. In addition, I am indebted to Christian Nuenlist of the Zurich Center for Security Studies for his detailed reading and thoughtful comments on the manuscript. I owe a great deal to my colleague at the National War College, James MacDougall, for the insights, understanding, and wisdom I gained from him in numerous discussions of relations between the United States and Russia and the future of European security. I also wish to thank my colleagues at the National Defense University, Cynthia Watson of the National War College, and Elena Pokalova of the College of International Security Affairs for their careful reading of and helpful comments on the manuscript.

Matthew Rojansky, director of the Kennan Institute, was kind enough to ensure me an especially conducive environment in which to bring this project to fruition. I owe a great debt and offer profound thanks to my research assistant at the Woodrow Wilson Center, Elisey Boguslavskii, who helped me locate and organize a wealth of high-level memoirs and policy statements from Russian and American officials and analysts during the period treated in this book. I am grateful to several other Kennan Institute colleagues and scholars—Will Pomeranz, Elizabeth Wood, Liz Malinkin, Joe Dresen, and Mattison Brady— for their help, encouragement, and advice during my tenure there. I owe an especial debt and am particularly grateful to the Wilson Center's Blair Ruble and Sam Wells for their consistent encouragement, intellectual inspiration, and wise counsel during the long time that I have known and worked with them.

To these and many others who helped to develop my knowledge and understanding of European security, I express my thanks. They have helped add to whatever virtues the reader may find in this volume; any flaws, errors, or omissions remain entirely my own responsibility.

Finally, no one writes a volume such as this in a vacuum. My wife, Joyce, and my children, Natalie and MacGregor, have offered me unconditional support, encouragement, and love over the course of many years that have enabled me to carry this project through to completion. I cannot ever thank them enough, but with these words at least I try.

Washington, D.C.
June 2017

*No Place for Russia*

# INTRODUCTION

The political crisis that began in Ukraine in late 2013, Russia's annexation of Crimea, and war between Russia and Ukraine shattered the political and security order that had prevailed in Europe since the end of the Cold War. The post–Cold War era began in 1989–90 with high hopes, expectations, and aspirations that we were witnessing the so-called end of history, with the emergence of a Europe undivided from Vancouver to Vladivostok.[1] The lines that had divided Europe for almost half a century were seemingly erased, and leaders of the states of Europe and North America agreed in Paris in November 1990 on democratic principles and humanitarian values that would henceforth guide their conduct. In summits at London and Rome, the United States and its Allies adopted a policy of integrating Russia and the nations of the former Soviet Bloc into an undivided Euro-Atlantic community, an approach that guided their relations with Moscow well into the next century. Yet twenty-five years after the overwhelming optimism of the end of the Cold War, Europe once again has been divided between East and West. By mid-2014, more and more observers spoke of a "new Cold War," with a new dividing line running through Europe between Russia and the West, only twenty-five years later and further to the east. A bitter and hostile Russia has seized territory and gone to war with its closest European neighbor, in the process trampling on some of the most important principles of the Helsinki Final Act and explicitly calling into question the basic principles and arrangements of the post–Cold War Euro-Atlantic security order.

How did the widely hailed "end of history" in Europe go sour so quickly, darkening the continent once again with division, mutual recriminations, and war? I trace the diplomatic, political, and institutional developments and decisions by the major European and North American actors from 1989 to 2016 with the aim of understanding how the optimistic peace of 1989–90 was transformed into the new Cold War of 2016. The narrative focuses special attention on the United States, Russia, Germany, the North Atlantic Treaty Organization (NATO), the European Union, and the Organization for Security and Cooperation in Europe (OSCE) as the most consistently crucial, but not the only, actors in this process. Although many mistaken, foolish, or self-serving actions can be identified during this period, in my view no single act or policy caused or explains Europe's current divisions and instability after such an optimistic end to the Cold War. The story I tell in these pages is, instead, one of many decisions and actions that seemed to make great sense at the time, and may have even enjoyed considerable success, but that also had second-order or unintended effects that led to the current predicament.

The most important security issue in Europe for most of the second half of the twentieth century was the threat of war posed by the division of Europe and the armed standoff between the Soviet Bloc and the Atlantic Alliance. Acting very much in the tradition of its Imperial Russian predecessor, in 1945 the USSR extended its control to the center of Europe. The West—the United States and its NATO Allies—spent the next forty years resisting further Soviet territorial advances. The Cold War ended in the late 1980s with an apparent victory for both sides. The Soviet Union under Gorbachev freed its Warsaw Pact satellites and agreed to remove its troops from Central Europe. The United States, NATO, and the USSR reached landmark strategic and conventional arms limitation agreements that dramatically reduced the threat of nuclear war that loomed over Europe and the world for half a century. The United States under George H. W. Bush and the Soviet Union under Mikhail Gorbachev embarked upon a new cooperative relationship that quickly produced a united front against Iraq's seizure of Kuwait and dramatic movement toward Arab-Israeli peace. For the first time in decades, global peace and great power cooperation seemed to be real possibilities.

For the quarter-century following the end of the Cold War, the United States and its European Allies pursued an overarching strategy of attempting to integrate Russia (as the major power and successor state to the Soviet Union) into global and Euro-Atlantic institutions and regimes. During the 1990s, when Russia was ruled by President Boris Yeltsin, this approach seemed to hold out the prospect of eventual success. However, under successive administrations of Vladimir Putin and his colleague Dmitry Medvedev, Russia has gradually grown more distant from, hostile to, and resentful of the United States and the EU. With the outbreak of war in Ukraine, Russia's annexation of the Crimea, and Putin's bitter denunciation at the September 2014 Valdai meeting of the international order fashioned and dominated by the United States, it appears that both the desire for and the intention of integrating Russia into the global order, and in particular the regional European security order, have vanished from both sides.

This book concentrates on Russia's place and role in European security institutions since the end of the Cold War, as part of a larger process of transforming and building an interlocking structure, or architecture, of institutions, in particular NATO, the European Union, and the OSCE. The basic argument in this volume is that neither Russia, the major European powers, nor the United States have been successful since 1989 in defining a place for Russia in the European or Euro-Atlantic security architecture or in integrating Russia into the major European security institutions. To make this case, I examine the development of NATO, the EU, and the OSCE from 1989 to the present. This volume also focuses on the major political developments, policies, and actions of key actors in the Euro-Atlantic area since 1989, in particular Germany, the Russian Federation, and the United States. The argument running throughout the historical narrative is that only by understanding the purposes, design, and growth of the European security order over the past two and a half decades can we adequately understand not only how but why it failed to integrate Russia.

With the fall of the Berlin Wall, the dissolution of the Warsaw Pact, and the unprecedented cooperation in the United Nations Security Council against Iraq in late summer and autumn of 1990, the Soviet Union ceased to be an enemy of the United States and its Allies. At the same time, individuals, groups, and nascent political parties in the Russian Federation advocating greater openness, economic freedom, and democratization were among the most important forces pushing the process of reform of the USSR. When the Soviet Union collapsed, the leaders of the Russian state that emerged from the wreckage committed themselves explicitly to building a democratic polity and a market economy. It is understandable that many observers and leaders in the West could have assumed in early 1992 that after more than four decades of a global nuclear standoff, peace and freedom had at last triumphed.

The end of the Cold War drastically reduced the prospect of great power conflict involving all of Europe, but the emergence of a nonimperial, democratic Russia did not solve all of Europe's security problems. Following the Cold War, most of the conflicts in Europe were regional and local, and—unfortunately—there were plenty of them. Soviet hegemony and the Warsaw Pact held together and kept quiet areas and nations in Central and Eastern Europe that had in fact not fared too well in terms of comity and stability during the interwar years following the Versailles Peace.

Fears concerning the security and stability of the former Warsaw Pact states were certainly not without justification, given their history between the two world wars. Poland, the land of the *liberum veto*, had a brief unsuccessful flirtation with democracy following World War I before lapsing into Marshal Józef Pilsudski's authoritarian regime. Hungary and Romania also were both unsuccessful with democracy, installing governments that were sympathetic to if not outright fascist by the end of the 1930s. The terms of the Trianon Settlement, giving Transylvania to Romania, also kept Budapest and Bucharest suspicious of and hostile toward one another. Indeed, this hostility began to reemerge as the Warsaw Pact began to fray in the mid-1980s. Czechoslovakia had territorial difficulties with Germany and especially Hungary, as well as its own democratic deficits. When the Warsaw Pact disappeared, there were legitimate fears and questions as to what might keep these and neighboring Central European states from lapsing once against into rivalries and conflicts with one another.

Indeed, history in Europe refused to end after 1989, and conflict soon returned to the old world, first of all in Yugoslavia. The Union of the South Slavs, first the brainchild of Croat Franciscan friars in Bosnia in the mid–nineteenth century, was the most troubled child of Wilson's Fourteen Points and the Versailles Peace, providing Europe with very little tranquility during most of the century that followed. By the late 1930s, the Kingdom of Yugoslavia had become a de facto Serb-Croat condominium, in which the main lines of the tripartite fascist-nationalist-socialist civil conflict during World War II were already evident. The post–World War II Yugoslav Republic was held together as much by the force of will of one man, Josip Broz, as by any commitment of the country's peoples to South Slavic unity. As reforms in the Soviet Bloc encouraged change in Yugoslavia during the decade after Tito's death in 1980, they brought not only democratization but also resurgent nationalisms.

Alas, Yugoslavia was not fated to experience a miracle similar to the peaceful dissolution of the Soviet Union. Beginning with the secession of Slovenia and Croatia in June 1991, Yugoslavia broke apart with extreme violence. The conflict in Slovenia was short, but war in Croatia and Bosnia-Herzegovina lasted for more than three years. Repression, tensions, and instability increased in Kosovo and Macedonia in the south. The conflict produced massive refugee flows into much of Europe and provoked increasing disagreements among European, North American, and world powers on how to respond. Diplomatic and military responses organized under the leadership of the emerging European Union and the United Nations failed to contain or resolve the conflict. Finally, the United States and NATO led a military intervention that ended hostilities, and the United States brokered a diplomatic settlement at Dayton. The Russian

Federation, which had participated in the unsuccessful UN response to the conflict, joined with the United States in implementing the terms of the Dayton Agreement in Bosnia-Herzegovina.

The former Yugoslavia's troubles (and the tension and instability it caused for Europe) did not end with the Dayton Agreement and peace in Bosnia and Croatia. By late 1998 Serbian president Slobodan Milošević's bloody response to an ethnic Albanian insurgency in Kosovo sent streams of refugees into Macedonia and Albania and provoked Western intervention. This time, however, the response came solely from NATO, led by the United States, without UN or Russian participation or approval. Despite Russia's involvement in brokering a cease-fire and initial involvement in the peacekeeping operation in Kosovo, the 1999 NATO war against Serbia-Montenegro also produced confrontation and ultimately lasting disagreement between Russia and the major Western powers. NATO's bombing of Belgrade in effect ended a decade of partnership first forged by presidents George H. W. Bush and Mikhail Gorbachev in Malta in December 1989 and foreign ministers Eduard Shevardnadze and James Baker at the UN Security Council from August to November 1990.

Although the new Russian Federation under President Yeltsin emerged with a remarkable lack of violence in late 1991, the Soviet Union did experience conflict in several places around its periphery during the process of dissolution. Most notably, from 1988 on Armenia and Azerbaijan contested with increasing violence the ethnic Armenian majority Autonomous Province of Nagorno-Karabakh in Azerbaijan, descending into outright war from 1991 to 1994. As Georgia began to assert its independence from the USSR, ethnic minorities in South Ossetia and Abkhazia sought to escape Georgian rule, producing conflicts that were ended only after Russian intervention in the early 1990s. As the majority in Moldova asserted its Romanian heritage and links at the end of the 1980s, the left bank Transdniestrian region, with a Slavic majority, sought first to proclaim a separate Soviet republic and later an independent state. A brief military conflict between Moldovan and Transdniestrian forces was halted in July 1992 by intervention of a large remnant of the Soviet Army stationed in the republic and taken over by Moscow after the USSR's demise. Competing factions in the political elites in Tajikistan began a struggle for power as the USSR collapsed, starting a war the ended only after some seven years of Russian and Iranian efforts. In fighting almost as bloody as that in Moldova, the North Caucasus Republic of Ingushetia attempted to recover territories given to neighboring North Ossetia by Stalin almost fifty years earlier. Other potential conflicts, such as Crimean concerns over its status within an independent Ukraine, were resolved eventually without the resort to force.

The other major conflict arising out of the breakup of the Soviet Union was inside the Russian Federation, in the North Caucasus Republic of Chechnya, which first declared independence in 1991. By late 1994, President Yeltsin was persuaded to send the Russian army into Chechnya to suppress the push for independence. Contrary to the expectations of senior Russian defense officials, the war demonstrated the rot and weakness within the Russian army. By 1996 Moscow had effectively lost the war and was forced to accept a humiliating peace. A largely unintended and fateful consequence of the First Chechen War was to reduce the authority of the secular nationalist proponents of independence, who had initially led the push to separate from Russia, and to strengthen Islamist advocates and fighters, both in Chechnya and elsewhere in Russia's North Caucasus republics.

In most of these conflicts on the territory of the former Soviet Union, the major Western powers had neither the desire nor the political will to intervene. In arguably the most serious, the face-off between Azerbaijan and Armenia over Nagorno-Karabakh, the United States proposed in early 1992 that the OSCE organize a peace conference, an initiative that eventually became the so-called Minsk Group, which after twenty-four years still seeks to resolve the conflict. In South Ossetia, Abkhazia, and Transdniestria, the United States and its Allies followed events and participated in some multilateral diplomatic interventions, but basically trusted and even supported Russian interventions on the ground to end the fighting and prevent recurrences. These were places—this was, in fact, a region—where Russian forces were already present and had been present for decades. Moscow had an obvious interest in the restoration of peace and stability in these areas, and clearly presumed a right to a leading, perhaps dominant, role. Given Western elation over the success of democratization in Russia and a commitment to Yeltsin as a reformer, the United States and its Allies did little to question or oppose, and at times even offered to support Moscow's role and actions in these conflicts in what quickly came to be called its "near abroad." Despite the horrific violence in the 1994–1996 war, Western leaders similarly largely gave Yeltsin a pass for his actions in Chechnya, the most notorious instance being perhaps US president Bill Clinton's comparison of the Russian president's actions to those of Abraham Lincoln against the southern secessionists in the United States.[2]

At some point between 1999 and 2014, the popular Western image of Russia as a democratic (or democratizing) partner was transformed into one of authoritarian rival, or even enemy. This change was gradual, nonlinear, and marked by reversals and disconnects. In addition, these popular perceptions of Russia were not and are not universally shared. In mid-2017 there are still plenty of experts and informed citizens who see Russia as a normal if somewhat embattled country that is simply pursuing its own legitimate interests, just as in 1999 there were a decent number of observers who called attention to the contradictions and flaws in Yeltsin's "democratic" Russia. But even if the picture is painted in shades of gray rather than stark blacks and whites, relations between Russia and the major Western partners have moved significantly from the cooperative end of the spectrum toward the adversarial. And even though Russia in 2017 remains freer and more open than it was in Soviet times, it is also a fact that the country is more closed and authoritarian now than it was when Vladimir Putin assumed power at the turn of the century.

There are many factors, domestic and external, behind the apparent failure of the democratic experiment begun in Russia as the Cold War was drawing to a close. The process of authoritarian restoration in Russia since 2000 has been accompanied by an apparent growth in nationalism and a sense of historical grievance demonstrated or expressed with steadily increasing frequency against the Western "victors" in the Cold War for allegedly taking advantage of Russia's weakness to seek either to destroy the country or at least to deny Moscow its rightful place in the European and global state system. Such sentiments have existed in certain circles of Russia's intellectual and political elites since the collapse of the USSR.[3] However, the growth in their extent and appeal and the rise of authoritarianism in Russia appear to relate to one another in chicken and egg fashion. A growing sense of grievance lends credence and support to populist authoritarianism, and would-be authoritarian demagogues encourage nationalist grievances to enhance their own political power.

The general area in which this narrative of a Russia neglected, excluded, denigrated, and weakened by its Western partners finds a major portion of its alleged facts and supporting materials is in the development of European security institutions and the conduct of Euro-Atlantic security affairs since 1989. Europe during the Cold War was divided between two major alliances. At the end of the Cold War, one of them—the Warsaw Pact—disappeared, but the other did not. The survival of the North Atlantic Treaty Organization after the end of the conflict for which it was founded, and its subsequent enlargement to include most of the countries of Europe except Russia, including most of Russia's former satellites and some former Soviet republics, is now advanced by many Russians as prima facie evidence of Western, especially the United States', intent to attain geopolitical advantage and perhaps even hegemonic domination of Europe.

At the same time that a security organization dominated by the United States gradually came to encompass most of Europe's territory, another Western-inspired and born organization, the European Union, gradually expanded to manage the political, economic, and social affairs of most of the continent, and it also implicitly and explicitly excluded Russia. The process was gradual, as at various times using its own terms the EU concentrated on getting either "deeper" or "wider." When Brussels explained that Russia was simply too big to be integrated successfully into the growing "united Europe," Moscow understood it to mean too alien, too eastern, too Soviet, too "Russian." Economic issues, particularly with respect to energy, increasingly became contentious between Moscow and Brussels, especially after the mass 2004 wave of both EU and NATO expansion. Moscow's suspicions and resentments were further deepened by the EU's steadily growing and increasingly close coordination and cooperation with NATO.

Russia clearly expected that security affairs in the new, undivided post–Cold War Europe would be handled in some new pan-European forum. The obvious candidate was the Conference for Security and Cooperation in Europe (CSCE); as the Cold War drew to a close, the CSCE was already the setting for the negotiation and adoption of groundbreaking agreements such as on-site inspection in confidence- and security-building measures, the Open Skies Treaty, and the Treaty on Conventional Forces in Europe. Beginning with the November 1990 Charter of Paris, the CSCE participating states began a process of building security and human rights institutions, culminating in the transformation in 1994 of the CSCE into the OSCE, the *Organization* for Security and Cooperation in Europe, a formal pan-European regional organization as envisioned under Chapter VIII of the UN Charter.

However, the OSCE never worked as the Russians hoped it would, and as statements by figures such as US Secretary of State James Baker suggested in 1991 that it might, hailing the emerging organization as the harbinger of a Europe whole and free, from Vancouver to Vladivostok.[4] Like the UN Security Council, the OSCE worked on the basis of consensus, and when there were disagreements among major powers, the organization was unable to act. The United States and its Allies gradually found it easier to take important security, political, and economic issues to institutions with which they were familiar and comfortable, such as NATO and the EU. Both of these institutions also worked on the basis of a consensus, but given a more restricted and likeminded membership, the absence of objection was easier to obtain. For this and other reasons discussed in the course of this narrative, the OSCE never attained the potential attributed to it by most of its participating states in the early 1990s.

The overriding features in the development of the European security landscape in the two and a half decades since 1989 have been the rapid development and then equally rapid atrophy of the once ambitious OSCE; the growth in size, reach, and power of NATO and the EU; and the effective exclusion of Russia from deliberation on important European security issues by the fact of its exclusion from membership in the latter two institutions. To be sure, both NATO and the EU developed liaison mechanisms with Russia, but—in the words of NATO—these were designed to give Moscow "a voice, not a veto." A weakened Kremlin may initially have been willing to accept this "half a loaf," but a resurgent, wealthier, more powerful, more confident Russia was not.

Russia's relations with NATO, the EU, and the United States and its Allies, especially since 2000, have been increasingly dominated by Moscow's efforts to be accorded greater, more meaningful participation in deciding European political and security affairs and growing complaints at the refusal of its interlocutors to do so.

Since 2000 Russia, under Vladimir Putin, has made several attempts at reaching an understanding and building better, more cooperative relationships with NATO, the EU, and the United States. Putin went out of his way to offer support and assistance first to the United States and then to NATO in the effort to fight al-Qaeda and the Taliban in Afghanistan. Putin offered minimal objections to the second, "big bang" enlargement of NATO and maintained a relatively constructive approach to broad military and political cooperation in the new NATO-Russia Council. Western support for the "color revolutions" in Georgia, Ukraine, and Kyrgyzstan, and Western indifference to Russian objections to Kosovo's march toward independence from Serbia, soured Putin's relations with his Western partners. Russia's 2008 war with Georgia brought a real break in these relations, especially with the United States, but the Obama administration's "reset" policy brought yet another warming. Meanwhile, Russia never flagged in its cooperation with the NATO war effort in Afghanistan and on some key nuclear nonproliferation issues, such as Iran's nuclear program.

Nonetheless, strains rapidly reappeared in Moscow's relations with the United States, NATO, and the EU. Russia's Western partners shunted aside a 2008 proposal from Dmitry Medvedev for a new, comprehensive treaty on the European security architecture following the Russia-Georgia war. Moscow's attempts at building a special relationship with Germany and Chancellor Angela Merkel bore little fruit. Meanwhile, Medvedev's agreement not to oppose a Western-sponsored UN resolution to protect civilian populations in Libya led to NATO intervention and regime change, prompting visible anger from Putin. Vocal Western support for antigovernment and anti-Putin demonstrators in Russia in 2011–12 appeared to be the final straw in convincing Putin that the United States, NATO, and the EU would never accept a truly equal partnership with Russia and were in the end after regime change, including his removal.

Russia has not been simply a blameless victim of Western ambition or deception in this roller coaster ride leading to the current crisis in relations between Russia and the West. From the very beginning of the post–Cold War era, Russian foreign and security policy in Europe contained a considerable element of the classic geopolitical approach to its neighboring states and regions as a Russian sphere of influence. As early as 1991, some of Russia's central European neighbors speculated about closer association with the North Atlantic Alliance as a hedge against renewed Russian expansionism. Several of the former

Soviet states that gained their independence with the collapse of the USSR in December 1991 complained repeatedly of difficulties in getting Yeltsin's Russia (to say nothing of Putin) to treat them as fully independent. Indeed, the Russian term *blizhnoe zarubezhe* (near abroad) reflects a view that the former Soviet states are somehow different from other sovereign states. Russia's claim to a special status or *droit de regard* with respect to its former satellites and Soviet republics has been a constant and growing hindrance to its integration into European institutions during the two and a half decades since 1989.

This volume looks at the process through which this all happened, the path along which the states of Europe and North America moved from the ideal of a Europe undivided from Vancouver to Vladivostok to the stark divisions of the summer of 2014 between Europe and North America on one side and Russia on the other. My argument is that this result was neither inevitable nor intended. In fact, many of the important decisions on European security issues and institutions during the past twenty-five years were made by some or all of the actors for specific reasons that made very good sense at the time, and indeed may still make sense. Sometimes the results that led in the direction of today's divisions were the product of a conscious choice between important alternatives. At other times, the consequences of decisions were unforeseen and unintended. And at times, many states and institutions were simply carried along their existing courses by inertia, or followed the path of least resistance. I do not seek either to indict Russia for abandoning democratic ideals or to accuse the United States and its Allies of ignoring vital, legitimate Russian interests (although many in each party may sincerely believe the other has done so).

My aim in this narrative is instead to examine and analyze how the states of Europe and North America got to where they are today, when they began with a wholly different intention and ambition, in the hope of understanding both how the tensions and animosities in the current situation might be alleviated and how the major actors might avoid similar mistakes in the future. Although I trace the development of NATO, the EU, and the OSCE from the late 1980s to the present— their structures, membership, and capabilities, and their relationships and interactions with one another—this book is not meant to be a comprehensive or definitive study or history of any one of them. I have defined as my primary task to set out the major security issues in the Euro-Atlantic area following the end of the Cold War; how the major states of this area chose, individually and collectively, to address these issues; and how the issues, the institutional structures, and the perceptions, intentions, and policies of these states have developed and changed over time.

I define the Euro-Atlantic area as that covered by the membership, or territory, of the OSCE's participating states. Some might prefer to restrict the term to the territory of NATO member states. Although I acknowledge such a preference, to avoid finding and using another term in this book, I include Russia and the rest of the former Soviet Union in the Euro-Atlantic area.

This narrative also deals with the domestic affairs and foreign policies of a number of important individual states—especially Russia, the United States, and Germany. But again, it is not meant to be an exhaustive political, diplomatic, or security history of any one of these states or of Europe as a whole. In each of these three major powers, as within all the states of Europe, important political, social, economic, demographic, and other domestic factors shaped their internal development and the policies they adopted in dealing with the outside world. I attempt only to identify and discuss the importance and influence of these key factors and those states that were important for the development of the Euro-Atlantic security order; this is not an exhaustive study of the respective post–Cold War histories of these states. By recounting the history of the major issues in European security since 1989, I hope to explain how a period that began with the optimistic, peaceful end of half a century of division ended in war and renewed division and mutual recriminations.

# 1. FROM A EUROPE DIVIDED TO A EUROPE WHOLE AND FREE

From 1945 to 1989, European geopolitics and the system of European security were relatively easy to describe. Europe was split, territorially and ideologically, between two giant blocs: the North Atlantic Treaty Organization (NATO), led by the United States; and the Warsaw Pact, headed by the Union of Soviet Socialist Republics, the twentieth-century manifestation of the Russian empire. For some forty years, the political and security landscape in Europe was constant and predictable, if not stable, and Russia's place as the second global power and chief rival to the United States was clear and undisputed.

The Cold War and the division of Europe into two separate military and ideological camps ended with unexpected rapidity and lack of violence in the late 1980s and early 1990s. The date most commonly cited as the symbolic end of the Cold War was the "fall" of the Berlin Wall on the evening of November 9, 1989, when East German guards at the border first refused to fire on demonstrators climbing and then dismantling the structure; by dawn on November 10, the guards seemed to have simply disappeared. Many US officials and academics cite the summit meeting between presidents George H. W. Bush and Mikhail Gorbachev in Malta in December 1989, which was followed by hitherto unthinkable US-Soviet cooperation, as the real end to the Cold War's hostility and competition between Moscow and Washington. Whatever importance is assigned to interim dates and events, it is an indisputable fact that the ideological, political, and military rivalry that characterized relations between the United States and the Soviet Union when Gorbachev came to power in February 1985 was clearly gone by early 1992, and neither the Soviet Union nor the Warsaw Pact existed any longer.

Although Europe from 1945 to 1989–1991 was dominated by the conflict and competition between the American and Soviet spheres of control and systems, after the collapse of the Soviet Bloc and the USSR itself, it was not immediately clear what would be the nature of the political and security order in Europe. During the waning days of the Cold War, a number of American political leaders and spokespeople described the ideal of "a Europe whole and free, from Vancouver to Vladivostok."[1] In the euphoric atmosphere following 1989, European and North American leaders and populations presumed and hoped that ideology and politics would no longer be employed to divide the states of Europe and to hinder or prevent contacts and commerce between the peoples across the continent.

Although evocation of the ideal of a Europe whole and free had an appealing ring to nations and peoples weary of a half century of nuclear standoff, there was no clear definition or consensus on what this abstract ideal might actually mean in practice. How should relations be constructed between states that for decades had been enemies, or at the least members of opposing camps? Who would provide for security of the many European states that were either formerly members of a larger military alliance or newly independent of the Soviet empire? Would the United States remain as deeply committed and involved in Europe's security now that its chief global geopolitical rival had disappeared? And if the United States did not remain a dominating presence in Europe, how would the states of Europe organize themselves and provide for order and security among themselves? The answers to these and similar or related questions were neither self-evident nor preordained.

The political and security landscape of post–Cold War Europe was shaped in large part by three major institutions that traced their beginnings well back into the height of the Cold War. NATO was founded in 1949 to continue the wartime US-UK alliance and to enlist American involvement and support in preventing Soviet expansion further to the West in Europe. The European Community, originally the European Coal and Steel Community, was born in 1950 out of a desire to prevent the recurrence of war on the continent, in particular by mending the relationship between France and Germany. The Helsinki Process, or the Conference on Security and Cooperation in Europe (CSCE; after 1994, the Organization for Security and Cooperation in Europe, the OSCE), grew out of a Soviet initiative to ratify the changes in borders in Europe imposed de facto by the territorial advances of Soviet troops by the end of World War II. These three institutions all survived the end of the Cold War, and their growth, permutations, and interactions basically constitute the history of the post–Cold War Euro-Atlantic security architecture. The Warsaw Pact, the fourth key institution in Europe's East/West standoff in the second half of the twentieth century, did not survive the end of the Cold War.

The transformations of two major European states, Germany and Russia, and the decision of the North American great power, the United States, to remain present and involved in Europe also played crucial roles in shaping the post–Cold War political and security environment in Europe. It was the emergence of a Prussian-dominated united Germany in the mid–nineteenth century that upset the prevailing European state system and brought almost a century of total war to the continent. The Western and Soviet Allies solved this problem from 1945 to 1990 by maintaining two separate German states, but most Germans clearly never fully accepted this solution.[2] Meanwhile, the Soviet experiment during most of the twentieth century to remake the Russian empire along ideological lines failed spectacularly by the end of the 1980s.[3] Following the unexpectedly swift and peaceful collapse of the Soviet Union, a new Russian nation-state emerged, occupying much of the territory of the old Russia, but in an almost entirely new form. Along with the emergence of a new Russia, the appearance of fourteen other new or newly independent states from the wreckage of the USSR arguably provided the new Europe's greatest challenge.

For Germans, then, the end of the Cold War brought a major opportunity: the possibility of reunification into a single German nation-state. For Russians, conversely, the post–Cold War era began with trauma—the loss of empire, some parts of which had been with Russia for almost four centuries—and then the challenge of constructing and living in a nation-state where ethnic Russians make up the majority, though with numerous, significant ethnic and religious minorities.[4] If that were not enough, Russians also aspired to move from a command to a market economy and from a closed, authoritarian political system to a more open, pluralist, democratic model. For Americans, it was not immediately obvious that the United States would or should maintain a deep involvement and significant physical presence on the European continent now that the aim of four decades of nuclear stalemate had apparently been so fully achieved. For both Europeans and Americans, the end of the bipolar Cold War confrontation also brought the problem of how to integrate into the new Euro-Atlantic political and security order the two largest states on the continent, each of which had undergone a transformation sufficient in size or in kind to make it essentially a new state, fundamentally different from the that which had occupied its space in Europe during the Cold War.

After the momentous events from November 9, 1989, to December 25, 1991—from the fall of the Berlin Wall to the final lowering of the Soviet flag over the Kremlin—Europe and its North American partners faced at least four key political and security questions. First, which of the Cold War–era institutions would survive: NATO, the European Community, the CSCE? Second, in what form might they survive, and which, if any, would assume primacy in the Euro-Atlantic space? In other words, what would be the guiding principles of international political and security relations in Europe, and how would these principles be implemented and enforced? Third, with the disappearance of the Soviet threat, which had been the major factor in ensuring continued US participation in and support for the Cold War Euro-Atlantic security system, would the US commitment and level of participation continue? And fourth, would a reunited Germany and a smaller, nonimperial Russia survive and develop as stable prosperous states, and how would they be integrated into the European or Euro-Atlantic security architecture?

## NATO

In the famous phrase of Lord Ismay, NATO's first secretary-general, the transatlantic Alliance aimed to keep "the Americans in, the Russians out, and the Germans down."[5] NATO was important not just for the commitment it institutionalized for the collective defense of Western Europe against Soviet domination but also, more crucially perhaps, for the American decision it represented to remain actively involved in European political and security affairs, which was in stark contrast to the US rejection of an international leadership role after World War I. Although the Alliance's broad strategic purpose—defending the territory of its member states against Soviet attack and domination—remained constant from its founding in 1949 through 1989, NATO during those four decades underwent significant changes in membership, strategy, and tactical response to the Soviet threat.[6] The upshot of these changes was to produce an international organization that, by 1989, in addition to collective territorial defense of its immediate members, had developed significant experience in coordination and collective response on political and security issues that sometimes extended considerably beyond the territorial boundaries of the Allies.

Turkey and Greece were added in 1952 to the original twelve members of the Alliance, giving broader institutional substance to the Truman Doctrine's guarantee of their independence and sovereignty.[7] The addition of new members, along with the heightened sense of threat engendered by the Korean War, focused attention on the Alliance's military capabilities and military posture and responses to deter or repel aggression, which were reflected in a new strategic concept and NATO's "new look," placing more emphasis on nuclear weapons.

The addition of West Germany to the Alliance in 1955 was seen by the Soviets as a greater and more direct threat to their Eastern European satellites than the initial formation of NATO, and it prompted establishment of the Warsaw Pact to solidify and institutionalize Soviet military and political domination in the region.[8] In 1954, the Alliance formally adopted a strategy of massive retaliation, which was seen as the best way to compensate for the significant Soviet advantage in conventional forces and armaments deployed on the continent and thus deter possible Soviet attack in Europe. However, many leaders and analysts within the Alliance grew increasingly dissatisfied with this strategy, and it proved comparatively ineffective in responding to relatively limited Soviet threats and actions in Berlin from the late 1950s through the construction of the Berlin Wall in 1961.

NATO then went through several simultaneous upheavals in the 1960s. Charles de Gaulle's rise to power as president of the Fifth Republic and his insistence on a greater role for France in European security affairs and structures led to France's withdrawal from the Alliance's unified military command in 1966 and the moving of NATO Headquarters from Paris to Brussels in 1967. Stemming directly from France's withdrawal from the Alliance's military structures, in 1967 NATO adopted a new strategy of flexible response, which envisioned countering aggression at the level of force on which it initially occurred and escalating the level of force only if the initial response proved insufficient or unsuccessful. Finally, looking ahead to the twentieth anniversary of the Alliance in 1969—when, according to Article XIII of the Washington Treaty, members would be theoretically entitled to withdraw—in 1967 the Allies also adopted the "Report of the Council on the Future Tasks of the Alliance," or the "Harmel Report," named for Belgian foreign minister Pierre Harmel, who spearheaded the effort.[9] The Harmel Report called for the Alliance to work toward reducing East/West tensions and resolving the underlying political problems behind the division of Europe into competing blocs, while still affording appropriate attention to military defense. The Harmel Report developed and built upon the idea first expressed in the 1956 "Report of the Three Wise Men" that NATO should engage in political and diplomatic, as well as military, coordination.

The Harmel Report came at the beginning of a long period of détente, lasting until the Soviet invasion of Afghanistan in December 1979, during which Allies collectively and individually sought to put their security, political, and economic relations with the Soviet Union on a new, more cooperative basis.[10] The United States conducted strategic arms limitation talks with the Soviet Union, which produced the 1972 Strategic Arms Limitation Treaty (SALT), the Anti–Ballistic Missile (ABM) treaties. and the unratified 1979 SALT II accord. The period also saw the birth and heyday of West Germany's strategy of Ostpolitik, building a more cooperative relationship with Moscow in order to normalize and improve contacts and relations between the two Germanys. Finally, as the Western Allies joined Moscow's initiative to launch the Conference on Security and Cooperation in Europe, NATO sought to reduce tensions and the threat level by entering negotiations with the Warsaw Pact on mutual and balanced conventional force reductions in Europe, the Mutual Balanced Forces Reduction talks.

It was not just Afghanistan that led to the end of détente with the USSR for NATO. By the mid-1970s, Soviet development and deployment in European Russia of SS-20 ballistic missiles threatened to change the strategic balance decisively against the Alliance in favor of the Warsaw Pact, especially because Soviet and Warsaw Pact conventional forces still maintained a significant advantage over those of NATO. In 1979, NATO adopted the so-called Dual-Track Decision, to negotiate limitation of medium- and intermediate-range ballistic missile systems in Europe with the USSR, and to deploy Pershing and cruise missiles in Europe if the Soviets failed to respond. The decision produced a prolonged hostile propaganda response from Moscow, widespread protests from peace groups and nervous publics across Europe, and considerable debates within the Alliance as the 1983 deadline for deployment approached. During this ongoing debate, NATO brought a newly democratic Spain into the Alliance in 1982 and maintained solidarity through the actual deployments in 1983. As Mikhail Gorbachev assumed the post of general secretary of the Communist Party of the Soviet Union in February 1985, NATO was demonstrating impressive solidarity, vitality, and staying power well into its fourth decade.

## THE EU

Many sights and experiences graphically and dramatically demonstrate the enormous changes—mostly for the better—that have occurred in Western Europe since the end of World War II. Perhaps one of the most impressive is driving across the bridge over the Rhine from Germany into Strasbourg, capital of the territory that lay at the heart of the bloody Franco-German rivalry for some three-quarters of a century. As one crosses the river into Alsace, there is little evidence that one is in formerly disputed territory, or indeed a different country, except that the signs at the first gas station are in French rather than German, though the currency is the same. If one contemplates the long history of dynastic, religious, ethnic, and national wars that plagued Europe for at least a millennium, the long peace and integration over much of the Western and Central parts of the continent since the mid–twentieth century is truly miraculous. This peace is partly the result of NATO's provision of collective defense against external threats, but it also is the product of an unprecedented experiment in economic, social, and political integration, a process that has been ongoing since the late 1940s.

Although the Washington Treaty of 1949 contained provisions and obligations aimed at the preservation and propagation of democratic institutions and free market economic principles, NATO was aimed primarily at countering an external military and ideological threat from the Soviet Union, not at rebuilding the societies and economies of its Western European members nor at promoting peaceful relations and amity between states that only recently had been at war with one another.[11] The European Coal and Steel Community, the brainchild of the French foreign minister Robert Schuman and French businessman and economic adviser Jean Monnet, brought France, West Germany, Italy, Belgium, Luxembourg, and the Netherlands together in a common effort to rebuild Western European prosperity, and in the process pursue peace and reconciliation among some of the most important World War II combatants. The development of Schuman's Coal and Steel Community into the broader European Community not only brought economic recovery to Western Europe but also finally ended the rivalry between Germany and France that had brought major war to the continent three times in less than a century. By the beginning of the next century, the European Economic Community had become the European Union, extending territorially over much of the continent and deepening the economic and political integration between its member states into an increasingly united Europe.

Although there were many aspirations and various proposals for greater political and economic cooperation and unity in Europe in the years immediately following the end of the war, it was not obvious that the result would be anything resembling today's European Union. Winston Churchill's speech in Zurich in September 1946 called for the establishment of a "United States of Europe." The US proposal of the Marshall Plan lent added impetus to leaders in Europe, urging a process of consultation, cooperation, and integration. However, the Congress of Europe held in The Hague in May 1948 witnessed a debate between those, such as Churchill, who favored a looser union of European states, and the continental advocates of greater integration and European federalism.[12]

The present-day European Union grew out of the aspirations and proposals of the continental federalists, and especially Jean Monnet. While working for the British and Free French governments during World War II, Monnet apparently concluded that an end to Franco-German rivalry could be attained only through the economic integration of the two countries, and, more broadly, that peace in Europe could be guaranteed only by limiting the national sovereignty of the European states in some sort of federation. However, after the war Monnet did not join the European federalist movement but instead took charge of France's national modernization and development plan. From this vantage point, he provided much of the intellectual inspiration for the May 1950 "Schuman Declaration," which was the genesis of the European Coal and Steel Community.

Thus, although European aspirations for greater unity that surfaced in the years immediately after World War II involved security, politics, and values, it was in the nuts and bolts of concrete economic cooperation and integration where the seeds of prospective European unity actually took root and sprouted. Advocates of European federalism such as Monnet steadily pressed to add areas where the members of the Coal and Steel Community might cooperate and integrate, and this organization progressively evolved into the European Economic Community, the European Community, and finally the European Union. This was basically the process of building a "deeper" union, that is, of expanding cooperation from only aspects of the member states' national economies to include the whole economy, agriculture, trade, social policy, justice, political coordination, and even foreign and security policy. This process of deepening has undergone fits, starts, and occasional reversals, but it has basically continued since Schuman's original proposal in 1950.

The other side of European unity emphasized by some advocates has been and is "widening," that is, including more countries in the project. The push for a wider union is often juxtaposed with that for a deeper union, although the two goals do not always contradict or impede one another. Over time, the original six member states increased to nine, then twelve, fifteen, twenty-five, twenty-seven, and now twenty-eight (although Britain's impending exit will lower the membership to twenty-seven). The first big debate over enlargement occurred over the candidacy of the United Kingdom, because both British and continental leaders had mixed feelings and opinions on the desirability of including Britain. De Gaulle memorably vetoed British membership repeatedly in the 1960s, and at various times both Labour and the Tories have been equivocal about UK membership. Subsequent enlargements in the 1980s and 1990s proved relatively less difficult. The one big exception to the EU's open door policy has been Turkey, which has been seeking membership for decades and which a number of important EU leaders consider not to be a European country.[13]

The contrast between the visions of Schuman and Churchill epitomizes the debate between the ideas of a deeper or wider Europe, a discussion woven through the development of a united Europe since 1950 and continuing today. As the Cold War began to draw to an end in the mid-1980s, the European Community both underwent a significant enlargement, adding Spain and Portugal in 1986 (Greece had joined five years earlier), and undertook a process of significant political and economic integration. The Single European Act was signed in 1986, which led directly to the formation of a political union, the European Union, with the 1992 Maastricht Treaty. This process eliminated borders between many of the member states and integrated their economies and populations, and it brought coordination and common policies on a much broader range of financial, social, economic, political, and security issues. Thus the end of the Cold War did not just raise the question of whether and which states might join with the EU in making a wider Europe. The question also arose to what extent the newly deeper European Union might handle political, foreign policy, and defense issues that had hitherto been the exclusive province of Cold War institutions such as NATO.

## THE OSCE

NATO and the European Community addressed the security and prosperity of Western Europe, but they did not include the states east of the Oder-Neisse line. In February 1954, Soviet foreign minister Vyacheslav Molotov proposed to his counterparts from France, the United Kingdom, and the United States that they draft a treaty on collective security in Europe—in fact, a pact that would have formally ended World War II and recognized the de facto territorial changes in Europe, including the division of Germany, resulting from that conflict.[14] The Western Allies were not interested at the time, so the Soviets shelved, but did not forget, this initiative. The Nixon administration's pursuit of détente and arms control agreements with the USSR, the emergence of West Germany's Ostpolitik, and the September 1971 Quadripartite Agreement on Berlin all helped to establish the preconditions for a broader settlement and easing of East/West tensions in Europe.

In late 1972, after President Richard Nixon's visit to the USSR and the signing of SALT I, the Western Allies agreed to the Soviet push for a European security conference. The Conference on Security and Cooperation in Europe, which opened in Helsinki in July 1973 and then continued in negotiations in Geneva for two years, concluded with the Helsinki Final Act, which was signed on August 1, 1975. The Helsinki accords not only recognized the existing borders in Europe but included commitments by all the European states (except Albania, which acceded only in 1991), Canada, and the United States to observe basic human rights and fundamental freedoms, and to include these in the basic principles governing the conduct of their relations with one another. Although full implementation was delayed and spotty, the Final Act and follow-on Helsinki Process provided a common political framework, guiding principles, and rules of conduct for all states in the Euro-Atlantic area.

The Helsinki Final Act was subjected to fierce criticism from some political quarters in the United States as a capitulation by the West to the division of Europe and the domination of Eastern Europe by the Soviets. Much to the surprise of these critics, almost immediately after the Final Act was signed, independent Helsinki monitoring groups formed in the Soviet Union and most of its Warsaw Pact satellites; these groups were dedicated to publicizing failures to observe provisions of the Helsinki accords and insisting on their implementation. The focus of these groups was generally the Helsinki provisions on fundamental freedoms and human rights, such as freedom of speech, assembly, association, and movement. The same general emphasis characterized an unexpected initiative in the United States, the establishment of the joint House-Senate Commission on Security and Cooperation in Europe, or the CSCE Commission, as it soon became known.[15] It turned out that the Helsinki accords offered a powerful tool to promote democratic change in the closed societies of the Soviet Bloc, from both within and outside.

The CSCE adopted an explicitly comprehensive definition of security that accorded equivalent, if not explicitly equal, importance to all three baskets of the Final Act, covering, respectively, security and principles (that is, norms of conduct or behavior of states); economics, science and technology, and the environment; and humanitarian and other fields, including human contacts, information, culture, and education. To get the terms it desired on territorial boundaries and integrity and military security, the Soviet Union was forced to accept obligations involving basic human rights. The Final Act also provided for regular follow-up meetings, at which the participating states were to report on and discuss implementation of the accords and to examine possible new areas of agreement. In between these follow-up meetings, the CSCE organized experts' meetings devoted to specific subjects or aspects of the Final Act's three baskets. The United States and its Allies insisted on discussion of and progress in all three baskets in the follow-up meetings and balance among the baskets in the experts' meetings, thereby ensuring the injection of continuing exchanges on human rights in the overall East/West dialogue. The Soviets demonstratively hated the human rights elements, but they went along, apparently finding sufficiently important those aspects of the CSCE that addressed military security. ·

The human rights dialogue between the CSCE's participating states was both vigorous and unprecedented. The authorities in the Soviet Bloc states quickly dispersed the indigenous Helsinki groups and incarcerated the members. These actions meant that a wealth of inquiries and complaints related to human rights were raised in CSCE meetings by Western states, which already were not short of critical ammunition. At the first Follow-Up Meeting in Belgrade in 1978, the head of the US delegation, former Supreme Court justice Arthur Goldberg, created a sensation and provoked an avalanche of Soviet criticism by naming individual victims of alleged Soviet human rights violations and repression. To show how unprecedented such US actions were in diplomatic practice at the time, one should note that he named only eight specific individuals during the entire meeting, which lasted for weeks. By the 1980s, at the Madrid and Vienna follow-up meetings, the United States' delegation, and other Western delegations, routinely named and inquired about that many specific individuals in the course of one week, if not one day. By the time the CSCE's Vienna Follow-Up Meeting opened in November 1986, the human dimension and human rights had become such an accepted part of the diplomatic dialogue that Soviet leader Gorbachev had his foreign minister, Eduard Shevardnadze, propose holding a CSCE human dimension meeting in Moscow.

Although its contribution in making human rights a part of the European security debate was clearly groundbreaking, the CSCE also played an essential role in the evolution and direction of European conventional arms control and military security affairs. The Helsinki Final Act's major contribution in the realm of military security was the introduction of transparency, in the form of confidence-building measures between the defense ministries and military forces of the participating states. The Final Act called for the participating states to notify all the other CSCE states about major military maneuvers and to invite observers. It also called on those states involved in arms control negotiations (the Mutual Balanced Forces Reduction talks) to keep the other CSCE states informed about these activities. Though the size of maneuvers initially requiring notification was quite large, over the course of a decade the participating states negotiated steadily lower limits. At the Madrid Follow-Up Meeting, the CSCE states agreed to hold an interim Conference on Disarmament in Europe, which met in Stockholm from 1984 to 1986. It was at this Stockholm meeting where the Soviet representatives first accepted the West's proposals for on-site inspections to verify military transparency and arms control agreements. This was one of the most important steps that set the stage and enabled the process that brought the Cold War to an end.

# REUNITED GERMANY

The emergence in the mid–nineteenth century of a united Germany, growing in wealth and power and seeking its place in the European and global state system, proved impossible to accommodate on the European continent without repeated, evermore destructive wars with its neighbors. The World War II Allies finally solved the problem of Germany for a few decades simply by reducing and dividing the country, giving some territory to its neighbors, and eventually forming two distinct states where there had been one. Western acceptance of East Germany was a key element in the Soviet proposal for a European security conference, which would ratify the Allies' utilitarian resolution of the German threat. This solution worked for a time, but German longing for a unified nation-state was sufficiently resilient and strong that it reemerged with the first major geopolitical upheaval in Europe.[16]

Soviet policy with respect to Germany rapidly diverged from that of its three major Allies and co-occupying powers. Moscow was leery of any measures that might be seen as leading to the restoration of German economic and military power, jealous of any initiatives that might compromise its rights and influence in its occupation sector, and suspicious that the United States, Great Britain, and France might collude with one another against what the Soviet Union perceived to be its interests in Germany. The Berlin blockade and airlift of 1948, whereby the Soviets attempted to push their former Allies out of their zone in Germany, ended in 1949 with the formal establishment of two German states, the Federal Republic of Germany (commonly known as West Germany; created by combining the United States', the United Kingdom's, and France's zones) and the German Democratic Republic (commonly known as East Germany; fashioned out of the Soviet zone).

The East German socialist state presented difficulties for Moscow from the very start.[17] Soviet retribution, in the form of harsh occupation policies and severe economic reparations, did little to endear the new pro-Soviet government to the East German population. The contrast with developments and conditions in the Western occupation zones and then West Germany also indubitably affected popular attitudes in the East, particularly given the possibility of contacts and movement between East and West through Berlin. In 1953, East Germany witnessed the first of recurring popular uprisings in the Eastern European satellite states in protest against Soviet rule. Most important, the enclave in the middle of East Germany of a free West Berlin provided a constant source of irritation to Soviet power and a challenge to East Germany's legitimacy. The problem of West Berlin was finally stabilized, at least from the Soviet point of view, by the construction of the Berlin Wall, after Khrushchev's lengthy confrontation with the West from 1958 to 1961 over the issue. By 1968–69, Moscow had succeeded in ending mass emigration from East Germany to the West, installing a highly repressive security apparatus to control the population, and ensuring in East Germany a reliable Warsaw Pact ally to offer support against attempts to reform the prevailing regime in Eastern Europe, such as the 1968 Prague Spring.

Meanwhile, in the two decades after its establishment in 1949, West Germany thrived. With the benefit of Marshall Plan assistance and integration with its Western European neighbors in the European Coal and Steel Community, the West German economy took off, bringing rapid recovery and increasing prosperity to its population. Much to Moscow's consternation, West Germany adamantly refused to accept the division of Germany and the loss of former German territory to the USSR, Poland, and Czechoslovakia. Until the late 1960s, West Germany's relationship with the USSR was generally noncooperative, and its relationship with East Germany was hostile to nonexistent.

By the early 1970s all this changed with the coming of détente and Ostpolitik. Following Willy Brandt's election as West German chancellor in September 1969, West Germany negotiated and signed treaties with the USSR, Poland, Czechoslovakia, and East Germany recognizing the post-1945 changes in Europe's borders and renouncing the use of force in their bilateral relations. Brandt explicitly pledged continued allegiance to West Germany's aim of reunifying the two Germanys, but he acknowledged that this would not occur any time soon. He also undertook real and symbolic political actions aimed at demonstrating Germany's desire for reconciliation in Europe. After reaching the September 1971 Quadripartite Agreement on Berlin with its former wartime allies, the Kremlin engineered the replacement of hard-line East German leader Walter Ulbricht, who objected to the Berlin accord, with Erich Honecker. Brandt also began a policy that continued through the 1980s of expanding West German economic ties with the USSR, East Germany, and other states in the Soviets' Eastern European orbit.

Although the details of West Germany's Ostpolitik changed under Brandt's successors, Helmut Schmidt and Helmut Kohl, the basic direction continued with remarkably little wavering or alteration. West Germany cultivated economic ties throughout the countries of the Soviet Bloc and sought to increase people-to-people contacts not only with fellow Germans in East Germany but also with those concentrated in the USSR and Romania, in particular. But détente, recognition of the new borders, and inter-German rapprochement did not prevent West Germany from remaining a staunch member of NATO, as the extended debate over the deployment of Pershing missiles and cruise missiles in response to Soviet SS-20 deployments ultimately demonstrated. Most important, both the left and right ends of the political spectrum in West Germany remained explicitly dedicated to the eventual reunification of the two Germanys, irrespective of their differences over other issues or tactics.

The accession of Mikhail Gorbachev to the post of general secretary of the Communist Party of the Soviet Union (CPSU) in February 1985 was the key step that set in motion the chain of events leading to German reunification in 1990.[18] Neither Gorbachev nor his closest colleagues and supporters even dreamed in the early years of glasnost and perestroika of changing the status quo between the two Germanys. However, the logic of reform within the Soviet Union and its bloc of satellites in Eastern Europe led steadily and inexorably to change in Germany. The hostility of the Honecker regime to reform, the discontent of the East German population and desire to escape to the West, and the opening of the political systems and borders in neighboring states as the effects of perestroika spread through the Soviet empire all combined to put pressure on the East German regime that ultimately could not be resisted. The reemergence of a united German state was not a development that was either planned or foreseen in 1985, but it was a result that the peaceful end to the Cold War made increasingly likely and difficult to avoid. Furthermore, it was a result that had enormous implications for the development of European and Euro-Atlantic institutions in the post–Cold War period.

## RUSSIA AS A NATION-STATE

Europe had both longer experience but arguably even less success in dealing with the question of how to include or integrate Russia into the European state system. Starting in the sixteenth century—which saw Tsar Ivan the Terrible's diplomatic and military encounters with Poland, Lithuania, and Sweden and his proposals of marriage to England's Elizabeth I—Moscow was an increasingly formidable but not entirely welcome actor on Europe's eastern edges. Peter the Great established the Russian empire as a European power, and Alexander I helped save the continent from domination by Napoleonic France. However, as either the imperial Russia of Nicholas I or the Soviet Russia of Lenin and Stalin—zealous champions of diametrically opposed ideologies in strident, authoritarian fashion—Moscow was an ominous, unsettling, threatening presence in Europe. Western Europeans were both contemptuous of Russian backwardness and ambivalent about the size and power that Russia brought to European political and security affairs. For their part, the Russians sought both to emulate and be included in Europe and to ensure inclusion through coercion and domination. As the old cliché has it, Russia ensured good relations with its neighbors by invading and incorporating them, a maxim containing enough truth that Russia during most of its history has never had many real friends on its borders.

Unlike Germany, the Russia that emerged from the Cold War had never really been a nation-state.[19] From the time that Muscovy threw off the last vestiges of the Tatar yoke in the sixteenth century, Russia was a multinational state with multiethnic elites and population. The Russian empire at the turn of the nineteenth and twentieth centuries was less than 50 percent ethnic Russian, both peasantry and nobility. In the wake of the 1917 revolutions, many of the imperial peripheries with non-Russian ethnic majorities broke away. However, within less than a decade, the Bolsheviks were successful in bringing most of them back under Moscow's control and in re-creating a multinational Russian empire in the form of the Soviet Union. The ideology and mechanics of Russian control in the Soviet empire were perhaps more subtle and sophisticated than under the Romanovs, but ethnic discontent in the USSR's non-Russian republics remained the Achilles heel of the Soviet state.

As early as the 1950s, when Stalin's successors assumed power, Soviet leaders were privately aware of the considerable political and economic flaws in their system. Perhaps the most vital and immediate issue was how to manage a complex, modern state and economy without physically eliminating competitors for power and authority or those who expressed different or dissenting opinions on technical issues, while maintaining the ban on dissent and factions within the CPSU first instituted at the Tenth Party Congress in 1921. Nikita Khrushchev's policy of de-Stalinization, announced at the Twentieth Party Congress in February 1956, began the process of renouncing extreme repression as the means of political and socioeconomic management in the Soviet system. However, unrest in Poland and revolt in Hungary in autumn 1956 demonstrated the dangers of attempting to liberalize Soviet style political systems.

There were also serious economic challenges to the Stalinist economic system in the USSR. Although the command economy—relying on investment derived primarily from collectivizing and exploiting the rural labor force and emphasizing the development of heavy industry—worked sufficiently well to produce a military-industrial plant that could defeat Nazi Germany, by the 1950s this system experienced increasing difficulty in both keeping pace with more complex Western industrial technology and—even more important—feeding the growing Soviet population. Khrushchev attacked the latter problem in classic Stalin era style by sending thousands of "volunteers" east to cultivate virgin lands in Siberia and Kazakhstan. Despite impressive successes in some fields, especially nuclear weapons and heavy rocket motors, Soviet science and technology generally lagged in industrial applications, in particular in the production of consumer goods.

By the 1960s, the Soviet leaders had a pretty clear understanding that their political and economic system was not working—not just in their competition with the West but also in being able to satisfy their own people's physical demands and aspirations. The problems were not just technical; they were also both structural and political, and most vexing, they were interconnected. The denial or repression of market principles, in particular the absence of a satisfactory mechanism for freely setting prices, essentially skewed decisions on supply and demand throughout the Soviet economy, producing incredible inefficiencies and retarding or preventing growth. Even modest remedies, such as the Liberman or Kosygin reforms, proved politically impossible to implement, because such actions might both challenge the leading role of CPSU cadres in managing the economic and political system and possibly lead to the encouragement and emergence of political dissent.

Even such an apparently conservative figure as Yuri Andropov—who became infamous for leading the repression of the 1956 revolt in Budapest when he was the Soviet ambassador to Hungary and was later the KGB chief most dedicated to repressing dissidents in the 1970s—during his stint in the 1960s as head of the International Department of the CPSU's Central Committee, gathered around him cadres of young, innovative thinkers who sought to address these dilemmas of reforming the Soviet system and making the economy more productive and competitive. Many of these thinkers later reemerged as key advocates of Gorbachev's policies of glasnost and perestroika. Meanwhile, however, fate and the innate caution of most of the USSR's senior leadership combined to postpone reform of the Soviet system. By the late 1960s, Leonid Brezhnev's party *apparatchiki* gained the ascendance over Kosygin's technocrats, especially after the Prague Spring in Czechoslovakia once again exhibited the dangers of attempting liberal reforms in Soviet-style systems. An unexpected and unprecedented rise in the world price of oil in the 1970s enabled the Soviet Union to earn sufficient foreign exchange to purchase grain and technology from the West, which was willing to sell both of these, as well as to negotiate political détente and arms control agreements with its ideological rival.[20]

Soviet foreign exchange earnings from commodity sales, in particular oil and gas, enabled the Soviet leaders under an increasingly infirm Brezhnev to keep a lid on political and ethnonational dissent in the USSR. However, the funds not spent on simply purchasing food from abroad were invested largely in the military and not the civilian economy. Thus both the quantity and quality of foodstuffs and consumer goods deteriorated slowly but steadily throughout the 1970s, but production of conventional and strategic weapons systems remained impressive. Dissent was endemic, if repressed, throughout the USSR. Although the KGB was able to jail or intimidate the most visible and vocal dissenters, a lack of belief and confidence in the system, evidenced most visibly in widespread cynical political humor, grew steadily. The outward unity of the diverse Soviet population, the so-called multinational Soviet people, was also largely a mirage. Though many Western readers dismissed the dissident Andrei Amalrik's *Will the Soviet Union Survive Until 1984?* as little more than a fantasy, Amalrik was off by only seven years.[21] His argument that the discontent of the subject nationalities and ethnic minorities constituted one of the major vulnerabilities of the Soviet system was both prescient and underappreciated by those outside this system.

Unfortunately for the Soviet leadership, neither détente nor high oil prices would go on forever. Détente ended first, as the steady production and deployment of new strategic weapons systems first provoked suspicion and finally produced a Western response with the NATO Dual-Track Decision in 1979 and deployment of Pershing and cruise missiles in 1983. The SALT II accords, which were already in trouble over Soviet missile deployments and support for pro-Marxist forces in several developing countries, were abandoned after the ill-fated Soviet invasion of Afghanistan in December 1979. By 1980, the entire structure of détente was unraveling, as the United States suspended exchanges, embargoed further grain sales to the USSR, and led a boycott of the 1980 Summer Olympics in Moscow. East/West relations arguably reached a low point in the wake of the Soviet shooting down of a Korean Airlines 747 civilian passenger aircraft in September 1983.

Since 1991, a narrative has developed in the West, in particular in certain circles in the United States, that the American arms buildup conducted by the Reagan administration strained the Soviet economy and system to the breaking point and thus produced the Soviet collapse.[22] Unfortunately for advocates of this theory, whatever the merits of Reagan's policies, the disintegration of the Soviet Union was in fact almost entirely the result of internally inspired and domestically driven attempts to reform the system from within.[23] Convincing research and analysis by leading Soviet and Russian participants indicates that the most influential external shock in this process was probably the collapse of the world price of oil, which made the Brezhnev approach of propping up the system untenable.[24] In early 1985, the newly chosen CPSU general secretary, Mikhail Gorbachev, and his foreign minister and old friend, Eduard Shevardnadze, allegedly agreed in a private conversation that they "cannot go on like this."[25] It was Gorbachev's attempts to bring about international change and domestic reform that really played the greatest part in launching the processes that ended the Cold War and destroyed the Soviet Union.

## THE UNITED STATES IN EUROPE: STAY OR GO?

The key difference between the post–World War I era and the post–World War II era was arguably the United States' decision by 1950 to maintain a massive presence and involvement in Europe, in contrast to the US Senate's rejection of membership in the League of Nations, one of the most important elements of the Versailles settlement. It took another quarter century after the Senate's rejection of Woodrow Wilson's vision of the League of Nations for American political elites to comprehend the importance of peace, security, and stability on the European continent for the United States' security and prosperity. It is not the purpose of this volume to answer definitively why Washington made one decision in the early 1920s and a diametrically opposite choice in the late 1940s. However, it is difficult to overestimate the importance of this choice for European and world history. The emergence of the USSR as a major rival and both physical and ideological threat was clearly the most important factor in American thinking starting in the late 1940s. During the Cold War, the American purpose was stated not in terms of dominating the world (which American economic and military might were clearly capable of attempting) but of countering the Soviet challenge to the West's security and way of life. Thus a strong sense of mission provided both the motivation and the explanation for US involvement in Europe and around the globe.

Although President George H. W. Bush took great pains to avoid the appearance of triumphalism as first the Warsaw Pact and then the Soviet Union disintegrated, nonetheless, most Americans, elites and public alike, perceived the events of 1989–1991 in Europe as an unequivocal victory for the United States and its Allies in their four-decade struggle with the Soviet Bloc.[26] In rapid succession, first the conventional and strategic military threats posed by the Warsaw Pact and the Soviet Union disappeared; then Moscow adopted a fully cooperative stance on some of the world's most difficult international political issues, such as the Iraqi invasion of Kuwait; and finally the Soviet Union and the ideological challenge it embodied vanished. Even with the benefit of twenty-five years of hindsight, it is difficult to see how anyone in the United States might see these events as anything less than a welcome triumph.

"Victory" in the Cold War brought widespread expectations in the United States of a substantial "peace dividend." For years, America had expended large sums to maintain a global military presence, including some 250,000 ground troops as a deterrent to Soviet advances in Western Europe. Indeed, the Soviet threat had been the justification for US overseas military bases and deployments, in particular those in Europe. When this threat disappeared, the question arose naturally for both Americans and Europeans whether and why the US military commitment and presence would continue. Europeans who recalled their history from the first decades of the twentieth century presumed that chances were good that the United States might substantially withdraw from Europe, as it did after Versailles. Americans who hoped for a peace dividend and saw no significant threat also assumed that most of their troops could come home and that the funds hitherto spent on overseas commitments could now be used for domestic needs.

Both Americans and Europeans thinking along these lines quickly turned out to be wrong. Although the size of the US military was reduced considerably during the 1990s, as early as 1991–92 it was becoming clear that some US soldiers might be moving to new locations, but many of them were not coming home. Many troops and large quantities of equipment based in Europe could be used for the 1990–91 Gulf War because they no longer faced a threat from the Soviets. A small deployment in Somalia and larger deployments in the Balkans followed during the 1990s. By the end of 1991, the Bush administration decided to support the continued existence and activities of NATO and committed to maintaining the Alliance's troop strength and material resources. Unlike after the Versailles peace, the absence of a specific threat did not dissuade American political leaders and the American public from maintaining their nation's internationalist policy and continuing overseas presence. In turn, the continuation of the US commitment, presence, and participation in European security affairs was a crucial factor in how the Euro-Atlantic security order and Euro-Atlantic security institutions developed after the Cold War.

## SETTING THE STAGE:
## FROM GENEVA TO CHECKPOINT CHARLIE

In addition to Soviet general secretary Gorbachev, the other key individual in the process of unraveling the Cold War was US president Ronald Reagan, not because he mandated the US military buildup that allegedly brought the Soviet Union to its knees but because he and Gorbachev provided each other with the partner each needed to pursue their different but overlapping visions of reform, disarmament, and peace.[27] Coming to office in 1981, Reagan inherited a program of increasing US conventional and strategic military capabilities already begun by President Jimmy Carter. Reagan also brought to the presidency a sincere belief in the desirability and feasibility of eliminating nuclear weapons, a conviction he demonstrated in forcing the so-called "zero option" on a reluctant US government bureaucracy preparing for Intermediate Nuclear Forces in Europe (INF) negotiations with the Soviets envisioned in the 1979 NATO Dual-Track Decision. The INF talks with the Soviets went nowhere while Brezhnev, Andropov, and Chernenko were in power. However, once Gorbachev took command, a process began that led in fewer than three years to the signing of the INF Treaty, the first of the major agreements ending the Cold War.

Contemporary observers and even senior government officials involved in US-Soviet relations foresaw little of what was to come as preparations were made for Reagan's and Gorbachev's first meeting in Geneva in November 1985. Before his encounter with President Reagan in Geneva, Gorbachev announced a halt to INF deployments on Soviet territory and a counterproposal to the United States' opening position in February 1985 in the Nuclear and Space Talks. The United States made a counterproposal just before the meeting of the two leaders, and by early 1986 real negotiations had begun. Even more important, the two leaders were able to take the measure of each other in Geneva, and apparently found that they both liked each other and—echoing Margaret Thatcher's earlier appraisal of Gorbachev—believed they could do business with one another. The Reagan and Gorbachev arms control initiatives found strong support in many quarters throughout Europe, and many states pushed for progress on arms control across the board, both strategic and conventional, not just with intermediate-range nuclear systems. The ambitious proposals, near agreement, and then dramatic failure at the October 1986 summit in Reykjavik produced short-term despair and disillusionment.[28] Ironically, however, in the long run the Reykjavik discussions showed both American and Soviet negotiators what the other side considered possible and acceptable, which opened the way to much further-reaching agreements than most officials might have considered possible even a few years before.

One of the key steps that made possible the dramatic progress in arms control, relaxation of tensions, and political reconciliation in the later 1980s took place in an obscure context quite removed from the nuclear arms negotiations. As the conventional arms negotiators in the Mutual Balanced Forces Reduction (MBFR) talks in Vienna contemplated the start of a second decade of mind-numbing exchanges on the technical details of the precise definitions of weapons systems, troop units, movements, and deployments, the CSCE Stockholm Conference on Confidence- and Security-Building Measures and Disarmament in Europe (CDE) made a breakthrough in early 1986.[29] Mandated by the Madrid CSCE Follow-Up Meeting, the CDE met from 1984 to 1986 with the aim of negotiating more intrusive and extensive transparency and confidence-building steps than called for in earlier CSCE documents, such as reporting movements and exercises by ever-smaller military units and more detailed data exchanges of weapons and military forces. One of the major obstacles to reaching agreement on significant confidence- and security-building measures (CSBMs) was the same as for disarmament pacts: the refusal of Soviet negotiators to agree to significant verification measures, in particular on-site inspection.

Indeed, the US proposal of intrusive on-site inspections and the Soviet refusal to accept on-site verification provisions was a constant feature of US-Soviet arms negotiations since at least the 1950s. Irrespective of whether such proposals were always made with serious intent or refused with substantive cause, a deep lack of trust was a prominent feature and serious obstacle in US-Soviet relations and negotiations as Reagan and Gorbachev met for the first time in Geneva. Soviet SS-20 deployments only five years after the signing of SALT I and the public revelation in the summer of 1983 of the construction of a phased-array radar system in Krasnoyarsk, an apparent violation of the 1972 ABM Treaty, were some of the most prominent reasons for mistrust cited by the US side. Bipartisan criticism of the United States' détente with the USSR from the Congress and private organizations, led by prominent former officials such as the members of the Committee on the Present Danger, nurtured fears of Soviet cheating, ambitions for unilateral advantage, and alleged plans for surprise attack. All this ensured that any significant agreement on arms limitation or reduction with the Soviets would require ironclad verification provisions involving more than "national technical means," that is, satellite observations.

For his own purposes of domestic reform within the USSR, Gorbachev believed he needed a significant relaxation of tensions with the West. Arms control agreements that would enable him to divert resources to civilian sectors of the Soviet economy were certainly part of his calculus, but ending the war in Afghanistan, increasing trade, and procuring investment and technology from the West also figured prominently in his thinking and approach. In any event, conventional arms control talks in the CDE offered him the first convenient venue to make a significant breakthrough.[30] Soviet CDE ambassador Grinevskii and later Russian prime minister Evgeniy Primakov have left us accounts of bitter Politburo debates in which Gorbachev and proponents of reaching agreements overcame objections from the military, in particular Marshal Sergei Akhromeev, and then required Akhromeev to announce the change in the Soviet position in Stockholm in August 1986. Though the Soviets initially indicated willingness to accept one or two on-site challenge inspections per year, both Grinevskii and Gorbachev soon after indicated the Soviets might well be more forthcoming on verification provisions.

The breakthrough at the CDE truly opened the door for productive negotiations on almost all fronts. NATO and Warsaw Pact representatives at the OSCE Vienna Follow-Up Meeting, which opened in November 1986, worked out a mandate for two conventional arms negotiations: one involving all thirty-five CSCE participating states to pursue agreement on further CSBMs, and a second involving only the twenty-three NATO and Warsaw Pact member states to succeed the MBFR negotiations in pursuit of reductions in conventional forces in Europe (leading to the CFE Treaty). At the same Vienna CSCE meeting, the Soviets proposed to hold an experts' meeting on human rights in Moscow, and the United States and its Allies demanded progress on key Western issues, such as human contacts, Jewish emigration, the jamming of

Western broadcasts, and other human rights and fundamental freedoms. In December 1986, Gorbachev ended the internal exile of Andrei Sakharov and his wife, Elena Bonner, and Soviet representatives promised US diplomats significant progress on Jewish emigration, divided families, and other key issues. These pledges were soon fulfilled.

Gorbachev undertook these steps and others not simply or primarily because he desired rapprochement with the West but because he deemed them essential to his primary goal of reforming the Soviet system.[31] By 1985, the Soviet consumer economy was in catastrophic shape. According to the personal experiences of Westerners who lived in the USSR at various times from the late 1960s through the 1980s, the goods offered in Soviet diplomatic stores in the mid-1980s were inferior in quality, quantity, and even availability to those in normal Soviet shops in 1970. By the early 1980s, it was difficult to find a Soviet citizen who would assert in private that the system was working or who did not repeat anecdotes making fun of Brezhnev's infirmity.[32]

The question for Gorbachev was where to start. There was considerable discussion of the current situation and possible actions in the government and party press, all masked by traditional Soviet rhetoric and indirection. One of the first visible public indicators of real change was the Kremlin's insistence on making public the fact, details, and causes of a Volga River passenger boating disaster in mid-1986, coming soon after the Soviets endured waves of international criticism for concealing the fact and scope of the Chernobyl disaster. The report of the Volga River tragedy quickly became the policy of glasnost, or more open reporting and discussion or the less positive aspects of soviet history and contemporary life. The result was like opening the valve on a pressure cooker, and Soviet intellectuals and professionals from all walks of life began to write, speak, and read evermore open, daring, and critical reporting and commentary without censorship or reprisals from the authorities.

Although the focus of this study is the genesis and development of European and Euro-Atlantic security institutions from the late 1980s to the present and Russia's relationship to and place in such organizations, Gorbachev's approach to European security in the second half of the 1980s was inextricably intertwined with his domestic political reform initiatives. Thus a discussion of Soviet foreign and security policies after Gorbachev's accession must be informed by and at least acknowledge the contemporaneous internal political struggles developing within the USSR. Once Gorbachev acquiesced on the key position that from the Western point of view had been blocking progress on arms control, negotiations on disarmament, transparency, and confidence building took off with astounding speed. Within two to three years, fundamental strategic agreements were reached on significantly limiting or eliminating entire classes of conventional and nuclear arms. The irony is that far greater success was achieved in altering Europe's security landscape than in attaining the goal that was more important for Gorbachev—transformation and thus preservation of the domestic Soviet social, economic, and political system.

Although the United States negotiated some of these basic security accords bilaterally with the Soviet Union and took the lead in the other major negotiations, Washington continuously and consistently informed and involved its NATO Allies in both the strategic and intermediate nuclear arms and conventional arms negotiations.[33] Since the December 1979 NATO Dual-Track Decision, the United States had consulted its Allies on the formation of its negotiating approaches and proposals and reported on the progress of the negotiations. Such an approach was crucial in maintaining the Atlantic Alliance's consensus on the 1983 Pershing deployments, but it continued after the nuclear and space talks were restructured in 1984 and reopened in 1985. The US approach on conventional arms control was similar. In 1986, NATO established a high-level task force devoted to conventional arms control, which coordinated the Allies' approach to the transition from the MBFR talks to the CFE negotiations set within the larger context of the CSCE. The reasoning behind this link was that after acceptance of the Stockholm CDE Document, conventional arms control, transparency, and confidence building were concerns of all thirty-five European and North American CSCE participating states. However, setting the levels of national holdings and deployments of troops and conventional arms was also a concern of the two military alliances on the continent, NATO and the Warsaw Treaty Organization, neither of which would agree to direct involvement of alliance nonmembers in formulating the alliance positions and determining agreements with the other military bloc.

NATO delayed formal agreement on the two negotiations within the framework of the CSCE process until Soviet acceptance of some major human rights proposals at the Vienna Follow-Up Meeting in late 1988. As agreement on the mandate for the CFE talks approached, Gorbachev announced unilateral Soviet and Warsaw Pact conventional troop and weapons reductions in a December 7, 1988, speech at the United Nations. As senior Soviet officials subsequently explained, the cost of maintaining large conventional forces was much higher than the strategic forces, and the funds expended on the conventional presence in Eastern Europe were increasingly needed elsewhere in the floundering Soviet economy.

The first major success came in the INF negotiations, and as in other forums, Gorbachev played a key role.[34] Seizing upon one of the possibilities obscured by the wreckage of Reykjavik, in February 1987 Gorbachev delinked the Soviet position on INF from the questions of Reagan's Strategic Defense Initiative and ABM. Within months, the United States and the USSR exchanged draft treaties, accepted total elimination of short- and long-range INF systems, and agreed on an intrusive system of on-site inspection and verification. The United States obtained agreement from West Germany to eliminate its Pershing systems also. On December 8, 1987, the INF Treaty was signed in the White House in Washington, D.C. The INF pact also resulted in the establishment of a fledgling infrastructure for strategic transparency and confidence building. In September 1987, US secretary of state George Shultz and Soviet foreign minister Eduard Shevardnadze agreed to establish Nuclear Risk Reduction Centers in Washington and Moscow. In January 1988, the United States established the On-Site Inspection Agency, which became responsible for monitoring the INF and subsequent arms control agreements.

Conventional arms limitations and reductions took a little bit longer to achieve.[35] In January 1989, the Vienna CSCE Meeting agreed on mandates for the negotiations on Conventional Forces in Europe and a new round of CSBM negotiations. The CFE talks opened in March and moved rapidly; the Warsaw Treaty Organization's representatives quickly accepted NATO's proposed approach of parity in troop and weapons levels between the two blocs. In May, President Bush revived and expanded President Dwight Eisenhower's 1955 Open Skies Treaty proposal, calling on both sides to agree to open their airspace to periodic unarmed inspection flights. By early 1990, the Warsaw Pact states joined in the Open Skies talks, as well as the CFE negotiations. Meanwhile, CSBM negotiations continued separately in Vienna, and by November 1990 reached agreement on the so-called Vienna Document, representing a quantum leap in advancing the scope and intrusiveness of confidence-building and transparency measures such as data sharing, snap inspections, and announcement of exercises and troop movements.[36] The Open Skies Treaty was signed in Helsinki in March 1992 and included many of the CSCE participating states. And at the same time, the CFE Treaty was agreed on during 1990 and signed at the November 1990 Paris CSCE Summit; it took more than eighteen months of further negotiations for this treaty to enter into force.

The problem with presenting a simple chronology of the major security agreements that were reached as the Cold War drew to a stunningly rapid and dramatic end is that this process of successful negotiation occurred simultaneously with the disintegration of two of the major protagonists in the Cold War: the Warsaw Pact and the Soviet Union itself.[37] As soon as Gorbachev eased domestic controls within the Soviet Union, Eastern European leaders and dissidents tested the limits of the new Soviet liberalization. In October 1986, Hungarian officials quietly but openly mourned the victims of the 1956 Budapest uprising against Soviet power. Polish negotiators told their US counterparts they intended to use Gorbachev's preoccupation with domestic affairs "to move as far west as possible." By 1988 grumblings of discontent and calls to follow or emulate Gorbachev's policies of glasnost and perestroika could be heard throughout the Soviet Eastern European satellites. Not all of these grumblings were positive or welcome. Tension increased quietly but perceptibly between Hungary and Romania over the long-resented award of Transylvania to Bucharest in the 1923 Trianon Treaty.

By 1988, Gorbachev was allowing unprecedented freedom of speech and association in the Soviet Union. Small private enterprises in the form of cooperatives were springing up, and there were calls for much further-reaching economic reforms. Gorbachev was on the cusp of ending the CPSU's monopoly on political activity and moving toward adoption of open, free elections. In such an atmosphere one could hardly expect the Warsaw Pact satellites to remain immune to the virus of reform and liberalization. The process of disintegration started in Poland, where support for the union called Solidarity and its aims was still strong, despite a lengthy period of martial law and repression. The Roundtable established in late 1988 to negotiate differences between the ruling party and opposition elements of society by May 1989 brought an election whose results would produce a government without communist representation. Gorbachev, the CPSU, and the USSR took no action to reverse these steps.

Meanwhile, a reform communist government came to power in late 1988 in Hungary, which in the spring of 1989 in effect opened its border with Austria. Discontented East Germans began to flood into the West through Hungary. When East German leader Honecker convinced his Czechoslovak counterparts to block travel through that country to Hungary, great masses of German refugees built up in Prague. By September, Czechoslovak authorities relented, and the flow of Germans fleeing to the West increased even more. In an early October visit to Berlin, Gorbachev warned Honecker that Soviet forces would not intervene to halt or reverse the process. In a little over a week Honecker's colleagues replaced him, but the move was too late and too little to head off the uprising already under way in the East German population.

The discovery on November 9, 1989, by venturesome East German protestors that East German guards would not shoot demonstrators who crossed into West Berlin and the ensuing celebrations throughout Berlin were carried worldwide on television, and the "fall of the Berlin Wall" has become the best-known and most popular symbol of the end of the Cold War. In reality, the drama of November 9 in Berlin was one of a series of remarkable events during the fall of 1989 that rivaled those that followed the taking of the Bastille in Paris two centuries earlier. On November 10, reform-minded Bulgarian Communist Party colleagues removed Todor Zhivkov from power; a month later, communist rule in Bulgaria came to an end. On November 17, massive student demonstrations in Prague led to the resignation of General Secretary Jakes within a week; by December 10, 1989 a noncommunist government took power in Czechoslovakia. Finally, on December 21, jeers and calls of protests greeted Romanian dictator Nicolae Ceauşescu in Bucharest. By December 25, Romanian party colleagues arrested and executed Ceauşescu and his wife and established a new, reform government. By December 31, 1989, the party was over in Eastern Europe.

It will remain one of history's great mysteries why Soviet leaders did not do more to try to prevent their system of Eastern European satellites from crumbling so quickly. Former Russian prime minister Yegor Gaidar, in his *Gibel' Imperii* (*Collapse of an Empire*), has provided a fairly convincing explication of how the Soviet Union's increasingly strapped economy simply did not provide Moscow with the means to subsidize the states in its Eastern European orbit, which made the process of separation increasingly easy from both sides. However, this explanation does not account for the failure of Gorbachev or any of his Soviet colleagues to resort to force; Soviet military and security forces in the late 1980s arguably still possessed sufficient resources to attempt a fairly substantial effort at repression of the indigenous revolts. By the accounts of many who worked closely with him, Gorbachev simply did not think it worthwhile to try to hold on to the reluctant satellites, especially if it would involve significant, expensive conflict. And finally, as became apparent also in his response to the Soviet collapse, Gorbachev seemed to have a moral aversion to the use of oppressive force, a feature of personal character that in the end may well have spared the lives of countless Eastern European and Soviet citizens.

Irrespective of Gorbachev's motivations, it was clear as 1989 drew to a close that the iron curtain Winston Churchill saw descending across Eastern Europe from Fulton, Missouri, in 1946 had disappeared. Western diplomats who repeated the slogan "A Europe whole and free" largely as a goal to be pursued suddenly found that aspiration now within reach, if not already attained. With political pluralism, freedom of association, freedom of speech, and freedom of movement now apparently realities in the Warsaw Pact states, the Cold War was clearly coming to an end. However, it was not at all clear what would replace the East/West standoff that had defined the Euro-Atlantic security order for more than four decades. Following the revolutions of 1989, events in Europe moved with unimaginable speed. Decisions would be made during 1990–91 in reaction to these events that would define the post–Cold War order in Europe and the world for the next quarter century. A new era was clearly dawning, but there was not yet enough light to make out the landscape.

## 2. BUILDING THE NEW WORLD ORDER, 1990–1991

As the revolutions in Eastern Europe neared a close in early December 1989, Mikhail Gorbachev met with President George H. W. Bush on board a Soviet and then an American ship in Marsaxlokk Harbor in Malta.[1] Although the two sides did not issue a formal declaration or enumerate the specific results of the meeting, many of the participants and observers call this meeting the real end to the Cold War. The discussions between the two leaders and their delegation members were breathtakingly open and constructive, especially considering the past four decades of unremittingly hostile bilateral relations. The two leaders discussed not only key security issues, such as strategic and conventional arms limitation and reduction, but also a wide range of political and normative issues, including (but not limited to) German reunification, free elections, self-determination, and free choice of social and economic systems. The spirit of accord and cooperation between the two sides was such that near the end of the final plenary session, in response to Gorbachev's objection to labeling democracy, openness, and free markets "Western values," Bush accepted the Soviet leader's point, and the US secretary of state, James Baker, suggested they be referred to as "democratic values."[2]

Whether this meeting or any other specific event might be seen as the end point of the Cold War, the discussions at the Malta summit opened a window onto dramatic changes that took place in European institutions and in many European states over the next two years. First, both Bush and Gorbachev spoke openly and dispassionately about the prospects for and pace of German reunification. Gorbachev speculated on the possible evolution of NATO and the Warsaw Pact into more political rather than military organizations (few at that time could anticipate the dissolution of the Warsaw Treaty Organization), and—more astounding for old Cold Warriors—emphasized the current Soviet view of the US presence and role in Europe as necessary and constructive. Referring to a conversation with Valéry Giscard d'Estaing on European integration, which the context makes clear involves negotiations that resulted in the Maastricht Treaty, Gorbachev welcomes such movement toward a new Europe, which he sees leading to a "common European home" that includes Russia. Finally, Gorbachev stresses the Soviet desire to pursue a consensus-based approach to deeper European integration, specifically by continuing the Helsinki Process, with all signatories of the Final Act, including the United States and Canada, by reaching a Helsinki II agreement to cover the changes in Europe since 1975.

The two years between December 1989 and December 1991 witnessed the formation of the most important elements of the post–Cold War European political and security architecture. It is crucial to keep in mind that these two years constituted not only a period of creation and integration but also a time of disintegration and destruction. The liberation of the Soviet Eastern European satellites led inexorably to the collapse and abolition of the Warsaw Pact, even as a landmark conventional arms control agreement was reached with the partici-pation of the Warsaw Treaty Organization's member states. The political map of Europe changed even more dramatically through 1991 as Tito's Socialist Federa-tive Republic of Yugoslavia (or, simply, Yugoslavia) and then the Soviet Union fell apart, the former with the worst fighting on the continent since World War II, and the latter with astounding speed and lack of violence. On the formative, integrationist side, the two Germanys reunited with unforeseen rapidity, with the West simply assimilating the East. In a process not without serious debate, NATO Allies decided to preserve and transform the Alliance, adapting and add-ing new institutions to address emerging security concerns in a transformed Central and Eastern Europe. The process of economic and political integration of Western Europe grew deeper as the European Community began transform-ing itself into the European Union and launched the process of eventual mon-etary union. Finally, the European and North American states participating in the Conference on Security and Cooperation in Europe (CSCE) were able to agree unequivocally on a comprehensive set of universal values, including free elections and freedom of speech, association, conscience, and movement, and established formal institutions aimed at transforming the Helsinki Process into a pan-European collective security organization. As the new year dawned in 1992,

Cold War Europe was gone, with the main features of the post–Cold War era already in place.

## REDUCING THE DANGER OF WAR

The first concern of the post–Cold War European and North Atlantic leaders was to reduce the danger of armed conflict in lasting fashion. For the duration of the Cold War, most of Europe was taken up by two armed camps faced off against one another. That situation began to change with the signature and ratification of the Intermediate-Range Nuclear Forces Treaty in 1987 and agreement between NATO and the Warsaw Pact in 1989 to begin serious negotiations aimed at reducing conventional forces in Europe. The vastly improved US-Soviet relationship following the East European revolutions of 1989 allowed accelerated progress in the talks on the Treaty on Conventional Armed Forces in Europe (CFE Treaty). The negotiations also were facilitated by unilateral Soviet reductions in the relatively more expensive conventional weapons and troop units and the beginnings of withdrawals of Soviet forces from the former Eastern European satellites. Conversely, the negotiations were complicated by the clear disaggregation and then disappearance of the Warsaw Pact. Thus the CFE Treaty was signed by twenty-two states at the CSCE Summit in Paris in November 1990 (down from twenty-three; the two Germanys that had begun the negotiations were by that time united), but it covered only five categories of conventional military equipment. The so-called CFE 1A talks, covering manpower limitations, continued well into 1991, even as the Warsaw Pact fell apart and some states began implementing CFE Treaty provisions covering equipment.[3] By the time the CFE Treaty formally entered into force on July 17, 1992, the Soviet Union had fallen apart and the treaty was ratified by thirty states, including eight former republics of the USSR with territory west of the Urals covered under the area of application.

The CFE Treaty was based on the principle of parity at reduced levels between NATO and the Warsaw Pact, not on limits on the troops and weapons of individual states.[4] Regional limits were established within each bloc to prevent undue concentrations of troops and equipment. The treaty covered five basic categories of conventional military equipment: tanks, armored vehicles, artillery, attack helicopters, and combat aircraft. Naval forces were not included, primarily at the insistence of the United States, which argued that its naval units stationed or operating in or near Europe had obligations outside the area of application of the CFE Treaty, such as the Middle East or Africa. The

CFE Treaty was a significant confidence-building and transparency agreement because the pact included extremely intrusive verification provisions, calling for extensive, regular exchanges of detailed data, on-site inspections, and challenge inspections.

The paradox of the CFE Treaty was that it was obsolete even before it was implemented; by mid-1992 Europe was no longer divided between two blocs. From the Western side, one of the chief motives behind the CFE Treaty negotiations was the desire to reduce the danger of conventional war with much stronger, more numerous Warsaw Pact forces. With the Warsaw Treaty Organization disintegrating by the time the treaty negotiations were nearing completion, it was already clear that the danger of war was substantially reduced. Nonetheless the Western Allies in particular pushed for completion and signature of the pact based on the general bloc-to-bloc approach agreed-on in what already seemed another era, even though it was only a short time ago, largely out of the fear that to seek too many or too sweeping changes in the approach might result in no agreement at all.[5] Indeed, almost all of the states that were parties to the CFE Treaty welcomed the pact and fairly faithfully adhered to almost all of its provisions, even though the aggregate figures and limitations for the Warsaw Pact were meaningless by the time it entered into force.

Once the United States and the Soviet Union significantly reduced tensions, almost all of the states of Europe embarked on significant reductions in their very expensive conventional forces. Other signatories, such as the United States, had other uses for troops stationed in Europe, as substantial numbers of US forces redeployed from Europe to the Gulf in 1990–91 for Operation Desert Shield and Operation Desert Storm. The CFE Treaty process thus reflected and provided a framework for verification, transparency, and confidence building in a political process that was increasingly proceeding for reasons and with a momentum not caused by or directly connected with the arms control negotiations themselves. There were complaints from some parties about some provisions of the CFE Treaty—in particular from Russia, over the so-called flank limits, once the war in Chechnya began in late 1994—but these problems were generally resolved without undue difficulty using the mechanism provided for in the agreement even though the treaty was out of date. In essence, the CFE Treaty's success for so many years is a testimony not simply to the effectiveness of confidence-building and transparency measures in technical negotiations but also to the extraordinary degree of political collaboration, trust, and confidence that had developed between American and Soviet leaders in the few short years following 1985.

The states involved in the CFE Treaty negotiations were participants in a larger confidence-building and transparency negotiation as well, which was conducted by the CSCE in Vienna and involved all the states of Europe (including Albania, which finally joined the CSCE in 1991, six years after Enver Hoxha's death).[6] The negotiations on confidence- and security-building measures (CSBMs) were mandated by the CSCE's Vienna Follow-Up Meeting, which closed in January 1989 and represented a continuation of the CSCE's transparency and confidence-building efforts begun in Basket I of the Final Act and continued in particular in the 1984–1986 Stockholm negotiations of the Conference on CSBMs and Disarmament in Europe. As in the CFE Treaty negotiations, the end of the East/West confrontation in Europe after the 1989 Eastern European revolutions and the Malta Summit enabled the CSCE delegations to make exceptionally rapid progress. Many European states had begun shrinking their militaries, and there were no longer objections to on-site inspections and other intrusive verification and transparency measures.

The Vienna Document 1990 (hereafter, VDOC 1990) was agreed on in time to be signed at the CSCE Summit in Paris on November 17, 1990.[7] VDOC 1990 is not a treaty, but similar to almost all agreements reached in the CSCE — and later, the framework of the Organization for Security and Cooperation in Europe (OSCE) — it is politically binding; that is, it entails nontreaty obligations undertaken by the CSCE's participating states. VDOC 1990 obligates all participating states to an annual exchange of detailed military information, including levels of military equipment and personnel, plans for future deployments, and military budgets. The document further provides for notification and observation of a wide variety of military activities, such as exercises, and for annual exchange of calendars for exercises and other military activities. VDOC 1990 further obligates each participating state to accept three on-site inspections on its territory by any other participating state and provides means for evaluation, communication, and an annual assessment meeting. Finally, in VDOC 1990, the participating states agreed to a significantly more intrusive transparency measure, the mechanism for unusual military activities. According to the provisions of this mechanism, any participating state has the right to inquire about any unscheduled or unusual military activity in any other participating state that might cause it concern. The state receiving the inquiry is required to reply within forty-eight hours. The mechanism for these unusual military activities mirrored similarly intrusive provisions with respect to human rights adopted in other CSCE meetings.

The Vienna Document 1990 was the first in a series of agreements negotiated within the framework of the CSCE (and, after 1994, the OSCE) aimed at strengthening peace and enhancing security on the continent through an ever-deeper degree of transparency and more intrusive confidence-building measures.[8] The CSBM negotiations were the other, less well-publicized half of the CSCE's approach to "hard" or military security. Senior American officials and the US press and public paid much more attention to questions of arms limitations and reductions, but processes of building trust by increasing transparency and predictability were essential to strengthening peace and maintaining stability in a Europe undergoing tectonic political changes. Although the CFE Treaty talks involved only the member states of the NATO and Warsaw Treaty Organization alliances, the CSBM negotiations included and affected all the states of Europe. This holistic approach to arms control and military security was one of the chief considerations motivating many of the European states as they discussed how to adapt the continent's political and security institutions to reflect the new, post-1989 political and security realities at a series of high-level meetings during 1990, in particular the June NATO Summit and the November CSCE Summit.

## CENTRAL EUROPE RESTORED: THE REUNIFICATION OF GERMANY

Once it became clear the Soviet Union would not use force to prop up or preserve the East German government, it was only a matter of time before the two German states united. However, it was not clear on November 10, 1989, how fast and in what fashion that unification would be accomplished. The formal incorporation of East Germany into the Federal Republic of Germany, or West Germany, in less than a year stunned most observers, and even many participants, with its swiftness. The inclusion of a unified Germany in NATO was a result even harder to imagine, given how hard the Soviet Union had battled over four decades against just such an eventuality. Although I will not provide an exhaustive account of or explanation for the rapidity and terms of Germany's unification during 1990, it is important to identify the major reasons contributing to such an outcome here and to speculate on the implications of that result for broader European politics and security.[9]

Neither West Germany nor the United States ever abandoned the ultimate goal of unification of the two Germanys, although during most of the Cold War this was seen as something that would occur in the far-off, indeterminate future. The events of October and November 1989 changed all that. According to the minutes of the Malta meeting, by early December even Gorbachev conceded the prospect of eventual German unification, although he cautioned against proceeding too quickly.[10] By February 1990, Gorbachev was convinced to give a green light to the process of unification for several important reasons. First, although West German chancellor Helmut Kohl initially spoke of self-determination for the German Democratic Republic, the flood of Germans fleeing East Germany rapidly demonstrated the intention of East German citizens to live in West Germany, if not by unification then by migration. By early 1990, it became increasingly apparent that a separate East German government had practically no popular support and that the cost of keeping alive an East German state would be prohibitive. Second, growing instability in East Germany and the need to preserve good relations with Western Europe and the United States convinced Gorbachev and his closest advisers that to preserve and advance perestroika—his primary aim of the domestic transformation of the Soviet Union—it would be necessary to agree to German unification sooner than the Soviet leadership would otherwise prefer. Third, the role played by the United States, and in particular by Secretary of State Baker and President Bush, appears in most accounts to have been crucial in convincing Gorbachev and his colleagues not only to accept rapid unification but to agree that all of Germany should remain in NATO.

For the future of European political and security institutions, it is the fact of a united Germany within NATO, and not simply a single, large Germany, that is of paramount importance. This is not to argue that the reappearance of a united Germany in and of itself was without effect. Indeed, both British and French leaders expressed clear doubts and misgivings during the process of reunification and were convinced not to oppose or block it through the efforts of their US counterparts. Rivers of ink have been spilled discussing the pledge by Secretary of State Baker that NATO's jurisdiction would not move "one inch to the east."[11] The major participants in the process disagreed among themselves at the time, as a letter from Bush to Kohl suggesting a special military status for the territory of the former East Germany seemed to contradict Secretary Baker. In any case, it took a while for Gorbachev and his closest colleagues to become convinced that—as Baker had phrased the matter—it was better to have a united Germany in NATO with the United States still present in Europe than a neutral Germany outside NATO, without US forces present. Although Gorbachev agreed that it would be best to have a united Germany remain within European structures, NATO was not a structure favored by many of his colleagues in Moscow. Soviet negotiators tried to play upon differences among and within their negotiating partners in the Two-Plus-Four process to win a better deal. Ultimately, they were unsuccessful.[12]

It appears that Moscow and Washington, then and to this day, emerged from that key Moscow meeting and from the process of German unification with different understandings about what had been agreed on vis-à-vis NATO. It is clear that nothing was put in writing concerning the possibility or prospect of expanding NATO to the east.[13] That was natural because the discussion concerned the future security orientation and affiliation of a united Germany, not NATO. However, US participants also report that Gorbachev expressed opposition to "any extension of the zone of NATO," and Secretary Baker agreed.[14] It would seem that each side was certain not only of what it said but also that this was what the other side heard. If such certainty ever existed, the fog of time and memory has certainly eroded it.

US leaders and negotiators were clearly aware of Soviet sensitivities to NATO in general and membership of a unified Germany in NATO in particular. The CFE Treaty negotiations over equipment and manpower levels, in particular those in Germany, provided clear insights into Soviet security concerns as the process of unification proceeded. The actions taken and decisions adopted at the June 1990 London NATO Summit, in which NATO's purpose was redefined and a new institutional relationship established with the states of the former Warsaw Pact, also may be seen in part as evidence of the desire of the United States and its Allies to alter Soviet perceptions of NATO as an enemy and a threat. As for the Soviets, Gorbachev and Shevardnadze had to overcome significant domestic criticism of and resistance to Germany's unification and continued membership in NATO. By their own accounts, their chief concern during this process was the fate of reform, or perestroika within the USSR.[15] Gorbachev, Shevardnadze, and the reformers in the Kremlin appear to have been operating on the premise that for both economic and political reasons maintaining good, cooperative relations with Europe and the United States was essential for continued domestic reform. This was a happy coincidence that facilitated German unification. Unfortunately for them, it was a premise that with respect to the future of reforming the Soviet Union turned out to be wrong.

## THE COLLAPSE OF THE LAST EUROPEAN EMPIRE

As Gorbachev was negotiating groundbreaking strategic and conventional weapons agreements with NATO, his country was falling apart under him.[16] As resistance to his proposed domestic reforms and conciliatory foreign policy course mounted within the USSR in 1987–88, he gradually but surely reached the conclusion that far-reaching economic reforms and revival of the Soviet Union would be impossible without accompanying political changes. The most crucial innovations were arguably the introduction of openly competitive elections and the authorization of political organizations separate from and in competition with the ruling Communist Party of the Soviet Union (CPSU), both coming in 1989. Gorbachev had already opened Soviet politics and society to free expression, uncensored reporting, and discussion and criticism of the repressions and abuses of the Soviet past. The decision to open the country's politics to competitive elections meant that critics of the Soviet system could now organize, win elections, and participate in Soviet institutions of government. Although the initial reforms still gave the CPSU substantial advantages, nevertheless a significant number of prominent critics and activists, such as Andrei Sakharov, managed to win election to the new Soviet Parliament (Congress of People's Deputies) and garnered great publicity via both domestic and international media.

Gorbachev manipulated the new legislature and overrode opposition criticism of the lack of openness in the process in order to have himself elected to the new post of president of the Soviet Union and sought to use the new parliament to adopt a series of economic reform initiatives.[17] Gorbachev turned to the institutions of government largely because he could not be certain of full, or even majority, support in the CPSU for his program of increasingly radical reform. Ironically, in the institutions of the legislative and executive branches of the national and republic governments, he rapidly lost the initiative and then, in some cases, control to more militant and radical advocates of far more extensive changes in the USSR's economic and political system. This process took place with astonishing speed, so that by the end of 1990 he found himself unsure of his political base in both the USSR national government and the CPSU.

Most critically, as the limits on political expression and competition gradually eased across the USSR, many of the non-Russian nationalities took advantage of the thaw to elect nationalist leaders in their respective republics who sought not reform of the Soviet system but secession from the USSR itself.[18] Like its predecessor, the Russian Empire, the Soviet Union was a multinational, multiethnic imperium in which the proportion of ethnic Russians in the population hovered at about 50 percent. The Soviets were arguably more adept than their Imperial Russian forefathers in managing the non-Russian territories of the Soviet Union, but that did not mean that the desire of many of the non-Russian peoples of the USSR for independence had been eradicated. Political manipulation and repression only suppressed these ambitions, and as the Soviet political system opened up under Gorbachev, they reemerged with a vengeance. Passions for national independence were particularly evident in the Baltic Sea states and Moldova, whose peoples joined in a human chain in August 1989 to protest the fiftieth anniversary of the Molotov-Ribbentrop Pact. Armenia, Azerbaijan, and Georgia, which were all independent states briefly between 1917 and 1921, rapidly fielded growing movements in support of independence. Most important, pronationalist and proindependence sentiment began to gain ground rapidly in the USSR's second-largest republic, Ukraine, in particular in the western regions acquired after World War II.

In his superb study of the collapse of the Soviet empire, Yegor Gaidar, independent Russia's first prime minister, points to the collapse of world oil prices during the 1980s as the single most important factor in making the Soviet system of Eastern European satellites and the Soviet economic system itself unworkable.[19] Gaidar makes a compelling case for the economic causes of the growing misery and incoherence of the Soviet system, but one might argue that this could have just as easily have led to violent repression by a beleaguered leadership as to dissolution of the union. The multinational composition of the Soviet population and the federal division of the USSR into constituent national republics were crucial in pointing the country toward disintegration as the ideology on which it had been based evaporated. As early as 1970, the Soviet dissident Andrei Amalrik cited the nationalities question as a likely cause of the demise of the USSR.[20] As the Western historian Steven Kotkin has pointed out, the CPSU was the one truly integrated federal institution in the Soviet Union.[21] When Gorbachev shifted power from the party to institutions of government, he inadvertently deprived the country of the glue that had been holding the federal units together. With the authority of the CPSU diminished, there were few if any impediments to national republic leaders who wished to break away from the Soviet Union. And many of them so wished.

One of the most fateful developments for Gorbachev's and the Soviet Union's future was the rise of the Russian Republic as a separate source of pressure for democratic reforms in the USSR and the joining of Boris Yeltsin to this Russian reform movement.[22] Yeltsin's enlistment brought significantly more votes if not ideological support to the Russian Republic's legislative and executive organs of government and gradually established Yeltsin and the Russian Republic government as an alternative to Gorbachev and the Soviet center. The success of the Baltic states in pushing the envelope of independence from Moscow encouraged other republics, and during the course of 1990 there was a series of declarations of national sovereignty by Soviet republics. Gorbachev and Soviet national officials were simply unable to stem the tide of growing assertiveness and separatism in the Western and South Caucasus Soviet republics without resorting to forcible repression, a step Gorbachev remained unwilling to take. Instead, Gorbachev continued his negotiations with Western leaders on security issues, arms control, and economic assistance, while his government's authority within his country gradually slipped away.

Gorbachev attempted to reverse this process during the first months of 1991.[23] Under increasing pressure from conservatives within the CPSU and the military and security agencies of the government in Moscow, Gorbachev hedged on support for reform in early 1991. Advocates of more forceful responses to national separatists managed to mount bloody repressive actions against demonstrators in Latvia and Lithuania in January 1991. Gorbachev repudiated such applications of force, and instead proposed a referendum on continuing the Soviet Union and a new treaty of union that would grant considerably more authority to republic governments, in fact turning the USSR into a confederation. Most of the USSR's republics—but not all of them, in particular, the three Baltic states—joined in the referendum. When the vote went in favor of continuing the union, these republics agreed to the pact, which was to be signed and formally adopted on August 20, 1991. In the interval between April and August, Yeltsin campaigned and won election to the post he had helped create, president of the Russian Republic, on May 29, 1991.

The story of Gorbachev's attempted removal on August 18–19, 1991, by opponents of the Union Treaty; of Yeltsin's defiant resistance to the coup; and of Gorbachev's eventual triumphant return to Moscow and the failure of the coup is well known and does not need to be retold here.[24] President Gorbachev returned on August 23 to a country that was essentially already dead, although it took another four months for its demise to become official. Soviet legitimacy was already waning, and Yeltsin's actions during that fateful week in August established his Russian government as the real authority in Moscow. During a few weeks of *dvoevlastie* (dual power) in the autumn of 1991, power gradually passed from the Kremlin to the "White House" on the Moscow River near the new US Embassy. The Belovezhskaya Agreement on December 8, 1991; the vote of the Soviet Parliament abolishing the Union of December 21, 1991; and Gorbachev's resignation on December 25 were the formal markers of a process moving inexorably toward the end of the Soviet Union once the coup failed.

There were several key factors in the process of the dissolution of the USSR and the emergence of the Russian Federation as its formal successor state, along with fourteen other independent states. Above all, this process was a largely unplanned and chaotic competition for power between Gorbachev and Yeltsin, and thus between the Soviet center and the Russian Republic reformers. The public debate in this competition focused almost exclusively on issues of domestic policy and internal political structures and relationships. Yeltsin and those in the Russian government handling foreign relations for him generally did not challenge Gorbachev's basic foreign policy and security line. The relative lack of discussion of these issues meant that there was also a significant absence of planning for the military, security, and diplomatic issues that would arise upon the dissolution of the USSR.

Until practically the very end of the Soviet Union, Gorbachev continued to conduct negotiations with his Western partners on serious arms control and security issues, such as the CFE Treaty, the Open Skies Treaty, the Strategic Arms Reduction Treaty (START), and the package of CSBMs that became the 1992 Vienna Document. Western governments, especially the United States, pressed Soviet and then Russian and other former Soviet Republic representatives to continue these negotiations and to support and respect the agreements reached in them.[25] Yeltsin and Russian foreign minister Andrei Kozyrev were particularly accommodating in supporting Western—and, in particular, American—desires for continuity in arms control and security policies. During the first months of 1992, both the CFE Treaty and START were adjusted to reflect the increased number of state parties after the Soviet breakup and to alter the terms appropriately to reflect changes in holdings, manpower, and other areas covered by the pacts.[26]

However, the fact that Boris Yeltsin in Russia, Leonid Kravchuk in Ukraine, and Stanislav Shushkevich in Belarus all agreed to continue the basic principles of Gorbachev's policies vis-à-vis the West and to respect the agreements he had negotiated did not mean that Gorbachev's new thinking in foreign policy had finally and completely triumphed in the former Soviet area. Western leaders such as George H. W. Bush developed great friendships with and trust in Gorbachev, a friendship and trust that successors such as President Bill Clinton transferred to Boris Yeltsin. However, those Central and Eastern European leaders who were closer to the Soviet Union were not nearly as confident that the changes wrought by Gorbachev were lasting or irreversible. The crackdown in the Baltic states in early 1991 and the attempted coup in August were proof to many former satellites that Soviet and Russian behavior could easily revert to the expansionist, imperialist norm feared and loathed by many of Russia's neighbors. Thus, from the very beginning of the post–Cold War period, the security perceptions, preferences, and choices of the Eastern European states differed substantially from those in Russia, and also in Western Europe.

Moreover, time and events would quickly show that the victories of Yeltsin and other reformers were indeed incomplete and fleeting. In the Russian Federation in particular, strong, fundamental challenges to Yeltsin's policies and authority arose almost immediately. Critics appeared within Russia of both his role in the destruction of the Soviet Union and his continuation of Gorbachev's accommodating policies toward the West. Although Yeltsin emerged as the victor following the August 1991 attempted coup, the change in Russia's foreign and security policies begun by Gorbachev and continued by Yeltsin was much less deep and thoroughgoing than contemporary Western encomiums to Yeltsin's defiance of the coup plotters suggested.[27] Because Yeltsin won the trust, friendship, and support of important Western leaders, these deeper facts of the mood and orientation of the Russian public remained in eclipse for much of Yeltsin's time in office, only to become more visible after Putin's accession.

Finally, though the larger republics of the Soviet Union generally came through the breakup without serious violence, several of the smaller republics on the Soviet periphery were not so fortunate.[28] In February 1988, demonstrations against Azerbaijan's rule of the largely ethnic Armenian enclave Nagorno-Karabakh set off a process that led to open war between newly independent Azerbaijan and Armenia by early 1992. Brief civil conflicts between Georgia and its minority area of South Ossetia, largely provoked by President Zviad Gam-sakhurdia's policy of "Georgia for the Georgians," erupted again in early 1992 into open fighting, followed by hostilities in Abkhazia, another discontented minority region, in August 1992. Moldova successfully defused an incipient revolt by the Orthodox Turkic Gagauz area in the country's south, but was not able to prevent secession of the eastern region of Transdniestria (or Transnistria) in the autumn of 1990. In the spring of 1992, Moldova and the Transdniestrian enclave engaged in a brief but bitter war. Such conflicts arising from the Soviet breakup all affected Russia significantly, whether directly or indirectly, and also posed security challenges for wider Europe. The manner in which Europe addressed these challenges would be one of the most important early factors in the restructuring and development of the continent's security institutions.

## DEEPENING EUROPEAN INTEGRATION: THE EC BECOMES THE EU

The unification of Germany and the disintegration of the Soviet empire took place against the background of a Europe that was moving steadily toward closer economic, monetary, and political integration. As president of the European Commission (EC) from January 1985, former French finance and economy minister Jacques Delors pushed constantly for policies and measures that would turn the European Community into a true union, along the lines envisioned by the tradition of European federalism from which he sprang. The addition of Spain, Portugal, and Greece to EC ranks in the 1980s and the end of the East/West divide in Europe with the revolutions of 1989 held out the alluring prospect of also attaining a much wider European union. The adoption and implementation of the Single European Act in 1986–87 launched the concrete movement toward a single market, common currency, and political union that were realized in the 1992 Maastricht Treaty.[29]

The epochal political changes in Europe and the movement toward the European Union also revived long-standing European aspirations for an independent defense capability and a common foreign and security policy. As far back as the late 1940s, a UK initiative had called for the formation of a European Defense Community.[30] Although this Defense Community faltered ultimately on French objections, the 1955 end of the Western Allies' occupation and the admission of West Germany into NATO also resulted in modification and augmentation of the 1948 Brussels Treaty on European Security to form the Western European Union (WEU). Events conspired to render the WEU dormant in its

London headquarters almost from the hour of its birth, but the organization did remain a wholly European security organization and an alternative to NATO, if the states on the continent should wish to pursue security in the absence of US participation.

Although movement toward a single market and Economic and Monetary Union might not impinge on the relationship with NATO, the Single European Act called for external policy positions adopted by the EC and in European political cooperation to be consistent. The march toward closer political union and the need for the EC states to react in concert to the looming political changes in Europe in 1989 both strengthened the push within the EC for coordination of security and defense policies and a perceived need for some sort of independent institutional capability in these areas.[31] Debates within the EC on foreign policy and security aspects of the Maastricht Treaty were conducted simultaneously with discussions on the future of NATO, and it is thus almost impossible to separate examination of the genesis of the EU's Common Foreign and Security Policy from that of NATO's post-1989 transformation. Indeed, in the years 1990 to 1992, the idea of transforming the CSCE into a pan-European security organization that might supplant the roles of NATO and the Warsaw Pact also gained considerable traction in a number of European states, making the period one when the future institutional structure for European security truly hung in the balance.

The process of forming the European Union proceeded with astonishing speed following the EC's December 1989 decision to hold an intergovernmental conference on Economic and Monetary Union.[32] By mid-1990, the EC added another conference on political union, and France, Germany, and the Benelux countries reached the Schengen Agreement on freedom of movement. The Bush administration was generally supportive of the progress toward greater economic and political integration in Europe. In November 1990, the EC and the United States adopted the Transatlantic Declaration on EC-US Relations, which stressed the dedication of the two signatories to common values, common goals, and a close partnership in addressing the challenges and opportunities presented by a newly undivided Europe. The United States acknowledged that the European Community was "acquiring its own identity in economic and monetary matters, in foreign policy, and in the domain of security," while also noting the commitment of both the United States and the EC member states to the North Atlantic Alliance.[33]

The agreed points in this statement obscured a deep disagreement between Washington and a number of its European partners, in particular Paris, over the security role and structures of the projected European Union.[34] French political and diplomatic elites found it hard to imagine a deeper, united Europe without its own security structures and capabilities. Although French president François

Mitterrand told the Bush administration that he wanted a continued US and NATO role in Europe, French explanations indicated that this role should remain limited to the Alliance's initial purpose of territorial defense against external attack.[35] This position was not always consistent with US thinking that NATO should evolve to reflect the fundamental changes in the European security environment (see below). The French saw two other important reasons to pursue development of a separate, independent EU security capability. First, France was unwilling to return to NATO military structures, which after 1966 were heavily dominated by the United States, without substantial changes in the command and staffing arrangements of these structures. Also, and perhaps more important, many French people believed that with the overwhelming Soviet threat gone, the United States would be increasingly reluctant to provide human and material resources needed for purely intra-European security problems. Irrespective of the presence or absence of any empirical evidence at the time, this position (or suspicion) grew out of a long Gaullist tradition that perceives both the need for and rightness of French leadership in Europe.[36]

The EC settled on the WEU as the most appropriate, or at least the most convenient, vehicle with which to pursue a security structure and capability independent of the United States. As the Rome intergovernmental conference opened in December 1990, Kohl and Mitterrand floated a joint proposal that the EC should absorb the WEU as the security and defense mechanism of the future European Union. WEU secretary-general Willem van Eekelen suggested that the organization could serve as a "bridge" between NATO and the EC, and EC Commission president Delors simply suggested that the WEU's treaty obligations be formally included in the Maastricht Treaty establishing the EU. Washington reacted strongly and negatively in the February "Bartholomew Message," warning explicitly against the establishment of any separate European security organization that might compete or conflict with NATO.[37] Disagreements among the EC member states, with the United Kingdom and the Netherlands much closer to the US position, ultimately facilitated Washington's push to have its European partners recognize NATO's primacy in consultation and coordination for all issues involving security and defense in the Alliance's territory. The urge to establish separate European defense capabilities did not disappear, as demonstrated by a proposal later in 1991 to form a joint Franco-German corps. Only the fundamental, thoroughgoing changes in NATO agreed on and proclaimed at the November 1991 Rome Summit and during subsequent years of negotiations with the French and then EU representatives eased the contradiction between US support for NATO as the vehicle for the American presence and leadership in Europe and the desire of a broader, deeper, more united Europe to develop its own, separate security and defense institutions and capability.

## TOWARD A COMMON EUROPEAN HOME:
## TRANSFORMING THE CSCE

With Germany unifying, the Warsaw Pact disappearing, and the EC in the process of transforming into the European Union, the states of Western Europe and their representatives in NATO and the EC debated how Europe could transform its institutions to include its former foes to the east and provide for its own security.[38] Germany showed particular concern for integrating the former Soviet Warsaw Pact satellites and the USSR (later the former Soviet states) into pan-European institutions. In addition, the Central and Eastern European states helped provide much of the initial impetus for institutionalizing the CSCE — the one all-European institution to which they already belonged.[39] France also saw the CSCE as a possible wholly European alternative institution to serve, inter alia, as the continent's provider of security.[40]

Gorbachev and Shevardnadze demonstrated similar aspirations for the CSCE, or the Helsinki Process, as they worked during this same period with President Bush and other Western leaders to completely refashion the European security system. Despite Gorbachev's eventual acquiescence to the reunification of Germany in NATO, the negotiating record makes clear the aversion that he personally and almost all his Soviet colleagues had for the Atlantic Alliance. Although many of Moscow's political elite might accept the desirability of a continued American presence in Europe as insurance against possible revanchism or instability, they saw NATO as an instrument dominated by the United States and not as a desirable forum for future collaboration or partnership between Washington and Moscow.[41] Similar to their Eastern European counterparts (although often with different motives), Soviet and subsequently Russian diplomats saw the CSCE as an all-inclusive forum where they had equal standing and rights with the United States. Thus the Soviets and then the Russians saw the CSCE as one of the potentially key institutions in a reformed, post–Cold War security architecture for an undivided Europe.

Beginning in late 1989, the CSCE underwent dramatic normative and institutional changes. In accordance with procedures first established during the 1973–1975 Geneva and Helsinki negotiations, the CSCE had a set of procedural rules, but no formal structures. The Final Act provided for periodic follow-up meetings; the host of each follow-up meeting provided an executive secretariat for the CSCE until the host of the next follow-up meeting was designated. Similar procedures were followed for interim experts' meetings agreed to at each follow-up meeting. The Vienna follow-up meeting, which closed in January 1989, continued the traditional practice and mandated a number of interim meetings in all three baskets: security, economics and the environment, and the human dimension.[42] The security meetings—the CFE Treaty negotiations for twenty-three states and the CSBM talks with all CSCE participating states— began to show promise fairly quickly, but results from the other baskets were slower in coming. The Sofia Environmental Forum, which met in Bulgaria in October 1989, in addition to substantive deliberations on its intended subject matter, served as a focal point and inspiration for civic opposition in that country, resulting in the fall of its communist government only weeks later.

Three interim human rights or human dimension meetings were mandated in the Vienna Concluding Document—one in Paris in 1989, another in Copenhagen in 1990, and a third in Moscow in 1991 (this last one was agreed on only after intense, last-minute bargaining and trade-offs). Although the influence of Gorbachev's new thinking was clearly visible in the approach and actions of Soviet arms control delegations, there was little such evidence of change for much of 1989 in Soviet negotiators on human contacts and human rights. The Soviet and Eastern European delegations to the Paris Human Dimension meeting in June 1989 were disappointingly unforthcoming and defensive, with much of the discussion focusing on failures to comply with previous CSCE human rights commitments, as opposed to discussions of new norms or mechanisms.[43]

The true breakthrough for the CSCE came at the June 1990 Copenhagen Human Dimension meeting. The 1989 revolutions had removed from power all the obstructive governments that had resisted the adoption by the CSCE of more far-reaching commitments and standards with respect to human rights and democratic institutions. The Bush-Gorbachev summits, in Malta in December 1989 and in Washington in May 1990, demonstrated quantum leaps in the Soviet leader's willingness not only to meet Western concerns but to adopt common positions long resisted by Soviet representatives. Gorbachev apparently took seriously the oral commitment he made at Malta to democratic values; this political change was reflected in the behavior of Soviet delegations at CSCE meetings beginning in early 1990.[44] First, at the CSCE Human Dimension meeting in Copenhagen in June 1990 and then at the CSCE Summit in Paris in November 1990, Soviet representatives joined with their counterparts from all the participating states in adopting documents with normative commitments on democracy, political freedoms, and human rights about which US and Western leaders had only dreamed during the forty-five years since the end of World War II.[45]

The Copenhagen Document and Charter of Paris are truly stunning products. Although the CSCE Final Act contains statements of value and lasting commitments to human rights and fundamental freedoms, the United States and its Allies had to fight for months with the Soviet Bloc's representatives for almost every word. The Copenhagen and Paris documents were achieved with almost breathtaking speed and cooperation, and the commitments are absolute.

The heads of state proclaimed, "We undertake to build, consolidate, and strengthen democracy as the only system of government of our nations."[46] Further, the CSCE leaders declared, "Every individual has the right to: freedom of thought, conscience, religion, or belief; freedom of expression; freedom of association and peaceful assembly; freedom of movement."[47] The Copenhagen Document and the Charter of Paris constitute an unequivocal statement of and commitment to democracy, fundamental freedoms, the rule of law, and basic human rights by all European states, as well as the United States and Canada. The two documents taken together constitute a normative achievement and commitment unmatched since the adoption by the United Nations General Assembly of the Universal Declaration of Human Rights in 1949.

The Copenhagen Document, in particular, also extended the principles of transparency and confidence building previously employed in CSCE negotiations and agreements primarily in the area of military security to the human dimension.[48] To encourage implementation of commitments with respect to open political campaigning, freedom of expression, and free and fair elections, the Copenhagen Document calls on all CSCE states to invite and permit observers at their elections not only from other participating states but also from nongovernmental organizations. The delegates at Copenhagen also adopted an obligation for all CSCE states to accept as observers at their court proceedings representatives from other participating states, nongovernmental organizations, and "other interested persons." Finally, numerous provisions of the Copenhagen Document include commitments to ensure the free flow of information, contacts between persons and private organizations, and other international organizations on a range of human rights and human contacts issues, all of which constitute an unprecedented acceptance by all CSCE states of extensive transparency throughout the human dimension.

The political changes in Europe gave rise not only to new statements of universal values but also to new institutions to reflect and manage relations between the states of a newly undivided continent. Leaders from Europe's east in particular turned to the CSCE and the Helsinki Process as the source of new political and security institutions for a new Europe. Many of the Soviets, and later the Russians, saw the CSCE as a logical successor to and replacement for NATO and the Warsaw Pact. Gorbachev, in particular, thought it was logical that both military blocs of the old Europe should disappear and be replaced by the European organization with universal membership and equal participation by all states. Other Eastern European leaders, such as Czechoslovak president Václav Havel, Polish prime minister Tadeusz Mazowiecki, and Czechoslovak foreign minister Jerzy Dienstbier all at various times in 1989 and 1990 entertained similar ideas.[49] French president Mitterrand, German chancellor Kohl and foreign minister Hans-Dietrich Genscher voiced similar thoughts to US leaders in the White House.[50] Although Bush administration leaders had reservations about investing too great an amount of responsibility or authority for European security in the CSCE, the United States also offered clear, consistent, and significant support for institutionalizing the CSCE and investing it with operational capabilities.[51]

Once the Cold War's ideological ice jam in the CSCE was broken with the unqualified statement of common values at Copenhagen in June 1990, European and North American representatives worked with astonishing speed to develop proposals to operationalize the CSCE. Consultations continued in the summer and fall of 1990 at a preparatory meeting in New York, and the agreements reached were ratified by the heads of the CSCE's participating states at the Paris Summit in November.[52] With old historical grievances and disagreements reappearing in the Eastern European states newly freed from Warsaw Pact restraints, and with rumblings of impending violence growing evermore audible from Yugoslavia, European leaders worried about how to avert possible conflicts or defuse them in their early stages. The proposal to establish the CSCE Conflict Prevention Center, to be located in Vienna, found general agreement among CSCE states. European leaders also sought to give the CSCE a more permanent deliberative and administrative structure than the practice of rotating conferences afforded. The CSCE states thus agreed to set up a regular schedule of meetings—regular gatherings of heads of state as follow-up meetings to the Summit in Helsinki in 1992. The CSCE's foreign ministers would meet once a year as a council, which would serve as the chief organ for CSCE political consultations. Between Ministerial Council meetings, a Committee of Senior Officials would serve as the chief forum for operational political consultations and for carrying out decisions reached by the ministers. The CSCE Secretariat was established in Prague to provide administrative support for these structures. Reflecting the importance accorded by many Western states, in particular the United States, to free and fair elections, an Office for Free Elections was to be established in Warsaw. Finally, in an effort to broaden the CSCE beyond its traditional home in the foreign and security policy agencies of the participating states' executive branches of government, the heads of state directed that a CSCE parliamentary assembly be formed, using models from similar international organizations. The CSCE's foreign ministers were to review progress on the implementation of these organizational decisions at the first meeting of their council, which was to take place in Berlin in June 1991.

The actual process of establishing and developing the CSCE's institutions was not as clear or straightforward as the prose of the Charter of Paris would make one believe.[53] The Prague Secretariat, for one, never really got off the ground. Because all the CSCE participating states were already maintaining delegations in Vienna for the CSBM negotiations, in practice these CSBM ambassadors were quickly double-hatted and with increasing frequency convened as the Committee of Senior Officials when events required it. Participating states also found maintaining the Secretariat in Prague and the Conflict Prevention Center in Vienna to be inefficient and wasteful. Because the CSBM talks (and thus the Committee of Senior Officials) were also already in Vienna, that city soon also became the site of the bulk of the Secretariat's work, although a minimal presence was retained in Prague. The mandate for the Office for Free Elections was extremely vague, calling for facilitation of contacts and exchange of information without specifying the nature of those contacts or the content and extent of information. As this office found real estate in Warsaw and recruited personnel, preparatory discussions for the 1992 Helsinki Summit would expand its mandate beyond just elections to human rights in general, eventually producing the present-day Office for Democratic Institutions and Human Rights (ODIHR), with a heavy emphasis on election observation as one of its chief operational activities.[54]

The CSCE constructed its new institutions and fleshed out their mandates and competencies against a global background of war and disintegration of old borders and major states.[55] CSCE experts met in Valetta, Malta, in January 1991 to develop a mechanism for the peaceful settlement of disputes, a long-time dream of the CSCE and a task agreed on at the Paris Summit, just as coalition operations commenced against Saddam Hussein's forces in Kuwait. The Valetta meeting produced a complex, legalistic procedure for adjudication of disputes between participating states that has yet to be employed in the twenty-six years since the meeting. A cultural forum in May 1991 in Krakow, and then an experts' meeting on national minorities in Geneva in June and July, focused attention on the political, social, economic, linguistic, and cultural positions and rights of people belonging to national minorities, reflecting the status and grievances of ethnic and national minorities as one of the chief concerns of many European states.

These fears seemed increasingly well founded as the CSCE gathering in Switzerland proceeded against the backdrop of the secession of Slovenia and Croatia from Yugoslavia and the outbreak of war. CSBM negotiators in Vienna donned their Committee of Senior Officials hats frequently in the final days of June to consider what action their nascent organization might take. Anticipating the results of the Maastricht Treaty, EC representatives assured other CSCE states that "Europe" could handle the emerging Yugoslav crisis and handed the job over to the incoming Luxembourg presidency with a midnight toast on the island of Brioni on June 30–July 1, 1991. The third CSCE Human Dimension meeting opened in Moscow in September 1991, while tanks, armored vehicles, and other assorted military equipment left over from the failed coup still remained in parks and on street sides. The first official act of the ministers attending the Moscow meeting was to recognize the independence of Estonia, Latvia, and Lithuania and to admit them to the CSCE, actions to which even a reluctant Soviet delegation agreed.[56]

By the final months of 1991, Europe was not as secure, peaceful, and hopeful as it had seemed to be when the New Year dawned in January 1990. The euphoria of an enthusiastic consensus on democracy and fundamental freedoms was gradually replaced by old grievances, political rivalries, and fears of ethnic violence and territorial changes. Although Soviet representatives uniformly joined the consensus at each successive CSCE meeting, the adoption of new commitments and the construction of operational structures was not their highest priority by far. For Soviet leaders—and their immediate Russian successors—the CSCE offered an opportunity to retain a voice, however much reduced, in Central and Eastern European security affairs now that their exclusive sphere of influence through the Warsaw Pact had vanished. More than anything, however, Soviet leaders and representatives were concerned with the political drama playing out at home as their country crumbled and disappeared. Moscow's primary concerns did not change materially during the first few years of the independent Russian Federation as the legal international successor to the USSR. The CSCE continued to offer Moscow a forum: aside from the UN Security Council, in fact, the CSCE was the only international forum in which Moscow retained equal status with the United States and other major Western powers.

For the United States, the CSCE was important more because it mattered in various ways to Washington's European partners than for its intrinsic attributes or potential.[57] Washington's political elites generally saw the CSCE as one of a number of interlocking Euro-Atlantic institutions that should work cooperatively with an appropriate division of tasks and responsibilities to address the political, security, and economic changes in Europe brought on by the end of the Cold War. One of the best expressions of the prevailing US view at that time is found in Secretary of State Baker's speech in Berlin on June 18, 1991, "The Euro-Atlantic Architecture: From West to East," delivered the day before the first CSCE Ministerial Council. Baker notes that "CSCE, the Helsinki Process, remains the one group that brings together all the countries of Europe and North America on the basis of a common commitment to human rights and democratic principles."[58] Baker called for the OSCE to build "appropriate capabilities" in all three baskets, including a security capability focusing on conflict prevention, mediation, and resolution. However, Baker made clear the need for NATO's strong defensive military capability to ensure peace and facilitate arms control and the growing role of the EC in European economic and political integration. Baker laid out a number of confidence-building, transparency, conflict prevention, and nuclear nonproliferation measures that future CSCE activities might implement or support. Baker stressed that "our objective is both a Europe whole and free, and a Euro-Atlantic community that extends east from Vancouver to Vladivostok." This would be, however, a community in which security would be provided and ensured by a set of interlocking institutions, and the United States envisioned that NATO would continue to play a central role.

## THE THREAT IS GONE: WHY NATO?

The processes of making the key decisions on the CSCE, the European Union, and NATO were intertwined during the crucial period from 1989 to 1992. During the same period that the CSCE was reaching its ultimate statement of common values in the Charter of Paris and the EC was transforming itself into the modern-day EU with the Maastricht Treaty, the United States and its NATO Allies were engaged in a process of self-examination that produced fundamental decisions that had far-reaching effects not only on the future of the North Atlantic Alliance but also on the entire security order in Europe. With the Berlin Wall disappearing, Germany reuniting, the Warsaw Pact dissolving, and Soviet troops returning home from their bases in Central Europe, one heard discussions in the media and public forums increasingly asking questions such as these: Do we need NATO any more? What is its purpose now that the Soviet threat is gone? Can we more usefully spend the funds formerly allotted to NATO? Many political leaders throughout much of Europe, and in particular those in the East, including Gorbachev, questioned the need for military alliances now that the divisions in Europe were rapidly being eliminated.[59]

Although the need for change in Europe's security structures to account for the political transformation of Europe in 1989–90 was apparent to almost anyone observing events during that period, it seems clear that the Bush administration never entertained the idea of abandoning the North Atlantic Alliance. President Bush and his closest advisers were committed Atlanticists and thus saw NATO as more than a military alliance; it was also the primary vehicle for continued American involvement in Europe.[60] Thus the administration fairly rapidly settled on a strategy of preserving and adapting NATO—both structure and mission—to reflect the changing Euro-Atlantic political and security environment, while also offering support for the development and strengthening of other European institutions seeking to respond to the changes in the East.[61] Given the rapid progression of events and constant changes in the situation in Europe, US leaders were called upon to make frequent tactical adjustments. However, their strategic approach with respect to NATO and European security remained remarkably consistent. Furthermore, this general strategic approach survived—with requisite tactical changes—throughout the administrations of Bill Clinton, George W. Bush, and Barack Obama.

For the United States, NATO was not simply an instrument for military defense of the territory of the Allies but the primary venue for coordination of political, security, and defense policies with its most important European partners. The United States used the NATO caucus to work out common positions with its Allies in negotiations in other bodies, such as the CSCE, and consulted closely with NATO as it conducted bilateral arms negotiations with the Soviet Union. The major priorities emerging from the high-level policy review in the first year of the Bush administration were to support reform in Eastern Europe and get Soviet troops out.[62] Speaking to the NATO Allies immediately after his Malta meeting with Gorbachev, President Bush pointed to NATO's origins as "a political alliance of nations sharing the same fundamental values" and expressed his conviction that NATO should continue to play a key political role in supporting continued reform in Eastern Europe.[63] In an address in Berlin just over a week later, Secretary Baker spoke evocatively of the advances of freedom in Eastern Europe, and called for the West to respond with "a new architecture for a new era."[64] Baker called for this new architecture to build upon old, valuable structures such as NATO, but using them for "new collective purposes." Baker called upon NATO to help construct a new European security environment in which the nonmilitary component would grow and to facilitate reconciliation with its former enemies in the east by demonstrating a fundamentally different approach to security. Finally, Baker offered extensive thoughts on how NATO should cooperate with and support the European Community and the CSCE in building an overlapping structure of institutions in this new security architecture.

Although the American vision of the new European security structures, as elaborated by President Bush and Secretary Baker, was relatively clear and direct, the operational path to fleshing out this new architecture was filled with twists and turns, advances and retreats. Management of the negotiations involving the reunification of Germany during 1990 was a task that consumed tremendous time and energy and that afforded leaders in the Four-Plus-Two grouping who did not fully share the Bush-Scowcroft-Baker vision the opportunity to push their own preferred variants—as Gorbachev, Thatcher, and Mitterrand all did at one time or another.[65] The CFE Treaty and START negotiations also remained top US priorities, and they absorbed a disproportionate amount of the time and attention of the most senior administration officials.[66] The other priority for the Bush administration, which dovetailed closely with the arms control and German reunification issues, was the adaptation and thus preservation of NATO.

As part of the effort to demonstrate to the Soviets that a reunified Germany inside NATO was no threat, Bush set about showing that NATO was indeed transforming itself.[67] Bush established a senior-level European Strategy Steering Group to provide a reassessment of the United States' NATO strategy and operational recommendations. At the same time, the White House quieted uneasy British and French nerves over a unified Germany, resisting both Thatcher's inclination to leave some Soviet troops in Germany for a time and Mitterrand's efforts to restrict NATO to its traditional role of territorial defense. In a May 4 speech at Oklahoma State University, Bush called for a NATO Summit to reexamine the Alliance's role for the 1990s, including review of its core military and political missions, rapid progress in the CFE Treaty talks, and strengthening the CSCE.[68] At a meeting in Turnberry, Scotland, on June 7–8, 1990, the NATO foreign ministers echoed many of President Bush's points, welcomed the changes in Eastern Europe, noted the "far-reaching changes in the political and military fundamentals of European security," and promised that the Alliance would adapt to reflect these changes.[69] The Turnberry Communiqué applauded the political exchanges between the two former opposing blocs and noted recent visits to NATO by the Soviet, Czechoslovak, and Polish foreign ministers, an unprecedented symbol of the easing of tensions. In a move signaling their intention to change, many of the NATO representatives in Turnberry then boarded a plane to pay a return visit to the capitals of the former Warsaw Pact countries.

By the accounts of most participants, NATO's adoption of the London Declaration on a Transformed North Atlantic Alliance at the July 5–6, 1990, summit was a true turning point in the history of the Alliance.[70] Shevardnadze told Baker that the declaration would be crucial in convincing the Soviet public that a reunited Germany inside NATO was acceptable.[71] Nonetheless, Bush and Baker needed to overcome last-minute doubts from Thatcher and Mitterrand over the declaration's phrasing with respect to nuclear policy before a consensus could be achieved.[72] In the declaration, the NATO leaders proposed to their Warsaw Pact counterparts a joint statement recognizing that they were no longer adversaries and promised to enhance the political component of the North Atlantic Alliance. The NATO heads of state invited Gorbachev and representatives of other Central and Eastern European states to visit Brussels and address the North Atlantic Council. The London Declaration vowed quick progress in arms control negotiations and promised fundamental change in NATO's military posture and defense policy. Finally, the London summit endorsed both the changes envisioned at the upcoming CSCE summit and also the institutionalization of the CSCE process.

As one reads the accounts of many of the participants in the events of the spring and summer of 1990, it is easy to form the impression that the negotiations over NATO's role, doctrine, policies, and relationship with the East served more as means to the ends of German unification and fundamental reform in the Soviet Union, than to ends in and of themselves. It is indisputable that the changes and promises made with respect to NATO were essential in overcoming resistance from the USSR to Germany's unification. The steps taken to begin NATO's transformation also may have enabled Gorbachev to combat domestic Soviet resistance to his program of reforms, but in the end they were not sufficient to keep Gorbachev in power or to ensure the success of his project for changing the nature of the USSR. Irrespective of their other purposes, the aims set out in the London Declaration were important in and of themselves insofar as they constituted essential first steps in ensuring the survival of the North Atlantic Alliance. To be sure, the repeated assertions by President Bush and other Allies, culminating in the London Declaration, that NATO would enhance the political component of the Alliance constituted a crucial indication of NATO's future direction, but they also tended to obscure an essential fact. From its very inception, NATO was the most crucial political instrument for the United States in managing its relations with its most important partners in the world: the democratic nations of Western Europe. The London Declaration thus represented, first and foremost, a decision with two intertwined, inseparable elements: the United States would remain present and deeply involved in Europe, and NATO would survive as the primary means for the United States to do so.

The Alliance's decisions announced in the London Declaration began a process of adaptation and reform that culminated at the NATO Rome Summit in November 1991. The results of this process included a fundamental redefinition of the Alliance's purpose, a restructuring of Europe's security architecture, and a sweeping reconstitution of NATO's relations with the countries of Central and Eastern Europe, in particular the Soviet Union. At Rome, NATO took a decisive step—reflected especially in the new Strategic Concept adopted at the Rome meeting—toward becoming a collective security organization, in addition to its original identity as an institution dedicated to collective territorial defense.[73] This transformation of NATO's identity and purpose was essential for establishing the basis for out-of-area operations, in which it would engage within a few years. NATO made more explicit its dedication to the tripartite, overlapping security architecture suggested in Secretary Baker's first Berlin speech with distinct, cooperative, reinforcing roles envisioned for the European Community and the CSCE. With respect to the Soviet Union and the countries of Central and Eastern Europe, the NATO allies proposed establishment of a formal institution, the North Atlantic Cooperation Council (NACC), to manage the new relationship between these countries and NATO.[74]

Events in Europe, especially the political changes in the former Warsaw Pact countries and the battles over reform within the Soviet Union, continued to move with exceptional swiftness throughout the second half of 1990 and 1991 as internal NATO consultations proceeded to flesh out the London decisions. Democratic, noncommunist governments consolidated power in most of the former Warsaw Pact states. As arms control talks progressed, many US troops transferred from Europe to the First Gulf War did not return to their former bases. The high-sounding democratic commitments at the Paris CSCE Summit were followed soon after by the attempted Soviet crackdown in the Baltic states. As the Soviet economy sank to ever-newer lows, Gorbachev's political struggle with Yeltsin sharpened and his proposal to revise the center-republics relationship in the USSR ended instead in the failed August coup. Indeed, the Soviet Union was not the only state in Europe that was falling apart; Yugoslavia erupted into war between Serbia and Croatia by June 1991 and promised further violent disintegration.

Against this background of reform, upheaval, and disintegration, NATO—as well as the EC and CSCE—tried to keep up with extraordinary events operationally while also devoting sufficient high-level time and attention to fundamental questions of reform for all three institutions. The decisions about NATO's purpose and structures ratified in the Rome Declaration were heavily influenced and conditioned not simply by the fast-paced events in Europe but also, perhaps even more fundamentally, by the simultaneous efforts under way aimed at redefining the roles, structures, and powers of the European Community and the CSCE. The French, in particular, pushed for acknowledgment of a European security identity and separate defense capability as part of NATO's recognition of the impending transformation of the EC into the European Union, with the signature of the Maastricht Treaty the following month. Although the United States was willing to accept references to the growing European Security and Defense Policy, or European pillar within NATO, as noted in the Rome Declaration by several specific favorable references to the WEU, Washington insisted that such bodies remain subordinate to NATO as a whole. Many observers, both then and subsequently, claimed that the presence and potential within NATO of a newly united Germany was a crucial factor in many Allies' support for a continued American presence and leadership in Europe.[75] The sharp debates and political struggle over this issue are reflected in the solution hammered out for the heads of state at Rome:

> The Alliance is the essential forum for consultation among its members and the venue for agreement on policies bearing on the security and defence commitments of Allies under the Washington Treaty. Recognising that it is for the European Allies concerned to decide what arrangements are needed for the expression of a common European

foreign and security policy and defence role, we further agree that, as the two processes develop, we will develop practical arrangements to ensure the necessary transparency and complementarity between the European security and defence identity as
it emerges in the Twelve and the WEU, and the Alliance.[76]

Although it would take more than a decade for NATO and the EU to work
out the "practical arrangements" referred to in the Rome statement, by the end
of 1991 the basic directions had been set. The United States would remain a
leading security presence in Europe, NATO would remain the primary instrument of this presence, and the emerging European security identity would be
coordinated with and subordinated to NATO.

The NATO Rome Summit came less than a year after the CSCE Paris
Summit, where many of the same participants accepted fundamental commitments to common values and wide-ranging institutional changes for the
CSCE, some of which were difficult to coordinate or reconcile with specific
decisions made by NATO at Rome. NATO's Rome Declaration specifically
lists and welcomes the institutional reforms to be adopted by the CSCE,
including conflict prevention, crisis management, arms control, and other
security capabilities to be invested in the institutionalized Helsinki Process.[77]
NATO, in particular, welcomed the CSCE-based security achievements such
as the CFE Treaty and the ongoing CSBM negotiations. Some European
leaders—such as Gorbachev, Havel, and Dienstbier—had already expressed
aspirations for an institutionalized CSCE to have a more extensive collective
security role; but as of late 1991, discussion of such ambitions and specific proposals had not advanced very far. As violent conflicts multiplied and spread
in the former Yugoslavia and in several states on the periphery of the former
Soviet Union starting in 1992, proposals multiplied for an expanded military
security capability and role for the CSCE, and with them discussions of the
relationship, coordination, and precedence between the CSCE and NATO.

The most serious conundrum created and left unresolved by NATO decisions
in November 1991 involved NATO's efforts at outreach to the Soviet Union and
former Warsaw Pact states of Central and Eastern Europe. To strengthen and
perpetuate new patterns of political contacts, exchanges, dialogue, and possible
cooperation with their former antagonists to the east, the NATO Allies sought to
institutionalize these activities and the overall relationship. The result was the
proposed establishment of the North Atlantic Cooperation Council (NACC),
building on an ambitious program to develop partnerships with these nations
set out at a NATO ministers' meeting in Copenhagen in June 1991. The NACC,
as proposed at Rome, was basically intended to be a regularized consultative
process, involving periodic meetings at all levels on military, political, and economic matters.

The NACC had two basic problems from its very beginning. First, its membership largely duplicated that of the CSCE, and it was not clear how consultations on security issues in the NACC would differ appreciably from possible discussions on the same subjects in the CSCE. Because exchanges in the NACC would be entirely consultative, and because some states had ambitions to operationalize the CSCE's security role, the NACC had considerably less value to some states than the CSCE, and in fact might be an impediment toward achievement of a pan-European security structure. Second, the prospective Eastern members of the NACC had very different ideas about what they wanted out of their contacts and relationship with NATO. Gorbachev and his colleagues, in what was left of the Soviet Union, tended to visualize some sort of relatively equal partnership between the two sides and two major former adversaries, perhaps along the lines of the US–Soviet collaboration in the UN Security Council during the 1990–91 Gulf crisis and war. However, the crackdown in the Baltic states, a conservative backlash against reform in the USSR, and then the failed August coup all pushed Central and Eastern European states formerly under Soviet tutelage in the Warsaw Pact and the Baltic states independent since September 1991 to look to NATO more for possible membership and protection. Even in early 1990, in the glow of the 1989 revolutions in Eastern Europe, trust in promises from Moscow was low, and individual, largely unofficial calls for some sort of association with or membership in NATO could be heard.[78] Once the Soviet Union disintegrated, most of the Western and Caucasus former republics shared this knee-jerk distrust of Moscow.

Although the thought of NATO membership for the Central and Eastern European states that later eventually joined or have applied seemed far-fetched in late 1991, from the very beginnings of the post–Cold War transformation of Europe's security order, Russia was at a disadvantage with its most immediate neighbors and former allies. This disadvantage was arguably not insurmountable, if the process of reform were to continue within the newly independent Russian Federation, and if Russian foreign policy and behavior were able to allay the fears, traditional suspicions, and animosities of its surrounding states. However, given the disparities between Russia and its former allies and Soviet compatriots in threats perceived and aims for their relationship with NATO, the NACC was probably dead on arrival. The institutional duplication and competition with the CSCE as a security forum made the NACC seem even more superfluous.[79]

As 1991 drew to a close, several important political and institutional decisions with respect to the post–Cold War order of European security had been made. First, the political division of Europe of the preceding four decades had ended, and the dismantling of the military confrontation between the two opposing blocs was already well under way. Even if this was not yet a Europe whole and

free, it was no longer a Europe divided and poised to launch nuclear Armageddon. One could already see on the horizon the nature of future violent conflict
in Europe, which would arise from within, with the disintegration of existing
states, rather than from disagreements and competition between opposing
states. Second, the unification of Germany produced a new European geography deceptively reminiscent of that before World War II and posed the question
of whether Europeans after 1991 could find a place for a united Germany at the
heart of Europe more swiftly and successfully than their ancestors had done
between 1870 and 1945. A quarter century later, the answer to this question is
still being decided. Third, though movement toward a united Europe would
continue and even accelerate through the vehicle of a transformed European
Community, Europe's security would continue to be ensured primarily through
a US presence and leadership, with a transformed NATO as the instrument. As
before the end of the Cold War, the United States maintained global responsibilities in addition to its key role in Europe. However, the United States explicitly decided that its relationship with Europe and European security were key
American interests and committed to continuing participation in NATO as the
primary way to pursue and defend these interests.

Neither Americans nor Europeans may have fully recognized it at the time,
but between 1989 and 1991 they indeed made the most crucial decisions and
steps in crafting a new post–Cold War world order. When President George H.
W. Bush spoke about a "new world order" at the conclusion of the Gulf War and
the end of the Cold War, he was criticized by many because he allegedly never
fully articulated what this concept entailed.[80] Indeed, the post–Cold War Euro-
Atlantic security architecture was constructed during the crucial period before
and after this speech as a set of apparently ad hoc reactions to unforeseen and
unprecedented events and opportunities, in particular responses to sudden conflicts and emergencies. The decisions to continue NATO with a US presence
and leadership, to transform the EC into the EU, and to create a pan-European
institution out of the Helsinki Process were all seminal steps that determined the
basic character and subsequent lines of development of European politics and
security. Nonetheless, however important and prescient each of these decisions
may have been, they did not work out the details of the relationships between
these three overlapping and competing institutions. These fundamental decisions also did not foresee and arguably could not have foreseen the effects on
the perceptions and policies of European leaders wrought by rising nationalism,
democratization, political disintegration, economic transition, and violent conflict in at least two major European countries: the Soviet Union and the Socialist Federal Republic of Yugoslavia. The events in these two European states
were the key factors in shaping the development of the EU, the CSCE, and
NATO—both at the dawning of 1992 and in the years immediately afterward.

## 3. BUILDING THE NEW INSTITUTIONS

## NATO, the EU, and the OSCE

Between June 1991 and June 1992, twenty new states appeared in Europe, replacing two existing states—the Soviet Union and Yugoslavia. The addition of eighteen additional entities to the European and United Nations state and political systems would have been hard enough at any time. The violent breakup of Yugoslavia and a series of conflicts between and within some of the new states on the periphery of the USSR presented an especially daunting challenge for peace and stability in the rest of Europe, given the recent end to the East/West military confrontation and the untried capabilities of Europe's fledgling post–Cold War security institutions. It soon became apparent that both the European Union and the Conference on Security and Cooperation in Europe (CSCE) lacked the mechanisms and institutional capabilities to prevent, suppress, or mediate the conflicts that arose in Yugoslavia and the former Soviet area. Although the North Atlantic Treaty Alliance may have possessed the requisite military capabilities, it lacked the internal consensus that would give it the political will and authority to undertake such tasks. Faced with the growing violence in Yugoslavia and the post-Soviet periphery, states participating in the CSCE hurried to endow the emerging institution with the requisite capabilities for conflict prevention, management, and mediation, in particular the ability to deploy CSCE operations directly to the field. Meanwhile, the EU devoted considerable attention to ratification of the Maastricht Treaty and to deepening the institutions of the new Union as mandated by that pact, including a common foreign and security policy. The EU also began a simultaneous process of widening that would ultimately lead to three new members in 1995 and ten more by 2004. NATO worked through a process of internal debate that ultimately led to its first out-of-area operations in Yugoslavia, moving the Alliance from a collective defense toward a collective security organization. Once that issue was settled by deployment of NATO peacekeepers to Bosnia to enforce the Dayton settlement, in the mid-1990s NATO focused its attention on enlargement of the Alliance to the east.

## THE CONFLICTS OF THE POST-SOVIET PERIPHERY

The core republics of the Soviet Union—Russia, Ukraine, Belarus, and Kazakhstan—emerged from the breakup of the USSR with remarkably little violence. Indeed, aside from the civil war in Tajikistan, most of Central Asia departed the Soviet Union tranquilly, if somewhat reluctantly.[1] After the attempted violent repression of independence advocates in the Baltic Sea republics in January 1991, Estonia, Latvia, and Lithuania also escaped from the Soviet Union cleanly, early, and peacefully. There was some grumbling in the Russian Federation about leaving Crimea with an independent Ukraine, surely not a possibility that Khrushchev envisioned when he transferred the peninsula from the Russian Soviet Federative Socialist Republic to the Ukrainian SSR in 1954.[2] Nonetheless, the population of Crimea voted by a small but clear majority to remain with Ukraine, and dissenters did not resist this choice.

However, in the Soviet republics to the south and west—specifically, Armenia, Azerbaijan, Georgia, and Moldova—ethnic divisions, national minority and language issues, and artificial political boundaries that had existed prior to Soviet times produced violent conflicts in these newly independent states. The first of the conflicts to emerge was between Armenia and Azerbaijan over what was then the Autonomous Region of Nagorno-Karabakh, inhabited largely by ethnic Armenians but under the jurisdiction of Azerbaijan.[3] As glasnost and perestroika loosened the restrictions on the Soviet population, demonstrations with crowds estimated up to the hundreds of thousands broke out in Yerevan in February 1988 protesting the subordination of Nagorno-Karabakh to the authorities in Baku and calling for its transfer to the jurisdiction of the Armenian republic. Hostile reactions from the authorities and the population in the Azerbaijani Soviet Socialist Republic culminated in a pogrom against ethnic Armenians living in the city of Sumgait, north of Baku. This tragedy in turn sparked a reaction against ethnic Azeris in Armenia; the result was massive refugee flows from both sides, as Azeris and Armenians sought refuge among their ethnic kin. Mediation and conflict prevention efforts from Moscow between the two Soviet republics were intermittent and half-hearted. Small-scale clashes, ethnic violence, and slaughters continued. By late 1991, Azerbaijan and Armenia were essentially at war with one another, using sizable stores of weapons and ammunition available to local forces as Soviet authority in the region waned. Soviet troops stationed in the South Caucasus, increasingly on their own as the government in Moscow disintegrated, intervened unpredictably and intermittently in favor of one and then the other side, depending on circumstances and payment.

As Armenia and Azerbaijan gained independence at the end of 1991 and applied for membership in the United Nations and the CSCE, the other participating states were faced with the dilemma of what to do about a budding war between two CSCE states. Czechoslovakia assumed the CSCE Chair from Germany in 1992, and at the Prague Ministerial Council meeting, it decided to send several fact-finding missions to the region both to assess the situation and to attempt to head off more extensive hostilities between Azeris and Armenians.[4] CSCE representatives were additionally motivated by the knowledge that both Yerevan and Baku would soon inherit the extensive stores of Soviet weaponry located on their respective territories, which would increase both their capabilities and the destructiveness of the fighting between them. With the reports of the fact-finding missions in hand, CSCE ministers meeting in Helsinki in March 1992 endorsed a proposal to hold a peace conference between Armenia and Azerbaijan, with the participation and mediation of several interested CSCE participating states. The ministers unexpectedly settled on Minsk as the proposed venue for the conference and ordered the deployment of an advance CSCE civilian monitoring mission to both countries.[5]

Italy was awarded the Chair of the group of CSCE states preparing the Minsk Conference, and representatives from Baku and Yerevan met in Rome separately, but never with each other, during the summer of 1992. As both countries acquired more and better weapons, the process of negotiation broke down, and by mid-1993 serious combat broke out. Armenian forces soundly defeated Azerbaijan's army, but Baku was also preoccupied by an internal political crisis that led to the assumption of the presidency by Heydar Aliev in October 1993. Armenia seized extensive chunks of territory around Nagorno-Karabakh in Azerbaijan proper, including a land connection between Karabakh and Armenia. By early 1994 the proposed Minsk Conference was on its way to becoming the CSCE Minsk Group; Russian efforts led to agreement on a cease-fire, monitored by the Organization for Security and Cooperation in Europe (OSCE), which still holds, and peace negotiations began between Baku and Yerevan, which continue to this day.[6]

As Soviet control in the South Caucasus became increasingly less effective, the Georgian Soviet Socialist Republic also moved quickly in the late 1980s and early 1990s to assert its independence.[7] An upsurge of Georgian national- ist feeling in 1990 led to the election of Zviad Gamsakhurdia, a member of the 1980s Georgian Helsinki group and scion of an old Georgian literary family, as the republic's president. Once in office, Gamsakhurdia took a strong nation- alist line, epitomized by the phrase "Georgia for the Georgians." Efforts to impose Georgian-language usage in the autonomous region of South Ossetia led eventually to communal violence in March 1991; Soviet troops stationed in the republic intervened to restrain attacks by ethnic Georgian militias on the ethnic Ossetian population.[8] The situation in Georgia was further complicated by a violent falling-out among the factions making up the government in Tbilisi, resulting by early 1992 in Gamsakhurdia's flight to his home district and civil war (including major fighting in the capital) between the militias of several warlords.

Georgia began to stabilize only when several of the competing warlords were able to agree in early 1992 on an invitation to former Soviet foreign min- ister Eduard Shevardnadze to assume the presidency in Tbilisi and attempt to establish order among them. Shevardnadze was able to restore a functioning government in Tbilisi but could not end the conflict in South Ossetia, which had asserted its independence from Georgia. In addition, Georgian nationalist intervention in the autonomous region of Abkhazia along with encouragement from Moscow produced resistance from the Abkhaz minority and yet another internal conflict in the late summer of 1992. Moscow successfully ended the fighting in both breakaway entities, but at great cost to Tbilisi. The two enti- ties remained de facto separate from Georgia, with Russian troops present as peacekeepers and Russia as the chief mediator in political settlement and rein- tegration talks in both cases. In addition, to win Boris Yeltsin's "support" in the Abkhaz conflict, Shevardnadze was obliged to agree to Georgian membership in the Commonwealth of Independent States.[9]

Ethnic Moldovan opposition to long-term Russification in the Soviet Repub- lic of Moldova by the late 1980s produced widespread popular support for separation from Moscow. Two major opposition strains appeared in the eth- nic Moldovan, Romanian-speaking population: a movement of pro-Romanian nationalists advocating the transfer of Bessarabia back to Romania, and a larger "Moldovanist" movement favoring recognition of the distinct (in particular from Russian) Moldovan cultural and linguistic identity.[10] On August 31, 1989, Moldovan nationalist deputies in the republic's Supreme Soviet passed the so- called language law making "Moldovan" (i.e., Romanian) in Latin script the republic's official language and requiring all government employees to pass a written language test within five years. This legislation sparked resistance from the Orthodox Christian Turkish, Russian-speaking enclave of Gagauzia in the

south and in particular from the eastern regions of the Moldovan Soviet Socialist Republic on the left or east bank of the Dniestr (Nistru) River, so-called
Transdniestria.[11] Deputies from Transdniestria walked out of the Moldovan legislature in mid-1990. When Moldovan nationalists asserted the republic's sovereignty from Moscow, Transdniestrian leaders proclaimed a separate Soviet
republic in September 1990.

Attempts by the Moldovan authorities in Chisinau to establish political and
physical control of the breakaway Transdniestrian region led to small-scale
clashes of police and militias through much of 1991.[12] Transdniestrian leaders in
Tiraspol received support from Gorbachev's opponents in Moscow, who sought
to derail the Union Treaty and eventually to topple Gorbachev in the August
coup. When the Soviet Union disintegrated, Tiraspol proclaimed Transdniestria to be an independent country. The rest of the world, however, following the
general rule of recognizing only the established constituent Soviet republics,
considered it a part of Moldova. Taking advantage of the windfall of Soviet Army
equipment left on its territory, Moldova attempted to restore its control over the
left bank militarily in the late spring and early summer of 1992. Unfortunately
for Chisinau, there were even greater amounts of Soviet military equipment,
more personnel, and greater expertise in the Transdniestrian region. The Soviet
Fourteenth Army, headquartered in Tiraspol, although ostensibly a Russian unit
from April 1992 and neutral in the conflict, in effect supported the separatists. Its
intervention in the fighting between Chisinau and Tiraspol in June 1992 turned
the tide in favor of the latter, and military hostilities ended in a stalemate with a
cease-fire brokered by Yeltsin on July 21, 1992.

One dog that did not bark in this series of conflicts along the Soviet Union's
southwestern periphery was Crimea. The Belovezhskaya agreement, Alma Ata
declaration, and general principles of international recognition embraced by
the West established that existing Soviet republic boundaries would be the basis
for the borders of the newly independent states, but there was considerable discontent in some circles in Russia over the fact that Crimea would remain with
Ukraine.[13] The transfer of Crimea from the Russian to the Ukrainian Soviet
republic in 1954 by Soviet Communist Party leader Nikita Khrushchev seemed
immaterial as long as the USSR existed, but many Russian nationalists considered (and still consider) Crimea as fundamentally Russian land since its incorporation in the empire by Catherine the Great in 1783. However, Yeltsin's need
for the support of Ukrainian leader Kravchuk in his project to defeat Gorbachev
by dismantling the Soviet Union meant that the new Russian government
would not push the issue of Crimea.[14] A referendum held on the peninsula in
1992 indicated majority popular support for remaining with Ukraine, and subsequent negotiations over several years produced agreement on an autonomous
status within Ukraine that appeared to settle the issue.[15]

Although Russia itself remained largely untouched by the fighting over borders and territory of the newly independent states, there was one major exception—Chechnya. After helping to ensure that Estonia would remain unaffected by military actions related to the August coup, Soviet general Dzhokar Dudaev returned in 1991 to his native Republic of Chechnya to head a secular nationalist government that sought to assert the region's independence from Russia.[16] Neither Moscow nor any foreign state recognized Chechnya's claim to independence, but Dudaev and his colleagues had widespread support within the republic and for almost three years the government in Moscow felt too weak and preoccupied to take action against them. By the mid-1990s this would change and Chechnya would become a major Russian security problem.

Notwithstanding any real or apparent similarities between them, these conflicts on the Soviet periphery arose, erupted into violence, and developed to considerable degree because of local grievances, animosities, conditions, and aspirations. In this sense, the issues and conflicts were not manufactured by Moscow or by Russian government policies. However, the factors common to them all—proximity to Russia and the involvement of ethnic Russians and Russian speakers—ensured that Moscow would be concerned with them and would seek to be involved in how they were resolved. Furthermore, there was no consensus among the political elite in Russia over the preferred nature of Russia's involvement in each of these countries and conflicts or the terms on which they should best be settled. Events in this region and these countries, however, constituted a continuing, primary security concern for Russia, irrespective of the policies or any general line adopted toward them by Moscow at any particular time. Given the disintegration of the USSR, what once might have been internal Soviet problems were now international issues between newly recognized state actors in the European security system. Yet Western interlocutors often did not fully understand the depth of Russian concerns or the importance of these countries and issues in Russian foreign and security policy.[17]

# THE VIOLENT BREAKUP OF YUGOSLAVIA

The disintegration of the Soviet Union, one of the two global powers for more than four decades, was potentially the more cataclysmic event, but the violent breakup of the much smaller Socialist Federal Republic of Yugoslavia arguably had a far more profound effect on major Euro-Atlantic powers and European security institutions.[18] According to a number of observers, the dissolution of Yugoslavia had been coming on for some time since the death of Josip Broz

Tito in 1980. Whatever the post-Tito prospects of the multinational, multieth-nic Balkan federation might otherwise have been, Serbian president Slobodan Milošević's use of Serb nationalism, inflamed by the explosive Kosovo question, to seek political primacy and control over the other republics of the federation almost certainly ensured the country's disintegration. By mid-1990, Milošević had asserted firm control over Yugoslavia's southern federal units (Serbia, Montenegro, Macedonia, Kosovo, and Vojvodina), with Slovenia and Croatia actively resisting Belgrade, and Bosnia-Herzegovina caught in the middle. Milošević used the ethnic Serb populations in Croatia and Bosnia to establish fifth columns and breakaway entities within these republics. By the end of May 1991, the country was on the brink of war.

US secretary of state James Baker visited Belgrade immediately after the inaugural meeting of the CSCE Ministerial Council in Berlin in June 1991, met with representatives of all the Yugoslav republics, but did not succeed in convincing the Serb, Croat, and Slovene leaders to avoid secession and violence.[19] War broke out when Slovenia and Croatia proclaimed their inde-pendence from the Yugoslav federation on June 25, 1991. Essentially under the control of Serbia and Milošević personally, the Yugoslav National Army (Jugoslovenska narodna armija, JNA) attacked both republics. After two weeks of fighting, Slovenia successfully fought off the JNA attacks and escaped from Serb control. Croatia was not as fortunate. Serb-supported local ethnic-Serbian forces controlled most of the Krajina, a mountainous crescent in central Croatia along much of the border with Bosnia. JNA armor and infan-try forces loyal to Belgrade attacked major Croatian population centers near Serbia in eastern Slavonia.

War in Yugoslavia broke out while CSCE representatives were meeting on national minorities in Geneva. In discussions among senior delegation rep-resentatives in Geneva and emergency sessions of the Committee of Senior Officials—the other hat of the Vienna negotiators for confidence- and security-building measures—the CSCE debated how to deal with the Yugoslav conflict, the first real security crisis in Europe since the groundbreaking CSCE summit in Paris the previous November. Weary from the nine-month effort at coalition building to oust Saddam Hussein from Kuwait, US leaders in the Bush adminis-tration were reluctant to get involved. Secretary Baker's reported comment that "we don't have a dog in that fight" seemed to sum up the American attitude. However, leaders of some states from the soon-to-be European Union, with the Maastricht Treaty only months away, were eager to use the Yugoslav crisis as an opportunity to demonstrate the potential of an independent European foreign and security policy. The European Community (EC) Troika stepped in and inserted observers in Croatia but ultimately failed to curtail the current fighting or prevent expansion of the war.[20]

External efforts to halt the conflict in Yugoslavia or to contain the effects were largely ineffective. Fighting in Croatia subsided a bit toward the end of 1991 following deployment of the EC Monitoring Mission (ECMM). However, this lull may have occurred more because Serb forces had captured most of the territories inhabited by their co-ethnics than because of EC and UN intervention; fighting renewed after the winter in early 1992. In February 1992, the United Nations inserted a peacekeeping force—the United Nations Protection Force (UNPROFOR)—whose mandate was primarily to protect the civilian population and not to halt the conflict. In any case, UNPROFOR was not strong enough to restrain the determined combatants, and some observers joked that the ECMM's white uniforms simply made mission personnel better targets.[21]

At first, the United States and some of its Allies hoped to keep Yugoslavia together, but they soon abandoned this aspiration. Nonetheless, Washington saw recognition of former Yugoslav republics as a card to be played in seeking to stop or restrain the fighting. Unfortunately, the haste of some European leaders sympathetic to Serbia's victims to recognize first Slovenia and Croatia, and then Bosnia, exemplified by German foreign minister Hans-Dietrich Genscher, arguably gave Milošević even more reason to grab territory when and where he could.[22] The war spread to Bosnia-Herzegovina immediately after recognition by the United States and EU states on April 6–7, 1992. The Serb bombardment of Vukovar, the gratuitous shelling of Dubrovnik, and then the ethnic cleansing and Serbian concentration camps discovered in Bosnia and shown by international media in the summer of 1992 brought increasing calls for intervention. International reaction was loud but ineffective. The UN expanded UNPROFOR from Croatia alone to include Bosnia-Herzegovina, but with a mandate to protect civilians and deliver humanitarian aid. Following the killing of dozens of civilians by a mortar shell in a Sarajevo market in May 1992, the United States successfully pushed for the imposition of UN economic sanctions on Serbia. After a personal appeal from President Bush to President Yeltsin, Russia went along. The revelation of war crimes and concentration camps prompted the first steps in the establishment of the eventual International Criminal Tribunal on Yugoslavia, which works to this day in The Hague.

Diplomatic efforts at intervention and mediation also were unsuccessful. An international conference in London in August 1992 assembled representatives of the belligerents (including one of Radovan Karadzic's last appearances in Western Europe until his arrest in Belgrade and transfer to The Hague in 2008), the EU, UN, and the United States. The ensuing peace process led by UN special representative Cyrus Vance and EU special representative Robert Owen (a former UK foreign secretary) produced a plan for a loose confederation of Serb, Croat, and Muslim areas, which was torpedoed by the incoming Clinton administration. Secretary of State Warren Christopher's trip to the region in mid-1993 and subsequent multilateral efforts in the UN did no better. The UN Security Council solemnly established six UN protected areas for Muslim enclaves in Bosnia, but UN states were unwilling to provide sufficient troops or rules of engagement to defend these areas militarily. As the fighting and slaughter continued (gruesomely chronicled by CNN and the BBC) and the flow of refugees to Western Europe intensified, cries for intervention intensified.[23]

The whole sad story of the Balkan wars of the 1990s and the failed attempts at international intervention are recounted elsewhere. It is sufficient here to note the quick demonstration of the insufficiency of EU foreign policy and defense capabilities to manage the Yugoslav crisis, and the longer, more agonizing process of the failure of UN intervention. By late 1993, public pressure to "do something" had grown enormously in many European states and in the United States. In particular, a number of US senators—including the 1996 Republican presidential candidate, Robert Dole—called on the Clinton administration to arm the Bosnians and Croats in their fight against the Serbs.

The Clinton administration was not interested in direct military intervention in the Balkans, especially following the October 1993 "Blackhawk Down" debacle in Mogadishu, but domestic and international pressure gradually prompted diplomatic and indirect military responses. As UNPROFOR continued to display an inability (and on the part of senior UN leadership an apparent unwillingness) to defend the safe areas, many critics pointed more and more to NATO as a possible instrument with which to respond. Theoretical discussions begun at London and Rome over provision of security by NATO in areas near but not in the territory of member states took on a more operational tone. The international community was then galvanized by another Serb mortar slaughter of Muslim civilians in Sarajevo in February 1994, which convinced NATO to deploy troops to enforce a zone around Sarajevo that would exclude Serbian heavy weapons. Russia agreed and joined in enforcement of this Sarajevo exclusion zone.[24]

For a while, the NATO intervention in Sarajevo halted the Serb shelling, and no-fly zones over the protected areas with NATO participation had some effect. In 1994–95, Serb forces pushed the envelope until the infamous capture of Srebrenica (over the ineffectual resistance of the hapless Dutch UNPROFOR detachment) and the slaughter of about 7,000 Muslim civilians. This time the United States and NATO took decisive military action, conducting an effective air campaign against Serbian forces in Bosnia and lending support to Croat ground forces that recaptured territories in Croatia and Bosnia long held by Serbian troops and separatist authorities.[25]

It was US and NATO action that brought Milošević to Dayton and obtained the opportunity for peace in Croatia and Bosnia-Herzegovina. Once the terms of the peace were agreed on, the Clinton administration was determined that

they would not be implemented by what Washington saw as a thoroughly ineffective, discredited UN headed by the weak and waffling secretary-general,
Boutros Boutros-Ghali.[26] The United States and its Allies agreed to divide civilian administration of the peace in Bosnia-Herzegovina between a high representative and staff from the European Union and a civilian OSCE mission,
headed by an American. Peacekeeping would be provided by an International
Force (IFOR) led by NATO countries, the United States first and foremost.
Russia agreed to participate in implementation of the Dayton Accords, including the peacekeeping forces. However, unlike other national detachments
participating in IFOR, the Russians declined to put themselves under the command of the NATO Supreme Allied Commander Europe. Instead, US secretary
of defense William Perry reached agreement with Russian minister of defense
Pavel Grachev that Russian troops in IFOR would be under the command of
the American commander wearing his other hat as commander in chief of the
US European Command.[27]

The lengthy crisis and wars in the former Yugoslavia played a crucial role in
the institutional development of NATO, the EU, and the OSCE when all three
were in formative stages of their post–Cold War redefinition. One might argue
that all three were already headed in the general direction in which the events
in the Balkans in the first half of the 1990s ended up pushing them. Nonetheless, the violence in the former Yugoslavia and the destabilization it spread
through much of Europe lent a sense of urgency to the process of change of
the European security architecture and produced many decisions taken out of
perceived operational necessity rather than reasoned institutional analysis and
debate. The apparent result by 1995 was that NATO went out of area, and in
the process reinforced its primacy as the leading provider of military security
in Europe. The European Union became deeper financially and economically
but temporized on developing its security capability. The OSCE developed a
large but haphazard set of field operations and capabilities as its participating
states used it to respond in a largely ad hoc fashion to the burgeoning number of
crises besetting southeastern Europe in the early 1990s. The overall and considerably unplanned result was to establish many of the main lines of the development of Europe's security architecture for the next two decades.

## NATO: OUT OF AREA OR OUT OF BUSINESS

The redefinition of NATO that took place between the June 1990 London
Summit and the November 1991 Rome Summit was primarily conceptual and

political. The transformation of the Alliance from a collective defense organization to a collective security organization played out in an operational sense, defined by the actions as much as the statements of NATO Allies, in its response to the Yugoslav wars from 1991 to 1995. The documents worked out and adopted by the Allied heads of state at the London and Rome gatherings presented far-reaching, fundamental, programmatic statements on the changes in the theoretical bases of the Alliance necessitated by the end of the Cold War and the disintegration of the Soviet empire. Had Yugoslavia not descended into chaos and produced instability requiring a military response, however, the changes in NATO's purpose and mission could easily have remained largely on paper. Instead, the need to stem the expanding conflict in the Balkans eventually led NATO into action and out of area.

Over the course of its entire forty-year existence during the Cold War, NATO successfully deterred any Soviet attack on its Western European member states, but NATO countries under the aegis of the Alliance did not conduct a single combat operation against an external foe.[28] The NATO countries' armed forces trained together and conducted joint exercises, and NATO's military committee and military leadership agreed and adopted joint standards, procedures, and equipment. Ironically, the First Gulf War against Saddam Hussein in 1990–91 offered the first large-scale opportunity for NATO to test its combined forces and procedures in real life in harm's way. NATO countries participating in the Gulf War coalition performed superbly in both logistical preparations and combat operations. In addition, NATO command, control, and communications standards and procedures proved to be convenient and efficient guidelines for integrating non-NATO participants into the coalition. Indeed, one of the major lessons of the Gulf War was that NATO had a purpose extending not only after the end of the Cold War but beyond the territory of its member states. The US ambassador to NATO noted in May 1991:

> Among the new lessons we learned from the war were:
> - The desirability of streamlined decisionmaking among European states to respond to crises on the periphery of NATO's territory; and
> - The need for an integrated European force for deployment out-of-area.[29]

NATO's new Strategic Concept, which was adopted at the November 1991 Rome Summit, reflected broad consensus within the Alliance that the recent fundamental changes in the European and global strategic situations had altered both the nature of the threats against NATO Allies and the range of political and military responses required from the Alliance.[30] The 1991 Strategic Concept asserts that collective defense remains the primary purpose of the Alliance, but how NATO might be involved in the prevention, management, and resolution of crises on its periphery that affect the Allies' security also is discussed at some length. The document envisions possible Alliance responses to global threats, such as the proliferation of weapons of mass destruction, disruption of the flow of vital resources, or terrorism.

The war that broke out in Yugoslavia in June 1991 fairly obviously constituted the most immediate crisis and threat to stability in the NATO region. However, the Alliance was slow to intervene, not simply because the guiding rules and operative mechanisms for out of area activities had not yet been fully worked out and agreed upon, but even more because many Allies were deeply divided in their analyses of the causes of the crisis and in their sympathies toward the various parties to the conflict. In a very rough way, Europe's divisions over the Balkan wars of 1991 mirrored those of the summer of 1914 after the Serb nationalist Gavrilio Princip assassinated Archduke Ferdinand. Although it was nearly impossible to find any leader or state that directly supported Serb leader Slobodan Milošević, former central and Habsburg powers such as Germany and Austria were clearly more in sympathy with Slovenia's and Croatia's efforts to separate from Yugoslavia, whereas traditional Serb sympathizers such as the United Kingdom were far more reluctant to agree to the breakup of the Yugoslav federation.[31] Thus, although NATO offered verbal support to UN peacekeeping and reconciliation efforts, the Alliance at first took no steps to intervene itself.

Furthermore, even as the Yugoslav crisis deepened from late 1991 into 1992 and the war expanded to Bosnia, NATO had to take care of important institutional and capacity-building business. In particular, NATO leaders faced questions regarding the possible use of forces or resources of NATO Allies in CSCE or EU operations, and the relationship of these institutions to the Alliance. At the Oslo Ministerial Meeting in June 1992, NATO foreign ministers expressed support for the CSCE's development of crisis management and peacekeeping capabilities (see below).[32] The Oslo Ministerial also expressed support for designation of the Western European Union (WEU) as the defense component of the European Union, formally adopted at Maastricht in December 1991, calling the action a "means of strengthening the European pillar of the Alliance."[33] Such declarations of principle called for more practical decisions on how to designate which forces of which Allies belonged to NATO, which to the WEU, and under what conditions such forces might be made available to WEU or CSCE operations. In principle, the United States supported the development of a European defense identity but feared that in practice designation of a specific European force might weaken overall NATO strength, which the United States considered crucial to ensuring European security. And finally, there was the question of what forces NATO itself should possess and use to respond in post–Cold War crisis missions.

To answer such questions, during 1992 the Alliance began to develop standing rapid reaction forces. Then, in 1993–94, the Alliance worked out and adopted the Combined Joint Task Force concept, which in practice allowed specific forces to be designated for use either in NATO or WEU operations, squaring the circle of a separate European defense identity with NATO unity and primacy. Discussions in NATO's Defense Planning Committee by mid-1992 produced "particular progress" on establishing new reaction forces called for in the most recent Strategic Concept.[34] Within a few months, the Allies agreed to use one of these newly adapted forces, the Standing Naval Force in the Mediterranean (STANAVFORMED), to assist in enforcement of UN economic sanctions against Serbia-Montenegro (at the time, the Federal Republic of Yugoslavia) adopted in May 1992.[35]

As the war in the former Yugoslavia intensified and spread to Bosnia in 1992, the concerns of NATO Allies about the situation in the Balkans intensified dramatically. Beginning with Rome in November 1991, the conflict in the Balkans featured prominently in NATO heads of state and ministerial meetings.[36] However, NATO as an institution remained officially uninvolved in the Balkan conflicts. Instead, the Allies used NATO meetings for coordination of national policy toward the former Yugoslavia and employed the United Nations for actual intervention. In fact, the NATO Allies made up a large portion of the forces dedicated to UNPROFOR in Bosnia and Croatia, with commanders drawn from Canada, France, and the United Kingdom.[37] NATO's slowness to become formally involved in the former Yugoslavia might be explained partly by institutional inertia, but fundamental differences over analysis of the situation and proper policy responses probably played at least as great or a greater role in the slow and limited response. The deep disagreement over recognition of the former republics of Yugoslavia is a prime example of such discord, with German foreign minister Genscher according unilateral recognition to Croatia and Slovenia in December 1991 over sharp objections of some European colleagues and the United States.[38] During much of 1992 and 1993, both the Bush and Clinton administrations sought, in different ways, to encourage the European Allies to take a primary role in containing the conflict. Nothing worked, and the situation kept getting worse.

The NATO Allies lurched from crisis to crisis as the Alliance gradually became involved as a whole, and not simply through its individual members, in responding to the conflict. By the end of 1992, NATO was not only using STANAVFORMED to help enforce the UN arms embargo on the region and sanctions on Serbia-Montenegro, but also had supplied assets and equipment to UNPROFOR in Sarajevo, was using NATO aircraft with E-3A airborne warning and control systems to monitor the UN no-fly zone over Bosnia-Herzegovina, and expressed a willingness to contribute to enforcement of the no-fly zone.[39] When the UN designated six cities and towns in Bosnia-Herzegovina as "safe areas," to be free from the threat of military activities, NATO ministers offered

Alliance air power to enforce the decision.[40] The "dual-key" command structure, requiring any NATO enforcement action also to be approved by a senior UN official — in effect, the secretary-general, Boutros-Ghali — rendered NATO involvement somewhat less than impressive.[41]

Another mortar attack on the central Sarajevo marketplace on Saturday, February 4, 1994, killing sixty-eight and wounding more than two hundred civilians, provided the impetus for deeper NATO military involvement.[42] Humanitarian outrage from Western publics at atrocities portrayed on television news remained the one constant among the NATO Allies throughout the conflict, and for the longest time it was the single strongest motivating factor for the Alliance. Led by a terminally ill secretary-general, Manfred Woerner, on February 9, 1994, NATO finally went out of area on the ground, declaring an exclusion zone for heavy weapons around Sarajevo, to be enforced by Allied troops, and giving the Bosnian Serbs ten days to comply.[43] The Bosnian Serbs barely made the deadline around Sarajevo; then, on February 28, NATO aircraft shot down four Serb jets that were in violation of the safe area around Gorazde in eastern Bosnia.[44]

The Sarajevo exclusion zone initially provided encouragement to those in Europe and North America who desired more decisive intervention to halt the fighting in Bosnia. However, the reluctance of UN leaders to authorize more direct attacks on Serb forces besieging Muslim populations and continuing disagreement among NATO Allies over whether to pursue negotiations or military actions soon allowed the situation to ease back into the cycle of fighting, slaughter, and ineffective response that had characterized the war in Bosnia from the beginning. The infamous UN dual-key authorization system proved spectacularly ineffective, and Serb forces attacked Muslims in Gorazde, Bihac, and elsewhere. It finally took another set of disasters in the summer of 1995, including the capture by Serbs and binding of UNPROFOR peacekeepers to posts to ward off NATO air strikes and the Srebrenica slaughter, to galvanize the Alliance into action. Even then, only a confluence of developments and actions largely resulting from US leadership produced the September 1995 NATO intervention, which led eventually to the Dayton Agreement and NATO peacekeeping in Bosnia.

## NATO: THE ROLE OF US LEADERSHIP

NATO was seized with the crisis in the Balkans by early 1992, but it took a long time for the Alliance to develop a coherent political response. From the very beginning, when Secretary Baker proclaimed that "we don't have a dog in that fight," the Bush administration attempted to avoid direct US involvement. Bush offered only lukewarm support to the August 1992 Conference on Yugoslavia and to former secretary of state Cyrus Vance's joint mediation effort with former British foreign secretary David Owen. Presidential candidate Bill Clinton roundly criticized President Bush for his insufficiently robust response to the war in Bosnia. However, once Clinton assumed office, he rejected the Vance-Owen proposed settlement plan and promptly sent Secretary of State Warren Christopher across the Atlantic to try to get the Europeans to take the lead. For months, political debate in the United States focused on helping the Bošniaks by lifting the arms embargo, the so-called lift and strike. However, a number of Washington's closest US Allies, in particular those with forces deployed in UNPROFOR, opposed supplying more arms to the region and pressed for more negotiations.

Growing public and political pressure from Capitol Hill as the news from the Balkans continued to be unremittingly bad eventually moved the Clinton administration to a more activist stance. In addition, the first steps toward support for NATO enlargement—including the genesis of the Partnership for Peace (see chapter 4), supported in particular by the US national security adviser Anthony Lake—made it imperative that the Alliance remain an active and viable policy tool. Washington was one of the more vocal supporters of NATO's role in the Sarajevo exclusion zone. Within Bosnia, the United States played a central role in brokering a truce between the warring Croat and Bošniak forces, resulting in the early 1994 formation of the Bošniak-Croat federation, which enabled full attention to be turned to defeating the Bosnian Serbs.[45] The Clinton administration provided significant assistance through private contractors in training the new Bosnian and especially Croatian armed forces. Also, in the spring of 1994, the US administration turned a blind eye as arms began to flow from suppliers in the region to the Croats and through Croatia to the Bosnians. Finally, the return of the US ambassador to Germany, Richard Holbrooke, to Washington to assume the post of assistant secretary of state for European affairs proved to be a crucial step in energizing the Clinton administration to intervene actively in stopping the conflict.[46]

None of the Allies was strong enough to lead NATO action on Bosnia on its own, and in any case few were inclined to do so.[47] For most of the war the United Kingdom, the second-largest military power in the Alliance, was opposed to what it considered undue stress on military action, favoring the provision of relief to civilian populations and negotiations. France, the other major military power in the Alliance, was just beginning its two-decade post–Cold War journey back into NATO's military structures and vacillated on how forcefully to intervene and in what manner. Secretary-General Manfred Woerner, a strong proponent of NATO going out of area, was far out in front of his own country, still burdened with paying for reunification and limited by Cold War era restrictions on military action outside its borders. Though not without occasional difficulties, the United States and NATO maintained cooperation with Russia throughout the war in Bosnia. It took a personal letter from President Bush to President Yeltsin to get Moscow to go along with adoption of UN economic sanctions against Serbia-Montenegro in May 1992.[48] Russian foreign minister Andrei Kozyrev joined Western ministers in the Joint Action Program in the spring of 1993, and Russian forces supported and participated in the Sarajevo exclusion zone. In April 1994, Russia joined the United States, the United Kingdom, France, and Germany in the Contact Group established to steer negotiations for a settlement in Bosnia.

Policy disagreements among Contact Group members and Allies continued to prevent decisive action against continued fighting throughout Bosnia into mid-1995, creating a crisis of credibility for the Alliance and producing realistic moves in the US Senate to lift the embargo over the objections of the White House. Continued Serb attacks on safe areas, massacres in Srebrenica and Sarajevo, and public humiliation of Allied peacekeepers finally produced a sense of crisis in the Alliance and political peril in the White House sufficient to move the United States and the Alliance to action.[49] NATO air strikes combined with effective ground campaigns by Croat forces in both Croatia and Bosnia brought the Bosnian Serbs and Serbian president Milošević to the table. Three weeks of negotiations in November 1995 at Wright-Patterson Air Force Base in Dayton produced agreement on reunification, political structures, territorial divisions, and military enforcement in Bosnia-Herzegovina. In December 1995, NATO ministers agreed to deploy Alliance troops to enforce the terms of the Dayton settlement.[50] The ministers in particular welcomed Russian participation in the military implementation force to be deployed in Bosnia-Herzegovina.[51]

NATO's history of involvement in the former Yugoslavia from 1991 to 1995 was troubled, but the result for Europe's security architecture was profound. Driven as much by events as by any overarching guiding vision, the Alliance revised and renewed its force structures and dramatically altered and augmented its overall mission by deploying forces outside the national territories of its own member states to provide stability and security to the broader region. To employ the terminology of political scientists, NATO became a collective security organization as well as a collective defense organization. The experience in the former Yugoslavia in the first half of the 1990s also showed that NATO remained essentially a vehicle for American involvement and leadership in European security affairs. Other Allies were unquestionably important in the process of transformation NATO underwent in the Yugoslav crucible, but it was essentially American vacillation and then American decisiveness that determined in the end both when and how the Alliance would act. This was certainly one of the most basic lessons US political elites drew from the experience of Bosnia—NATO must be activist, and the United States must lead to ensure a proper response to crises and maintain stability in Europe and the world. Although such an outcome may not have been surprising, it is nonetheless both material and important for understanding subsequent events to recognize these basic conclusions that American thinkers and policymakers drew from the lengthy crisis in the Balkans.

Finally, it is important to note that Russia remained throughout an active and integrated member of the Euro-Atlantic policy community in addressing the wars in Croatia and Bosnia-Herzegovina. To be sure, Moscow was not always cooperative or easy to convince, but neither were Paris, London, Bonn, and a number of other Allies and partners. Russia participated in negotiations, deliberations, and decisionmaking, and generally observed whatever consensus may have been reached. As IFOR began to deploy in late 1995 and early 1996, the dream of a Europe whole and free from Vancouver to Vladivostok might well still seem to be alive.

## MAKING A EUROPEAN UNION: MAASTRICHT AND BEYOND

In June 1991, the European Community, in expectation of soon becoming the European Union, volunteered to take the lead in responding to the war that had just erupted between Serbia, Croatia, and Slovenia in Yugoslavia. The capabilities with respect to foreign policy and security of the nascent united Europe soon proved not to be up to the task. Between 1991 and December 1995, the EU continued efforts to develop the European Security and Defence Policy and to assert a distinct role for the EU in European security affairs. However, the demands of reaching agreement and creating the institutions intrinsic to the other aspects of the European Union, along with some unexpected events and setbacks, repeatedly diverted the attention of EU states and leaders from the issues of the European Security and Defence Policy and the EU's role in European security affairs. By the end of the Dayton negotiations and implementation of the agreement in Bosnia-Herzegovina, the EU had carved out a significant political, foreign policy role in European security affairs, but for the time being it had clearly ceded primacy in defense and military issues to NATO.

After discussions at CSCE meetings in Geneva and Vienna in late June 1991 on how to respond to the war in Yugoslavia, the EC troika resolved to exercise

Europe's foreign and security policy capabilities anticipated under the Maastricht Treaty by sending a monitoring mission to prevent widening of the conflict (see above). At a July 7, 1991, meeting with representatives of the Yugoslav republics, agreement was reached on the European Community Monitoring Mission under the authority of the EC troika to encourage cessation of the fighting in Slovenia and Croatia.[52] The war in Slovenia ended before the mission could be deployed, and the ECMM had no apparent effect on reducing the fighting in Croatia. Some ECMM personnel became casualties when they were caught between the belligerent parties. Although the ECMM continued its operations for a considerable time after UNPROFOR was deployed in Croatia and Bosnia-Herzegovina—and even extended its activities into Hungary, Bulgaria, and Albania—it was deemed a failure by most observers because of the EC's inability to deploy a sufficiently large and robust force to halt hostilities in Croatia and to prevent expansion of the war to Bosnia.

Meanwhile, the European Council's meeting in Maastricht in December 1991 completed work on the treaty, which was formally signed on February 7, 1992. As an integral part of creating the European Union, the Maastricht Treaty—or the Treaty on European Union—expanded the earlier European political cooperation into the Common Foreign and Security Policy and also envisioned that the EU might have a common defense policy, possibly leading eventually to a common defense.[53] The Maastricht Treaty called the WEU "an integral part of the development of the European Union" and singled out the WEU as the primary institution to implement EU decisions with defense implications.[54] For its part, the WEU at Maastricht invited EU member states to become WEU members or observers. The EU–WEU relationship had been carefully agreed on in principle with NATO and the United States, and the move was welcomed by the Alliance's heads of state in the Rome Summit Statement.[55] The Maastricht language and provisions on security and defense constituted a key compromise in an ongoing battle between the Europeanists, led by France, who sought to create a separate, independent European defense capability, and the Atlanticists, led by the United Kingdom and the United States, who sought to maintain NATO's primacy.

The ratification and implementation of the Maastricht Treaty, as well as the development of the Common Foreign and Security Policy and the WEU, took considerably longer than anticipated and absorbed a great deal of political attention that might otherwise have been turned toward operations in the Balkans. The process of transforming the EC into the EU ran suddenly off the rails in June 1992, when 50.7 percent of Danish voters rejected the treaty in a referendum.[56] Fears for the process of European integration intensified when a bare majority of French voters accepted the Maastricht pact in a September 1992 referendum. With much of Europe mired in recession in the years

1992–93, voters in many countries were prone to populist and anti-incumbent appeals that threatened to leave the Treaty on European Union as one of the casualties. European political leaders were forced to turn inward, paying more attention to the popular moods in their own countries, to ensure continuation of the process of European integration. While holding the EU presidency in the first half of 1993, the Danes held a second referendum, this time winning popular approval for the Treaty on European Union.

Perhaps no European country suffered as much domestic political difficulty over the treaty as Germany, where a reluctant population and political elite were extremely hard to persuade to give up the deutsche mark for monetary union.[57] The expenses of integrating the states of the former East Germany turned out to be considerably greater than initially expected in the euphoria of late 1989 and 1990. Furthermore, the disappearance of the Soviet threat with the end of the Cold War loosed significant pacifist and antimilitarist sentiment in opposition to Germany's hesitant participation in the first Gulf War and NATO involvement in the Yugoslav conflicts. Chancellor Helmut Kohl made a number of concessions to his French counterpart on trade and economic issues in seeking to make the newly united Germany a responsible partner in the nascent European Union. However, Kohl's domestic political colleagues and German institutions, particularly the Bundesbank, had a number of red lines on how monetary union must be implemented in return for abandoning Germany's strong national currency. It was not until Kohl obtained agreement on full independence of the European Central Bank from political influence and its location in Germany that he could agree to ratify Maastricht. Germany did so on October 11, 1993, and the treaty entered into force on November 1, 1993.

The debate over the proper nature and development of a European defense capability and its concrete expression in the WEU also required considerable attention and energy from European and North American political and security officials. The French in particular pushed for the WEU to develop distinct roles and capabilities. In June 1992, at a meeting at Petersberg Castle near Bonn, the WEU ministers adopted the so-called Petersberg Tasks, an enumeration of the purposes for which WEU forces might be used:

- humanitarian and rescue tasks;
- peacekeeping tasks; and
- tasks of combat forces in crisis management, including peacemaking.

The WEU member states also established committees and centers designed to support field operations, and they drew up a list of national forces from member states on which the organization could call. The WEU deployed several small operations in the Balkans, supporting NATO's STANAVFORMED monitoring operation in the Adriatic (1993–1996), the OSCE Sanctions Assistance Missions along the Danube (1993–1996), and a police contingent in Mostar in Herzegovina (1994–1996).[58]

Washington was particularly concerned that French-led attempts to assert a separate identity and role for the WEU, including designation of specific European military units to the WEU, would end up eroding NATO military capabilities and political solidarity. American fears struck sympathetic chords in a number of more Atlanticist EU member states, in particular the United Kingdom. The course of international attempts at intervention and peacemaking in Bosnia from 1992 to 1995 demonstrated to all but the most diehard Europeanists the continuing desirability of a US presence in Europe and NATO for European security. Nonetheless, the often acrimonious dialogue with Paris and like-minded Europeans over a European defense identity and burden sharing eventually brought Washington to a better understanding that at times some European Allies might wish to engage in military or security operations in which the United States had neither a desire nor need to participate. US officials found a solution to the dilemma in the concept of the combined joint task force (CJTF; also see chapter 4), which was first suggested to NATO Allies by US secretary of defense Les Aspin in the autumn of 1993 and elaborated and adopted over the next couple of years.[59] The United States found it particularly difficult to reach agreement with France on the precise terms and composition of CJTFs, a situation that was almost certainly exacerbated by the continuing French separation from NATO's formal military structures. In fact, the debate over the theory and practice of CJTFs in many respects may be seen as one of the first important steps on the part of Paris toward eventual reintegration over a decade and a half later into the Alliance's military structures.

As the Maastricht Treaty's ratification process lurched slowly toward completion, the EU devoted an increasing share of its attention to widening Europe (chapter 4 examines the establishment of formal criteria for enlargement and the first wave of EU expansion in the 1990s). However, EU aspirations to exercise the new institutions and policy competencies of the union remained strong, even though the United States increasingly dominated the debate and response to the war in Bosnia in 1994–95. Evidence of continuing EU ambitions may be seen in the events that accompanied and followed immediately after the conclusion of the Dayton negotiations. Although the agreement is known by the name of the Ohio city in which it was reached, the treaty that embodies the accords was signed in Paris. Furthermore, though the United States and NATO took the lead in implementing the military aspects of the settlement, the EU assumed primary responsibility for executing the political provisions, with the creation and appointment of an EU high representative to oversee the process.[60]

## FROM CSCE TO OSCE: THE HELSINKI PROCESS
## BECOMES AN ORGANIZATION

The United States, Russia, and other non-EU states participated in the political side of conflict prevention and conflict management in Europe through the other major actor in the European security pantheon—the CSCE—which during this same period also developed new and significant security competencies, institutions, and capabilities in response not only to the wars in the former Yugoslavia but also to the conflicts on the post-Soviet periphery. A number of the decisions made at the November 1990 CSCE Paris Summit showed that even at that time most of the participating states were already exploring ideas about how the Helsinki Process might be used to prevent or manage some of the conflicts visible on Europe's post–Cold War horizon.[61] During the second half of the 1980s, the CSCE had slowly and painfully come to agreement that participating states might legitimately express concern about unusual or emergency situations in another participating state, and in some cases might even offer to assist.[62] However, the mechanisms agreed to for such expressions of concern or assistance were cumbersome, consensual, and slow. The Charter of Paris for a New Europe had established the Conflict Prevention Center (CPC), but as war broke out in Yugoslavia in June 1991, there was no detailed operational guidance on what this center should be doing.[63]

The conflicts in the former Yugoslavia and the periphery of the former Soviet Union quickly posed a threat to the stability and security of large portions of the CSCE area, and the urgent need for decisive responses accelerated the process already under way of giving the CSCE both the authority and the operational capabilities to intervene in crises in other CSCE participating states. At the first meeting of the newly created Ministerial Council in Berlin in June 1991, the ministers adopted the so-called Berlin Mechanism, which enables any CSCE participating state that perceives an "emergency situation" to have arisen in another participating state to require the CSCE to address that situation.[64] In October 1991, participating states reached agreement at the CSCE Moscow Human Rights Meeting on strengthening the human rights mechanism first agreed on in 1989 in Vienna and expanded in Copenhagen in 1990 to enable any group of six or more CSCE states to require another state to accept CSCE intervention to investigate human dimension issues.[65] The Vienna Document (VDOC) mechanism on Unusual Military Activities, and the Berlin and Moscow mechanisms all were circumscribed by the Final Act's principle of noninterference in the internal affairs of another state but reflected a clear movement in Europe and in the CSCE toward greater activism and intrusiveness as conflicts loomed and Europe's stability was threatened.

When the war in Yugoslavia broke out, the CSCE delegates at the Geneva Meeting on National Minorities and VDOC negotiators in Vienna welcomed the decision of the European Community to send to monitoring mission to help limit the conflict.[66] As the fighting in Croatia continued without significant abatement, the CSCE's Committee of Senior Officials (CSO) discussed the issue regularly, and by autumn it sent a human rights rapporteur mission to the region.[67] Becoming convinced through the autumn that Yugoslavia could not be put back together, the states of Europe and North America debated how and when to recognize the new states emerging from the Socialist Federal Republic of Yugoslavia. German foreign minister Genscher preempted this debate with his decision on German unilateral recognition of Croatia and Slovenia in December 1991.[68]

As the CSCE foreign ministers gathered in Prague in late January 1992, they were faced with multiple emergencies. There was a lull in the fighting in Croatia but no end in sight to the crisis in the former Yugoslavia. Armenia and Azerbaijan, having become independent barely a month before, were already effectively at war, with the fighting between the two Soviet republics now transformed into a state to state conflict.[69] Georgia had descended into civil war, as President Gamsakhurdia fled the capital, conflict raged between competing warlords, and the ethnic enclaves of South Ossetia and Abkhazia were asserting separatist claims.[70] Tensions were high in many other locations in the Balkans and the former Soviet area. Both the Paris Summit and the Berlin Ministerial had tasked the ministers with developing detailed plans for CSCE institutions, which would then be formally adopted at a summit in Helsinki in the summer of 1992. However, violence and instability appeared to be spreading rapidly in Europe, and the CSCE representatives gathered in Prague clearly felt the need to fashion operational responses right away in addition to their long-term institution building.

With respect to their institutional mandate, the CSCE delegations at Prague made considerable progress in defining and fleshing out in greater detail the CSCE institutions first mentioned in the Charter of Paris. The most urgent tasks facing them clearly involved crisis management and conflict prevention. The Prague Document called for the Helsinki Follow-Up Summit to pursue instruments of at least five types: fact finding and rapporteur missions, monitor missions, good offices, counseling and conciliation, and dispute settlement.[71] The Prague delegates also called for consideration of possible CSCE peacekeeping and authorized the chairman-in-office and the CSO to delegate ad hoc tasks to the CPC. A relatively detailed set of instructions for the CPC was included in the Prague Document, and it also expanded the mandate of the Warsaw Office for Democratic Institutions and Human Rights well beyond elections to include regular reviews of implementation of CSCE human rights commitments. Most striking, the CSCE ministers at Prague adopted a "consensus minus one" procedure that authorized the Ministerial Council or the CSO to take action against a state guilty of "clear, gross and uncorrected violations of relevant CSCE commitments," even in the absence of agreement from the state concerned.[72] By the time of that decision, many of the CSCE foreign ministers (and their heads of state) had Serbian president Slobodan Milošević squarely in their sights as the foremost candidate for the initial application of this rule.

Another important order of business at Prague was the admission of all the states emerging from the USSR and Yugoslavia. The three Baltic Sea states had already achieved recognition and admission to the CSCE at a special ministerial meeting held at the start of the Moscow Human Rights Meeting in September 1991.[73] After the USSR fell apart, Russia was accorded the right of succession to the Soviet Union. The admission to the CSCE of all the remaining Soviet republics except Georgia was formally blessed at the Prague meeting, and the Prague Document contains the template of the pledges they submitted to observe CSCE norms and commitments, including the Final Act, the Charter of Paris, the VDOC, and the Treaty on Conventional Armed Forces in Europe.[74] Georgia rapidly gained CSCE membership once Eduard Shevardnadze assumed the presidency and restored a functioning government in Tbilisi. Because of political disagreements among major European and Atlantic powers over how recognition might affect the Balkan wars, the former Yugoslav republics had to wait somewhat longer for recognition and admission than their former Soviet counterparts.

Although it was natural that a pan-European security organization should readily include all newly recognized states appearing in the region, the recognition and admission of the new states did more than just make the CSCE a bit larger and more unwieldy. Rivalries and disputes that formerly had been subsumed (and arguably, repressed) within the boundaries and institutions of a single state now assumed the character of international issues demanding inclusion on the CSCE's agenda and attention from the participating states. Furthermore, the addition of the new actors brought new crises, such as the conflict between Armenia and Azerbaijan, and gave the opportunity for former Soviet subjects—such as the Baltic republics, Moldova, Georgia, and Ukraine—to express long pent-up resentment of Moscow. Given their particular and often less than pleasant histories with Russia, the Central and Eastern European states—including Poland, Hungary, the Czech Republic, Slovakia, Estonia, Latvia, Lithuania, Romania, and Bulgaria—were all inherently suspicious of Russia and tended to gravitate toward the West, in particular the United States, and Western institutions, such as NATO. Conversely, the Yeltsin administration believed with some justification that Russia had played an essential role in the end of the Cold War and democratic reform in Eastern Europe, and he expected that Russia would be a full partner, most likely through the institutionalized CSCE, in the post–Cold War councils of European security.[75] These conflicting perceptions and aspirations complicated political dialogues within the newly expanded CSCE almost from the very beginning. Such problems only increased once the former Yugoslav republics were also admitted to the CSCE. The CSCE family not only grew suddenly and dramatically larger; its quarrels grew more numerous and contentious, and the process of reaching consensus even more laborious.

Because the UN and the EC were already engaged operationally in attempting to end the conflict in the former Yugoslavia, the CSCE ministers in Prague limited themselves to granting Slovenia and Croatia observer status in the CSCE. (Belgrade still held the Yugoslav CSCE seat, and Bosnia-Herzegovina had not yet formally seceded from Yugoslavia.)[76] However, the CSCE's ad hoc responses to the crisis over Nagorno-Karabakh were in fact major steps in developing operational conflict management and resolution capabilities. With the admission of Armenia and Azerbaijan, the CSCE instantly acquired a war between two participating states. The incoming Czechoslovak Chair and several other CSCE states, in particular the United States, had already been following the growing violence over Nagorno-Karabakh in the fall of 1991, and the CSCE in early 1992 decided to send several high-level fact-finding missions to the region (see above). With the situation between Armenia and Azerbaijan not improving, the United States proposed to a gathering of CSCE ministers in Helsinki in March 1992 (which began preparations for the summit later that year) that the CSCE organize a peace conference between Armenia and Azerbaijan over the disputed territory. The ministers endorsed the proposal, and almost a dozen states expressed a desire to attend the conference as facilitators or mediators. The CSCE had difficulty deciding where to hold the conference because both Yerevan or Baku suspected that most CSCE states were partial to one or the other. At a ministerial lunch, the choice fell unexpectedly on Belarus, which ended up offering Minsk as a venue.[77]

The CSCE ministers further decided to send to the region an advance team of several dozen CSCE observers to gather information and make recommendations for a civilian monitor mission to support any agreement that might be reached. Using ad hoc procedures and resources via the CSO and the CPC, within days the CSCE had a force of some fifty monitors deployed throughout Armenia and Azerbaijan. The Advance Team remained on site into mid-May and presented a thorough report and deployment plan for a monitoring mission to follow the peace conference.[78] The CSCE established an Initial Operations Planning Group (renamed the High-Level Planning Group in 1994) to help prepare for a possible peacekeeping mission related to the conflict over Nagorno-Karabakh. Working in Vienna, the group engaged in fairly detailed planning, but a political consensus on a settlement necessary for deployment of a mission never materialized. In the end, it did not matter because Armenia and Azerbaijan declined to cooperate with either the Italian chair or the US special negotiator seconded to Rome to prepare for the Minsk Conference. Instead, both states made use of the former Soviet weapons and ammunition acquired through the Tashkent reallocation of the property of the Soviet army to prepare for evermore-serious hostilities. By mid-1993, a major war raged between the two countries, with Armenia the clear winner, occupying large swaths of Azerbaijan territory bordering on Nagorno-Karabakh. Starting in mid-1992, Russia increasingly sought a more dominant or unilateral role for itself in the Caucasus, and finally succeeded in brokering a cease-fire between the belligerents in early 1994. The CSCE remained involved, with the states supporting the Minsk Conference transformed into the Minsk Group, which to this day remains the principal forum for political contacts and settlement negotiations between Armenia and Azerbaijan.[79]

The Nagorno-Karabakh Advance Team deployed while CSCE delegations were gathered in Helsinki preparing the major institutional decisions to be adopted at the summit in early July. The wars in the former Yugoslavia also did not wait for the CSCE to finish its Helsinki Document and form its crisis management instruments. As the Helsinki Follow-Up Meeting opened, Bosnia-Herzegovina declared its independence from Milošević's rump Yugoslavia, the United States and most of its European Allies recognized the new state on April 7, 1992, and Milošević's forces invaded. With renewed fighting in Croatia and a more serious war in Bosnia, the representatives of the Euro-Atlantic states in Helsinki were obliged to divide their attention between CSCE institution building and a crisis response. The international community continued to give the UN the lead in responding to events in Yugoslavia. However, the CSCE reacted to the overall crisis in the former Yugoslavia with important operational initiatives, which were instrumental in defining the institutional role and capacity of the organization in the future.

The savagery of the war in Bosnia-Herzegovina stunned Europeans, who had become used to having the proxy conflicts of the Cold War fought far from their own territory. In addition to concerns with genocidal slaughter, ethnic cleansing, concentration camps, and destruction of cultural monuments, European and North American leaders worried that the Yugoslav conflict—or other, similar ethnonational conflicts—might spread elsewhere in the Balkans or further into Europe. Proposals designed to provide conflict management to prevent immediate spillover and early interventions to forestall ethnic violence therefore found immediate resonance and support among the CSCE delegations gathered in Helsinki. The activities of the UN, EU, and the ad hoc International Conference on the Former Yugoslavia left little room for CSCE operational involvement in Bosnia-Herzegovina. However, just as the war had spread quickly and disastrously into Bosnia, there appeared to be a real danger in the spring of 1992 of further spillover of the conflict to the remaining portions of the former Yugoslavia. Serbia, in particular—with its long history of unrest and recent brutal repression of the overwhelmingly majority-ethnic Albanian population in its Autonomous Province of Kosovo—appeared to be sitting on a powder keg.

The United States and several of its European Allies were especially worried about the potential consequences for the region and Europe as a whole if the fighting were to spread to Kosovo. As the unrelenting stream of bad news from Bosnia-Herzegovina stretched the resources of other international institutions, some US officials wondered whether the CSCE might be brought in to prevent possible spillover. In May 1992, the United States proposed to the ongoing CSCE conclave in Helsinki a combination of a monitoring and good offices mission to Kosovo that might establish an ongoing international presence and thus encourage local dialogue and prevent the conflict from spreading. The proposal found unexpectedly enthusiastic support from almost all delegations. Hungary and Turkey proposed that the mission be expanded to include the ethnic minority areas of Vojvodina and Sandjak; neither addition evoked any significant opposition. The result was the so-called Mission of Long Duration to Kosovo, Vojvodina, and Sandjak, as CSCE delegations in Helsinki decided to send international monitors to the region for one year.[80] Working out the modalities of the Mission of Long Duration took slightly more time than initially expected when the proposal was first broached, so the final decision was adopted and personnel were deployed only in August 1992, after the close of the Helsinki Summit.[81]

The Helsinki decision to establish the Mission of Long Duration to Kosovo was a significant leap beyond what seemed to be contemplated in the CSCE ministers' decision in Prague only a few months earlier. All the CSCE missions envisioned in the Prague Document might be characterized as essentially short-term visits. The Mission of Long Duration in effect established a continuing operational field presence of the CSCE in a potential conflict zone, going beyond the short-term operational monitoring presence mounted in Armenia and Azerbaijan that spring. Although the security concerns and motivations for the CSCE responses in Prague and Helsinki were basically the same, the character, ambition, and scope of these responses were substantially different. In crafting this ad hoc reaction to potential spillover in Kosovo, the CSCE at the same time made a much further-reaching institutional decision both on becoming an operational organization in the field and on the manner in which this would be done.

Once the decision was made that the OSCE could and should deploy and maintain constant presences in the field, there were plenty of trouble spots in

Europe that warranted such attention, and CSCE field missions multiplied rapidly through 1992 and 1993. There were reasonable fears that the war in the north could also extend to the former Yugoslavia's southernmost republic, Macedonia.[82] At the same August 1992 CSO meeting that authorized the Mission of Long-Duration to Kosovo, Sandjak, and Vojvodina, the CSCE adopted a mandate for a spillover mission of much the same character to Macedonia in the hope that an international presence might contribute to stability and peace.[83] The Spillover Mission to Skopje was deployed in conjunction with expansion of the EU monitoring presence as well as an eventual small UN preventive military deployment.[84] In September 1992, the CSCE chairman-in-office, Jirí Dienstbier, sent Adam Rotfeld, a senior Polish official (and later foreign minister), to Moldova as his personal representative to report on the recent conflict with Transdniestria.[85] On the basis of Rotfeld's reports to the CSCE in November and December 1992, in early 1993 the CSCE authorized and deployed a small mission to Moldova charged with assisting in efforts to reach a political settlement. In November 1992, the CSCE established a mission to Georgia aimed at encouraging negotiations with the country's breakaway regions in hope of reaching a political settlement.[86] Responding to concerns expressed by Russia about the condition of the ethnic Russian minority in the Baltic states, in December 1992 the CSO agreed to establish a mission in Estonia to "promote integration and better understanding between the communities in Estonia."[87] In September 1993, the CSO established a similar mission to Latvia to assist in addressing "citizenship issues."[88] When Latvia and Russia signed an agreement on April 30, 1994, on the removal of the Skrunda Radar Station, the CSCE provided representatives to a committee set up by the parties to monitor and coordinate implementation.[89]

The war in the former Yugoslavia also spurred the CSCE to develop operational capacities in cooperation with other international organizations. In August 1992, the International Conference on the Former Yugoslavia in London determined, in consultation with the states involved, that the countries bordering on the Federal Republic of Yugoslavia could use assistance in enforcing the UN economic sanctions adopted after the May 1992 bombing of the main Sarajevo market, in addition to the 1991 UN embargo on arms sales and deliveries to all the former Yugoslav republics.[90] CSCE and EC representatives met in Vienna in September 1992 to determine what assistance their institutions might provide. The EC established a communications center in Brussels, and by October 1992 sanctions assistance missions were already in place in Bulgaria, Hungary, and Romania; missions were subsequently also deployed in Albania, Croatia, the former Yugoslav Republic of Macedonia (FYROM), and Ukraine.[91] The WEU joined the EC and CSCE in monitoring riparian enforcement of the sanctions on the Danube. The United States provided a significant number of personnel to the missions, and the EC/CSCE and the United States established senior-level positions of sanctions coordinators.

In its ministerial meetings in Prague and Stockholm and at the Helsinki Summit in 1992, the CSCE made the transition from norm setting to policy, and from principles to operations. By the end of 1992, the CSCE was no longer a conference devoted primarily to discussing and adopting norms, especially with respect to human rights, and to reviewing the implementation of these norms. It had become a political and operational body engaged in discussing current events and in formulating and executing decisions in response to them. The January 1992 Prague Document included specific conclusions reached in the ministerial discussions of the Yugoslav crisis, an action new to CSCE practice.[92] At the Helsinki Summit some six months later, the declaration referred to the wars that had broken out in the CSCE area and specifically mentioned the need for withdrawal of former Soviet forces from the Baltic states.[93] By the time of the Stockholm Ministerial Meeting at the end of 1992, the concluding document contained extensive, specific political discussion of the situations in Bosnia-Herzegovina, the Baltic states, Moldova, Georgia, and Nagorno-Karabakh.[94] By 1993, irrespective of the intentions of the participating states when the process began, the CSCE was engaged in real-time political discussion of current events and crises and the formulation of operational responses.

The CSCE representatives meeting in Helsinki from April through June 1992 also engaged in comprehensively constructing the basic structures and institutions of a proposed pan-European arrangement for a newly undivided continent. The Helsinki delegations declared the CSCE to be a "regional arrangement in the sense of Chapter VIII of the Charter of the United Nations," an assertion that effectively claimed for the CSCE overall responsibility for Europe in the global security order.[95] On security, the Helsinki meeting established the Forum for Security Cooperation, which was to be the institutional home for all CSCE confidence-building, transparency, and arms control efforts, including further negotiations on confidence- and security-building measures (CSBMs) and on arms reduction following up on the Treaty on Conventional Armed Forces in Europe.[96] The Helsinki meeting spelled out more detailed procedures and responsibilities for the CSO and the CPC, which would make them more effective organs for political dialogue, early warning, and preventive action.[97] Finally, the Helsinki Document provided authorization for the CSCE to engage in civilian or military peacekeeping, except for enforcement actions.[98]

One of the most important and innovative actions of the Helsinki Meeting was establishment of the CSCE position of the high commissioner on national minorities (HCNM).[99] The post–Cold War conflicts in Europe, in particular those in the Balkans, had raised the consciousness and sensitivities of many European leaders to the problems posed by questions of ethnic minority rights and maintaining stability and peace in multiethnic societies. The ethnic conflicts of the 1990s were already becoming visible by the late 1980s at the Vienna Follow-Up Meeting, which mandated a special CSCE meeting on national minorities, held in Geneva in June and July 1991. The Balkan wars showed that more than meetings were necessary, and the Netherlands advanced a proposal at Helsinki to establish a separate high-level OSCE office to deal solely with questions of national minorities.[100] The idea behind the proposal was to provide early warning and early intervention, before ethnic, religious, linguistic, or other communal differences could grow extreme enough to provoke civil conflict. In establishing the post of HCNM, the Helsinki delegations characterized the office as "an instrument of conflict prevention at the earliest possible stage."[101] At the end of 1992, at the CSCE Ministerial Council meeting in Stockholm, former Dutch prime minister Max van der Stoel, the most important inventor and advocate of the idea of the HCNM, was formally appointed the first occupant of this office.[102] In almost a decade as HCNM, van der Stoel more than fulfilled the hopes and expectations of those who had advocated for the post.

Not every initiative considered at Helsinki enjoyed great success or impact. The CSCE peacekeeping capability authorized at the meeting has never been used. A number of European member states desired to increase the CSCE's attention to and activities in the second basket, devoted to economic and environmental cooperation. Other states, in particular the United States, objected that the international financial and economic system founded at Bretton Woods already contained more than enough established institutions, whose work did not need to be duplicated by the CSCE. Delegations at Helsinki eventually reached a compromise in agreeing to give greater content to the CSCE Economic Forum first agreed to at the Prague meeting. The Economic Forum was to meet regularly, under the auspices of the CSO (and thus not at an overly senior level), to consider specific topics of current interest to participating states. Despite occasional ambitions from various participating states, the CSCE and its Economic Forum have never become major actors in international economic affairs.[103]

Perhaps the CSCE's greatest labor of unrequited love came in the field of the peaceful settlement of disputes. The Helsinki Summit advanced and the Stockholm Ministerial Council six months later completed a CSCE mechanism and agreement on the peaceful settlement of disputes that has never been employed. From the beginning of the Helsinki process in 1973, a number of CSCE states, in particular Switzerland and France, advocated for establishment within the CSCE of a mechanism for the peaceful, binding resolution of disputes. The United States in particular was resistant to the pursuit within the CSCE process of treaty obligations, as opposed to politically binding agreements.[104] Meetings on the peaceful resolution of disputes were held in Montreux in 1978 and in Athens in 1984, but without significant results. An experts' meeting in Valetta in January 1991 managed to overcome the traditional lack of a consensus sufficiently to produce agreement on a limited dispute resolution mechanism.[105] France and Germany pushed for a treaty on dispute resolution during the Helsinki meeting but were able to get consent only for a further meeting on the subject in Geneva in October.[106] At this meeting, the CSCE states succeeded in expanding the Valetta mechanism into a formal Convention on Conciliation and Arbitration, which was duly included in the Stockholm Document by the CSCE ministers in December 1992. However, the Stockholm decision also reflected the reluctance of members such as the United States to accept binding arbitration by leaving the convention merely "open for signature by interested participating states."[107] The OSCE convention and the Court of Arbitration and Conciliation have never been used, despite the duty accorded the CSO at Stockholm to instruct states that were parties to a dispute to do so. There has never been a consensus within the CSO or its successor, the Permanent Council, to issue such an instruction.

The Helsinki Follow-Up Meeting and Summit on July 7, 1992, also represented the high-water mark for the OSCE's efforts to make decisions on any basis other than a full consensus, defined in its most liberal sense as the absence of objection. By May 1992, international opinion had hardened against the Federal Republic of Yugoslavia (FRY) and President Milošević into almost universal condemnation. Even a reluctant Russian president Yeltsin had been brought into the consensus against the FRY.[108] On May 12, spurred by graphic news of atrocities in Bosnia, the CSO exercised the consensus-minus-one provision adopted at the Prague meeting and suspended Serbia-Montenegro's participation in the CSCE, first until October 1992, and then indefinitely. The heads of state confirmed this suspension in July; cynics claimed the decision was made so none would be forced to be photographed together with Milošević.[109]

Although the suspension of Serbia-Montenegro from CSCE meetings lasted for the rest of the decade, the results of this action were by any standard unimpressive. When the mandate for the Mission of Long Duration to Kosovo, Sandjak, and Vojvodina came up for renewal in the summer of 1993, Milošević refused to renew it, and the international monitors were forced to leave. The war did not spread to Kosovo, but the conflicts in Bosnia-Herzegovina and Croatia continued well into 1995, irrespective of Milošević's exclusion from the OSCE, and ended only with NATO intervention. Serbian representatives were not fully available in OSCE institutions and discussions as the crisis in Kosovo lurched toward war in 1998. Most of all, a number of CSCE participating states had time to contemplate the treatment and position of the FRY; many of them seemed to conclude that the requirement for a consensus on any action was in the end a valuable tool for self-preservation. In retrospect, the unanimity in condemning Milošević was a rare moment in European diplomatic history. Within six months, Russian foreign minister Andrei Kozyrev's two interventions at the Stockholm Ministerial Meeting—the first a mock statement designed to reflect the views of powerful political actors in Russia who had a good chance of replacing the current administration in Moscow—provided a glimpse of a future Europe in which Russia would demand greater understanding and latitude with respect to its actions in the former Soviet space and Eastern Europe.[110]

## PUTTING OSCE FLESH ON THE CSCE SKELETON: FROM STOCKHOLM TO BUDAPEST

Although the CSCE did a tremendous amount of work both in the field and in further constructing its own institutions from the Ministerial Council in Stockholm in December 1992 to the CSCE Summit in Budapest in December 1994, the most important structures and approaches to European security in that body were essentially already established during the course of these seminal debates and meetings during 1992. During the two years following Stockholm, the CSCE centralized and rationalized its political consultation and conflict management and prevention functions in a largely integrated Secretariat in Vienna. The post of secretary-general was established to provide overall administrative management of the CSCE's operational activities.[111] The chairman-in-office still provided overall political direction on behalf of the CSCE Council (renamed the Ministerial Council after the 1994 Budapest Summit); the secretary-general served as the chairman's chief administrative agent.[112] German ambassador at large Wilhelm Hoynck was appointed the CSCE's first secretary-general in early 1993, and he served until mid-1996.[113]

From 1992 to 1994, the CSCE's operations gradually migrated from Prague and were centralized in Vienna. The Charter of Paris originally distributed CSCE institutions around Europe—with the Secretariat in Prague, the CPC in Vienna, and the Office for Free Elections (quickly expanded into the Office for Democratic Institutions and Human Rights) in Warsaw. The Netherlands quickly claimed the HCNM, which set up its headquarters in The Hague, and the OSCE Parliamentary Assembly was located in Copenhagen. The Helsinki Summit Document provided an agreed-on scale of country-by-country contributions to the CSCE budget to support all these institutions, which required more than the host nation's funding for meetings and sending-state funding for temporarily relocated personnel and delegations, which had been sufficient for the Cold War–era CSCE. The CSCE's participating states—especially the newer, less wealthy ones—rapidly questioned the need to support multiple institutions in multiple capitals. The Czechoslovak Chair found it convenient to continue holding CSO meetings in Prague, but the CSCE states maintained large CSBM delegations in Vienna (which, for many, also were concerned with the Treaty on Conventional Armed Forces in Europe). With the CPC also located in Austria's capital and with the rapid proliferation of field missions in 1992–93, once Sweden assumed the CSCE Chair in December 1992, the CSCE states rapidly concluded that it made more sense to also locate both the Secretariat and the CSCE's regular political consultations in Vienna.

These decisions, which were made during the course of 1993, were recognized and formalized by the ministers at the Council meeting in Rome in December 1993.[114] In addition to blessing the establishment of the CSCE's Secretariat in Vienna, at Rome the CSCE ministers established the Permanent Committee, which was to be "a permanent body consisting of representatives of the participating States for political consultations and decisionmaking in Vienna."[115] The Permanent Committee was mandated to conduct "regular and comprehensive consultations" and to make decisions on CSCE issues when the CSO was not in session. In reality, the Permanent Committee by and large simply replaced the CSO because few CSCE participating states had enough diplomats and money to support the maintenance of so many separate deliberative bodies. Within a year, at the December 1994 Budapest Summit, the CSCE representatives transformed the CSO into the so-called Senior Council, which was to meet twice a year in Prague (recommended at the level of political directors), once shortly before the annual ministerial meetings and once as the Economic Forum.[116]

The Budapest Summit culminated the process of formally making the CSCE an organization—an institution with multiple departments, permanent staff members and headquarters, and operational responsibilities—begun with the Charter of Paris and shaped by the multiple crises that confronted European and North Atlantic states after 1991. The Budapest Summit Document first and foremost recognized what had happened in this process, and thus it renamed the CSCE the Organization for Security and Cooperation in Europe (OCSE).[117] The meetings and procedures of this organization were to be rationalized: summits would be held once every two years, and council meetings—henceforth, the Ministerial Council—would generally be held in the capital of the Chair near the end of the year. The Permanent Committee was renamed the Permanent Council and was designated the CSCE's "regular body for political consultation and decisionmaking."[118] The Forum for Security Cooperation's competencies were also made more precise with respect to CSBMs and transparency, arms control, and other military security measures.

It would not make much sense to proclaim the CSCE henceforth an organization without also prescribing what that organization was for, and the heads of state did so in Budapest. The Budapest Summit Document directs that the future roles and functions of the OSCE will include the following:

- to make vigorous use of its norms and standards in shaping a common security area;
- to ensure full implementation of all CSCE commitments;
- to serve, based on consensus rules, as the inclusive and comprehensive forum for consultation, decisionmaking, and cooperation in Europe;
- to enhance good-neighborly relations by encouraging the conclusion of bilateral, regional, and potentially CSCE-wide agreements or arrangements between and among participating states;
- to further strengthen the CSCE's capacity and activity in preventive diplomacy;
- to further the CSCE's principles and develop its capabilities in conflict resolution, in crisis management and peacekeeping, and in postconflict rehabilitation, including assistance with reconstruction;
- to enhance security and stability through arms control and disarmament efforts and CSBMs throughout the CSCE region and at regional levels;
- to develop further CSCE work in the field of human rights and fundamental freedoms, and other areas of the human dimension;
- to promote cooperation among participating states to establish strong, market-based economies throughout the CSCE region; and
- to further enhance the CSCE's problem-solving activities and abilities, taking into account the whole spectrum of its responsibilities as they have developed since the adoption of the Helsinki Final Act, in order to meet the new challenges and risks.[119]

The third bulleted item in this ambitious list is perhaps the most important in understanding the disparity in aspirations for the fledgling organization among the participating states. The phrasing reflects the ambitions for the Helsinki Process held especially by Russian representatives and first seen in Gorbachev's musings during his meeting with Bush at Malta.[120] Such broad ambitions for the organization were shared in some degree by representatives of a number of participating states, particularly some of the smaller, newer, or less-aligned nations on the continent. However, none of the other participating states would accept proposals from Moscow, such as according the OSCE a de facto right of review over NATO's activities in Europe and giving the Commonwealth of Independent States the lead in security affairs in the former Soviet space. Thus the phrasing in the Budapest Summit Document explicitly stops short of according the OSCE any preeminence or exclusivity. In this, it unmistakably reflects the position of the United States and some of its most Atlanticist Allies—ready to recognize the usefulness of the OSCE, and thus to say good things about it, but nonetheless considering it a secondary tool and junior partner to more important institutions and organs.[121] All the NATO and EU member states joined the consensus expressed in the Budapest Summit Document, including its assertion of the lofty, comprehensive role of the OSCE. Yet this consensus masked deep divisions over the real place and relationship of the OSCE vis-à-vis the other major components of the European security architecture. For though they were endorsing the OSCE's utility, almost all these states were at the same time at the initial stages of a policy of enlarging these other institutions, a course that would eventually counteract and call into question assertions of the OSCE's inclusivity and comprehensiveness.

Some two decades later, many contemporary political figures and analysts, particularly from Europe, questioned whether the United States ever took the OSCE seriously. Solely from this narrative of US involvement in OSCE meetings, structures, and field activities, it is clear that from the beginning Washington desired a continued, important role for the Helsinki Process. However, senior US officials also sought to prevent the CSCE from developing a large and costly bureaucratic structure, a continuing American tendency that can be seen in Washington's long-standing opposition to European proposals for granting the OSCE a legal personality.[122] Although finding a use for some OSCE functions, Washington fought against the creation of another UN-style bureaucracy in Europe. Moreover, from the very beginnings of the post–Cold War era, it is clear that the Bush administration was also committed to the preservation of NATO as *the* key instrument for a continuing American presence and role in European security affairs. Both the Bush and the succeeding Clinton administrations attempted to construct an integrated European security architecture in which institutions such as NATO, the EU, and the OSCE played complementary and mutually supporting roles. In the years immediately after the Soviet collapse and outbreak of war in the Balkans, operational requirements were so extensive that it was possible for each of these entities to assume plenty of responsibility and work without substantially infringing on the others' turf. As the EU and in particular NATO began to expand during the 1990s, the interrelationship among these three security institutions began to change, inexorably raising the questions of whether one would be preeminent and, if so, which one it would be. In considering these questions during the next two decades, the United States and Russia ended up with diametrically opposed answers.

## 4. NATO AND THE EU MOVE EAST

### Extending Stability or New Divisions?

From the time of their founding, both NATO and the European Union (and its predecessors) were open to new members. Indeed, from the late 1940s to 1990, several members were added to each organization. During the Cold War, however, enlargements of both the EU and NATO were limited due to Soviet control or influence over half of Europe's territory. Once the Warsaw Pact disbanded and the Soviet Union dissolved, this impediment to broader NATO and EU membership effectively disappeared. In addition, the numerous wars and widespread economic hardship in the post–Cold War, post-Soviet transitions raised serious questions for many Central and Eastern European states as to where and how they could provide hard military and economic security for themselves. The emerging Conference on Security and Cooperation in Europe (CSCE) offered the advantage of comprehensive membership, which could ensure that the concerns and positions of all interested states would be heard on any particular issue. However, the CSCE's capabilities lay largely in providing transparency, impartial separation of antagonists, and mediation. The CSCE possessed neither NATO's military capabilities for hard defense and deterrence nor the EU's economic and financial resources that might help achieve economic stability and sufficiency. The European political and security environment during the first half of the 1990s encouraged Europe's states, especially those emerging from the Soviet orbit, to seek concrete, existing security and economic capabilities It was this environment and the understandable response to it that provided much of the attraction of NATO and the EU to aspiring new members.

Looking back from the vantage point of more than two decades later, it is easy to see the enlargements of NATO and the EU as processes of simply moving the Cold War dividing line in Europe further to the east, until it seemed that only Russia might be left out of the integrated European security and economic structures. Although Moscow in particular may perceive this to have been the aim from the start, it was not the stated purpose of the processes of enlargement. The aims expressed by those states already members of NATO and the EU were often more limited and specific to individual aspiring member states, or to small groups of them. Such aims included providing political and military stability, promoting democratic political change, and assisting in transitions to market economies. These goals were normative and ideological, involving the transformation of political and economic systems, rather than solely achieving territorial expansion or geopolitical advantage. To be sure, most of the states of Central and Eastern Europe had chafed under the domination or direct rule of the Soviet Union, and these states ardently sought to escape Moscow's orbit for that of Western Europe. In this sense, it was extremely difficult with respect to the states to the east of the former Iron Curtain for the processes of NATO and EU enlargement not to take on an anti-Russia, geopolitical aspect. Nonetheless, many North American and Western European proponents of NATO's and the EU's expansions attempted for a long time to keep these processes from calling into question the original ideal of "a Europe whole and free, from Vancouver to Vladivostok."

## RUSSIA: EURO-ATLANTIC INTEGRATION, DISINTEGRATION AT HOME

Russia was exceptionally weak during much of the 1990s and focused most of its attention on developments within the borders of the Russian Federation or the neighboring post-Soviet states. For President Boris Yeltsin, no foreign policy issue was as important or urgent as ensuring the transition of the new Russian state from Soviet power to a pluralist political system and a market economy. The policy of shock therapy adopted in 1992 by acting prime minister Yegor Gaidar's government arguably deepened the economic hardship Russia had experienced in 1990 and 1991, but it appeared to achieve its aim of forestalling any attempt to return to a Soviet-style command economy.[1] The political battles of 1992 and 1993, through which Yeltsin eventually triumphed over his communist and nationalist critics, ensured the preservation of a friendly, pro-Western administration in the Kremlin, but it also left Russia with a superpresidential political system, which was enshrined in the December 1993 Constitution. This system allowed Yeltsin to govern over the objections of the red-brown forces (the communist-nationalist coalition) that dominated the State Duma but provided few institutional checks on an ambitious head of state once Boris Nikolaevich left office.

Yeltsin's victory over his opposition in 1992–93 and his continued control of the executive branch ensured that the Russian government would be relatively well disposed to the West and fairly cooperative in the elaboration of the European security architecture during the 1990s and in reaching and implementing collective responses to most European security problems. The extremely pro-Western Andrei Kozyrev stayed on as foreign minister until late 1995. Even then, his replacement, Evgenii Primakov, though more Soviet in his thinking and more suspicious of the West, was a pragmatic interlocutor for Russia's European and North American partners when he judged it in Russia's interest. Prime Minister Viktor Chernomyrdin, who succeeded Gaidar in that post, was also a practical, results-oriented manager who got along well with a wide variety of foreign interlocutors.[2]

However, there were deeply conservative, nationalist, neo-Soviet, and anti-Western political forces in Yeltsin's Russia, all of which enjoyed considerable popular support.[3] Kozyrev's first, mock speech to the December 1992 Stockholm CSCE ministerial meeting provided clear insights into the thinking of many of those involved with these forces and a warning of the ease with which they might replace the Yeltsin administration.[4] Yeltsin and his administration were absorbed during most of 1993 in a bitter battle with the president's opponents both outside and in the government, many of whom followed the "national-patriotic tendency" cited by Kozyrev. Yeltsin won his battle with the opposition only at great cost—with an internationally televised tank artillery barrage on his own parliament.[5]

Many of Yeltsin's and Russia's most important international interlocutors supported the Russian president in this struggle as the best hope for lasting democratic and market reform in Russia. However, the dramatic events in Moscow during October 1993 had quite a different effect on the voting public inside Russia. Vladimir Zhirinovskii's unexpectedly large vote in the December 1993 parliamentary elections, followed by strong performances from his Liberal Democratic Party (it was neither) and the Communist Party in the 1995 elections, demonstrated both deep disillusionment with Yeltsin and his colleagues and strong, ongoing opposition inside Russia to the president's reform program. Following the 1993 elections, Yeltsin and his administration governed largely by executive order because he found it inadvisable and impossible to obtain the legislation he desired from a far more conservative and nationalist legislature.[6]

Debates over whether and what the West may have done wrong in support- ing Yeltsin and the small band of reformers around him will likely continue as long as histories of Russia are written, but they are not this study's pri- mary subject matter. With respect to Russia's role in the construction of the European security order during the 1990s, the most immediate and impor- tant consequence of Russia's internal political struggles was the continuation through much of the 1990s of a regime that was basically accommodating and cooperative with the major Western powers. However, this cooperative stance arguably resulted less from a real convergence of views on European security structures and issues than from Yeltsin's need to focus on the domestic politi- cal struggle and not to alienate his international supporters. As soon became apparent with the issue of NATO enlargement, when Yeltsin had the time (and capacity, some might argue) to focus on security questions, or when these ques- tions had great domestic political import, the Russian president could be a very difficult, obstinate interlocutor.

To be sure, Western leaders, in particular US president Bill Clinton, cul- tivated Yeltsin and made concessions in return for Russia's cooperation, such as inclusion in the Group of Seven (G-7) or negotiation of favorable terms for Russian military deployments to the North Caucasus in the 1996 Flank Agree- ment for the Treaty on Conventional Armed Forces in Europe (CFE Treaty).[7] The United States established a special, complex bureaucratic structure to manage its relationship with Russia: a bilateral presidential commission headed by Vice President Al Gore and Prime Minister Viktor Chernomyrdin, which in its heyday included representatives from most of the executive branch agencies of both governments.[8] However, Western support for Yeltsin had long-lasting, largely counterproductive effects on the image held by the Russian public of the West and Western motives. The means whereby domestic and external support was marshaled for Yeltsin's reelection in 1996 left a particularly bitter aftertaste and considerable doubt as to the real nature and purposes of West- ern democracy promotion in Russia.[9] The collaboration of a small group of Russia's wealthiest oligarchs to raise money for Yeltsin's campaign and fund a media blitz to revive his popularity and vilify his opponents contributed to the growth of cynicism among Russian elites about the nature of market economics and press freedom. The presence of US campaign advisers, or "political tech- nologists," advising the Yeltsin campaign from a posh Moscow hotel did little to convince Russian voters of the value of Western democracy in Russia.[10] Well- publicized scandals—for example, insider trading by American advisers work- ing with the Yeltsin administration to build a Russian stock exchange—helped convince many Russians of the West's alleged venal, self-interested motives in supporting "reform" in Yeltsin's Russia.[11]

US policy toward Russia in the early 1990s placed special emphasis on arms control and nuclear issues. Even as the Soviet Union began to crumble, the US Congress adopted the Nunn-Lugar Cooperative Threat Reduction legislation, which offered extensive financial and technical assistance to the Russian Federation and other former Soviet republics in maintaining control of nuclear weapons, delivery systems, and nuclear materials, and in providing work for nuclear scientists who might otherwise contribute to proliferation in the employ of aspiring nuclear powers.[12] Washington mounted extensive bilateral and multilateral diplomatic efforts with Russia, Kazakhstan, Belarus, and Ukraine to obtain the agreement of all four either to destroy or to transfer all the nuclear weapons and delivery systems of the former USSR to the territory and control of the Russian Federation. This activity resulted in particular in the December 1994 Budapest Memorandum — signed by the United States, the United Kingdom, and the Russian Federation — containing security assurances for Ukraine in return for renouncing its status as a nuclear weapons state.[13] During the 1990s, the United States continued to make first negotiation and then ratification and implementation of the 1993 Strategic Arms Reduction Treaty (known as START II) a major item on the US-Russian strategic bilateral agenda.[14] The US military particularly valued the extensive contacts provided by the Nunn-Lugar Cooperative Threat Reduction program with the Russian military and the armed forces of other post-Soviet states as essential transparency and confidence-building activities.

With generous financing behind the Nunn-Lugar program, the concentration of all former Soviet nuclear weapons and delivery systems on the territory of the Russian Federation, and continued pursuit of bilateral strategic arms reduction negotiations, Washington in effect continued to deal with Moscow as though it were still the other major power in the old bipolar world. The essential elements on Washington's bilateral agenda with Moscow included strategic issues such as nuclear nonproliferation, in particular containing Iran's nuclear program and regional security in the Persian Gulf, especially limiting Iran's conventional military strength, countering Tehran's support for terrorism, and enforcing UN sanctions against Saddam Hussein.[15] During the 1990s, the United States also sought Russia's support for security initiatives and operations in Europe, in particular in the Balkans. The Yeltsin administration's support for — or, at least, lack of objections to — key Western initiatives masked the ambivalence or opposition to Western actions that was widespread in Russian society.[16] The United States also cut Yeltsin's government considerable slack vis-à-vis Moscow's involvement with its so-called near abroad, going so far as to offer support for Russian mediation in some of the local conflicts in Georgia,

Moldova, Armenia-Azerbaijan, and Tajikistan.[17] Because the United States made global, strategic nuclear issues its top priorities in dealing with Russia, Washington ended up paying relatively less attention to its emerging differences with Moscow over regional concepts and issues in European security.[18]

Russia in the 1990s may have retained some of the external attributes of a great power — it had the largest territory of any state in the world, the largest nuclear arsenal, and a permanent seat on the United Nations Security Council — but in reality it was engaged in a process of state building that taxed its government's resources to the breaking point. Many of the Russian Federation's constituent federal units — taking seriously Yeltsin's injunction to seize "as much sovereignty as they could swallow" — paid little heed to directives or commands from the Kremlin. The second wave of privatization in the notorious "loans for shares" program was a desperate measure to fund the government against the backdrop of massive tax avoidance by Russian citizens and corporations alike. Organized crime and corruption were rampant throughout the country, and firms spent sizable portions of their revenues on private security, given the apparent inability or unwillingness of the government's law enforcement and security agencies to preserve order and observe the law.[19]

Perhaps the most stunning indication of the thoroughgoing weakness of the Russian state came during the First Chechen War, from 1994 to 1996.[20] Led by former Soviet general Dzhokhar Dudaev, starting in late 1991, the secular republic authorities in Chechnya proclaimed their independence from Russia. For several years, with more pressing domestic issues to resolve, Yeltsin largely ignored the breakaway Chechen authorities in Groznyi. However, Moscow steadily increased its surreptitious efforts in Chechnya until matters came to a head in late 1994. As one narrative would have it, after Defense Minister Pavel Grachev allegedly claimed he could eliminate the breakaway Chechen regime in some two weeks, Yeltsin gave the go-ahead to attack in December 1994. The performance of the Russian armed forces in the war that followed was shockingly bad; they resorted to extremely brutal tactics, including mass slaughter of civilians, that provoked widespread repugnance outside Russia. Russian troops deserted, sold their weapons to the enemy, and fought unpredictably and usually badly when they could not avoid combat.[21] A small, determined Chechen force essentially fought the much larger Russian army to a standstill. With the 1996 elections looming, Yeltsin recruited his political rival, General Aleksandr Lebed, as national security adviser and had him make a humiliating peace that gave Chechnya independence in all but name.[22] Then, once Yeltsin was safely reelected, he wasted little time in ditching Lebed.

The United States' support for Yeltsin extended so far that President Clinton at one point likened Yeltsin's war against a rebellious Chechnya to that of Lincoln against the South in the US Civil War.[23] Washington also took more practical, concrete steps to assist Moscow in fighting this domestic conflict. Under the CFE Treaty, Russian military deployments in the Caucasus region, even though inside the territory of the Russian Federation, were limited by provisions affecting the so-called flanks, regions in the north and south of Russia around Turkey and Norway.[24] At the 1996 Review Conference for the CFE Treaty, the US delegation led an effort to revise the treaty's so-called Flank Agreement limitations to permit larger temporary deployments, which in effect would have legalized the concentration of Russian forces fighting the Chechens in the North Caucasus. The United States then took the lead in 1996–97 in obtaining the Flank Agreement's ratification and entry into force, over the misgivings of many of Russia's smaller neighbors in the Caucasus and Eastern Europe.[25] Washington maintained a close and steady dialogue with Moscow on a wide range of issues pertaining to conventional and nuclear arms control, including adaptation of the CFE Treaty to reflect the elimination of the Warsaw Pact.[26]

Russia's foreign policy concerns were generally much closer to home, mostly involving the situations in and relations with the countries of the former Soviet Union. Moscow collaborated with Tehran in mediating a settlement to a protracted, bitter civil war in Tajikistan that dragged on into the late 1990s.[27] In addition to joining the United States and the United Kingdom in assuring Ukraine's security in the Budapest Memorandum, Moscow engaged in a difficult dialogue with Kyiv over Crimea, in particular over the status and future of Russia's Black Sea Fleet. Moscow participated in reaching cease-fire agreements in Georgia's conflicts with Abkhazia and South Ossetia and obtained Western agreement and support (including from the United States) for its role as the sole military peacekeeper for both. Russia also obtained Moldovan acquiescence to Russian peacekeepers in the Transdniestrian region after Yeltsin brokered a cease-fire to the conflict there in 1992 and served as a mediator in the political settlement talks. Moscow also paid considerable attention to the overall structure and purpose of the Commonwealth of Independent States and the roles each of these post-Soviet neighbors might play in that organization.

Thus, while the United States and at least some of its Allies in the mid-1990s were thinking globally, Russia was thinking locally, or at best regionally. To be sure, Western policy supported the independence, sovereignty, and territorial integrity of all the post-Soviet states; but in practice, Western attention and concern collided and conflicted with Russian interests and activities in this region relatively infrequently. To some extent, this relative Western inattention to Russia's so-called near abroad may be explained by greater concerns elsewhere—for example, Iraq, the Arab-Israeli peace process, and peacemaking and postconflict reconciliation and reconstruction in the former Yugoslavia. The "Blackhawk down" incident in Somalia certainly did not make the Clinton administration eager for foreign involvement, and it arguably helped delay eventual US involvement in Bosnia. In addition, the Yeltsin administration enjoyed considerable trust in major Western capitals, and the United States and many of its Allies were content to give Russia the benefit of the doubt in assessing its role and activities vis-à-vis many of its post-Soviet neighbors. Both NATO and the EU were still relatively far away from the territory of the former Soviet Union and were deeply engrossed with important internal institutional issues. Thus, during the 1990s, Moscow enjoyed relatively less scrutiny and considerably more tolerance from its Western interlocutors than it would after the turn of the century. Similarly, in the early 1990s the Russian authorities had considerable trust in American and Western European intentions and were relatively open to reaching agreements and engaging in cooperation with the EU and even NATO. As both these organizations began a process of expansion to the east, this situation would change.

## IN NATO OR WITH NATO? FROM NORTH ATLANTIC COOPERATION COUNCIL TO PARTNERSHIP FOR PEACE

By transforming the fundamental purpose of the Atlantic Alliance, the London and Rome NATO summits answered in the affirmative the question of whether the Alliance should survive. Subsequent decisions during the next few years, in particular with respect to NATO's involvement in the Balkans, altered the nature and geographic scope of the Alliance's activities. However, some Allies and neighboring European states argued that these transformations by themselves would not be sufficient responses to changes in the European political and security environment unless NATO's composition also was changed by adding new members. The leaders of a number of the Warsaw Pact's member states expressed interest in closer association with or membership in NATO, even as the Soviet-dominated alliance was crumbling.[28] Meanwhile, the expanding war in the Balkans and the woefully insufficient responses of the EU and CSCE to this conflict accentuated the sense of insecurity in the states of Central and Eastern Europe and the need for security arrangements involving established, reliable hard military capabilities. Domestic developments in Russia during 1992–93 also gave the former Soviet republics and Warsaw Pact members a strong impression that democratic changes in Moscow might not be irreversible and made them newly motivated to insure themselves against autocratic backsliding by their large eastern neighbor.

At the same time that NATO gradually made the decision to embark on out-of-area operations to contain the wars in Bosnia and Croatia, the Allies came to the fateful decision to address the perceived "security vacuum" in Central and Eastern Europe by offering the former member states of the Warsaw Pact and Soviet republics not just association with but also formal membership in the Alliance. Although NATO's enlargement eventually found enthusiastic support from a number of Allies, the most consistent advocates and the driving force for the initiative from within the Alliance were the United States and Germany.[29] The United States exercised leadership at almost every stage of the process. Furthermore, in almost all the states located between Germany and Russia, substantial elements of civil society and government elites expressed strong desires to join NATO and thereby obtain for themselves assurances of hard military security. Although Russia's attitude toward this decision and its effects on relations with Russia were considered steadily throughout the process, NATO adopted enlargement primarily for its potential benefits for the states lying between Russia and the eastern borders of the Alliance at the end of the Cold War. In the end, the policy of enlarging NATO was justified not only because of the bad things it would prevent by addressing the security vacuum in Central Europe but also for the good things it would produce by promoting democratic change and market economies in the former Soviet satellites and republics.

The George H. W. Bush administration committed itself to retaining NATO as the main vehicle for the US presence and influence in Europe, but it took no position on enlarging NATO's membership. However, by late 1992 at least two senior administration officials—Secretary of Defense Dick Cheney and Secretary of State Lawrence Eagleburger—speculated in public on possible expansion of NATO to the east.[30] Outside the government, in the summer of 1992, former national security adviser Zbigniew Brzezinski publicly called for making Poland a member of the Alliance.[31] By the end of 1992, it was clear that the North Atlantic Cooperation Council (NACC) did little beyond bringing representatives of the former Warsaw Pact and former Soviet states into the same room with the Allies.[32] The NACC contained no provision or mechanism for operational military cooperation between NATO and the former Soviet satellites and republics to the east. In this respect, there was nothing to distinguish it as a forum for political and security dialogue from the CSCE, and there was no added benefit from its association with NATO. Meanwhile, the deepening of the wars in the former Yugoslavia accentuated fears that other long-standing territorial and national rivalries in Central Europe—such as Hungary/Romania, Romania/Moldova, and Hungary/Slovakia—might also degenerate into instability and even violence.

Against this backdrop of instability and regional conflict in Europe, the arrival of the Clinton administration in Washington in January 1993 presented opportunities to incoming officials at various levels who advocated for change in the US approach to European security in general and NATO in particular. Clinton's national security adviser, Anthony Lake, favored rapid expansion of NATO membership as part of an effort to promote the transition to democracy and market economies in Central and Eastern Europe.[33] At the State Department, Secretary Warren Christopher's chief of staff, Thomas Donilon; the undersecretary for international security affairs, Lynn Davis; and several members of the Policy Planning Staff were enthusiastic proponents of rapid NATO enlargement.[34] Advocates inside the US government for enlarging NATO received important intellectual support and ammunition for their arguments from RAND Corporation analysts who had been tasked after the revolutions of 1989 with developing analyses and proposals for post–Cold War security in Central and Eastern Europe.[35]

During the course of these debates within the US government in 1993, three of these RAND analysts—Ronald Asmus, Richard Kugler, and Stephen Larrabee—went public with an article in *Foreign Affairs*, "Building a New NATO"; this piece is worth examining closely because it contains the seeds of many of the arguments advanced by proponents of NATO expansion in debates within the US government during the crucial first year of the Clinton administration.[36] The article asserts the need to reach a new transatlantic bargain that will extend "NATO's collective defense and security arrangements to those areas where the seed of future conflict in Europe lie: the Atlantic Alliance's eastern and southern borders."[37] Although the authors acknowledge that support for democracy in Russia is a key US and Western interest, they argue that post–Cold War Europe's strategic challenges are found "almost exclusively" in the area between Germany and Russia and along the Mediterranean in North Africa. They further assert that "East-Central Europe is littered with potential mini-Weimar republics, each capable of inflicting immense violence on the others."[38] The authors then argue that NATO's expansion to the east can provide the security, stability, and conditionality necessary to promote transition of the countries of the region to democracy. A relatively comprehensive discussion of how to transform the Alliance is also provided, including changed roles for the United States, France, and Germany and the need for out-of-area operations. As for specific policy recommendations for the region, the authors call for integrating the Visegrad countries ("Poland, Hungary, the Czech Republic, and possibly Slovakia") into both the European Community (EC) and NATO. As for Russia, Asmus, Kugler, and Larrabee argue that extending NATO to the east will be a step toward partnership with Russia, not against it, as long as Russia continues on a path of democratic reform.[39] However, the authors argue vigorously that Russia should not be given any *droit de regard* over the West's policies with respect to Central and Eastern Europe.

There were plenty of skeptics and opponents to NATO expansion within the US government. President Clinton himself envisioned building a special relationship with Russia as he prepared to assume office, and he recruited his graduate school friend and Russian and Soviet expert, Strobe Talbott, for a special position in the State Department devoted to US-Russian relations.[40] Senior administration officials—including the secretary of defense, Les Aspin; the deputy secretary (and later secretary) of defense, Bill Perry; and the Supreme Allied Commander Europe, and later Joint Chiefs of Staff chairman, General John Shalikashvili—were all reportedly inclined toward developing relations with Russia as most important for ensuring America's security.[41] Aspin, Shalikashvili, and other senior Department of Defense officials also feared that expansion would dilute and weaken NATO, adding states that would be "consumers" of security without bringing additional capabilities to the Alliance and making it harder to reach a consensus and implement decisions.[42] Finally, State Department officials charged with handling NATO affairs and relations with Russia feared that NATO's enlargement would both make the Alliance more difficult to manage and damage relations with Russia.[43]

The opportunity to promote new policies going beyond the Bush administration, timely pressure from high-level Central European advocates of NATO enlargement, and an increasingly urgent need to provide security and stability to a region threatened by war combined during 1993 to push the debate in Washington toward a decision in principle to expand the Alliance and to propose the Partnership for Peace (PfP) as the instrument to begin this process. Russian cooperation in the Balkans had been essential in imposing economic sanctions on the Federal Republic of Yugoslavia, excluding Slobodan Milošević from the CSCE, and mounting efforts to achieve a settlement formulated at the London Conference. US defense officials in particular hoped to cultivate a military-to-military relationship with Russia that could include operational cooperation in the former Yugoslavia. In the late summer of 1993, in the midst of comprehensive discussions about transforming NATO, Charles Freeman and Joseph Kruzel—respectively, assistant secretary of defense and principal deputy assistant secretary of defense for regional security affairs, whose responsibility included NATO affairs—came up with the idea of a program associating other European countries operationally with NATO that eventually became PfP. Freeman and Kruzel developed the PfP proposal while participating simultaneously in discussions involving their Department of Defense bosses and colleagues—Shalikashvili, Aspin, Perry, and the assistant secretary for international security policy, Ashton Carter—on the Combined Joint Task Force concept and NATO's relationship with Russia.[44]

The PfP was both a bureaucratic ploy advanced to defend turf in US interagency debates over NATO's future and a substantive response to several policy and operational concerns. At the June 1993 meeting of the North Atlantic Council in Athens, Secretary Christopher raised the possibility of extending the NACC's agenda to include operational cooperation—perhaps even peacekeeping—between former communist states and NATO Allies. After that meeting, a working group led by the staff of the US National Security Council forced the issue of NATO expansion in Washington bureaucratic discussions.[45] Advocates for NATO enlargement in the executive branch received key support from Senator Richard Lugar, who as early as June 1993 spoke publicly in favor of NATO undertaking out-of-area operations and adding Poland, Hungary, and the Czech Republic to the Alliance.[46] There was continuing pressure from several quarters in Europe in favor of enlarging the Alliance. From Germany, the defense minister, Volker Ruhe, and NATO secretary-general, Manfred Woerner, both spoke in favor of enlarging the Alliance to the east, to address both current and potential instability. Czech president Vaclav Havel and Polish president Lech Walesa used meetings with President Clinton in conjunction with the April 1993 opening of the Holocaust Museum in Washington to lobby bluntly and vigorously for their countries to join NATO.[47] In August 1993, during a visit by Yeltsin to Poland, Polish president Lech Wałęsa reportedly plied his Russian visitor sufficiently with alcohol so Yeltsin told reporters that Moscow would have no objection to Poland becoming a NATO member.[48] Although Russian presidential and Foreign Ministry staff members quickly walked back their leader's indiscretion, the incident supported those who argued that Russia could be brought around to approve of enlarging NATO.

The issue came to a head in Washington in a mid-October 1993 meeting of the National Security Council's Principals Committee (which consisted of council members minus the president) to prepare the US position for the NATO summit coming in January 1994. Clinton's senior advisers were clearly divided, with Lake pushing for early enlargement of the Alliance whereas Defense Secretary Aspin sought to delay consideration of the issue. The State Department was divided within itself, with Russia hand Strobe Talbott arguing that a proposal for early NATO enlargement would severely damage relations with Russia.[49] The result was a decision that Talbott later characterized as "kicking the can down the road." In accordance with this decision, at the January NATO summit President Clinton formally proposed only PfP, but he also said something about NATO's eventual expansion.[50]

The October 18 Principals Committee meeting was the only formal session at which all the most concerned senior US government officials debated the issue of whether to expand NATO. Although the decision made at this meeting was in principle only a recommendation to President Clinton, in fact, after the meeting, there was no more significant senior-level debate within the US government's executive branch over whether NATO should add new members. Only Clinton himself could state definitively when he made up his mind to support NATO enlargement and how enthusiastically he embraced the October 18 recommendation. From both his own memoirs and Talbott's account, as the latter visited Europe in January 1994, the issue was "no longer whether NATO will take on new members, but when and how."[51]

As an interim solution, PfP enjoyed considerable immediate success. Defense Secretary Aspin first presented the idea to a NATO defense ministers' meeting in October 1993, and the proposal was formally adopted at the NATO Summit in Brussels in January 1994.[52] The invitation from NATO heads of state, which was addressed to NACC participants and other CSCE member states, envisioned participation in NATO's political and military organs, providing for political consultation on security matters similar to that envisioned under Article IV of the Washington Treaty and for operational military cooperation with NATO Allies in a number of areas, in particular peacekeeping.[53] The invitation also specifically welcomed the possibility of "NATO expansion that would reach to democratic states to our East," but without offering any further clarification, criteria, or timetable for expansion.[54] The PfP Framework Document adopted along with the invitation allowed each partner country to establish its own individual program of cooperation. Supporters of the initiative praised this provision as a means for allowing each country to determine the degree of its association with the Alliance. Critics of PfP denounced the program as a ploy to divert attention from the real issue — to provide hard security to states that needed it by including them in the Alliance.[55]

Notwithstanding such criticism, response to the initiative was generally quick and positive. Almost all the European countries quickly prepared and submitted applications, both those that desired eventual NATO membership and others that desired closer cooperation and interoperability with the Alliance in responding to real security emergencies, in particular the ongoing wars in the Balkans. The Pentagon and US military leaders in particular were highly supportive of PfP because it gave them a framework for establishing and deepening operational military-to-military relationships with the defense establishments of most of the former Soviet allies and republics.[56] The PfP, along with the Combined Joint Task Force concept developed and adopted at the same time, gave US military and security officials new and better tools, adapted to the post–Cold War European political landscape, for responding to pressing operational security concerns.

Russia was initially happy with the PfP initiative, but for reasons exactly the opposite of those countries that saw it as a way station on the road to NATO membership. Talbott provides a memorable description of Yeltsin's reaction to the proposal when he and Christopher briefed the Russians on it immediately after the October 1993 Principals Committee meeting. Yeltsin interrupted Christopher to shout: "Genial'no! Zdorovo! Tell Bill this is a wonderful decision!"[57] However, the US record of the conversation shows that Yeltsin may have missed, and Christopher may have downplayed, the proposal's dual-track nature, and that PfP would not replace or preclude NATO enlargement.[58] Talbott's message for Yeltsin's subordinates, such as Foreign Minister Kozyrev and Deputy Foreign Minister Mamedov, was more explicit and nowhere near so welcome—namely, that PfP was merely a postponement of an inevitable enlargement of NATO.[59]

Thus, by the beginning of 1994, the decision to enlarge NATO had been made in principle. To be sure, the important questions of who, when, and how remained unresolved, but these were arguably less momentous than the strategic issue of whether to proceed with expansion at all. In analyzing the reasons for and the effects of this decision, several points stand out. First, the role of the United States was enormous, if not exclusive. The governments and publics of all the European Allies had diverse views on the subject, not all of which were in accord with those of Washington. Yet the United States dominated the debate and carried the day without either serious or prolonged opposition from within NATO.

Second, the motivating factors and stated explanations for the decision to enlarge the Alliance almost all involved the security and stability of the states on NATO's immediate periphery at the time—that is, the former Warsaw Pact states of Central and Eastern Europe. For the United States and some of its major Western European Allies, the wars in the former Yugoslavia appear to have had considerable influence in making more persuasive arguments concerning the effects of a security vacuum in Central Europe on the potential spread of ethnic conflict and instability. For Germany in particular, the desire to move NATO's frontier to the east, away from Germany's borders, had considerable attraction. However, for many of the Alliance's potential new members, the most persuasive argument for joining NATO remained their geographic proximity to Russia and a lingering historical sense of the threat emanating from the east.

For the Russians, NATO remained an anachronism and anathema. Beginning with Gorbachev and Shevardnadze, Soviet and then Russian leaders had accommodated and learned to live with the Alliance. However, Gorbachev and then Yeltsin aspired to participate as equals with their Western counterparts in building security structures and deciding security issues in Europe. Pro-Western Russian officials such as Kozyrev repeatedly drew attention publicly to the hostility felt by "national patriots" in Russia to the rapprochement with the West effected by the reformers in power in Russia.[60] Talbott recalls that his message about eventual NATO enlargement in October 1993 drew highly unfavorable reactions from both Mamedov and Kozyrev, probably the most pro-Western officials in the Russian government.[61] Perry and Carter recalled that their Russian military interlocutors, even at a time of exceptionally close cooperation, had a highly unfavorable, even hostile view of NATO as an unwanted relic of the Cold War and a sign that Western Europe would never accept Russia as a true partner.[62]

The basic strategic question that US and NATO leaders had to face after the Cold War was how to overcome the continent's previous divisions and to promote democracy, security, and stability in Europe as a whole. The idea of a Europe "whole and free" presumed the absence of dividing lines. Yet Clinton summarized the problem facing him in January 1994 in the following way: "I left for a long-planned trip to Europe to establish a process for opening NATO's door to Central European nations in a way that wouldn't cause Yeltsin too many problems in Russia. I was determined to do everything I could to create a Europe that was united, free, democratic, and secure for the first time in history. I had to make sure NATO expansion didn't simply lead to a new division of Europe farther to the East."[63]

Although one of the aims expressed in this statement—to avoid new dividing lines in Europe—is clear and praiseworthy, the distinction drawn between Central Europe and Russia with respect to eventual NATO enlargement leaves open the potential for such new lines, if it does not actually draw a new dividing line. Those who advocated enlarging NATO as a means of building democracy, market economies, ethnic peace, and stability in Central and Eastern Europe essentially hoped to have their cake and eat it too. Those who pushed the process convinced themselves, despite repeated warnings from their most pro-Western interlocutors in Moscow, that Russia could somehow be reconciled to and included in the process, without irreparable damage to relations with Russia or the process of reform within Russia. To a significant degree, this hope ignored the considerable historical fear of and animosity toward Russia that motivated the states seeking to join the Alliance. Perhaps deft management of the process of deciding who, when, and how in enlarging NATO might have produced a less divisive result. Or perhaps other factors and developments were instrumental in producing the mutual NATO-Russia animosity of 2017. Irrespective of subsequent events and causes, the very substance and justification of the 1993 decision to enlarge NATO at the very least greatly increased the possibility, and perhaps the likelihood, of an eventual new political and security division in Europe. Although by no means inevitable, such a division was far more likely on January 1, 1994, than it had been just one year earlier.

# THE EU ADDS COPENHAGEN TO MAASTRICHT

Although joining NATO seemed the best option for many of the former Warsaw Pact states and Soviet republics in order to provide for their own security and regional stability, the prospect of membership in a wider and deeper European Union appealed both to these states and to the former neutral and nonaligned nations as a rapid route to prosperity. Indeed, relatively early in the Cold War, a number of Western and Central European nations saw the benefit of establishing more liberal trade relations with the European Economic Community (EEC), even if at the time they did not share that bloc's aspiration for deeper economic and political association. The result was the founding in 1960 of the European Free Trade Association (EFTA), which initially included Austria, Denmark, Norway, Portugal, Sweden, Switzerland, and the United Kingdom.[64] The EFTA rapidly reached agreement on duty-free trade in industrial products with the EEC, and over the next three decades it reached free trade agreements with many other states in and beyond Europe. New members joined the EFTA as some left to join the EC. As the Cold War drew to a close in 1989, the EFTA began negotiations that concluded in 1992 with an agreement with the EU on a European Economic Area (EEA), which allowed EFTA states to participate in the benefits of the EU's common economic space.

For some of the EFTA states, simply reducing barriers and increasing access to the EU market was then, and to this day, remains sufficient. However, a larger number of the EFTA's members and other unaffiliated European states ultimately desired all the economic and political benefits of EU membership. As East/West tensions dissipated, between April 1987 and November 1992, Turkey, Austria, Cyprus, Malta, Sweden, Finland, Switzerland, and Norway applied for EU membership.[65] In 1994, a wave of applications began from the former Warsaw Pact states and the three Baltic republics. There were clearly special cases among the aspiring members. Turkey took years to decide to apply, and the EU took almost as long to accept and begin formal consideration of a Turkish candidacy.[66] Norway actually applied twice, and in 1992 and 1994 the Swiss and Norwegian publics rejected EU membership in popular referenda. NATO member Iceland as of 2015 was still debating whether an EU bid would be worth the effort.

By the early 1990s, with the disappearance of the Soviet Bloc, and thus of the major dividing line in Europe, it was obvious that the ambitious EU project for a united Europe, set in motion by the Single European Act and embodied in the Maastricht Treaty, was going to involve far more than the twelve countries that had launched the process in the 1980s. The real question was how the EU would develop its relationships with the rest of the countries in Europe.

The EEC and the EC had already developed elaborate bureaucratic procedures for establishing and conducting relations with nonmembers and for
processing applications and admitting new members. American diplomats,
frustrated by years of negotiations with the EC over meat and bananas, could
testify to the plenitude and complexity of EC/EU regulations and procedures.
After the disappearance of the Soviet Union and signature of the Maastricht
Pact, the EU faced at least three basic issues: (1) how far to expand the EU, that
is, which countries to accept as potential members; (2) what requirements to
set for aspiring members; and (3) what should be the framework and substance
of relations with nonmembers in Europe, especially those countries no longer
under Moscow's thumb.

The post-Maastricht environment in Europe was not particularly conducive
to orderly and deliberate consideration of future integrative efforts. The prolonged economic hardship, political chaos, and eventual September–October
1993 violence in Russia's transition, combined with the waves of refugees and
potential for spillover from the wars in the Balkans, created a background of
uncertainty and instability. A prolonged economic recession throughout much
of Western Europe in 1992 and 1993 created further domestic distraction for
and political pressure on European national leaders. The increasingly burden-
some demands for diplomatic and military personnel to staff the growing sanctions and peacekeeping missions in the Balkans placed strains upon even those
European powers with the greatest resources and expertise. Finally, against this
difficult background, the major powers within the EU did not see eye to eye on
a number of crucial issues, making the processes for both deepening and widening the EU even more complicated.

Germany in the mid-1990s was still devoting significant resources to the
efforts to bring its recently reunited eastern states closer to the economic level
of the former West Germany. Nonetheless, by 1994 Germany was still doing
better than many of its EU partners, with lower unemployment and economic
growth of almost 3.0 percent.[67] Despite the difficulty with accepting eventual
abandonment of the deutsche mark for European monetary union, which led
Germany to be the last to ratify the Maastricht Treaty, Chancellor Helmut Kohl
and his administration remained committed to the common economic space
(formally introduced on January 1, 1994) and even chided their EU colleagues,
in particular the French, for moving too slowly in deepening the union.[68]
Germany was especially well disposed to expanding the EU, particularly to the
east, given the discomfort German leaders felt at being on the frontier of both
NATO and the EU. With much the same reasoning, Germany paid greater attention and attached greater significance to building a constructive relationship with
Russia than did many of its EU colleagues.[69] Germany also was deeply involved
in addressing the crises and wars in the Balkans, from the infamous premature

recognition of Slovenia and Croatia by Foreign Minister Hans-Dietrich Genscher to Manfred Woerner's push for NATO to go out of area to assume responsibility for the Sarajevo exclusion zone. However, many Germans were not as willing to have their military follow Woerner into the Balkans, and the issue of German participation in foreign military operations, even peacekeeping, remained a sore subject in German domestic political debate for a long time.

France, meanwhile, was challenged by how to maintain its old role as one of the two leaders of the EU in partnership with a reunited, far more power-ful Germany. For decades, French thinkers and political leaders had provided the inspiration for and served as the drivers of the process of deepening the European political and economic union. In 1990, French president François Mitterrand clearly harbored fears about the effect of a reunified Germany on the balances of forces and French influence within the European Community. Some four to five years later, Mitterrand and his colleagues in Paris feared that adding new members from the north and east to the EU would serve to increase German influence at France's expense.[70] Ironically, although Paris had been a strong advocate for monetary union in the Maastricht Treaty negotiations, in the mid-1990s it appeared that the French might have more difficulty than the Germans in meeting the basic criteria for monetary union. In addition, the French had long-standing, traditional interests and concerns in the Mediter-ranean and Maghreb regions and believed that rapid EU expansion to the east would divert attention and resources from those regions. Finally, French leaders began a process at this time that came to fruition only years later of gradually abandoning their emphasis on the Western European Union as the European pillar of Euro-Atlantic security and returning to full participation in NATO's military structures. These were uneasy processes, punctuated at times by unilat-eral assertions of French sovereign power, such as Jacques Chirac's insistence on conducting widely condemned nuclear tests in the South Pacific.

The United Kingdom was another often uneasy spectator to the processes of German reunification, EU deepening and expansion, and the development of a European security and defense identity. Prime Minister Margaret Thatcher was both reluctant to see Germany reunified after the fall of the Berlin Wall and a dyed-in-the-wool Eurosceptic in managing the United Kingdom's relationship with the EU.[71] Indeed, her opposition to important elements of the draft Maas-tricht Treaty, along with polls showing the Labour Party consistently ahead of the Tories by a wide margin, reportedly played a role in her replacement as prime minister by John Major in November 1990. The United Kingdom under Major was less resistant to the process of European integration, although Major and his Tory colleagues still emphasized NATO and the transatlantic relation-ship and proved unwilling to adopt fully all the provisions of the Maastricht Treaty, in particular monetary union.[72] Britain under Tory leadership, whether

Thatcher or Major, continued to stress the preeminence of NATO in debates over the European Security and Defence Identity and the role of the Western European Union. The United Kingdom, though it recognized early on that NATO's enlargement to the east was probably inevitable, favored keeping this enlargement as small as possible, fearing that NATO's decisionmaking capabilities, power, and influence might be adversely affected by adding new members.[73] And though Major's more favorable stance than Thatcher toward the emerging EU may have played a role in the Tory victory at the polls in 1992, the United Kingdom still insisted on the "opt-out" and "subsidiarity" provisions in the Maastricht Treaty, which reflected continuing British ambivalence about fully joining the process of European integration.[74]

European Union bureaucrats expected that the creation of the European Economic Area (EEA) in the spring of 1992 would allay demands for rapid expansion of the EU beyond the borders of those member states in the process of finalizing the Maastricht negotiations.[75] However, similar to the roles envisioned and played by PfP with respect to NATO, the EEA rapidly became a waiting room for EFTA member states seeking EU membership. Of the seven EFTA members at the turn of the decade, Austria, Finland, Sweden, Norway, and Switzerland pursued EU membership. Advocates of membership argued, for the most part successfully, that even though the EFTA states were part of a large European market together with the EU, they had no effective voice in the development of rules for this integrated market without formal membership in the EU. The process of candidacy for all these states went very quickly (especially by EU standards) because they had already adopted large portions of the EU's *acquis communautaire* during the EFTA's negotiations during the 1980s with the EC over establishment of its single market. Formal membership negotiations with Austria, Finland, and Sweden began in early 1993 and finished thirteen months later in March 1994. On January 1, 1995, the three states joined the EU, bringing its membership to fifteen. Switzerland and Norway dropped out along the way, with the Swiss populace rejecting the EEA in a December 1992 vote and Norwegian voters refusing the EU in a November 1994 referendum.[76]

The Swiss and Norwegians were Europe's outliers. Almost all the remaining Central and Eastern European states, whether from the former Soviet orbit or among the so-called neutral nonaligned countries, found the attraction of joining the giant, growing, integrated economic and political bloc in Europe irresistible. Even before the accession negotiations of the first new members from the EFTA's ranks had begun, during 1992 EC officials reviewed the possible criteria that the EU might use in evaluating the candidacies of potential new members.[77] Although there were many bureaucratic and technical requirements for aspiring members, from the very start EU political leaders and officials stressed the importance of common or shared values, including human rights, democratic political systems, market economics, and the rule of law. At its June 1993 meeting in Copenhagen, the EU Council adopted what has become known as the "Copenhagen criteria," the most basic requirements for any prospective EU member. These include:

- Stable institutions guaranteeing democracy, the rule of law, human rights, and respect for and the protection of minorities;
- A functioning market economy and the capacity to cope with competition and market forces in the EU; and
- The ability to take on and implement effectively the obligations of membership, including adherence to the aims of political, economic, and monetary union.[78]

These criteria were aimed essentially not at the first three new members, which joined in 1995, but at the wave of Central and Eastern European nations that would apply in 1994 and 1995 and eventually become members a decade or more later. From very early on, the EU's leaders saw the enlargement process as a means of promoting democracy and market reform and cooperative international relations in Central and Eastern Europe.[79] Thus expansion of the EU into the former Soviet area from the start was envisioned as a strategy for supporting and achieving positive changes and results in the states involved, and not as a means of geopolitical expansion or drawing new dividing lines further to the east. However, unanticipated events in Europe and changes in the geopolitical context, along with the manner in which this strategy was elaborated and implemented for more than a decade and a half, ultimately produced additional, unforeseen consequences to the political and economic benefits envisioned by those who launched the process.

The EU's decision to expand and its bureaucratic response to assist aspiring members in making the economic, social, and political changes required in the application process also had an institutional effect on Europe's architecture of international organizations. The PHARE initiative (originally established in 1989 as the EC Poland and Hungary: Assistance for Restructuring their Economies program) was redirected in 1993 to assist applicants from Central and Eastern Europe, with a complete preaccession schedule of activities in place by 1997.[80] Similarly the Technical Assistance to the Commonwealth of Independent States (TACIS) program, established in 1991 to aid the non-Baltic former Soviet states in the transition to democratic market economies, gradually became one of the chief vehicles for these states to build a closer relationship with the EU.[81] With the enlargement of the EU and the development of institutional connections with Central and Eastern European states, Brussels became in essence the bureaucratic, institutional center for economic affairs in Europe. Although this process was of relatively little import to NATO, whose growing membership in any case would closely mirror that of the EU, it was of decisive significance for the economic and environmental dimension of the Organization for Security and Cooperation in Europe (OSCE). And though the second was never the strongest of the Helsinki Process's three baskets, the growth of the EU by the mid-1990s made the OSCE's economic dimension all but irrelevant.


## THE OSCE ADDS POSTCONFLICT
## RECONSTRUCTION AND RECONCILIATION


Despite the ambitious rhetoric of the concluding document, many of the participants considered the December 1994 OSCE Budapest Summit an overall failure for two important reasons.[82] First, as the United States made increasingly clear during the course of 1994 that it was intent on pushing for NATO enlargement in the relatively near future despite Russian objections, the encounter between presidents Clinton and Yeltsin in Budapest was one of their least pleasant and least successful meetings.[83] Angry at NATO's announcement that it would be proceeding with a study of enlargement, Yeltsin warned publicly at the summit of a coming "cold peace."[84] At the same time, the war in Bosnia seemed to be in one of its bleakest stages, and deep disagreements had appeared within NATO over how to deal with the continued fighting, widely reported atrocities against civilians, and the seeming inability of the international community, in particular the UN and NATO, to respond effectively.[85] Finally, shortly before coming to Budapest, Yeltsin issued an ultimatum to the leaders in Chechnya and subsequently ordered Russian military forces to "restore constitutional order" in that constituent republic.[86] At the time of the Budapest Summit, the Russian military had begun aerial bombardment of Chechnya, but Russian ground forces had not yet officially or overtly entered the republic.

Despite the apparently grim news and prospects as it began, 1995 ended better than expected for both the conflict in Bosnia and the OSCE. After military intervention by NATO and negotiation of the Dayton Agreement, the OSCE was entrusted—in tandem with the EU—with some of the most important aspects of postconflict reconciliation and reconstruction in the Balkans.[87] Furthermore, as the war in Chechnya developed, Moscow surprised almost everyone involved by agreeing to accept an OSCE field presence (called an Assistance Group rather than a mission) in Chechnya. The OSCE sustained or increased the activities of its existing field operations and looked to increase their number and scope, thereby significantly increasing and deepening its conflict prevention and management role and capabilities.

As described in chapter 3, the decisions on the role of the OSCE at the Budapest Summit left unresolved major disagreements between some of the larger participating states over the OSCE's place in the structure of the European security architecture. At least partly in response to Russian disappointment at not having the OSCE formally designated by the heads of state at Budapest as the leading European security institution, the OSCE participating states launched an ongoing dialogue on a comprehensive security model for Europe in the twenty-first century, which eventually led to the elaboration and adoption of the comprehensive Charter for European Security at the Istanbul Summit in November 1999. The push for an all-inclusive agreement and document on European security was a logical outgrowth of and heir to the aspirations for an undivided Europe and comprehensive definition of security embodied in the Charter of Paris and other immediate post–Cold War documents and proposals. Russia was especially keen to make the role and capabilities of the OSCE broader and stronger, essentially giving the OSCE preeminence over NATO, the EU, and other European multilateral security actors.

The debate over a security model for Europe mandated by the Budapest Summit was in reality an ongoing discussion between the OSCE's participating states about its preferred place, role, and powers in the European security architecture. As the Dutch observed in late 1994, "Their rhetoric notwithstanding, states do not seem too sure about the particular role of the CSCE in Europe or, if they are, how far they want to take that role."[88] The Hungarian Chairmanship in 1995 began discussion of the security model for Europe among delegations in Vienna but also organized several external seminars, including one in Moscow. The OSCE states agreed to embrace the OSCE's existing comprehensive concept of security, thus including human rights, national minority questions, and economic issues, among others, along with hard military security.[89] OSCE representatives also agreed that a security model should be inclusive, in the sense that it should include other participants—such as international organizations, nongovernmental organizations, and the like—and not be limited to the structures and roles of the OSCE. The debates launched by the Hungarian Chair also sought to identify the major threats and challenges for European security in the new post–Cold War milieu.

Discussions under the Swiss OSCE Chair in 1996 became more institutionally specific and operational, especially as preparations for the Lisbon Summit at the end of the year grew more intense. During 1996, a rough consensus formed around a model of common and cooperative security, in which interlocking institutions in the OSCE area would collaborate in a nonhierarchical fashion on the basis of comparative advantage.[90] This approach reflected a general assumption that the major security problems Europe would face after the end of the Cold War would come from conflicts not between states but within states. In particular, ethnic and national minority issues and the disintegration of states were identified as major challenges.[91] The principle of cooperation between mutually reinforcing institutions became the central theme of the OSCE's approach to the new security model for Europe. The heads of state and government at the Lisbon Summit endorsed this approach and mandated further work aimed at developing the "Platform for Cooperative Security."[92] The concluding document at Lisbon reflected an approach of "co-operative security based on democracy, respect for human rights, fundamental freedoms and the rule of law, market economy and social justice. It excludes any quest for domination. It implies mutual confidence and the peaceful settlement of disputes."[93]

Several different national approaches to European security structures and their interrelationship were in play in the discussion of the OSCE security model. After failing at Budapest in 1994 to establish a UN Security Council–style structure within the OSCE and to assert the OSCE's preeminence over other European security institutions, Russia tried other approaches to assert its major power status, and in particular to obtain recognition of what it saw as its sphere of influence in its former Soviet neighborhood.[94] For example, Moscow sought the OSCE's imprimatur for its national or Commonwealth of Independent States (CIS) peacekeeping operations in Georgia and Moldova, and its role as a mediator in conflicts in the former USSR region. Russia also sought to maximize the role of the OSCE in European security affairs as a means of ensuring that it had a contributing and deciding role in major European security issues. It was at this time that Moscow's use of the phrase "no new dividing lines in Europe" began to be understood as opposition to NATO's expansion.[95]

The major EU states also continued to hold very different views and had trouble defining the desired role and importance of the OSCE. Germany, France, and the United Kingdom were all deeply committed to the Helsinki Process, but the creation of the EU and the attempts to give content to its declared common foreign and security policy produced varied conceptions from London, Paris, and Bonn on the OSCE's future. Germany and the Netherlands sought to emphasize the OSCE's link with the UN declared in the 1992 Helsinki Document and to enhance OSCE peacekeeping and conflict resolution capabilities as a means of addressing conflicts in Eastern and Southeastern Europe.[96] Paris favored giving the OSCE a legal personality and emphasizing its potential for peaceful resolution of disputes, arms control, and disarmament, while reserving potentially more muscular security capabilities for the EU. The United Kingdom came up with the idea of the Platform for European Security as a way of emphasizing the OSCE's role in coordinating and providing an imprimatur or legitimacy to operations conducted by other security actors. For the British, the transatlantic connection and NATO were still the most important elements of European security.

The Central and Eastern European states by this time were already looking toward enlargement of NATO and the EU as the path to strengthening their own security as much as any increased role for the OSCE. The United States basically reinforced this tendency because Washington saw NATO as the most important structure in the European security architecture, while at the same time supporting an increased role and capabilities for the OSCE in addressing specific issues. US support for the OSCE's post-Dayton role in overseeing elections and implementing the disarmament and confidence-building provisions of that agreement testify to Washington's willingness to make major use of the organization. The chief US condition in this and similar cases was that the OSCE should not be strengthened instead of—or at the expense of—NATO. It is in this sense that one should read provisions in the Budapest Summit and Ministerial documents and in the Lisbon declaration to the effect that each country should be free "to choose or change its security arrangements, including treaties of alliance, as they evolve."[97] The United States stood firmly and consistently with the Central and Eastern Europeans on the overriding importance of enlarging the Atlantic Alliance.

The OSCE in the mid-1990s after the Budapest Summit was defined as much by the growth and character of its field operations as by the conceptual discussion of the European security model. With the agreement of Azerbaijan and Armenia to a cease-fire in 1994 in their conflict over Nagorno-Karabakh, the OSCE's Minsk Group and the High-Level Planning Group in Vienna resumed serious discussions on a possible OSCE peacekeeping operation in that region.[98] The field missions in Georgia, Moldova, and the former Yugoslav Republic of Macedonia remained busy, with varying degrees of success, through the mid-1990s. In mid-1994, the OSCE sent experts on constitutional law and economics to Ukraine to support its newly elected president, Leonid Kuchma, in his attempt to reach an agreement on power sharing with local Russophone authorities in Crimea.[99] The OSCE established a field mission in Kyiv to support the work of these experts and other efforts aimed at resolving the issue of Crimea's status within Ukraine. Although the Serbian authorities refused permission to reopen the original Mission of Long Duration in Kosovo, Vojvodina, and Sandjak—not the least because the Federal Republic of Yugoslavia remained suspended from the OSCE—the OSCE continued to play a key part in the deployment and operation of Sanctions Assistance Missions in the region.[100] Finally, the CSCE deployed field missions to Estonia and Latvia in 1993, in part to address Russian concerns about the status of Russian speakers in these states.[101] Although the missions were mandated primarily to address national minority and citizenship issues, their presence arguably also helped ensure Russia's continued fulfillment of its commitment to withdraw its military forces from the Baltic states, a process that was essentially complete by late 1994.[102]

One of the most striking developments of 1995 was Moscow's acceptance of an OSCE presence in its war-torn Republic of Chechnya. The motivation for the Russian decision was a complex mix—a desire to promote the status of the OSCE (as opposed to NATO) as a leading European hard security institution, a related aspiration for OSCE endorsement of Russian peacekeeping operations and initiatives in the CIS region, and a need to deflect a storm of criticism from Europe over human rights abuses in the brutal Chechen campaign.[103] Moscow increasingly needed a neutral broker in the North Caucasus as well as a visible concession to international opinion after the Council of Europe delayed its application for membership and the EU suspended its interim trade accord after reports of atrocities from Chechnya. In any event, the OSCE agreed in early April to send an Assistance Group to Russia to help with the conflict in Chechnya by promoting human rights, facilitating the delivery of international assistance, aiding with the return of refugees and internally displaced people, promoting resolution of the conflict, and supporting the rule of law.[104]

The OSCE field presence deployed to Chechnya in late April 1995, a remarkably short time after the mandate was adopted.[105] The work of the mission was exceedingly difficult. Negotiations on a settlement organized by the OSCE opened on the heels of the notorious hospital hostage taking in Budennovsk. Hostilities continued through 1995, and the OSCE had occasion to criticize the Russians for brutality and the Chechens for hostage taking.[106] Assistance Group personnel departed the region temporarily in December 1995, when elections for the Chechen head of state were held, contrary to the recommendation of the mission. The Russian authorities cooperated, but without much apparent enthusiasm, with efforts by the OSCE to mediate the conflict. However, as the presidential elections in Russia approached and the fight continued to go badly for Moscow, Yeltsin eventually softened his stand, dispatched his newly appointed security adviser, General Aleksandr Lebed, to negotiate, and in August 1996 accepted the Agreement of Khasavyurt, signed in the presence of the head of the OSCE Assistance Group, and providing for a cease-fire and final resolution of Chechnya's status by 2001.[107] This proved to be the high point for the OSCE's activities in Chechnya, as the deterioration of the security situation, growing Russian resentment of external involvement in what it regarded as a wholly domestic matter, and the outbreak of the Second Chechen War led to evacuation of the mission to Moscow, a brief return, and eventual closure in 2003, as President Putin found another path to resolving the conflict.

The greatest operational expansion in the OSCE's responsibilities and activities came at the end of 1995, in conjunction with the signature and implementation

of the Dayton Agreement ending the war in Bosnia. Conscious of European political sensitivities and aspirations after successfully forcing an agreement among
the warring former Yugoslav parties, American leaders deliberately accorded the
leading role in implementing the political provisions of the Dayton Accord to
the European Union.[108] The agreement provided for the appointment of a high
representative to oversee implementation of all civilian aspects of the accords.
The first to hold the office was Carl Bildt, former prime minister of Sweden;
in practice, the high representative was always from an EU country, with the
principal deputy from the United States.[109] The primary US concern was that
NATO lead the military force that guaranteed fulfillment of the agreement, but
Washington was not certain about EU capabilities to handle civilian implementation on its own. In addition, the United States was willing to obtain a formal
UN mandate authorizing the Implementation Force (IFOR), but after years of
what it saw as UN mismanagement of the international effort in the Balkans
during the war, Washington was leery of any operational UN involvement in
post-Dayton Bosnia.[110]

Washington settled on the OSCE as the logical choice, in cooperation with
the Office of the High Representative, to implement the civilian provisions of
Dayton. This allowed the United States to participate extensively in the process,
while also involving EU personnel, other Europeans, and the Russians. On
December 8, 1995, the Budapest OSCE Ministerial Council adopted the mandate for the new Mission to Bosnia-Herzegovina, with the tasks of supervising
the preparation and holding of the first postwar elections, monitoring human
rights and the rule of law, and facilitating the implementation of arms control and confidence- and security-building measures.[111] An American diplomat
was appointed head of mission, with deputies from the EU and Russia. With a
staff of more than 230 mission members in addition to support personnel from
many other international organizations, the Bosnia Mission was by far the largest field operation mounted by the OSCE. The Bosnia Mission quickly ended
up coordinating efforts with an array of international actors, including the EC/
EU Monitoring Mission, the Office of the High Representative, the Council
of Europe, the International Monetary Fund, the World Bank, and a host of
nongovernmental organizations.

The two most pressing tasks faced by the OSCE in Bosnia immediately after
Dayton were agreeing on and implementing confidence- and security-building
measures (CSBMs) and guiding the process leading to elections. Special representatives of the OSCE Chair from Hungary and Norway successfully brought
the three parties to Dayton to agreement on CSBMs and regional arms control (Articles II and IV of Annex 1B of the Dayton Agreement) and launched
implementation.[112] The process of getting Bosnia-Herzegovina to the point of
successfully holding elections proved even more difficult. The OSCE set up

a Provisional Election Commission, chaired by the OSCE head of mission, who had the authority to resolve any disputes within the commission. Despite widespread misgivings about lack of adequate preparations and suitable conditions, the OSCE decided there was no good alternative to holding presidential and parliamentary elections in September 1996; municipal elections were postponed until November. The OSCE fielded about 1,200 election supervisors and 900 international observers, and provided a lukewarm but controversial endorsement of the vote.[113] The elections demonstrated the depth of lingering ethnic animosity in Bosnia-Herzegovina, and the OSCE was severely criticized both for going ahead with the vote and for accepting the results. Given the high-profile role of the American head of mission, some OSCE staffers even began to joke that the institution should be renamed the "Organization to Secure Clinton's Election."[114]

While the Dayton negotiations were going on, an OSCE fact-finding mission visited Croatia, in part to investigate local conditions after the summer's battles, which had eradicated the breakaway Krajina Serb entity.[115] This visit launched a dialogue with the Croatian authorities that eventually produced agreement in April 1996 on the establishment of an OSCE mission in Zagreb, which would cover all of Croatia's territory and would coordinate the postconflict reconciliation and reconstruction efforts of an alphabet soup of international organizations.[116] Given concerns expressed particularly by Russia over the fate of Serb populations and refugees, the Croatia Mission was tasked with assisting Croatian authorities with human rights, national minority issues, the rule of law, and development of democratic institutions. The Mission to Croatia, like its counterpart in Bosnia-Herzegovina, also began with a much larger staff than all previous OSCE field operations, and then grew even more during the initial years of its activity. Together, the missions to Bosnia-Herzegovina and Croatia provided a model for postconflict reconstruction field operations subsequently deployed by the OSCE at various times and in various forms throughout the Balkans, including Albania, Kosovo, Serbia, and the former Yugoslav Republic of Macedonia. More than twenty years after Dayton, some of these missions are still operating, including (sadly) the one in Bosnia-Herzegovina.

Finally, during the mid-1990s the OSCE's Office for Democratic Institutions and Human Rights (ODIHR) worked out and put into practice the methodology for election observation that eventually became its trademark and—in the words of one senior American official a decade later—the "gold standard" for assessing whether elections were free and fair.[117] The new framework called for ODIHR to focus attention on the periods before and after elections in participating states, which allowed election experts "to make more thorough enquiries into the situation as regards the political rights of citizens."[118] ODIHR election monitoring and support activities were significantly expanded to meet the demands placed on the OSCE by the Dayton requirements in Bosnia. However, it is also from this time that one observes the routine deployment of short- and long-term ODIHR election observation missions to a growing number of OSCE participating states. Among those elections observed and evaluated were the Russian Federation's parliamentary elections in December 1995 and both rounds of the presidential elections in Russia in the summer of 1996. At the time, few observers objected to ODIHR's conclusion in July 1996 that "the OSCE ODIHR Observer Mission believes that the declared result of the election accurately reflects the wishes of the Russian electorate on the day, and congratulates the voters of the Russian Federation for participating in a further consolidation of the democratic process in the Russian Federation."[119] Whatever one thought of the substantive judgments in Bosnia and Russia in 1996, the precedent of ODIHR commenting on and evaluating election practices and results was clearly established. A decade later, it would create controversy.

## THE OSCE: ARMS CONTROL AND HARD SECURITY

During the mid-1990s, the United States also used the OSCE as a platform to address some of Russia's most pressing security concerns. As the war in Chechnya intensified, Russia found it necessary to move significant military assets, both troops and heavy armor, to the North Caucasus. The fighting in Chechnya was taking place in a portion of the Russian Federation that was covered by the so-called Flank Agreement restrictions of the CFE Treaty, with limitations imposed on the deployment of troops and treaty-limited equipment (TLE) in northern and southern regions of the USSR near to NATO Allies Norway and Turkey as an additional protection for those countries against attack by overwhelming Soviet forces.[120] After the dissolution of the Soviet Union, the southern flank region was divided among a number of the former Soviet republics and Russia's volatile North Caucasus region. Russia complained repeatedly that the Flank Agreement limits in the treaty were outdated and hampered its response to the present day security problems presented by the conflict in Chechnya. Finally, in November 1995, the thirty states parties agreed to consider revising the flank provisions.[121]

From May 15 to 31, 1996, at the first of the review conferences required by the CFE Treaty to be held every five years, the states-parties adopted changes to the areas included as part of the flank and agreed upon what amounted to more generous allotments for Russia for permanent and temporary deployments of troops and TLE in the region.[122] The United States took the lead both in negotiating the changes to the Flank Agreement provisions of the treaty and in convincing the states-parties to ratify the agreement, especially Russia's former Soviet neighbors to the south, who were wary of permitting even temporary accumulations of Russian military equipment near their borders. To allay such fears, the Flank Agreement also provided for additional regular inspections and exchanges of information on TLE in Russia and Ukraine. The revisions were duly ratified by all parties (100–0 in the US Senate!) and entered into force by mid-1997.

Another Russian concern with respect to the CFE Treaty involved the change in the balance of conventional forces in Europe between the time the treaty was adopted and the mid-1990s. The original CFE Treaty signed in 1990 provides for parity between the conventional forces of the Warsaw Pact and those of NATO deployed in Europe. At that time, the conventional forces of the Soviets and their allies were still somewhat larger than those of the NATO Allies. By 1996, the Warsaw Pact no longer existed, and the combined conventional forces of the Atlantic Alliance significantly outnumbered those of Russia. It was also evident by 1996 that when NATO expanded its conventional advantage over Russia would increase even more. In light of the changes in circumstances and the military balance in Europe, the states-parties at the review conference agreed to begin negotiations on revising the treaty.[123] Also notable, especially in retrospect, was the specific inclusion at the review conference of a provision in the Flank Agreement that requires host nation consent for foreign military deployments, already a concern of several former Soviet states with Russian troops still present.

Similar to the negotiation of the original CFE Treaty, the CFE review conferences and the negotiation of an adapted treaty took place "within the context of," but not formally as part of, the OSCE. The CFE's standing Joint Consultative Group met regularly in Vienna, so that the CFE negotiators were generally part of their nations' OSCE delegations, and sometimes actually one and the same. The process of CFE review and adaptation thus remained closely linked with the OSCE. The May 1996 review conference noted that "the States Parties recognize that the Treaty and the Concluding Act are essential contributions to the achievement of the goals and purposes of the Organization for Security and Co-operation in Europe (OSCE), in particular the promotion of confidence, stability and security in an undivided Europe."[124] At the Lisbon OSCE Summit in early December 1996, the OSCE participating states adopted a framework for arms control that placed the CFE Treaty in a broader context of arms reductions, transparency, and CSBMs, also including the Vienna Documents, Open Skies Treaty, and OSCE Code of Conduct.[125] At the same time, the CFE parties formally advised the Lisbon Summit of agreement to begin negotiations on adapting the CFE Treaty from its existing bloc-to-bloc structure to a system of national and territorial limits that would better reflect current and future conventional military and political realities in Europe.[126] Formal negotiations on adapting the treaty began in the Joint Consultative Group in January 1997.

The process agreed on for adapting the CFE Treaty and the overall Framework for Arms Control were very much in the spirit of the emerging Common and Comprehensive Security Model for Europe also endorsed at the Lisbon Summit. These decisions and concepts all reflect the approach to the developing European security architecture of the United States and its major Western European Allies, in which a framework of cooperative, overlapping, and interlocking institutions could be seen to allow for an expansion of NATO and the EU that would not come at the expense of other states or institutions. Although Washington obtained a consensus among the NATO Allies for the Flank Agreement and the CFE Treaty's adaptation proposals before negotiating them with Moscow, the initiative to accommodate the CFE regime to Russian concerns clearly came from the United States, whose efforts both brought the flank revisions into force and provided the fundamental concepts for the Adapted CFE Treaty eventually signed in Istanbul in November 1999.[127] These actions by Washington were part of an overall US strategy aimed at keeping Russia inside and supportive of the changing security architecture in Europe, in particular directed at diminishing if not eliminating Russia's objections to NATO expansion.

## NATO EXPANSION: HOW, WHEN, AND WHO

Despite renewed discussions of possible OSCE peacekeeping in Nagorno-Karabakh after the cease-fire between Armenia and Azerbaijan in mid-1994 and the subsequent activities of the OSCE's Minsk Group, the establishment of the Partnership for Peace and the initiation of formal military activities under the aegis of that program rapidly ensured that the OSCE would have no military forces or military activities beyond observation, information exchanges, and CSBMs. During 1994 the Central and Eastern European states were almost all quick to sign on to PfP, to establish military-to-military contacts with the Alliance, and to work out formal programs of activities.[128] The enthusiasm for PfP did not mean that many of these states had changed their minds about seeking NATO membership; most understood that PfP provided the best path for pursuing membership and acted accordingly.[129] By September 1994, the first PfP military exercise was held in Poland, including troops from six NATO Allies, six former Warsaw Pact members, and Ukraine.[130] By late

1994, almost all the new partners had missions at NATO headquarters in Brussels, and the Alliance established a Partnership Coordination Cell at Supreme Headquarters Allied Powers Europe (known as SHAPE) to help coordinate training and exercises; in 1995, SHAPE added an International Coordination Cell to provide briefing and planning for all non-NATO countries contributing to NATO's peacekeeping operations.[131]

The Russian response to PfP was less positive; Moscow quickly understood that the initiative was not only no guarantee against enlargement of the Alliance but would most likely actually facilitate it. Clinton's first discussions of the subject with Yeltsin in Moscow after the January 1994 NATO Summit gave hints of the coming disagreement, despite Yeltsin's apparent endorsement of PfP.[132] Yeltsin's remark to Clinton that Russia should become the first new member of an enlarged Alliance began a year during which Moscow alternately attempted to assert a special status in its relationship with NATO or to block enlargement. The Pentagon's leadership expended special effort to convince their Russian counterparts to take advantage of PfP to build a special military-to-military relationship with the United States, but there was bitter opposition from deep within Russia's bureaucracy and political elites. When Kozyrev signed the agreement for Russia's participation in PfP in June 1994, the Alliance agreed to a joint statement emphasizing the importance of NATO-Russia cooperation.[133] However, in December 1994, as Russia appeared finally ready to sign its PfP program of action, NATO's announcement of the proposed *Study on Enlargement* right before Clinton's travel to the Budapest OSCE Summit brought further delay and Yeltsin's warning about a cold peace in Europe.[134]

During much of 1995, Washington devoted considerable effort to repairing the US-Russian relationship after the crockery broken at the December 1994 NATO and OSCE gatherings, and NATO itself worked out a definitive set of criteria for admitting new members. With Russia, the United States expended extensive high-level diplomatic energy in preparing the ground for the Yeltsin-Clinton summit in Moscow in May 1995, at which the Russian president agreed to participate fully in PfP in return for launching a special NATO-Russia dialogue.[135] In private, Clinton promised Yeltsin that in return for Russia's engagement in dialogue with NATO and participation in PfP, actual enlargement of the Alliance would be held off until after presidential elections in both countries in 1996.[136]

Meanwhile, the war in Bosnia became the central question with respect both to NATO's expansion and its viability. Arriving in Washington in late 1994 from his post as ambassador to Germany, Richard Holbrooke used his new post as assistant secretary of state for Europe to push for greater US and NATO involvement in the Balkan conflicts. As disasters continued into mid-1995, Holbrooke won his bureaucratic battles in both Washington and Brussels; by summer's end, NATO air strikes combined with Croatian ground offensives in both Croatia and Bosnia-Herzegovina brought Milošević to the negotiating table and posed the very real questions of the mandate and composition of a NATO-led peacekeeping force to enforce any settlement reached at Dayton.[137] The Clinton-Yeltsin discussions at the October 1995 Hyde Park Summit and ongoing contacts between US secretary of defense Perry and Russian minister of defense Grachev eventually produced a formula for Russian participation in IFOR, with the Russians agreeing to serve under the overall commander in his capacity as US commander in Europe rather than commander of NATO forces.[138]

While US and NATO leaders dealt with the simultaneous problems of vocal Russian opposition to NATO's enlargement and the seeming inability of external efforts to end the fighting in Bosnia, the bureaucratic process of examining "how NATO will enlarge, the principles to guide this process and the implications of membership," mandated by the December 1994 NATO Ministerial, provided a bureaucratic mechanism for keeping the process of enlargement moving while postponing some of the most sensitive internal political decisions involved.[139] The *Study on NATO Enlargement*, released by the Alliance on September 3, 1995, is a bureaucratic document that reflects the lowest common denominator among all of the Allies, the fundamental political principles and realities that had to be reflected in any decision on enlargement in order to maintain unanimous support within NATO.[140] The Enlargement Study claims that an enlarged NATO will be part of a European security architecture that contributes to stability and security while threatening no one. Although the study refers to NATO's purpose under the Washington Treaty of collective defense, it makes no mention of any particular threats, specifying only that the Alliance must be prepared to respond to new risks and challenges, yet to be determined. Instead, the document refers to the 1991 revised Strategic Concept, which stated that "the threat of a simultaneous, full-scale attack on all of NATO's European fronts has effectively been removed." The study asserts that the "architecture of European security" includes European institutions, such as the EU and Western European Union; transatlantic institutions, such as NATO; and Euro-Atlantic bodies, such as the OSCE, which were especially important because they provided the framework for agreements such as the CFE Treaty regime.

At the top of the list for how NATO enlargement will contribute to stability and security, the Enlargement Study places "encouraging and supporting democratic reforms, including civilian and democratic control over the military."[141] The study reiterates several times this commitment to democracy, individual liberty, and the rule of law, in particular as enshrined in the UN Charter. The document reflects explicitly the conviction that security and peaceful international relations are strengthened by the spread of free institutions. The study also asserts the contribution enlargement will make toward peaceful cooperation and integration throughout Europe. Notably, the study explicitly requires states that have ethnic disputes, external territorial disputes, or internal jurisdictional disputes to settle these issues peacefully, in accordance with OSCE principles, as a factor to be considered in determining whether they will be invited to join the Alliance.

Finally, the Enlargement Study addresses Russia's relationship with NATO and opposition to enlargement directly, in some detail.[142] The study notes that Russia has an important role to play in European security and calls for a special NATO-Russia relationship to be developed through the dialogue already begun. The Enlargement Study envisions a special NATO-Russia relationship as one of the basic building blocks of a comprehensive European security structure, but crucially notes that Russia cannot be given a veto or *droit de regard* on Alliance decisions. In effect, the study explicitly promises that NATO will address Russian concerns with respect to enlargement, but implicitly makes clear that these concerns could not block enlargement.

As American, Russian, and other European troops deployed in IFOR throughout Bosnia-Herzegovina in early 1996, the real political processes began of determining which countries would join the Alliance, when, and what the arrangement with Russia would be. Political forces within the United States strongly pushed the Clinton administration on this issue; after the Republican electoral victories in November 1994, both the Senate and House were vocal in support of enlargement.[143] As the 1996 presidential elections approached, Clinton was mindful of large Central European diasporas located in key states such as Pennsylvania, Ohio, Michigan, and Illinois, for whom NATO enlargement was an important issue. Beyond domestic politics, for US officials NATO enlargement became part of the *raison d'etre* for maintaining the Alliance as the primary vehicle for America's continued presence and involvement in European security affairs.[144] Germany particularly favored both NATO and EU expansion into central Europe, both to move the borders of the Alliance to the east and to forestall the reemergence of historical rivalries between Central European states.[145] French support for NATO enlargement gradually increased, both as it became apparent that support was minimal within the EU for strengthening the Western European Union, and as the newly elected president, Chirac, began to explore more seriously reintegrating France into the Alliance's military structures.[146] The United Kingdom was also relatively slow to warm to NATO's enlargement, fearing dilution of the Alliance and its transatlantic relationship, but grew more supportive with the deployment and successful role of IFOR in the Balkans.

The candidates for membership almost all remained enthusiastic. Poland, Hungary, and the Czech Republic had the inside track, as all three had more successfully than most of their neighbors implemented democratic and market reforms. Hungary also helped its case by extensive cooperation with NATO operations in the former Yugoslavia in the second half of 1995 and logistical assistance with IFOR deployments.[147] The Slovak Republic, once considered a shoo-in for membership in the first wave, was gradually separated from its Visegrad partners because of the erratic and antidemocratic behavior of its prime minister, Vladimir Meciar. Slovenia and the three Baltic states made impassioned applications for membership but were each judged a bridge too far for inclusion in the first round of enlargement. The surprise result of the 1996 presidential elections in Romania, with the victory of opposition candidate Emil Constantinescu, brought Bucharest strong support from some European states, particularly France. In part because of domestic political reasons, Clinton announced US support for NATO expansion by the Alliance's fiftieth anniversary in 1999 at a September 1996 campaign rally near Detroit.[148] Also for domestic reasons, fearing that the US Senate would not ratify a NATO enlargement with too many candidates, the Clinton administration made public its endorsement of only three candidates—Poland, Hungary, and the Czech Republic—more than a month before the NATO summit at which the formal decision was taken. There was grumbling among some Allies at the manner in which Washington short-circuited and essentially predetermined the results of the debate, but the rest of the Alliance duly fell into line. On July 8, 1997, the NATO heads of state met in Madrid and formally invited Poland, Hungary, and the Czech Republic to begin the process of formal accession to the Alliance, which would be completed in Washington in April 1999.[149]

Just as it directed the pace and determined the results of the first enlargement, the United States also led the process of negotiating a special relationship between NATO and Russia. This endeavor became significantly more complicated after Clinton reached his understanding with Yeltsin at Hyde Park in the autumn of 1995. With parliamentary elections in December 1995 producing yet another Duma dominated by communists and nationalists, Yeltsin replaced Kozyrev as foreign minister with foreign intelligence chief Yevgeniy Primakov, who had a considerably more suspicious, less forthcoming attitude toward the West. Yeltsin then suffered a heart attack during his reelection campaign in mid-1996 and was not healthy enough to work or meet with foreign interlocutors for several months, which meant that US and NATO negotiators for a time had to deal almost exclusively with Primakov.[150]

Starting with the December 1995 NATO Ministerial, Secretary of State Christopher made several public statements pushing forward the process of consultations with those states seeking membership.[151] After Yeltsin's reelection in the summer of 1996, in a speech in Stuttgart in September, Christopher proposed that a NATO summit be held in the spring or summer of 1997, at which new members would be invited to join, and that at the same time NATO negotiate a formal charter with Russia. Christopher's initial encounters with Primakov were difficult and unproductive, but the United States persevered. At the December 1996 North Atlantic Council meeting, Christopher made the famous statement of the "three nos": that NATO had no need, no plans, and no intention of extending nuclear deployments in Europe. After a meeting in Lisbon between Vice President Gore and Prime Minister Chernomyrdin and agreement on adapting the CFE Treaty, Moscow indicated it was ready to negotiate a charter with NATO and that Primakov would be the one to cut this deal. The United States supported the designation of NATO secretary-general Javier Solana as the principal negotiator with Primakov, although in fact Solana worked closely with a US National Security Council official, Sandy Vershbow, and closely coordinated the text of the NATO-Russia Charter with Washington.

Negotiations on a charter continued, but were still extremely difficult until Clinton and Yeltsin met in Helsinki in March 1997.[152] Clinton's promise of support for Russia's integration into global institutions, epitomized by undertaking to turn the G-7 into the G-8 by including Yeltsin in the next meeting, did a great deal to overcome Moscow's resistance to NATO's enlargement. The promise by NATO that "in the current and foreseeable security environment" there would be no "additional permanent stationing of substantial combat forces" in the new members of the Alliance also was important in overcoming Russian objections.[153] Finally, the prospect of holding a summit in May exclusively for signing the charter also appealed to Yeltsin. In any event, by the accounts of almost all participants, Primakov became more amenable after the Helsinki summit — or at least it became easier for the Western negotiators to get Yeltsin to overrule him. The NATO-Russia Charter, or "Founding Act," was completed with Russia, agreed on within NATO, and signed in Paris on May 27, 1997.

The Founding Act is at the same time both a bureaucratic and a strategic policy document.[154] On the bureaucratic, operational side, the document establishes the Permanent Joint Council as the mechanism for cooperation between Russia and NATO, with formal rules of procedure and specific substantive areas enumerated whereby NATO and Russia will cooperate. Some of these areas are ambitious, such as peacekeeping, theater missile defense, and nuclear safety. Others seem more mundane, such as air traffic control and disaster relief. And still others seem vague and probably unattainable, for example, conversion of defense industries. As for the political or policy aspects of the document and the strategic understanding between Russia and NATO that this document reflects, the extensive discussion of the CFE Treaty, the need for its adaptation, and the possible effects of enlargement on the existing correlation of conventional military forces within Europe all reflect real Russian concerns about the ongoing political-military changes and realignment going on in Europe since 1989, in particular Russia's military weakness and its political inability to halt or affect the basic direction of these changes. The opening paragraphs of the Founding Act express the Alliance's political commitment to a peaceful, cooperative relationship with Russia. The introductory paragraphs also describe a comprehensive, cooperative security architecture developing in Europe, a vision similar to that outlined in contemporary OSCE documents, such as that adopted at the Lisbon Summit. However, a key feature of this document is that it is a political commitment, not a formal treaty obligation. As with the promise about possible deployments on the territory of new members, the rest of the document, in the end, is dependent upon "the current and foreseeable security environment." The Founding Act successfully mitigated Russia's opposition to the first wave of NATO enlargement and created the possibility of decent working relations between Brussels and Moscow. However, the Allies—and the United States, in particular—retained the possibility of adjusting the terms of these relations if the security environment became something unforeseen. It did not take long for this to happen.

# 5. WAR OVER KOSOVO

## The Parting of the Ways

The Paris and Madrid NATO summits of mid-1997 seemed to be great victories for the Atlantic Alliance and for the advocates of NATO enlargement. Democratic stability and security would be spread to Central and Eastern Europe, and a special relationship with Russia might help promote the continuation of reform in that country. Arms control, confidence, and transparency in Europe were being strengthened and extended, in particular as an adaptation of the Treaty on Conventional Armed Forces in Europe was launched. A new, post–Cold War, comprehensive, cooperative security architecture for Europe was gradually taking shape, with the component structures of this edifice developing their capabilities, increasing their memberships, and refining their missions. European integration, with the addition of three new members of the European Union and gradual movement toward a single currency and a common defense, was becoming both wider and deeper. Finally, the Organization for Security and Cooperation in Europe (OSCE) — the pan-European security organization — was growing in capabilities and increasing the amount and scope of its activities aimed at conflict prevention or resolution and postconflict reconciliation and reconstruction.

Alas, from other angles, the picture looked much less rosy. Resentments lingered and festered in Russia at the weakness and the inability of the former global power to deflect or deter NATO's geographic growth. The effects of incomplete economic reform, corrupt privatization, and the erosion of state authority and with it law and order led eventually to a dramatic economic collapse in Russia.

An increasingly ailing President Boris Yeltsin ruled by decree, appointing a merry-go-round of prime ministers to make it less attractive to a hostile legislature to impeach him. In the Balkans, peace was achieved in Bosnia-Herzegovina and Croatia, but at the cost of neglecting Kosovo, a powder keg of suppressed (and oppressed) ethnic Albanian resentments. Irrespective of progress on arms control and common security in the OSCE framework, or collaboration for regional stability with the European Union, the decisive event for European security and security institutions at the end of the 1990s was again conflict in the Balkans. The revolt of ethnic Albanians in Kosovo against Serbian rule, Belgrade's brutal response, and NATO's unilateral intervention over Russia's objections in the end cast a pall over NATO-Russia relations that has still not lifted.

In fact, for Europe the last years of the twentieth century were beset by security contradictions and paradoxes. Although Moscow's Western partners claimed to see and support continuing democratic and market reforms, Russia under Yeltsin was never as open, stable, or pro-Western as his supporters might have wished. Washington's attention was increasingly diverted by a global agenda, and the top concerns were containing Saddam Hussein, stopping Iran's nuclear program (after failing to do so with Pakistan and India), and managing China/ Taiwan tensions. After the Labor landslide victory in 1997, Germany, France, and the United Kingdom took significant steps toward resolving some of the basic issues that had been holding up creation of a European security and defense identity, and Germany and France led the way toward implementation of monetary union. In November 1999, the Istanbul OSCE Summit reached agreement on a comprehensive model for European security and a revised conventional arms control regime. However, the Istanbul achievements were predicated upon continuation of Russia's withdrawal of its military forces from neighboring states, in particular Moldova and Georgia, a process that could not be guaranteed. At the same time, however, the United States and its key Allies led a NATO military attack on Serbia, without United Nations authorization, over Russian protests. As Yeltsin handed over power to Vladimir Putin at the turn of the century, the new Russian president might well ponder the utility of these impressive achievements in arms control and a European security architecture in the face of NATO's growing power, territorial reach, and unilateralism.

## MOSCOW AND WASHINGTON: INCREASINGLY AT ODDS

Despite recovering from an approval rating in the low single digits and winning a second term with a handy majority in the second round of the 1996 presidential vote, Boris Yeltsin was in political trouble for most of his second term in office. The legislature elected in 1995 contained more communists and nationalists and even fewer supporters of reform than that chosen in 1993.[1] Yeltsin was reduced to ruling by decree with the assistance of a few close advisers because there was little prospect of getting any legislation passed by the hostile Duma. Only three months after his reelection, Yeltsin fired General Aleksandr Lebed, his former opponent and then national security adviser, who had made peace with Chechnya, apparently because he viewed Lebed's high profile and popularity as a threat.

Similarly, Yeltsin's relations with Prime Minister Viktor Chernomyrdin cooled after 1996 because the latter's competence and visibility also endangered the president's hold on his office. Indeed, under the Russian Federation's 1993 Constitution, any premier would be a threat to a beleaguered president, given that the prime minister was first in line for the presidency if the incumbent were to be removed by death, illness, or impeachment. Starting in 1997, Yeltsin's opponents in the Duma frequently threatened impeachment and refrained from carrying through less from lack of votes than from other tactical political reasons.[2] Yeltsin was also increasingly uneasy with his prime ministers because of growing accusations of corruption, which threatened to end in prosecution of members of his administration and his immediate family. By his final year in office, scandals had engulfed Yeltsin's daughter, Tatyana; her husband, Valentin Yumashev; the head of the Kremlin property management office, Pavel Borodin; and others. Russian procurator general Yuriy Skuratov was in the midst of consultations with Swiss prosecutors (including Carla del Ponte, later of renown at the International Criminal Tribunal on Yugoslavia) over possible cases of money laundering and credit card fraud when he was driven from office by a video purporting to show someone "similar" to him with two prostitutes.[3] If the Skuratov investigation had continued to its conclusion, there could have been a real possibility that Yeltsin's associates, family, and even he himself might have faced charges.

Economic reverses, domestic scandals, and sheer misfortune also plagued Yeltsin's second term. Western supporters of reform cheered when Anatoliy Chubais, the architect of the loans for shares privatizations, became Yeltsin's chief of staff. He was joined by Boris Nemtsov, a former reform mayor of Nizhnii Novgorod, as deputy premier and the other chief economic adviser. However, the privatization program had not solved the Russian government's chronic shortage of revenues and had helped create a highly visible class of fabulously wealthy oligarchs in an economy characterized by extreme inequality.[4] The system also was plagued by lax or nonexistent regulation, cronyism, and the absence of rule of law. The highly publicized 1997 scandal involving insider trading by Harvard Institute for International Development personnel, who had been funded by the US Agency for International Development to assist Russia in establishing its securities exchange, was one of the most visible, egregious cases of perceived Western involvement in and tolerance of the abuses of Russia's emerging "crony capitalist" system.[5] Then, just as it appeared the Russian economy might have started to emerge from its prolonged post-Soviet slump, the Asian financial crisis that had started in Thailand spread inexorably to Russia, and in August 1998 Russia's overextended financial structures collapsed spectacularly. Matters were made even worse as some $16 billion in a rescue package from the International Monetary Fund evaporated within days; the ruble crashed, and millions of Russians saw many of their assets become worthless.[6]

Western leaders and economic advisers were not responsible for the abuses, shady and risky practices, lawlessness, and extreme economic inequality that emerged in Russia in the 1990s, irrespective of how good or bad their policy advice may have been. However, large segments of Russia's public and political elites blamed outsiders, in particular the West, as they perceived these foreigners expressed continuing support for the Yeltsin administration's "reforms" and publicly defended controversial programs such as "loans for shares" and other measures that primarily benefited Russia's small emerging clique of superrich oligarchs. Indeed, Clinton administration officials may well have relied too much on assurances from Chubais, Nemtsov, and their colleagues with respect to the soundness of the Russian economy. However, one might also argue that by 1997–98 the Russian economic system had descended so far into speculation, insider trading, corruption, and lawlessness that practically no external actors or policies could have averted some sort of crisis or collapse. In fact, along with the well-known negative consequences, the 1998 crash brought some positive economic results for Russia. With the sharp devaluation of the ruble, domestic production rose at the expense of imports, particularly food products, and exports also felt a boost. Russia's gross domestic product grew by more than 3 percent in 1999, and growth accelerated as the price of oil rose after 2000.[7]

The crisis of 1997–98 and the crash of August 1998 had far-reaching political consequences. Under increasing pressure from the legislature, Yeltsin dismissed Chernomyrdin in March 1998 for alleged corruption and replaced him with the thirty-five-year-old Sergey Kirienko, who was portrayed as an advocate of economic reform.[8] With a hostile Duma and the impending crisis, Kirienko never really had a chance. After the August crash, Yeltsin at first tried to bring back Chernomyrdin as premier; when the Duma withheld its agreement, Yeltsin faced the inevitable and promoted Yevgeniy Primakov from foreign minister to the premiership.[9] Primakov turned out to be more moderate and more competent than many Western critics had feared. He cut government expenditures drastically, raised revenues somewhat, and brought Russia out of the crisis and through the winter. The only problem—at least for Yeltsin—was that Primakov's popularity with the Duma and the public was also rising, and by early 1999 he was often mentioned as a logical candidate to succeed Yeltsin after the 2000 elections. In contrast, Yeltsin was increasingly ill, erratic, distracted, absent, and beset by scandal.[10] Primakov also refused to cut off the Skuratov investigation of the Yeltsin family, and in April 1999 Yeltsin replaced him with Sergey Stepashin, a former security official and minister of the interior. Stepashin also did not last long; Yeltsin replaced him on August 10, 1999, with Vladimir Putin—a candidate whom the president identified as his chosen successor.[11]

The economic scandals and crash, along with the spectacle of musical chairs in the Russian White House (the site of the prime minister's office), had a demoralizing effect on Washington's support for reform in Russia and for Yeltsin personally.[12] Although Russian reform and NATO-Russia relations were important for the United States, the Clinton administration had other crucial regional and global equities on which it desired cooperation from Moscow. For example, Iran's nuclear program and support for terrorism played a major role in Clinton's conversations with Yeltsin in Helsinki in March 1997 and the Group of Seven (G-7) in Colorado that summer and continued to be an important item on the US agenda for most high-level bilateral meetings.[13] In June 1998, Clinton vetoed legislation sanctioning Russia for arms transfers to Iran, but he later adopted trade restrictions against some Russian firms. As the economic crisis peaked in Russia, Clinton was in the throes of the Monica Lewinsky scandal, which had a lengthy, paralytic effect on the higher levels of the US executive branch. As he emerged from his own personal crisis and reengaged, Clinton felt that he had little alternative but to continue support for Yeltsin as the best hope for reform in Russia, but he also had significantly less optimism and excitement about the direction in which Russia was heading.[14] The Clinton administration, Vice President Al Gore, and the president personally also came under increasing attack from Republicans in the Congress as the 2000 election campaign drew closer, with charges that Clinton's Russia policy had led to failed reform, corruption in Russia and elsewhere, and aid to Iran and other rogue states.[15]

The US-Russia relationship had been dominated in the early 1990s by the public display of friendship between the leaders of the two nations: the "Bill and Boris show." By the end of the decade, however, although the bureaucratic structures put together during the Clinton administration remained, there was little of the optimistic spirit that had animated earlier days. US-Russian bilateral and multilateral contacts often continued as if on automatic pilot. Each country was distracted by domestic political crises. Washington increasingly seemed to view its ties with Moscow as a means for achieving other goals rather than tending and improving the relationship itself. Already smarting from its inability to prevent NATO's enlargement, Moscow was increasingly frustrated by its obvious lack of influence on US and NATO policies and actions in the Balkans as the crisis in Kosovo deepened. Despite the continuation of cooperation in forums such as the OSCE and on issues such as arms control, it was Kosovo and NATO intervention that were decisive in shaping Russia's attitudes toward European security and security structures as the new century began.

## THE EU: WIDER AND DEEPER

With the addition of Sweden, Finland, and Austria in 1995, the European Union grew larger; but it was clear that before long it would become much bigger. It also was clear that the former Soviet Bloc states of Central and Eastern Europe would be much more difficult to assimilate than the Austrians and Scandinavians. Similar to its position on NATO enlargement, Germany favored expansion of the European Union to the east to provide a buffer beyond its own eastern border. Germany used its 1994 term as EU president to launch a "structured dialogue" with applicant countries from Central and Eastern Europe.[16] At the request of the EU Council, the European Commission produced a white paper on EU accession in May 1995 that laid out detailed guidelines. After working closely with all the Central and Eastern European applicants, the Commission reported in mid-1997 on the status of democracy, the rule of law, and market institutions in all of them, recommending that accession negotiations begin in early 1998 with the Czech Republic, Poland, Hungary, Estonia, Slovenia, and Cyprus.[17]

Although the EU's *acquis communautaire* imposed extremely detailed technical requirements on all the Central and Eastern European states seeking membership, the Council's and Commission's statements and decisions in the mid-1990s make clear that they saw the process of enlargement as a way of encouraging democratic and market transition in the former Soviet Bloc. The EU conducted the actual accession negotiations with each applicant on a bilateral basis, but the first of the overall criteria for membership iterated by the Council in December 1997 was a "precise commitment" to democracy.[18] Fears that the six "fast-track" countries that began accession negotiations in early 1998 would leave their neighbors far behind or be excluded altogether turned out to be unfounded. Latvia, Lithuania, Slovakia, and Malta caught up with the fast track, and Bulgaria and Romania in the end were only two to three years behind.

In addition to launching a complex process of enlargement that took almost a decade to complete, the EU in the mid-1990s continued the process of deepening the union, both implementing and augmenting the Maastricht Treaty. One of the major milestones in the process was the Amsterdam Treaty, which was agreed to at the end of a 1996–97 intergovernmental conference. Although some critics lamented that the Amsterdam Summit could not accomplish more, it did reflect a process of German-French cooperation that, though rocky at times, kept movement toward European monetary union on track. After Germany elected a Social Democratic–led coalition government in 1998 under Chancellor Gerhard Schröder, the country showed fewer reservations about merging the deutsche mark and its economy into a larger European whole.[19] The Amsterdam agreements also addressed ongoing British reservations about its relationship to Europe by formally including the principle of subsidiarity, calling for decisions in the EU to be made at the lowest appropriate level, thus introducing some provision for national flexibility and variation, although not the full opt-out that some in the United Kingdom desired. Finally, the Amsterdam decisions called for the adoption of common strategies but also established some instances in which the EU's decisions on the Common Foreign and Security Policy could be made with less than a full consensus.[20] The landslide Labour victory in May 1997 significantly lessened British recalcitrance and obstructionism in inner EU negotiations, as the new prime minister, Tony Blair, brought to the office a strong commitment to move the United Kingdom closer to Europe.[21]

Amsterdam also marked a milestone in the development during the second half of the 1990s of the institutional bases for the Common Foreign and Security Policy and for a closer EU relationship with NATO. After his election in 1995, French president Jacques Chirac sought acceptable arrangements under which he might return France into NATO's unified military structures. Although these efforts ultimately failed in 1997 over an inability to agree on allocating the post of NATO's deputy military commander in Europe to France, the negotiations did prompt more specific agreement on the concept of a combined joint task force, with its key idea of "separable but not separate" forces, which was crucial for the development of a distinct European defense identity.[22] At the Amsterdam Summit, the EU's leaders inserted the so-called Petersberg Tasks into the basic EU Treaty and also called for eventual merger of the Western European Union into the EU.[23] Finally, to manage the new capabilities of EU foreign and security policy, the EU created the post of high representative for the Common Foreign and Security Policy, and within a few months it recruited NATO secretary-general Javier Solana for the position.[24]

The changes adopted at Amsterdam were extremely important for advancing the EU's institutional scope and capabilities as a security organization, but Blair's election and his personal chemistry with Chirac may have been even more significant. The differences between the United Kingdom and

France on Europe's institutional provisions for its security and defense for decades had been one of the main obstacles to creating a European security and defense identity and an understanding and satisfactory working arrangement between NATO and the EU. After Chirac, the Gaullist, made a real step toward NATO, Blair then sufficiently softened the United Kingdom's uncompromising Atlanticism under a succession of Tory governments to bring the United Kingdom under a European security umbrella. Meeting in Saint-Malo, France, in December 1998, Blair and Chirac issued a joint statement that in effect announced British agreement that the EU should have the military capability to act in cases in which NATO preferred not to intervene.[25] The EU would act through the Western European Union but "will also need to have recourse to suitable military means (European capabilities predesignated within NATO's European pillar or national or multinational European means outside the NATO framework)."[26] The Saint-Malo declaration also called for strengthened European armed forces and a stronger European defense industry.

The Saint-Malo joint statement was one of the more dramatic steps during 1998–99 in a significant British change of direction with respect to European security and defense policy. UK prime minister Blair and UK defense secretary Robertson first announced the new British policy approach at EU meetings in the autumn of 1998 and characterized it as a way to increase the EU's institutional capacity and physical defense capabilities as a means of strengthening NATO as the primary instrument for Europe's defense.[27] This was a crucial change from the United Kingdom's traditional position, at least under recent Tory governments, of perceiving any growth in EU defense capabilities as a de facto diminution in NATO's capacities. The "New Labour" government was able to present the NATO-EU relationship as a win-win proposition rather than a zero-sum competition, combining the United Kingdom's traditional emphasis on NATO and the transatlantic relationship as the primary pillar of the United Kingdom's security with an understanding of the EU's European Security and Defence Identity (ESDI) as a means of strengthening the defense capabilities of both. The previous long-standing Tory position had left the United Kingdom increasingly isolated from the deepening EU across the English Channel, while the Blair government's shift enable the United Kingdom to assume a leadership role in the construction of a European Security and Defence Policy.

Prime Minister Blair's redirection of British policy played out against the backdrop of turmoil, discord in Europe and across the Atlantic, and eventually conflict over Kosovo. According to a number of his British colleagues, Blair was frustrated "throughout 1998 as he struggled to formulate a policy on the Balkans."[28] American hesitation and vacillation over the manner and

forcefulness with which to respond to Serbian actions and the growing crisis in Kosovo eroded the long-standing Cold War British assumption that the
United States would automatically and unilaterally provide for Europe's security. From the time the crisis began brewing in 1997, with destabilization in
Albania and the flow of arms to ethnic Albanian resistance forces in Kosovo, it
became increasingly evident that even if able to muster the collective political
will to intervene the EU did not possess sufficient independent operational
military capabilities to do so.[29] Some critics of the NATO campaign against
Milošević noted that European nations were prepared in principle earlier than
the United States to deploy ground forces in Kosovo, but in reality they were
unable to field a sufficient number of troops.[30]

The British change of course in 1998 established a United Kingdom–France
axis on defense and security policy within the EU somewhat analogous to the
France-Germany axis that was the main driver in the development of EU financial integration and establishment of the common currency. Paris locked up
the support of the new German government of Chancellor Gerhard Schröder,
so the major EU capitals were in basic accord on the European Security and
Defence Policy after the Saint-Malo meeting.[31] Washington responded in a
reserved but basically positive fashion, characterized by some as "yes, but." An
op-ed piece by US secretary of state Madeleine Albright and US national security adviser Sandy Berger offered formal support to the initiative but cautioned
against "duplication, decoupling, and discrimination"—the so-called three Ds.
In this, the United States warned the Europeans not to duplicate efforts already
being handled by NATO, or to delink European defense efforts from NATO and
US activities and capabilities in Europe. The United States also was concerned
that EU defense activities should not exclude countries that belonged to NATO
but were not EU members, in particular Turkey, but also Norway, Canada,
Iceland, and the United States itself.[32] These were the same basic concerns
Washington had expressed since the end of the Cold War about the EU's push
to develop a separate, independent security and defense identity and capability.

Washington's position on ESDI remained basically unchanged, but the
volte-face in British policy finally gave the EU the internal consensus it needed
to go beyond abstract debate and make real progress on the subject. The decisions and statements adopted at the Washington NATO Summit in April 1999
basically supported the European aspirations, especially insofar as they would
result in strengthening European defense capabilities, but reiterated that
changes must be consistent with the three Ds.[33] During much of 1999, British
diplomats shuttled frequently between Washington and Paris as they attempted
to keep the process of EU security and defense reform moving forward in a
manner that satisfied French ambitions while allaying American fears. An EU

consensus was reached in support of the Saint-Malo agreement at the June 1999 European Council meeting in Cologne, at which the EU accepted in principle the need to create an autonomous military capability to respond to crises and also created a new set of internal security and defense decisionmaking structures.[34]

By the time of the Helsinki Summit in December 1999, the EU was able to adopt agreed-on basic targets on collective military capabilities in the so-called Headline Goal:

> By the year 2003, cooperating together voluntarily, [EU member states] will be able to deploy rapidly and then sustain forces capable of the full range of Petersberg Tasks as set out in the Amsterdam Treaty, including the most demanding, in operations up to corps level (up to 15 brigades, or 50,000–60,000 persons). These forces should be militarily self-sustaining with the necessary command, control, and intelligence capabilities, logistics, other combat support services and additionally, as appropriate, air and naval elements. Member states should be able to deploy in full at this level within 60 days, and within this to provide smaller rapid response elements available and deployable at very high readiness. They must be able to sustain such a deployment for at least one year.[35]

The Helsinki decisions also promised to provide for full consultation, cooperation, and transparency between the EU and NATO and to make appropriate arrangements for participation in EU military crisis management by non-EU European NATO countries and others.

The December 1999 Helsinki EU Summit resolved, in principle, one of the most basic security issues that the process of European integration had faced during the first post–Cold War decade: the relationship between an integrated Europe's own defense resources and decisionmaking procedures and the security organization — NATO — that ensured and embodied the continued US presence and role in European security affairs. The dilemma had always been simple: how to ensure that the United States would be involved and able to participate in Europe's defense (the British desire) but also to enable Europe to respond in cases when the United States might prefer not to act (the French concern). The Helsinki solution was equally simple, although politically hard to reach; the United Kingdom would interpret an enhanced EU defense capability as strengthening NATO and thus the transatlantic connection, whereas France would view the same development as giving Europe the capability for possible independent action. The process of implementing this decision in practice was neither simple nor easy, and continues so to this day.

## NATO STRUCTURES: THE ROAD TO WASHINGTON

The signing of the NATO-Russia Founding Act and the invitations to the Czech Republic, Hungary, and Poland to begin negotiations to join the Alliance dominated public and press attention to NATO during much of 1997. Setting the basis for the relationship with Russia and taking the first specific step in the process of adding new members were indeed major milestones, but at the same time the Alliance faced a number of other significant issues and tasks. With the development of the Partnership for Peace (PfP)—including actual partner deployments in the NATO-led Implementation Force, and the launch in practice of enlargement—the North Atlantic Cooperation Council (NACC) no longer made sense as the sole forum for managing the Alliance's relations with non-NATO European states. The moves by France to return to NATO military structures, the development of the combined joint task force concept, and the experience of fielding and maintaining a combined peacekeeping force in the Balkans all required attention to, and some rethinking of, command and force structures, procedures, and requirements. NATO's initial experience in the Balkans also demonstrated a great disparity between the military capabilities of most of the European Allies on one hand and the United States on the other hand. This disparity became more evident through the remainder of the decade, and the lack of sufficient European military capabilities in key areas was a continuing, major US concern. Finally, with Russia explicitly a partner and not an enemy, with NATO forces deployed out of area, and with the Alliance about to take on new members, leaders in many NATO capitals (and elsewhere) began to ask once again what the Alliance was for.

The NACC was conceived when the Soviet Union still existed, and its membership and purpose were quickly and deftly adjusted when the USSR fell apart.[36] But by 1996–97, the European security landscape had changed so drastically that the NACC as originally structured no longer made any sense. First, the nations that were PfP members were engaged in cooperative activities with NATO, such as exercises or peacekeeping, that had not been envisioned or provided for under the NACC. Second, a number of European states had joined PfP that were not NACC members and thus had no institutional platform for political contacts and cooperation with NATO. Third, the ongoing development of the EU security and defense identity and capability could bring other countries that were not members of NATO or PfP into the mix. One of the most compelling complaints at the time was that non-NATO PfP member states that were cooperating with NATO operationally in the field needed a better mechanism for consultation and coordination with the Alliance.[37]

The Clinton administration chose to address the disconnect between PfP and the NACC not by reforming the latter but by establishing an entirely new NATO-affiliated institution, the Euro-Atlantic Partnership Council (EAPC). The proposal for the EAPC was developed and circulated among the Allies and partner states at the same time the Founding Act and the Paris Summit were being prepared, and NATO's foreign ministers formally established the EAPC at their meeting in Sintra, Portugal, on May 30, 1997.[38] NACC and PfP members automatically became EAPC members, if they wished, and the organization was open to any other state that wished to join PfP. The EAPC retained the crucial PfP principle of self-differentiation; although the entire organization was to meet once a month, EAPC members could choose to meet in smaller groups or individually with Allies. EAPC members also were offered great flexibility in choosing the type and frequency of their joint activities with NATO.[39] At the same time, PfP was augmented with the establishment of the Partnership Coordination Cell at NATO Military Headquarters in Mons, which provided for closer operational consultation and collaboration of partner nations with the Alliance.

In practice, the EAPC was so large, with almost as many members as the OSCE, as to be unwieldy. In addition, among the member states there were vastly differing levels of interest in collaboration with NATO, so plenary meetings of the EAPC at any level quickly turned out to be largely ceremonial, boring, and unproductive. Russia and Ukraine, the two large former Soviet states with special relationships with the Alliance, not surprisingly turned out to favor meeting with NATO Allies in the format of their separate councils. Although the EAPC Basic Document called for the organization to "take account of and complement" the activities of the OSCE, the EU, the Western European Union, and the Council of Europe, a number of observers claimed to see considerable overlap, particularly with the OSCE. Some former Soviet states, particularly Russia, also perceived the EAPC as giving NATO Allies an advantage in their ability to determine the agenda, and thus these states preferred the OSCE because it accorded equal status to all participating states. The EAPC thus appealed more to those NACC and PfP members that desired a closer relationship with the Alliance, while appearing to other states to supplant more inclusive, pan-European structures.

Although the initial effort of French president Chirac to bring his country back into NATO's military structures apparently ended with the decision by Paris in June 1997 not to rejoin the Military Committee and joint command, the issue of France's participation in NATO's military affairs and operations never really went away. The basic sticking point was the American reluctance to cede to the French one of NATO's major subordinate commands, Allied Forces Southern Europe (AFSOUTH). The French argued that allocating this slot to a European (read French) commander was not simply a national gesture to France but also meant recognition of the importance of the emerging ESDI.[40] Washington welcomed the prospect of full French participation in NATO's military affairs; Paris was a major troop contributor, and having a full French presence in Alliance structures would ease coordination. However, AFSOUTH also included the Mediterranean region, where the United States kept major military—in particular, naval—assets whose missions included more than just NATO defense. Changes in the global and European security environments and consequent adjustments in US and NATO commands for military reasons made it easier to accommodate the French more than a decade later when Paris made its next real move to return to the Alliance's integrated military structures.

NATO's experience on the ground in Bosnia-Herzegovina also had effects on both the dispute with the French and the concern about European military capabilities. The US-French standoff was probably not helped by the fact that the US commander of AFSOUTH was also the overall commander of the Implementation Force, and the French had a major deployment and regional command in the Implementation Force. The Clinton administration's promise to the US Congress that American forces would be deployed to the former Yugoslavia for no more than one year immediately set the clock ticking and did little to convince skeptics such as the French of Washington's commitment to European security. Conversely, although there were clear national differences, European nations' overall performance as part of NATO's operations in the Balkans starting in 1995 demonstrated basic lacks of a number of key military capabilities, such as intelligence, communication, reinforcement, and resupply.[41] During the Cold War, the United States relied on most of its Allies to provide little more than territorial defense in place, with the United States augmenting or providing Alliance capabilities in most other areas. When NATO began to go out of area in the 1990s, it soon became apparent that few of the European Allies had any capacity to project power outside their national territory.

After the November 1996 US presidential elections, when fighting broke out that same month in Bosnia between Serbs and Muslims, the Clinton administration accepted the need for a longer military presence in Bosnia-Herzegovina, and NATO's Implementation Force was transformed into the still-robust Stabilization Force, with a broader mandate to cover civil affairs and reconstruction. As the crisis deepened in Kosovo throughout 1998, and NATO embarked upon military action against Serbia-Montenegro in 1999, the need for stronger and more balanced Alliance military capabilities, especially among many of the European Allies, became increasingly apparent. Discussions of European defense reforms and defense capacities increased within the Alliance during 1997–98. At the Washington Summit in April 1999, the NATO heads of state announced the Defense Capabilities Initiative, which was explicitly intended to improve deployability, mobility, sustainability, command and control, and interoperability.[42] A High-Level Steering Group was to be created to oversee follow-through on the initiative. Although the immediate results were mixed, one enduring outcome has been continuing attention within the Alliance to the need for more a robust and balanced European military capacity.

NATO also continued firmly on its course of enlarging itself. At Madrid in July 1997, NATO's heads of state emphasized that it remained open to new members, noted that twelve had already applied, and singled out Romania and Slovenia as showing particular progress in developing democracy and the rule of law.[43] In the Madrid Declaration, NATO promised intensified dialogues to states aspiring to membership, and during the next year and a half the Alliance worked out a template of systematic requirements and procedures that could constitute the basis for individual national programs aimed at preparing a country for membership. This comprehensive procedural guide was adopted at the Washington Summit in April 1999 as the Membership Action Plan.[44] The Washington Declaration again praised Romania and Slovenia but also offered encomiums of varying warmth for Estonia, Latvia, Lithuania, Bulgaria, Slovakia, and even the former Yugoslav Republic of Macedonia (footnoted, because of Greece), and Albania.[45] Thus, by the end of the century, the major questions about NATO enlargement involved where and how it would end, not whether it would continue.

Among the many questions that faced the North Atlantic Alliance as the first post–Cold War decade drew to a close, perhaps the most important was what the Alliance was for. NATO's new Strategic Concept, adopted at the November 1991 Rome Summit, proclaimed the transformation of the Alliance from a collective defense organization to an institution with multiple missions, reflecting the changes taking place in the European security environment.[46] Whatever the merits of that 1991 document may have been, many of its good and bad points had clearly been overtaken by events. For one, the Soviet Union still existed when it was written. In addition, NATO by the late 1990s had out-of-area experience, new members and more on the way, and a very different formal relationship with Russia and Ukraine. As early as the middle of the decade, many Allies recognized the need to update NATO's basic statement of purpose, and the 1997 ministerial and summit meetings at Sintra and Madrid launched a review process that was completed with the adoption of yet another Strategic Concept at the Washington Summit.[47]

By NATO's own account, the Alliance's Strategic Concept adopted by heads of state in Washington was the sixth overall, and the second unclassified definition of the fundamental purpose of the Alliance.[48] The document approved in Washington contains large verbatim portions of the Alliance's 1991 Strategic

Concept.[49] In general, the Washington text defines NATO as both a collective security and collective defense organization; as in the 1991 Strategic Concept, responsibility for the European security environment comes before deterrence and defense of member states in the enumeration of the Alliance's basic tasks. The major difference between the two documents in enumerating the organization's fundamental tasks reflects NATO's engagement by 1999 in major out-of-area operations and the effects of enlargement on its relations with the countries to the east. In 1991, the fourth and final NATO task was "to preserve the strategic balance within Europe."[50] By 1999, this final task had been transformed to include both crisis management, including conflict prevention and crisis response operations, and partnership with other countries in the Euro-Atlantic area—all "in order to enhance the security and stability of the Euro-Atlantic area."[51]

The Washington Strategic Concept devotes considerable attention to recent changes in the overall security environment and emerging challenges and threats. Instability, ethnic and religious discord, territorial claims, and the dissolution of existing states were cited as the Alliance's main concerns; this was not surprising given the history of the 1990s. The description of and guidance for the Alliance's conventional force posture contained considerable change in areas where Allies had mounted out-of-area stability operations, which again was understandable in light of NATO's experience in the field during the past few years. The biggest changes involve NATO's relations with other European non-NATO states. In 1991, the Alliance focused especially on dialogue, some cooperation, and eliminating the vestiges of the Cold War through arms reductions and arms control. Although the Washington Strategic Concept acknowledged the impending adaptation of the Treaty on Conventional Armed Forces in Europe (CFE Treaty), it accorded greater space to new elements such as partnership and enlargement, reflecting both an increase in the territory covered by the Alliance and a significant change in the character of many NATO activities.

The Washington Strategic Concept explicitly committed the Alliance to "a broad approach to security, which recognizes the importance of political, economic, social and environmental factors in addition to the indispensable defense dimension."[52] This comprehensive definition of security, viewed together with the explicit aim of its partnership and outreach activities to "support and promote democracy," suggests that the Allied consensus reached in 1999 still viewed enlargement as a means of promoting democratic and market transitions in the Allies' former adversaries to the east. The document leaves unanswered the question of why such democracy promotion was seen as desirable and potentially effective for some of the former Warsaw Pact states, but not for others, such as Ukraine and—in particular—Russia. The answer at the time, and perhaps today, that Russia had a special relationship with NATO enshrined in the Founding Act begs the question. If NATO's expansion was truly or primarily for promoting democratic transitions, then certainly Russia should have been included. If Russia was not included, then one might easily conclude there were other reasons behind the expansion. It did not take long for such suspicion to become evident in Moscow.

## THE OSCE'S SEARCH FOR COMPREHENSIVE SECURITY

The OSCE truly flowered in the late 1990s, perhaps reaching the zenith of its activity and influence. It deployed and managed a plethora of important field missions, including a high-profile presence in Chechnya and the largest field operation in its short history in Kosovo. OSCE field operations dealt with early warning, conflict prevention, management and resolution, and postconflict reconstruction and reconciliation. Continuing the CSCE's and OSCE's traditional focus on conventional arms control, negotiations were held within the framework of the OSCE, producing the Adapted CFE Treaty (ACFE), which was signed by heads of state at the OSCE's Istanbul Summit in November 1999. Finally, discussions on a security model for Europe continued, resulting in the adoption of a comprehensive Charter for European Security, also at the Istanbul Summit.

By 1997, and continuing until at least the end of the decade, the OSCE had developed sufficient experience, institutional capacity, and credibility among all its participating states that the European countries' response to almost any local crisis or dispute where they did not wish to send troops was to send an OSCE Mission. OSCE field operations remained engaged in aspects of conflict resolution in Moldova, Georgia, and Chechnya. The Minsk Group, mediating between Armenia and Azerbaijan over Nagorno-Karabakh, reorganized itself, with Russia, France, and the United States becoming cochairs and working together surprisingly well. The special representative of the chairman-in-office for the Karabakh Conflict maintained a small field presence in Armenia and Azerbaijan. An OSCE mission in Kyiv took part in negotiations that successfully produced an agreement on autonomy between Kyiv and local authorities in Crimea. As domestic political freedoms began to be curtailed in Belarus under President Aleksandr Lukashenko, Minsk accepted the presence of the OSCE Monitoring and Advisory group, which was to focus exclusively on implementing human dimension commitments.[53]

The OSCE continued to support extremely large missions in Bosnia-Herzegovina and Croatia, and the work of both presences on reconstruction and reconciliation proceeded by and large successfully—for example, with marked improvement in the 1997 local elections in Bosnia-Herzegovina. When Albania began to destabilize in 1997 with the crash of a countrywide pyramid scheme, a visit by the special representative of the OSCE Chair, former Austrian prime minister Franz Vranitzky, was followed by a resident OSCE presence. Some critics complained that the OSCE squandered a chance to deploy its first-ever peacekeeping mission as envisioned under the 1992 Helsinki Document when an ad hoc group of EU states led by Italy responded to an Albanian request for assistance in keeping order after the collapse. Perhaps most impressive, in response to an agreement to avert growing violence between Serb authorities and ethnic Albanians in Kosovo, the OSCE rapidly organized and deployed an observation and verification force with more than 1,000 members.[54]

Behind this apparent facade of widespread activity and considerable success in the field, significant differences were beginning to emerge, or at least to become more apparent between some of the major participating states on the OSCE's proper and desirable role in European security affairs. Russia had not lost its earlier ambition to make the OSCE Europe's overarching, umbrella security organization, with de facto if not de jure superiority over NATO and the EU's emerging ESDI. Although it was clear that Moscow was unlikely to win agreement for proposals such as to establish a guiding security council within the OSCE, the Russian approach to negotiating the Charter for European Security aimed at making the OSCE one of the, if not *the*, deciding institutions in European security. The United States, the United Kingdom, France, Germany, and many other NATO and EU member states found the OSCE a useful institution, but largely for addressing specific issues on an ad hoc basis. The United States, the United Kingdom, and the Netherlands clearly held an Atlanticist view of NATO primacy. France and Germany were concerned with growing the EU's security and defense capabilities. Many of the countries in the OSCE that were formerly neutral and nonaligned, former Warsaw Pact members, and former Soviet states aspired to join either NATO or the EU, or both. Thus the circle of states supporting Russia's aspirations for OSCE preeminence shrank to a very few by the end of the century.

One of the OSCE's major projects in the three years between the Lisbon and Istanbul summits was the elaboration of a comprehensive security model, which eventually became the Charter for European Security.[55] Although it would be inaccurate to assert that other participating states did not support the effort or did not find elements of value in the exercise, the strongest push behind the negotiation of the charter came from Russia's efforts to make the OSCE the leading or preeminent European security institution, dating at least from Moscow's proposal to the Budapest Summit for an OSCE security council.[56] Once the OSCE heads of state at Lisbon decided to develop a "common and comprehensive security model for the twenty-first century," it was to be expected that multiple national visions, projects, and aspirations for the OSCE would be advanced. Indeed, in the course of the negotiations, Moscow proposed that the OSCE develop a standing peacekeeping capability and play a "leading" or "coordinating" role in cooperative efforts with other European institutions. Washington (also unsurprisingly) rejected a military peacekeeping role for the OSCE and stressed the organization's role in civilian operations, such as monitoring and policing. France was one of those members that advocated developing a formal legal personality for the OSCE, an idea that Washington had resisted from the OSCE's earliest days. During 1998, the Polish Chair floated the idea that not all OSCE decisionmaking needed to be done by reaching a consensus.[57]

Moving from the 1997 Copenhagen Ministerial and 1998 Oslo Ministerial meetings, the document changed from the "Charter on" to the "Charter for" European Security. Like most documents negotiated by a large number of participants, there were items, often unrelated and sometimes contradictory, from and for everyone. On the essential issues, the nature and role of the OSCE, the participating states mostly overcame their fundamental differences by inserting elements from almost all the competing visions for its future. Thus the document represents less a decision or set of decisions on its future direction than a review of all the things it was doing in 1999 and all the things it might do in the future. In the short run, this made the charter easier to sign; in the long run, it made the charter much less useful.

The Charter for European Security reviews some of the major changes in Europe's security environment during the past decade, noting in particular that threats can emanate from conflicts within states as well as between states.[58] The charter enumerates newer or emerging threats—such as international terrorism, violent extremism, organized crime, and drug trafficking—and emphasizes the OSCE's comprehensive concept of security by noting the role that economic and environmental issues can play in security.[59] The document reaffirms previous OSCE norms and commitments, singling out the Final Act and Charter of Paris, and asserts a role as "the inclusive and comprehensive organization for consultation, decisionmaking, and cooperation in the region."[60] However, the charter leaves the OSCE as one of several important organizations in the web of interlocking European institutions, the model that most of the leading Western participating states had adopted by the mid-1990s.

The charter also includes an addendum, the so-called Platform for Cooperative Security, inserted at the behest of the European Union, that in essence constitutes a framework and guidance for how the OSCE should cooperate with other European security organizations.[61] The platform is both normative, requiring institutions that collaborate with the OSCE to accept basic OSCE principles, and operational, with an explicit set of suggested modalities for cooperation. Thus Russia's aspiration for OSCE exclusivity or preeminence did not make it into the charter.

The Charter for European Security also calls for strengthening the OSCE's capabilities, but the functions and responsibilities enumerated in the document are wide-ranging and eclectic and thus do not reflect any particular national agenda for the organization. The charter reflects Russia's repeated push for an OSCE role in peacekeeping, though one heavily conditioned by reservations and caveats, which allows for the possibility of a lead role for the OSCE in a peacekeeping operation or the provision of the mandate for an operation carried out by others. At the same time, the document gives a nod to the more limited view pushed by the United States and some others that the OSCE should expand its capabilities in the general areas of policing and the rule of law. In light of the OSCE's recent experience in Kosovo, the charter aims to strengthen the OSCE's operational capacity through establishment of an Operations Center at the Vienna headquarters and by instituting a standing personnel pool of experts available for quick deployment to field missions (Rapid Expert Assistance and Cooperation Teams, or REACT). Finally, the charter seeks to improve the work of the OSCE's chief organ for political discussion and decisionmaking, the Permanent Council, as well as establishing clearer guidelines for making and implementing decisions in other OSCE bodies.

Like almost all other major OSCE documents, the Charter for European Security and the attached Platform for Cooperative Security are politically binding commitments and provide for no means of juridical or physical enforcement. The charter certainly merits praise, to the extent that it explicitly recognizes the changes in Europe's security environment and lessons learned through the bitter conflicts during the past decade. However, the document also remains aspirational and hortatory. It provides improved coordinating and operational mechanisms for the OSCE to respond to current and foreseen security issues, but only if a consensus can be reached within the organization's deliberative political decisionmaking bodies. The United States and the EU member states shared a broad view of where they wished to take the OSCE and European security institutions as a whole. For Washington and Brussels, the Charter for European Security constituted a blueprint for how the OSCE, the EU, and NATO could overlap and cooperate, while at the same time maintaining distinct competencies and capabilities for separate action when necessary.[62] What was not clear in November 1999, as the charter was adopted, was how far beyond the US-EU borders consensus on such a vision extended. As one EU analyst observed at the time, "It is true that the OSCE will not work and will not develop without a real partnership with Russia. One can only hope that the new Russian leadership agrees and will act accordingly."[63]

## THE OSCE'S APOGEE:
## ISTANBUL AND ARMS CONTROL

The OSCE Istanbul Summit registered two major accomplishments in addition to the Charter for European Security, both in the general field of hard security and arms control. First of all, continuing the OSCE's dedication to promoting confidence and transparency, the Istanbul meeting capped some five years of negotiations with formal adoption of the Vienna Document 1999, a modest but real expansion and deepening of the commitments of all OSCE participating states with respect to information exchanges, visits and inspections, and other transparency measures.[64] By the time of the Vienna Document in 1999, the negotiation, implementation, and monitoring of confidence- and security-building measures had become an ongoing process and one of the major functions of the OSCE's Forum for Security Cooperation. Although not treaty-based and thus not legally binding, the OSCE's confidence- and security-building process was the only arms control regime that included all European states and was thus the ultimate, basic repository for military transparency in Europe.

The other major achievement of the Istanbul Summit was the completion and signing of the Adapted Treaty on Conventional Forces in Europe. The institutional arrangements for handling the ACFE Treaty negotiations bore a very similar relationship to the OSCE, as had the original CFE negotiations. The talks were held among the thirty states that were parties to the original treaty within the Joint Consultative Group in Vienna, the body set up to implement and monitor the treaty. The original CFE Treaty was an incredibly important achievement in reducing the levels of conventional arms throughout Europe and thus diminishing the danger of war, but it was obsolete even before it formally entered into force in November 1992. The arms levels specified in the treaty were based upon numerical parity at each step within a set of nested zones between the forces of the Warsaw Pact and NATO. Although individual national holdings were reported, it was the alliance totals that were crucial. When Russia lost its Warsaw Pact alliance and NATO continued to exist, it was clear that the parity established by the original treaty no longer had any real meaning. Once it became clear that NATO would be joined by states that had previously been counted in the Warsaw Pact totals, the sense of imbalance on Russia's side became more acute.

Although the danger of conventional war between Russia and the West seemed remote by the mid-1990s, the United States, its Allies, and their partners all recognized that a more rational arrangement for limiting conventional arms in Europe needed to be found that would take into account both Russia's sense of diminished security by the loss of its Allies and NATO's perceived need for flexibility to respond to possible out-of-area contingencies. All the parties to the original treaty also recognized the great value of its legally binding provisions for information exchanges, challenge inspections, monitoring, contacts, and visits. Also, given the independence of the Baltic states, the likelihood that they might join NATO in the relatively near future, and the fact that they were not covered by the original CFE Treaty after the collapse of the USSR, Russia was eager to have them included in a revised conventional arms control treaty regime. Finally, the principle that military deployments must have the consent of the receiving state, which was not an issue while the Soviet Union existed, was increasingly emphasized by those post-Soviet states where Russian military units still remained, especially Moldova and Georgia.[65]

The ACFE Treaty constituted a wholesale conceptual restructuring of conventional arms control in Europe.[66] This treaty replaced the old treaty's bloc-to-bloc, nested zone structure with a system of national and territorial ceilings, all using the same five basic categories of treaty-limited equipment established in the original treaty. The adapted agreement reflected NATO's concerns for flexibility by providing extra room for temporary deployments or transit of forces. Although there were no formal collective alliance limits, the ACFE Treaty also responded to Russian concerns by providing, through the system of territorial ceilings, that a significant portion of NATO's military equipment would remain far from Russia's borders. Reflecting other considerations, including domestic political expectations in a number of Allies and a low estimate of any conventional threat, ceilings in many NATO countries were set low (and actual force levels even lower). The adapted agreement also strengthened transparency, with stiffer requirements for inspections and information exchanges.

Most crucial, however, both for the negotiation of the ACFE Treaty and for its possible ratification was the issue of a host nation's consent for a foreign military presence. Given the nature of Soviet military deployments under the terms of the Warsaw Pact, the issue of a host nation's consent was not a central element in negotiating the initial CFE Treaty. Furthermore, once the Warsaw Pact crumbled, the Soviet and then the Russian authorities rapidly completed withdrawal of their troops from Central Europe and, a bit later, from the Baltic republics. However, after the Soviet Union fell apart, it was difficult to find a single formula to resolve questions with respect to the responsibilities of the Russian Federation under the CFE Treaty and the presence of Russian troops on the territory of several former Soviet republics. In the May 15, 1992, Tashkent Agreement of the former Soviet states in the CFE Treaty area, Russia assumed responsibility for those Soviet troops that remained in Estonia, Latvia, Lithuania, Poland, and Germany.[67] Thus the Baltic states were effectively left outside the CFE Treaty's regime. Russian troops eventually all left Azerbaijan. Belarus and Armenia did not object to Russian troops; after about five years of difficult negotiations, Ukraine also agreed to a substantial Russian military presence in conjunction with the Black Sea Fleet.

However, Moldova and Georgia, whose governments charged Russian troops with supporting separatist enclaves in their countries, called for the complete withdrawal of Russian military forces from their territory. Although Moscow had explicit bilateral agreements with both Chisinau and Tbilisi for the presence of its troops for peacekeeping, Russian diplomats in principle agreed with Moldovan and Georgian demands for troop withdrawal (without specifying a date), and by the mid-1990s did not object to the insertion of language to that effect in yearly OSCE Ministerial statements. Moldovan and Georgian frustration with Russia's dilatory tactics mounted in the late 1990s, and both countries sought to use the ACFE Treaty negotiations as a lever to force a Russian troop withdrawal. They were generally supported by Ukraine, which along with Moldova adopted highly restrictive constitutional provisions regarding the presence of foreign military forces. Along with Azerbaijan, they formed the GUAM group—whose name is an acronym for the Organization for Democracy and Economic Development in Cyrillic—in the Joint Consultative Group in early 1997 to push for treaty restrictions on foreign military deployments.[68] Thus the ACFE Treaty talks rapidly subsumed a secondary negotiation or set of negotiations between Russia and the several countries belonging to the Commonwealth of Independent States that had Russian troops, separatist conflicts, or both on their territories.[69]

It was no mean feat to balance successfully the concerns of Russia and nineteen NATO members over national and territorial limits, but the toughest (and last) issues to be settled concerned the timing of Russian troop withdrawals from Georgia and Moldova. Tbilisi finally agreed to a commitment from Moscow to reach agreement by the end of 2000 on a withdrawal schedule from the two Russian bases in Georgia not covered under bilateral peacekeeping agreements.[70] Moldova wrangled a Russian promise to remove all its treaty-limited equipment from Moldova by the end of 2001 and to withdraw all its troops by the end of 2002.[71] According to US negotiators, the agreement on Russian troops in Moldova was reached only six hours before the agreement was to be signed by the heads of state.[72] The ACFE Treaty was duly signed on the morning of November 19, 1999, and the heads of state committed themselves to rapid ratification of the agreement.[73]

The signing of the ACFE Treaty was the crowning success of the Istanbul Summit and a landmark conceptual achievement. The ACFE Treaty successfully recast a complex arms control regime along a totally different set of organizing principles, all while preserving and achieving the fundamental goals of limited and lower levels of conventional arms in Europe. As far as theory was concerned, the organizing principles and numerical limits of the adapted regime adequately reflected the immense changes that had taken place in Europe's security landscape since 1990. Openness, transparency, and confidence were fully preserved by the terms of the adapted regime.

The fatal flaws in the ACFE Treaty were less evident. The agreement apparently provided for Russia's desire to include the Baltic republics, as prospective NATO members, and thus provide treaty-based protection for Kaliningrad and the Saint Petersburg region against potential NATO deployments there. However, the old CFE Treaty had no provision for accession of new signatories, so the ACFE Treaty needed to enter into force before the Baltic republics could join. Yet the adapted agreement's entry into force would require Russia to fulfill its agreements with Moldova and Georgia. In practice, this turned out to involve more than simply removing troops; it also required settling the bitter separatist conflicts in South Ossetia, Abkhazia, and Transdniestria. This turned out to be a much longer, more complicated, and more difficult proposition than any of the treaty signatories at Istanbul anticipated.

For much of the 1990s, the Russian Federation repeatedly expressed a special interest and asserted a *droit de regard* with respect to security questions in the former Soviet area. Beginning with the Charter of Paris, Russia's Western partners asserted the right of every country to determine its own security arrangements, implicitly (and often explicitly) rejecting the idea of spheres of interest anywhere in Europe. While Russia was ruled by the relatively cooperative Boris Yeltsin and was often too weak to object or obstruct Western actions effectively, collisions with its Western partners over actions and events in Central and Eastern Europe were less frequent and less severe. Preoccupied with the Balkan wars in the first half of the decade, Russia's Western partners frequently turned a blind eye or even supported Russian intervention in the conflicts in the former Soviet area. As Western attention to the countries of the former Soviet Union beyond Eastern Europe gradually grew more intense, the possibility of disagreements with Moscow increased, especially given the presumption by many Russian officials that there would be Western assent to their special interests and exclusive rights in the region.

In linking the ACFE Treaty to the withdrawal of Russian military forces from Georgia and Moldova, the other signatories, in particular the United States and its Allies, gave Tbilisi and Chisinau a very large say in whether the new regime would succeed. The decision to do so may well have seemed just, but it ended up linking the resolution of three separatist conflicts to the new treaty's entry into force. Irrespective of the rights and wrongs in the individual cases of Georgia and Moldova, the approaches and decisions of the ACFE Treaty's signatories at Istanbul uncovered fundamental differences in perception and principle between Russia on one hand and the United States and the EU on the other hand over Russia's security interests, influence, and role in the former Soviet area. These differences existed below the surface and were left unresolved throughout the 1990s until increased NATO and EU proximity and activity and returning Russian wealth, power, and confidence brought them out into the open and often into conflict. This discussion is not meant to assert that conflict between Russia and the West over Russia's near abroad was inevitable. It does seem the case, however, that these real differences were ignored, suppressed, or rationalized during most of the 1990s, which made them more difficult to reconcile or resolve when they reemerged at the end of the decade.

## NATO'S WAR FIGHTING TRUMPS THE OSCE'S MONITORING: THE ROAD TO PRISTINA

Institutional reform in NATO and the OSCE collided with the march of events in Kosovo in 1998–99. Both organizations had been honing their capabilities for intervention in conflict prevention and management. Finally, the long-feared descent into ethnic violence of the most bitter of the rivalries in the former Yugoslavia, between Serbs and ethnic Albanians in Kosovo, presented the opportunity and the need to use those capabilities in practice. The OSCE mounted the largest field mission in its short history in support of frantic diplomatic attempts to head off full scale war in Kosovo. As these efforts at conflict prevention proved increasingly ineffective, NATO stepped in first to provide a credible threat and then to employ military force against Serbia in an avowed defense of the civilian ethnic Albanian population in Kosovo. The buildup to NATO's intervention in Kosovo demonstrated significant differences in approach within the Alliance. The actual intervention shattered any semblance of unity among the major powers in Europe, leaving Russia isolated and bitter. Although Moscow was subsequently mollified sufficiently to assist in ending the war and joined the OSCE consensus at Istanbul, the NATO war with Serbia had lasting negative effects on the attitude toward the Alliance of large segments of Russia's political elite. The extent of these effects and their consequences for Russia's relations with the West are still being felt.

The crisis in Kosovo was building steadily at the same time that the rest of Europe, the United States, and Canada were engaged in the initiatives already chronicled in this chapter: the initial post–Cold War enlargements of NATO and the EU; the reorientation and reform of the military structures of the Alliance; the development of a more concrete ESDI; the development of a comprehensive security model for Europe; and the transformation of the continent's fundamental conventional arms control regime. It seems to be a chicken-and-egg argument as to which influenced the other more. Did the growing crisis and war in Kosovo condition the development of Europe's security institutions, or did the ongoing changes in these institutions determine the pace and nature of the response to the crisis in Kosovo? My argument is that events and institutional changes developed together, each influencing and conditioning the other, making it impossible to isolate a single reason why events and institutions turned out the way they did.

Kosovo had been troubled since it was awarded to Serbia by the great powers in 1913.[74] The home of the first medieval Serbian kingdom, containing some of the most cherished sites and monuments of Serbian history, Kosovo by the mid–twentieth century had a population of some 90 percent ethnic Albanians. Kosovo was made an autonomous province of Serbia in Tito's Yugoslavia, but Kosovo's Albanians wanted full republic status. The province revolted against Serbian rule in 1966 and 1980, and in 1989 Milošević revoked its autonomy and installed repressive colonial-style rule. Although Albanian resentment of Serb rule was deep, the largest opposition force in Kosovo, the Democratic League of Kosovo (Lidhja Demokratike e Kosovës), led by Ibrahim Rugovo, adopted an approach of nonviolence and noncooperation with Serb rule. The province thus escaped violent conflict during the wars in Bosnia and Croatia.

However, the ethnic Albanian population of Kosovo (to say nothing of Rugovo himself) was deeply disappointed when the Dayton agreement did not address Kosovo's status. Holbrooke argued that to include Kosovo in the negotiations would have lessened the chances of getting a deal in Bosnia.[75] In any event, calls for violent resistance to Serb rule in Kosovo began to multiply during 1996 and 1997. When civil order in Albania collapsed in mid-1997, some 800,000 weapons disappeared from military depots; many of these weapons found their way to Kosovo, thus arming the resistance.[76] Armed groups began attacking Serbian police and soldiers; the most prominent of these was the Kosovo Liberation Army (Ushtria Çlirimtare e Kosovës, UCK, or in English KLA). The KLA's tactics and attacks provoked reprisals by Serbian police and soldiers, often against civilians, which were then publicized widely in the West and prompted predictable pressure on Milošević.

The danger of conflict in Kosovo had been a serious concern for years, and European and North American leaders were determined not to repeat what they saw as the mistakes of Bosnia by waiting too long, until the violence grew too bad and too widespread to stop easily. After an apparent massacre of dozens of ethnic Albanian civilians by Serb forces was discovered in Kosovo in March 1998, the six-member Contact Group—the United States, France, the United Kingdom, Germany, Italy, and Russia—was able to agree only on modest sanctions against Serbia. Russia was particularly reluctant to endorse harsh measures or to link them directly to Kosovo. The United States, the United Kingdom, and Germany endorsed stronger action, and France and Italy favored more moderate steps. In any event, the measures taken in the spring of 1998 had no apparent effect on the rising level of violence in Kosovo. Worried by the threat of war on their borders, both Albania and Macedonia requested consultations with NATO as envisioned under PfP. In June 1998, the NATO defense ministers expressed concern about the growing danger of war in Kosovo and ordered their military authorities to develop a range of options for NATO intervention to halt the violence against and expulsion of the ethnic Albanian population in Kosovo.[77]

Meeting the next day, the Contact Group's foreign ministers demanded that Milošević agree to a cease-fire and withdrawal of his troops from Kosovo, grant free access for international monitoring and aid, allow the return of displaced persons, and begin talks on a settlement with ethnic Albanian leaders in Kosovo. Milošević acceded to some of these demands; for example, he admitted an OSCE technical assessment mission in mid-July.[78] However, violence between Serbs and ethnic Albanians continued sporadically as the summer stretched into autumn, along with periodic threats and recriminations from various NATO Allies. By mid-October, the United Kingdom, France, and the United States were frustrated enough to begin pursuit of a UN mandate and an order within NATO for air strikes against Serbia.[79] The Clinton administration sent Richard Holbrooke to press Milošević, who appeared to cave when faced with the threat of force, promising to return autonomy and a local police force to Kosovo, with local elections within nine months. Before the end of October, the OSCE mandated the Kosovo Verification Mission (KVM) to help ensure "compliance of all parties in Kosovo with the requirements set forth by the international community with regard to the solution of the crisis in Kosovo."[80] The OSCE aimed eventually to have 2,000 monitors on the ground in Kosovo; by the end of October, 150 were already in place.

Although Milošević initially appeared to comply with the promises he made in October, NATO kept the threat of air strikes on the table. Within weeks, the situation in Kosovo once again began to deteriorate. In mid-January, a massacre of forty-five ethnic Albanians was discovered in the small town of Racak, which the head of the KVM, US ambassador William Walker, immediately attributed to Serb forces.[81] As fighting and the expulsion of ethnic Albanians mounted, the

Contact Group invited Serb and Kosovo Albanian representatives to Rambouillet, a chateau outside Paris, in an apparent attempt to replicate the successful Dayton negotiations over Bosnia. However, this time Milošević did not attend, there were no air attacks or ground forces threatening the Serbs, and the conference failed to reach agreement between the two parties. The security situation in Kosovo grew steadily worse. The KVM was withdrawn on March 20 after reaching a total strength of 1,500 international members, and its headquarters were temporarily moved to Skopje. Recriminations and calls for military measures against Milošević abounded, but disagreement both within the Contact Group and between NATO Allies forestalled any action. Important leaders in the US Congress also were skeptical about the need for military intervention, thus making it harder for the Clinton administration to take the lead. It took another visit to Belgrade by Holbrooke, and continued defiance by Milošević as his forces continued the ethnic cleansing of Albanians from Kosovo, before NATO finally began bombing on March 24, 1999.

There were many reasons behind NATO's Hamlet-like hesitation over the course of almost a year before at last employing military force against the Federal Republic of Yugoslavia. There were disagreements within NATO, and not all Allies maintained the same position on Kosovo and the use of force throughout the crisis. Originally hesitant to go beyond rather moderate sanctions, France by late 1998 and early 1999 pushed not only for air strikes but also for the insertion of ground troops. The United Kingdom also favored keeping open the option of ground troops. Indeed, Prime Minister Tony Blair's reported growing frustration with Washington's wavering on taking military action against Milošević was cited by many of his colleagues and subordinates as a major factor in his agreement with Chirac at Saint-Malo on developing a more robust EU military capability.[82]

Washington's approach was shaped by numerous and conflicting motives. Like most of their NATO colleagues, US leaders were mindful of their experience in Bosnia, with refugees, camps, and mass slaughters such as the one at Srebrenica in 1995. Some in the Clinton administration also still harbored the memory of Rwanda, where the failure to intervene may have cost the lives of hundreds of thousands.[83] Conversely, as the Kosovo crisis built up during 1998, the White House was distracted by the Lewinsky sex scandal, which became public in August. Clinton was then impeached by the Republican-majority House of Representatives in December, and the Senate did not reach its verdict failing to convict him until mid-February 1999. When one considers, in addition to these events, the legislative branch criticism his administration experienced with respect to the US deployment in Bosnia, Clinton's reluctance to commit US ground troops to an operation in Kosovo hardly seems a surprise, irrespective of the friction it caused with the United Kingdom and France.

The odd man out in the run-up to war in Kosovo was Russia. Moscow's representatives participated up to the last minute in the work of the six-nation Contact Group and consistently advocated less stringent measures against Serbia. Prime Minister Primakov reportedly argued that severe sanctions would provoke nationalists in Serbia and pointed to the attacks by Albanian resistance groups as provoking Serb reaction.[84] Primakov, Foreign Minister Igor Ivanov, and other Russian representatives argued repeatedly against military action in Kosovo, and thus it was obvious to all that there was no hope that any NATO action could receive UN Security Council approval. The Russian disapproval was so well known and so strong that US leaders were willing to inform Primakov of the impending NATO strikes only a couple of hours in advance, when it was already too late to warn Belgrade. Primakov, who was already on his way to Washington for a visit, turned his plane around over the Atlantic and went home.[85]

NATO's two-and-a-half-month war against Serbia is a case of the proverbial half-full and half-empty glass.[86] On the half-full side, NATO's nineteen members were able to reach a decision on a non–Article V military action against another European state and to see that operation through to completion. NATO's operations were carried out with minimal losses, and the French participated even though they were not part of the integrated military structures. On the half-empty side, the air strikes did not appear to have a dramatic effect on Serb actions on the ground, and arguments emerged within NATO, especially at and after the Washington Summit, over expanding the range of permissible targets and whether ground forces would eventually be employed. As the bombing campaign failed to procure Milošević's capitulation and discord within the Alliance became more apparent, the Clinton administration faced the prospect that inserting ground forces might be the only way to achieve the original goals of the war. Instead, Clinton was rescued by Boris Yeltsin, who in late April appointed former prime minister Viktor Chernomyrdin as his special representative for the conflict. Chernomyrdin, who was joined by Finnish president Martti Ahtisaari, eventually convinced Milošević to bend sufficiently to bring a settlement.

With Russia back in the game, the deal ending the war was adopted in the form of a UN Security Council resolution.[87] Serbia agreed to withdraw its military and police forces from Kosovo, with only a small number allowed to return under international auspices, and to accept UN-led military and civilian missions. The resolution also demanded that the KLA and all other Kosovo Albanians cease offensive military actions and cooperate with the peacekeeping force. A UN special representative would supervise implementation of all the civilian international missions in Kosovo and coordinate with the commander of the military mission. The peacekeeping force would include "substantial North Atlantic Treaty Organization participation . . . under unified command

and control," and thus it ended up being led by NATO. The return of refugees and internally displaced persons (IDPs) was to be facilitated, and cooperation of all parties was required with international war crimes investigations and prosecutions. Finally, the resolution called for establishment of a political process leading to "substantial self-government for Kosovo," but also "taking full account of . . . the principles of sovereignty and territorial integrity of the Federal Republic of Yugoslavia."

Thus the Kosovo Albanians received international guarantees of their physical safety, the right to return to their homes, the prospect of considerable self-government, and the promise that those guilty of mass killings and ethnic cleansing might be punished. For Serbia, the key provision was that Kosovo would remain a part of the Federal Republic of Yugoslavia, a formal written commitment accepted by all members of the UN Security Council. Russia played an indispensable role in achieving the war's eventual settlement, helped the Serbs retain Kosovo as part of their country and retained a strong element of control over the nature of any eventual settlement in Kosovo by placing that process under the UN's political control. The United States and its NATO Allies could claim victory in the end of hostilities, the withdrawal of Serb forces, the return of the ethnic Albanian population, and eventual NATO leadership of the peacekeeping process.

Milošević's acceptance of the G-8's terms on June 3, however, was only the start of a process that revealed deep, bitter disagreements within Russia's political and military leadership over collaboration with NATO against Serbia and offered Western nations a preview of a far more difficult relationship with Russia in the future.[88] There was little opposition, except in Belgrade and Moscow, to a NATO-led force in Kosovo, and NATO for some time had detailed operational plans ready for inserting the Kosovo Force (KFOR), with or without local resistance.[89] Negotiations with the Serb military for a handover to NATO forces entering Kosovo began on June 5, and Allied representatives sought to deploy quickly to avoid a security vacuum and possible reprisals by Albanian groups as Serb forces withdrew. The negotiations with the Russians, conducted by the United States for the Atlantic Alliance, were difficult and punctuated by the apparently uncoordinated and perhaps unauthorized rapid deployment of a Russian peacekeeping unit from Bosnia to Pristina Airport. A dramatic standoff between Russian and NATO troops around Pristina nearly provoked a broader confrontation, and only after sustained, high-level intervention were the modalities for Russian participation in KFOR finally agreed on between the Russian minister of defense, Igor Sergeev, and the US secretary of defense, William Cohen, just before the June 1999 G-8 Summit in Cologne.[90]

An examination of the political background in Russia and the motives of various actors with respect to NATO's war with Serbia, the terms of the settlement,

and the confrontation as KFOR deployed is appropriate here, not just for understanding the events themselves but also for illuminating the broader divisions
and currents in Russian society and the political elites that would shape the
development of Moscow's view of the European security landscape and its foreign and security policies for the immediate future. First, Russia was in the midst
of a serious political struggle that may not have been adequately appreciated at
the time in the West. Yeltsin's replacement of Primakov as prime minister with
Sergey Stepashin in mid-May 1999 may have made it easier for Chernomyrdin to negotiate with NATO and Milošević, but it did not achieve what arguably may have been Yeltsin's chief objective, to protect him and his family from
political and personal enemies in the Duma. Yeltsin remained in real domestic
political trouble for the rest of 1999, and Primakov remained a formidable threat
to the president's political and perhaps even personal fate until Putin's eventual
triumph in early to mid-2000.

Second, NATO's actions in Bosnia, NATO enlargement, and the Alliance's
war against Serbia were all deeply disturbing and extremely unpopular with
many Russian military officers at all levels. In addition, serious divisions existed
within the Russian foreign and security policy establishment over issues such as
cooperation with the West, the structure of Russia's military forces, and proper
allocation of the defense budget. Foreign Minister Ivanov and Defense Minister
Sergeev participated in the NATO-Russia Permanent Joint Council, yet the General Staff's head for international cooperation, General Leonid Ivashov, stead-
fastly resisted operational military-to-military cooperation and contacts with the
United States and NATO. Sergeev and the chief of the General Staff, Anatoly
Kvashnin, came, respectively, from the missile and infantry forces and disagreed
deeply on how to manage and rebuild Russia's heavily eroded military. Russian
officials confirm the lack of cooperation and coordination between the Foreign
Ministry and General Staff observed by the US deputy secretary of state, Strobe
Talbott, in Moscow in June 1999 while discussing civilian and military arrange-
ments in Kosovo.[91]

Finally, Russia's eventual cooperation with the United States and NATO in
ending the war with Serbia was ultimately the result of decisions made at the
presidential level, and not the product of a broad, solid working relationship
between those at lower levels of government. One of Yeltsin's motives in replacing Primakov may have been improving relations with the West before the June
G-8 Summit, but both a successful G-8 and Primakov's ouster were crucial first
and foremost to Yeltsin's domestic political standing. Yeltsin and Chernomyrdin
worked effectively with their Western interlocutors, but many of their subordinates and colleagues were increasingly open in their resentment of Western
actions and consequently more difficult to deal with. Those who met Yeltsin
at the G-8 in Cologne and at the OSCE Summit in Istanbul in November

describe a man in markedly deteriorating health and with declining vigor. The days of Yeltsin overruling his bureaucracy and political opponents in order to cooperate with Washington were clearly numbered.[92]

It is difficult to overstate the effects of the Kosovo war on Russia's view of and relations with the West. Russia's anger at the West, in particular the United States, was profound and prompted many resentful reactions, ranging from Primakov turning his plane around to Moscow's representatives abandoning the Russia-NATO Permanent Joint Council.[93] Russia was humiliated by its inability to prevent NATO from going to war against Serbia, and it was frustrated by the result, with Serbia defeated and NATO troops in Kosovo.[94] However, there were serious longer-term consequences of the Balkan conflict as well. The damage to NATO's reputation in Russia (and in some other parts of the Commonwealth of Independent States) was immense. What the Alliance justified as a humanitarian action to protect civilians and restore stability, many Russians perceived as a cynical exercise in geopolitical aggrandizement, especially coming at the same time as completion of the Alliance's first enlargement.[95] The Kosovo war was the final straw in discrediting and marginalizing most of the aspiring politicians and leaders in Russia who favored domestic reforms and foreign policies along Western lines.[96] Even as well disposed a Russian official as Yeltsin, who cooperated with his friend Clinton to end the war, later speculated bitterly in his memoirs that the US president authorized bombing Serbia in the spring of 1999 to distract the public from his domestic political troubles.[97]

For many Russian officials and analysts, the 1999 Balkan war constituted a tectonic shift in the European security system. Foreign Minister Igor Ivanov charged that "the United States' real motive was to impose its will through NATO bypassing the United Nations. This is when the United States laid the foundation of a unipolar world."[98] Another senior Russian political analyst characterized the effects of NATO's war in Kosovo in the following fashion: "The Kosovo crisis was not only a distinct watershed in relations between Russia and the West, but begins a qualitatively new stage in the development of the whole system of international relations and the formation of Europe's security system."[99] However, this same analyst also called for Russia to build its future security system in cooperation with and not in opposition to NATO, and Ivanov continued pragmatic cooperation with the West while railing at NATO's actions for making Russia's domestic situation more difficult for him. Thus the effect of Kosovo was not so much to end Russian cooperation with the West as to fundamentally change Russian perceptions of Western motives and approaches to European security structures and issues.

Many Western accounts of this period, in particular the Kosovo crisis and war, emphasize the lengths to which the United States and its Allies went to include Russia in the process and to take into account Russian interests and views.[100] Such accounts point to the indisputable fact that Russia was a full member of and participant in the contact groups that managed negotiations with Milošević during both the Bosnian and the Kosovo wars. Seen in this light, Russia indeed had a voice in the management of Balkan security affairs during the 1990s. However, by the time NATO went to war with Serbia in March 1999, Russia had "a voice, not a veto" in the decision. As US deputy national security adviser James Steinberg recalled, "For those of us who wanted to do something, the worst outcome would be not to do something because Russia didn't want us to do it. It would have been bad for us, bad for the Balkans, and bad for Russia. . . . The whole security of Europe would be thrown into question if Russia's sense of its interest precluded the international community addressing this serious question."[101]

Moscow was not convinced that either Washington or Brussels had the right to determine what "the international community" should think or do. The reasoning behind Moscow's 1994 proposal to create a de facto security council within the OSCE, an initiative it revived several times during the 1990s, was to ensure that Russia had a veto over fundamental decisions of war and peace in Europe, and especially in regions where it had important interests or close historical ties. Indeed, the Contact Group on Kosovo often functioned like a European security council, but Russia's participation in this ad hoc arrangement conferred no institutional or juridical rights.

Yeltsin's critics in 1999 warned him "Belgrade today, Moscow tomorrow!" Although this claim clearly seemed then and seems now wildly exaggerated, Russia had no institutional or treaty guarantees against such an eventuality. The structures and relationships that made up the European security system in which Russia participated after 1989 were all based on documents that contained politically binding commitments—that is, promises and not treaties. As long as a high degree of mutual trust existed between the nations of Europe, institutions and arrangements based upon such politically binding documents were sufficient to provide for security and stability in much of Europe. However, both NATO and the EU are treaty-based institutions. Neither organization includes Russia; and although they have been expanding, neither has aimed to include Russia. For a time, Russia was satisfied with political commitments such as those in the Helsinki Final Act, the Charter of Paris, and the NATO-Russia Founding Act. NATO's attack on Serbia in 1999, ignoring Russia's objections and bypassing the United Nations, was by far the single greatest act and the single most important factor in eroding the trust that served as the basis of Russia's relations with the West and the European security system in the 1990s. As the new millennium began, Russia, Europe, and the United States would need either to find a way to restore this trust or to construct a new institutional basis for managing Europe's security.

## 6. NEW MILLENNIUM, NEW THREATS

NATO's war in Kosovo provoked a thoroughgoing reassessment by Russia's governing elites of the fundamental nature of the Atlantic Alliance and what its expansion meant for their country's security. However, this altered Russian perception was some time in taking shape and finding recognizable expression in the form of changes in Russian policies. In the meantime, significant leadership transitions took place in both Russia and the United States, and domestic developments and internal political rivalries considerably overshadowed foreign policy concerns. At the same time, both the European Union and NATO routinized, institutionalized, and bureaucratized the processes of their outreach to nonmember states in Europe and the expansion of their membership. The third major pillar of the European security establishment, the Organization for Security and Cooperation in Europe (OSCE), was fully occupied in implementing the major decisions made at Istanbul and deploying resources to address ongoing and new conflicts arrayed throughout Eastern Europe and the former Soviet Union. In some of these conflict resolution efforts, increasing signs appeared of Russia's unease with the Western presence and activity in areas of the post-Soviet space (and former Russian empire) that Moscow had long considered its own sphere of special interest.

Unforeseen events, however, would soon shatter any illusion that European security institutions could develop smoothly along well-established lines in response to already familiar and well-understood threats. When war broke out once again in late 1999 in the North Caucasus, this time rebellious Chechens were mobilized more by radical Islamic ideology than by militant secular nationalism. US forces and installations in the Middle East and East Africa had suffered a series of attacks by radical Islamic terrorists during the 1990s as well, but on September 11, 2001, the United States experienced the stunning, coordinated attacks on the World Trade Center towers and the Pentagon. Moscow reacted with a brutal assault on Chechnya; Washington responded with a global war on terror. Although terrorist actions inspired by radical Islamic ideology had been growing steadily during the 1990s, these events abruptly and dramatically altered both Russian and American perceptions of the major contemporary threats to their security. These major shifts in threat perceptions in Moscow and Washington of necessity also altered in turn European thinking about threats and how European security institutions should respond. One of these new responses, ballistic missile defense, began to emerge as an ongoing, increasingly contentious global and regional security issue.

These dramatic changes in the global security environment at the beginning of the new century unavoidably had serious effects on the inseparably intertwined European security environment. The new century began with the United States and NATO watching with disapproval the brutal Russian campaign in the North Caucasus, wondering about the mettle and intentions of a new Russian ruler, and hoping to implement the major revisions in the conventional arms control regime agreed to at Istanbul. In less than four years, by August 2003, NATO had formally taken command of a multilateral military operation in Afghanistan fighting against the terrorists who had attacked the United States in 2001 and those who had harbored them. Meanwhile, American (and some British) troops occupied Iraq after invading and toppling Saddam Hussein over the vocal objections of Russian president Vladimir Putin, French president Jacques Chirac, and German chancellor Gerhard Schröder. Both Washington and Moscow claimed to be battling radical Islamic-inspired terror and called upon allies and partners around the globe to help them in the fight.

## PUTIN CONSOLIDATES HIS POWER

To many observers, Putin looked small and ill at ease next to Boris Yeltsin when the president appointed him prime minister and called Putin the best qualified to follow him (Yeltsin) as president.[1] Even to seasoned Russia watchers, Putin seemed an unlikely choice for Russia's highest office, although in retrospect he clearly was not anywhere near as inexperienced as contemporary Western press accounts suggested; he was instead less well known and unexpected. The sudden, seemingly quixotic attack into Dagestan by Chechen forces under Shamil Basaev and the unexplained bombing of several apartment buildings in southern Russia and Moscow provided the opportunity for a patriotic campaign in Russia's broadcast media in support of the new prime minister.[2] Putin's relative youth, vigor, and toughness—epitomized by his infamous promise "to whack [the terrorists] in the outhouse"—won him rapidly escalating public support. Yeltsin's allies, in particular the oligarch Boris Berezovskii, helped organize and publicize a pro-Putin political party, Edinstvo (Unity), which unexpectedly took second place in the December 1999 parliamentary elections. Eclipsing what had seemed to be formidable rivals only weeks earlier—in particular former prime minister Yevgenii Primakov and Moscow mayor Iurii Luzhkov—Putin won the presidency in his own right on the first ballot in March 2000.

Putin's primary concerns during his first year or two in office were clearly domestic. First and foremost came the war in Chechnya, and along with it the state of the Russian military and security services.[3] Years later, during his 2011–12 presidential campaign, Putin reported that in September 1999, when attempting to organize a response to Basaev's incursion into Dagestan, the Kremlin was able to assemble a force of barely 60,000 troops capable of combat operations in the field, out of an armed force of allegedly more than 1 million men.[4] Even with somewhat improved although still brutal tactics, Russian military forces in the North Caucasus made headway against the Chechen insurgents only slowly and with difficulty. Putin's unpleasant experiences with the capabilities, command, control, and reliability of the military were dramatically illustrated by the string of events, excuses, explanations, and recriminations involved in the sinking of the attack submarine *Kursk* and the deaths of its crew in August 2000.[5] Before the end of his first year in office, Putin found Russia's defense forces both weak and unreliable; he would devote considerable effort over the next decade and a half in addressing these deficiencies.

Putin also needed to remedy the extreme decentralization, deterioration of government capacity, and running battle between the executive and legislative branches that characterized most of the later Yeltsin years. Putin successfully overcame the worst of the legislative dysfunction by negotiating the merger of Unity with Primakov and Luzhkov's Fatherland-All Russia (Otechestvo-vsia Rossiia) to form the reliable ruling party United Russia (Edinaia Rossiia). He managed considerable resubordination of local authorities to the center with the construction of his "power vertical" (*vertikal' vlasti*), especially through the establishment of seven regions each headed by a personal representative of the president. In one of his most widely known moves, he invited the leading oligarchs to his official residence outside Moscow and laid out the terms of his future relations with them—he (Putin) would not challenge the legality of the privatization processes during the 1990s that produced their wealth; in return they would refrain from participation in politics. Those that appeared to think about challenging this arrangement, such as Boris Berezovskii and Vladimir Gusinskii, quickly had their media holdings seized and eventually fled into exile. When he attempted to intervene in politics a couple of years later, Yukos owner Mikhail Khodorkovskii suffered a similar, but harsher fate.

Contrary to how he has come to be portrayed in many Western writings about contemporary Russia, Putin was responsible for introducing considerable, serious, necessary reforms in Russia, especially during his first term. Surrounding himself with economic experts, some of them old colleagues from Leningrad / Saint Petersburg—such as the minister of finance, Aleksei Kudrin; the minister of the economy, German Gref; and an economic adviser, Andrei Illarionov—Putin instituted fundamental changes, such as a universal flat tax of only 13 percent, greatly increasing the government's revenue collections, and the right to buy and sell land, introducing a true real estate market and facilitating the growth of investment in the country.[6] Where Westerners saw openness and competition in the Russian government under Yeltsin, many Russians had seen chaos, corruption, and collapse. Large segments of the population and the elite were delighted to see the country headed by a young, firm, purposeful *khoziain* (boss).[7] Westerners perceived the adoption of the melody of the Soviet national anthem, with new words, as a sign of neo-Soviet revival; Russians explained the move as preservation of better elements of the country's recent history rather than a wholesale return to the past.[8]

In his first years in office, Putin also largely sought accommodation and not confrontation with the European Union, the United States, and NATO. Soon after becoming president, Putin reached out to NATO; and its secretary-general, George Robertson, became the first high-level Western visitor to the new head of state. Putin expressed a desire to Robertson to repair Moscow's relationship with NATO and noted decisively his view that Russia was a part of Europe.[9] Prime Minister Tony Blair followed Robertson to Moscow almost immediately, successfully warming both political and economic-commercial ties.[10] By the late summer of 2000, Putin had also established warm personal relations with French president Chirac and German chancellor Schröder, whom Putin reportedly charmed in a long tête-à-tête in German.[11] In addition to the obvious political advantage in establishing good personal ties with the new Russian president, the major European leaders had a strong desire to repair the damage done to relations with Moscow by the war in Kosovo and to bring Russia under Putin back into greater participation in European political and economic affairs. For some time during the early years of the 2000s, the

Europeans were stronger advocates of integrating Russia into European institutions than were their counterparts in Washington.

Putin's relations with the Clinton administration were initially a bit testy. Strobe Talbott describes a meeting in December 1999 at which Putin expressed a desire for good relations with the United States but was unyielding on sensitive issues such as Chechnya or Georgia.[12] Putin's subsequent meetings with President Clinton during 2000 were not terribly successful. Although Clinton had basically given his friend Boris Yeltsin a pass with respect to Russia's actions in Chechnya, neither the US president nor members of his administration were anywhere near as forgiving of Putin's tactics in the North Caucasus some five years later.[13] The United States also took a far more active stance in defending the sovereignty and independence of Russia's smaller former Soviet neighbors, such as Georgia and Moldova. By late 1999, Russian accusations of Tbilisi's tolerance or support for Chechen fighters finding sanctuary across Russia's border with Georgia were already a source of friction with Washington.[14]

The issue of missile defense reemerged in the last year of the Clinton administration as perhaps the most difficult bilateral security issue between Moscow and Washington, and for more than a decade and a half it has remained a major source of discord and tension between Russia and the United States.[15] Washington enthusiasts of President Ronald Reagan's Strategic Defense Initiative had never given up the hope that technological advances would someday provide an answer to the country's vulnerability to ballistic missile attack. By the late 1990s, advances in missile technology by rogue states such as North Korea made the issue more pressing for Washington at the same time that Pentagon researchers began to report significant progress. The 1998 congressionally mandated Rumsfeld Report trumpeted the threat from rogue states (fortuitously supported by a failed North Korean launch six weeks later) and gave political support to Republican advocates of missile defense.

The major achievement of the Clinton administration with respect to strategic arms control in its relations with Moscow was completion of the consolidation of all former Soviet nuclear weapons and delivery systems in Russia. With a good relationship at the highest levels between Washington and Moscow, during the 1990s the world was arguably the most secure against nuclear war than at any time since nuclear weapons were invented. However, Clinton's strategic understanding with Russia did not extend very far beyond the Kremlin. The State Duma repeatedly refused to ratify the Strategic Arms Reduction Treaty (known as START II) agreement, thereby precluding further progress on strategic arms control or reductions. As work progressed in the United States on ballistic and theater missile defense, Clinton was unsuccessful in making any headway with Yeltsin on what aspects of missile defense might be permissible and acceptable to Moscow under the Anti–Ballistic Missile Treaty.

Clinton raised the subject again with Putin in the summer of 2000 but found little understanding on Putin's part of US concerns and little willingness of the Russians to explore possible compromises on the subject.[16]

The Russians basically decided to wait out the lame duck Clinton administration and pinned their hopes on George W. Bush, whose victory they apparently anticipated more accurately than many in the United States itself.[17] Despite a rocky start, when the United States expelled some fifty alleged intelligence operatives in the Russian Embassy's staff in Washington, Putin was soon rewarded in his efforts to cultivate a better relationship with the United States. Bush and Putin hit it off at their first meeting in Ljubljana, when the American president famously got a sense of the Russian's soul. Putin's quick expression of support for the United States after the September 11 attacks and his override of his advisers' objections to the United States' use of military facilities in Central Asia for the attack on Afghanistan cemented his ties with Bush. Putin was rewarded with an invitation to the Bush ranch in Texas as part of an official visit to the United States in November 2001.[18]

Putin apparently hoped for greater American understanding of Russia's war against the Chechen rebels and Islamic extremists, whom the Russians considered very similar if not identical to the individuals and groups that had attacked the United States.[19] According to Putin's aspirations, a joint effort against terrorists around the globe might serve as the launching mechanism for a truly equal partnership between Moscow and Washington. In pursuit of this partnership, Putin supported and facilitated a number of American actions that provoked often severe objections from his colleagues. Moscow helped the United States arrange a military presence in Uzbekistan and Kyrgyzstan as part of the war in Afghanistan. In the early months of that war, Moscow shared what some Americans called "valuable intelligence" on some of the forces in Afghanistan.[20] Putin countenanced (at least in public) the unilateral US withdrawal from the Anti–Ballistic Missile Treaty and signed a vague United States–proposed strategic arms agreement with no provisions for verification. Finally, Moscow accepted with a minimum of public protest NATO's 2002 decision on the second wave of NATO enlargement, including offering membership to the three Baltic Sea states. Putin and his colleagues pronounced themselves satisfied with the creation of a NATO-Russia Council, which purportedly would give Russia an even more special relationship with the Atlantic Alliance.

In return for going along with these American initiatives, Putin received a mixed lot of benefits and concessions.[21] At the Bush ranch in November 2001, the United States announced a planned reduction of strategic nuclear warheads during the next decade (an action that might have been taken anyway). Bush promised Putin to try to abolish the Soviet-era Jackson-Vanik Amendment, still hampering US trade with Russia, and to forgive the Soviet debt assumed by Russia in 1991. Washington also promised to support economic reform and growth in Russia by backing the country's early entry into the World Trade Organization. US criticism of Russian operations in Chechnya was muted, at least in comparison with the Clinton administration's stance during 2000, but Washington nonetheless annoyed Moscow by refusing to extradite and even meeting unofficially with representatives of Chechen exile groups that Russia labeled terrorists.[22] American criticism of the Russian security forces' assault on Chechen terrorists holding hostage several hundred spectators at Moscow's Dubrovka Theater in October 2002 also was muted when the use of an anesthetic gas result in the deaths of dozens of hostages.

More than a decade later, a common narrative offered to Western interlocutors by senior Russian officials claims that the United States never fulfilled its side of the bargain with Putin when the latter offered Russia's help in the war on terror.[23] US officials generally deny that there was any explicit deal with Putin; many in the Bush administration apparently presumed that Moscow would understand that US actions in Afghanistan (and beyond) would also result in improved security for Russia. From the Russian perspective, the US military presence and operations in Central Asia and the Caucasus, although largely related to the war in Afghanistan, made it hard to see future trade or strategic arms benefits as a fair exchange. In addition, as the Kremlin's political control within Russia strengthened and the economy began the long stretch of remarkable growth during the 2000s, Moscow began to approach international affairs, in particular security, stability, and conflict resolution in the former Soviet states on its periphery with increased confidence and correspondingly less tolerance of Western involvement there. Russia's increasingly critical stances toward the OSCE Chechnya Assistance Group and the OSCE Border Monitoring Mission in Georgia are prime examples of this gradual change in Russia's approach to its so-called near abroad.[24]

Whatever Putin hoped to gain by accommodating George W. Bush's major international initiatives, it was evident by early 2003 that his expectations were unlikely to be met. Strains in various aspects of the relationship became more and more apparent, in particular with respect to the American march toward war in Iraq. Putin joined with Chirac and Schröder in efforts to avert a US attack on Saddam Hussein; and when the war began, he called it "a big political mistake."[25] Although a cooperative facade was maintained throughout much of 2003, Moscow and Washington were growing steadily further apart. The arrest of Mikhail Khodorkovskii in October 2003 and the start of the process of dismantling Yukos prompted considerable dismay in the West and confirmed the predisposition of many of Washington's neoconservatives with respect to Putin's alleged "true character." The Kremlin's orchestration of the 2003 parliamentary elections in Russia, in particular the use of the right-wing nationalist party Rodina (Motherland) to attract enough votes to keep the independent right-center democratic parties out of the Duma, also tarnished Putin's credentials as a reformer and acceptable partner among many in the West. By the autumn of 2003, Russia was growing evermore distant from the United States and Western Europe, although the cracks were not yet showing clearly.

## WASHINGTON'S GLOBAL WAR ON TERROR

The most important events for the development and direction of European security institutions in the early twenty-first century arguably occurred on the other side of the North Atlantic, in Washington and New York, on September 11, 2001. The terrorist attacks on the Pentagon and the World Trade Center launched the George W. Bush administration, which had come into office disavowing intervention and state building, onto a course of global intervention, unilateralism, and democratic transformation. For many observers, the path of the future Bush administration was predicted in a January–February 2000 *Foreign Affairs* article by Condoleezza Rice, who would become Bush's foreign policy adviser, in which she sharply criticized as overly ambitious the Clinton administration's interventionist foreign policies.[26] Yet the new administration also contained major neoconservative figures, such as Vice President Dick Cheney, which meant that the urge to use US power to remake the world would never be far below the surface.[27]

Since 1945, the United States had always had global interests and commitments, but the attacks of September 11 prompted a rapid and marked shift of a considerable portion of US attention and resources away from Europe and toward South Asia and the Middle East. Some contemporary historians might argue that such a change had already begun at the time of the First Gulf War, as US assets remained in the Persian Gulf region even after successful conclusion of the conflict. Even so, US diplomatic and military resources were also heavily committed to Europe during the 1990s in the international responses to the Balkan crises and the wars in Bosnia and Kosovo. Europe was never the only game in town for Washington, but as the Bush administration took office, it was still relatively high on the United States' global agenda.

Senior Bush administration officials frequently remarked that the September 11 attacks "changed everything."[28] In fact, the global strategic environment was not appreciably different on September 12, 2001, from that prevailing in the previous days, months, or even a few years. However, the spectacular fall of the Twin Towers and the feeling experienced by senior officials of being under possible attack in their own offices in Washington changed US perceptions of the nature, importance, and immediacy of the threats facing the nation. Terrorism had been a problem for at least two decades, but attacks had generally been conducted against US assets, personnel, and citizens overseas, and rarely in the continental United States. The demonstration that Islamic radicals could stage significant operations on US soil, combined with existing fears on the part of senior administration officials about the spread of weapons of mass destruction and missile technology to rogue states, produced a White House decision to seek out and destroy at the source not only those who had conducted the attacks on Washington and New York but also those who might have the capability and intent to mount further attacks. A series of anonymous attacks with anthrax powder sent through the mail enhanced the sense of siege in Washington and likely contributed to the urgency and scale of the US response.[29]

Indeed, Washington's response to the September 11 attacks was global and unlimited. It included immediate retaliation against the al-Qaeda cells in Afghanistan, which had almost immediately been identified as the authors of the operation, and the Taliban hosting them. Having apparently been surprised by al-Qaeda's plans and especially capability to reach US territory, the Bush administration sought to ensure that no such incident of any sort could be repeated, often invoking the specter of a nuclear, chemical, or biological attack. Washington's attention focused almost immediately on Iraq and Saddam Hussein. Responding to assertions that Saddam had been contained and his own denials that Iraq possessed weapons of mass destruction, administration officials such as the national security adviser, Rice, countered that the risk was too great—the proof of being wrong might be a mushroom cloud.[30] Within a few months, Washington's concerns expanded from responding to al-Qaeda's destruction of the twin towers to confronting an "Axis of Evil" comprising Iraq, Iran, and North Korea.[31] The US policy shift in the wake of September 11 in the end included responses to almost all the threats, enemies, and rogue states identified and described by senior neoconservative members of the Bush administration—in particular, Dick Cheney, Donald Rumsfeld, and Paul Wolfowitz—as early as the 1992 Defense Planning Guidance.[32]

The response of America's Allies to September 11 was immediate and supportive, with NATO invoking Article V for the first time in its history. To those who remembered the Cheney Pentagon's (and Wolfowitz-authored) Defense Planning Guidance, it would come as no surprise that the Bush administration's reply to NATO's offer of assistance in crafting a collective plan of actions was essentially "thanks, but no thanks." The same current and former Pentagon officials who were determined unilateralists and intent on preserving American supremacy in 1992 were now in charge of formulating American defense and security policy.[33] The importance of this factor lies not simply in the criticism that the refusal of Allied assistance in the autumn of 2001 might have been more gracious (although that is probably the case). Starting in October 2001, the Bush administration pursued a new global agenda—the global war on terror—with the objectives determined almost entirely by the United States through widespread application of America's overwhelming military power. These efforts were multilateral almost solely in the sense that the Bush administration welcomed friendly nations to join the cause in supporting and subordinate roles. If its friends or Allies objected, the United States proceeded anyway on the course it had determined, with objections noted and long resented (the US Capitol's restaurants served "freedom fries" for a long time).

In terms of how this all affected US views and actions with respect to European security, Washington was primarily concerned with obtaining support for its broader, global objectives. The United States sought Allies and friends that would contribute forces to coalitions in Afghanistan and Iraq. The administration found cooperative capitals that would not object to the incarceration, transit, or questioning of suspected terrorists. Washington pushed nuclear nonproliferation concerns, in particular apparent attempts by Iran to develop a nuclear weapons capability. Finally, first citing Iraq and then Iran, the United States pushed research on and the development and testing of ballistic missile defense systems and discussed with many different interlocutors the possibility and consequences of deploying ballistic missile defense systems.

The United States remained the unquestioned leader in European security, but after September 11 it was leading Europe in directions that had steadily less and less to do with the defense of European territory or security and stability on the continent. Instead, Washington mostly sought to enlist both European institutions and its European Allies and friends in pursuit of its global goals and antiterror campaign. In the early part of the decade, well into the first year of the Iraq War, Bush's global campaign was expressed chiefly in military actions to counter terrorist threats. By the beginning of Bush's second term, this global quest blossomed into a full-blown neo-Wilsonianism, as the president's second inaugural address committed the United States to the defense and spread of democracy around the world.[34] The results vis-à-vis Europe and Russia were mixed: cooperation on some issues, and criticism and opposition on others. The institutional changes that took place during this same period, especially NATO and EU enlargements, would eventually alter the political balance within these organizations and thus also in Europe, setting the stage for serious collisions in the middle of the decade.

## EUROPE GETS A PHONE NUMBER

Moving from the twentieth into the twenty-first century, the European Union continued its steady development along several lines that had been clearly established during the 1990s. Adhering remarkably closely to the timetable for Economic and Monetary Union set out by the Maastricht Treaty, the EU pegged all participating national currencies to the new common currency, the euro, on January 1, 1999. Precisely three years later, euro coins and bills were introduced, and a dozen historic European currencies vanished into history. In further developing its institutional capacity, the EU established the post of high representative for the Common Foreign and Security Policy, along with appropriate political and military committees aimed at both formulating and implementing policy. These newly established EU bodies and representatives reached agreement with NATO on procedures for using national assets also dedicated to NATO in EU operations, and EU peacekeepers were deployed in Africa and Europe. Finally, EU representatives pressed ahead with enlargement negotiations with at least a dozen applicants and reached agreement, in late 2002, for ten new members to join the EU in 2004.

The provisions of the Maastricht Treaty and the subsequent relentless push to establish and implement the euro zone reflected the thinking of the substantial school within the European integration movement that political union would be a natural and necessary by-product and follow-on to a closer economic union. With a retrospective view of well more than a decade, it seems foolish at best to adopt a common monetary system and common currency in a body with only a relatively weak central bank and in which fiscal policy was still jealously reserved for national jurisdictions.[35] The stability and growth pact adopted in Amsterdam in 1997 obliged all euro zone member countries to keep budget deficits below 3 percent of gross domestic product, and the euro countries lost all control over monetary policy. There were other demanding institutional and policy requirements for joining the euro included in the Maastricht Pact, and only the United Kingdom and Denmark had a formal opt-out clause. The EU officials and bureaucrats who set and put into practice the rules for the euro clearly understood there was little appetite in European publics for supranational political institutions that might adopt common policies on taxation or spending. The parents of the euro were clearly closer to Hayek than to Keynes, and the Maastricht Treaty makes clear that price stability (that is, avoiding inflation) is a central task of the European Central Bank.[36]

At the time of the euro's introduction, almost all economic analysts would probably have named excessive spending, borrowing, and inflation as the greatest dangers to European economies. EU officials were dismayed when the euro dropped some 30 percent against the US dollar almost immediately after its introduction, from an original peg of $1.20 to €1 to a low of just over 80 cents, and they were embarrassed when the Federal Reserve and other central banks had to intervene to prop up the euro. In the longer run, the fact that the Mediterranean EU countries were inside a common monetary system with larger EU economies, such as Germany, ultimately made it easier for them to borrow to finance growth and to purchase goods within the EU market. All this eventually produced a relatively long period of growth and prosperity in the 2000s, until the global economic crisis of 2008.

Proponents of the view that closer economic union would lead to corresponding political union found some support for their position in the push for further institutional reform marked by another EU treaty update agreed at the Nice Summit in December 2000. The Nice Treaty, signed in February 2001, took a large amount of work for relatively meager results, such as revised voting weights in the European Council, representation in the European Commission, and size of the European Parliament.[37] The Nice Treaty was almost immediately rejected by a decisive 64 percent majority by Irish voters, and EU officials went back to the drawing board. With the prospect of a large number of additional members in the relatively near future, and the need for better developed political institutions and procedures, the EU embarked upon yet another intergovernmental conclave, called the Convention on the Future of Europe, which would undertake to adopt fundamental reforms, but this time in the form of a complete EU constitution.[38] More than two years of negotiations, beginning in early 2002, were needed to reach agreement on a constitutional treaty for the EU, which was signed on October 29, 2004. Although the treaty would never be ratified and implemented due to decisive rejections by French and Dutch voters in 2005, the impetus to fashion closer and more capable political institutions for the EU, launched at Nice in 2000–2001, continued unabated throughout the 2000s.

One area in which national representatives and officials made considerable progress in deepening the EU and strengthening its institutions was foreign and security policy. As the European Council adopted its first common strategy in June 1999 — aimed at a consensus EU approach to Russia — the EU also plucked Javier Solana away from NATO to become the council's first secretary-general and the high representative for the EU's Common Foreign and Security Policy.[39] In pursuit of the Helsinki "Headline Goals" by early 2000, the EU set up its Political and Security Committee as the main working-level, decisionmaking body for the EU Council on issues related to the Common Foreign and Security Policy.[40] At the same time, the EU established the EU Military Committee to provide military advice, along with the EU Military Staff to support the

Military Committee. Before the end of the year, these committees sponsored the EU Military Capabilities Conference, which produced a comprehensive review of EU members' personnel and equipment resources.

The big issues were how these EU political and military institutions would relate to NATO in both theory and practice, and how these EU military resources might be employed if not as part of a NATO operation. The debates within the EU over these questions were quite familiar to all. France called for more extensive development of the European Security and Defence Policy before initiating formal discussions with NATO, thus seeking to avoid what Paris saw as Washington's undue influence over EU security structures and policies. Not surprisingly, London pushed for what NATO secretary-general Lord Robertson called "a NATO-friendly European defense."[41] By September 2000, the EU's Political and Security Committee and NATO's North Atlantic Council began to hold joint meetings, and four joint working groups began to work on the security of sensitive information, military capabilities, institutional arrangements, and EU contributions and operations. The last was called Berlin-Plus, because it followed on discussions held between NATO and the EU in Berlin in 1996.[42]

The process worked better than might have been expected, due to the friendly and effective collaboration of NATO secretary-general Robertson and EU high representative Solana, each of whom had a deep understanding of and commitment to the success of both institutions. The United States also was remarkably supportive, with the Clinton administration enthusiastically endorsing the development of an autonomous European defense capability. At the NATO Defense Ministers' Meeting in October 2000, US secretary of defense William Cohen stated that "we agree with this goal — not grudgingly, not with resignation, but with wholehearted conviction."[43] At the same time, Cohen stressed that the United States had no intention of withdrawing from Europe, and he called for a collaborative approach and relationship between the EU and NATO. However, a final agreement on a NATO-EU package proved unattainable in 2000 because Turkey objected to providing EU access to NATO planning, and EU negotiators thus had to persuade the incoming Bush administration to accept the nearly completed package. In a February 2001 visit to Washington, UK prime minister Blair convinced the new US president that the arrangement would not weaken NATO and ensured that the United States would remain at least benevolently inclined, if not supportive.

In fact, the new Bush administration was considerably more concerned with convincing the Allies — and Russia, and China, among others — of its positions on the necessity for developing and deploying missile defense systems. After September 11, 2001, Washington's focus fell almost entirely on the fight against

terror, first the effort in Afghanistan, and then increasingly the buildup to eventual war against Iraq. As calls from senior Bush administration officials grew
in frequency and intensity for action against Saddam Hussein, disagreements
and tensions mounted with many of the closest European Allies, particularly
Germany and France. The supportive role of Blair's Britain in Bush's march to
war has been well chronicled elsewhere, but London also remained an important interlocutor on European Security and Defence Policy. US and UK persuasion overcame the Turkish objection to the new NATO-EU relationship
in December 2001; the accession to office of a far more EU-friendly Adalet ve
Kalkinma Partisi (AKP; Justice and Development Party) government in Turkey
in 2002 made the process of final approval easier.[44]

The final agreement was formally announced in the "EU-NATO Declaration on European Security and Defence Policy," issued by Robertson and
Solana on December 16, 2002.[45] The more detailed institutional arrangements
for EU-NATO cooperation were issued in written form on March 17, 2003.
The Berlin-Plus arrangements embodied three key points in this document: (1)
NATO guarantees that the EU has access to NATO planning; (2) the EU may
request a NATO European Command option for an EU-led operation; and (3)
the EU may request the use of NATO assets and capabilities. In a working document on EU-NATO consultation, planning, and operations adopted later in
2003 by the EU Council, EU representatives noted that "NATO is the forum for
discussion and the natural choice for an operation involving the European and
American Allies."[46]

With this, the long struggle over a separate European defense and its relationship to NATO was apparently over. The United States paid relatively little
attention to the final steps in the process, and those involved from Washington
were satisfied with the result. In fact, the Bush administration spent more
effort browbeating reluctant Allies that did not support the war in Iraq, and was
not at all reluctant to permit the European Union to take over rather routine
European security operations, such as the peacekeeping and police operations
in the Balkans. In mid-2003, the EU formally assumed control of Operation Concordia, the stabilization presence in Macedonia; in 2004, in Bosnia-Herzegovina,
NATO'S Stabilization Force in Bosnia and Herzegovina became the European
Union Force, as the EU assumed responsibility for what had been NATO's first
major out-of-area operation. Washington by this time had other, far more distant
and more pressing priorities.

One final, important result of the shift in American concerns and priorities
and the discord between the United States and many of its European Allies
over the Iraq war was the EU decision in 2003 to adopt a common security strategy. The European Council requested High Representative Solana to come up
with a draft, which was then adopted at the December 12–13, 2003, council

meeting.[47] The initiative was prompted explicitly by the recent transatlantic discord, and the reasoning was that in light of the experience with Iraq EU members needed to ensure that they were operating on the basis of a common strategic vision. Solana's strategy enumerated five basic threats: terrorism, proliferation of weapons of mass destruction, regional conflicts, state failure, and organized crime. The document emphasized diplomacy, preventive engagement, and broad multilateral cooperation, as it was clear that the EU could not address all these threats by itself. At the time the document was drafted, one might infer that regional conflict referred in particular to the Balkans. The EU enlargement of 2004 expanded its territory, extended its borders, and ultimately made new regions, conflicts, and threats greater concerns for Brussels and its member states.

The EU also doggedly continued work on the project it had begun in the mid-1990s to prepare the states of Central and Eastern Europe for membership, a process that culminated in 2002 with formal agreements on admission with ten candidates, which all became full members in 2004.[48] By 2000, all ten Central and Eastern European candidates, plus Cyprus and Malta, were fully engaged in accession negotiations, although it was unclear how quickly these states would meet all the requirements for full membership. Romania and Bulgaria gradually fell behind the others in closing chapters of the *acquis communautaire*, and it became clear they would gain membership somewhat later. During its 2001 presidency, pro-enlargement Sweden managed to force a European Council decision that all the candidates that successfully completed negotiations by December 2002 could join in 2004.

When the accession talks first began in 1997–98, the EU was enthusiastic about the positive effects on reform that enlargement might have, and the applicant countries were more or less willing to accept any conditions imposed by the European Commission, which managed the negotiations. As the process developed and dragged on into the next century, some of the candidate countries—in particular, Poland—became irritated with what they saw as discriminatory treatment. Enlargement issues and the rights of new members became entangled with debates within the EU over deepening the union and strengthening existing institutions. For example, Austria and Germany lobbied for some limitation on freedom of movement for residents of the new members, fearing an influx of cheap labor to compete for jobs with their own workers. The size and distribution of agricultural subsidies and voting weights in EU bodies were sore subjects among existing members in the debates both before and after Nice, and these arguments spilled over into the accession talks. A last-minute agreement on the Common Agricultural Policy in October 2002 enabled the accession talks to finish by the end of the year, and in March 2003 ten candidates signed formal treaties of accession. After successful ratification, ten new members—Estonia, Latvia, Lithuania, Poland, Hungary, the Czech Republic, Slovakia, Slovenia, Cyprus, and Malta—joined the European Union on May 1, 2004.[49]

The massive enlargement of May 2004 was an impressive political achievement and changed the EU in many ways, both foreseen and unanticipated. Citizens of the new member states gradually obtained the considerable benefits of the four freedoms, with the ability to travel, work, live, and own property over much of the continent. However, the long and difficult debates within the EU and in the accession talks left a residue of bitterness and "enlargement fatigue." Right-wing nationalist parties in a number of longtime EU member states (France was a particularly prominent example) used fears of mass immigration from Europe's East to ride to worrisome electoral showings. Even with the accomplishments of the Amsterdam and Nice treaties and the constitutional negotiations, the EU was not prepared institutionally to cope immediately with the addition of ten new national jurisdictions (and languages) and more than 100 million people. Even though enlargement has continued at a more moderate pace, it is hardly surprising that after May 2004, the European Union entered a long period of internal consolidation during which issues of domestic EU governance were of paramount importance to the national authorities of almost all the member states.

As the EU simultaneously completed more than a decade of negotiations with NATO and the United States over an autonomous defense capability for Europe, the process of enlargement produced deep changes in the manner in which the EU as a whole contemplated the use of this capability. Although the United States after September 2001 pushed its European Allies toward greater engagement in a global campaign against terror, European attention retained considerable focus on domestic and regional concerns. The EU first agreed to use its military not to defend against external threats, but to assume responsibility for local European peacekeeping and police missions that the United States no longer wished to conduct. US secretary of defense Rumsfeld's perception of a divide between "old" and "new" Europe had some basis in reality, manifested more in the attitude of the new EU members from Eastern Europe toward NATO and the United States. Poland and the Baltic republics, for example, had quite a different perception of Russia's nature and role in European security than did many of their Western European colleagues. The sudden and mass inclusion of Central and Eastern European countries in the EU and NATO changed the underlying consensus, threat perception, and nature of the discussion in both institutions. These changes eventually had quite profound effects on the relationship of both institutions with Russia, a subject explored in more detail in the discussion of NATO later in this chapter.

# THE OSCE: MOVING FROM THE BALKANS
## TO THE NEAR ABROAD

The OSCE concluded the twentieth century with a major programmatic document, the Charter for European Security, the most important and ambitious provisions of which were then never really implemented. The OSCE continued to serve as a jack of all trades, troubleshooting mechanism for the states of Europe and North America, with a particular emphasis on placing individually tailored operations in the field to address specific needs and threats in different regions and particular states. The OSCE also served as the central institution for conventional arms control in Europe, actively managing the confidence-building and transparency regime established by the Vienna Document series and providing a platform for the smaller group of OSCE states that were parties to the Treaty on Conventional Armed Forces in Europe (CFE). Largely in response to other processes and developments under way in Europe, the OSCE's troubleshooting focus shifted gradually during the early 2000s from the Balkans and Central Europe toward the peripheral areas of the former Soviet Union. The process of seeking ratification of the Adapted CFE Treaty concentrated this focus on particular areas of Russia's "near abroad" and on "frozen conflicts" in Moldova and the Caucasus.

Whatever its flaws, by 2000 the OSCE had become a large, mature, diverse institution with extremely broad responsibilities and a growing bureaucracy. The Permanent Council in Vienna served as the chief forum for political consultation within the OSCE. For an institution that required a consensus of its fifty-plus members to take any action, the OSCE's effectiveness depended heavily on the depth (or absence) of disagreements between its participating states. There were periodic, perennial proposals to improve the work of the Permanent Council, which were doomed to fail less because of inefficiency than due to a lack of comity among the states of Europe. The Forum for Security Cooperation also met in Vienna and busied itself largely with the technical details of arms control and confidence building—highly detailed, unpublicized, but nonetheless valuable work. The OSCE also expanded its Secretariat and other headquarters operations in Vienna and fleshed out and rationalized the bureaucratic structures that supported its work in the field. Secretary General Jan Kubis, who was appointed in 1999, embarked on a multiyear management reform effort to provide basic rules and procedures to an institution that for much of the 1990s operated on a largely ad hoc basis, the result of the hope of some of its largest participating states that the OSCE could avoid becoming unduly large and bureaucratic. In yet another sign of its maturity and institutionalization, the OSCE's delegations in Vienna increasingly argued over budgets, both the level of contributions from participating states and the allocations to various OSCE institutions and operations.

The Office for Democratic Institutions and Human Rights (ODIHR, or OSCE/ODIHR) in Warsaw managed an annual review of the human dimension, which was gradually becoming a kabuki exercise and a pale echo of the Cold War–era human rights debates in the CSCE. However, ODIHR also ran a largely autonomous election observation section, which developed an approach that became the model for government and nongovernment election monitoring operations around the globe. ODIHR's election reports were generally so accurate and impartial that only large states ventured to complain when they found the substance of the report uncomfortable. The high commissioner on national minorities, headquartered in The Hague, accumulated a sizable staff and was extremely active in dozens of states in the OSCE area, engaged largely in quiet, preventive diplomacy. The OSCE also had an increasingly active Parliamentary Assembly, which met in plenary session twice a year and in the 2000s began to establish ad hoc groups of parliamentarians to involve themselves in various conflicts and problems around the OSCE area. The weakest of the OSCE's original three baskets was the economic and environmental dimension. The OSCE held a yearly Economic Forum, at which annual priorities were set and discussed. However, for many reasons, most of the OSCE's member states preferred other international financial institutions for serious economic projects.

The heart of the OSCE's operations, and what distinguished it from other international security and human rights organizations in Europe, were its field operations—primarily, its individually mandated and designed missions deployed in more than fifteen participating states.[50] These OSCE missions might be grouped into several distinct categories. There were (and are) the missions dedicated to conflict prevention or resolution, mostly established in the early 1990s, such as those in Georgia, Long Duration in Kosovo-Vojvodina-Sandzak, Moldova, Ukraine, and Macedonia. The missions in Estonia and Latvia, including representatives for Soviet military pensioners and the Skrunda radar, were aimed at assisting the social, political, and military transition from Soviet to independent rule. There was a wave of missions established in the Balkans following the wars in Bosnia and Croatia, and before and after the NATO war in Kosovo. Most of these field operations focused on ethnic and social reconciliation and postconflict reconstruction. In the late 1990s and early 2000s, the OSCE's impulse to deploy field operations reached its zenith, with missions (or "centers," as some were called) established in Armenia, Azerbaijan, and all five states in Central Asia. The mandates of these offices generally called for them to assist their host states in implementing their OSCE commitments, convenient shorthand for facilitating or promoting the transition to democratic political systems and market economies.

In the years immediately following the Cold War, deployment of an OSCE field mission was often welcomed by host countries that were hard pressed to cope with domestic or external crises. However, as time passed, such an intrusive international presence became generally less welcome. Aside from Slobodan Milošević's Serbia, which remained a special case, the first countries to push back against an OSCE presence were Estonia and Latvia. Both Baltic states considered that an OSCE presence would hurt their bid for EU membership; they also perceived, rightly or wrongly, that an OSCE presence constituted a sign of continuing, unwelcome Russian influence on their domestic political affairs. Both obtained withdrawal of their OSCE missions by the end of 2001, although smaller, military-related presences remained. Moscow was not pleased but took advantage of the Baltic example to rid itself of the OSCE presence in Chechnya a year later.[51]

Belarus and Chechnya became the best examples of OSCE field operations that became increasingly unwelcome by their host countries for a variety of political reasons. Amid growing reports of political repression and human rights violations in Belarus after Aleksandr Lukashenko assumed the presidency, Belarus was pressured in 1997 into accepting a small OSCE Advisory and Monitoring Group headed by a senior German ambassador, with a mandate to "assist . . . in promoting democratic institutions and in complying with other OSCE commitments."[52] The Advisory Group had constant clashes with the Belarus authorities, and in 2002 was finally closed and replaced by an OSCE Office in Minsk, which had a less intrusive mandate, calling for assistance "in further promoting institution building, in further consolidating the rule of law," and also economic and environmental activities.[53] The Minsk Office lasted until the end of 2010, when its mandate expired shortly after an almost complete rupture of Belarus-EU relations in the wake of the regime's crackdown on civil society following the presidential elections. It was clear early on that Lukashenko, perhaps the most open if not the first authoritarian in the former Soviet space, was simply unwilling to tolerate foreign intervention in how he ran his domestic politics, irrespective of OSCE commitments. Some seasoned OSCE hands also noted the role of some Western participating states in exacerbating the situation by frequently urging the heads of mission in Minsk to take a more critical, confrontational posture toward Lukashenko and the Belarus authorities.[54] This pattern of behavior was repeated more broadly and more often in a number of participating states that hosted OSCE field operations after 2000.

The fate of the OSCE Assistance Group to Chechnya also epitomizes the decrease after 2000 in the desirability of hosting OSCE missions, along with a fundamental shift in the Russian Federation's attitude toward field operations and the OSCE itself.[55] From the very beginning, Moscow had mixed feelings about the involvement of the OSCE mission in resolution of the conflict in

Chechnya. After the Khasavyurt Agreement, Russia asserted that the Chechnya Assistance Group thereafter need only attend to humanitarian and human dimension issues, but as part of the overall compromise at the Istanbul Summit reaffirmed the group's full mandate, including assistance with conflict resolution. As security deteriorated in Chechnya in late 1998, the group's diplomatic staff relocated to Moscow; after the second war began, the Putin administration for a long time obstructed the group's return to the North Caucasus.[56] Although the group was permitted to return to Chechnya in June 2001, Moscow resisted any political mediation role for the group as Russian forces prosecuted the war against the Chechen resistance. In 2002, during discussions on renewal of the group's mandate, the Russian delegation insisted on restricting the mandate to humanitarian affairs. When almost all other delegations refused this proposal, Moscow opposed any further extension of the group's work, which ended on December 31, 2002.[57]

After 2000, the OSCE continued to be deeply involved in the Balkans and responded in an ad hoc fashion to problems and crises as they arose. The OSCE deployed an enormous mission to Kosovo, which in keeping with the approach adopted with the Platform for European Security was explicitly designated as one of the pillars of the total international effort at reconstruction under the aegis of the UN Mission in Kosovo.[58] The Kosovo Mission was given special responsibility for preparing local elections, and the EU undertook special responsibility for promoting the rule of law.[59] The Austrian Chairmanship closely followed the September 2000 elections in Serbia-Montenegro and the October 5–6 uprising that resulted in Milošević's removal. Subsequently, the Austrians took the lead in promoting Serbia-Montenegro's readmission to the OSCE and the deployment of an OSCE mission to Belgrade by the end of the year to assist with the transition.[60] The OSCE's quick action in response to events in Belgrade was facilitated when, after a night of hesitation and waiting, the Russian delegation received instructions from Moscow to support the new government in Belgrade.[61]

The Balkan region also had its share of countries eager to graduate from having an OSCE mission on their territory. Croatia, in particular, chafed at a continuing OSCE presence until President Franjo Tudjman left office, after which Zagreb and the OSCE conducted a long but amicable process of completing the tasks set out by the mandate.[62] Macedonia tried several times in the late 1990s to wind up the OSCE field operation, arguing that its job was done. However, an armed revolt of ethnic Albanians in the country's north and west put an end to such assertions of stability. The OSCE special representative appointed by the Romanian Chair, US ambassador Robert Frowick (the first head of the OSCE Mission to Bosnia-Herzegovina), worked out a sweeping decentralization and power-sharing agreement. The Macedonian government initially rejected the proposal and declared Frowick persona non grata. The EU's Solana and the United States stepped in, and in August 2001 Macedonians and ethnic Albanians accepted much the same agreement, the Ohrid Framework, which has served as the basis of ethnic cooperation and shared government since that time.[63] The OSCE Mission to Skopje was increased to more than 200 international members by the end of 2001 and cooperated with the EU Monitoring Mission (left over from the Balkan wars) in supervising implementation of the Ohrid Agreement. The history of the negotiation of the Ohrid Accord and the initial implementation served as an early example of overlap and competition between the OSCE and an EU in the process of developing a more robust foreign policy and defense capability.[64]

The OSCE also continued its determined pursuit of resolution of the four "frozen conflicts" on the periphery of the former Soviet Union: Moldova-Transdniestria, South Ossetia, and Abkhazia in Georgia; and Nagorno-Karabakh, between Azerbaijan and Armenia. The Karabakh conflict appeared near resolution at least twice—in the autumn of 1999, via a territorial swap; and in the spring of 2001, in the context of a meeting of the Minsk Group mediators and presidents Heidar Aliyev and Robert Kocharian in Key West, Florida.[65] The three cochairs of the Minsk Group—France, Russia, and the United States—cooperated remarkably well, given other issues that divided them, but were unsuccessful in overcoming the bitter enmity between Baku and Yerevan. Debate in the Permanent Council became so acrimonious that it became impossible even to gain a consensus on the geographical name for the conflict, which for some time has been referred to in OSCE documents as "the Conflict Handled by the Minsk Group."[66]

In Moldova and Georgia, the OSCE, along with other mediators, in particular representatives of the Russian Federation, appeared from 2000 to 2002 to be making headway on some of the issues involved in these intractable conflicts. The OSCE established a Voluntary Fund of contributions from several participating states to assist Russia in the destruction or withdrawal of its large stores of Soviet-era military equipment from Moldova, and Russia successfully met the first deadline established by the agreements at Istanbul by eliminating all its CFE Treaty-Limited Equipment before the end of 2001.[67] In Georgia, responding to Russian claims that Chechen fighters were finding refuge across the border in the mountains in Georgia, the OSCE in 2000 expanded the mandate of the mission to Georgia to deploy a border monitoring force under the command of a senior Austrian officer and specifically tasked the force "to observe and report on movement across the border between Georgia and the Chechen Republic of the Russian Federation."[68] Moscow found it hard to take yes for an answer and continued to complain that the OSCE border monitors were not catching all the Chechen terrorists hiding in the mountains. As part of antiterror cooperation after September 11, President Eduard Shevardnadze accepted a small number of US troops to help train his forces, which then effectively cleaned out the Pankisi Gorge. The presence of foreign forces in Georgia under the OSCE flag, and the bilateral presence of US troops, were extremely unwelcome to Russia.

Russia under Yeltsin had always viewed the Commonwealth of Independent States as an area of special Russian interest and influence, but it was generally willing to accept a certain amount of Western involvement there, especially under multilateral auspices such as the OSCE and as trade-offs for other things Moscow wanted. However, after Putin became president, Russia began to push back hard against what it portrayed as discriminatory Western use of the OSCE as an instrument for exerting influence or control primarily in the countries of Eastern Europe and the former Soviet Union. Moscow also complained about an undue Western emphasis on the human dimension, human rights and elections, while neglecting hard security and stability. For the first time since the Cold War, an OSCE ministerial meeting failed to reach consensus on a final document in Vienna in November 2000. The head of the Austrian delegation concluded that "the Russian Federation under Vladimir Putin is acting with increasing self-confidence vis-à-vis Western demands. Russia wants to be taken as a serious and equal partner. Its inclusion in the consultations does not suffice, Russian interests have to be acknowledged. . . . Russia is clearly sending out a signal that the OSCE has developed in a direction that does not correspond to Russian interests."[69]

The dividing lines between East and West for the new century were already becoming visible in Vienna that November. Washington rejected Moscow's criticisms of overemphasis on the human dimension but also demurred from overwhelming Western European sentiment in favor of granting the OSCE a legal personality, preferring a less structured, unbureaucratic institution responding to issues and crises on an ad hoc basis.[70] The Austrian chair's view of the overall US stance at the Vienna ministerial was not much more flattering than its comments on Russia: "The US, the most 'uncompromising' country within the Western realm, insisted on a harsh assessment of the Belarus elections and demonstrated next to no flexibility towards a surprisingly far-reaching offer by the Russian Federation on the return of the Assistance Group to Chechnya and in support of Georgian interests."[71]

This deep, fundamental split on the objectivity and appropriateness of OSCE activities between Russia on one hand, and the United States and many of its Allies on the other hand, continued through most of 2001. During the course of the year, Russia made a number of sweeping proposals and demands for OSCE reform; the United States and like-minded Western states denied there was any OSCE crisis or need for drastic change.[72]

A true crisis or showdown within the OSCE between East and West was averted largely because of Vladimir Putin's cooperative, forthcoming approach to the United States after the September 11 attacks. In the OSCE, the Russian delegation wholeheartedly supported American initiatives to have the OSCE turn its attention and do more to respond to international terrorism. During the autumn of 2001, the Permanent Council prepared and the Ministerial Council at Bucharest adopted a comprehensive OSCE Action Plan Against Terrorism.[73] The goal of the Action Plan was to promote comprehensive action in those areas where the OSCE could provide added value. The plan urges all OSCE states to review their commitments and join those international antiterror agreements or instruments to which they are not already parties, as well as coordinating with other international institutions. In addition, the plan mandates all OSCE institutions to take actions within their mandates to prevent terror or conditions that might support terrorism—for example, support for human rights and the rule of law, and preventing movement of funds or persons to support terror.

Although relatively modest, agreement on these steps set the tone for the Bucharest meeting and overshadowed fundamental differences over many other questions. For example, the Bucharest Ministerial Statement makes no mention at all of Chechnya, where Russian military actions against the rebels were at their height; instead, Moscow received considerable praise for destroying and withdrawing its CFE Treaty-Limited Equipment from Moldova some two months before the Istanbul deadline at the end of the year.[74] In addition, neither Russia nor other participating states that had engaged in a rather acrimonious dialogue during the year over OSCE reform pushed any of their more controversial proposals at the ministerial, opting for solidarity in the face of terrorism and agreeing to disagree for the time being about the future of the OSCE.

The OSCE's discussion and cooperation against terrorism continued through 2002, although the results were hardly spectacular. At the ministerial meeting at the end of 2002 in Porto, the OSCE adopted the three-page "OSCE Charter on Preventing and Combating Terrorism," which consisted largely of expressions of support for measures taken in other international venues and a relatively modest number of steps to be taken by the OSCE.[75] As a normative political commitment, this charter certainly addressed important tasks, but it contained no real indication of practical ways in which it might lead to effective actions. The Porto Ministerial Document also contained a programmatic declaration on trafficking in human beings, which during the remainder of the decade (and beyond) would become a major concern and action item for the OSCE. Finally, reflecting broader cooperation between Russia and the United States during 2002, the Porto declaration gave the Russian Federation a one-year extension to the deadline set at Istanbul, until the end of 2003, for the complete removal of its military forces and equipment from Moldova. This was the last time Moscow would be given such a pass by other participating states; it also was the last time for almost a decade that the OSCE would be able to reach a consensus on a comprehensive ministerial statement.

The clouds of Russia's discontent gathered steadily during 2002, both with the OSCE and with Russia's role in it. The enlargements NATO and the EU agreed on during the year would clearly change the nature of debates and decisionmaking within the OSCE, and not to Moscow's advantage. One Russian analyst noted that within a few years, thirty-one out of the fifty-five OSCE participating states would belong either to NATO or the EU, and many to both.[76] Many Russians concluded that the OSCE had ceased to matter because NATO and the EU (with its Common Foreign and Security Policy) now essentially made European security policy decisions: "Russia was wrong to hope that the OSCE would take the lead in the European security system, thus protecting Russia's political interests. The failure of the OSCE to assume the leadership position has created yet another institutional problem for Russia's ongoing interaction with other European states."[77]

This same senior foreign policy analyst suggested forming a Russia-EU "security council" to coordinate policies on weapons of mass destruction, terrorism, organized crime, and so forth. Writing in late 2002, when cooperation between the Bush and Putin administrations was at its height, another senior foreign policy adviser stated bluntly that "NATO has instead been made the European security system" and called for a US-Russian condominium similar to the Concert of Europe.[78] Moscow complained that its Western partners increasingly reserved important questions for decisions in NATO or the EU, where Russia has no vote and no chance of ever getting one: "It is impossible to be fond of a club to which you do not belong and which you have no chance of joining, even if you are allowed to attend the club's bar and order soft drinks."[79] Some Russian diplomats fastened on a German idea that Russia, the EU, and the United States might become the three pillars and equal partners in a revitalized and rebalanced OSCE.[80] However, the widespread perception among Western leaders of Russia's weakness and thus lack of relevance made the idea of a Russian leg in any tripod farfetched at best.

The Netherlands assumed the chairmanship of the OSCE in 2003, with a determination to make resolution of the Transdniestrian conflict in Moldova its highest priority. In the process, the Dutch hoped both to revive the OSCE's standing as an instrument for conflict resolution and to use the EU's emerging Common Foreign and Security Policy institutions in cooperation with the OSCE in this process. If The Hague had been able to carry off this plan, it would have been a real triumph and a boost for both institutions. Instead, the Dutch ran into Moldova's inability to choose between East and West, Georgian civil society's thirst for change, and Russia's desire to have the final say on political and security affairs in its near abroad. These factors, shown in key events during 2003, would begin the unraveling of outward East-West comity and cooperation not only within the OSCE but also within the broader European security architecture.

## NATO: BEYOND THE "BIG BANG" TO AFGHANISTAN

The NATO Allies had considerable broken crockery to clean up in the wake of the war with Serbia over Kosovo. Serious friction arose between the Allies over both political issues involved in the decision to go to war and the terms of the settlement and the conduct of the campaign.[81] The Alliance also faced the dual challenge of ameliorating lingering Russian bitterness about the unilateral decision to attack Milošević over Moscow's objections and to smooth out more recent suspicion and resentments aroused by Russia's attempt to unilaterally stake out its own peacekeeping zone and integrate the Russian detachment into the Kosovo Force. At the same time, NATO preparations for a second wave of enlargement continued steadily, along with growing debate over which nations this tranche should include. Russian sensitivities were exacerbated as it became increasingly likely that the three Baltic states would be among those gaining Alliance membership. In the first years of Putin's presidency, NATO first worked out a new institutional structure for managing the NATO-Russia relationship that suited Moscow sufficiently to enable not only renewed but also enhanced cooperation and, moreover, to overcome (outwardly, at least) Russian reservations about a second, extensive NATO enlargement that included the three Baltic states.

The actual military campaign against Serbia-Montenegro over Kosovo left a bitter aftertaste with many NATO participants. The United States and some of its closest Allies were badly split over whether or how quickly to resort to sending ground troops to augment the air campaign. Both Washington and a number of European capitals were displeased with the high percentage of air operations that needed to be executed by US forces. Command arrangements were uneasy at times as well, reflecting diverging views from almost a decade of discussion within the Alliance of possible changes in military structures. The needs of an out-of-area war-fighting campaign—in terms of planning, logistics, force structures, and command—were quite different from those of the expected Article V defensive missions for which the Atlantic Alliance had long prepared or even the peacekeeping operation in Bosnia after the Dayton Accords.

Although much was done well in the Kosovo war, the experience clearly exposed questions of organization, doctrine, and command relationship that had not been addressed or resolved at the Washington Summit.[82] The terrorist attacks of September 11 and the US global war against terrorism, manifested quickly in two major wars in Afghanistan and Iraq, drew NATO even further out of area and placed additional demands on the Alliance's military structures and capabilities. The debates on NATO military responsibilities and capacities that had begun by the mid-1990s enlarged their purview in the two to three years following the Kosovo war. NATO's movement toward a global role and greater expeditionary capabilities came almost entirely at Washington's behest, the result of the US shift to an emphasis on international terrorism as the overwhelmingly greatest threat facing the Alliance and its members.

In many instances, the Bush administration acted largely according to its unilateralist principles, preferring to construct coalitions of the willing under unquestioned US dominance for specific international missions. To the extent that it called on the Alliance, the United States pushed NATO to act in concert with and in support of its global military agenda, pushing the Allies to operate in areas far removed from Europe and to increase their contributions of troops and equipment to participate in these far-flung campaigns. Constant working-level attention was placed on the Defense Capabilities Initiative agreed on at the Washington Summit.[83] This process rapidly assumed many of the aspects of a decades-long kabuki play, which still continues in the Atlantic Alliance meetings more than fifteen years later: the United States calls upon its European Allies to spend more on modernizing and increasing their military capabilities, the Allies agree to do so, but nothing noticeable changes, and the process is repeated at the next set of high-level NATO meetings.

The problem was not that America's NATO partners were mendacious or slackers. The issue was that by the early 2000s the United States and most of its European Allies had developed clearly distinct perceptions of what were the most immediate threats to their security and what should be the nature of their response.[84] Although both the Americans and the Europeans saw terrorism as an extremely serious threat, the United States mounted a global military response, whereas many European states and leaders leaned toward policing responses closer to home. Leading US defense strategists increasingly pushed for a new transatlantic bargain in which the United States would rely on multilateral operations involving the Europeans to respond to terrorism; in return "the Europeans [would] assume greater security responsibilities outside Europe."[85] The United States was particularly concerned that even those Allies that possessed significant military capabilities generally did not have the requisite combination of assets, particularly logistics and transportation, needed to project power. By November 2002, at the Prague Summit, the NATO Allies had accepted an idea advanced by US defense secretary Rumsfeld to create a NATO Response Force, which would be a combined, joint force of some 21,000 troops "ready to move quickly to anywhere needed."[86] The Response Force reached its initial operational capability in October 2004; after a demanding exercise in the Cape Verde Islands, it was declared fully operational at the November 2006 Riga Summit.[87]

At the Prague Summit, the NATO Allies also approved basic reform of the Atlantic Alliance's command structures, which had been under discussion at least since 1999. There would be one operational command, designated Allied Command Operations, based in Belgium and commanded by the Supreme Allied Commander Europe, who would continue to be an American general double-hatted as commander of the United States European Command.[88] The Allied Command Operations was to have two subordinate joint force commands capable of generating land-based combined joint task forces, and a standing joint force headquarters capable of generating a sea-based joint task force. At the same time, the Allied Command Atlantic was stripped of its operational responsibilities and became the Allied Command for Transformation, still headquartered in Norfolk and responsible for coordinating the development of military capabilities and the interoperability of NATO's forces. In addition, the Prague Summit made the 1999 Defense Capabilities Initiative more specific and farreaching, including protection against chemical and biological attacks, in what was dubbed the Prague Capabilities Commitment. Finally, the heads of state in Prague called for this Capabilities Commitment to be compatible and coordinated with the EU's European Capabilities Action Plan.

NATO's capabilities were tested almost immediately, individually and collectively, in Afghanistan. After the initial US invasion and removal of the Taliban government, the International Security Assistance Force was authorized by UN Security Council Resolution 1386 in December 2001. The force was made up largely by contributions from NATO's member states and was commanded in six-month rotations by the United Kingdom, Turkey, and then Germany and the Netherlands. The Atlantic Alliance provided considerable assistance and eventually assumed formal command of the operation in August 2003.[89] The United States continued its own national, unilateral military operation in Afghanistan but also successfully involved its major Allies in a coordinating, supporting role in a projection of power, expeditionary military operations, and nation-building exercises that could hardly have been envisioned by the NATO heads of state who signed the London Declaration only thirteen years earlier, let alone the signatories of the Washington Treaty in April 1949.

The transformation of NATO's command structures, the strengthening of its military capabilities, and the deployment of NATO forces and assumption of command in Afghanistan taken all together constitute an eloquent testament to the underlying strength of the transatlantic bond and the cohesiveness

of the core of the Alliance, irrespective of outward signs of discord or inefficiency. The agreements at Prague and the deployments to Afghanistan, after
all, were achieved during a time of profound crisis in transatlantic relations
over the American rush to war in Iraq. The profound divisions of that time are
perhaps best illustrated by the dilemma of Prime Minister Tony Blair, perhaps
the most European of British leaders since the formation of the European Economic Community, who found himself in bitter disagreement with his French
and German counterparts, Chirac and Schröder, over his support for President
George Bush's campaign against Saddam Hussein.[90] Washington did not return
to the UN for a second resolution on the use of force before the start of the war,
largely out of the realistic fear that not only Russia but also France would use its
veto.[91] Less well-remembered but equally damaging was the refusal of key Allies
that opposed a war against Iraq to offer formal guarantees of support to Turkey
in case of Iraqi retaliation.[92] Turkey, in one of the most controversial votes of the
newly installed AKP parliament, subsequently declined to authorize American
use of Turkish bases for US operations against Iraq.

Relations between the United States and Europe were indeed in a crisis in
late 2002 and 2003, emanating and spreading from a collision of differing world-
views and policy approaches of the heads of government at that time. European
leaders such as Chirac, Schröder, and Putin genuinely disagreed in principle
with the unilateralist, preemptive approach to security reflected in George
Bush's 2002 National Security Strategy and in practice with the preemptive
attack on Iraq in March 2003. Many Europeans also disagreed for a variety of
reasons with the Bush administration's conduct of the war on terror, in particular harsh interrogation procedures, extrajudicial renditions, secret prisons, and
a refusal to apply the laws of war, such as Common Article 3 of the Geneva
Conventions. Transatlantic disagreements and discord over these and related
issues have persisted, in some instances to this writing in 2017. These disagreements inevitably involved NATO, especially when the issue concerned how the
Alliance should or should not contribute to or be involved in American global
counterterrorist efforts.

However, the crisis in transatlantic relations at about the time of the Iraq
War's start did not extend to the issue of NATO's continued existence or status as the main pillar of Europe's security architecture. Although the disagreement over Washington's attack on Iraq was severe, there had been other serious
differences within the Alliance over the course of its existence, such as the
controversy in the early 1980s over the deployment in Europe of intermediate
range nuclear missiles or in the early 1990s over the need and desirability of
military intervention in the Balkans. During the Cold War, the central global
strategic aim of the United States had been to contain the expansion of Soviet
power. The most important theater in this conflict by far was in Europe, so the

strategic threat perceptions and goals of the United States and its European Allies coincided almost perfectly. The terrorist attacks of September 11 and the US response brought abruptly into view a strategic shift that had been a decade in developing: namely, the emergence of the United States as an unchallenged global power with threats, interests, and responsibilities extending far beyond Europe. For Washington's NATO Allies, conversely, the chief security interests remained maintenance of stability and avoiding armed conflict within Europe.[93]

This difference between Europe and the United States in scope and area of interests is a fundamental feature of the post–Cold War European security landscape. The United States has not abandoned Europe, and as of mid-2017 appears still to be adhering to that commitment, but it has interests and perceives threats beyond Europe and frequently attempts to enlist Europe in ventures outside its immediate area to address these threats and help defend these interests. Europe's perceived interests and the threats against them no longer so closely coincide with those of the United States. This does not mean that Washington and its European Allies will not frequently find common ground and engage in common action. It means, instead, that one should also expect somewhat more divergence and disagreement across the Atlantic than was the case during the Cold War. The United States and most of the states of Europe for the foreseeable future still have a large reservoir of values and interests in common and may well remain partners and allies of first choice, irrespective of events that may occasionally divide them.

The durability and strength of the transatlantic bond (whether by inertia or by choice) was vividly demonstrated by the simultaneous processes in 2000 to 2002 of fashioning a new relationship between NATO and Russia under Putin and agreeing on the admission of seven new members to the Atlantic Alliance. The two were not dependent upon one another, although the successful rapprochement with Moscow in the first half of 2002 indubitably made the crucial decisions on enlargement in the second half of 2002 easier and smoother. Putin clearly pursued improved relations with NATO from the very start of his presidency. More than once he raised the possibility of Russian membership in the Alliance—initiatives that many Russian interlocutors insist were serious.[94] According to some accounts, the idea even received consideration in some quarters of the Bush administration.[95] After marking time rather than deal with a lame duck Clinton administration, Putin made a concerted turn to the West, away from the post-Kosovo denunciations of NATO, to seek a cooperative partnership with the United States and its Allies in the fight against terrorism.[96]

At the highest levels of government, among other events, Putin hosted Robertson and Blair; allowed Bush to get a "sense of his soul"; and wooed Silvio Berlusconi, Jacques Chirac, and Gerhard Schröder. At working levels, the Russia-NATO Permanent Joint Council resumed meeting regularly during 2000. In addition to operational issues involving Russian participation in the Kosovo Force, the discussion gradually included exchanges on strategy and doctrine, arms control, nuclear issues, infrastructure, search and rescue, and similar topics, many of which might be considered areas for practical cooperation.[97] At a meeting of foreign ministers at the end of 2000, NATO and Russia agreed to open a NATO Information Office in Moscow in 2001. These substantive, working-level discussions continued in 2001 and gained considerable velocity when Putin supported the United States after September 11 and opened Russian air space to Alliance flights to support the campaign in Afghanistan. By early 2002, NATO-Russia discussions included possible military cooperation in the fight against terrorism, which was also the subject of a separate NATO-Russia conference in Rome in early February.

Russia's cooperative stance and Putin's courtship of key Allied leaders convinced most of the latter by the turn of the year that the NATO-Russia relationship needed to be placed on a new, closer, more equal basis. Tony Blair was reportedly the first to float the idea of a NATO-Russia Council to replace the Permanent Joint Council, the key difference being that sessions would be at 20 rather than 19+1—meaning, in practice, that Moscow could bring up subjects and discuss them before the Allies had reached a common position on them.[98] At a May 2002 NATO-Russia Summit held in Rome (at Berlusconi's insistence, for his friend Vladimir), Putin and his NATO counterparts inaugurated what they called a "qualitatively new relationship between NATO and the Russian Federation."[99] The struggle against terrorism was at the top of the list of areas for cooperation enumerated in the Rome Declaration, but the comprehensive list also included crisis management, nuclear nonproliferation, arms control, theater missile defense, search and rescue, military-to-military cooperation, and several other topics. The tone set by the leaders at the summit was sober but optimistic, not the least by Putin: "The problem for our country was that for a very long period of time it was Russia on one side, and on the other practically the whole rest of the world. And we gained nothing good from this confrontation with the rest of the world. The overwhelming majority of our citizens understand this only too well. Russia is returning to the family of civilized nations. And she needs nothing more than for her voice to be heard, and for her national interests to be taken into account."[100]

The note of optimism struck by Putin at Rome was not shared by many senior Western officials with long experience working with Russia, particularly in Washington. But the solution blessed by the heads of state at Rome did establish sufficient comity in the Alliance's relations with Moscow to allow other, controversial business to proceed without disruption from that quarter.[101] The decision process for NATO's first enlargement was ad hoc and chaotic in some aspects, and the Allies had adopted the Membership Action Plan (MAP) process at the Washington Summit to make both the preparation of applicant countries and decisionmaking by the Allies more thorough, systematic, and predictable.[102] The MAP process covered all the key criteria for membership enumerated in the 1995 NATO Enlargement Study and added more systematic evaluation of civil-military relations, defense reform, threats, and capabilities than had been the case with the first three successful applicants. The MAP also provided a convenient institutional channel for preparing the political decisions on which countries to admit, a decision that the Clinton administration essentially preempted in 1996–97.

The process of preparing nine applicant nations through the MAP exercise took on a bureaucratic continuity at the working level through 2000–2001 as debates raged at the political level over which should be admitted. The most controversial applicants were the three Baltic states—Estonia, Latvia, and Lithuania—with the United States, Nordic, and newly admitted Central Europeans most enthusiastic in favor, and much of "old Europe" (including the United Kingdom) more cautious.[103] In the end, Washington and the arguments against "selective enlargement" carried the day. At the Prague Summit in November 2002, NATO opted for the "big bang," admitting the three Baltic republics, three former Warsaw Pact members (Slovakia, Romania, and Bulgaria), and one former Yugoslav republic, Slovenia.[104] Russia's reaction was generally muted, but not pleased. As one Westerner with close ties to the Kremlin noted, this was probably not the sort of equality Putin had in mind when he signed the Rome Declaration only six months earlier.[105] In May, Russian Foreign Ministry spokesman Yakovenko asked rhetorically against whom NATO was preparing its new members. Commenting to the press in June 2002, Putin allowed that Baltic states' membership in NATO would be "no tragedy" for Russia but also noted that he did not think NATO enlargement improved anyone's security.[106]

Western views of the second NATO enlargement generally stressed the positive effects on the transition to democratic institutions and market economies in the nations joining the Alliance and the contribution to regional stability.[107] As with the first NATO enlargement, the second enlargement in 2002 was supported most vocally by those senior officials, in Washington in particular, who focused first and foremost on the stabilization, security, and democratization of Central and Eastern Europe.[108] As one highly placed American observer put it: "Together with its European partners, Washington set out to create a peaceful, undivided, and democratic Europe. NATO evolved from a collective defense organization into Europe's main security institution—helping to stabilize the Balkans, to transforming military practices with no less than twenty-seven partnership countries and forging new relationships with erstwhile opponents. . . . As a result of these efforts, Europe is today more peaceful, more democratic, and more united than at any time in history."[109]

Such a view of Europe and European security institutions at the end of 2002 makes the key assumption that Russia's discomfort with and opposition to NATO enlargement have been overcome once and for all. Unfortunately, this was clearly not the case, irrespective of any other considerable benefits the transformation and enlargement of the Atlantic Alliance might have brought to its members and to the world.

NATO had in fact been transformed into a collective security organization by the end of 2002, and it was clearly the dominant security institution in Europe. However, during the process of enlargement, NATO did not renounce its original purpose of collective defense, which was much of the attraction for the new members located closer to Russia. In addition, NATO had developed a considerable expeditionary military capability, a capacity to project power globally, particularly in missions conceived and conducted primarily under American leadership. NATO had waged one out-of-area campaign against Serbia-Montenegro and was in the midst of another, arguably more ambitious effort in Afghanistan. Although Moscow supported the war in Afghanistan, it had opposed the war against Milošević but had been unable to deter it, and Russia still had no veto in the new NATO-Russia Council. Even with Putin's rapprochement in 2001–2, it is not surprising that not all in Russia saw the enlargement of NATO territory and the enhancement of its ability to project military power as benign. Military commanders traditionally look hard at capabilities because intentions often change, even those of current friends. Very few senior Russian leaders could view the increase in NATO's reach and power with equanimity.

In contrast, for most Western leaders, the enlargements of NATO and the EU were generally seen as major steps in building a peaceful, stable democratic Europe. To those constructing the larger NATO and united Europe, these institutions are composed of like-minded states dedicated to common democratic ideals. Many of these leaders and advocates of enlargement would present the EU and NATO as evidence of the truth of their understanding of Kant's idea of the democratic peace—that democracies do not go to war against one another, and thus the best way to ensure peace is to increase the number of democratic states. After the Cold War, NATO and the EU indeed successfully contributed to expanding the democratic space in Europe and had defended endangered populations from murderous dictators in the Balkans. With new, extended borders coming into place in 2004, this question arose: How would this process now play out with the Atlantic Alliance's and the EU's new neighbors?

## 7. COLORS OF REVOLUTION, RIVALRY, AND DISCORD

The US-Russian and NATO-Russian rapprochements of 2001–2002 did not last long. Western involvement and influence in the foreign and domestic affairs of the states of the former Soviet Union, which Russians frequently called the "near abroad" or "post-Soviet space," were viewed with increasing discomfort by Russia. Western leaders and publics watched with growing alarm what they perceived to be a retreat from openness, competitive politics, and the rule of law in Russian domestic affairs. Moscow perceived the "color revolutions"—a series of popular and elite revolts in Georgia, Ukraine, and Kyrgyzstan broadly supported by Russia's European and North American partners—as evidence of Western intentions to promote regime change throughout the former Soviet Union, including in Russia itself, all under the guise of democracy promotion and support for civil society. Many Western political leaders and area specialists interpreted Vladimir Putin's consolidation of power in himself and a small group of close advisers as a form of neo-Soviet or neo-imperial authoritarian revival, which they inferred to include aspirations to restore some or all of the lost territories of the USSR or Imperial Russia.

The development and work of Europe's major security institutions were not outwardly hampered by the tensions mounting between Russia and its Western partners, although the growing discord was reflected from time to time in engagement and discussion of specific issues. Both the EU and NATO continued to focus particular attention on combating terrorism, with European concerns heightened after attacks on the Madrid rail station in 2004 and a London city bus and subway in 2005. NATO concentrated attention on recruiting contributors and sustaining that portion of the military effort in Afghanistan that it commanded. The EU took over peacekeeping operations in Macedonia and Bosnia from NATO and undertook other military and police interventions in Europe and Africa. After protracted labor by its political elites to draft a formal constitution for the European Union, the Brussels bureaucracy suffered a stinging setback as voters in France and the Netherlands rejected the document, sending their leaders back to the drawing board.

The transatlantic relationship was poisoned for several years as a result of the US rush to war with Iraq in 2002–2003. Bad feelings were especially noticeable between Bush and Chirac and Bush and Schröder, and relations between the French, German, and British leaders were strained due to Blair's steadfast support for Bush. Against this backdrop of top-level resentments and ill will, a remarkable amount of transatlantic working level cooperation continued within NATO and between the Alliance and the EU. The most notable area of discord was the issue of Europe's deficiencies in many military capabilities, particularly those necessary for projecting power beyond the immediate territory of NATO or the EU. During much of this time, discussion between Washington and its European allies (that continues as of this writing) was characterized by the United States continuously badgering the Europeans to spend more on defense, with most of the latter promising yet failing to do so.

Both NATO and the EU continued their programs of outreach and cooperation with nonmember states in their neighborhood, the Alliance through the by now well-established Partnership for Peace program, and Brussels through the newly established European Neighborhood Policy. After the enlargements of the EU to twenty-five members and NATO to twenty-six, discussions within both institutions took on a distinctly more wary and suspicious tone with respect to Russia. Moscow quickly became aware of this change, not only through its direct dealings with both Brussels-based institutions but also in political exchanges and debates in the headquarters of the Organization for Security and Cooperation in Europe (OSCE) in Vienna. Both NATO and the EU had always coordinated the positions of their members in OSCE discussions, but the EU's enlargement in 2004 had a particularly great impact on the OSCE because EU member states and aspirants for membership (which also coordinated their positions with the EU) now made up more than half the membership of that organization. The OSCE continued to manage a large number of field operations and to address a mix of generally second-order security, political, and human rights issues that the NATO and EU member states did not wish to reserve for those institutions. As cooperation among participating states flagged, particularly between East and West, the OSCE's approaching thirtieth anniversary in 2005 was met with increasing criticism of its ineffectiveness and predictions of its imminent demise.

One key thread weaving together the growing tension between Russia and its Western partners, the OSCE, and NATO was the ongoing debate over ratification of the Adapted Treaty on Conventional Armed Forces in Europe (ACFE) and, by implication, the future of the conventional arms control and security regime in Europe. Western states that were parties to the ACFE Treaty refused to ratify it until Russia fulfilled the commitments undertaken at Istanbul to withdraw its troops from Georgia and Moldova. Russia claimed to have complied with these obligations and accused the West of using Georgia and Moldova as a pretext to avoid implementing the new treaty, which would cover the new NATO members in the Baltic Sea region and recognize the post–Cold War political changes in Europe. The standoff grew evermore bitter and reflected the growing, larger political polarization in Europe between Russia on one hand and most of the NATO and EU member states on the other hand.

## THE UNITED STATES: BUSH'S SENSE OF MISSION

As the Bush administration moved into its second term, the missionary zeal of the president and his neoconservative advisers both intensified and somewhat redirected from the global war on terror to worldwide promotion of democracy. The highly ideological bases of the administration's foreign policy were already evident in the president's January 2002 State of the Union Address, in which he called on his countrymen and allies to combat the "axis of evil"—Iraq, Iran, and North Korea. His response to September 11 was not simply to find and punish those responsible for the act but also to hunt down and eliminate terrorists and their supporters wherever they might be. In this same address, he evoked a long tradition of volunteer service in the United States, calling on his compatriots to join the USA Freedom Corps (a coordinating office in the White House, later called the White House Office of Social Innovation and Civic Participation) by enlisting in a local or federal volunteer program. Bush combined a sense of idealism and service with a doctrine of preemptive action, which was clearly reflected in the administration's 2002 National Security Strategy that called for eliminating terrorists before they attacked rather than responding to what might be catastrophic damage.[1]

The initial US attack on one of the members of the "axis of evil" went very well at first, and Saddam Hussein was toppled in little more than a month.

However, the transition to an acceptably stable post-Saddam Iraq went exceptionally poorly, and Bush, Rumsfeld, and Cheney were pressed to explain what went wrong. The president's answer was not that the war against Iraq might have been a step too far, despite the failure to find any weapons of mass destruction. Instead, Bush apparently concluded that simply toppling the Baathist regime was not sufficient; one also needed to install democracy in Iraq to ensure it would not become a haven for terrorists. In other words, the ultimate answer to terror was the spread of freedom because the lack of freedom had created the conditions in which terrorists were formed. As the president explained in January 2005,

We have seen our vulnerability—and we have seen its deepest source. For as long as whole regions of the world simmer in resentment and tyranny—prone to ideologies that feed hatred and excuse murder—violence will gather, and multiply in destructive power, and cross the most defended borders, and raise a mortal threat. There is only one force of history that can break the reign of hatred and resentment, and expose the pretensions of tyrants, and reward the hopes of the decent and tolerant, and that is the force of human freedom.[2]

President Bush made clear his determination to support freedom in all countries in all parts of the globe:

The survival of liberty in our land increasingly depends on the success of liberty in other lands. The best hope for peace in our world is the expansion of freedom in all the world. . . . Across the generations, we have proclaimed the imperative of self-government, because no one is fit to be a master, and no one deserves to be a slave. Advancing these ideals is the mission that created our nation. It is the honorable achievement of our fathers. Now it is the urgent requirement of our nation's security, and the calling of our time. So it is the policy of the United States to seek and support the growth of democratic movements and institutions in every nation and culture, with the ultimate goal of ending tyranny in our world.[3]

By the time his second National Security Strategy was released in 2006, Bush referred to the war in Iraq as the removal of a dictator rather than a struggle against terrorism. Indeed, the 2006 document envisions the protection of American security not so much through neutralization of military threats as in expanding freedom and democracy throughout the world:

Our national security strategy is founded upon two pillars. The first pillar is promoting freedom, justice, and human dignity—working to end tyranny, to promote effective democracies, and to extend prosperity through free and fair trade and wise development policies. Free governments are accountable to their people, govern their territory effectively, and pursue economic and political policies that benefit their citizens. Free governments do not oppress their people or attack other free nations. Peace and international stability are most reliably built on a foundation of freedom. The second pillar of our strategy is confronting the challenges of our time by leading a growing community of democracies.[4]

President Bush's national security and foreign policy appealed to the purest strains of American idealism, combining Woodrow Wilson's sense of mission with Theodore Roosevelt's commitment to action. Bush's assertion of worldwide freedom and democracy as the ultimate national security aims of the United States went far beyond Madeleine Albright's characterization of the United States as the indispensable nation. It is a breathtaking view of the role of the United States in the world, perhaps the apotheosis of American exceptionalism.

The Bush "freedom agenda" received mixed reviews around the world. Fellow believers, of whom there were many, signed on and offered enthusiastic support. For others, including many Allies and partners, the United States was overwhelmingly the greatest military power in the world, and in this the ultimate guarantor of the global commons and international order. Some more cynical rulers may have given lip service to these ideals, hoping for the support of the United States against threatening neighbors or troublesome domestic opponents. In any event, the democracy promotion industry, which has been well developed in the United States since the 1980s, enjoyed perhaps its greatest public support and was at the height of its worldwide activity during the two terms of the George W. Bush administration.

Those who did not share the idealism of the Bush administration, or those who feared they might be the objects of America's democracy promotion, had distinctly different perceptions during this time. First of all, many saw the United States as neglecting the fight against the Taliban and the remnants of al-Qaeda in Afghanistan while getting bogged down in a predictable and avoidable insurgency in Iraq. Sectarian massacres in key Iraqi cities and towns belied American claims for the progress of democracy in that country. Second, skeptics heard Washington speak about support for freedom, human rights, and democracy, which they contrasted with reports of harsh interrogation techniques used on suspected terrorists incarcerated without due process, secret prisons, rendition of suspects to countries with poor legal protections, harsh treatment of prisoners at the Abu Ghraib prison and the Guantánamo Bay prison in Cuba, and strong support for highly undemocratic governments, such as Saudi Arabia, Egypt, and several other less-than-democratic friends of Washington.

There has long been an inherent contradiction in American foreign policy between traditional, principled support for human rights and democracy and the need to do business with foreign leaders and governments that fall far short of these ideals. However, the ideological component of American foreign policy has rarely been as pronounced as it became during the George W. Bush presidency. As a result, the contradictions between high ideals and actions dictated by raison d'état have rarely been as stark and the charges against the United States of hypocrisy and double standards as easy to make. In addition, as the Bush administration intervened around the world with the strongest military ever seen while calling for the spread of democratic regimes, it was not surprising for less-than-democratic rulers to wonder whether they might be next. As popular revolts occurred in Georgia, Ukraine, and Kyrgyzstan from 2003 to 2005 and Washington continued to fund several democracy promotion nongovernmental organizations in Russia itself, it should have come as no surprise (at least with the benefit of hindsight) that Vladimir Putin (or at least some of those around him) might question what the United States was up to in the near abroad and what future the Americans contemplated for Russia.

## PUTIN SHUTS DOWN THE OPPOSITION

For Putin, the fight against terrorism was a continuing, real, and bloody war inside Russia. On October 23, 2002, about forty to fifty armed Chechens took hostage an audience of more than 800 at a performance of the play *Nord-Ost* at a theater in Moscow's southeast Dubrovka quarter. After a siege of two and one-half days, Russian security forces pumped an unidentified anesthetic gas into the building and shortly thereafter stormed the theater, killing all the terrorists. More than 130 hostages died, all but two from the effects of the gas.[5] Despite the loss of life among the hostages, Western governments condemned the hostage takers and generally expressed understanding for the Russian actions in retaking the theater.[6]

This seeming Western solidarity with Russia in the fight against terrorism was already beginning to show cracks, however, even as condemnations of the *Nord-Ost* terrorists poured in. During the night of October 25–26, shortly before Russian security forces stormed the theater, the terrorists received an appeal for moderation from Akhmed Zakaev, an exiled associate of Chechen president Aslan Maskhadov, whose extradition Moscow had sought unsuccessfully several times from Western countries. More than once, senior Russian officials, including President Putin, railed at their Western counterparts for refusing to hand over Zakaev as a wanted terrorist and instead accepting his claims to be a political refugee. Despite George Bush's and Tony Blair's friendship with and understanding approach to Vladimir Putin, many senior American and British officials took a hard line on Russian actions in Chechnya. The United States particularly infuriated Putin by allowing a senior working-level State Department official to meet informally with a Zakaev colleague in a Washington coffee shop.[7]

Putin was continually frustrated by the insistence of many of his Western partners in seeing the conflict in Chechnya as a human rights issue rather than an egregious case of international terrorism. Starting in the late 1990s, Russian officials claimed that in the North Caucasus Russia was fighting some of the same people and groups as the United States and its Allies in the Middle East and South Asia were fighting.[8] For a long time, Putin apparently considered Western failure to understand these similar threats and coincidence of interests as signs of obtuseness and incompetence. At some point, influenced by other actions and statements from his Western partners, Putin came to a less charitable, more paranoid view of Western intentions. If his Western partners, so consumed by their own antiterror campaigns, would not offer full cooperation and assistance against those terrorists who were attacking Russia, then these Western partners must hope that such attacks might weaken Russia and make it less of a threat.[9] Discussing the Chechen terrorist attack on the school in Beslan in September 2004, Putin portrayed the tragedy as part of a larger threat to Russia:

> In general, we need to admit that we did not fully understand the complexity and the dangers of the processes at work in our own country and in the world. In any case, we proved unable to react adequately. We showed ourselves to be weak. And the weak get beaten. Some would like to tear from us a "juicy piece of pie." Others help them. They help, reasoning that Russia still remains one of the world's major nuclear powers, and as such still represents a threat to them. And so they reason that this threat should be removed.[10]

In response to the attack, Putin promised entirely new approaches to crisis management and law enforcement. In practice, he continued and accentuated the process of restoring central control in the hands of the Kremlin by abolishing the election of governors of all of Russia's federal units, making them all appointive offices. The measure seemed an incongruous reply to the events in Beslan and appeared to most Western observers to bear little or no relationship to the basic security and law enforcement issues raised by a major terrorist incident.

In fact, in Putin's view and that of many of his Russian colleagues, the Russian president's steady consolidation of authority in the Kremlin from the time he took office had everything to do with fighting crime, terrorism, instability, and the disintegration of state institutions, which in their minds dominated the Russian domestic landscape during most of the 1990s.[11] The reimposition of government control on the press, in particular the broadcast media, was explained as an attack on corrupt oligarchs, especially Boris Berezovskii and Vladimir Gusinskii. Restrictions on the political activity of the leading oligarchs met with little serious popular opposition given the widespread belief that their wealth had been acquired through corruption and favoritism. The October 2003 arrest of Mikhail Khodorkovskii and the breakup of Yukos, considered by many in the West to be the clearest of many signs of autocratic revival in Russia, drew few protests within the country given Khodorkovskii's checkered business history during the 1990s and widespread reports that he was busy purchasing political support among willing Duma deputies.

In fact, Putin was engaged from the time he assumed office in reducing the scope for independent political opposition in the country and in this the extent of truly competitive electoral democracy. The 2003 parliamentary elections were deftly managed so that the progovernment United Russia party won a clear majority and the remainder of the seats were taken by so-called official opposition parties, that is, those willing to collaborate in the pretense of independent political activity while remaining ready to support key Kremlin initiatives when instructed. Putin's chief political adviser, Vladislav Surkov, coined the terms "sovereign democracy" and "managed democracy" to describe the system. Western analysts used terms such as "virtual politics" and "competitive authoritarianism."[12]

Putin was supported in his consolidation of personal political authority by Russia's remarkable economic performance. First of all, his economic reforms of 2001–2 had the salutary effects of restoring many activities to the overt, legal economy and greatly enhancing the collection of government revenues. Second, as the decade wore on, the price of oil and natural gas rose dramatically, fueling a period of incredible economic growth. Gross domestic product in Russia grew at rates of 7 to 8 percent a year, real wages increased several times over, and Russia's current account accumulated an enormous positive balance.[13] Burdened by growing government and private debt during the 1990s, some of it left over from the Soviet era, by 2005 Russia had paid off all its state debt, and in mid-2006 it settled its obligations to the Paris Club, while accumulating a large surplus of foreign currency reserves.[14]

Domestically, economic prosperity solidified and enhanced popular support for Putin and facilitated his consolidation of semiauthoritarian power by the middle of the decade. In foreign policy, Russia was no longer obliged to or dependent on foreign creditors or assistance. Putin and his colleagues thus felt themselves considerably freer to take a much more assertive and even confrontational approach with Western interlocutors and partners who they felt were ignoring or acting against Russia's interests. This growing self-confidence and assertiveness led to increasingly frequent collisions with the West, in particular over Russia's energy policies and over political and security developments in the near abroad, especially in Central Asia, Georgia, Moldova, and Ukraine. By 2006, the outward attributes of a cooperative relationship still existed between Russia and the major Western countries and institutions, such as NATO and the EU, but the substance and essence of cooperation were increasingly missing.

## BEYOND BERLIN-PLUS: THE EUROPEAN SECURITY AND DEFENCE POLICY IN ACTION

The process of negotiations crowned by agreement on the Berlin-Plus formula settled, in principle, the basic question between the United States and some of its major European allies, especially France, on the relationship between NATO capabilities and those that would support an autonomous European defense identity.[15] However, Berlin-Plus was ultimately an agreement on modalities, and it did not settle practical questions of implementation such as where and why Europe might wish to intervene independent of the United States. Berlin-Plus also did nothing to ensure that there would be sufficient military capabilities for the Europeans to intervene, should they ever decide on such a course. As the war of words over the war in Iraq escalated across the Atlantic, the EU's leaders, already divided by this acrimonious debate, needed to find an agreement on the general type of desirable EU-led operations as well as specific missions to be undertaken in the immediate future. They also needed to reach an accord on which of their number would provide the human and material resources for these missions, never an easy task even in times of harmony and overall agreement.

The 1999 Helsinki Headline Goal called for the achievement by 2003 of an EU army corps of 50,000 to 60,000 troops, capable of mobilizing within sixty days and deploying to the field for at least a full year.[16] The intention was that this should give the EU the capability of conducting simultaneously one "heavy" mission involving the potential application of military force, such as separating combatants, and another "light" mission such as humanitarian disaster relief or evacuation.[17] Despite these good intentions, an EU review conducted shortly after the September 11 attacks on the United States showed considerable delay in many areas in meeting the overall goal. The European Capabilities Action Plan was drawn up to address deficiencies identified in this review; in December 2003, the Capability Development Mechanism was adopted as an institutional instrument for achieving the goals that had been identified. Nonetheless, EU reports in May and November 2004 indicated that little more than 10 percent of the deficiencies identified in 2001 had been successfully remedied.[18]

In late 2003, the United Kingdom and France pushed through the so-called battle groups initiative, which aimed at creating small, more deployable EU groups of about 1,500 troops that would be able to respond to a crisis within fifteen days and sustain a deployment for thirty days.[19]

The EU responded to the lack of progress by setting new goals. The June 2004 European Council meeting adopted the so-called Helsinki Goal 2010, a capabilities plan calling for the EU "to be able by 2010 to respond with rapid and decisive action applying a fully coherent approach to the whole spectrum of crisis management options covered by the Treaty on the European Union."[20] Almost simultaneously, the council established the European Defense Agency (EDA) in July 2004, with the aim of both improving operational defense capabilities and strengthening the EU's military industrial base.[21] The EDA was to provide overall guidance and direction to governments conducting projects under the European Capabilities Action Plan and to provide for use of the Capability Development Mechanism. In addition, the EDA would provide supervision and coordination for multilateral defense projects such as the Eurofighter.

Many European leaders and officials tended to place greater emphasis than their American counterparts on civilian aspects of conflict management and prevention. Indeed, European governments have consistently tended to view terrorism as a police rather than a military problem and to place more emphasis on policing as part of preconflict or postconflict interventions. At the same time as it addressed the development of its military capabilities, the EU identified the need to increase its common civilian intervention capacity in the areas of policing, the judiciary, civilian administration, and civil protection.[22] Goals were set in 2001 for the EU to have the capacity to provide up to 5,000 civilian police within thirty days for a crisis intervention. In 2004, the EU also adopted a civilian capabilities Headline Goal, this one for 2008, addressing planning and administrative functions as well as policing.

The EU's goals for military and civilian capacity to support the autonomous European Security and Defence Policy (ESDP) have been consistently more impressive than the actual results achieved. By perusing year after year of internal EU debates and reports, it can be seen that goals are constantly being set, results fall short, and new goals are established further out in the future. Similarly, policy, professional, and scholarly analyses and journals on both sides of the Atlantic during this period are filled with descriptions of Europe's shortfalls in specific defense areas and recommendations for remedies. However, during this same period, the EU as an aggregate was the largest economic power in the world, and the total defense budgets of its member states made it on paper the world's second-largest military power, next to the United States (if military power depended on budgets alone). As related below, beginning in 2003 the European Union conducted, on its own, a steady number of short- and long-term security operations in Europe and Africa. So the question arises, were EU defense and military capabilities truly insufficient for the threats and operations it needed to address, or were they simply not as robust as Washington would have liked in order to provide support for American operations around the globe?

Similar transatlantic disagreements arose throughout much of the Cold War over the amounts spent on European defense respectively by the Americans and their European Allies. Although discord over the percentage of gross domestic product spent on defense may not be new, the post–Cold War era brought far greater disagreement over the nature of the threats and the ways and in particular the size of the means needed to address them. With a far less identifiable enemy and much less agreement on how to counter that enemy, it was almost inevitable that Europeans in the first decade of the twenty-first century would find it even more difficult than before to resolve the always contentious questions of how much to spend on defense, and for what. The differing proclivities on the opposite sides of the Atlantic toward military and civilian responses to crises also ensure that the United States and its Allies will have differing opinions on the proper amounts and types of defense expenditures. Judging by the history of the post–September 11 world, these differences will have to be managed without any realistic expectation that they can ever be fully eliminated.

The push by some EU states, in particular France, for an independent European defense force caused great concern from the United States and the more Atlanticist EU members, such as Britain, during the run-up to and initial stages of the Iraq war. A joint Franco-German statement in January 2003 calling for a defense union and security guarantee within the EU raised fears that by duplicating NATO such moves could weaken or marginalize the Alliance. The so-called Chocolate Summit of April 2003—at which France, Germany, Belgium, and Luxembourg called for a European Security and Defence Union and an independent EU headquarters—threatened to split the member states over the question of a common security policy and defense capability.[23] The US ambassador to NATO, Nick Burns, called this summit "the most serious threat to the future of NATO."[24] Fears of the decoupling of Europe from the United States and tension between the EU and NATO lasted for most of the year and were relieved only by the NATO-EU agreement in December 2003, which worked out details of implementing the Berlin-Plus arrangements.[25]

Despite these deep divisions, great strains, and open disagreements both within the EU and across the Atlantic caused by the US war in Iraq, the EU was able to make clear progress in developing the institutions of an independent ESDP first formalized in mid-1999 and in giving the ESDP real physical capabilities. France and the United Kingdom took diametrically opposite stands on the US attack on Iraq in 2003, but the experience reaffirmed the beliefs of both nations and their leaders of the necessity of strengthening a separate European military capability.[26] Although President Jacques Chirac and his colleagues maintained the public line that improved EU military capabilities would strengthen NATO and not detract from it, the French position was clearly consistent with Paris's long-standing advocacy of an independent European military capability. In the spirit of his Saint-Malo initiative, Prime Minister Tony Blair supported the development of a European capability to act independently in crises that were important to Europe when the United States did not wish or choose to intervene. Blair also apparently hoped to increase UK and EU influence in Washington by making the EU a more capable defense partner. Although Germany was far more reluctant than Britain or France with respect to the application of military force, the German EU presidency had been crucial in launching the ESDP at the 1999 Cologne Summit. Berlin tended to favor civilian intervention—by the police, or under the rule of law—but was supportive of a broad-based strengthening of the EU's capabilities.

Even as the strains in the transatlantic relationship seemed to reach near-crisis levels, the EU began to make use of its fledgling military and civilian capabilities in the field. In fact, despite fears of Europe's decoupling from America, the United States was eager for the EU to assume a number of military and police missions in the Balkans because Washington wished to use American and NATO military resources for what it considered more important kinetic missions in Iraq and Afghanistan. Working with the United States and the OSCE in the Dayton framework, in January 2003 the EU deployed a police mission to Bosnia-Herzegovina that took over from the earlier United Nations Police Mission established to assist the development of a professional democratic national police force.[27] In March 2003, following discussions that continued steadily following the 2001 Ohrid Agreement, Operation Concordia, an EU military mission, took over from the NATO force that had been in place since late 2001.[28] As the first-ever EU military mission, Operation Concordia was exceedingly modest, and France initially attempted to have it run using solely EU resources without reference to NATO. However, Germany and the traditionally Atlanticist EU members insisted that Berlin-Plus procedures be used (even though they had not been formally ratified) to clearly show that the ESDP would be a supplement to rather than a substitute for NATO. As such, the political significance of the mission far outweighed its military importance.

Following the deployment to Macedonia, the EU rapidly organized and dispatched a series of military, police, and rule-of-law missions to various locations in the Balkans, the Middle East, and Africa. The most important of these missions was arguably the European Union Force Althea, which took over from the NATO-led Stabilization Force SFOR in Bosnia-Herzegovina in December 2004. Because most of the EU personnel in the new Bosnia mission had previously served in the Stabilization Force, in December 2004 many of the members of the new force simply changed the patches on their uniforms.[29] The European Union Force in Bosnia concentrated on tasks such as preventing the accumulation or use of hidden caches of arms, bringing war criminals to justice, and combating organized crime, which freed US forces for combat operations in Afghanistan and Iraq. The EU also dispatched first a military and then a police mission to the Democratic Republic of Congo (DRC) in 2003–2004, a Palestinian Police Support Mission in 2005, and rule-of-law missions to Georgia and Iraq in 2004 and 2005.[30]

The success of the small French-led EU mission to the DRC—Operation Artemis—reinforced the EU priority since 2000 for combined civilian and military responses to crisis management and conflict resolution, with less reliance on military force than the United States. The DRC operation also demonstrated for many European political leaders that the EU could act independently of NATO and that success would not always depend on the availability of very large military forces. The EU preference for an integrated political and military approach was visible in its approach to combating terrorism as well, calling as much for preventive police action within the EU as for military action against threats in third countries.[31] The EU's initial successes and increased activities did not quiet all critics of the need for a separate European defense capability or an independent ESDP.[32] However, the formalization and implementation of the ESDP reflected the prevailing sentiment among EU leaders and elites on the need to give both institutional structure and substance to the long-standing concept of a common foreign and defense policy as part of the movement toward a true political union, best represented in the drafting and adoption of a formal EU constitution going on at that same time.

Another key step in the institutionalization and formalization of the common foreign and security policy, prompted both by the transatlantic and internal disagreements over the Iraq war and by the constitutional process, was the drafting of the European Security Strategy (ESS), published as *A Secure Europe in a Better World*, and directed by EU high representative Javier Solana (see chapter 6). The ESS, completed by Solana and approved by the European Council in December 2003, was the first-ever programmatic analysis by the EU of its overall security environment, along with a comprehensive approach for responding to the identified threats and challenges.[33] The ESS identified five basic threats to Europe: terrorism, proliferation of weapons of mass destruction, regional conflicts, state failure (due to bad governance), and organized crime. Remarkably, the ESS made no mention of any danger of major interstate conflict in Europe; in fact, the document explicitly noted that, in contrast to the Cold War era, none of the threats was purely military.

The ESS formulated three overarching strategic objectives for the EU. First, there was the need to address the threats identified by the document.

The authors noted that in a globalized world, distant threats could be of equal or greater concern than local ones, and "the first line of defense will often be abroad."[34] The second objective was "building security in our neighborhood." The ESS stressed that "it is in the European interest that countries on our border are well-governed."[35] The document noted that enlargement would bring the EU nearer to troubled regions and urged attention to problems and conflicts both to the east and in the Mediterranean, specifically calling for resolution of the Arab-Israeli conflict. As its third strategic objective, the ESS called for the development and maintenance of an international order based on effective multilateralism, specifically referring to the World Trade Organization, NATO, the OSCE, and the Council of Europe. Reflecting the importance of values in the overall approach, the document noted that "the best protection for our security is a world of well-governed democratic states."[36]

The overall result was a document and an approach that shared much of the Bush administration's dedication to the promotion of democracy, but little to none of the Americans' unilateralism and advocacy of preemptive military action. Despite these differences between Washington and Brussels, Solana's successful work on the ESS gave the EU a shared strategic vision, which was crucial for the further development of the common foreign and security policy, and in so doing helped considerably to alleviate the tension between the United States and the EU. The adoption of a common strategy that overlapped Washington's sufficiently to provide for common interests and common actions, as well as the nature and conduct of initial EU military and civilian missions, reduced to manageable levels some of the greatest fears and the most intense resentments in Washington at the height of Franco-German criticism of the Iraq war. The transatlantic discord took a long time to abate, but by early 2004, the United States, the EU, and NATO seemed to have overcome the worst and faced other challenges.

One of the greatest of those challenges facing the EU was the second strategic priority identified by Solana in the ESS: building security in an EU neighborhood that was about to undergo dramatic change with the 2004 enlargement. The addition of ten new members brought the EU much closer to the troubled regions of the Middle East and North Africa, as well as right up to the borders of Russia and other states of the former Soviet Union. The infusion of new blood in the EU accentuated the traditional divisions between its member states with respect to the relative importance of its neighboring regions. As one might expect, the southern tier called for priority to be given to problems of the Mediterranean and North Africa. Northern and eastern member states stressed the importance of relations with Russia and other former Soviet states. The 2004 enlargement brought in seven new members that had been either members of the Warsaw Pact or—in the case of the Baltic Sea republics—part of the

USSR, which augmented the number of member states that were already more concerned with relations with Russia and added to the EU's internal debates a sizable bloc that was far more hostile to and suspicious of Moscow than many of the EU's older members.

The European Neighborhood Policy (ENP), which was worked out and adopted during 2003–2004, was the result of and the EU response to the geopolitical changes brought about by the massive 2004 enlargement. In the 1990s, the EU paid relatively little attention to its more distant neighbors to the east (or the south, for that matter), as the bulk of Brussels' attention was concentrated more on those immediate neighbors that were candidates for membership. When it became clear in late 2002 that enlargement would occur in 2004 and would include almost all the candidates, the EU's members suddenly seemed to realize that its borders would expand dramatically and a host of formerly distant former Soviet and Mediterranean states would become immediate neighbors. This change in borders provoked a host of political and practical questions requiring significant changes in or additions to EU policy, subsequently provided by the ENP.[37]

The first calls for greater attention to some of the countries eventually included in the ENP came from the British, who in early 2002 called for a "wider Europe" initiative, having in mind in particular Russia, Ukraine, Belarus, and Moldova. By the time the question was debated at the December 2002 Copenhagen European Council (the same meeting at which the May 2004 enlargement was confirmed), at the insistence of the southern tier of EU countries, Ukraine, Belarus, and Moldova had been joined by the "Southern Mediterranean countries" as objects of the new policy.[38] The EU contemplated enhancing relations with its new neighbors "on the basis of shared values, . . . to be based on a long-term approach promoting reform, sustainable development and trade."[39] In the words of European Commission president Romano Prodi in December 2002, the idea was to offer the new neighbors "more than partnership and less than membership, without precluding the latter."[40] In March 2003, the Commission transmitted a lengthy proposal to the Council that included most of the basic provisions of the eventual ENP, which was formally adopted during a series of meetings in late 2003 and early 2004.

The ENP was offered in 2004 as a framework for relations with the EU to sixteen neighbors from the Western Newly Independent States, the South Caucasus, the Eastern Mediterranean, and North Africa, including the Palestinian authority.[41] The EU already had either partnership and cooperation or association agreements with all these countries except Libya. The largest of these neighbors, the Russian Federation, decided early in the process that the ENP was not an appropriate framework for developing its relations with the EU. At the May 2003 summit in Saint Petersburg, the EU and Russia decided "together" to further develop their strategic partnership by creating four common spaces—economics; freedom, security, and justice; external security; research and education—in essence attempting to accord Russia a status distinct from and more important than the EU's other neighbors.[42] In substance, the ENP framework is basically a collection of sixteen separate bilateral action plans separately concluded between the EU and each of its neighbors. There are common elements among these agreements, most notably an emphasis on respect for human rights and democratic principles.[43] Many of the ENP countries were explicitly unqualified for EU membership due to their location outside Europe. However, no promise of eventual candidacy (let alone membership) was offered to the six Western Newly Independent States and the South Caucasus states.

The ENP in essence was an ungainly compromise among the fifteen EU member states before the 2004 enlargement to provide an institutional structure for conducting debates over and relations with states brought right up to the EU's borders by that enlargement. The ENP was at best a very general overall approach to achieving the ESS's second strategic goal—stability in the immediate neighborhood of a significantly larger EU. The policy reflects a basic assumption that fostering a process whereby shared values would be embraced by the EU's immediate neighbors is the best guarantee of long-term security—a highly political and ideological approach.

The mutual decision by both Moscow and Brussels to pursue a separate "strategic partnership," distinguishing Russia from the EU's other neighbors, demonstrates the EU's continuing ambivalent attitude toward Russia. Even for those individuals and states within the EU that might consider Russia to be a European country and thus implicitly eligible to apply for membership, the practical effects of joining a country of the size and population of the Russian Federation to the EU dispelled any thoughts of actual admission. EU rules would give Russia enormous subsidies and outsized voting power in many EU institutions. After adopting a special strategy for Russia in 1999, as one of the first actions of this sort under the new common foreign and security policy, most EU leaders and states explicitly dismissed any thought of Russian membership and were more than content to deal with Moscow as a special, important partner.

For its part, Russia tentatively welcomed the EU's establishment of the ESDP in 1999 in a "mid-term strategy on relations with the EU," which was adopted and made public in October 1999.[44] The initial positive Russian response to the ESDP, and to greater activism and initiative on the part of the European Union in general, can be explained partially as reflecting lingering Russian anger at the United States and NATO in the wake of the war with Serbia. The Putin administration's attempts to expand dialogue and practical cooperation with the EU vis-à-vis security issues also may have partly reflected the traditional Russian approach of attempting to delink Europe from the United States as a means of increasing Russia's influence on the continent. As US unilateralism became more pronounced in the run-up to the war in Iraq, some Russian leaders argued for closer cooperation between Russia and Europe, if not integration into Europe, as a means of balancing against Washington.[45] However, in the end the EU was not prepared for the degree of operational military cooperation apparently envisioned by some on the Russian side.[46]

Relations between the EU and Russia became considerably more difficult after the 2004 enlargement. Of the new member states, Poland, Estonia, Latvia, and Lithuania were, for various reasons, particularly suspicious and critical of a number of Russian actions and policies in the former Soviet space, now a subject of the ENP. Although Putin still had relatively well-disposed interlocutors and colleagues in Rome, Paris, and Berlin, the addition of these new members made for a much sharper tone in internal EU discussions of relations with Russia, particularly as the retreat from free political competition and the rule of law became more apparent inside Russia. Brussels and Moscow avoided collision over one sensitive issue raised by the enlargement, the transit of people and goods between Kaliningrad and Russia proper, as agreements were successfully reached and implemented in 2002 and 2004.[47]

After the enlargement, however, issues that had earlier been peripheral became more important due to the change in borders and membership and soured relations. EU-appointed special representatives became more involved in the so-called frozen conflicts in Moldova and Georgia, and the EU's member states grew more critical of what was widely perceived as Moscow's use of its position as a mediator to bring pressure on Chisinau and Tbilisi.[48] Differing approaches to the color revolutions in Georgia, Ukraine, and Kyrgyzstan further cooled overall EU-Russian relations. Russia's January 2006 cutoff of natural gas deliveries to Central and Western Europe through Ukraine and Belarus then severely soured the view of many in the EU of Russia as an economic and political partner. Although the institutional process of conducting EU-Russia relations, replete with semiannual summits and countless lower-level meetings, continued to grind on, due in part to the considerable inertia of the bureaucracies involved, after mid-2004 the trajectory was slowly but inexorably downward.

## NATO: FAR, FAR OUT OF THE AREA

By 2003, less than two years after the terrorist attacks on New York and Washington, D.C., NATO and the EU had both made strategic decisions to defend their territories and ensure their security by conducting operations outside their immediate area—in fact, anywhere in the world. At the Prague Summit, the NATO Allies expressed determination to "deter, disrupt, defend, and protect against any attacks on us." In order to do this, the Prague Declaration vowed that "NATO must be able to field forces that can move quickly to wherever they are needed . . . to sustain operations over distance and time."[49] The Prague decisions to create the NATO Response Force, reform NATO's military command structures, adopt the Prague Capabilities Commitment, and embrace a military concept of defense against terrorism all flowed from this agreement, on the principle that security and defense require the development and employment of expeditionary capabilities to confront threats at their source, anywhere in the world.[50]

The apparent agreement in principle between NATO and the EU (and, as such, between the United States and its major European Allies) on the need for expeditionary capabilities and out-of-area operations did not avoid or eliminate the continuing, deep disagreements over the nature and gravity of particular threats, the appropriate nature and size of the response to these threats, the order of priorities among these responses, or the types and amounts of military and civilian capabilities that needed to be stockpiled to ensure adequate responses. The differences of opinion between the EU and NATO on these practical operational questions resulted largely from the fact of the United States' membership and leadership in the latter organization, though it could hope only to exercise influence over the former. As Washington became increasingly beleaguered in its efforts in Afghanistan and Iraq, it sought ever-greater assistance from its NATO Allies and from partners that were outside but cooperating with the Alliance. America's unique capabilities for heavy lifting, global logistical support, and global intelligence were sorely strained by the growing demands of massive deployments and combat operations on the other side of the globe. As a consequence, Washington made steady, increasingly outspoken statements on the need for its European Allies to devote more resources to defense capabilities and to make greater contributions to the far-flung US and NATO operations.

NATO was deeply troubled during the years immediately following the American invasion of Iraq by the slow and difficult process of healing the rift between the United States and some of its most important Allies, in particular France and Germany.[51] Strong differences between European members of the Alliance did not help the process of reconciliation, given that newer Allies— such as Poland, Romania, and the three Baltic states—were strong supporters of Washington and were generally critical of Paris and Berlin. Even statesmen with long experience, such as Henry Kissinger, depicted the situation in grave terms: "The transatlantic relationship is under greater strain today than at any point in at least a generation. Many Europeans assume malign intent on the part of the United States. Many Americans resent European behavior and dismiss European perceptions of today's threats. The conviction that the United States is a hyperpower to be contained has become fashionable in Europe. Reliance on coalitions of the willing to act when the United Nations and the North Atlantic Treaty Organization (NATO) will not has become the policy of the United States."[52]

Depictions in Europe of George W. Bush as an ignorant cowboy and warmonger were countered on the other side of the Atlantic with references to Europeans as cheese-eating surrender monkeys. The transatlantic atmosphere in 2003–2004 was probably more acrimonious, mutually hostile, and vituperative than at any time since the Euro-missile crisis of the early 1980s.

Events facilitated the process of bringing the United States and "Old Europe" back closer to one another. As already noted, the adoption of the European Security Strategy in December 2003 explicitly aligned the EU more closely with Washington's prevailing view on the need to ensure security by attacking threats at their source. In addition, the rise of the insurgency in Iraq and the growing burden imposed on US human and material resources by the twin efforts in Afghanistan and Iraq moved the Bush administration away from its more strident assertions of unilateralism and, more gradually, from its initial deprecation of civilian intervention and "nation building."[53] In the words of one experienced observer at that time, "Washington is learning the hard way that even the world's sole superpower needs Allies."[54] Stripped of the rhetoric on unilateral and preemptive action, US threat perceptions and security priorities coincided considerably with those identified in the ESS, particularly with respect to the threat from international terrorism and the importance of stability in the greater Middle East.

This confluence of perceived interests, when added to considerable historical and institutional inertia, facilitated the practical reconstruction of transatlantic relations and cooperation. This process was easier in Afghanistan than in Iraq, as there had been far less European dissension over the US incursion into Afghanistan following the September 11 attacks. In both Afghanistan and Iraq, the United States initially built ad hoc coalitions of the willing, which included a varied collection of old, new, and prospective NATO members as well as some other partners. In Afghanistan, the United Kingdom, Turkey, Germany, and the Netherlands, acting in their national capacities, successively commanded the UN-authorized International Security Assistance Force (ISAF), which operated in cooperation with the US national military effort.[55] In August 2003, NATO took formal command of ISAF under a German general officer, a move that changed little in terms of the composition and mission of the force but represented a significant increase in NATO's collective commitment to the effort. After ISAF's mandate was expanded by the UN in October 2003 to cover all of Afghanistan, NATO increased the number of Provincial Reconstruction

Teams (PRTs) it supported in 2004–2005 and extended operations in the northern and western parts of the country.[56] NATO forces were generally deployed to ensure security in less threatening areas, and the practice of national "caveats" employed to restrict availability of some forces for combat operations eventually became a serious source of dissension within the Alliance. Conversely, even though the United States infused the PRTs with a hefty dose of military staffing and direction, their mixed civilian-military composition and the significant civilian reconstruction portions of their mandates represented a considerable step toward the sort of mixed or civilian intervention favored by the EU.

NATO's involvement and role in Afghanistan became more extended and complex deeper into the decade. In October 2004, NATO completed deployment of PRTs to all the country's northern provinces, shortly after deployments to Herat and other western centers, thereby taking responsibility for more than 50 percent of Afghanistan's territory. In mid-2005, NATO deployed an additional 2,000 troops to help provide security for Afghan local and parliamentary elections. This growth of NATO's presence and responsibilities coincided with the Taliban resurgence, which has generally been dated from late 2004 or 2005, and which began gradual destabilization of the country and a steady rise in security incidents and casualties.[57] The United States pressed for greater NATO contributions in Afghanistan as the situation in Iraq worsened throughout 2005 and 2006 and demanded ever-greater commitments of American troops and material. US entreaties apparently found a sympathetic ear in NATO secretary-general Jaap de Hoop Scheffer, who continued during most of his term to make Afghanistan the Alliance's chief priority.[58] In response to increasing attacks, in February 2006 NATO's ISAF troops adopted more robust rules of engagement. In June 2006, the NATO defense ministers began a practice of special meetings of ISAF contributors and agreed to expand NATO's ISAF operations into nine southern Afghan provinces.[59] On the eve of the November 2006 NATO Riga Summit, ISAF took over command of international military forces in the east from the United States–led coalition; at the Riga gathering, NATO's leaders agreed to remove some of the national caveats attached to their troops participating in ISAF.[60] This progression toward full-scale NATO involvement over all of Afghanistan unfortunately was not matched by increasing success, and the conflict there would remain a major NATO concern and headache for years to come.

The road toward NATO's involvement in Iraq was much tougher. Secretary-General de Hoop Scheffer, the former Dutch foreign minister, who assumed the office in January 2004, consistently stressed the Alliance's strategic interest in the success of US operations in Iraq but did not fully convince harsh critics of the US invasion, in particular, France. However, a number of Allies, most notably the United Kingdom and Poland, were participants in the American-led

coalition in Iraq. Discussions of how NATO might contribute to stabilization and reconstruction in Iraq during 2004 threatened to reopen the split
between Paris and Washington. De Hoop Scheffer helped broker a compromise
whereby a Dutch assessment team would visit Iraq and report on possible forms
of NATO assistance.[61] The ensuing Dutch report was instrumental in reaching agreement at the NATO Istanbul Summit in June 2004 that the Alliance
would provide training for the new Iraqi government's security forces, an action
explicitly couched as a response to the appeal in UN Security Council Resolution 1546 requesting the assistance of the international community and regional
organizations in the transition from the occupation to the new interim sovereign government in Iraq.[62] The transition from US occupation to national rule,
supported by the United Nations, gave the French sufficient political cover to
agree to Alliance participation. A small NATO contingent deployed to Iraq in
the summer and expanded modestly over the next few years. In the end, the
NATO Training Mission–Iraq remained in country for more than seven years,
withdrawing only at the end of 2011 after failing to negotiate a status-of-forces
agreement with the new Iraqi government.[63]

Much like the expanded European Union, NATO after the 2004 "big bang"
enlargement cast its gaze much further into the countries and regions on its
periphery than before. In addition, as the Alliance's leaders noted at the June
2004 Istanbul Summit, the emerging threats such as international terrorism and
proliferation of weapons of mass destruction "emanate from a far wider area than
in the past."[64] Given the strong overlap of EU and NATO member states and
the recent US experience in Iraq and Afghanistan, it was hardly surprising that
NATO should identify the Mediterranean and the greater Middle East as two
areas of primary concern in the Alliance's increasingly global portfolio. Reflecting both the broader scope and need for greater resources in the fight against
terrorism, the Alliance began to seek new partners outside of the area encom-
passed by the Euro-Atlantic Partnership Council and Partnership for Peace; it
also encouraged greater participation by old and new partners in NATO-led
operations. This tendency toward more numerous and far-flung operations with
the participation of more states, some of them far outside NATO's traditional
area, was reflected in several important actions taken at or on the margins of the
Istanbul Summit.

First, Allies adopted an updated, more comprehensive, and more ambitious
program for the Euro-Atlantic Partnership Council and the Partnership for
Peace, which reflected both the new threats and NATO's broader geographic
area of concern.[65] At the same time Allies issued a broader, more ambitious
Partnership Action Plan against Terrorism, which was to be approved at the
Istanbul meeting.[66] Though comprehensive, these new arrangements put
increased importance on military cooperation and interoperability as the

goals of partnership. Geographically, Alliance leaders at Istanbul laid particular emphasis on partnership ties with the Caucasus and Central Asia and appointed a relatively senior special representative for these two regions from the international staff.[67] Looking beyond the established Euro-Atlantic Partnership Council space and partners, Allies at Istanbul agreed to expand the Mediterranean Dialogue, a political dialogue with five Mediterranean states first established in 1994 and expanded modestly in subsequent years.[68] The initiative not only called for enhancing the existing political dialogue but also envisioned supporting defense reform in partner countries and achieving some degree of interoperability, all with the aim of joint efforts in the fight against terrorism. Finally, the leaders at Istanbul proclaimed a new Alliance effort directed at the greater Middle East, the "Istanbul Cooperation Initiative," to establish partnerships for practical cooperation in that region. Directed initially at the six Gulf Cooperation Council member states, the initiative was nonetheless explicitly open to all states in the region, and it specifically mentions defense reform, military-to-military cooperation, and fighting against terrorism as possible activities for the partnership.[69]

Aside from these specific initiatives and decisions, the mid-2004 NATO Summit in Istanbul was a landmark in several respects. First, the deepest cracks in the Alliance between some of the oldest and most important members seemed to have been successfully papered over, although not entirely eliminated, with what one expert called "the shared perception that projecting stability beyond the Euro-Atlantic area is essential to the security of NATO member states."[70] Although this may be a somewhat overly optimistic characterization of the state of the Alliance, the results of Istanbul also belie contemporary predictions of NATO's imminent demise. Istanbul was the first summit for NATO at twenty six, with the seven "big bang" new members joining other relatively recent additions to the Alliance from the former Warsaw Pact. Of the ten new members since the mid-1990s, only one—Slovenia—did not have relatively recent, direct, close, and unpleasant experience with Russia, a fact that did not substantively influence the results of Istanbul but was to be increasingly significant over coming years.[71]

Finally, the substance of the Istanbul initiatives and the very fact of holding the meeting there went a long way to repairing damage done in relations between the Alliance and Turkey in the disputes in late 2002 and early 2003 over Turkey's relationship to Berlin-Plus operations and use of Turkish bases for the US attack on Iraq. Despite the setback in the spring of 2004 of Greek Cypriot rejection of Kofi Annan's plan for resolving the long-standing division of Cyprus, an initiative Ankara successfully convinced Turkish Cypriots to accept, the government of Recep Tayyip Erdoğan held to an overall line of cooperation with NATO and the EU. Turkey continued its program of reforms and after decades of waiting became a formal candidate for EU membership in 2005. In mid-2005 a Turkish general assumed command of ISAF, the second time a Turk held that post. Thus Istanbul may be seen as important in smoothing relations with the Alliance's easternmost, as well as westernmost, member.

Matching NATO capabilities to current and possible future operations remained a constant concern of the Alliance throughout the decade. The lack demonstrated by most European Allies of many of the military capabilities necessary to conduct operations in the Kosovo War was even more pronounced in the post–September 11 campaigns in the Middle East and South Asia. The changes adopted in the command structure and establishment of the NATO Response Force at the Prague Summit were well under way by Istanbul, but the Alliance's Supreme Commander nevertheless noted in mid-2004 that "most of the force structure promised to the Alliance is of little use in dealing with the threat that member nations face today, since the units are not sufficiently mobile, deployable, or sustainable."[72] By the time of the Riga Summit in November 2006, NATO was conducting six active operations in Europe, Africa, and the greater Middle East. In addition to Afghanistan, Kosovo, and the Iraq training mission, the Alliance continued its naval operations in the Mediterranean, Operation Active Endeavor, monitoring and accompanying shipping to deter and counter terrorism.[73] In 2005, NATO joined the EU in offering support to the African Union's mission in Darfur in Sudan, both by airlifting peacekeepers to the region and providing training in intelligence and headquarters operations. Finally, the NATO Response Force was deployed at least twice in disaster relief operations, airlifting supplies to the United States after Hurricane Katrina and providing more sustained relief to Pakistan after the 2005 earthquake.

The increased number and tempo of NATO operations provoked constant discussion within and between NATO capitals of the proper amount and structure of forces needed to mount and sustain these efforts.[74] Without delving into the details of the analysis, amounts and types of equipment and forces, and so forth, in general NATO's capabilities were always in the process of catching up to the Alliance's perceived needs and ambitions. Four years after the Prague Capabilities Commitment was adopted, NATO heads of state at Riga concluded that "in order to undertake the full range of missions, the Alliance must have the capability to launch and sustain concurrent major joint operations and smaller operations for collective defense and crisis response on and beyond Alliance territory, on its periphery, and at strategic distance."[75] In this guidance adopted at Riga, NATO's leaders enumerated ten demanding requirements that might be expected for NATO forces over the next ten to fifteen years, first among them "the ability to conduct and support multinational joint expeditionary operations far from home territory with little or no host nation support and to sustain them for extended periods."[76]

The ongoing debate over the shortfall in NATO capabilities was not simply a reflection of the reluctance of European publics to spend as much on defense as was required or, at least, as their US partner might desire. This discussion of capabilities and new operations also reflected the significant changes in the Alliance's strategic environment since the last Strategic Concept was adopted in Washington in 1999. Although that document pointed to instability and state failure within Europe rather than massive invasion by a hostile power as the greatest danger, after September 11, the chief threats to NATO countries were seen to emanate from outside Europe. The Comprehensive Political Guidance adopted at the Riga Summit was an attempt to acknowledge this fundamental change in the strategic context without wholly reworking the Alliance's basic strategic document. Even as he asserted the continuity of NATO values and efforts, Secretary-General Jaap de Hoop Scheffer nonetheless acknowledged on the eve of the Riga meeting that the Alliance was in fact "a dynamic agent of change."[77] In the Riga Summit Declaration, the NATO leaders noted that the major threats in "today's evolving security environment," such as terrorism and proliferation of weapons of mass destructions, are "increasingly global in scale."[78] De Hoop Scheffer stressed the global scope of the Alliance's concerns and called for building relations with partners as far-flung as Australia, New Zealand, South Korea, and Japan.[79]

Despite NATO's adaptation, enlargement, and increasingly global reach, doubts were still being raised on the margins of the Riga Summit about the fundamental purpose of the Alliance. Both Americans and Europeans remained in agreement that NATO overall had contributed to democratic change and greater security over much of Europe during the past decade and a half, but there was considerable discord over more specific ways in which the Alliance should pursue these objectives. The French parliamentarian Pierre Lallouche, who was then president of the NATO Parliamentary Assembly, asserted that "the raison d'être of our organization is in question."[80] He noted German chancellor Angela Merkel's public query in early 2006 whether the Alliance still was "the primary venue" for discussing European security issues and himself asked whether NATO should welcome countries such as Australia, Japan, or Israel as partners or even members, as suggested by de Hoop Scheffer and some others. A senior US diplomat noted the self-defeating tendency of the United States to assert a very broad role for NATO and then to use the Alliance only on an "a la carte" basis, and concluded that "the real problem is that the United States does not really know what it wants from NATO."[81]

At least one country took NATO at its word with respect to its goal of promoting the spread of democracy and its aspiration to attain a global military reach—Russia. On the surface, following the establishment of the NATO

Russia Council at the 2002 Rome Summit, working relations between the Alliance and Moscow seemed to prosper. By 2004–2005, the accomplishments and agreed tasks and activities on the NATO-Russia agenda on paper were impressive. NATO expanded its presence in Moscow and even held a NATO-Russia Council meeting there in 2003.[82] Russia agreed to participate in Active Endeavor in the Mediterranean and invited NATO observers to a nuclear weapons accident response exercise near Murmansk. In December 2004, NATO and Russia agreed on a joint action plan against terrorism that, among other actions, called for improving the capability of Russian and NATO militaries to work together and leading to the signing of a NATO Status of Forces agreement with Russia in early 2005.[83] In June 2005, a meeting of NATO and Russian defense ministers called for developing interoperability between their military forces.[84] Also in 2005, Russian sailors participated in a major NATO search and rescue exercise at sea, and UK sailors helped to rescue Russian sailors trapped in a submarine off of Kamchatka.

The casual observer might be forgiven for thinking that relations between Russia and NATO had been fully restored after a hard patch following the war in Kosovo. However, there were significant clouds on the horizon. The issue of missile defense was one enduring bone of contention between Russia and the West, in particular the United States, since Reagan's "star wars" initiative in 1983. Bush administration advocates of missile defense, in particular Defense Secretary Rumsfeld and Vice President Cheney, successfully removed the United States from the Anti–Ballistic Missile Treaty with the USSR in 2002 and pressed forward ballistic missile defense and theater missile defense research and development, also arguing for near-term deployment.[85] The NATO Allies commissioned a study on missile defense feasibility at the Prague Summit and received a positive report at Riga, where Alliance leaders mandated continued work on the technical, security, and political implications, including an updated assessment of the threat.[86] Russia and NATO began cooperation in missile defense almost immediately after establishing the NATO-Russia Council. A feasibility study was commissioned in 2003 on possible interoperability of NATO and Russian theater systems, and three NATO-Russia command post exercises were held annually from 2004 to 2006.[87] Alas, familiarity did not bring agreement or acceptance, and Moscow remained deeply suspicious of and strongly opposed to NATO and US plans to develop and deploy missile defense systems in Europe. The issue would become increasingly pressing and even more divisive in the years following Riga.

Russia was moving with seeming inexorability toward confrontation with the United States and its European Allies over democracy promotion. In a comment typical for that time, NATO PA President Lallouche lamented, on the eve of Riga, the lack of success of NATO parliamentarians in establishing closer relations with their Russian counterparts:

> We cannot fail to notice the increasingly anti-democratic and anti-Western tone of statements made by our Russian colleagues, something that mirrors what has been described as a growing "values gap." And while the rhetoric is deteriorating, there has also been a worrying divergence of interests on a wide range of issues affecting Russia's domestic and foreign policy, including the lack of an independent judiciary, attacks on freedom of the press, growing concerns over energy security, the Iranian nuclear issue and Moscow's attempts to re-establish its influence—often in a very brutal manner—over its former empire. It is time for us to wake up and face the facts, however unpleasant they may be. We must now develop a common strategy as to how we can best promote and support democracy, in and around Russia, in order to reduce these tensions.[88]

Moscow could not fail to hear such criticisms of the direction of Russia's domestic political institutions. Russian leaders also were keenly aware of NATO's professions to support democratic change, as well as its continuing aspirations to increase both the magnitude and territorial reach of its military capabilities. Notwithstanding ongoing, extensive, active NATO-Russia cooperation, this was not a combination of intentions and capabilities that Russian military and political leaders could contemplate with equanimity.

## THE OSCE AND THE COLOR REVOLUTIONS

Russia's competition with the West over influence in and the geopolitical direction of the states of the former Soviet Union first came to a head from 2003 to 2006, in particular, over the activities of the OSCE in the region more than the enlargement or activities of NATO and the EU. The OSCE was particularly prone to producing conflicts between Moscow and its Western partners because of the large number of OSCE field operations active in the region, generally with a majority of their staff from the Western participating states. OSCE representatives successively clashed with Moscow over a settlement plan for the Moldova-Transdniestria conflict sponsored by Russia, support for the Rose Revolution in Georgia replacing President Shevardnadze with Mikheil Saakashvili, negative OSCE / Office for Democratic Institutions and Human Rights (ODIHR) evaluations of elections in former Soviet states, including the 2004 presidential vote in Russia, support for Viktor Yushchenko's complaint that the presidential election in Ukraine was stolen (the Orange Revolution), the 2005 Tulip Revolution in Kyrgyzstan replacing President Askar Akaev, and violent repression of a popular demonstration in Andijon, Uzbekistan. Moscow complained that the Western nations also ignored issues important to Russia, such as ratification of the Adapted Treaty on Conventional Armed Forces in Europe in order to bring the new Baltic NATO members into this key European conventional arms control regime.

To be sure, these issues were discussed in other forums, including EU-Russia and NATO-Russia settings, but operational responsibility for addressing these questions was primarily located within the OSCE, and it was within the various bodies of that organization that the real clashes between Russia and its Western partners first played out. NATO and the EU were generally involved less directly. After their 2004 enlargements brought them right up to the former Soviet borders, both organizations took a more active interest in developments in the former Soviet space. Western staff members in OSCE bodies received more frequent queries and more expressions of concern from their home countries, and even without being directly instructed they quite naturally acted less passively concerning issues and places in which many had been content before 2004 to accord Moscow greater leeway. Enlargement engendered greater political interest in the post-Soviet region in NATO and EU capitals, which in turn sent more activist instructions to their delegations in Vienna. This process was not necessarily fully conscious or premeditated, but to one working over a long stretch of time in the OSCE, it was noticeable.[89]

Fresh from the significant east-west compromises at the 2002 OSCE Porto ministerial meeting, the 2003 Dutch Chairmanship announced that it would set as one of its top priorities settlement of the Moldova-Transdniestria conflict, according to accepted wisdom at the time the "easiest" of the four "frozen conflicts" on the periphery of the former Soviet Union.[90] The Dutch appointed a high-level special representative for the conflict and made great headway during the year in promoting significant withdrawals of Russian military equipment and ammunition from the Transdniestrian region during the year, bringing the Moldovans and Transdniestrians together in a joint commission to draft a new, federal constitution for a reunited state, and reaching agreement with Ukrainian and Russian negotiators on a mediators' document that settled most of the issues needed to support a federal solution to the conflict.[91] However, as a direct result of Moldovan president Vladimir Voronin's appeal to Russian president Putin for assistance in reaching a settlement, from mid-2003, the deputy head of the Russian presidential administration, Dmitri Kozak, conducted a parallel negotiation with Chisinau and Tiraspol that won the agreement of both to a memorandum describing a federal solution very similar to that embodied in the OSCE mediators' document, but with several key differences.

Kozak asked the OSCE to join in supporting his so-called Kozak Memorandum. The Dutch Chairmanship concluded that the document had flaws that were too serious to allow support, but—because it was apparently accepted by the Moldovan government—concluded that the OSCE could not oppose it. That position changed two days before the memorandum was to be signed in Chisinau in the presence of Putin, when the OSCE became aware of three additional articles added to the Kozak Memorandum providing for a significant Russian military presence in the country until 2020. The security revisions to the memorandum left Russia with the only peacekeeping forces in the country; Western participation might have been allowed, but Russia would have had control over the type and amount of Western involvement, including the final say. The OSCE, the EU, and the United States all spoke out against the revised Kozak Memorandum, and Voronin withdrew his agreement to the document only hours before Putin was to fly to Chisinau for the signing. The Russian president was furious and blamed the West, in particular, for sabotaging a successful Russian effort in conflict resolution. Years later Putin still nurtured a resentment of the United States for its role in the matter.[92]

At the same time the political settlement in Moldova apparently attained by the Kozak Memorandum was starting to unravel, Georgian president Shevardnadze was being carried out of the parliament in Tbilisi barely ahead of an angry band of demonstrators calling for his removal from office. The Rose Revolution, which replaced Shevardnadze with the young, stridently pro-Western Saakashvili, came on suddenly and rather unexpectedly as the former attempted to convene a new parliament installed by a highly disputed election whose results were widely believed to be falsified by the authorities.[93] However, the relationship between Moscow and Tbilisi had been rocky for some time. With the renewed outbreak of war in Chechnya in 1999, Moscow made frequent complaints that Chechen rebels were finding refuge in the mountains over the border in Georgia. An OSCE border monitoring operation was added to the OSCE's Georgia Mission in December 1999 to cover the border with Chechnya, and later also Ingushetiia and Dagestan.[94] This monitoring operation lent some transparency and may have helped deter some Chechens who might otherwise have sought refuge in Georgia, but Russia was clearly unhappy with the additional number of official Westerners it brought to the country. Moscow was even more displeased when after the September 11 attacks Shevardnadze in 2002 agreed to an offer by Washington to send US troops to Georgia as part of an antiterrorist train-and-equip program, even though the Americans helped the Georgian clean out the Pankisi Gorge of armed Chechens.[95] From that time on, the United States retained a small military presence in Georgia.

Although Shevardnadze had never been a favorite of Moscow (many Russian officials actively detested him), Russian officials were uneasy with the manner in which a popular uprising had replaced him. The fact that Saakashvili was at least as pro-Western as Shevardnadze and more outspoken about it was also deeply unsettling for Moscow. Foreign Minister Igor Ivanov, born and raised in Georgia, was initially sent to establish relations with the new Georgian leader, and Putin tacitly assisted Saakashvili in taking back the wayward province of Ajaria from local strongman Abashidze.[96] However, most of Moscow's political elites were suspicious of and hostile to Saakashvili from the start, and Putin's seeming efforts to build a better relationship with the new Georgian leader rapidly soured with the latter's efforts to continue fulfilling his pledge to restore Georgia's territorial integrity by taking full control of South Ossetia during the summer of 2004.[97] Saakashvili's strident pro-Westernism, punctuated by the extremely warm welcome accorded George Bush in his May 2005 visit, eventually turned Russian leaders further against the Georgian leader and deepened their cynicism about the geopolitical purposes of popular revolutions.[98]

The OSCE Ministerial Council met in Maastricht barely a week after the tumultuous events in Georgia and the Moldovan rejection of the Kozak Memorandum. The split over Moldova colored all the discussions at the meeting, which ended without agreement on a final document.[99] (In fact, Maastricht marked the first of a string of seven straight ministerial meetings that ended without a consensus concluding document.) The disagreement over the Kozak Memorandum versus the Mediators' Document reflected a far more fundamental divide between Russia and most of its Western partners over their respective roles in the former Soviet space. During 2003 the Dutch pushed hard to follow up on a 2002 mandate for an evaluation of the status of OSCE peacekeeping by mandating an OSCE peacekeeping operation for Moldova as part of the envisioned political settlement. Russian representatives flatly refused to discuss the Dutch proposal, which would have fielded an OSCE-mandated, EU-led force.[100] The late additions to the Kozak Memorandum providing for a unilateral Russian military presence reflected an apparent Russian desire to maintain precedence, if not close to exclusive rights, to mediation and peacekeeping in the former Soviet states. Western OSCE states were unwilling to agree to such exclusive rights for Russia, which they generally saw as a serious infringement on the independence and sovereignty of the former Soviet states in question. The United States, Britain, and France (and by inference the EU) had been willing in 1994 to endorse a unilateral Russian peacekeeping force in Abkhazia. Ten years later, they were not willing to accept such a Russian force in Transdniestria. Times and circumstances had changed; the Commonwealth of Independent States (CIS) would no longer be seen as primarily Russian turf.

Maastricht also marked a turning point of sorts in Europe's conventional arms control regime, constituting—in retrospect—the start of a long, slow decline for the CFE Treaty. Russia, Ukraine, Belarus, and Kazakhstan all ratified the

Adapted CFE Treaty signed in Istanbul in November 1999 almost immediately, whereas Western states-parties waited for Moscow to fulfill the commitments it undertook at Istanbul to withdraw its military forces from Georgia and Moldova. Russia had actually made good progress in Moldova and some in Georgia, and Western interlocutors were generally favorably disposed at least as late as the Porto OSCE Ministerial Meeting in December 2002, agreeing to a one-year extension of the deadline for Moldova.[101] By December 2003, at Maastricht, Western states attempted to insert into a final document language criticizing Russia's failure to meet these commitments, comments that Moscow vetoed and angrily denounced.[102] Following Maastricht, the Western OSCE states attempted every year to adopt statements criticizing Russia's failure to fulfill the Istanbul commitments, and every year Russia angrily rejected the criticism. None of the Western states-parties ratified the ACFE Treaty. Without this the treaty could not enter into force and be joined by the Baltic states, now NATO members, much to Russia's frustration. Russia withdrew one more trainload of ammunition from Moldova's Transdniestrian region in March 2004. After that withdrawals ceased, and Russian armed forces remain to this day in both Moldova and Georgia.

Meanwhile, OSCE/ODIHR also played a distinct role in the events leading to the Rose Revolution, with its judgment that the November 2003 parliamentary elections fell short of international standards, contributing to the popular upsurge that swept Shevardnadze from power. During 2004 the OSCE's election observation practices would run seriously afoul of Russian sensibilities and interests in at least two important cases. In the March 2004 Russian presidential election, in which Putin easily triumphed, the OSCE Election Observation Mission report was distinctly negative:

> The 14 March 2004 Presidential election was generally well administered. The Central Election Commission (CEC) demonstrated professionalism in the technical preparations for the election. However, the election process overall did not adequately reflect principles necessary for a healthy democratic election process: essential elements of the OSCE commitments and Council of Europe standards for democratic elections, such as a vibrant political discourse and meaningful pluralism, were lacking. The election process failed to meet important commitments concerning treatment by the State-controlled media on a non-discriminatory basis, and secrecy of the ballot.[103]

The head of the observation mission, Bruce George—a British member of Parliament and president of the OSCE Parliamentary Assembly—was blunt in responding to those who defended the election: "They haven't ever seen a good election and wouldn't know one if it hit them in the face."[104] However, Putin thought he knew an unfriendly act when he saw one. The Russian president and his colleagues grew increasingly frustrated as they perceived that the United States and the OSCE applied double standards, criticizing Russia harshly while turning a blind eye to significantly greater electoral abuses in states such as Azerbaijan and Kazakhstan.[105]

OSCE institutions and officials played important roles in Ukraine's Orange Revolution, which further turned Russian elite opinion against that organization.[106] Having already endured two unpleasant surprises in Georgia and Moldova in late 2003, Moscow took care to ensure that outgoing Ukrainian President Leonid Kuchma would be followed by a congenial successor. Russia sent a bevy of advisers to assist the campaign of Kuchma's chosen successor, Viktor Yanukovych, and made a number of economic and financial concessions aimed at wooing Ukrainian public opinion. As the election neared, Putin visited Ukraine and personally campaigned with and for Yanukovych. Dirty tricks were also involved, as the leading opposition candidate, Viktor Yushchenko, was poisoned, saved by treatment in an Austrian hospital, and seriously disfigured. Nonetheless, Yushchenko did well enough in the first round to face Yanukovych in a run-off in late November.

The ODIHR election observation mission was highly critical of the run-off election on November 21 and cited a number of election day abuses that might have been used to inflate Yanukovych's vote totals.[107] Putin congratulated Yanukovych immediately, even though exit polls and parallel counts conducted by many nongovernmental organizations (NGOs)—many of these financed by Western foundations—showed Yushchenko to be a narrow victor. When the Central Election Commission announced that Yanukovych had won, angry crowds occupied and stayed in Kyiv's Independence Square (Maidan Nezalezhnosti, thus giving the movement the name Maidan) during the dead of winter, blocked government offices and demanded a new vote. After negotiations of almost a month and interventions by Poland, Lithuania, the OSCE, the EU, Russia, and the United States, a repeat election was held on December 24, which Yushchenko won. More negotiations followed, brokered by international mediators, including OSCE secretary-general Jan Kubis, which produced key agreement on a revised division of power between the president and prime minister (the latter subject to closer control by the legislature, still dominated by Yanukovych's party), that in turn finally allowed Yushchenko to take office in early 2005.

The Orange Revolution was a stunning defeat for Russia and for Putin personally. The open intervention of many Western countries and organizations such as the OSCE and the EU for a level playing field (and thus in effect against his candidate) was interpreted by the Kremlin as de facto support for Yushchenko and regime change. Russian officials found confirmation of this conclusion through sights such as the Ukrainian ambassador to the OSCE (later a foreign minister under Yushchenko) handing out orange buttons in the Hofburg in Vienna. Many Russians reached the conclusion that Western governments, in particular the United States, had engineered the popular uprising in Kyiv and the eventual defeat of Yanukovych.[108] The significant presence of and support for the orange demonstrators by Western-sponsored NGOs and some Western NGOs was used by bitter Russian critics to buttress these claims. The events in Ukraine (especially after Tbilisi in 2003 and Belgrade in 2000) convinced the Kremlin that the West—especially the United States—had embraced a policy of supporting regime change in the Balkans and the CIS, and that if it could happen so close to home, it could happen in Moscow.[109]

Two events in Central Asia in the first half of 2005 cemented many Russian officials in this belief. In Kyrgyzstan, President Askar Akaev, once seen as a democratic oasis in a desert of despotic rulers, had become increasingly corrupt and authoritarian and reportedly desired to install a "tame" parliament in the 2005 elections in order to change the constitution to allow him to run for another term.[110] Public protests in the capital and other urban centers after two flawed rounds of voting in February and March eventually drove Akaev into exile in Russia. He was replaced in a July vote by former prime minister Kurmanbek Bakiev (who ironically suffered the same fate in 2010). There were no strongly pro-Western parties in Kyrgyzstan, and the United States was most interested in preserving rights to its air base in Manas.

However, the Tulip Revolution in Kyrgyzstan both confirmed the widespread impression in Russia that a wave of regime change was sweeping the former Soviet area and worried at least one ruler in the region. When a band of armed men seized the local prison in Andijon, Uzbekistan, on May 13, 2005, freed a number of prominent businessmen held prisoner on charges of radical Islamism, and then took control of the town, Uzbek authorities and President Karimov reacted with extreme violence.[111] Uzbek troops dispersed large numbers of demonstrators in regaining control of the town, and killed hundreds. Years later there are still widely contradictory accounts of what occurred. The United States in the end chose to side with human rights observers and activists who claimed that the businessmen were innocent of charges of radicalism and terrorism, and that Uzbek forces had fired on and killed scores to hundreds of innocent civilians. Harsh criticism from Washington caused Karimov to cut off US access to the air base at Karshi-Khanabad (K-2), making Manas all the more crucial for operations in Afghanistan.[112]

To Western supporters, in the short run the color revolutions seemed to signal the spread of popular activism and democracy into the former Soviet area. These hopes were never real in Kyrgyzstan and Uzbekistan; in the longer run, they were sorely disappointed in Ukraine and Georgia. However, for Moscow it certainly seemed that the United States was bent on challenging and perhaps replacing Russian influence in the near abroad through the use of popular movements and demonstrations, and the Kremlin set about pushing back in the same fashion. The Russian government began adopting legislation restricting the activities and funding of independent NGOs, a process that continues within Russia today over a decade later. The Kremlin also stepped up the practice of using GONGOs (government-organized NGOs) to challenge demonstrators on their own turf. The real rise of the pro-Kremlin youth group Nashi ("Ours" in Russian) and the appearance of pro-Russian groups in Ukraine and Moldova with the same name, Proryv ("Breakthrough"), reflected a determination to fight fire with fire.[113]

The fallout from the color revolutions was particularly apparent in the OSCE at the Ljubljana Ministerial Meeting in December 2005. There was rancorous debate over Russia's continuing failure to satisfy the Istanbul commitments, the refusal of Western states to ratify the ACFE Treaty, and the lack of progress on the "frozen conflicts."[114] For the third ministerial meeting in a row, there was no consensus concluding document, although there were more limited, specific statements adopted on Georgia and the Karabakh negotiating process. The Russian delegation and some of its CIS colleagues also subjected OSCE election observation procedures and practices to harsh criticism, accusing ODIHR of double standards, unbalanced composition of observation missions, and nonobjective reports. Russia called for uniform criteria for judging elections to be adopted (without specifying what those might be) and for submission of observation reports for approval by the Permanent Council before making them public, thus giving the observed state a veto over any criticism.

By 2005, the OSCE was thought to be in crisis by most of its participating states, and Russia was the organization's harshest critic. In July 2004 Russia prompted a statement of nine CIS presidents at an unofficial summit in Moscow complaining of violation by the OSCE of some of its basic principles, such as state sovereignty and noninterference in internal affairs.[115] Moscow followed up in September 2004 with the so-called Astana Appeal of eight CIS foreign ministers complaining of imbalances, discrimination, and double standards in the work of the OSCE.[116] Moscow voiced three major complaints about the OSCE: (1) there was an undue emphasis on the human dimension, especially human rights and elections, and a concomitant neglect of the first basket security issues; (2) the OSCE focused on domestic developments in states "east of Vienna," largely the Balkans and former Soviet Union, and ignored issues in Western participating states; and (3) OSCE institutional structures were weak and the organization was thus dominated by ad hoc demands and interests of the largest blocs, the EU and NATO.[117] As Russian deputy foreign minister Vladimir Chizhov put it: "The OSCE appears to have found itself on the sidelines of the processes of the EU and NATO enlargement and started to play an even less noticeable role in the dialogue on key security issues linked to the changing European architecture."[118] In addition to the complaints enumerated above, Chizhov saw the OSCE's weakness linked to the failure to turn it into a true regional international organization "in the meaning of Chapter VIII of the Charter of the United Nations." In such a reformed OSCE, wayward institutions such as ODIHR would be placed firmly under the control of a stronger secretary-general, under the supervision of something that looked like the perennial Russian proposal for a European security council.

Ultimately, Moscow criticized the OSCE because it perceived the organization as pushing a political agenda of reform and regime change favored by the West. In the words of one Russian expert:

> The political change that has taken place over the past two years in Georgia, Ukraine, Kyrgyzstan, and the erosion of the political regime in Uzbekistan fuel the fear in Moscow that the forthcoming change may not only question the role of Russia in the former Soviet Union but, indeed, can spill over to Russia proper. The OSCE is (correctly) perceived as an institution that does not help Russia to solidify the status quo but rather often becomes an agent of change. It is largely perceived as an institution that promotes and encourages the change on behalf of the "Western states" by pushing the human dimension agenda and by challenging manipulated elections by publicly blaming them as being unfair and even not free.[119]

Russian officials generally identified two possible solutions to the crisis in the OSCE and their disaffection with the organization. One approach was to place all of the far-flung institutions, offices, and field operations of the organization under firm political control on the basis of a consensus among the representatives of the participating states. The other solution was simply to abandon the organization. In Russia there were numerous advocates for each approach.

Western officials and analysts also realized there was a growing crisis in the OSCE, but they had no clear vision as to what to do about it. At their meeting in Sofia in December 2004, the OSCE foreign ministers called for the establishment of a "Panel of Eminent Persons on Strengthening the Effectiveness of the OSCE," that is, a group of senior former officials to provide advice. The Slovenian Chairmanship followed up, and just before the thirtieth anniversary of the Helsinki Final Act it received the document "Common Purpose: Towards a More Effective OSCE," which contained dozens of specific recommendations for enhancing the political profile and concrete work of the OSCE.[120] This eminent persons' report contained many sensible, in places far-reaching and imaginative proposals for reforming the OSCE. However, the report's fundamental weakness was that these proposed reforms were almost all within the framework of the OSCE's current structures and its established place in the overall European security architecture.

The real problem, as noted at the time by several European specialists on the OSCE, was that Russia was dissatisfied not so much with the OSCE per se but with the overall structure and hierarchy of the European security architecture as it had developed by 2005. One European diplomat working in the Balkans for the UN reflected that Russia's original aim of making the OSCE "into the security organization in Europe, because in this organization Russia and the US were on an equal footing," had been frustrated by the primacy accorded NATO and the EU in military, political, and economic affairs by almost all European states.[121] Moscow's unhappiness with NATO enlargement and the expanded EU's neighborhood policy did not, unfortunately, translate into increased support for the OSCE, which Russian officials also perceived in mid-decade to be an agent for the Western, NATO, and EU agenda.[122] European and American leaders increasingly perceived Russia to be attempting to use its position in the OSCE to defend great power, hegemonic aspirations in its near abroad. Frustrated by Western criticism of both its domestic and foreign policies as inconsistent with OSCE principles, Moscow became steadily more resentful and less cooperative within the organization. Western (including OSCE) support for the color revolutions accelerated this process of Russian alienation from the OSCE:

> The changes of regime in Georgia, Ukraine, and Kyrgyzstan (and Russia's role in them) are telling examples. The Russian Federation has reacted defensively to these changes, trying to shore up the old regimes rather than participating in the management of change. Russia perceives the changes in these and other post-Soviet countries as a zero-sum game, where Western influence rises as Russia's falls. The OSCE, and the way it is used by Western states, is seen as one of the agents of change. This is the core of Moscow's criticism of the OSCE's alleged geographical and substantive asymmetries.[123]

By 2006, Russia considered not just the OSCE but the entire European security architecture, including NATO and the EU, to be working against its interests. The West, conversely, still used the model of comprehensive, cooperative security of interlocking institutions developed in the mid-1990s, but with the role of the OSCE growing less important as NATO and the EU enlarged and strengthened. To be sure, Moscow continued its everyday participation in OSCE structures and affairs and its broad working-level cooperative efforts with NATO and the EU. However, this was due as much to bureaucratic and policy inertia as to any conviction that such activities and collaboration were truly in Russia's vital interests. At the same time, increased prosperity and economic power brought to Russia by oil and natural gas riches made Moscow more self-confident and therefore more assertive in challenging a European security order it believed to have been constructed to Russia's fundamental disadvantage. This Russian pushback, already quite noticeable by 2006, dominated the European political and security landscape during the next few years, ultimately resulting in a head-on collision in the war in Georgia.

## 8. RUSSIA LEAVES THE WEST

### From Kosovo to Georgia

From 2006 to 2008, the European security order gradually broke down in a process culminating in Russia's four-day war with Georgia. Russian dissatisfaction with the European security architecture as it had developed since the end of the Cold War was the root of the problem, but many factors contributed to bringing Moscow's disaffection to the point of military hostilities with a small neighbor. Vladimir Putin's consolidation of his authority and domestic reaction to the color revolutions led an even greater number of his Euro-Atlantic colleagues to express concern with or disapproval of Russia's growing democracy deficit. Moscow's attempts to exert influence in the former Soviet neighborhood, and especially its use of the so-called gas weapon and embargoes of other goods, stoked fears in Europe and North America that Putin was bent on some sort of neo-Soviet or imperial restoration.

Russia's building frustration with the existing security order in Europe led Putin to make an unprecedented programmatic complaint about the behavior of his Western interlocutors at the February 2007 Munich security conference. Russian foreign minister Sergei Lavrov expanded on Putin's litany of grievances in a long article later in 2007, but Western responses failed to satisfy Moscow's chief complaints. The election of Putin's longtime assistant and protégé, Dmitry Medvedev, to the presidency and Putin's assumption of the prime minister's slot in 2008 had no apparent effect on Russia's sense of grievance and assertiveness.

The United States continued to pursue its efforts to develop and deploy missile defense systems. Western signatories of the Adapted Treaty on Conventional Armed Forces in Europe continued to condemn Russia's failure to fulfill its commitments for withdrawal of its military forces from Georgia and Moldova and consequently maintained their refusal to ratify the updated conventional arms regime. Western negotiators in the contact group for Kosovo overrode Moscow's protestations that Belgrade and Pristina needed more time for talks on a possible status agreement and pushed resolution of the issue toward independence for Kosovo.

The United States continued to push NATO toward an ever more global reach, with global partners and responsibilities far removed from Europe. By mid-2006, the United States was in the midst of a combined foreign and domestic crisis. The war in Iraq was going very badly, requiring continued and larger deployments of US troops, but the security situation in Iraq continued to deteriorate. Taliban operations were increasing in Afghanistan, causing security in much of the country to deteriorate and leaving Washington hard pressed to find additional US troops to send to that theater and requesting often reluctant Allies to send more troops for combat roles that dubious publics in many NATO states were not keen to accept. All the while, the bureaucratic wheels of NATO enlargement continued to turn, with candidacies for membership from several Balkan states at various stages of the process, but with possible candidacies looming from two countries that would without doubt provoke heartburn in Moscow—Georgia and Ukraine.

Meanwhile, the European Union's steady march from a common foreign and security policy toward a "deeper" union and a more integrated European security and defense policy took an unexpected detour. From the beginning, European integration had been primarily an elite-led process, but two of the original EU publics—France and the Netherlands—spoke up in referenda in 2005 rejecting a proposed EU constitution which would establish new posts of president, foreign minister, and other offices and institutions of common governance and which was the result of a convention of high officials lasting almost two years. EU leaders regrouped, and in the space of some four years fashioned a treaty with many of the same provisions as the draft constitution that they were able to get ratified and implemented by 2010. Popular disillusionment with the EU getting "deeper" also applied to it getting "wider," and the addition of ten new members was instrumental in producing "enlargement fatigue." Romania and Bulgaria were already far enough along in the process to gain admittance in early 2007, but prospects for further enlargement dimmed drastically, with eventual effects on relations with Turkey and the Western former Soviet states.

Europe's descent into crisis in 2008 began with the February unilateral declaration of independence by Kosovo and recognition from most of the EU and

NATO member states. Putin was furious and hinted at some sort of eventual action in response. The NATO Summit in Bucharest followed in April, and the United States pushed for a membership application process to be started for Ukraine and Georgia over the strong objections of key Allies such as Germany and France (to say nothing of Russia, with Putin in attendance). The compromise reached at Bucharest was perhaps even worse than starting the formal application process; it promised both Georgia and Ukraine eventual membership in NATO some day, without offering any guarantee of protection against attack before that happened. Putin's bilateral summit with George W. Bush in Sochi immediately following the NATO meeting did nothing to resolve the differences over NATO enlargement to the near abroad. Tensions built into the summer until early August, when Russia was able to take advantage of Georgian president Mikheil Saakashvili's impatience to restore Georgia's control over South Ossetia to draw the Georgian into war with Russia, which he lost quickly and decisively.

In the aftermath of the Georgia war, Russia explicitly asserted a "privileged sphere of interest" in the neighboring countries of the former Soviet Union. Moscow solidified its military presence in Georgia's breakaway regions of Abkhazia and South Ossetia, and then—in a move that was clearly revenge for Western recognition of Kosovo's independence—recognized the two as independent states. The war in Georgia brought a further decline to the standing of the Organization for Security and Cooperation in Europe (OSCE). Despite being perhaps the only entity that provided balanced reporting during the war from both sides of the front, the OSCE Mission to Georgia was closed within months after the end of active hostilities. French president Nicolas Sarkozy, acting on behalf of the French presidency of the EU, mediated a cease-fire agreement between Moscow and Tbilisi, and at Sarkozy's behest the EU subsequently became the chief mediator in the process aimed at resolution of the conflict between Georgia and Russia. Despite all the talk of NATO membership, the war showed that both the Alliance and the United States were unwilling to intervene militarily in a conflict with Russia in Moscow's backyard.

## EUROPE: NEW BLOOD FOR DISILLUSIONED VOTING PUBLICS

The European Union marked time for several years in the middle of the decade, at least from the rejection of a proposed constitution for the union by French and Dutch voters in 2005 until the Russo-Georgian war. This is not to claim that nothing was happening in Europe during that period or that EU institutions and their enormous bureaucracies were idle. Rather, EU leaders and countries were devoting most of their time, attention, and energy during this period to internal institutional and political questions, in particular to how a drastically expanded union would be governed. The EU's leaders were faced with the challenges of integrating many new states and large populations into the union's existing institutions at the same time they attempted to adapt those structures. They also faced a rising tide of disillusionment and resentment from the voters of established EU member states who were disenchanted by what many perceived as the distant elitism of the Brussels bureaucracy and were fearful of the effects of enlargement on jobs, economic benefits, and social stability. All this left little time for attending to the EU's role as an international security actor.

As early as 2000, European leaders, such as German foreign minister Joschka Fischer, recognized the need to prepare for the strains that ten more member states and more than 100 million new citizens would place upon EU institutions.[1] EU officials and national leaders were generally unimpressed with the results of the December 2000 Nice Summit, so they eventually agreed to prepare for the next intergovernmental conference by convoking a constitutional convention under the leadership of former French president Valéry Giscard d'Estaing, which opened in Brussels in February 2002. The convention witnessed a protracted battle between large and small EU member states (with Giscard favoring the former) over issues such as the size of the European Commission, requirements for qualified majorities, replacement of the rotating Council presidency by an elected president, and writing the Charter of Fundamental Rights drafted at Nice into the constitution. The most significant change with respect to foreign and security policy was the merger of the positions of high representative and commissioner for external relations into the position of secretary-general of the European Council in charge of foreign and security policy, in effect the EU foreign minister.

The draft constitutional treaty was completed in June 2003 and debated for a year in the ensuing intergovernmental conference. Inept leadership under Silvio Berlusconi's Italian presidency, along with deep disagreement between France on one hand and Spain and Poland on the other, delayed approval of the draft well into 2004. Changes in government in Madrid and Warsaw in the first half of 2004 (along with a more consistent Irish presidency) helped EU members reach consensus and put the treaty out for ratification in October 2004.[2] However, the EU's leaders had not foreseen the reaction of Europe's disaffected voters in those states that chose to seek ratification through referendum rather than parliamentary vote. Within days of one another in May and June 2005 voters in France and the Netherlands rejected the treaty by 55 and

62 percent, respectively.[3] Faced with the prospect of an unfavorable referendum in the United Kingdom as well, in June 2005 the European Council put the issue of the treaty on hold for a year.

Most observers perceived at least three factors behind the surprisingly strong negative reaction to the treaty. First, critics of EU governance had called attention for years to the so-called democracy deficit in the Union, and the remoteness that many citizens felt from institutions, policies, and decisions made in Brussels. Second, and related, many critics saw the EU as elite-driven and high-handed, rarely asking the citizenry of the member states whether they approved of or desired further European integration. Third, almost all observers tended to see the vote as evidence of "enlargement fatigue," in particular, fear of an influx of large numbers of alien foreigners. The notorious example of the "Polish plumber" taking jobs from French workers typified objections of this sort. Domestic politics within countries such as France, fear of immigration, and the rise of nationalist, right-wing parties all contributed to anti-EU sentiment.[4]

After a lengthy period of due deliberation, EU officials and political leaders decided to move forward in precisely what one seasoned observer called "the least credible scenario": to hold another intergovernmental conference.[5] There was a general reluctance among European political elites to lose many of the substantive reforms reflected in the constitutional treaty; the problem was how to adopt them without provoking further popular backlash.[6] The process was pushed especially by Germany, whose recently elected chancellor, Angela Merkel, wanted to make a demonstration of German leadership during her country's presidency in the first half of 2007. The United Kingdom, France, and the Netherlands all wanted to save provisions of the constitutional treaty, but in a fashion that would not require going to the voters again. The solution was to have the intergovernmental conference that met during 2007 amend the existing overall EU treaty with individual items from the constitutional treaty, thus achieving a similar result, but allowing the argument that revisions to the existing EU text did not require referenda. The final product—the Treaty of Lisbon—was signed in December 2007, and it was ratified and entered into force two years later, in December 2009.[7]

The changes introduced by the Lisbon Treaty promised significant effects for EU domestic policies and governance, as well as for its foreign and security policies.[8] The European Council indeed received a president, and the posts of high representative and commissioner for external relations were merged, with the title of high representative and vice president of the commission. The EU itself acquired a formal legal personality, and with this the ability to enter into treaties and official agreements as an entity in and of itself, and not a collection of individual states. Less than a year later, the European External Action Service was established, constituting a formal EU diplomatic service. These changes continue to affect and facilitate the conduct of foreign affairs and security and defense policy by the European Union in 2017.

However, the largest effects of the failure of the constitutional treaty and the long hiatus while EU member states debated alternative paths to similar reforms were arguably on EU enlargement and neighborhood policies. Accession negotiations with Romania and Bulgaria were far enough along by mid-2005 that the two received full membership without serious delay on January 1, 2007.[9] It was clear to most EU political leaders and outside observers by 2005–2006 that further enlargement of the union was likely a long way off.[10] Even though the impressive record of reform of the first government of Recep Tayyip Erdoğan led the EU to open accession negotiations with Turkey after almost four decades as a candidate, there was little prospect of success for Ankara given significant opposition in France and Germany to Turkish membership.[11] The European Neighborhood Policy also became significantly less ambitious and forthcoming because there was little realistic prospect of holding out possible membership even to the European states in the western part of the former Soviet Union.[12] The EU set up "action plans" for improving conditions in and relations with many of its eastern neighbors, but the emphasis now was clearly on enhancing security and stability on the EU's perimeter rather than enlarging the territory or membership of the union.

The other significant developments associated with the failure of the constitutional treaty and its eventual replacement by the Treaty of Lisbon were the beginnings of the real rise of German power and influence within the EU and—connected with this—the reversal of roles in the partnership between Paris and Berlin, along with the ebb of pro-EU sentiment within the United Kingdom and the decline of the political fortunes of Tony Blair. Germany had already begun to participate in EU security and military missions under Chancellor Gerhard Schröder, but Berlin's growing economic clout and Merkel's more balanced relationship with Washington gave her increased leverage in EU councils. Meanwhile, French president Jacques Chirac's break with the United States over Iraq, his mishandling of the constitutional treaty ratification, and his continuing domestic political difficulties all weakened France's standing in Brussels. Tony Blair was perhaps the most pro-European British leader in decades, but by 2006–2007 his luster had been badly tarnished by his close association with George W. Bush in the Iraq war. His role in 2007 in preparing the Lisbon Treaty was really his swan song on the European stage before being replaced by Gordon Brown. The 2008 global economic crisis and the rise of right-wing, nationalist parties in England subsequently sharply boosted anti-EU sentiment in the United Kingdom.

## THE UNITED STATES: BUSH FATIGUE

By 2006, the Bush administration was in trouble both at home and abroad. First, the war in Afghanistan was not going particularly well, and the conflict in Iraq was an ongoing and growing disaster. Insurgencies gripped significant portions of Iraq, forces loyal to al-Qaeda held substantial patches of territory in the country, Iranian influence in Iraq had greatly increased, and US troops were suffering continuing high numbers of killed and wounded. US military forces were under increasing stress, with repeat lengthy deployments to combat zones, widespread use in combat of National Guard units not originally intended for such a purpose, and the mandatory retention of many military personnel after their terms of service had expired. The costs of America's two major foreign wars had greatly expanded and—even though hidden somewhat in separate, supplemental appropriations—were driving a federal budget that had been in surplus when Bush first took office in 2001 deeper and deeper into deficit. Profound popular disillusionment with the Bush administration resulted in disastrous reverses for the Republican Party in both chambers in the November 2006 legislative elections, producing a substantial Democratic majority in the House and a bare majority in the Senate.

Washington also had suffered enormous reverses in popularity in Europe since the Allies had rushed to proclaim their solidarity with the Americans after the September 11 attacks. The Bush administration's defiant unilateralism, the 2003 attack on Iraq (and subsequent failure to find any weapons of mass destruction), practices such as rendition and secret prisons for detainees, the use of the Guantánamo Bay prison in Cuba to evade due process, and abuses such as those at the Abu Ghraib prison all contributed to dramatic declines in public opinion favorable to the United States and concomitant growth in unfavorable opinion in most of America's European Allies and partners.[13] The unpopularity of the United States and of Bush personally in much of Europe did not prevent Washington from working productively in bilateral and multilateral contexts with old and newer European partners, but it did affect the enthusiasm in many European capitals for US initiatives, especially those more distant from and less relevant to European governments and publics.

Bush's second term became a mixture of ideology and pragmatism. As noted above, his second inaugural address and his second National Security Strategy, issued in 2006, contained unequivocal support for the proposition that America's security is best ensured by worldwide support for the spread of democracy.[14] Vice President Dick Cheney, perhaps the strongest adherent to this general position, remained in the administration until it left office in 2009. However, by mid-2006

Bush's greatest practical problem was what to do to reverse the situation in Iraq. To address this issue, he replaced one of the other major ideologues of his administration, Secretary of Defense Donald Rumsfeld, with Robert Gates, a veteran of his father's administration, and adopted recommendations for a "surge" in Iraq, a widely criticized but ultimately successful significant increase in combat forces and their activity. Bush held firm on the surge in Iraq in the face of fierce criticism at home and abroad. With the help of favorable internal developments in Iraq—such as the "Anbar awakening," a local Sunni reaction against the excesses of al-Qaeda insurgents—the security situation in the country slowly but significantly improved.

Other personnel changes in the second Bush term—in particular, Condoleezza Rice's move to secretary of state; the elevation of Steve Hadley to national security adviser; and the eventual departure of neoconservatives such as John Bolton, Douglas Feith, and Paul Wolfowitz from key Washington policy positions—may have made internal policy deliberations somewhat easier, but they did not entirely remove the messianic element from Washington's approach to the world. To be sure, the crusade against the "axis of evil" subsided, and the post-2005 Bush administration even agreed to nuclear nonproliferation negotiations with both Iran and North Korea. However, democracy promotion remained a major element in the Bush team's foreign policy (it is difficult to see how else Secretary Rice's "transformational diplomacy" might have been perceived), and this element was particularly prominent in Bush's approach to Russia and the former Soviet area.

The Bush-Putin friendship, widely traced in popular press accounts from the "sense of his soul" moment in Ljubljana, was growing strained as both presidents moved deeper into their second terms. Their meeting in Bratislava in 2005 was not particularly warm, but each continued to speak well of the other in public. Their subordinates were not so restrained; Vice President Cheney was an egregious example on the US side. At a May 2006 summit of Baltic Sea and Black Sea leaders hosted by Lithuania, Cheney blasted Putin's Russia for its lack of democracy in its domestic affairs and for using "energy blackmail" against its neighbors.[15] Cheney's speech in Vilnius brought sharp replies from Moscow, but what truly annoyed the Russian leaders, in particular Putin, was Cheney's subsequent trip to Kazakhstan for a bilateral meeting with and warm words of praise for President Nursultan Nazarbayev, hardly an exemplar of democratic governance.[16] In the years following the color revolutions, US officials steadily criticized domestic legislation and actions in Russia that restricted the media and independent civil society organizations, along with many of Russia's policies and actions vis-à-vis its immediate neighbors in the former Soviet space. As the White House noted in announcing Cheney's travel to Lithuania and

Kazakhstan, his trip was "to advance the President's Freedom Agenda" and "to promote democratic reform and development."[17]

Continuing US support for democracy in the countries of the former Soviet Union was not the only Washington policy that by mid-decade Moscow might perceive as aimed directly against it. For some time, US officials and political leaders had publicly worried about the degree to which many European and former Soviet countries depended on Russia as their primary or a major source of energy. Russia's monopoly on pipeline transportation of natural gas from the territory of the former Soviet Union—including Kazakhstan, Turkmenistan, and Azerbaijan—to customers in Europe also worried US policymakers and policy analysts, who warned of the potential that afforded Moscow to exert political pressure on many European states. A number of Western countries, in particular the United States, offered growing public support for key energy companies involved in exploiting hydrocarbons in the South Caucasus and Caspian region that joined together in the late 1990s to construct a pipeline from Azerbaijan through Georgia and Turkey to the Mediterranean Sea, bypassing existing pipelines to Europe through Russia. The idea received support from both the Clinton and Bush administrations. This Baku-Tbilisi-Ceyhan (BTC) Pipeline was endorsed in principle at the margins of the 1999 OSCE Istanbul Summit, the BTC Corporation to construct the pipeline was formed in 2002, and the first oil began to flow in 2005. Although BTC was originally constructed to carry oil, there has been considerable discussion about the transmission of natural gas from the Caspian Sea via the same route.[18]

After 2000, the United States became one of the most vocal and constant supporters of the BTC project and other proposed pipelines to bypass Russian territory and Russian-controlled infrastructure to deliver oil and natural gas from Eurasia to Europe. US government officials and nongovernmental analysts have generally perceived the question as one involving the security of America's European Allies and partners against possible political coercion by Moscow by withholding energy supplies at crucial times, such as natural gas for heating during the coldest months of the winter.[19] Such a position was not new to Washington. The Reagan administration had taken a similar stance in the early 1980s against Western Europe's cooperation with the Soviet Union to construct the "friendship" natural gas pipeline through what is now independent Ukraine. As Russia's use of its de facto energy monopoly in parts of Europe became more pronounced in the mid-2000s, the US response was once again to make energy more a security than a commercial issue. On May 1, 2006, the US Senate adopted a resolution calling upon NATO to protect the energy security of its member states.[20] Such calls were repeated from time to time in the following years, evidence of growing distrust of Russia and a tendency to see Europe's considerable energy trade with Russia as a security threat.

# RUSSIA LEAVES THE WEST?

As Russia was about to pay off the last of the foreign debts it had accumulated during the late Soviet era and the 1990s, was experiencing unprecedented growth in gross domestic product and real incomes, and was preparing to host a Group of Eight (G-8) Summit in President Putin's native city, Western calls for more democracy in Russia and sharing of energy infrastructure with those who had not paid for it were perceived as hypocrisy and sour grapes.[21] Western support for groups and organizations that opposed the existing system and government in Russia and efforts to reduce Russian energy revenues through support for alternate suppliers and delivery routes seemed directly aimed at weakening or even changing the existing regime in Russia. What Western political leaders perceived as attempts to influence and change Russian behavior, the Kremlin perceived as direct challenges to its very existence and hold on power. In Putin's view, Russia had experienced similar Western encroachments on its domestic and foreign affairs during the Yeltsin era, but it had been too weak and disorganized to make any effective response. But by 2006, Russia had recovered enough of its wealth, power, and confidence to push back against the West, and Putin did so—hard.

By 2006–2007, the Kremlin's domestic response to the threat it perceived from the color revolutions was well under way. Youth groups such as Nashi were by that time well organized and staffed out, and members were deployed to demonstrate against domestic or foreign critics of Kremlin policies.[22] Legislation was adopted giving the government greater control over the establishment, funding, and operations of nongovernmental organizations. Requirements for the establishment of political parties, their appearance on the ballot, and their representation in local and national legislative bodies were stiffened. Independent media received increased attention and screening, and individual journalists and print and broadcast outlets that were critical of the Kremlin were pressured. The space available for competitive, pluralist politics and open, independent civil society was considerably circumscribed and continued to narrow.

Putin devoted considerable attention not only to making the domestic political system less susceptible to challenges from independent actors but also to the question of how to preserve his own authority. According to the Russian Constitution, he was limited to two terms of office; if he respected the law of the land, he would have to depart the Kremlin in early 2008. Speculation flourished in Russia and abroad in 2006–2007 about whether Putin would leave office, would change the Constitution to permit a third term, or would simply ignore the law and remain in office. Putin remained silent on the subject, but he clearly did not discourage competition between two possible successors, deputy prime ministers Sergei Ivanov and Dmitry Medvedev, or gossip over which one was the favorite.[23]

In retrospect, it is easier to understand where Putin thought he was going. He presented his overall political course as working to repair the severe damage done to Russia during the 1990s, in the aftermath of the Soviet collapse. In May 2006, he explained his vision in his annual submission to the legislature:

> As we plan the continued development of our state and political system, we must also take into account the current situation in society. . . . The changes of the early 1990s were a time of great hopes for millions of people, but neither the authorities nor business fulfilled these hopes. Moreover, some members of these groups pursued their own personal enrichment in a way such as had never been seen before in our country's history, at the expense of the majority of our citizens and in disregard for the norms of law and morality: "In the working out of a great national program which seeks the primary good of the greater number, it is true that the toes of some people are being stepped on and are going to be stepped on. But these toes belong to the comparative few who seek to retain or to gain position or riches or both by some short cut which is harmful to the greater good." These are fine words, and it is a pity that it was not I who thought them up. It was Franklin Delano Roosevelt, the president of the United States of America, in 1934. These words were spoken as that country was emerging from the Great Depression. Many countries have faced similar problems, just as we are today, and many have found worthy ways to overcome them. At the foundation of these solutions was a clear understanding that the state's authority should not be based on excessive permissiveness, but on the ability to pass just and fair laws and firmly ensure their enforcement.[24]

Putin's answer to his Western critics is clear: "I am not doing anything very different from what you have done, when faced with similar problems." By this time, Putin's chief domestic political strategist, Vladislav Surkov, had formulated the idea of "sovereign democracy," or "managed democracy," to explain and justify the differences between Russia's current system of governance and concepts of democracy generally promoted by Western representatives. Surkov, and Putin, argued that historical experience and present conditions in Russia required a different, and at times slower, path toward the common aim of democracy than Western leaders and thinkers might choose for their own countries or wish for Russia.[25]

Putin fired back at Western criticisms of Russia's domestic political system, labeling them as self-serving attempts to gain geopolitical advantage. Answering Cheney's criticism in his same annual address to the legislature, Putin charged that US defense spending was twenty-five times that of Russia. And as for the United States' defense of human rights, Putin continued,

This means that we also need to build our home and make it strong and well protected. We see, after all, what is going on in the world. [Comrade] wolf knows who to eat, as the saying goes. It knows who to eat and is not about to listen to anyone, it seems. How quickly all the pathos of the need to fight for human rights and democracy is laid aside the moment the need to realize one's own interests comes to the fore. In the name of one's own interests, everything is possible, it turns out, and there are no limits.[26]

The significance of Putin's remarks is not simply that he was critical of the West, and particularly of the United States. Many Russian political leaders since the end of the Cold War had expressed such sentiments and similar criticism. Equally important, or perhaps even more important, was the fact that Putin and his colleagues now possessed the self-confidence to make such criticisms directly and confrontationally, demanding for Russia a status and rights in the international order equal to those of the West.[27]

In addition to responding sharply to Western critics, Moscow stepped up efforts to bolster its authority and counter Western influence in its near abroad. The most notorious action was the cutoff of Russian natural gas shipments through Ukraine to much of Europe on January 1, 2006, in a dispute over the pricing of and payment for Russian natural gas used by Ukraine.[28] Moscow's relations with the new "Orange" government in Kyiv had been difficult during most of 2005, and Kyiv's unwillingness to agree to a higher price for natural gas and alleged failure to pay for past deliveries was only one of a number of sore points in Russo-Ukrainian relations. Although some Gazprom, Russian, and Ukrainian oligarchs' commercial interests were indubitably involved in the Russian action, Putin clearly also had political aims, in particular pressuring Ukraine's leadership to take a more pro-Moscow course. Russia had used its "gas weapon" for political purposes against other former Soviet states in the past, but Putin and his colleagues greatly underestimated the side effects in Western Europe during one of the coldest Januarys in years.[29]

Russia took other steps to bring pressure in various ways on Georgia, Moldova, and Ukraine in the first months of 2006. Relations with Tbilisi had been rocky for some time, in particular over Georgian efforts to reassert control over the breakaway entities of Abkhazia and South Ossetia. On January 22, 2006, an unexplained explosion shut down the main natural gas pipeline from Russia into Georgia. In the wake of the gas crisis with Ukraine, almost no one in Tbilisi believed this was an accident. At the same time, Moscow imposed an embargo against the importing of wine, bottled water, and other food products from Georgia, allegedly for sanitary reasons.[30] In early March 2006, Ukraine and Moldova cooperated in closing the section of their border controlled by the breakaway Transdniestrian entity, sparking a crisis in the political settlement process. Russia placed an embargo on the importing of Moldovan wines, fruits, and vegetables similar to that with Georgia and threatened various actions against Ukrainian firms doing business in and with Russia. In all these cases, the disputes were eventually settled and commerce was restored, but hard feelings remained and mistrust of Moscow deepened. The image of Russia bullying its former Soviet neighbors out of neo-Soviet or neo-imperial ambitions spread widely through Western Europe and North America.[31]

Russia's natural gas crisis with Ukraine and various embargoes somewhat tarnished the June 2006 G-8 Summit in Saint Petersburg, which an increasingly confident Russian political leadership had intended to be a showpiece for their country's leadership in international affairs. Russian analysts contrasted the 2006 Petersburg meeting with a 1996 special summit of the G-7 in Russia to demonstrate Russia's return as a serious player on the world stage, with a serious agenda led by energy and nuclear nonproliferation.[32] The G-8 session actually went relatively well despite Western criticism of Russia's human rights record and George W. Bush's separate meeting with Russian rights activists. After the G-8, Moscow sought another bilateral meeting with Bush to pursue a broad agenda, including the World Trade Organization and nuclear nonproliferation issues. However, during a November 2006 stopover by Bush on his way to the Asia-Pacific Economic Cooperation Summit, Putin found his counterpart preoccupied with Iraq and either unfocused or unwilling to engage on substance of interest to the Russians. Both Russian and American participants agreed the meeting was a lost opportunity.[33]

Events again intervened in the final months of 2006 to tarnish Russia's image in the West and complicate relations. In September, hostilities erupted between Georgian and South Ossetian forces after a Georgian push during the summer to resolve the dispute and reassert control over the entity. Russian criticism of Saakashvili and economic pressure on Tbilisi increased. On Putin's fifty-fourth birthday, October 7, 2006, the renowned opposition journalist Anna Politkovskaia was killed at the entrance to the elevator in her apartment building in Moscow. Chechen leader Ramzan Kadyrov was widely believed to be responsible for the killing; Putin compounded the public relations damage when, in response to inquiries by journalists, he showed little regard for Politkovskaia's work or sorrow for her untimely death.[34]

Finally, the strange, slow death by polonium poisoning of former KGB and FSB agent Alexander Litvinenko in London in November 2006 dominated Western coverage of Russia for weeks. Litvinenko's deathbed charge that Putin was responsible for his death and oligarch-in-exile Boris Berezovskii's subsequent exploitation of Litvinenko's murder in his own ongoing campaign against Putin made dispassionate public comment about Russia almost impossible in the West for weeks, if not longer.[35] Relations between Russia and the United Kingdom were damaged for half a decade, and Putin's personal image in the West suffered substantially.

Russia's defiant reaction—refusing to cooperate with the British inquiry by extraditing the suspects, and electing one of them to the State Duma in late 2007—further entrenched widespread, highly negative Western views of the Kremlin and Russia's political system. The finding by British investigators that Litvinenko's death was a "state-sponsored assassination orchestrated by Russian security services" remains, after almost a decade, a still-unanswered indictment of Moscow's apparent lack of commitment to international cooperation and the rule of law.[36]

At some point during these events and developments during 2006, Putin seems to have decided that his Western interlocutors were unlikely to accept Russia's integration into the Euro-Atlantic political and security order on any but their own terms. These included the requirement that Russia adopt political institutions consistent with Western definitions of pluralist democracy and an economic system based on Western market principles. Writing on the eve of the Saint Petersburg G-8 meeting, the widely respected Russian analyst Dmitri Trenin claimed that "Russia's leaders have given up on becoming part of the West and have started creating their own Moscow-centered system."[37] Irrespective of whether Trenin's metaphor of Russia leaving the West is accurate, statements and actions from Putin and his colleagues in 2006–2007 make clear that Russia's criticism of its European and North American partners by this time had gone beyond objection to individual actions or specific policies and represented a critique of the basic structure of the Euro-Atlantic international security order.

The essence of Putin's and Russia's position is clearest in his "broadside" delivered at the annual Munich security conference (formerly Wehrkunde) in February 2007.[38] According to a Western Kremlin adviser, in early 2007 Putin finally lost patience with his American interlocutors following a US decision to move ahead with plans for a missile defense system in Europe.[39] Whatever the proximate cause, Putin's frustration was apparent almost as soon as he began to speak, with his blunt complaints about the United States and the West in general clearly surprising many of the senior European leaders in the crowd.[40] The speech is basically a list of unvarnished complaints about the structure and major institutions of the post–Cold War international order, with Putin criticizing the United States, NATO, the EU, and the OSCE by name.

According to Putin, the first and major problem in the post–Cold War world is US unilateralism and "uncontained hyper use of force" without authorization from the United Nations, the only legal basis for such action—not NATO or the EU.[41] Citing the rising power of states such as China and India, Putin called for an international order that better recognizes the interests of all participants. He expressed disapproval of attempts to build and deploy new, more sophisticated weapons systems, and he cited US and Russian agreements on arms control and nuclear nonproliferation, presumably as potential casualties of a new arms buildup. He especially blasted his Western partners for failing to ratify the Adapted Treaty on Conventional Armed Forces in Europe (ACFE Treaty), and he dismissed as artificial pretexts their complaints about Russian troops in Georgia and Moldova. The Russian president blasted NATO's expansion as having nothing to do with improving European security and as actually decreasing Russia's security. He accused Russia's partners of setting unfair conditions and using double standards in judging Russia's bid to join the World Trade Organization. Finally, he excoriated those who would "transform the OSCE into a vulgar instrument designed to promote the foreign policy interests of one or a group of countries," an apparent reference to the OSCE's election observation and human rights activities. When challenged by one questioner that Russia itself had a "unipolar" domestic political system, Putin retorted that many nongovernmental organizations were funded by outside powers seeking to carry out their own policies inside Russia.

Putin's comprehensive blast created a press sensation, but much of the international reaction, in particular that from the United States, was restrained. Newly appointed US secretary of defense Gates declined to engage in a point-by-point rebuttal, wryly noting that one cold war had been enough for him.[42] Reaction from the White House was also muted, as Washington apparently decided that Moscow's cooperation on Iraq, Afghanistan, Iran, and other pressing international issues was more important than a debate over governance and human rights in Russia. German policy under Chancellor Angela Merkel (who sat in the front row listening to Putin's speech) was less chummy than under Schröder but still reflected substantial German interests in close economic and commercial ties with Russia.[43]

Putin's Munich speech did not signify an end to Russian cooperation with the West, but it did herald a new Russian independence and assertiveness. Some seasoned Russia observers connect Putin's heightened confidence and assertiveness in 2006–2007 with the liquidation of Russia's financial obligations to the International Monetary Fund and the Paris Club in 2005–2006.[44] Others note the effects of the country's remarkable economic growth from 1999 through 2006 in generally bolstering the self-esteem of Russia's political elites and engendering in them a sense of greater entitlement to equal participation in European and world political and security affairs. In this sense, Putin's Munich speech was not an announcement of obligatory opposition or hostility to the West, it was a declaration of Russia's independence—its freedom to set its own standards and determine on a case-by-case basis whether to align with or remain separate from the West. For many in Western Europe and North America who had become accustomed since 1991–92 to dealing with a more retiring and agreeable Russia, this change came as a shock and took getting used to.

Perhaps Putin's most important task during most of 2007 was preparing for legislative and presidential elections, and with that, determining who would succeed him when his second term ended in 2008. Speculation flourished both within Russia and abroad before the carefully scripted announcements that Putin would support Dmitry Medvedev as United Russia's candidate for president, and Medvedev promised to appoint Putin his prime minister.[45] Reflecting Putin's critical remarks about the OSCE at Munich, Russia imposed severe limits on the election observation operations of the OSCE Office for Democratic Institutions and Human Rights, essentially scuttling them. Putin appointed one of his oldest and most trusted friends from Leningrad, Viktor Zubkov, as prime minister during the final months before the election to ensure loyalty and stability from a bureaucracy and elite uneasy before the transfer of authority.[46] Both United Russia and Medvedev were big winners in the elections, so Putin's efforts were well spent in ensuring the results he wanted.

Developments in two fields during 2007 deepened Putin's discontent with the structure of the international order and his Western interlocutors. Russia had been increasingly frustrated by Western refusal to ratify the ACFE Treaty as long as a small contingent of Russian troops remained in Moldova. Meanwhile, four European states—Estonia, Latvia, Lithuania, and Slovenia—that had joined NATO were not parties to the existing CFE Treaty and thus were not covered by this key part of the existing European conventional arms control regime. This meant, for example, that NATO fighter air patrols over the Baltic Sea republics would not be counted or limited under the ACFE Treaty, although the existing treaty provided for limits on combat aircraft. Following Putin's remarks on the subject at Munich, Russia requested an Extraordinary CFE Review Conference to address the subject (the last regular Review Conference had been held in 2006).[47] When Russia's Western partners maintained their refusal to ratify the ACFE Treaty without the complete withdrawal of Russian troops from Moldova, Moscow announced in mid-July that it would suspend implementation of the treaty in 150 days unless the Western states changed their position. When this did not occur, Russia announced its suspension of the treaty in December 2007.[48] Although some scholars debated whether Moscow's action was legal (the procedure used was actually for withdrawal from the treaty; there was no provision for suspension), Russia ceased to participate in the transparency and confidence-building activities conducted under the treaty, such as information exchanges and challenge inspections. This left the non-treaty-based OSCE Vienna Document regime as the sole system functioning in Europe for conventional arms control, transparency, and verification.

The other major item on the Russian agenda that reflected extreme dissatisfaction with the West, particularly the United States, was missile defense.[49] This subject had been under discussion in US-Russian contacts since the beginning of the Bush administration when Washington informed Moscow of its intent to withdraw from the 1972 Anti–Ballistic Missile Treaty. Missile defense was also discussed with some regularity in NATO forums, but the major US effort under Bush was to develop and deploy a US national system of ballistic missile defense in Europe. American officials repeatedly assured their Russian counterparts that the system would be directed against the growing ballistic missile threat from Iran, but the Russians generally did not believe them and feared that any US system could eventually be used against Russia.[50]

The issue took on new urgency in 2007 as the United States began to move ahead with plans to deploy elements of a national missile defense system in Poland and the Czech Republic. Moscow tried bluster, and Foreign Minister Lavrov reportedly succeeded in putting off representatives of both "old" and "new" Europe with vague threats of Russian reactions to ballistic missile defense deployments at a NATO-Russia Council meeting in the spring of 2007.[51] The Russians then tried persuasion, and Putin made a detailed presentation, complete with charts and maps, to Bush at the G-8 Summit in Heiligendamm, Germany, in June 2007, reportedly demonstrating graphically why Russia felt threatened by the proposed system and how Bush's advisers were deceiving him.[52] Putin offered to drop Russian opposition to missile defense if the two countries could work cooperatively and followed up during an early July visit to the United States with a proposal to use radar installations in Azerbaijan and southern Russia, instead of the Czech Republic.[53] The United States sent a high-level team to Russia in early autumn to follow up on Putin's proposals. They found the radar installations unsuitable (which reportedly was welcome news to American neoconservatives), but Gates and Rice also found the Russians receptive to an informal proposal to cooperate by having Russian personnel present on the US sites in Europe, which would presumably increase confidence that the systems were not directed against Russia. However, the US bureaucracy contained enough skeptics about such a proposal (to say nothing of Poland and the Czech Republic) that Washington was unable to follow up.[54] Although the issue was regularly reviewed in bilateral contacts and meetings at NATO, no progress was made on finding common ground. At the April 2008 US-Russian Summit in Sochi, following the Bucharest NATO Summit, Putin affirmed that "our fundamental attitude to the American plans has not changed."[55]

## THE SYSTEM FAILS:
## KOSOVO'S DISPUTED INDEPENDENCE . . .

In 2008, the European security system failed. If the ultimate purposes of security institutions such as the EU, the OSCE, and NATO are to preserve peace, ensure the security of their members, and promote stability in their regions, then by most measures the growing crisis that culminated in war between Russia and Georgia marked a failure on all counts. First, the lack of success of the European and UN mechanisms engaged in the search for agreement between Belgrade and Pristina and a final status for Kosovo ended in the disputed declaration of independence by Pristina in February 2008, with majority but not full recognition by the international community. Second, conflict resolution mechanisms in Georgia failed to restrain a growing spiral of hostilities between Tbilisi and Tskhinvali, which eventually led to open war between Russia and Georgia. Although the independence and recognition of Kosovo by many Western states did not directly provoke the Russo-Georgian war, these acts did inflame already-existing Russian resentments and reinforce conclusions that the West was willing to cooperate with Moscow only on its own terms. Russia warned that recognizing an independent Kosovo could set a dangerous precedent, and then used this precedent to cement its de facto control over Georgia's breakaway regions.

As events first in Kosovo and then in Georgia progressed toward their denouements, neither the EU, nor the OSCE, nor NATO proved capable of producing universally acceptable resolutions or of heading off the march toward war. All three institutions were deeply involved in Kosovo's domestic postconflict reconstruction—with the EU promoting the rule of law, the OSCE overseeing elections, and NATO providing physical security and stability. However, reminiscent of how Bosnia was handled in the mid-1990s before the Dayton Accords, the process of negotiating a political settlement between the two local former combatants and an agreed-on status for Kosovo was conducted by a UN special representative working with the contact group of six important interested powers, an essentially ad hoc mechanism under overall UN auspices. In the end, neither the world organization nor the institutions that European leaders had built or transformed since the mid-1990s proved capable of bridging the differences between the region's major powers over this last, most disputed political issue in the Balkans.

The OSCE would have seemed the logical European forum in which to debate and decide Kosovo's future status. However, by late 2006 the OSCE was hopelessly split between the United States and Russia, with the EU and most other Western and Central European states with rare exception lining up with Washington, whereas Moscow could generally count on the support of a few (but not all) of its partners in the Commonwealth of Independent States.[56] One of Europe's leading experts on the OSCE called 2007 "a most inauspicious year," beginning with Putin's denunciation of the organization in his Munich speech as a tool of Western geopolitical interests and ending with Moscow's suspension of its CFE participation.[57] With Russia bitterly opposed to most Western initiatives within the OSCE, the organization was barely able to keep its existing operations going, such as conflict management, mediation, and reconstruction activities in the field, and unable to make any progress that required consensus.

In this light, the contact group and the UN remained the instruments that addressed conflict resolution and political status in Kosovo. NATO and the EU were deeply engaged in Kosovo, but the UN was presumed to be the lead organization for managing the international presence, which rested ultimately on UN Security Council Resolution 1244. Thus Russia's participation was necessary for reaching a settlement between Belgrade and Pristina, and Moscow was simply unwilling to do so in a NATO-Russia or EU-Russia forum. The UN, NATO, the EU, and the OSCE had all established large civilian and military (in the case of NATO) presences in the province. In late 2003, the UN Mission and the Kosovo government agreed on a set of standards for human rights, the rule of law, and governance that should be met in the province before the issue of status could be addressed (the so-called standards-before-status approach) and agreed on a UN evaluation in 2005.[58] The states in the contact group at the same time asserted that this 2005 review should provide the basis for beginning negotiations on status.

However, in March 2004 intercommunal violence broke out throughout the province, primarily in the form of ethnic Albanian attacks on Serb minority enclaves. The 2004 riots did not change the UN calendar for further evaluation but seemed to engender a sense of frustration and urgency in many of the Western governments involved in reconstruction in Kosovo. UN secretary-general Ban Ki-moon appointed a senior Norwegian diplomat with long experience in the Balkans, Kai Eide, to conduct the 2005 review. Eide's report, which was submitted on October 4, 2005, concluded that though "there will not be any good moment for addressing Kosovo's future status, . . . an overall assessment leads to the conclusion that the time has come to commence this process."[59] Eide made no recommendation as to what the final status should be, but he warned that without providing a political perspective by opening talks on status the province risked slipping back into "stagnation," and presumably violence.

In November 2005, UN secretary-general Ban Ki-moon appointed former Finnish president Martti Ahtisaari special envoy for the future status of Kosovo.[60] Working intensively with local representatives as well as with representatives of the contact group states, Ahtisaari came to the conclusion, presented in his March 2007 report, that the only viable alternative for Kosovo was "independence, supervised by the international community."[61] The reasoning behind this conclusion, shared by most Western states, in particular the United States, was that without settling the political question of status further violence in Kosovo and instability in the region was inevitable.[62] The history of previous intercommunal violence and the diametrically opposite positions of Belgrade and Pristina made it clear, according to this line of thought, that the only viable solution was to separate Kosovo from Serbia. According to this argument, the especially bitter history between Serbs and Albanians in this region made it impossible in this particular case for them to live together.

Russia was dead set against the solution offered in the Ahtisaari Report, and not just or particularly because of traditional Russian sympathy for their Orthodox brother Serbs.[63] First, even after almost a decade had passed, NATO's forcible separation of Kosovo from Serbia over Russia's objections still rankled, and continuing Western domination of the settlement process kept the spark of resentment alive in many of the Russian political elite. Second, the Russians had their own active and potential separatist entities and did not wish to establish with Kosovo anything that might serve as a precedent for Chechnya or other entities in the Russian Federation. Notwithstanding Western arguments that Kosovo was a unique case that could not be applied to other places or situations, Russians simply did not believe that.[64] Third, Russia expressed fears as to possible spillover from Kosovo to other states in the region. In particular, Moscow warned that Bosnia's ethnic Serb entity, Republika Srpska, might use the Kosovo case to argue for breaking away from Bosnia and joining Serbia, or that Macedonia's ethnic Albanians might seek to separate from that country. Finally, Russian representatives pointed to the separatist entities of the so-called frozen conflicts in Moldova, Georgia, Azerbaijan, and Armenia, which might also see in Kosovo a precedent allowing them to demand recognition.[65]

Recalling her discussions of the subject with Russian foreign minister Lavrov, US secretary of state Condoleezza Rice called the Kosovo issue one of the most contentious on the US-Russian agenda.[66] Moscow was adamantly opposed to granting Kosovo any sort of independence, calling this a violation of Serbia's territorial integrity, one of the basic conditions of UN Security Council Resolution 1244, which ended the 1999 conflict and constituted the basis for the international administration of Kosovo.[67] A troika of senior representatives from Russia, the United States (Frank Wisner), and the EU (German political director Wolfgang Ischinger) was itself unable to reach agreement on accepting the Ahtisaari Plan, let alone to convince Serbia and Kosovo.

With the prospect of a Russian veto in the UN Security Council, the United States and the European Union simply took the question of Kosovo's future out of the UN framework and unilaterally implemented the Ahtisaari recommendations. Kosovo declared its independence on February 18, 2008, and was immediately recognized by the United States and all the EU states except Romania, Spain, Slovakia, Greece, and Cyprus (all countries with concerns about actual or possible separatism). The EU and NATO took it upon themselves to assume the ongoing responsibilities for the international community in Kosovo, as envisioned in the Ahtisaari Report. US and EU representatives prompted the

Kosovo authorities to request that the Kosovo Force continue its mission and that the EU's International Civilian Office and Rule of Law Mission (known as EULEX) take over many of the tasks previously done by the UN Mission in Kosovo. Western leaders convinced UN secretary-general Ban Ki-moon to bless the deal, which he did, following a delay of a few months that he hoped would ward off Serbian anger.[68]

The Russian reaction was immediate and harsh. As soon as the Kosovo authorities' decision was announced but before it was formally adopted, a statement from the Russian Foreign Ministry denounced the step and demanded that the United Nations and NATO's Kosovo Force authorities take appropriate countermeasures, including annulling the Kosovo proclamation.[69] President Putin quickly described the Kosovo declaration of independence as a terrible precedent that would come back to hit the West in the face.[70] Within a week, the Russian State Duma called hearings on the "frozen conflicts" in Abkhazia, South Ossetia, and Transdniestria, inviting the leaders from the separatist entities to speak.[71] The Duma adopted resolutions recommending that Russia recognize the two Georgian breakaway entities as independent states, and Russian political leaders promised further, unspecified responses to the Western "perfidy" in Kosovo.

In considering whether the internal political, social, and economic situation and dynamics in Kosovo required or justified the course taken by the West in unilaterally implementing the Ahtisaari Plan, the jury is probably still out, with considerable data and decent arguments both for and against. However, given the Russians' complaints starting in 2005 and 2006 about the OSCE and NATO and that the structure of European security architecture was being stacked against them, it is hard to see how the United States, the EU, and NATO could have taken any other action better designed to justify these complaints in Russian eyes. Once again, Russia's major European and North American interlocutors ignored Moscow's substantive objections to a course of action in an area where Russia had expressed interest, and made decisions on that course of action outside the international institution where discussion had been going on and in which Russia had a vote. Russia's political leaders (and the Russian public) were hardly moved by arguments that Russia was being difficult, that its position on this issue was not well founded or supported by objective factors, and that this case of Kosovo was unique.

Even if all these Western positions and arguments were entirely justified and correct, the manner in which the Kosovo question was resolved ensured that there would be long-lasting Russian resentments and most probably adverse Russian reactions. The United States, the EU, and NATO simply assumed responsibility in Kosovo for functions that were being performed by the UN and had been authorized by the UN Security Council. The Western explanation that expedience necessitated and justified the measures taken in Kosovo may, in the long run, turn out to be correct. However, expedience is a two-edged sword, just as easily wielded by Moscow. Although many other conclusions might be drawn from the history leading up to Kosovo's declaration of independence, the chief lesson drawn by Moscow may well be that because the West—in particular the United States—does not appear to be bound by the existing rules and structures of the international order when it suits American purposes, why should Russia be bound by these same rules and structures? It would not take Moscow long to apply this lesson.

## . . . BUT NO NATO IN GEORGIA

By mid-2008, Russia was angry and hostile to Western policies and actions on a number of important issues, and the West's presence in a number of regions either close to or important to Russia, or both. However, circumstances combined as much by chance as by design or predestination to transform this hostility into open war in Georgia by midsummer. Georgia was in any estimation at considerable risk of experiencing another round of fighting in a number of places in and around its disputed areas. Neither Abkhazia nor South Ossetia had been completely quiet since the initial hostilities in 1991 and 1992. There had been episodes of serious fire fights between Georgian and South Ossetian forces in 2004 and 2006. There were regular confrontations and incidents between Georgian and Abkhaz forces in the disputed zones in the Kodori Gorge region. Georgian officials complained constantly that Russian peacekeeping forces in both entities favored the separatists. Although cease-fires had been in force in both conflicts since the early 1990s, there were regular individual cases of sniper, mortar, and artillery fire from all sides. This low-key but constant violence waxed and waned, generally not rising to a level to cause great alarm outside the region, but also rarely disappearing entirely.[72]

The special representative of the UN secretary-general was the chief international mediator in Georgia, and he conducted talks aimed at a political settlement of the Abkhaz conflict. The special representative was supported by the ad hoc "Friends of Georgia" group (later "Friends of the Secretary-General"), which included Russia and the major Western powers and met regularly in New York. The unilateral Russian peacekeeping force in Abkhazia, the result of a bilateral cease-fire signed by Boris Yeltsin and Eduard Shevardnadze, received a de facto UN blessing with the establishment of the UN Observer Mission in Georgia, which consisted of a small number of international personnel representing the UN who were deployed along with the Russian troops.[73] The OSCE Mission to Georgia, which was first mandated and deployed in late 1992, was the primary international mediator in the South Ossetia conflict, although Russian bilateral agreements with Georgia governed the peacekeeping force and the Joint Control Commission that supervised it.[74] In 2003, as part of the process of filling out institutions to be created by the constitutional treaty and reflecting growing interest in the post-Soviet region, the European Union created the post of special representative for the Caucasus and filled it with a senior Finnish diplomat with considerable experience in the region.[75]

Neither the OSCE nor the UN had any significant success in moving the parties in Georgia toward a political settlement. The official position of all the external mediators, including the Russian Federation, was that Abkhazia and South Ossetia remained parts of Georgia, and the purpose of the settlement negotiations was to restore Georgia's territorial integrity by reaching an agreement on some sort of special status for these entities within a reunited Georgia. As the talks dragged on through the 1990s and into the 2000s, the Russian position seemed increasingly to favor and protect the separatist entities, irrespective of Moscow's protestations to the contrary. Georgian sensibilities were particularly inflamed in 2002 when Russia issued passports on a mass scale to residents of Abkhazia and South Ossetia in conjunction with the adoption of revised Russian Federation passport legislation. Georgian officials, and leaders from many other countries, called this action a step by Moscow toward the gradual annexation of the two breakaway entities.[76]

As he assumed the office of president of Georgia in January 2004, Mikheil Saakashvili promised to make his first priority the restoration of Georgia's territorial integrity, which he vowed to complete by the end of his first term.[77] After taking back Ajaria with de facto support from Moscow, Saakashvili aggressively began to seek reincorporation of South Ossetia into Georgia. The impulsive Georgian's pressure tactics, his extensive courting of Western support, and his installation of an alternate South Ossetian leader, Dmitri Sanakoev, who was loyal to Tbilisi, all annoyed Moscow, which finally responded with political and economic measures of its own. The EU, and especially the United States, were consistently supportive of the Georgian position in international bodies such as the OSCE, particularly after George W. Bush's 2005 visit to Tbilisi. Efforts by the 2006 Belgian OSCE Chair to use joint infrastructure projects as a means of promoting reconciliation between Georgia and South Ossetia were counteracted by actions such as Saakashvili's support for Sanakoev's "election" and installation in a front-line village controlled by Tbilisi together with Moscow's March 2006 embargo on wine, water, vegetables, and other products; public campaigns against Georgians and Georgian businesses in Russia; Tbilisi's

September 2006 arrest of four Russian military spies; and Moscow's subsequent cutoff of all road, rail, and air traffic to Georgia.[78]

Georgia under Saakashvili increasingly sought support for its efforts to reunify the country through its relationships with the United States and NATO rather than in diplomatic venues such as the OSCE and the UN. Under Eduard Shevardnadze, who cast his lot clearly with the West, Georgia became an eager contributor to international peacekeeping efforts, such as the Kosovo Force. Tbilisi first expressed an explicit desire to join NATO in 2002, constructing an Individual Partnership Action Plan aimed at increasing its capabilities for joining NATO.[79] US troops helped the Georgian authorities clear the Pankisi Gorge of suspected terrorists, and a small contingent of US troops has remained in the country since then. Under Saakashvili, Georgia became proportionately one of the largest contributors of troops to Iraq and Afghanistan, at one time deploying about 2,000 troops in Iraq and later more than 1,500 in Afghanistan, out of a total force of about 45,000.[80] It was never made explicit whether Saakashvili or any of his colleagues expected a quid pro quo for these efforts, but Georgia's highly pro-Western, pro-American direction was clear for all to see, in particular Moscow.

In the meantime, neither NATO nor the OSCE had a particularly auspicious year in 2007. As the "surge" of American troops in Iraq began to turn the tide by the end of the year, the international effort in Afghanistan did not prosper. NATO was in the process of developing its so-called Comprehensive Approach, which was launched at its Riga Summit, but any effects from the application of integrated civilian and military components in establishing security and promoting reconstruction were still over the horizon in Afghanistan. Instead, the epithet "two-tiered Alliance" was beginning to be heard, referring to limitations placed by some nations on the exposure to combat of their troops deployed to ISAF.[81] Despite a large number of joint activities conducted under the auspices of the NATO-Russia Council, relations between Allies and Moscow became more and more strained because of deepening differences over key issues, in particular missile defense and the CFE Treaty.[82] In December 2007, Moscow carried through on its threat issued at the June 2007 Extraordinary CFE Review Conference and suspended its participation in the treaty, refusing to exchange information or to accept on-site inspections. The NATO Allies expressed regret at this Russian move but refused to ratify the ACFE Treaty until Moscow fulfilled its obligations undertaken at Istanbul to withdraw its troops from Moldova and Georgia.[83] The United States made bilateral approaches to Russia in an attempt to work out a face-saving compromise for Moscow, but the Russian leaders remained firm in their argument that they had fulfilled all their CFE Treaty–related obligations undertaken at Istanbul, and the ball was now in the court of the treaty's Western signatories.[84]

NATO had a lot on its plate as it approached its April 2008 Summit in Bucharest, but the most important question for Russia, and Putin personally, was whether there would be further NATO enlargement and, if so, which states would be the new members. Albania and Croatia were on track to become the Alliance's twenty-seventh and twenty-eighth members and, indeed, at Bucharest they received invitations to begin accession talks with little fanfare.[85] The real controversy was whether the NATO Allies would be able to agree on a Membership Action Program (MAP) for two former Soviet states, Ukraine and Georgia, which had both expressed interest in joining the Alliance. Although Georgia's aspirations toward the Alliance had been constant since 2002, Ukraine had vacillated in its intentions after the Orange Revolution coalition fell apart in mutual squabbling in 2005–2006. However, in January 2008 President Viktor Yushchenko, Prime Minister Iulia Timoshenko, and the speaker of Parliament, Arseniy Yatseniuk put aside their political differences long enough to sign a joint letter reviving Kyiv's request for membership.[86]

Putin was dead set against Ukrainian and Georgian membership in NATO. Saakashvili described a meeting with the Russian president shortly after Kosovo's declaration of independence at which Putin warned that the Kosovo decision was a dangerous precedent that would bring "an entire chain of unforeseen consequences."[87] Explaining that Georgia needed protection in a "risky region," Saakashvili told George W. Bush, in a meeting only a few days after his encounter with Putin, that giving Georgia a MAP would advance democracy and implement Bush's freedom agenda.[88] Bush ended up solidly behind Ukraine's and Georgia's bids for NATO membership, but there were important leaders besides Putin—Western leaders—who were against them, most notably French president Sarkozy and German chancellor Merkel.[89]

The Bucharest NATO Summit was unprecedented in two ways. It was the first time a Russian president had attended a NATO summit as opposed to a NATO-Russia summit. But the open disagreement between the heads of state of the oldest and largest members of NATO in full view of the head of state of the former greatest threat to the Alliance—now *that* was unusual. In fact, it was clear to Washington well before Bucharest that there was no consensus in the Alliance on granting Kyiv and Tbilisi MAPs, but the Bush administration nonetheless pushed ahead.[90] Arguments before and at Bucharest that neither Ukraine nor Georgia satisfied the criteria for membership set out in the NATO Enlargement Study proved utterly unpersuasive to advocates of Kyiv and Tbilisi. The leaders of NATO's newer members, such as Poland's president Lech Kaczyński, argued that the character of the Alliance as a force for democracy was at stake, and that in any case Russia should not be given a veto over internal NATO decisions.[91] In a compromise reportedly engineered especially by Merkel, the Allies declined to approve a MAP for either Ukraine or Georgia, but they did insert in the final declaration these fateful sentences: "NATO welcomes Ukraine's and Georgia's Euro-Atlantic aspirations for membership in NATO. We agreed today that these countries will become members of NATO."[92]

The Bucharest Summit confirmed a number of other elements in NATO's ongoing transformation, although these were overshadowed in public commentary by the compromise over Ukraine and Georgia. The Alliance continued its push to strengthen its operational capabilities, in particular with respect to its ongoing deployment in Afghanistan, which was highlighted by a separate statement on ISAF's strategic vision adopted by the heads of state.[93] The Bucharest gathering also expressed support for the Alliance's increasingly far-flung partnerships, highlighted by the attendance of UN secretary-general Ban Ki-moon. By early October, NATO secretary-general Jaap de Hoop Scheffer would sign a Joint Declaration on NATO–UN Secretariat Cooperation, which reflected NATO's aspirations to a global role.[94] The list of operations and partnerships enumerated, described, and praised in the Bucharest Summit Declaration is truly impressive and reflects the Alliance's growing aspirations and reach.

Putin had plenty to say about the results of the Bucharest meeting, and not all of it was bad. In a press conference on April 4, the Russian president lauded a number of the activities and achievements of the NATO-Russia Council.[95] First, Putin praised steps forward in practical cooperation in areas such as Afghanistan, counternarcotics, counterterrorism, and NATO-Russia interoperability, and he noted that "we have achieved much together and we intend to continue our active joint work." However, he then noted serious obstacles to this work: NATO enlargement, new military infrastructure close to Russia, the CFE Treaty, Kosovo, and ballistic missile defense deployments in Europe. He continued, saying that "the appearance on our borders of a mighty military bloc whose members' actions are governed by Article 5 of the Washington Treaty will be taken by Russia as a direct threat to our country's security." In this respect, Putin added that NATO's transformation into a global security actor, also concerned with new areas such as energy and cybersecurity, eroded trust, especially because NATO's criteria for the use of force were unclear and did not necessarily depend on the UN Security Council.

Putin did not raise the question of Ukrainian or Georgian NATO membership in his prepared remarks, but he had much to say on the subject in response to journalists' inquiries, and his resentments showed through more clearly. He asked rhetorically why NATO still existed, and he scornfully evaluated the Alliance as ineffective against contemporary challenges such as terrorism or the proliferation of weapons of mass destruction. To the assertion that NATO's enlargement had brought democracy and stability along with it, Putin expressed doubt whether Ukraine would become democratic the day after entering NATO and pointed to the continuing lack of citizenship rights of Russian speakers in

Latvia. Citing his own decisions to withdraw Russian forces and facilities from Cuba and Cam Ranh Bay, he pointed to the NATO facilities being established in Romania, Bulgaria, Poland, and the Czech Republic. Attributing the thought to Bismarck, Putin asserted that in the end what is important in such questions are not intentions but capabilities. For Putin, NATO's capability to fly fighter air patrols over the Baltic Sea member states was far more important, or relevant, than all the Alliance's statements on friendship, partnership, and cooperation.

Putin and Bush immediately moved from Bucharest to Sochi for a bilateral US-Russian summit. The tone of the meeting was deceptively friendly, although it did not mask the deep differences that still separated Washington and Moscow on issues such as missile defense and NATO enlargement.[96] US and Russian officials worked hard to assemble a Strategic Framework Declaration that enumerated a lengthy list of important areas in which the two sides already were cooperating or had expressed the intention to cooperate.[97] The Strategic Declaration did not hide the disagreements between the two sides, and most of the press attention went to the short section near the top on missile defense, on which Moscow and Washington could agree only to intensify their dialogue. Almost lost amid the shouting was a joint commitment to work out a post–Strategic Arms Reduction Treaty (START), a commitment that survived the deep crisis the bilateral relationship was about to undergo and eventually produced the Obama-Medvedev New START agreement of 2010.

Contemporary press coverage and subsequent expert commentary on the Bucharest and Sochi summits reflect the degree to which US-Russian and NATO-Russian relations had already been polarized. The vast majority of such coverage and analysis focuses on the sharp disagreements over NATO enlargement to Ukraine and Georgia, Kosovo's independence, and ballistic missile defense, whereas the more positive aspects of these relationships received relatively little attention. For example, the participants in Bucharest expressed particular satisfaction that agreement was reached on supplying NATO forces in Afghanistan through Russia via the Northern Distribution Network, yet this decision passed almost unremarked in public commentary.[98] In fact, the Bucharest Summit decisions and the US-Russian Sochi documents reflect extremely full agendas on which there is a great deal that is cooperative, forward-looking, and positive.

As for Putin, the Russian president's tone with international audiences was generally polite and measured, without some of the crude phrases and extreme metaphors he occasionally used with domestic audiences. However, he believed he had a clear set of justified grievances with the West; just as he had expressed these at Munich, he reiterated them clearly at Bucharest. The most common response from his Western interlocutors was to dismiss these complaints as unfounded, or as reflecting an uncooperative stance arising from malign, hidden motives. For example, American officials, including President Bush, could not believe that Russian fears about US missile defense plans were real, and they grew frustrated at Moscow's constant objections and often suspected ulterior motives.[99] Irrespective of the intrinsic merits of the Russian positions on NATO enlargement, missile defense, Kosovo, and the near abroad as expressed by President Putin, these positions were consistent and clear. One could ignore them only, as it turned out, at considerable peril.

## WAR IN GEORGIA

The term "frozen conflicts" applied to the long-standing disputes involving the separatist entities of South Ossetia, Abkhazia, Transdniestria, and Nagorno-Karabakh, in Georgia, Moldova, Armenia, and Azerbaijan was always a misnomer. The term "frozen" was used to reflect the fact that in each case the settlement process seemed stuck, incapable of reaching any agreement. In fact, there was never any guarantee that any one, or all, of them might not heat up unexpectedly. Sadly, that was what finally happened in South Ossetia in August 2008.

It is unclear what conclusions Saakashvili drew from the somber warning on the consequences of Kosovo's independence delivered to him by Putin in February 2008. His subsequent reference to Bush's "freedom agenda" in his meeting with the US president in Washington in March could have been a response to the Putin warning, but the move was also typical of tactics the impulsive Georgian had been using with Bush since 2005.[100] However, several sources confirm that Bush warned Saakashvili multiple times not to provoke the Russian president and stated that the United States would not be able to come to Georgia's rescue if Russia took action against it.[101]

Saakashvili was caught in a political spiral of his own making. Seeking to repair damage done to his and Georgia's image by security forces' harsh response to opposition demonstrations in November 2007, Saakashvili called for early presidential elections in January 2008.[102] He won a bare majority in the first round, and promised repeatedly during the campaign to restore Georgia's territorial integrity in a matter of weeks, or at most months. Following Kosovo's declaration of independence, Moscow began to increase pressure on Tbilisi via South Ossetia and Abkhazia. The March hearings in Russia's State Duma (which recommended recognition of the two entities) were followed by an "upgrading" of Moscow's relations with the two "mini-states" in April. During that same month, in a chicken-and-egg sequence, Georgian and Russian forces were reinforced in the Kodori Gorge and Abkhazia against a backdrop of mutual recriminations between Moscow and Tbilisi. Russia dispatched an additional 500 troops to Abkhazia in May to repair the railroad there, and Secretary of State Rice expressed fear that hostilities could erupt in the region.[103]

Saakashvili apparently derived some hope of a settlement from his initial meeting with Medvedev in Saint Petersburg in June 2008, but he was soon disappointed as Moscow demanded of him a written non-use-of-force pledge. Rice weighed in with Saakashvili, urging him during a private dinner in Tbilisi on July 9 to reject the use of force, warning that it could only backfire on him. As far as Moscow could tell, the only thing Saakashvili heard from the Americans were Rice's public remarks on July 10 in defense of Georgia's territorial integrity and her conclusion that America would continue its support for Georgia.[104]

Despite all efforts, diplomacy failed. Russia assembled a large concentration of troops across the border from Georgia in the North Caucasus and began a massive training exercise in June and July. Despite Russian objections, the United States went ahead with its long-planned military exercises in its Train-and-Equip Program in Georgia in July 2008. The Western military activity in Georgia may have lent an unintended context to Rice's proclamation that "we always stand by our friends."[105]

By July 2008, Georgian and South Ossetian security forces were already engaged in low-level hostilities against each other. July 3 attacks on Ossetian police and pro-Georgian leader Sanakoev were followed by Georgia's seizure of high ground on the edge of South Ossetia, mutual shelling, and Ossetian attempts to retake the heights.[106] The OSCE Mission to Georgia continued to work in the region, including in its office in Tskhinvali. The UN maintained its small presence in Abkhazia, but observers from the UN Observer Mission in Georgia had no ability to affect the growing violence in South Ossetia. The activities of the EU special representative and EU delegations in Georgia likewise had little or no effect on arresting the rising spiral of violence. Georgia had a promise of future NATO membership but no NATO military presence or assistance.

Irrespective of where the bulk of the blame for the conflict lies, the fact remains that the major European security institutions proved incapable of reducing tension between Moscow and Tbilisi in 2008 or preventing the outbreak of war. Indeed, one might argue that at least two of these institutions—NATO and the OSCE—actually contributed to the chain of events that led eventually to war. NATO's leaders were clearly aware well in advance of Bucharest of their own deep disagreement over the Georgian and Ukrainian candidacies and of the strident Russian objections. Yet these leaders went ahead and ended up giving Kyiv and Tbilisi more than a MAP—a promise of eventual membership. NATO heads seemed so agitated by the prospect that Russia might have an indirect veto over a NATO decision that they failed to consider whether that decision was actually a good idea. In the OSCE, for most participating states discussion of South Ossetia and Abkhazia involved primarily concerns for Georgia's territorial integrity to the exclusion of other factors, such as whether the "Sanakoev project" or Georgian drones over Abkhazia were constructive steps. For its part, Russia showed no flexibility in its aspirations for a special sphere of influence in the near abroad and appeared to give little thought to how it might cultivate friendly relations with truly independent states on its borders in the post-Soviet space.

The war itself was brief and tragic. It began with a Georgian attack on South Ossetia during the night of August 7–8 and ended with a massive Russian counterattack into Georgian territory with large forces assembled and ready well before the outbreak of war on Georgia's borders with Russia.[107] The Russian forces were much larger than those from Georgia opposing them, but Russian performance was not particularly impressive and in the end the Russians won more through size than because of superior equipment or ability.[108] The Russian military aim seems to have been to move Georgian forces away from the boundaries with Abkhazia and South Ossetia and to degrade Georgia's ability to conduct military operations against those two entities. Moscow did not seem bent on conquering Georgia or seizing control of substantial Georgian territory other than adjustments that would make the two separatist entities easier to defend and thus more secure. The Russians—in particular Putin—probably also had the political aim of removing Saakashvili, but they appear to have hoped that his own people would do that as a result of his losing the war.[109] The results of the war were most of all tragedy and futility: hundreds dead, thousands displaced, property destroyed, and dividing lines even more deeply etched inside Georgia.

In the immediate aftermath of the war, the EU became the most active external international actor in the region. Asserting his authority inherent as holder of the rotating EU presidency, French president Sarkozy flew to Moscow on August 12 to negotiate an end to the war. His meetings with Medvedev and Putin produced a six-point agreement for ceasing hostilities, which he then managed to sell to President Saakashvili.[110] The first three points of the Sarkozy Peace Plan were relatively clear: no resort to force, full cessation of hostilities, and free access for humanitarian aid.[111] However, the last three points of the plan, which concerned the withdrawal of military forces and follow-on discussions about international involvement, were far less clear and thus open to conflicting interpretations based on the desires of the protagonists. Russian and South Ossetian forces were slow in withdrawing and retained some territory beyond where their lines had been before the war. Moscow was sharply denounced by Georgia and its supporters for violating the Sarkozy agreement, but the Kremlin clearly considered international opprobrium an acceptable price to pay for consolidating the territory of South Ossetia and Abkhazia and thus making them more defensible.[112]

Moscow had another surprise for the international community. On August 26, Dmitry Medvedev announced that the Russian Federation was recognizing South Ossetia and Abkhazia as independent states.[113] Medvedev provided liberal references to international law and agreements and to Georgia's alleged violations of these norms and obligations as justification for Russia's decision, which he claimed was in response to referenda, parliamentary decisions, and direct requests from the "presidents" of South Ossetia and Abkhazia. To anyone who had closely followed the recent Western explanations of how the decision to recognize Kosovo was reached and justified, Medvedev's explanation sounded like a crude imitation and mockery. It is difficult to read Moscow's justifications for its recognition of these entities without suspecting that this step was planned long before Georgia's actual attack on Tskhinvali and was closely linked to the West's purposeful exclusion of Russia from the decision on Kosovo's independence.

For anyone who did not get the message, Medvedev gave an interview on the chief Russian state television channel on August 31 in which he iterated five principles that would govern Russian foreign policy during his administration.[114] Some of these principles were unremarkable; Medvedev asserted that Russia recognizes the primacy of international law and seeks conflict with no other state. However, he also proclaimed that a unipolar world is unacceptable, in which decisions are made by one country, even as "serious and influential a country as the United States of America. Such a world is unstable and threatened by conflict." Perhaps even more notable was Medvedev's assertion that, as is the case with other countries, there are regions in which Russia has "privileged interests." Medvedev professed to desire friendly relations with the states in those regions but made clear his belief that Russia also has special rights in such places. With the hindsight gained after later Russian actions in Ukraine, Medvedev's assertion that Moscow's actions were justified by the need and right to protect Russian citizens in these neighboring countries seems particularly important, if less remarked on at the time. Though Putin was gone from the Kremlin's presidential office, Russia's foreign policy stance did not seem very different under his successor.

Russia's actions during and after the war in Georgia stunned the rest of the world, even though it had been plain for months, if not years, that conflict was brewing. Moscow's invasion of Georgia polarized Europe, and most EU and NATO leaders vigorously denounced the Russian military action and supported Georgia and Saakashvili. A number of Western heads of state and government made a hasty, highly publicized visit to Tbilisi even before all the guns were fully silent.[115] In a highly publicized action, the United States also facilitated travel home for Georgian troops deployed in Iraq when the war broke out. However, neither the United States nor any other NATO member state provided any military or logistical assistance to Georgia in its fight against Russia. In Washington, the principals of the US National Security Council explicitly declined to contemplate putting "boots on the ground" as the battle raged.[116] Western rhetoric denouncing Russia during and immediately after the war was extreme; in contrast, Western military actions during that same period were extremely modest and relatively nonconfrontational.

The war also produced a shake-up in the structure of international involvement in Georgia. Russia, South Ossetia, and Abkhazia (the latter two acting as self-asserted independent states following Russian recognition) declared that the mandates of the OSCE and UN missions in those regions no longer made sense given recent events and their change in status. The UN Observer Mission in Georgia continued with a diminished presence until mid-2009 when Russia vetoed a UN Security Council resolution continuing the mission.[117] Moscow announced in October 2008 that it would station 3,700 troops each in Abkhazia and South Ossetia, based on bilateral agreements, and was no longer bound by the bilateral agreements with Georgia and the United Nations' resolutions that had served as the authorization for its peacekeeping forces in those regions from the early 1990s until 2008. Using the same line of reasoning (that with South Ossetian and Abkhazian independence the conflicts that occasioned the need for the OSCE Mission were over), Russia refused to agree to the extension of the mandate for the OSCE Mission in Georgia past the end of 2008.[118] The OSCE closed up shop and withdrew its last monitors from Georgia in mid-2009.

Meanwhile, in order to implement the Sarkozy Peace Plan, the EU established a Monitoring Mission in Georgia in early September 2008.[119] The EU Mission's main tasks were to include ensuring against any return to active hostilities, facilitating a normal life for inhabitants on both sides of the administrative boundaries between Georgia and the breakaway entities, and building confidence between the parties to the conflict.[120] The EU assembled and deployed more than 200 monitors to the region extremely rapidly. However, the EU monitors discovered, contrary to their understanding from a September 8 Sarkozy-Medvedev agreement, that Russian and separatist authorities on the ground would not grant them access to territory controlled by Abkhazia or South Ossetia. OSCE and UN personnel over the entire lives of their missions had regular, relatively unrestricted access to these territories. Thus the postwar switch to an EU presence left South Ossetia and Abkhazia essentially inaccessible to international officials and organizations and far more dependent on and controlled by Moscow.

The international mechanisms dealing with the resolution of the South Ossetian and Abkhaz conflicts also underwent a total transformation following the war.

The four-member Joint Control Commission dealing with South Ossetia and the UN-based Friends of Georgia ceased to operate. The EU, UN, and OSCE jointly sponsored peace talks between Georgia and Russia in Geneva, with the first meeting taking place in October 2008.[121] The first session broke down over Moscow's insistence that Abkhazia and South Ossetia be given seats at the table; in the end, the two were represented at subsequent rounds informally. By the end of 2008, the Geneva talks had accomplished little other than establishing official channels of communication between Tbilisi and Moscow, both having broken diplomatic relations as a result of the war. Given the widely different interpretations among all parties of what had taken place and the mutually exclusive demands advanced by Moscow and Tbilisi, the process of reconciliation and eventual settlement promised to be long and arduous.

The effects of the Russia-Georgia war were felt far beyond the two belligerent countries and the separatist entities over which the conflict was ostensibly fought. Moscow was first of all asserting through military action a right to preeminent influence in the states of the former Soviet Union that it had asserted since 1992, but which it had been powerless to enforce for most of the post-Soviet era. Thus the Kremlin's attack on Georgia prompted particular attention and raised special fears in Russia's closest neighbors, such as Ukraine, Moldova, Azerbaijan, and the Baltics. Russia's concerns for ethnic minorities, such as the Ossetians or Abkhaz, or its claims to protect large numbers of Russian citizens, could be applied to most of these adjacent states. Moscow's behavior vis-à-vis Tbilisi both before and during the conflict also suggested that there was little in the normative structure and commitments of Europe's interlocking security institutions that would restrain the Kremlin in pursuit of perceived Russian interests.

The structure and workings of those interlocking security organizations—overall, the European security architecture—also gave Russia less and less reason to think that it could pursue its perceived interests in cooperation with its partners in those institutions or that it had much to lose by acting outside existing organizations, in violation of established rules. Russia was a full participant in the UN and OSCE debates, decisions, and operations, and these institutions were less and less empowered and involved in security issues of primary importance to Russia. The OSCE in particular was perceived by the Kremlin to be most active only in areas and tasks that worked against Russia, such as critical election observation. The most important European security questions were handled more and more by either NATO or the EU, and sometimes by those two in cooperation with each other. Moscow had an active and rewarding program of activities with both organizations, but no right to participation in decisions made by either organization on the most critical security issues.

The Kosovo case was the proverbial straw that broke the camel's back with respect to all of these Russian concerns. Moscow had serious, principled objections to Kosovo's independence from Serbia and international recognition based on the precedent it would set and the possible effects in territories close to Russia.[122] With Kosovo, the United States, NATO, and the EU arrogated to themselves the right to make a decision on Kosovo's status without involving the UN Security Council and by overruling UN Security Council Resolution 1244, which up to that time had been the basis for the international presence in Kosovo. The EU and NATO then unilaterally assumed the bulk of international operations in Kosovo that had been performed by the UN. Western arguments that Kosovo was a unique, especially difficult case and thus needed special treatment might have had some substance. But the Western argument that a unilateral declaration of independence and international recognition would not serve as a precedent elsewhere was incredibly obtuse and shortsighted.

Russian positions on Kosovo were often difficult, obstructive, insensitive to human rights concerns, and overly solicitous of often unreasonable Serbian positions. Nonetheless, Moscow had made an important contribution to obtaining Serbian consent to ending the fighting in 1999 and introducing the international presence in Kosovo. However difficult Moscow's subsequent behavior may have been, UN Security Council Resolution 1244 contained substantive points that were important to Russia, and it is hard to see how Western leaders could have expected anything good to come of ignoring or overriding Moscow's concerns. It is also difficult to accept at face value Western arguments that *immediate* independence for Kosovo was the only realistic path available to avert greater instability in the region. Again, the view may have been correct that Serb-Albanian antagonisms were too deep and lasting to allow cohabitation in a single state, but there were many, varied, more gradual routes to a separate states solution than the one that was taken.

Both the substantive decision on Kosovo and the manner in which it was made by the EU, NATO, and the United States seemed almost designed to maximize Russian resentment. Similar to the argument that Moscow should welcome NATO enlargement, because it made the states on Russia's borders more secure and stable, the Kosovo decision in effect instructed Russian leaders what they should think about an issue of some importance to them. The decision also showed Moscow that, despite all the appealing rhetoric about cooperation and partnership, NATO and the EU believed it was their right to make any decision they desired, over Russian objections, if they believed this decision was justified or in their interests. At some point, one had to expect some sort of Russian reaction to this pattern of thinking and behavior. The war in Georgia was this reaction. This line of reasoning should not be taken as an argument that Russia's actions in Georgia were justified but that they certainly should not have been surprising.

NATO, the EU, and the OSCE all failed to keep the peace in Europe in 2008, but the Russo-Georgian war had negative consequences for NATO beyond this simple failure. At the Bucharest Summit, the leaders of the Alliance made an unequivocal commitment to Ukraine and Georgia. Although the protection explicit and implicit in Article V of the Washington Treaty extends only to members of the Alliance, it is hard to see how extending a commitment of eventual membership does not convey some sort of implicit security assurance. NATO's promise of membership to Georgia in April 2008, followed by its inaction in response to Russia's invasion of Georgia in August 2008, could lead to speculation about not only when but whether there would ever be a firm guarantee of Georgia's security. To be sure, NATO had no legal obligation to come to Georgia's defense. However, the deterrent value of Alliance membership is not rooted in legalities but in the conviction of foe and friend alike that the Alliance can and will take military action in response to an attack on one of its members. NATO's response to the Georgia war did little to buttress this conviction. Even worse, it may have led some of the newest NATO members to question how firmly the populations of the oldest member states were committed to defending its newest, most distant members. In the end, much of NATO's value is its credibility. The war in Georgia in 2008 left one to wonder whether NATO, in its enlargement to support democratic transformation, might have eroded the strength behind its initial, fundamental purposes of deterrence against attack and collective defense.

## 9. THE RESET

## One More Try

The movement of Russian armor and troops into Georgia in early August 2008 shocked the world, but events were already under way on Wall Street that arguably would have a far more profound and long-lasting effect on the world. The economic bubble that had fueled eye-popping growth around the globe since the turn of the millennium burst in North America and Europe in 2008, with drastic drops in asset and commodity prices, chain reaction failures of small and large enterprises, and a near collapse of the global financial system. The tale of the global financial and economic crisis has been told many times and need not be repeated here in any detail. However, it should be noted that the effects of that crisis are still being felt in Europe's economy and politics in 2017. Since 2008 the European Union has been divided into two camps: an economically stronger northern tier, in particular Germany; and an economically depressed and politically troubled southern, or Mediterranean tier. Since the crisis began, the euro has regularly been under siege, and Berlin's role in propping up and preserving the common currency has helped cement Germany's status as the EU's clear leader.

The EU heads of state and government, collectively and individually, have devoted much more attention in recent years to dealing with the economic crisis of 2008 and the political turmoil it produced. EU political leaders and officials also continued to spend considerable time and effort on internal consolidation, achieving agreement and ratification in 2009 of the Lisbon Treaty, which incorporated many of the changes in structure and rules of governance included in the failed draft constitution. As a result, the EU has had less time and political capital to spend on foreign and security policy in the wake of the global economic crisis. When the EU's leaders did turn to such subjects, they found that they had far fewer material and economic resources to employ in executing their policies.

Russia took one of the heaviest hits from the global economic crisis, watching its annual gross domestic product (GDP) drop some 8 to 9 percent in 2008–2009. However, Russia's accumulated economic growth since 1999 and its rich reserves of natural resources provided a cushion not available to the so-called PIIGS—Portugal, Ireland, Italy, Greece, and Spain—the EU states most affected by the crisis. Spending some $200 billion, one-third of its accumulated reserves, Russia was well on the road to recovery by late 2009 or early 2010. Under the new president, Dmitry Medvedev, together in "tandem" with Putin as prime minister, Moscow began to seek changes and a more influential role in the governance of the global financial system. Taking an active part in the Group of Twenty (G-20), Russian leaders also paid increasing attention to alternative international financial and security arrangements, such as the BRICS (Brazil, Russia, India, China, and South Africa—the world's largest fast-growing economies), the Collective Security Treaty Organization, and the Eurasian Economic Union. Medvedev also launched an attempt at revising the European security architecture, proposing an umbrella European security treaty that would provide a normative structure governing the actions of existing institutions such as the EU or NATO. Russia's Western interlocutors greeted the initiative coolly, combining discussion of the proposal into a more general examination of the Organization for Security and Cooperation in Europe's (OSCE's) reform in the Corfu Process, which was named for the venue offered by the 2009 OSCE Greek Chair for the first exchanges on the subject.

Both the United States and the EU attempted to repair relations with Russia that had deteriorated to a level of bitterness and mutual recriminations after the war with Georgia not seen since the end of the Cold War. Vice President Joseph Biden first suggested a "reset" of US-Russian relations at the February 2009 Munich security conference. Despite Secretary of State Hillary Clinton's gift to Foreign Minister Sergei Lavrov of an oversize switch that incorrectly read "overload" rather than "reset" in Russian, Moscow took up the offer, and presidents Dmitry Medvedev and Barack Obama made significant progress on nuclear and trade issues during the next two to three years.

The EU approach to Russia and the region was less straightforward than the direct US initiative to begin with a clean slate. EU-Russia relations already had a well-developed institutional base initially constructed in the 1990s. EU-Russia high-level meetings were often complicated and testy because of long-standing disagreements, especially in areas such as energy policy. Following on Germany's lengthy history of Ostpolitik, Chancellor Angela Merkel attempted to use bilateral contacts to improve both the German and EU relationship with Moscow, most notably in the so-called Meseberg Initiative, which promised increased EU dialogue on issues of importance to Moscow in return for Russia's assistance in resolving the Transdniestrian conflict in Moldova.[1] Conversely, in 2009 the EU launched the Eastern Partnership, an update of the European Neighborhood Policy for Belarus, Ukraine, Moldova, Armenia, Azerbaijan, and Georgia, pointedly excluding Russia. Just as within Germany, the wider EU was split between those members that favored a more cooperative stance toward Russia and those that were traditionally hostile to and suspicious of Russian motives and actions.

NATO faced yet another interlude of existential self-examination after the Russo-Georgian war exposed the hollow nature of the commitment made to Georgia at the Bucharest Summit. NATO leaders commissioned a high-level panel of former officials and experts to review the strategic environment and purpose of the Alliance, and in 2010 NATO Allies adopted yet another revised Strategic Concept. Meanwhile, NATO collaboration with the International Security Assistance Force in Afghanistan left much to be desired. The United States was increasingly frustrated both at the reluctance of some Allies to make their forces available for a full range of combat missions and the continuing failure of most Allies to maintain levels of defense spending sufficient to provide the resources of men and material needed by NATO to augment the US contribution.

NATO's involvement in Libya in 2011 was another example of both the strengths and deficiencies of the Alliance. With some Europeans, particularly the French, eager to intervene, the Obama administration adopted the policy of "leading from behind," letting European forces assume the most important roles in protecting civilian populations and attacking forces loyal to Muammar Gaddafi. However, Washington found that its European Allies (even some of the most capable) were still greatly dependent on the United States for key assets and capabilities, such as aerial refueling and intelligence.[2] As for Russia, Medvedev abstained on the key United Nations resolution authorizing the use of force for protecting civilians and suffered Putin's criticism as NATO used that authorization to effect regime change. Although there were other reasons for the move, NATO's campaign in Libya was a key factor in Putin's decision (announced in September 2011) to return to the presidency and his increasing emphasis on Eurasian integration for Russia.

# ALL BETS ARE OFF:
# THE GLOBAL ECONOMIC CRISIS

Around the turn of the millennium the global economy took off, ushering in a period of rapid economic growth and expanding prosperity on a geographic scale unprecedented in modern history. Commodity prices soared, and development and wealth seeped into parts of the world that hitherto had seen relatively little of either. The US consumer economy played a key role in this global spurt, providing much of the underlying demand with sustained growth in production around the world. Unfortunately, much of this US demand was sustained by credit, which in turn was based on steadily rising real estate prices. This US bubble began to burst in 2007; during 2008 it became clear the extent to which the United States and the global financial, securities, and economic systems had constructed their recent rapid expansion on a foundation of unsound unsecured loans, securitized and distributed through financial institutions around the globe.[3]

The United States was not the only country in the world in which an overheated real estate market and unwise overextension of credit created a bubble that eventually produced a spectacular crash. However, the crisis appeared first in the United States, and the size and reach of the US economy then influenced the economic severity and geographic spread of the crash. As it turned out, the euro zone also was constructed on an unsound fiscal basis: credit was easily obtainable in many states in the zone with less productive and resilient economies based on the presumed overall strength of the euro. EU member states such as Portugal, Italy, Ireland, Greece, and Spain experienced bubbles, including residential and commercial real estate construction booms far exceeding anything their individual national economies could support. When credit dried up in Europe in the wake of the near-panic in the United States, these states were left with failed enterprises and debts almost impossible to repay from their own resources.[4]

The economic crisis in the euro zone produced a fundamental rebalancing of political authority in Europe, with Germany emerging clearly as the EU's most powerful state. Benefiting from steady growth since the late 1990s and deft industrial policy under both the Gerhard Schröder and Angela Merkel administrations, Germany dominated the single European market. By 2008 Berlin oversaw the largest, most powerful economy in Europe. As the EU attempted to respond to the global economic crisis, the lack of wisdom in creating monetary union without a common fiscal structure became clear. It was far more difficult for Europeans than North Americans to rescue their enterprises and economies through the injection of resources such as bailouts and subsidies. In addition, most European leaders opted for austerity rather than stimulus as the preferred approach to reducing debt, which increased the economic pain for many European workers and consumers. Finally, Germany was the one EU country with sufficient economic reserves to prop up other, failing euro zone members, but it was a daunting political task to convince German leaders and the German public of the need to do so.[5]

The rules of the European Central Bank were eventually changed to give the institution the capability to address the euro zone's ongoing debt, liquidity, and credit crises. A number of the EU states hardest hit by the global crisis suffered through years of austerity and only recently have been restored to relative economic stability. In other places, in particular Greece, the crisis that began in 2008 is still playing out in 2017, with the ultimate result still uncertain. This study is not about economics, the global crisis, or the merits of austerity or stimulus as a response. Nonetheless, in examining European security institutions and policy after 2008, it is crucial to note the chief political result of the crisis: it made clear Germany's standing as the strongest economic power in the EU. Given the importance of economics for the EU's survival after 2008, Germany's political position was correspondingly strengthened into one of near primacy. Although France remained ambitious, its economic troubles after 2008 contributed to a reversal of roles for Paris and Berlin, with the latter clearly assuming greater authority in EU councils. Finally, Tony Blair's replacement by Gordon Brown, the defeat of Labour in 2010, and the fact that the United Kingdom remained outside the euro zone all contributed to sharply diminished British activity and influence within the EU. With the relatively close Scottish independence vote and UK prime minister David Cameron's ill-advised referendum on EU membership after his reelection, the surprise mid-2016 vote to leave the EU more or less completed the steady process over most of a decade of London's self-marginalization in Brussels.

In the United States, the single biggest result of the global economic crisis was arguably the election of Senator Barack Obama in November 2008 as the country's first African American president. George W. Bush remained highly unpopular because of the ongoing wars in Iraq and Afghanistan, lingering fallout from human rights issues such as the Guantánamo Bay prison in Cuba and enhanced interrogation of prisoners, and egregious failures such as the response to Hurricane Katrina. However, the dramatic deepening of the crisis during the height of the presidential campaign and the heroic measures needed to avert collapse of the financial system all but assured defeat of the incumbent party. Obama was popular in part simply because he was not Bush, but he came into office determined to alter several key policies of the previous Republican administration. First, he was committed to extricating the United States from both Iraq and Afghanistan, to curtail the abuses allegedly employed by the Bush administration, and to rely more on multilateralism than on preemptive unilateralism. Second, like his predecessor Ronald Reagan, Obama sincerely believed in the reduction or elimination of nuclear weapons, and he made nuclear reductions and nonproliferation a major goal as he entered office. Finally, Obama made reform of America's health care system, along with restoration of the economy, the chief priorities of his administration, which affected both the time and the political capital he had available to spend on international affairs.

Obama came into office with large enough majorities in both chambers of Congress to allow adoption and implementation of the key items of his agenda, regardless of Republican opposition. However, this felicitous situation did not last long. Massachusetts senator Ted Kennedy's death in August 2009, followed by his unexpected replacement by Republican Scott Brown in a special election in January 2010, meant that Obama would need Republican votes to avoid blockage in the Senate. The president used his short-lived legislative majorities in domestic policy to achieve health care reform and in foreign affairs to secure ratification of the New Strategic Arms Reduction Treaty (New START) with Russia. In November 2010, the Democrats suffered a stunning defeat in elections to the US House of Representatives, losing a record sixty-three seats, in part because of the rise of the populist right-wing Tea Party. For the remainder of his two terms, Obama would have to deal with divided government and stubborn Republican obstructionism on almost any issue that required legislative approval. This was not a political environment offering any real flexibility for an activist president, whenever and however Obama might choose to be one.

Russia suffered especially dramatic reverses as the result of the global economic crisis, but then rebounded relatively quickly. As Dmitry Medvedev took over the presidency in May 2008 and duly appointed Vladimir Putin prime minister, the Russian economy seemed to be sailing along on the crest of a nine-year wave of record economic growth.[6] By the end of the summer, the Russian economy seemed in free fall. In a matter of weeks, the world price of oil plummeted from well over $100 per barrel to $33 in mid-December, gutting Russia's main source of foreign exchange. Russia's stock markets collapsed, with trading suspended for a time in December, and lost about 75 percent of their value by the end of the year. Despite substantial state intervention, the ruble lost almost half its value, and (like elsewhere around the world) credit in the country dried up. The effects of the dramatic drop in earnings and credit spread through the rest of the economy, resulting in a precipitous decline in economic activity and output. Russia's GDP fell by more than 8 percent in 2009.

Over the course of the crisis, the Russian economy faced threats from several directions.[7] The fall in oil prices sharply reduced expected revenues for the state budget, which had to be replaced out of reserves to ensure funding of social benefits and key operations. The government also dipped into its reserves to moderate the decline in the value of the ruble. Although Russia had minimal sovereign debt, having finished paying off its major international creditors in 2005–6, many Russian corporations had assumed substantial debt during the boom years after 1999 to finance a wave of foreign acquisitions. Many of these purchases were on margin, with stock in the Russian enterprises as the collateral. When the bottom dropped out of European credit markets in 2008, many of these loans were immediately called due. Rather than allow foreign corporations and financiers to acquire substantial stock in Russian enterprises, the Russian government stepped in, providing significant sums from the state's foreign exchange reserves to satisfy these debts. The effect was to accelerate movement already under way toward increased state involvement in key industries and sectors in the Russian economy, an unsurprising result given Putin's long-standing inclination toward a national economy constructed around a set of "national champions."[8]

## RUSSIA UNDER THE TANDEM: THE TWO-HEADED EAGLE

One of the truisms about post-Soviet Russia's national emblem, revived from Imperial Russian times, was that it looked simultaneously both east and west. This seems a particularly fitting symbol for Russia under the joint rule of President Dmitry Medvedev and Prime Minister Vladimir Putin after the global economic crisis. Even after the onset of the crisis, the Russian leaders continued to project the same confidence in the strength of the Russian economy they had shown in early 2008.[9] Medvedev and Putin's team of economic advisers — including Kudrin, Dvorkovich, Shuvalov, and others — mounted a capable and generally effective technical response during the crisis, preserving the banking system and stabilizing the currency.[10] Russia experienced a deeper drop in GDP than its European neighbors as an immediate result of the crisis largely due to the greater dependence of its economy on oil and natural gas, but Russia's recovery was also considerably faster than that of most European states, due in part to Russia's substantial reserves and avoidance of the austerity measures that delayed Europe's return to economic growth.

Most experts — both Russian and foreign — drew at least two important lessons from Russia's experience in the global economic crisis: first, the degree to which the Russian economy had integrated into the world economy, unlike Soviet times, and thus was influenced by and vulnerable to global economic trends; and second, the unhealthy level of dependence of the economy on hydrocarbons, in particular, on world oil markets.[11] Medvedev and the liberal-technocratic Putin-Medvedev economic team (Kudrin, Dvorkovich, and others) clearly recognized the need to reform and diversify the country's economy, and they set about trying to achieve those ends. Medvedev's September 2009 online manifesto, *Rossiia, vpered!* (Go, Russia!), was a stunningly candid evaluation of Russia's economy and governance, characterizing the system as a "primitive economy based on raw materials and endemic corruption."[12] Unfortunately, Medvedev's policy prescriptions and initiatives were nowhere near as radical or far-reaching as his analysis. His best known project was probably the top-down attempt to promote innovation by establishing a Russian "Silicon Valley" in the village of Skolkovo outside Moscow.[13] Medvedev later proposed transforming Moscow into a global financial center, similar to the city of London, and launched construction of a high-rise district in western Moscow for that purpose. The young, energetic president continually sought to integrate and modernize Russia, especially by attracting foreign investment and expertise, but was consistently thwarted by the obstacles posed by Russia's failings in the rule of law and widespread corruption.[14]

However, Medvedev had a more serious, immediate problem than the endemic, historic, Gogolian nature of corruption in Russia: Vladimir Putin, Medvedev's colleague and, in the view of many observers, his de facto boss. According to the British representative of Russia's Western public relations firm, "Putin himself refused to accept that the crisis revealed any structural shortcomings in Russia's economy. He blamed it all on American recklessness and saw it as yet more proof of the iniquity of American hegemony."[15] Many of Putin's most publicized actions after the crisis typified the Russian government's practice of subsidizing many enterprises to preserve jobs and local economic activity, in effect moving in the opposite direction from Medvedev's efforts to modernize the economy. Putin's trip to save a cement factory in Pikalevo, near Saint Petersburg, and his March 2009 televised humiliation of an oligarch factory owner, Oleg Deripaska, was a classic populist response to an intractable economic problem. In that same month, Putin similarly promised a massive subsidy to the floundering AutoVAZ factory in Togliatti, and later in the year he issued a public ultimatum to the French investor Renault to help keep the plant afloat or see its investment reduced.[16] Such actions indubitably played well with workers at failing, outdated enterprises in Russia's heartland, but they did little to attract the foreign investment needed to transform the manufacturing sectors of the Russian economy and reduce its dependence on hydrocarbons.

Putin saw the global financial crisis as yet another example of the unipolar world dominated by American hegemonism that he had denounced in his Munich speech in February 2007. Cynics suggested that he was unduly influenced by an unfortunate investment by the Russian sovereign wealth fund in Fannie Mae and Freddie Mac, shortly before those mortgage lending institutions had to be bailed out by the government, with their bonds plummeting in value. The rumor mill at the time had it that some Russian officials believed the United States had engineered the debacle intentionally to cause the Russian financial losses.[17] In any event, it is clear that the global crisis reinforced Putin's view that the international financial system was unfairly and irresponsibly run by the United States for the benefit of a small American financial and economic elite. Putin's suspicions that the United States' intention was to marginalize Russia and to hamper its pursuit of prosperity through integration in the international economy were deepened by cases such as General Motors' reversal of its decision to sell its European Opel division to Russia in the fall of 2009. Putin was reported to comment at the time that "we will have to take into account this style of dealing with partners in the future."[18]

Putin's view of the United States and its more ardent Western Allies also was not improved by the Russia-Ukraine natural gas crisis of January 2009, which once again resulted in the cutoff of key energy deliveries to much of Europe during the coldest time of the year. When Moscow and Kyiv were once again unable to agree on prices for natural gas supplied to Ukraine and transit prices through Ukraine to Europe, Russia cut off natural gas deliveries to Ukraine on January 1, 2009, and subsequently transit deliveries to Moldova and more than a dozen EU states on January 6, 2009.[19] Putin was able to reach ten-year agreements on pricing and transit with Ukrainian prime minister Iulia Timoshenko, and gas deliveries resumed on January 20. (After coming to office in 2010, President Yanukovych lodged criminal charges against Timoshenko and jailed her on the basis of these deals with Russia.)

The issue of energy security, in particular the heavy dependence of some European states on Russian energy, tended to divide both the EU and NATO along the lines of "old" and "new" Europe. The percentage of energy supplied by Russian natural gas was much higher in several Central and Eastern European states, many of which were already suspicious of and hostile to Moscow for reasons other than energy. Since the late 1990s, Washington had expressed continuing concern about overly great European reliance on Russian energy deliveries, plugging the Baku-Tbilisi-Ceyhan pipeline and other alternate energy sources. The Bush administration also had been critical of the Russo-German Nordstream pipeline project; European critics of the Kremlin such as Polish foreign minister Radek Sikorski even likened the project to the Molotov-Ribbentrop Pact.[20] From the Russian vantage point, dealings with Ukraine on natural gas pricing and transit were a constant headache after 1991, and the Kremlin saw Western criticism of its actions as discriminatory attempts to restrict Russia's legitimate commercial interests. Putin and his colleagues apparently saw only the justice of their own grievances with Ukraine, demonstrating a tin ear to European protests over cutting off natural gas supplies in the dead of winter and turning a blind eye to the incredible cronyism and corruption built into the Russia-Ukraine commercial natural gas relationship.[21]

Putin's response to what he saw as the discriminatory, unjust, and treacherous international order constructed and maintained by the United States and its Allies was to seek integration into alternative institutions. Both Putin and Medvedev welcomed the emergence of the G-20 in late 2008 as an apparent substitute or replacement for the G-8 and the Bretton Woods international financial institutions as the chief venue for the world's major economic powers to manage the international financial and economic systems.[22] Putin seemed especially keen on turning the BRIC (now the BRICS, after the addition of South Africa), which began as a Goldman Sachs emerging markets investment category, into a real international organization. Medvedev hosted the BRIC Summit in Yekaterinburg in the summer of 2009, and Putin has continued to promote the organization as an alternative to Western-dominated institutions.[23] In 2009, Moscow suspended its efforts of a decade and a half to join the World Trade Organization, angered by Western denunciations of its war with Georgia but even more disillusioned with what it saw as constantly moving goalposts with new or stricter requirements in conjunction with the application process.[24]

In the wake of the global economic crisis and the war with Georgia, Putin in essence put into another gear Russia's long-standing, ongoing efforts to consolidate and increase its influence in the former Soviet area through various integration projects. Some Western observers, such as Hill and Gaddy in their study of Putin, characterize these efforts as largely defensive, designed to preserve Russian influence in the post-Soviet space against an encroaching West and to defend the Russian economy against external shocks.[25] Russian analysts, such as Dmitri Trenin or Fedor Lukyanov, argue that as early as Putin's second presidential term Russia abandoned its goal of integrating into the West, having failed to find a suitable place in the Western-built international order, and thus sought to create a "system of its own" as one of the world's major power centers.[26] Irrespective of the motives of Russian leaders (both these lines of interpretation may have considerable basis in fact), Moscow had been seeking to consolidate its influence and integrate the post-Soviet states under its wing ever since Yeltsin constructed the Commonwealth of Independent States (CIS) in late 1991. Yeltsin envisioned a far more robust role for the CIS than it ever achieved, but the organization and its institutional structures continue to function, although badly, in 2017. For example, an agreement on a CIS-wide free trade area was signed in 1994; although ostensibly still on the books, it has never been implemented.[27] Similarly, Yeltsin's attempt at a Russia-Belarus union in the late

1990s foundered on the inability of even Russian elites to stomach Lukashenko's authoritarian economic populism.

Soon after succeeding Yeltsin, Putin undertook his own post-Soviet area integration efforts, launching the Eurasian Economic Community in 2000, which aspired to create an area for free movement of goods and capital, a common transportation system, common energy market, and even a common currency.[28] This plan failed to gain any real traction with Russia's partners, especially in the sense of any meaningful economic measures, although the Eurasian Economic Community continued to provide a political platform for high-level meetings of the member states. In 2003 Putin followed up with the proposal for a Single Economic Space aimed chiefly at more closely uniting the economies of Russia, Belarus, Kazakhstan, and Ukraine. The Orange Revolution effectively ended any interest Kyiv might have shown in the project, but even Yanukovych after 2010 demonstrated little receptiveness when the proposal was revived by Moscow. Following suspension of Russia's bid to join the World Trade Organization, Moscow came up with its Customs Union with Belarus and Kazakhstan, duly established in 2010, with the thought of eventually adding Ukraine to the trio.[29]

Putin also attempted to promote security cooperation and integration within the post-Soviet area. The CIS originally envisioned (at least in the Russian imagination) considerable common security agencies and activities, but most of the post-Soviet states quickly attempted to free themselves of any Russian military or security presence, and cooperation remained more declarative than actual. The security content of the CIS was to be provided in particular by the Collective Security Treaty, signed in Tashkent on May 15, 1992, by Armenia, Belarus, Kazakhstan, Kyrgyzstan, Russia, Tajikistan, and Uzbekistan. (Azerbaijan and Georgia acceded to the treaty in 1993; Uzbekistan withdrew in 1999, as did Azerbaijan and Georgia.)[30] Putin sought to replace security cooperation and integration efforts through the CIS with an institution modeled on NATO and based on the Collective Security Treaty. Thus, in 2002, the Collective Security Treaty Organization (CSTO) was established, recognized by the UN in 2004, and sought cooperation with other international security organizations. The CSTO Secretariat and especially the military structures of the organization have been and remain heavily dominated by Russia, and NATO has declined all CSTO overtures for dialogue or cooperation.[31]

Russia's Central Asian neighbors showed more interest in another integration project, the Shanghai Cooperation Organization (SCO), which emerged out of the so-called Shanghai Five group in 2001.[32] The SCO was more congenial for the smaller members because it included both Russia and China, enabling the other members to balance between the two major powers. The major security goals of the SCO focused on antiterrorism, separatism, and "extremism" in the region, reflecting especially China's major concerns. In time, the SCO also developed considerable economic content and has added a number of observers—including Afghanistan, Iran, and Mongolia—and "dialogue partners." In July 2015, the SCO decided to include India and Pakistan as full members, a process that was completed at the June 2017 SCO summit. The SCO conducts regular military counterterrorist exercises but is not a formal military alliance as are NATO and the CSTO. As Russia's political relations and economic ties with China have become closer, the SCO has gained increasing importance in the Russian diplomatic toolkit. However, in terms of European security affairs, the CSTO remains Moscow's chosen multilateral security equivalent to the EU and especially to NATO.

Russian security policy vis-à-vis Europe during Medvedev's presidency was dominated by three major lines of development. First, the Obama administration's reset led to a reconstruction of bilateral US-Russian relations, an initiative that was not motivated solely by considerations involving Europe but that had significant effects on European security affairs. Second, Russia and the EU, increasingly led by Germany, attempted to fashion a more cooperative working relationship, exemplified by Merkel's Meseberg Initiative, which involved giving Russia greater access in policy deliberations with the EU in return for Russian cooperation in resolving outstanding security issues such as the Transdniestrian conflict in Moldova (see above). EU-Russian relations eventually foundered over the simultaneous attempt by Brussels to deepen its ties with Russia's immediate neighbors through the Eastern Partnership. Third, Moscow attempted to overcome what it saw as the structural and political flaws of a security architecture dominated by NATO (and a weak OSCE) through a proposal from Medvedev for a comprehensive European security treaty. Medvedev's proposal was duly welcomed by European and North American heads of state, and then sidetracked and buried in the OSCE's Corfu Process.

None of these initiatives enjoyed long-term success except, perhaps, the US-Russian reset, and even there the results are at best mixed. It is clear, however, that Russia's foreign interlocutors took Medvedev seriously as president and in many cases attempted to engage him in serious business. Medvedev had a similar record in Russian domestic affairs during his presidential term, with alluring statements critical of Russian reality and promising reform, but with generally modest to disappointing concrete actions and results. Despite his skimpy record of achievement, Medvedev's tenure had an important effect on a crucial segment of the Russian public, the emerging urban middle and professional classes that saw in him the prospect of change, reform, and modernization in Russia. In the end, the paucity of substantive achievements and the manner in which he left the presidency after arousing such hopes may have had a greater effect in Russia than anything he accomplished from his Kremlin office.[33]

# ONE MORE TRY: THE RESET

The failure of Secretary of State Hillary Clinton's State Department staff to recognize the difference between *perezagruzka* and *peregruzka* — "reset" versus "overload" — is an appropriate metaphor for the story of US-Russian relations in the Obama-Medvedev era.[34] It is certainly difficult to fault President Obama and his national security team for recognizing that Washington's relations with Moscow had deteriorated to a dangerously great degree, reduced to mutual recrimination and polemics by the end of George W. Bush's presidency. As Vice President Biden explained, the motivation for the initiative and the choice of the term "reset" was not necessarily for either Washington or Moscow to change or disown existing or previous policies or actions but to put aside the resentments and recriminations that had accumulated during the preceding years and to make a fresh start, much like one resets a computer to begin a task anew.

From the American point of view, a reset of relations with Russia made a great deal of sense. Washington had a global list of regional and functional issues on which cooperation with Moscow was essential: the war in Afghanistan; international terrorism, especially in the Middle East and South Asia; and nuclear nonproliferation, in particular the Iranian and North Korean nuclear programs. The existing US-Russian strategic arms limitation treaty was due to expire at the end of 2009. Although there was little reason to think that either country contemplated a drastic increase in its nuclear weapons or delivery systems, if no action were taken before the end of the year, there would no longer be any legal basis for inspection of either side's strategic arsenals, a potential real loss of transparency and confidence. There was also the long-standing issue of possible cooperation on civilian nuclear energy, never fully realized despite years of talks on the subject between Moscow and Washington. The possibility of resupplying US and NATO forces in Afghanistan through Russia and the former Soviet Union — the so-called Northern Distribution Network — took on added importance as delivery of supplies through Pakistan became increasingly difficult and dangerous. Moscow's assistance to the Western effort in Afghanistan through the Northern Distribution Network demonstrated the willingness of Russian leaders to put aside recriminations when they saw their own regional interests at stake. Ongoing cooperation in space, the United States' purchase of Russian heavy booster rocket engines, Russian contributions to Boeing's new 787 Dreamliner, and other technical and commercial projects all militated in favor of better relations.

Many of the issues that troubled US-Russian relations during the George W. Bush years did not seem to be a problem for Obama and his advisers. The Obama administration significantly toned down criticism of reported human rights abuses in Russia, continuing encroachments on democratic institutions and political pluralism, and Moscow's relations with its neighbors in the near abroad and Central Europe. The new president's apparently accommodating attitude toward Russia was so alarming to many in the region that in July 2009 twenty-two prominent intellectuals and former leaders from Eastern Europe, including former Czech president Václav Havel and former Polish presidents Lech Wałęsa and Aleksander Kwaśniewski, addressed an open letter to Obama calling for greater attention to the threat from a "revisionist Russia."[35]

President Obama's major objectives in resetting the relationship with Russia concerned bilateral and global issues. Most did not directly or primarily bear on European security. The centerpiece of the reset was the negotiation that produced the New START. Presidents Medvedev and Obama agreed to launch strategic arms talks during the latter's July 2009 visit to Moscow.[36] After fast-paced, stressful negotiations, the two presidents signed the treaty in Prague in April 2010, an extremely fast result for such a complex subject. New START lowered the limits for deployed strategic nuclear warheads of each side from 2,200 to 1,550 and included a broad set of verification measures that maintained the regimes of mutual confidence and transparency established with the original START. The pact was ratified by the Russian State Duma and the US Senate and formally entered into force in 2011.

New START was both a throwback to the major arms control negotiations that helped end the Cold War and a reflection of President Obama's dedication to the elimination of nuclear weapons, reminiscent of the similar desire of President Ronald Reagan, who helped with the first of those landmark arms control breakthroughs that ended the US-Soviet rivalry. During the negotiation process, Obama developed a close working relationship with President Medvedev, and it was his personal involvement that overcame the most significant disagreement between the two sides, missile defense.[37] Obama also demonstrated his deep personal concern for nuclear issues in hosting the April 2010 Washington Nuclear Summit, held under the auspices of the 2004 Global Threat Reduction Initiative. At this conference, the United States and Russia agreed to dispose of 68 metric tons of weapons grade plutonium, and the other countries participating in the summit agreed to work with the International Atomic Energy Agency to dispose of significant excess highly enriched uranium. Finally, the Obama administration was able to bring negotiations that had dragged on for years between Washington and Moscow on a civilian nuclear cooperation agreement (named after section 123 of the US Atomic Energy Act) to a successful conclusion, thereby establishing the two as the chief global partners in almost all aspects of nuclear safety and security.

The biggest stumbling block in the New START negotiations was also of the most immediate concern for European security—missile defense.[38] During the talks, Moscow insisted that reductions in strategic warheads and delivery systems must be linked to restrictions on development and deployment of US missile defense systems. A sufficient number of US senators to prevent ratification of the treaty were adamantly opposed to any such linkage or restriction on missile defense. US plans to deploy radars in the Czech Republic and interceptors in Poland made the issue an immediate concern. At his July 2009 meeting with Medvedev in Moscow, Obama promised to review the Bush administration's missile defense plans for Europe. Less than two months later, the new American president announced significant changes to these plans, with initial deployments on ships in the Mediterranean and land-based systems to follow much later. Republicans in the Senate, the Czech and Polish governments, and a number of other Eastern European leaders, harshly criticized the decision. However, Moscow, German chancellor Merkel, and NATO secretary-general Anders Fogh Rasmussen welcomed the move, and Washington pushed during the next two years to include first NATO and then Russia in a cooperative missile defense program.

The history of the missile defense negotiations, and in particular the decision to cancel the projected deployments in the Czech Republic and Poland, reflect the diminished importance of Europe for the Obama administration in comparison with the attention and significance accorded the region by previous presidents. Obama came into office committed to winding down the wars in Iraq and Afghanistan, and by 2010 announced a "pivot" or "rebalance" to Asia, involving the transfer of greater political attention and military resources to the region.[39] In addition to its intrinsic significance as the world's second nuclear power, Russia was of particular importance in this set of priorities for the support it could provide in continuing and gradually curtailing the effort in Afghanistan, as well as possible cooperation on other regional issues. Obama did not ignore Europe, but in contrast to the George W. Bush administration, the first Obama administration did not press Moscow on either its relations with the former Warsaw Pact satellites in Eastern Europe or its involvement in its former Soviet neighbors in the near abroad, such as Georgia, Moldova, or Ukraine.

## THE MEDVEDEV EUROPEAN SECURITY TREATY INITIATIVE

In terms of European security policy and the Euro-Atlantic security architecture, the Medvedev presidency took up where Putin had left off in his bitter complaint about NATO and the United States in Munich in February 2007.

Medvedev continued the quest to overcome what he portrayed as structural obstacles and outmoded attitudes of some interlocutors to gain Russia its rightful place as an equal partner in managing European security affairs by proposing a comprehensive treaty on European security. Medvedev's first initiative came after the April 2008 NATO Bucharest Summit and before the war with Georgia, but he then continued to push the proposal with surprisingly little change in content after that conflict. Although Medvedev clearly had some of his personal prestige invested in the initiative, it appeared to be coordinated among a number of senior foreign policy and security officials within the government, as indicated by the concurrent adoption of a new Russian foreign policy concept in July 2008 and subsequent statements of figures such as Foreign Minister Lavrov and Ambassador to NATO Dmitry Rogozin. Although his position as prime minister did not give him a formal role in foreign and security policy, Putin found ample opportunity to make clear that Medvedev's proposal was consistent with his views on how the European security order should be restructured.[40]

Medvedev's initiative struck a responsive chord in important circles in the West. Both Germany and France, the two Allies most dubious of the American push at Bucharest for NATO membership for Ukraine and Georgia, demonstrated obvious sympathy with the general direction, if not the particulars of the Russian initiative. However, Washington and many European Allies — especially those located closer to Russia — were suspicious of Moscow's motives and focused on the obvious downsides of the Russian proposal. Discussion of the Medvedev initiative was channeled into the OSCE and merged with an overall consideration of strengthening and reforming the OSCE, a development that Moscow proved unable to resist. The Russians nevertheless gained considerable understanding and a number of Western sympathizers with the substance of their analysis and complaints about the European security architecture, but they took an extremely long time to come up with a specific proposal. When Moscow finally tabled drafts of a comprehensive European security treaty in November 2009, the documents were so clumsy and simplistic that it was easy for Western critics to pick them apart and bury them in a process of endless debate.

On June 5, 2008, newly inaugurated Russian president Dmitry Medvedev spoke on bilateral relations and security issues to an audience of German political, parliamentary, and civic leaders in Berlin. The venue and subject matter had apparently been coordinated by Moscow with the German administration in the hope of finding "a new form of coexistence" between Russia and the major Euro-Atlantic security organizations, presumably NATO and the EU.[41] Medvedev's speech was a direct plea for Russia's full integration into Europe, asserting that "we cannot resolve Europe's problems until we achieve . . . an organic unity between all of its integral components, including the Russian

Federation."[42] Referring to Russia, the EU, and North America as three branches of European civilization, Medvedev claimed that Russia's return to Europe after its self-isolation of almost a century has been blocked by NATO, the concrete representation of the outdated Cold War principle of Atlanticism. The Russian president called for unity of the entire Euro-Atlantic area from Vancouver to Vladivostok and advocated for building a "genuine greater Europe." Alluding to the motivation behind the failed 1928 Kellogg-Briand Pact, Medvedev proposed that a general European summit begin drafting a regional security pact based on the principles of the UN Charter.

The Russo-Georgian war came before there was much chance for substantive international response to Medvedev's Berlin speech, but he returned to the subject in an address to a conference on world politics at Evian, France, on October 8, 2008.[43] At Evian, Medvedev enumerated Moscow's specific grievances with the West, in particular the United States, such as US unilateral military actions, NATO expansion, unilateral recognition of Kosovo's independence, and construction of military bases, including missile defense installations, close to Russia's borders. Fresh from the G-20 meeting in Washington on the global economic crisis, Medvedev expanded the scope of his remarks to include US economic unilateralism and the failings of the world financial order. On security, he pointed to the recent war in the Caucasus as evidence of the need for a new European security order based on a treaty that would enforce the principles of the UN Charter (fulfillment of international law and respect for sovereignty and territorial integrity of states), reject the use of force, and guarantee equal security, in particular, "no development of military alliances that would threaten the security of other parties to the Treaty." Seizing the opportunity, Medvedev praised the role of President Nicolas Sarkozy and the EU in mediating the cease-fire in Georgia and charged that the "NATO-centric" approach to European security had shown its weakness.

Moscow remained short on specifics about the Medvedev security treaty initiative but nonetheless conducted an energetic campaign in support of the idea. In a speech to Russian ambassadors in July 2008, Medvedev touted the newly adopted Foreign Policy Concept, which called for a new system of collective security in Europe that would properly recognize Russia's status as a great power.[44] On July 28, just before the war with Georgia, Russian ambassador to NATO Dmitry Rogozin explained the Medvedev proposal at a NATO-Russia Council meeting and denied the aim was to weaken NATO or the OSCE.[45] At the EU-Russia Summit in Nice in mid-November, Medvedev wangled support from his French counterpart, who agreed with the idea of convening a European conference in mid-2009, perhaps in the framework of the OSCE, to consider Medvedev's proposal.[46] At the December 2008 OSCE Ministerial Council in

Helsinki, Foreign Minister Lavrov continued Moscow's lobbying for a special summit of the OSCE, the CIS, the EU, the CSTO, and NATO to launch negotiations aimed at reaching such a treaty.[47]

Much to Lavrov's frustration, there was not sufficient support at the Helsinki Ministerial Meeting to support Sarkozy's proposal to convoke a special summit on the Medvedev initiative in mid-2009. Instead, at an informal lunch the OSCE ministers agreed that "the OSCE is the most suitable venue for these discussions."[48] The incoming Greek OSCE Chair then took up the idea and organized a special Ministerial Meeting in June 2009 on the island of Corfu to discuss the proposal, which produced a decision to continue broad, informal discussions in Vienna at the ambassadorial level seeking a "more structured dialogue."[49] During the rest of the year, the Greek Chair organized a series of discussion meetings that covered the entire agenda of the OSCE, not what the Russians originally had in mind. According to many participants in the process, a number of major Western powers favored the OSCE as the natural forum for a general discussion of the future of European security, including Medvedev's proposed treaty, because the venue could provide recognition of the Russian initiative without obligating other OSCE participating states.[50]

Medvedev continued to push the idea, in particular in a speech at Helsinki University in April 2009.[51] Sensitive to the venue, Medvedev gave special tribute to the OSCE, but he nonetheless made clear that what he had in mind was not reinvigoration of that organization so much as a treaty-based umbrella over all European security organizations. Meanwhile, at home Medvedev had some of Russia's liberal foreign policy thinkers hard at work on the general subject, a project that resulted in the Russian Institute of Contemporary Development's April 2009 report, *The Architecture of Euro-Atlantic Security*.[52] This report presents a comprehensive review of European security organizations—including the OSCE, the EU, NATO, the Council of Europe, the CIS, and the CSTO—and major arms control, hard security, and human rights regimes and obligations in Europe. Although clearly in agreement with Medvedev's assertion that the European security architecture is flawed and in need of fundamental reform, the authors present relatively calm and balanced analysis. Given that Igor Yurgens, the head of the Russian Institute of Contemporary Development, and the team he assembled were among the most internationalist and pro-Western thinkers in Russia's foreign policy elite, the document reflects the depth of dissatisfaction in Russia and disillusionment with the West.

Notwithstanding the criticisms of the current European security order, NATO, and the United States, the report also reflects continuing aspirations of Russia under Medvedev for European integration: "The authors base their judgments on the assumption that Russia is fundamentally—that is, historically, socially, culturally, economically, and intellectually—an integral part of Europe and its security space. It is in our common interest to integrate Russia as much as possible into this space on the basis of shared principles and values."[53]

When Russian representatives presented the draft text of a proposed treaty, it was both an anticlimax and a letdown. On November 29, 2009, just five days before the OSCE's Ministerial Council meeting in Athens, the Kremlin released on its website the draft of a Treaty on European Security.[54] On December 4, 2009, Foreign Minister Lavrov presented a similar draft agreement between Russia and NATO member states, which was not made public, at the Ministerial Meeting of the NATO-Russia Council.[55] The public version of the treaty declared its guidance by the UN Charter, the Helsinki Final Act, the Manila Declaration on the Peaceful Settlement of International Disputes, and the Charter for European Security. The pact was open to all states of the "Euro-Atlantic and Eurasian space from Vancouver to Vladivostok," as well as to the EU, the OSCE, the CSTO, NATO, and the CIS.[56]

The draft treaty obligates all parties to take into account the interests of other parties in taking "any security measures," and not to take any actions "significantly affecting the security" of any other party to the pact. The draft does not further define these terms, such as "security," "threat," or "significantly affecting." Any party to the treaty has the right to request information from any other party on "any significant legislative, administrative, or organizational measures" that it deems may affect its security. The pact provides a three-tiered set of responses: consultations among the parties, a conference of the parties, and an extraordinary conference of the parties. Any two states-parties to the treaty may require a conference. An extraordinary conference is envisioned in the case of armed attack (or presumably other such emergencies). The conference and extraordinary conference set their own rules; neither mechanism removes the right to self-defense under Article 51 of the UN Charter. A conference must be attended by two-thirds of the parties to the treaty, and decisions are to be by consensus; an extraordinary conference must be attended by four-fifths of the parties to the treaty, and decisions are to be taken "by unanimous vote."

Medvedev's proposed European security treaty is clearly a preventive, restraining document, designed to restrict the freedom of other Euro-Atlantic actors from undertaking actions or activities of which Russia did not approve. The draft pact chose selectively from the accumulated precedents and obligations under the UN and OSCE auspices, such as refrain from the use of force to resolve disputes and the right to inquire about the domestic actions of a state if those actions might seem to affect other states. Critics immediately noted that the initiative seemed to be an attempt to put a limiting umbrella over NATO and the EU, and it also equated these organizations with the clearly not equivalent CSTO and CIS.[57] The draft provides almost solely for management of disputes or conflicts and does not envision or include any provisions for promoting cooperation, increasing transparency, strengthening trust, or reducing tensions.[58] Perhaps most egregious was the complete absence in the Medvedev draft of the normative, humanitarian, and human rights content of the UN and OSCE documents to which it referred.

The Medvedev draft European security treaty reveals significant elements of continuity in the Soviet and Russian approaches to European security. First, the draft is as much declaratory as functional; it is difficult to see what the pact would do beyond adding venues for discussions and statements should one of the states-parties engage in truly threatening behavior. Second, the desire for a comprehensive European security treaty order clearly dates back at least to Soviet foreign minister Vyacheslav Molotov's 1954 call for a European security conference, which eventually became the CSCE.[59] One senior European politician and diplomat even traced the Russian initiative back to Prince Adam Czartoryski's 1803 memorandum to Emperor Aleksandr I suggesting establishment of an international order guaranteed by the European great powers.[60] Indeed, many non-Russian diplomats and analysts attributed the Medvedev proposal to Russia's aspirations to restore its pre–Cold War great power status and to retain (as Medvedev put it in August 2008) its "sphere of privileged interests" in the near abroad.[61] With proposals at Budapest in 1994 and Lisbon in 1996, Moscow had tried to fashion a European security council within which it would be a key member, within the OSCE. The negotiations leading up to the 1999 Charter on European Security also reflected this Russian ambition.[62]

Having failed in their aspiration in the 1990s to make the OSCE *the* primary European security organization, Russian leaders were attempting in the 2000s via the Medvedev proposal to establish a new mechanism they hoped would serve the same purpose they had desired for the OSCE—to regulate and limit the freedom of action of other key actors in Europe, in particular the United States, NATO, and the EU. At the same time, many Russian officials apparently hoped the new pact might rid them of many of the humanitarian, human rights obligations the Western OSCE participating states considered so crucial. In private, some Russian interlocutors confided that they were not sure that their country would be willing to accept all of the provisions of the Helsinki Final Act should that document be renegotiated today.[63] As Putin demonstrated in his 2007 speech in Munich, many Russians had come to consider the OSCE primarily as a forum and instrument used by the West to attack and weaken Russia through "color revolutions," democracy promotion, election monitoring, and the like. What they desired was a treaty-based international organization or regime that allowed Russia to protect its sphere of influence without outside interference.

The Western response did little to alter this markedly negative Russian view of its major Western interlocutors. Secretary of State Clinton responded to the Russian draft by asserting that the United States shared Russia's desire for a secure Europe but considered that this goal could best be pursued through existing institutions such as the OSCE or the NATO-Russia Council rather than with new treaties.[64] Major EU states such as Germany, France, and Italy may have been inclined to give the Russian proposal a slightly more sympathetic hearing, but the December 2009 Athens OSCE Ministerial Council meeting revealed a basic difference of approach between Russia and most of the other participating states. The Greek OSCE Chair presumed that the Corfu Process, begun in the summer of 2009, was a response to the Medvedev proposal. Lavrov's statements and conduct at the Athens Ministerial made clear that for Russia the Corfu Process was mainly about OSCE reform and was not a sufficient response to the proposed security treaty.[65] At Athens, the OSCE foreign ministers welcomed the establishment of the Corfu Process, mandated that it be continued in 2010 by their ambassadors in Vienna, and instructed that it consider, among other things, "the concept of comprehensive, co-operative and indivisible security, as enshrined in the OSCE fundamental documents [and] . . . OSCE norms, principles and commitments in all three OSCE dimensions, in full and in good faith, and in a consistent manner by all."[66]

For the Russian leaders, choosing the OSCE as the venue for discussing the draft European security treaty simply repeated their experience in the 1990s. Moscow sought a geopolitical pact on hard security that would restrain the United States and NATO and instead wound up with a comprehensive agreement with numerous intrusive provisions on governance and human rights. Lavrov's conversation a year earlier in Helsinki made clear the Russian desire to focus on hard security.[67] It is not clear whether Russian officials considered their Western interlocutors intentionally antagonistic to Moscow's professed desire for greater security or simply hopelessly dedicated to goals and standards that Russia did not share. In any case, the Russians never formally submitted any draft of the treaty for negotiations within the OSCE, and the Corfu Process ended up yet another disappointment for Moscow with the Helsinki framework.

A dispassionate observer might inquire why a large and important country such as Russia experienced such difficulty in persuading its major interlocutors to consider its stated interests seriously, and why these interlocutors appeared to mistrust and dismiss Russian initiatives. The fate of the Treaty on Conventional Armed Forces in Europe (CFE) regime serves as an instructive microcosm illustrating the growing gap between the two sides in the Euro-Atlantic community. At the OSCE annual security review conference in June 2009, Foreign Minister Lavrov presented a lengthy diatribe over the failure of NATO states to ratify the Adapted CFE Treaty because of "invented pretexts."[68] As part of the overall reset policy, by early 2010 the United States launched first consultations with its NATO Allies, and with Russia, on what might be done to revive the CFE regime

(Russia had suspended participation in verification and data-sharing activities in late 2007) and to ratify the Adapted Treaty.[69] The initiative failed due to Russian insistence that its Western partners ratify the Adapted Treaty, and the United States and its Allies demand that Russia respect the principle of host nation consent in the new pact and complete its withdrawal of military forces from Georgia and Moldova as agreed on at Istanbul in 1999. The complete inability of either side to find a practical resolution of the specific disagreement over a relatively small number of troops in two small states graphically illustrated the depth of disagreement and distrust that had grown up in relations between Moscow and its major Western partners. When taken in isolation, Russia's position of principle on its right to have a real vote (not just a voice) in European security affairs and the principled defense by many Western states of the independence and sovereignty of Russia's smaller neighbors are each equally defensible. However, neither Russia nor the West could manage to realize both of these principled objectives within the existing institutions of the European security order.

The Medvedev security treaty proposal and the Corfu Process ended up getting entangled with Kazakhstan's long-awaited, controversial OSCE Chairmanship and President Nursultan Nazarbayev's ambitions to host a summit during his country's year in charge of the OSCE. Kazakhstan's bid to chair the OSCE dated back to 2005, the time when Moscow was actively soliciting the support of its CIS and CSTO partners for its demands to reform the structures and rules of procedure of the OSCE. Many Western states, in particular the United States, opposed Astana's bid to head the organization until and unless it improved its own dismal human rights record. The issue, yet another divisive question on the extensive agenda of disputes between Russia and the West within the OSCE, was finally settled at the Madrid Ministerial Council meeting in December 2007. It was agreed that Kazakhstan would hold the OSCE Chairmanship in 2010, a year later than the original bid, in between the Chairmanships of Greece and Lithuania.[70] To obtain the Chairmanship, Kazakhstan promised to continue its own process of domestic reform and, in the OSCE, to continue to give priority attention to the human dimension, including participation by NGOs and preserving the OSCE's Office for Democratic Institutions and Human Rights with its present mandate.[71] This last point especially irked the Russians, who had been pressing criticism of this OSCE office and demands for its reform.

The Kazakhs assumed the OSCE Chairmanship against a backdrop of gridlock, acrimony, and mutual suspicions. The Greek Chairmanship's major accomplishment in 2009 had been the launch of the Corfu Process, which by the end of the year did not seem to be going anywhere. In the aftermath of the Russia-Georgia war, no progress was achieved in the settlement processes managed by the OSCE for any of the protracted conflicts in the former Soviet space. In the words of one longtime European analyst: "Those who have observed the

OSCE for a long time now know that the disappointment, if not the disenchantment, of some participating States stems from the perception that the security situation changed to their disadvantage and those who do not share the same perception do not even want to discuss this matter. This demonstrates that cooperative security has declined in the OSCE. Without regaining it, the OSCE will face similar troubles [to those] it experienced during the last decade or so."[72] Russia's most prominent action in the OSCE during 2009 was Lavrov's speech at the annual Security Review Conference in Vienna in June, in which (in addition to complaining about the CFE) he touted Medvedev's security treaty initiative.[73] The United States and its Allies focused on Lavrov's assertion in the address that NATO should have been abolished along with the Warsaw Pact and dismissed the speech as yet another instance of unconstructive Russian whining.

In this context, the Kazakhs' proposal to hold an OSCE summit in Astana during their Chairmanship was greeted with considerable skepticism. The Western attitude may have been best summed up by NATO's new secretary-general, Anders Fogh Rasmussen, while visiting Moscow in December 2009: "I don't see a need for new treaties or new legally binding documents because we do have a framework already."[74] However, Kazakh president Nazarbayev apparently made a favorable impression on President Obama on the margins of the April 2010 nuclear summit in Washington, and the Kazakh Chair's performance during the April 2010 crisis and change of government in Kyrgyzstan also apparently made a good impression on many Western interlocutors.[75] Kazakhstan also put Russia in an extremely awkward position by tying the proposal for a summit to the Corfu Process, and thus indirectly to the Medvedev initiative. In July 2010 the Kazakhs copied the Greek example, holding an informal Ministerial Council meeting in Almaty where a consensus was reached to hold a summit in Astana at the end of the year.[76] Although Moscow could hardly avoid joining the consensus in favor of its Kazakh ally, Russian leaders were clearly not pleased with the broad definition of the agenda as "the future of European security" rather than their proposed European security treaty.[77]

After all the buildup and debate on whether an important regional power with a poor human rights record such as Kazakhstan could or should hold the OSCE Chairmanship, the Astana Summit was an anticlimax.[78] In terms of protocol, the gathering was a success for the Kazakhs; more than half the OSCE participating states were represented by their heads of state and/or government. Although these high representatives of their countries gave laudatory speeches in the plenary hall, the meeting almost broke down due to disagreements over the content of the summit document. In the preparatory work for the summit, the final declaration was to include an "action plan" for addressing existing conflicts and major threats that were identified. At the summit, it proved impossible to bridge existing differences over Abkhazia, South Ossetia, Nagorno-Karabakh, and Transdniestria, and the proposal to include an action plan in the summit statement was dropped, much to the regret of Moldova and Georgia. Consequently, the eventual declaration included largely references to past commitments and general statements of aspirations for future cooperation.[79] The Astana document reaffirms the most important (at least from the Western point of view) OSCE documents, such as the Helsinki Final Act and the Charter of Paris, and explicitly notes the principle first explicitly iterated at Moscow in 1991 that "commitments undertaken in the field of the human dimension are matters of direct and legitimate concern to all participating States and do not belong exclusively to the internal affairs of the State concerned." The Astana declaration also includes a paragraph on conventional arms control, including a call to overcome existing difficulties in the CFE regime. The Corfu Process, however, is mentioned only in the eleventh paragraph of the document, and the text calls for realization of the "vision of a comprehensive, co-operative, and indivisible security community throughout our shared OSCE area," with no reference to the Medvedev security treaty proposal.

The result of the Astana Summit, though nowhere near as disastrous for human rights or the existing structures of the OSCE as some Western critics had feared, was very far from what the Russians envisioned when President Medvedev first advanced the idea of a new treaty-based comprehensive security regime for the Euro-Atlantic area. In his remarks at Astana, Medvedev wished the OSCE well, but Russian disappointment with the result was palpable.[80] Even though the host was a close ally and integral part of Russia's budding Eurasian integration projects, Moscow could not bear to make the significant political compromises on one or more of the protracted conflicts that could have given the summit a real political result. Instead, the Astana declaration instructed the incoming Lithuanian Chairmanship to carry on the existing formats for dialogue, including the Corfu Process. In reality, this was an initiative that was going nowhere. Having failed to get what it considered serious consideration of the Medvedev proposal, Russia would increasingly scorn and starve the OSCE and seek alternatives to the existing Euro-Atlantic security architecture.

## THE EU COMES OF AGE:
## FROM LISBON TO MESEBERG

The European Union completed the process of deepening its institutionalization, which it had launched at the beginning of the decade, after concessions by European leaders to the Czech Republic's recalcitrant president, Václav Klaus, permitted the Lisbon Treaty to enter into force on December 1, 2009.[81] The Lisbon Treaty established the post of full-time European Council president, and retained the system of rotating six-month national presidencies. The treaty also accorded the European Parliament greater powers, including greater participation and authority in foreign and security affairs. Most important for security policy, however, the pact transformed the post of high representative held since its inception by Javier Solana into a full-fledged EU foreign minister. The name remained similar—high representative for foreign and security policy—but the incumbent chaired a newly established Foreign Affairs Council, served as vice president of the European Commission with responsibility for foreign affairs, and directed a newly established European External Affairs Service, with a staff of several thousand diplomats.

The Lisbon Treaty also contains important though often overlooked security provisions. The pact completed the process of merging (and thus disappearing) the Western European Union into the EU and included a mutual assistance clause, based on Article V of the Western European Union Treaty, that calls on EU member states to come to the assistance of another member state that may become the victim of armed aggression.[82] The clause also contains the caveat that "commitments and cooperation in this area shall be consistent with commitments under the North Atlantic Treaty Organisation, which, for those States which are members of it, remains the foundation of their collective defence and the forum for its implementation."[83] The Lisbon Treaty established a system of "permanent structured cooperation" for defense and security tasks conducted under the direction of the high representative, designed to encourage enhancement of EU states' military capabilities and enable the EU to play a more assertive security role. Finally, the Lisbon pact expanded the so-called Petersberg Tasks to include "joint disarmament operations, humanitarian and rescue tasks, military advice and assistance tasks, conflict prevention and peacekeeping tasks, tasks of combat forces in crisis management, including peacemaking and postconflict stabilisation. All these tasks may contribute to the fight against terrorism, including by supporting third countries in combating terrorism in their territories."[84]

Appointment of the new EU officials and the working of the new institutions was—unsurprisingly—deeply entangled with and complicated by European politics. German chancellor Merkel and French president Sarkozy were perceived to exert decisive influence over the process, in which the relatively unknown Belgian prime minister Herman Van Rompuy was chosen as the first European Council president. Portugal's Jose Manuel Barroso remained as European Commission president, and the United Kingdom's inexperienced Catherine Ashton became the first post-Lisbon high representative.[85] These appointments, as others in the EU before and after, reflected a balance between left- and right-wing parties, small and large member states, and geographical distribution. As it turned out, Ashton's relative inexperience may have initially negated some of the structural advantages gained in the Lisbon provisions that eliminated much of the duplication of authority in the management of EU external relations. In any event, the changes introduced by Lisbon did not eliminate the national disagreements over foreign and security policy between EU member states. Because almost all decisions in these fields were still to be made by consensus, rather than qualified majority, one of the biggest obstacles to unified EU foreign and security policy remained.

Even before ratification of the Lisbon Treaty, the EU assumed an ever-increasing civilian and military security role in Europe, Africa, and the Middle East. The EU Rule of Law Mission in Kosovo (known as EULEX) formally began implementation of its mandate in December 2008, although it had begun to take over from the earlier UN mission by the middle of the year.[86] The EU Monitoring Mission in Georgia (known as EUMM) deployed in September 2008, almost immediately after hostilities ended between Russia and Georgia.[87] In December 2008, the EU began its first naval mission, Atalanta, promoted particularly by France, to fight piracy in the Gulf of Aden.[88] From 2008 to 2010, EU military forces deployed for training and stabilization missions in Chad, Guinea-Bissau, and Somalia, in addition to an ongoing civilian political mission in the Democratic Republic of Congo.[89] Although one might argue about the type and size of its military capabilities, it was indisputable by the time the Lisbon Treaty entered into force that the EU was clearly pursuing an activist foreign and security policy, well outside its own territory, clearly consistent with the strategy iterated in 2003 of promoting stability on its periphery.

As the Lisbon Treaty was being ratified, the leaders of the major EU states also appeared to be arriving at a new, more activist and muscular understanding of Europe's political and military role in the Euro-Atlantic security order. First, over the course of the first decade of the new century, Germany demonstrated increasing acceptance of its potential power and willingness to engage in military missions well beyond its borders.[90] Particularly striking was Germany's progression from Schröder's denunciation of the US invasion of Iraq in 2003 to Merkel's 2006 reconstitution of the German military's force structure and Germany's command role in the International Security Assistance Force. Second, after a major redefinition of national security strategy in a white paper issued in the summer of 2008, France returned to NATO's integrated military command and military structures after an absence of forty-three years.[91] Although the move by President Sarkozy was seen by many as largely symbolic because France had been making major contributions to NATO military operations since Bosnia in the early 1990s, Paris's full participation in the Alliance had important political effects and significance. Third, even though the

United Kingdom's most European of prime ministers, Tony Blair, was replaced by Gordon Brown, the United Kingdom remained strongly supportive of the development of the European Security and Defence Policy / Common Security and Defence Policy (ESDP/CSDP), symbolized by its agreement to take command of the Atalanta mission.[92] Finally, in a striking display of the solidarity that came to be known as "Merkozy," on February 3, 2009 (on the eve of the annual Munich Security Conference), Merkel and Sarkozy published a joint declaration on European security in several newspapers, in which they stated that they were "convinced that it is in our interest to make European integration and Atlantic partnership the two faces of the same security policy."[93] On paper, at least, NATO and the EU's ESDP/CSDP were now mutually reinforcing and complementary, and no longer mutually exclusive.

Although Merkel and Sarkozy seemed to personify the ideal of Franco-German cooperation within a united Europe, the dynamics of EU politics outside of the security sphere, particularly with respect to economics and finance, gradually pushed Berlin forward as the almost unchallenged first among equals in EU councils.[94] The beneficiary of reforms implemented by both the Schröder and Merkel administrations and an effective industrial policy, Germany recovered relatively quickly from the global economic crisis. France, conversely, was not as devastated by the crisis as the southern tier (Portugal, Spain, Italy, and Greece), Ireland, and some of the new Central and Eastern European member states, but France still remained in a prolonged economic slump, partially due to the crisis and partially because of structural factors. It is not part of the purpose of this study to examine in detail the structural economic and fiscal causes of the euro zone crisis or to analyze the various proposals advanced by EU countries to respond to this crisis. What is crucial for a study of European security is the fact that as a result of the crisis—to stress an assessment advanced above—Germany emerged as the most powerful actor within the EU by almost any measure. To be sure, old powers such as the United Kingdom and France still possessed power and influence, and newer actors such as Poland and Sweden were assuming more important roles, but they all increasingly depended on Berlin's agreement or acquiescence. Events also diminished the capacity of some to compete with Berlin. For example, despite unprecedented, open support from Merkel, France's economic woes led to Sarkozy's defeat at the polls in 2012. The new coalition UK government, elected in 2010 and led by the Tories, adopted a policy of economic austerity that reduced British defense and diplomatic resources and arguably either prompted or hastened a gradual withdrawal of the United Kingdom from Europe and the world.

Russia's increasing economic and political pressure on its common neighbors with the EU, and especially the 2008 Russia-Georgia war, convinced many EU officials that changes needed to be made in the European Neighborhood

Policy, which had assumed a more benign environment for building stability, especially toward the East, when it was adopted in 2004. In December 2008, the European Commission staff produced a proposed Eastern Partnership with Belarus, Ukraine, Moldova, Azerbaijan, Armenia, and Georgia, to be pursued "in parallel with the EU's strategic partnership with Russia."[95] The initiative called for deeper economic integration, closer energy cooperation, increased freedom of movement, and promotion of democracy and rule of law with the six post-Soviet states, ostensibly designed to give a "specific Eastern dimension within the European Neighborhood Policy," but clearly aimed at strengthening them to resist pressure from Moscow. Strongly supported by Sweden's Carl Bildt and Poland's Radek Sikorski, the proposal received an emphatic endorsement in February 2009 from Austria's Benita Ferraro-Waldner, the commissioner for external relations, who pointed to Russia's use of the energy weapon a month earlier as clear evidence of the need for greater EU support for these countries.[96]

The initiative called for individual bilateral cooperative projects with each of the six countries, aimed at eventually achieving Association Agreements that would cover economic integration, freer trade, visa-free travel, energy security, and closer cooperation in a number of other areas. The proposal called for summits to be held with the EU and all six countries every two years to review accomplishments and set future tasks. To launch the Eastern Partnership, the first summit was held in Prague in May 2009. The Eastern Partnership was clearly a means of offering closer cooperation and deeper integration with the EU to each country without holding out the prospect of membership. EU officials generally recognized that European publics were suffering from "enlargement fatigue," and the prospect of successful candidacy and admission of any new members in the near future was highly unlikely.[97] Although Moscow appeared to be paying more attention at the time to Medvedev's European security treaty proposal and the issue of NATO enlargement (a leftover from the Bucharest Summit and the Russia-Georgia war), Russia clearly perceived the Eastern Partnership as an attempt by the EU to extend its sway in Eastern Europe at Russia's expense. Foreign Minister Lavrov was said to respond: "What is the Eastern Partnership if not an attempt to extend the EU's sphere of influence? Is this promoting democracy, or is it blackmail?"[98] Although there were clearly other factors in Russian decisionmaking, the Eastern Partnership initiative indubitably helped convince Putin that Russia's relations with the EU were developing on a zero-sum basis, and helped push him along the path of Eurasian integration as a response and counter to the growth of the EU presence and activity in Russia's neighborhood.

The Russia-Georgia war and the Eastern Partnership slowed and complicated efforts by the EU to put its institutional relationship with Russia on a broader, sounder basis. An understanding reached at the June 2008

Khanty-Mansiysk EU-Russia Summit to negotiate a new basis for the relationship to replace the 1994 Partnership and Cooperation Agreement bogged down immediately, for obvious reasons. The Partnership for Modernization was eventually agreed on at a summit in Rostov in June 2010, covering the same "common spaces" that had constituted the bilateral agenda for some time — economy and the environment; freedom, security, and justice; external security; and research and education, including cultural aspects.[99] EU-Russia summits and other meetings grew increasingly testy, in particular because Moscow objected to EU efforts to counter or restrict Gazprom's position as a monopoly supplier of natural gas in Europe.

As Moscow's relations with Brussels grew increasingly difficult, one effort by Russia and Germany to perform an end run around the EU bureaucracy through a direct connection with Germany stands out as a graphic illustration of the widening difference in motives and goals between the two sides. In June 2010 Chancellor Merkel and President Medvedev produced a half-page memorandum at a meeting at Schloss Meseberg in Germany that purported to establish an EU-Russia mechanism for security cooperation and crisis management and to elicit Moscow's assistance in settling the Transdniestrian conflict in Moldova.[100] The memorandum proposed exploring the possible establishment of an EU-Russia Political and Security Committee, headed by Ashton and Lavrov. The Russian side presumed this committee would give them a vote (and thus possible veto) on EU security activities in the near abroad. The Germans presumed that Moscow would reciprocate by pressing the Transdniestrians to resolve the conflict; the Russians assumed that getting the stalled negotiating process going again would be sufficient from their side. As it turned out, Merkel made the proposal without prior consultation, not only with Brussels but also with her own foreign ministry. For their part, the Russians had no clear means of delivering either Tiraspol or Chisinau in order to fulfill their part of the ostensible bargain.

The Meseberg Initiative did not produce the result that either Germany or Russia envisioned in the memorandum, although it did result in greater German and EU attention to the Moldova-Transdniestria dispute, and less directly to the renewal after five years of inactivity of the "five-plus-two" political settlement negotiations. On a broader scale, the Meseberg affair illustrated the growing dilemma in EU-Russia relations and in the European security order as a whole. Germany, its EU partners, and the United States desired greater Russian cooperation in resolving the long-standing conflicts in the states from the former Soviet periphery because the unresolved disputes posed possible threats to the stability and security of an enlarged EU. The United States and the EU also desired to conduct relations with these states as fully sovereign, independent entities. Russia, on the other hand, desired to maintain its influence in this same post-Soviet periphery, and to acquire some sort of *droit de regard* on Western, EU, or NATO actions and influence in this area. The approaches of the two sides appeared increasingly incompatible, not susceptible to mutually acceptable compromise, perhaps even mutually exclusive.[101] The course toward collision in Ukraine was thus by this time largely set.

## NATO TRANSFORMS ITSELF — AGAIN

Some three months after the Bucharest Summit and a couple of weeks before war between Russia and Georgia broke out, NATO announced the hiring of an executive from the Coca-Cola Company to assist with a "branding policy for NATO."[102] In explaining the move, NATO officials noted that only a very small percentage of the population of NATO countries had any idea what the Alliance was for or deemed it necessary for security. With the failure to prevent a military attack on one of the countries promised eventual membership only months before and increasing difficulties in its major out-of-area operation in Afghanistan, NATO by early 2009 indeed seemed to face both operational and existential crises. The issue was not simply how to make the Alliance work better, or how to answer the latest wave of editorial pieces asking why NATO still existed, sixty years after its founding and twenty years after the end of the Cold War.[103] Both the character of the threats perceived by the Allies and the kind and scope of Alliance operations had changed significantly since adoption of the last Strategic Concept, NATO's raison d'être, in 1999. Open disagreements between Allies over how to respond to the Russia-Georgia war and what needed to be done in Afghanistan were clear evidence of the need for the Alliance once more to revisit its basic statement of purpose, both to resolve the discord within the Alliance and to ensure continuing support from NATO publics.

Afghanistan in early 2009 was not a pretty picture. Taliban attacks on International Security Assistance Force (ISAF) forces had grown dramatically in number, frequency, and severity.[104] The practice of some Allies that supplied forces to ISAF of placing caveats (that is, restrictions) on the use of their troops in combat created discord and resentments within the Alliance. A number of high-profile cases of collateral civilian deaths as the result of NATO combat operations both lost hearts and minds among the Afghan population and also soured some NATO publics and legislatures on the Alliance's activities in Afghanistan. Most important, the number of Allied forces in Afghanistan were simply insufficient to successfully achieve the mission goals of "clear, hold, and build" on territory held by the Taliban and training Afghan forces to take over these tasks at some time in the future.[105] In 2009, ISAF adjusted its command structure to better distinguish and manage its separate war-fighting and training activities, and newly inaugurated President Obama decided on a "surge" of 21,000 additional US troops, to be followed later in the year with 30,000 more, bringing the American military presence in Afghanistan to more than 100,000.[106] More than 10,000 additional Allied troops joined the American surge, at least giving the coalition a more reasonable chance of fulfilling its mission.

The causes for NATO's difficulties in Afghanistan were multiple, complex, and interactively related. Within both the US government and military, and NATO military and political organs, war-fighting doctrine seemed in a state of almost continuous adjustment to reflect lessons learned in the difficult campaigns in Iraq and Afghanistan. New US approaches and re-emphasis on counterinsurgency developed in Iraq were reflected in the new strategy introduced in Afghanistan by General Stanley McChrystal in 2009. The coalition experiences in both Iraq and Afghanistan relatively quickly convinced officials managing those campaigns of the impossibility of a purely military victory and the necessity of coordinating civilian political and military kinetic activities to gain lasting advantage over their adversaries. Relatively early in NATO's involvement in Afghanistan, in the run-up to the 2006 Riga Summit, Denmark and the United States launched NATO discussion of what became the Comprehensive Approach to complex operations, in essence an approach that calls for close cooperation and coordination between civilian and military conflict management operations.[107] At the 2008 Bucharest Summit, NATO leaders adopted an Action Plan for the Comprehensive Approach, and during 2009 the extensive NATO bureaucracy was busy working out how this might be implemented in NATO operations.

One of NATO's most serious difficulties was lack of resources. As US secretary of defense Robert Gates noted in 2011: "Despite more than 2 million troops in uniform—*not* counting the US military—NATO has struggled, at times desperately, to sustain a deployment of 25,000–40,000 troops, not just in boots on the ground, but in crucial support assets such as helicopters, transport aircraft, maintenance, intelligence, surveillance and reconnaissance, and much more."[108]Although NATO's Comprehensive Approach, combining military and civilian operations and resources, was much closer to the European Union's approach to conflict management than the more robust kinetic US dogma, European nations still were slow in providing either military or civilian resources to the NATO effort in Afghanistan. The disparity between NATO aspirations, on one hand, and the political will and physical ability of European Allies to augment the US contribution with commensurate military and civilian resources, on the other hand, dogged the Alliance's effort in Afghanistan from beginning to end.

One piece of good news for NATO's military capabilities and political solidarity was the return of France to the Alliance's military structures, announced on March 11, 2009, and formally accomplished at NATO's Sixtieth Anniversary Summit in Strasbourg and Kehl on April 3–4, 2009.[109] France almost returned to full participation in the Alliance under Jacques Chirac in 1996–1997, but the effort failed due to American unwillingness to accede to the French demand for the appointment of Europeans to NATO's subordinate command positions, in particular that Allied Forces Southern Europe, headquartered in Naples, be allocated to a French officer. Irrespective of France's continuing absence from the Military Committee and the formal command structure, the French made major contributions to NATO out-of-area operations in Bosnia, Kosovo, and Afghanistan. As of 2007, France was the third largest troop contributor and fourth largest financial contributor to the Alliance.[110] Although not a formal participant, Paris nonetheless maintained a substantial military contingent at both Supreme Headquarters Allied Powers Europe (known as SHAPE) in Mons and the Transformation Headquarters in Norfolk.

Upon assuming office in 2007, Sarkozy clearly put aside Chirac's deep disagreement with Bush over Iraq and in speeches in Paris and Washington in late 2007 announced his intention to bring France back fully into the Alliance.[111] At the Bucharest NATO Summit, Sarkozy upped the French troop contribution to Afghanistan, asserted the need for both NATO and a strong European defense, and won support from George Bush for his position. The 2008 French white paper and Sarkozy's understanding with Merkel brought Paris back to full participation in NATO.

France's rapprochement with NATO was brought about not so much by shifts in France or French thinking as by fundamental changes in Europe reflected in the composition and nature of both the Alliance and the EU. First, with the changes wrought by the Amsterdam and then the Lisbon treaties, in particular the merger and disappearance of the Western European Union into the EU together with the explicit connection of ESDP with NATO, it was not really possible to talk about European defense structures wholly separate from the Atlantic Alliance. Second, the enlargements of 2004 brought into both NATO and the EU a number of Central and Eastern European member states that were markedly pro-Atlanticist, if not pro-American, in their orientation. As Chirac's unhappy experience with respect to Iraq demonstrated, these new members would not "take the opportunity to be silent" and quietly follow the French lead. In the end, if France wanted to be more active in *European* defense, it had to be more active in NATO, and this was not possible without full participation in the Alliance's military structures. France's return to NATO's military structures offered the possibility for improving military planning and coordination, thus strengthening the Alliance. Ironically, by resolving the institutional competition between NATO and the EU, provoked primarily by Paris, the move also promised to remove one of the chief, if not the most important, obstacles to strengthening the European defense capability.

France arrived back in NATO's military structures just in time for yet another debate over the fundamental purpose of the Atlantic Alliance. NATO's previous statement of purpose, the 1999 Strategic Concept, basically offered a rationale for the out-of-area operations the Alliance had conducted during the 1990s in the Balkans. The document identified ethnic rivalries, internal instability, and conflict within states as the major threats. The terrorist attacks on the United States of September 2001, the involvement of Allies and the Alliance in wars in Iraq and Afghanistan, and the 2004 and 2005 bombings in Madrid and London had all brought a fundamentally different global security context with threats and operations simply unforeseen by the previous Strategic Concept. With skeptical publics and resources even harder to come by in the wake of the global economic crisis, Allies found an increasing need to come up with new, more relevant and convincing explanations of why NATO should continue to exist and to do what it was currently doing around the world, particularly in Afghanistan.

Anniversaries (especially those with a zero at the end) almost inevitably prompt reflection on the past achievements and future prospects of the person or institution celebrating the date. As NATO approached sixty, the uncertain course of the war in Afghanistan lent doubt and urgency to speculation over the future of the Alliance. Even some favorably inclined Western observers asserted that the indifferent performance and poor results in Afghanistan showed that NATO was near the end of the line.[112] Others noted that despite the seeming "make-or-break" nature of NATO involvement in Afghanistan, the Alliance's accumulated set of military standards and customary operational procedures provided bases for international interoperability that were simply too useful to be cast aside.[113] Some senior officials—notably the secretary-general, Jaap de Hoop Scheffer—remained dedicated to a global NATO that could "address security challenges at their source whenever and wherever they arise."[114] Former US national security adviser Zbigniew Brzezinski, writing on the occasion of the sixtieth anniversary, also envisioned a global security role for NATO, providing for the defense of the European core of the Alliance, continuing to help integrate Russia into a broader Europe, and helping to maintain stability among rising powers around the world.[115] Another longtime Washington analyst and Clinton National Security Council official went even further, calling for the Alliance to complete its transition from collective defense to collective security and the process of European integration by having Russia join NATO.[116]

It was clear by the middle of the decade that NATO operations had gone far beyond the stated purpose and tasks of the Alliance in both nature and geographic scope. The driving force in this process was the American war on terror, in particular the United States' need for coalition partners and support in the wars it had started in Iraq and Afghanistan. Washington gradually pushed individual Allies and then the Alliance as a whole into these conflicts. The bitter split within NATO in 2003 over Iraq made it inevitable that significant involvement of the Alliance in Afghanistan would be far easier. Even so, it was not easy to convince European publics to provide the financial or human resources for expeditionary combat forces to fight a threat thousands of miles from Europe's borders, far beyond even the neighborhoods in which the EU security strategy envisioned operating.

Thus the push for a new Strategic Concept came largely from the United States or from European countries and leaders with markedly Atlanticist views.[117] On the margins of the 2006 Riga NATO Summit, former UN ambassador Richard Holbrooke and Ron Asmus, one of the intellectual fathers of NATO's enlargement, lobbied for a redefinition of NATO to respond to new global threats.[118] The Comprehensive Political Guidance adopted by NATO leaders at Riga outlined the changes in the global security environment that had occurred since 1999 and noted what they might mean for the Alliance. By the time of the Bucharest Summit, figures such as Asmus were calling even more explicitly for a redefinition of NATO and its relationship with the EU: "We [the United States and Europe] must define a new sense of shared purpose, giving rise to a common strategic agenda."[119] Other Alliance thinkers struggled to find a way to define NATO's antiterror operations as a kind of "borderless collective defense."[120]

At the Sixtieth Anniversary Summit in Strasbourg and Kehl on April 3–4, 2009 (the first such meeting for the Obama administration), NATO leaders recognized the problem and kicked the can down the road. The summit first dealt with the operational issues crucial to the Alliance's credibility by endorsing the changes in command structure and NATO operations in Afghanistan, including establishment of the NATO Training Mission.[121] The summit also produced a lengthy, traditional declaration, basically a laundry list of the challenges, operations, contacts, commitments, and activities of the Alliance and the leaders' resolve to attain their stated objectives.[122] However, arguably the most important result of the summit (including France's return to the Alliance's military structures) was reflected in the shorter "Declaration on Alliance Security." Less than three pages in length, this document reaffirmed NATO as the "essential transatlantic forum for security consultations," and noted the appearance of "new, increasingly global threats" such as terrorism and proliferation of weapons of mass destruction, along with energy security, climate change, and failed states. NATO leaders committed themselves in this declaration "to renovating our Alliance to better address today's threats and to anticipate tomorrow's risks." To achieve this goal, the heads of state and government tasked newly appointed Secretary-General Rasmussen with convening a group of experts to develop a new Strategic Concept for possible adoption and implementation at NATO's next summit.[123]

The outgoing secretary-general, Jaap de Hoop Scheffer, and the incoming secretary-general, Anders Fogh Rasmussen, launched preparation of a new Strategic Concept at a NATO-organized security conference in Brussels in July 2009. An impressive group of experts, headed by former US secretary of state Madeleine Albright and former CEO of Royal Dutch Shell Jeroen van der Veer conducted an eight-month program of consultations and conferences in most NATO states and Russia. The group was assisted by a high-level group of military advisers, drawn from former NATO and national commanders, and a small group of civilian advisers featuring several American experts who had played prominent roles in NATO's transformation and enlargement in the 1990s and 2000s.[124] The talents, achievements, and experience of the group of experts were self-evident, but so was their commitment to NATO as the primary security institution and instrument of the North American and European states making up the Alliance. Thus their report—perhaps any document they might produce—was far more likely to address what objectives the Alliance could serve in the changing global security context rather than why NATO still should exist in the first place.

The group of experts presented its report in May 2010, as *NATO 2020: Assured Security, Dynamic Engagement*.[125] Noting the significant changes in the security environment since NATO's last Strategic Concept was adopted in 1999, and the rapidly changing nature of the contemporary environment, the report looks at the Alliance's future for the next ten years—hence the title. However, the experts asserted that certain basic ideas behind NATO remained unchanged, in particular that "NATO's central purpose is to safeguard—by political and military means—the freedom and security of all its members."[126] In addition, the document asserts that the Alliance constitutes the link that permanently ties the security of North America with that of Europe.[127] Describing what NATO should look like heading toward 2020, the experts reaffirmed collective defense of Alliance members as the core task but warned that unconventional threats, such as terrorism or cyber, would be of increasing concern. Other core tasks of the Alliance specified in the report include contributing to the broader security of the entire Euro-Atlantic region; serving as the means for transatlantic consultations and crisis management for the entire continuum of issues facing the Alliance; and enhancing the scope and management of partnerships.

To execute these core tasks, the report calls on Allies to develop guidelines for operations outside of the territory of Alliance members and recommends greater use of Article 4 consultations among Allies for conflict prevention and conflict management. The expert group envisioned greater use of partnerships with non-NATO and non-European actors, in particular in operations and activities under the "Comprehensive Approach to Complex Problems." With respect to Russia, *NATO 2020* recommends continued dedication to the NATO-Russia partnership and more effective use of the NATO-Russia Council, basically preservation of the status quo. The report categorically supports continuation of the Alliance's "open door" policy for new members, for states that wish to apply and meet the criteria. *NATO 2020* contains familiar language with respect to the need for the Alliance to acquire new and sufficient capabilities. The report calls for the Alliance to retain "secure and reliable" nuclear forces, while at the same time supporting ongoing nonproliferation and arms control efforts, in particular consultations with Russia for "increased transparency and further mutual reductions." The document contains a clear commitment to Alliance development of a missile defense capability, including specific praise for President Obama's recent decision on ballistic missile defense deployment and a call for cooperation with partners, especially Russia, in this area. The report also specifically identifies cyber as a rising security concern for Allies. Finally, *NATO 2020* calls for efforts by the Alliance to better explain its purpose and activities not only to the populations of NATO member states but to peoples around the world.

In the end, *NATO 2020* appears most of all to be a consensus document that resolves disagreements over the core tasks, priorities, and operations of the Alliance by including them all. As the group of experts began its work, one of the civilian advisers—the research director of the NATO Staff College, Karl Heinz Kamp—cited basic disagreement among Allies on at least four key questions: how to balance territorial defense and out-of-area provision of security; how to maintain credibility of Article V; when Article V applies; and how to provide for collective self-defense against new threats.[128] Speaking at one of the group of experts seminars in early 2010, Secretary of Defense Gates noted that the real transformation of NATO over the previous twenty years was the evolution from a static defense force to an expeditionary force.[129] Gates argued that the new and emerging threats in the changing global security environment necessitated NATO actions beyond its borders, and he launched into a familiar appeal for more resources and greater burden sharing. In essence, *NATO 2020* supports this conclusion, but with considerably more discussion of more specific issues and Alliance responses.

It was hardly a surprise that a large number of the recommendations of the group of experts were included in some form in a new Strategic Concept, "Active Engagement, Modern Defence," adopted at the Lisbon NATO Summit in November 2010. The document reorganizes and reduces the *NATO 2020* recommendations to three core tasks for the Alliance: collective defense, crisis management, and cooperative security.[130] The new Strategic Concept asserts that threats of conventional attack are low but still exist, but focuses attention on new and emerging threats such as cyber, and even mentions energy needs, health risks, climate change, and water scarcity. The document contains an impressive list of capabilities the Alliance should maintain or acquire to deter or defend against these threats. With respect to crisis management, the Strategic Concept reserves the right for Alliance intervention should the preferred approach of conflict prevention fail. The new document reiterates Alliance dedication to international cooperation in arms control, disarmament, and nuclear nonproliferation, and reiterates the importance of partnerships in pursuing security, particularly with the EU, Russia, and the Euro-Atlantic Partnership Council. Finally, the new Strategic Concept reaffirmed the Alliance's "open door" in support of "the eventual integration of all European countries that so desire into Euro-Atlantic structures."

The longer, more detailed Summit Declaration adopted by the NATO heads of state at Lisbon in November 2010 spelled out with far greater specificity the entire range of current NATO operations, activities, and concerns.[131] The document in this manner makes clear the continuing commitment of the Alliance to security operations around much of the globe, as well as to the combined application of civilian and military resources in conflict management in complex operations. In this connection, the heads of state tasked the North Atlantic Council to update the Bucharest Comprehensive Approach Action Plan in time for the NATO Foreign Ministers meeting scheduled for April 2011. The Lisbon Declaration also specifically instructed the secretary-general to work with the EU high representative on further development of the NATO-EU partnership, also to report to the foreign ministers in April. The Lisbon document reaffirmed the Alliance's commitment to eventual membership for Georgia and Ukraine and called for continued cooperation with Russia. In general, the Lisbon Declaration called for development of a more "efficient and flexible partnership policy," again to be presented at the Ministerial Meeting in April. Finally, the heads of state at Lisbon mandated an update of the political-military framework for NATO-led operations of the Partnership for Peace, to be presented to the defense ministers' meeting in June 2011.

The Lisbon Summit thus produced both a restatement of NATO's basic purpose and core tasks, presented in broad strategic outlines in the new Strategic Concept, and the beginnings of multiple processes aimed at defining these tasks and the ways and means of achieving them, as seen in the assignments made in the Lisbon Declaration. In these results, Allies first and foremost reaffirmed NATO's continuing evolution into an expeditionary security organization with a self-assigned global scope. To be sure, territorial defense remained among NATO's core tasks, but so many other tasks had been added that no non-NATO member could be expected to view the Alliance as simply a defensive security organization. The Lisbon Summit continued a process in NATO of at least a decade and a half of steadily adding tasks and increasing capabilities. Rhetorically, NATO's intentions were benign, dedicated to building a "community of freedom, peace, security, and shared values."[132] To those inside the Alliance, such statements of purpose seemed straightforward and reassuring. For those outside the fold, NATO's growing capabilities and expanding area of operation might well seem more important than good intentions.

The revolts of the Arab Spring and NATO's intervention in Libya came almost as an exclamation point to the Strategic Concept and Lisbon Declaration, connecting several threads running through the EU's development of ESDP and NATO's deliberation over a new statement of purpose. First, Moscow's abstention on UN Security Council Resolution 1973, despite open disagreement over the issue between Medvedev and Putin, could hardly be interpreted as wholehearted Russian support for NATO intervention in Libya, let alone removal of Gaddafi.[133] Second, even with the clear US desire that Europe take the lead in responding to the crisis in Libya, to the disappointment of ESDP enthusiasts the international action in Libya became rather quickly a NATO-led coalition.[134] Third, irrespective of the after-action claims by Secretary-General Rasmussen that NATO Allies do not lack military capabilities—and, in the case of Libya, that "any shortfalls have been primarily due to political, rather than military, constraints"—most observers considered the operation against Libya glaring evidence of the deficiencies of almost all European NATO Allies in key military capabilities such as intelligence, transportation, and logistics, to say nothing of combat air, sea, and land forces.[135] Fourth, the US position of "leading from behind" in the Libya operation could be seen by some as a harbinger of change in Washington's strategic security orientation. To be sure, President Obama may have been cautious about committing US forces abroad to a new conflict after the Democratic Party's shattering defeat in the November 2010 legislative elections and with ongoing efforts to extract US forces from Iraq and Afghanistan. Notwithstanding, the United States' reluctance to become involved in Libya came at roughly the same time as the announcement of its "pivot to Asia," leading many to wonder where Washington's priorities really lay.

In any event, NATO's intervention in Libya and support for the removal of Gaddafi apparently convinced one important observer of the direction in which the Alliance's capabilities and intentions were taking it. Vladimir Putin called the intervention in Libya "something akin to a medieval crusade" at the beginning of the operation. By the time Gaddafi was captured and killed, the Russian premier was thoroughly disgusted with his Western partners and apparently even more determined than before to return to the presidency.[136] In the process begun at Kehl/Strasbourg and culminating at Lisbon, NATO may have successfully restated its purpose and launched yet another transformation to adapt to the new security environment. It may also have addressed the deficiencies of its operation in Afghanistan and successfully mounted another operation in Libya, all the while maintaining other, lower-profile missions in Africa and the Middle East. With the reaffirmation at Lisbon of NATO as an expeditionary security organization with a global reach, followed by de facto support for regime change in Libya, the Alliance may have achieved important security objectives. However, by these same actions, the Alliance intensified and accelerated the deterioration of its relations with its largest and arguably most important European partner — Russia.

## 10. THINGS FALL APART—AGAIN!

In December 2010, a desperate fruit vendor in Tunisia set himself ablaze to protest unchecked corruption in his country. The protest that subsequently erupted spread rapidly through much of the Middle East, resulting in the fall of governments in Tunisia and Egypt and serious challenges to the prevailing authorities in at least another half dozen Arab states in the Maghreb and Levant. Many Western observers and pundits on the Middle East and nongovernmental activists were thrilled by the outpouring of popular protest and opposition in a region that had seemed the last, most stubborn bastion of resistance to the post–Cold War spread of democracy, the farthest reach of Samuel Huntington's "third wave."[1] After hesitation and bitter debate within the US government and those of other major Western powers, most Western leaders generally welcomed the revolts of what quickly came to be called the Arab Spring, pushed for democratic reforms in the countries affected, and recognized the new governments.

Some observers, both in the West and Russia, wondered whether the Arab world was witnessing a political transformation similar to that which swept Central and Eastern Europe in 1989.[2] Some Russian experts exhibited schadenfreude at the sight of US leaders first hesitating, and then abandoning, longtime American ally Hosni Mubarak.[3] However, the popular revolts and successful regime changes of the Arab Spring worried official and unofficial Russians on several counts. First, Russia's neighbors to the south, in particular the five

Central Asian states, appeared dangerously similar to the Arab countries of the Middle East experiencing popular revolts, with the population overwhelmingly Muslim and the governments almost without exception authoritarian and often repressive.[4] Second, the example of successful Muslim antiauthoritarian, prodemocracy revolts provoked worries about Russia's domestic political stability, with sizable Muslim populations in the North Caucasus, central Volga, and western Siberian regions. Third, Russia had close political and economic ties to some of the existing authoritarian rulers in the Middle East, especially Syria's Assad and Libya's Gaddafi, and the prospect of upheaval in the region was troublesome from the geopolitical standpoint.

In sum, the Arab Spring brought instability and the possibility of dramatic change to a region already turned upside down by the massive introduction of US power to oust Saddam Hussein. The United States and its major Allies by and large welcomed this change. Although President Obama was far less eager than his predecessor to intervene militarily, a number of influential senior figures in his administration were vocal advocates of America's duty to support the spread of democracy and to protect innocent civilian populations against violent, repressive regimes. Russian analysts and political leaders did not immediately charge the United States with fomenting or abetting the revolts of the Arab Spring, although such speculation was not long in coming.[5] It was bound to occur to both officials and opponents of the regime in Russia that what could happen in Cairo's Tahrir Square might also occur on Red Square in Moscow.[6] Even if the Arab Spring did not pose an immediate or direct threat to Russia's international interests and domestic stability, the widespread conflagration in the Middle East intensified a sense of insecurity already present in much of Russia's political elite and a suspicion of American and its Allies' motives in supporting popular movements that from Moscow's vantage point seemed likely to produce only conflict and terrorism.

In the United States and Western Europe, conversely, the Arab Spring seemed to rekindle appetites for democracy promotion and humanitarian intervention that had been considerably diminished by the difficult experiences of occupation and counterinsurgency in Iraq and Afghanistan. Given the long alliance with Mubarak, it took Washington some time to reach a decision to support the opponents of the old governments in both Tunisia and Egypt, and to endorse free and open elections, irrespective of the prospects for victory of pro-Islamic parties. The US attitude toward revolution and regime change was not uniform everywhere in the Middle East, given long-standing security relationships and alliances, such as those with Saudi Arabia and Bahrain. However, as popular unrest spread to Syria, the United States and many of its Allies sided with the demonstrators against President Assad, which would increasingly place them on the opposite side of the fence from Moscow. Finally, the harsh measures taken against demonstrators and the civilian population in eastern Libya, especially around Benghazi, by supporters of Muammar Gaddafi, aroused public indignation on both sides of the Atlantic and prompted calls for military intervention.

For the United States and its chief NATO Allies, the campaign against Gaddafi in Libya was a clear case of humanitarian intervention to protect an innocent population against murderous attacks from the side of its own rulers. The modalities of the intervention caused bitter debate at times within NATO and demonstrated continuing disparities in key military capacities between the United States and even its most capable European partners. Nonetheless, with the sociopolitical deterioration within Libya still far in the future, by the end of 2011 the NATO intervention seemed basically a success. From Moscow, the events in Libya appeared to be another classic case of Western duplicity and geopolitical aggrandizement, the kind of actions that seemed to threaten destabilization around the globe. For Russia, the Arab Spring was in the end an unwelcome, threatening spread of instability to a region close and important to Russia. The events there, in particular Western intervention in Libya and Gaddafi's fall, brought not only unwelcome geopolitical consequences but also important effects on Moscow's domestic politics.

## THERE WILL BE NO "MOSCOW SPRING"

During Dmitry Medvedev's presidency, or the time of the "tandem," a joke made the rounds of Moscow's political and diplomatic circles to the effect that in the Russian government there was a Putin camp, and there was a Medvedev camp. The only uncertainty was whether Medvedev was in the Medvedev camp. To those who followed Russian politics closely and seriously, it was obvious that differences of opinion existed between the president and the prime minister, and these sometimes were expressed publicly.[7] One clear example came in their comments on Khodorkovskii's second trial and sentencing in 2009.

Another glaring public disagreement between president and prime minister occurred over Medvedev's decision not to oppose Western intervention in Libya in March 2011, overruling his own foreign ministry in ordering abstention on UN Security Council Resolution 1973.[8] In public comments made during a factory visit, Putin likened the UN action to a medieval call for a crusade and complained that the action was simply the latest in a series of intemperate American military interventions around the globe. Within hours, Medvedev called a number of reporters to his dacha and provided a hasty, nervous justification of his decision. Subsequent events in Libya did little to move Putin closer to Medvedev's position. Gaddafi's defeat by the rebels damaged significant Russian business ties with Libya. Qaddafi's execution during capture by a rebel unit appeared to offend Putin personally and gave him yet another reason to be hostile to Western humanitarian interventions.[9]

Putin also may have had domestic political reasons for disagreement with his old friend and subordinate in the president's chair. Medvedev was clearly pushing an agenda and raising hopes in Russia for political and economic reform. In what was presented as an anticorruption measure, Medvedev forced those holding senior government positions to relinquish senior corporate positions that they held simultaneously. The most prominent target was Putin's old colleague Igor Sechin, who was then chairman of Rosneft and deputy prime minister. A Medvedev speech in Magnitogorsk in early 2011 proposing ten reform steps to improve Russia's investment climate was matched by a February 2011 speech by the finance minister, Alexei Kudrin, in Krasnoyarsk, in which Kudrin stated that real economic reform in Russia depended on the development of political pluralism.[10]

Such domestic political sentiments and international developments were clearly not to Putin's liking. In a speech to a rally in Volgograd in May 2011, Putin issued a surprise proposal to form an All-Russia Peoples' Front, which would include the United Russia party but also "non–party supporters," to prepare for the legislative elections at the end of the year.[11] The move was clearly aimed at maximizing Putin's personal political authority as well as improving the electoral chances of United Russia. Then, again in Volgograd, on September 24, 2011, at the United Russia convention a clearly conflicted Dmitry Medvedev announced that he would not run for another term and nominated Vladimir Putin to succeed him. Basking in the applause, Putin confided to the adoring crowd that he and Medvedev had agreed on the switch more than four years earlier, when they had first exchanged positions.[12]

Many Russians were stunned, not by the announcement of Putin's return but by the revelation that Medvedev apparently had never really been an independent actor during his term as president. As subsequent events in Russia made clear, the Medvedev presidency had mobilized substantial segments of Russia's growing urban middle and professional classes and raised hopes for change that would not simply dissipate after a couple of speeches at a political rally. Disillusionment with both Putin and Medvedev had been growing in key elements of Russian society, and it came out into the open in startling fashion after the September 24 Volgograd announcement. Speaking to reporters on the margins of the annual meetings of the International Monetary Fund and the World Bank in Washington, Minister of Finance Kudrin expressed displeasure with a prospective Medvedev government. He was subsequently fired by Medvedev in a government meeting shown on Russian television, underscoring the disarray in Russia's governing circles. Putin was unexpectedly jeered by spectators during an impromptu appearance at a mixed martial arts bout in Moscow.[13]

Public relations efforts to explain such incidents could not hide the popular discontent apparently crystallized by the revelation at the Volgograd convention that the voters' preferences did not really matter. Despite massive support from government administrative organs, United Russia's results in the December 2011 balloting were poorer than expected, not even reaching a majority of the popular vote. More important, the results were inflated through vote-rigging and other manipulation by the authorities; some of this was captured in a number of urban centers by citizens with mobile phones and tablets and disseminated swiftly and widely via social media on the Internet.

A storm of popular protest against falsified election results rapidly engulfed many of Russia's largest cities. Despite initial regime efforts at repression, protest information and arrangements spread through social media. By Saturday, December 10, six days after the election, tens of thousands of protestors filled the streets of Moscow, Saint Petersburg, and many of Russia's other large cities, from Kaliningrad to Vladivostok.[14] Police observed but generally did not interfere with the protests, and Medvedev and Putin both announced several reforms aimed at greater openness and transparency, promising to make registration of new parties easier and placing video cameras in all polling places to discourage cheating.

Putin, however, was still concerned about his own election in the presidential balloting in early March, and he took a harder verbal line against the demonstrators. Referring to criticism from US secretary of state Hillary Clinton in late 2011, he suggested that the United States had played a part in prompting the protests. He seemed to go out of his way to belittle the protestors, gratuitously explaining that he thought the white ribbons they were wearing were condoms. He played on the theme that the protestors were controlled by outside forces, likening them to the monkey people—bandar-logs—from Rudyard Kipling's *Jungle Book*. While Medvedev, Surkov, Kudrin, and others might seem to be engaged in an opening to critics of the regime, Putin turned to patriotic themes and the disgruntled electorate of Russia's old industrial centers, such as the massive Ural tank factory in Nizhnii Tagil.

With a vigorous campaign, extensive use of "administrative resources," and a hefty dose of flag-waving, Putin won almost 65 percent of the popular vote (although, worryingly, his share in Moscow was below 50 percent). However, Putin's tactics and campaign promises contributed heavily to an increasing polarization within Russian society, embraced a potentially difficult set of economic promises to the Russian population, and created a considerably testier political backdrop against which to conduct relations with the West. In a campaign article—one of a series—addressing Russia's position and role in the world, Putin evoked the tone and themes of his 2007 Munich speech, denouncing American unilateralism, NATO enlargement, and disregard for the authority of the United Nations.[15] To make sure Washington got the point, the newly arrived US ambassador, Michael McFaul, who was the architect of Obama's "reset" policy, was greeted with unprecedented public criticism and rudeness from the very beginning of his term in February 2012.[16]

Once reelected to the presidency, Putin's record demonstrated no clear policy direction. His April 18 postelection speech might be seen as a call for unity after a tough election campaign. His harsh response to protesters who came out into the streets on his inauguration day, including a brutal police response, arrests, and draconian prosecutions, seemed to indicate an intention to suppress rather than accommodate discontent within Russia's middle and professional classes. Immediately upon assuming office in early May 2012, Putin issued a set of directives (the "May promises") with respect to pensions, salaries, and social benefits that played to the working class electorate he had mobilized in his campaign but that promised to be expensive to fulfill. To the surprise of conservative and nationalist Duma deputies, in his last speech to the legislature before moving back to the presidency, Putin supported continued cooperation with NATO, including possible Alliance use of the airfield near Ulyanovsk, in the campaign against the Taliban in Afghanistan. Nonetheless, Putin snubbed Obama's invitation to the Group of Eight (G-8) at Camp David shortly after his inauguration, sending Medvedev instead, and sat through an apparently frosty meeting with the US president at the G-20 in Los Cabos in July. Yet American participants in the latter related that Putin told Obama he wished to focus on US-Russian economic relations after the US elections and later welcomed American assistance in finally gaining membership in the World Trade Organization.[17]

In addition to the crackdown on public protestors, Putin adopted a number of measures designed to reduce or eliminate foreign influences in Russian society and politics.[18] Nongovernmental organizations, already subject to several restrictive legislative and administrative measures during the preceding decade, were required by new legislation to register as "foreign agents" if they received any sort of public or private funding from foreign sources. This measure was in addition to any restrictions the government might place on the activities of nongovernmental organizations. One specially targeted class was independent Russian organizations that received foreign funding, assistance, or training to promote human rights or to monitor elections (activities Putin apparently found particularly unwelcome). Further, Moscow informed Washington that assistance funded through the US Agency for International Development was no longer necessary. To avoid expulsion of Russian diplomatic personnel in the United States, the American staff of the agency's mission was allowed to stay, but there would be no programs in which they might engage. Similarly, after over twenty years of joint work in the Nunn-Lugar Cooperative Threat Reduction initiative, Russian officials informed their US counterparts that they no longer required such assistance and would withdraw from the program. The Russians expressed willingness to continue work on counterproliferation, control of nuclear materials, and arms reductions but said they would finance their participation themselves. The most significant result of this step was the loss by the US side of the right to inspection and other verification measures, and thus a real loss of transparency.

In terms of military power, Putin continued and accelerated a process already under way of reforming and rearming the Russian military. The relatively poor performance of the armed forces in the 2008 war against Georgia provided the leverage for Defense Minister Anatoliy Serdyukov to implement thoroughgoing reforms in the military's force and command structures. The move toward a more professional army was augmented by an expensive multiyear plan to equip most of Russia's forces with new, improved weapons and equipment by 2020. Russia's nationalist ambassador to NATO, Dmitri Rogozin, was made deputy prime minister and given charge of the country's aging, ailing, military-industrial complex. Although Serdyukov fell victim to political intrigue (and his own human failings) in November 2012, his replacement—former Minister of Emergencies Sergei Shoigu, an able administrator and long-time Putin loyalist—continued the most important elements of the military reform. In one of his 2012 campaign articles, Putin noted that Russia had barely managed to find 60,000 troops able to be deployed at the start of the second Chechen war from August to September 1999. As he returned to the presidency in May 2012, he was already well on the way not only to remedying that deficiency but to restoring Russia as a serious regional military power.[19]

As Russian membership in the World Trade Organization finally approached in the summer of 2012, Washington had an increasingly urgent need to remove a Cold War relic in US-Russian trade relations, the Jackson-Vanik Amendment, which was adopted in 1973 and linked granting most-favored-nation status to allowing Soviet Jews freedom to emigrate. With the collapse of the USSR in 1991, free emigration became an everyday reality, but Jackson-Vanik continued to be applied to Russia and other former Soviet states. Promises from both the Clinton and then George W. Bush administrations to repeal the amendment went unfulfilled, and Washington even used the restriction in disputes with Moscow over imported US frozen chicken parts (*nozhki Busha*, or "Bush legs"). For many Russian officials, Jackson-Vanik came to symbolize what they saw as America's lingering Cold War mentality and constituted evidence of the US tendency to make promises that it would not keep.

Ironically, as the Obama administration began to mobilize political capital to end Jackson-Vanik, the US Congress acted independently in a way that called to mind the legislative reaction to the Nixon-Kissinger policy of détente that produced the amendment in the first place. Congressional critics of Russia's human rights record and backsliding on democracy, led by Senators John McCain and Ben Cardin (cochair of the Commission for Security and Cooperation in Europe), took up the cause of Sergey Magnitskiy, a Russian lawyer employed by British venture capitalist Bill Browder (a former US citizen and grandson of the head of the US Communist Party). Magnitskiy had been unjustly imprisoned and left to perish in prison when he called attention to fraud committed by Russian government officials in order to loot Browder's company.[20] Rejecting the pleas of the Obama administration, at the same time the Congress abolished Jackson-Vanik (December 2012) it adopted the so-called Magnitsky Act, which required the executive branch to impose travel (visa) and economic sanctions, including expropriation of property, on Russian officials who were found guilty of human rights abuses, including those implicated in the Magnitsky case.[21]

The Russians were livid when Obama signed the Magnitsky Act, and the Russian Duma soon found a legislative way to retaliate. Over several years Russian and American diplomats had painstakingly worked out an agreement that facilitated the process for Americans who desired to adopt Russian children while responding to Russian concerns about how some of these children had been treated in the United States. Russian legislators immediately jumped into the fray with the so-called Dima Yakovlev law, named after a Russian child who had perished in 2009 of heat stroke after being left in a car by his American adoptive parents.[22] This legislation forbade any further adoption of Russian children by Americans; the Russians also announced that they had their own list of American officials and other Americans who would not be allowed to visit Russia because they were guilty of human rights violations.

Although relations with Moscow were not the major issue, Obama's Russia policy came under steady attack during the 2012 campaign, with Romney at one point calling Russia America's "number one geopolitical foe."[23] For the most part, Obama appeared to try to keep the relationship out of the political battle, in particular because he had practical goals he wished to pursue with Moscow.[24] Although Republican (and some Democratic) critics attacked the reset policy as naive and blind to Russian human rights violations, Obama backers saw both the New Strategic Arms Reduction Treaty (New START) and the Northern Distribution Network as significant successes. The administration wanted (and needed) Russian cooperation in dealing with both Iran and Syria during a second term. Finally, Obama truly believed in the goal of a nuclear-free world and hoped to persuade Moscow to engage in another round of strategic arms cuts before he left office.[25]

Moscow, however, was not particularly interested in pursuing further strategic arms reductions. Russian interlocutors offered various reasons, but one of those unspoken was very likely Russia's extensive reliance on nuclear weapons as a counterweight not only against NATO's considerable superiority in conventional weaponry but also as a deterrent against a rising China.[26] The other obstacle to arms negotiations and security cooperation with Russia was America's and NATO's determination to press ahead with plans for developing and deploying a missile defense system.[27] Obama created a small furor when he was overheard at a March 2012 nuclear summit in Seoul to promise Medvedev that he could show more flexibility on missile defense after his reelection, but subsequent US and NATO statements in 2012–13 failed to convince Moscow. Obama twice sent senior officials to Russia during 2013—his national security adviser, Tom Donilon, in April; and a delegation from the National Security Council and the State Department, in December. Putin's national security adviser, Nikolai Patrushev, paid a much-publicized reciprocal visit to Washington in May 2013, but without immediate apparent results.[28]

The reciprocal visits of national security advisers produced agreement to hold an Obama-Putin Summit after the G-20 summit, to be held in Saint Petersburg in September. However, there was relatively little of substance in the bilateral relationship for the two leaders to discuss, and even less on which they might agree. US legislators and human rights activists continued to bash Moscow for its deficiencies in democracy and repression of civil society. The prosecution of three Pussy Riot band members who staged a "punk prayer" in protest against Putin in Moscow's Cathedral of the Savior illustrated the deepening political and cultural divide between Russia and the West. The harsh punishment meted out by Russian courts against what was not much more than scatological disturbance of the peace by counterculture performance artists drew howls of protest from Western intellectuals, while allowing Putin to appeal to a traditionalist, prudish Russian electorate outside the major urban centers. Putin and his colleagues similarly used Western criticism of Russian legislation and practices on gay rights to cast himself as a defender of traditional Christian values against a decadent West.

Thus, when Putin and Russian authorities decided to afford temporary refuge to Edward Snowden after he became stranded in the transit area of Moscow's Sheremetevo Airport, there was little doubt that Obama would forgo a bilateral summit with Putin. Putin's sudden and unexpected rescue of Obama later in September, when the United States faced the unpleasant prospect of going it alone in punishing Syrian president Assad for his use of chemical weapons against his own citizens, underlined the highly transactional nature of Putin's relationship with the West. The Russian president did not reject all cooperation, as the quick agreement reached on collecting and disposing of Syria's chemical weapons arsenal demonstrated. However, any cooperation—in fact, any substantive interaction—would be solely on Moscow's terms and based on Russia's perception of its own interests.

Somewhere between the NATO attack on Libya in March 2011 and his own return to the presidency in May 2012, it appears that Putin reached a personal conclusion that the West, in particular the United States, could not be trusted to carry through on any of the commitments it made to Russia. Therefore, Russia should rely on its own resources for its domestic political and economic development. This did not mean rejection of any external deals, as the 2012 Rosneft–ExxonMobil agreement showed, but rather that Russia should remain in control, able to leave and stand on its own if necessary. The same tendency can be seen in Russia's foreign relations. During this period Putin significantly increased his efforts to build his own Eurasian integration projects, initiatives such as the Eurasian Economic Union and the Collective Security Treaty Organization that would give Russia its own economic and security spheres as counterweights to NATO and the EU. This determination to make Russia fully sovereign, a major international actor in a multipolar world, and not dependent on any European or North American interlocutors, began to shape Russian policy toward and interaction with all of Europe's major security actors: the Organization for Security and Cooperation in Europe (OSCE), NATO, and the European Union.

## THE OSCE: GOING NOWHERE FAST

American officials who visited OSCE Headquarters in Vienna after 2011 often returned to Washington with the observation that, if the Helsinki Final Act were to be renegotiated at the present time, Russia would probably not sign it.[29] After the Astana Summit, one OSCE veteran wrote that "Astana will be considered a turning point in the history of the OSCE. Either it was the beginning of a new era, or the beginning of the end."[30] A year later, as the foreign ministers of the participating states gathered for their annual meeting in Vilnius, it seemed the OSCE was on the latter course. To be sure, Lithuania inherited the OSCE Chairmanship with detailed, ambitious plans, and the considerable number of OSCE structures and field missions were busy with an enormous amount of ongoing work in all three traditional dimensions (or baskets) of the Helsinki Process.[31] For example, OSCE officials or personnel seconded from participating states trained police, worked against smuggling and human trafficking, promoted media freedom, supported minority rights, and exchanged information and experience in the fight against terrorism. Hundreds of meetings, courses, trainings, exchanges, and other valuable activities were organized or supported by the OSCE every year.

However, when it came to debate or action on the most important security questions for the Euro-Atlantic area, the OSCE was paralyzed by fundamental, increasingly deep disagreement among its most important participating states. The divisions in the OSCE replicated those in Europe at large, with the EU and the United States on one side, and Russia and a few of its partners in the Commonwealth of Independent States on the other side. The two camps disagreed not just on the particulars of specific important security questions; they also increasingly diverged on the nature and desired future of the European security architecture. This divergence is vividly illustrated in the statements to the December 2011 Vilnius Ministerial Council of US secretary of state Hillary Clinton and Russian foreign minister Sergei Lavrov. Clinton stressed the American emphasis on human rights and the human dimension, with lengthy references to human rights cases in Belarus, Ukraine, and Russia. Clinton emphasized that "we must never lose sight of the truth at the core of our comprehensive security concept: Respect for human rights and human security is essential to the progress and security of all countries, here in the OSCE region and across the globe."[32] Speaking shortly before Clinton, Lavrov proclaimed that the OSCE had buried itself in a host of inconsequential and second-tier issues and had lost sight of its original and primary purpose: to serve as a collective instrument for providing security and cooperation.[33] Lavrov complained that "the mechanism of the OSCE that has developed is producing malfunctions, and the path of extensive development of a mass of documents and obligations has fully exhausted itself." In conclusion, Lavrov noted the need for mutual respect for others' interests, a clear suggestion that Russian interests were not being adequately represented and respected in the OSCE.

Sadly, the results of the Lithuanian and Irish OSCE Chairmanships in 2011 and 2012, respectively, were depressingly meager (through little or no fault of Lithuania or Ireland, one could plausibly note). The Vilnius Ministerial Council took place two days after the controversial parliamentary elections in Russia; against a backdrop of mounting East/West recriminations, the delegations in Vilnius were able to agree on almost nothing, not even uncontroversial antiterror, antinarcotics, antitrafficking initiatives that past ministerial gatherings had passed routinely.[34] The Vienna Document was updated for the first time in twelve years with new measures for confidence building and transparency, and a procedure was adopted for regular updates every five years, but lack of consensus prevented the adoption of all but technical fixes. A group of thirty-nine, mostly Western states added in an interpretive statement: "We had hoped for strategic direction that could lead to successful work on Vienna Document, to bring it into line with the realities of the political and military situation that pertains in Europe and across the OSCE space. These hopes remain unfulfilled. We would like to register our concern at a time when arms control and [confidence- and security-building measures] in Europe are under strain as never before, that we are unable to look up from our national agendas to engage on work that would benefit us all."[35] With Russia's 2007 suspension of its participation in verification and transparency activities for the Treaty on Conventional Armed Forces in Europe (CFE), the Vienna Document mechanisms were the sole remaining conventional arms control regime in Europe. The continued underlying disagreement over the CFE Treaty clearly had an inhibiting effect on the ability of the participating states to expand cooperation in the Vienna Document context.

On the protracted conflicts in Europe, to which the Lithuanians and the Irish both devoted considerable attention, the OSCE was able to achieve little more than maintain the current level of its activities. The cochairs of the Minsk Group—Russia, France, and the United States—surprisingly enough continued to work together relatively effectively and harmoniously, producing regular statements, one year with Armenia and Azerbaijan joining in, calling for continued work in the Minsk process.[36] On the Moldova-Transdniestria conflict, the Meseberg Initiative in 2010 led to several high-level meetings between representatives of both sides in Germany. However, Berlin was unable to deliver anything close to what Moscow wanted in the form of a special forum with the EU, and Russia clearly considered its side of the deal to consist of little more than to allow negotiations to get going again between Chisinau and Tiraspol.[37] Even then, it took the Lithuanians almost a full year of skillful diplomacy to convince the Moldovans and Transdniestrians to formally resume the "five plus two" political settlement negotiations in November 2011; they had not met since a Moldovan walkout in February 2006.[38] During 2012, the Irish managed to keep both parties to the conflict coming to negotiating sessions, to reach agreement on a ministerial statement on the conflict at Dublin in December, and to agree on dismantlement of an aged aerial tramway across the River Dniestr between Rezina and Ribnita, a relic of cement production on both sides of the river during the Soviet era.[39] The fact that such modest steps might be listed as accomplishments of an OSCE chairmanship visibly attest to the yawning divisions and lowered expectations in an organization increasingly forced to accept the lowest common denominator.

On the strategic level, the participating states were simply not able to agree on what the OSCE was or what they wished it to be. Russia's Western interlocutors had essentially channeled Medvedev's security treaty proposal into an effective dead end in the OSCE's Corfu Process. By the end of 2010 at the Astana

Summit that initiative seemed to peter out, with the heads of state agreeing that the OSCE was a "free, democratic, common and indivisible . . . security community," but without any specific explanation of what their concept of a "security community" was. Discussions continued in the Permanent Council and other institutions on OSCE reform, often a code word for transforming the organization so it might better conform to a particular national agenda. Looking toward the fortieth anniversary in 2015 of the adoption of the Final Act, the Irish were able to fashion consensus on a "Helsinki +40 Process," which would "provide strong and continuous political impetus to advancing work towards a security community."[40] Although the initiative was aimed at making the OSCE more effective and relevant, interpretative statements by Western and Eastern states, in particular the United States, make it clear the process would go nowhere except in their preferred direction. Work duly proceeded, with appropriate fanfare, on Helsinki +40 but—as one might have expected—demonstrated minimal accomplishments and was eventually overtaken by events in 2014.

The OSCE also remained stalemated on efforts to complete its transformation into a full-fledged international organization by acquiring a formal legal personality. After years of US foot-dragging and expression of doubts whether such a step was really necessary, in 2007 Washington agreed in principle and indicated it would accept a draft convention drawn up as a legal document to be ratified by the OSCE's participating states.[41] In discussions on the text of the proposed convention, however, a number of OSCE states expressed the view that an additional document was needed that would amplify the provisions of the convention and codify the organization's extensive rules of procedure.[42] Washington expressed continuing willingness to sign the 2007 draft convention, yet it adamantly opposed not only adoption but also even discussion of a constituent document, which it stated could be counterproductive. The US position derives from the suspicion that some states might use adoption of a constituent document to insert rules that would limit or inhibit the operations of OSCE's institutions, such as its Office for Democratic Institutions and Human Rights (ODIHR) and its Office of the High Commissioner on National Minorities. Irrespective of whether the US fears have any foundation, its unbending position means that the OSCE's acquisition of a legal personality remains stalled.[43]

The differing visions for and approach toward the OSCE of East and West, in particular Russia and the United States, are perhaps most clearly manifested in their views of ODIHR's approach to election observation.[44] Both ODIHR and the Russian government were mindful of their failure to reach agreement on observing the Russian elections of 2007 and 2008, and thus both parties were determined to avoid a repetition in the parliamentary and presidential elections in 2011–12. However, the requirements of each side were clearly far apart, as Russian authorities obviously desired to limit and control as much as possible any foreign presence, whereas ODIHR's leaders were dead set on avoiding any compromise of their existing logistical standards for mounting effective observation missions. ODIHR eventually agreed on roughly half the number of short-term observers (260 instead of 450) it had originally desired. However, with the addition of Parliamentary Assembly observers from the OSCE and Council of Europe, the number was deemed sufficient by ODIHR's election experts to provide an adequately founded, fair assessment of the elections. Meanwhile, the Russian authorities kept up a steady drumbeat of criticism aimed at Western election monitoring, claiming it was biased in favor of the West's geopolitical interests.[45]

ODIHR's evaluation of the parliamentary and presidential elections did little to dispel Russian criticism of election observations as geopolitically motivated. Under the direction and coordination of the Swiss diplomat Heidi Tagliavini, who had supervised a widely respected investigation of the 2008 Russia-Georgia war for the EU, the OSCE election observers' conclusions were artfully phrased, but unmistakable in their import: there were serious irregularities, particularly in the postelection counting, tabulating, and reporting of results.[46] The OSCE's conclusions simply confirmed what the Russian public was being shown on television and social media by its own domestic election observers, and this indubitably helped contribute to the popular outrage. The OSCE's comments on the presidential election in March 2012 were somewhat less critical, although the reports noted in particular some unfair practices and use of administrative resources during the campaign. The Russian reaction was pugnacious and unyielding. In a response to the ODIHR report and comments from some OSCE participating states, on March 8, 2012, the Russian ambassador to the OSCE pointed to comments from the Commonwealth of Independent States' observation mission and some individuals in the OSCE mission to the effect that the election was basically free and fair. The Russian representative added: "It is worth noting that the statement by the representative of the United States focused for the most part on the negative aspects of the findings by the OSCE/ODIHR mission. I should like to point out that violations occur in any country, including in the United States."[47] The message was clear: Moscow would decide what constituted objective commentary on Russian elections, and when violations needed to be acknowledged and addressed. The massive demonstrations after the Duma elections left the Kremlin feeling under siege, and ODIHR's criticisms were apparently perceived as joining the opposition, perhaps with ulterior motives. Just as the travails of the 2011–12 elections soured Putin's view of the United States, it did little to dispel his view of the OSCE as an instrument of Washington's geopolitical ambitions.

The continuing deadlock in the OSCE was illustrated starkly in the presentations of the Russian and American representatives to the Annual Security Review

Conference in June 2013, which the Ukrainian chairmanship dedicated toward providing content and direction to the Helsinki +40 process.[48] Russian deputy foreign minister Aleksey Meshkov called for the OSCE to pay more attention to security issues, rapidly citing the impending withdrawal of the UN-authorized International Security Assistance Force (ISAF) from Afghanistan and the "instability and unpredictability" in the Middle East and North Africa as examples of the type of problems he had in mind. He ran through a long list of hard security problems and called for interested participating states to focus on collective action "based on the strict observance of the norms and principles of international law." The American representative, US deputy assistant secretary of state Eric Rubin, conversely stressed the centrality of the Final Act's commitments on human rights and fundamental freedoms to the OSCE and European security. The differences in emphasis and direction were both obvious and immense. Clearly, the OSCE would not play any significant role in Euro-Atlantic security affairs as long as the OSCE's leading actors had such conflicting visions of what it should be.

## NATO: AN ALLIANCE IN SEARCH OF A MISSION?

Even though NATO proclaimed a new Strategic Concept in 2010, ostensibly providing an updated mission statement, the absence of any clear sense of direction nonetheless still seemed widespread among its many Allies. With the United States clearly eager to develop an exit strategy from Afghanistan, it was difficult to find Allies who were enthusiastic about ISAF. Europe's sluggish and uneven economic recovery and periodic crises within the euro zone made many European Allies even more reluctant than in the past to supply personnel for NATO's operations or to meet NATO's targets for national military spending. Arguments over the proper extent of NATO's expeditionary missions, in particular its mission in Afghanistan, developed into speculation that NATO was evolving into "a two-tier Alliance, where some do the (strategic, military, political, financial) heavy lifting while others just tag along, accomplishing menial tasks at best."[49]

The fears and recriminations expressed over an alleged "two-tier NATO" reflected a growing divergence within the Alliance in the nature, immediacy, and severity of the threats perceived by different allies and two distinct definitions of security (and how it might be ensured). For some allies, in particular the United States with its global reach and global concerns, international terrorism, instability, and failed states around the world remained serious threats, often demanding kinetic responses. For many of NATO's newest members in the East, and for a number of NATO partners from the former USSR, Russia constituted a continuing threat, which had grown in menace following the 2008 war with Georgia.[50] Yet some of the older NATO Allies—especially Germany, France, and Italy—contained substantial groups from business, society, and government that still pushed for cooperative relations with Moscow, hoping to make Russia a partner. Finally, NATO's southern tier of Mediterranean member states maintained a continuing concern about instability in the Middle East and North Africa, with the potential for prompting refugee flows, terrorism, and social and political instability in their own countries.

This diversity of views among NATO allies was not surprising given changes in the global strategic context since the end of the Cold War, and especially since 2001. In mid-2009, NATO's outgoing secretary-general Jaap de Hoop Scheffer noted that "in the Cold War, the threat we faced was both visible and measurable, and our responses were largely institutionalised. Alliance solidarity was near-automatic."[51] De Hoop Scheffer admitted that the contemporary security environment worked against such solidarity: "By contrast, many of today's challenges are regional in nature and do not affect all Allies in quite the same way. Many challenges also do not lend themselves to purely military solutions. And while some challenges require instant, perhaps even preventive action, others require long-term, costly, and risky engagement far away from our own borders."[52] The threats to post–Cold War Europe's security were multiple and variegated, and one's evaluation of which threat was most important depended considerably on where—from which capital—one viewed them.

The new Strategic Concept adopted at the Lisbon Summit attempted to overcome this divergence in perceptions of the changing strategic context and major threats by identifying three major objectives in describing the purpose of the Alliance: collective defense, crisis management, and cooperative security. Crisis management remained an ongoing concern for most Allies, given continuing low-level instability in the Balkans, but was no longer as vitally important to security and stability in the rest of Europe as during the 1990s. The trade-offs between collective defense and cooperative security, however, remained subjects of active debate after the Lisbon Summit. A number of factors were involved in this debate. Some European Allies, most notably Germany, perceived relatively few security threats to their own territory and were not persuaded that more distant foes—such as those in Afghanistan—placed their security and stability in immediate peril.[53] Other allies simply perceived threats from Moscow or the Maghreb as more immediate than the new and more distant dangers identified by American officials. One US military analyst identified missile defense, cyberwarfare, space operations, state-sponsored terrorism using weapons of mass destruction, conflicts in the Middle East or the Asia-Pacific region, and possible attacks arising from non–Article V operations as issues that argued for further development of NATO's expeditionary capabilities as part of collective defense in a globalized security environment.[54] In essence, even after adopting a new statement of purpose, NATO Allies remained basically divided on what the Alliance was for, what capabilities it needed, and how and where those capabilities should be used.

As Allies began the process of implementing their Lisbon decision to wind down their mission in Afghanistan, the Alliance was drawn into another conflict closer to home. When Muammar Gaddafi's troops threatened to slaughter Libyan opponents demonstrating against his regime, a group of Allied and Arab states, especially France and the United Kingdom, led a campaign to intervene to protect the civilian population. Although international intervention in Libya was managed by a multinational contact group and authorized by UN Security Council Resolution 1970 and Resolution 1973, the operation was NATO driven.[55] What began as a humanitarian operation was transformed relatively quickly into an exercise in regime change. Most of those participating in the operation (if not the so-called international community) argued that through his attacks on his own people Gaddafi had lost all legitimacy and had to go.[56] With support from NATO Allies and coalition partners, rebel forces captured Tripoli in August and killed Gaddafi in October, arrangements for a provisional government were established, and NATO announced a successful conclusion to Operation Unified Protector in October 2011.[57] Several years later, some might question characterization of the mission as a success, although immediately after Qaddafi's exit that seemed to be the case.

Whatever the judgments of historians concerning the ultimate success or failure of international intervention in Libya, several aspects of the operation were particularly revealing and of particular importance for NATO. With respect to capabilities, the United States supported the intervention and pushed for regime change but sought to allow European Allies to take the lead in military operations.[58] To the dismay of many allies (including Washington), European military capabilities proved insufficient for mounting, supporting, and sustaining the types and intensity of operations needed to have the desired effects on the ground. The coalition thus had to call on the United States to sustain the operation. In particular, the unique US capabilities in intelligence, surveillance, and reconnaissance; aerial refueling; and air defense suppression enabled Allies such as France and other coalition partners to make thousands of accurate attacks with relatively little acknowledged collateral damage.[59]

Although NATO secretary-general Rasmussen argued after the fact that any shortfalls in NATO's performance in Libya were due to political constraints, and not from lack of military capabilities, questions still remained whether NATO was really a two-tier alliance, with the United States and a few other allies making the lion's share of military contributions, or even simply a coalition of the willing in the form of an Alliance.[60] Although the US strategy of "leading from behind" seemed to work, one result of the Alliance's performance in Libya was further US disillusionment with the willingness of allies to contribute, epitomized by a speech given by US secretary of defense Robert Gates to NATO in June 2011.[61] Given Germany's abstention on UN Security Council Resolution 1973 and the unwillingness of some European Allies (Spain, the Netherlands, and Turkey) to participate fully in the operation, serious questions also arose whether Europe could realistically claim to have any sort of real common defense.

Russia, in particular Vladimir Putin, was extremely unhappy with NATO's intervention in Libya. Paradoxically, the Kremlin's displeasure with Operation Unified Protector did not seem to be reflected in the range or level of activities carried on under the aegis of the NATO-Russia Council. In his first speech after assuming the office in mid-2009, Secretary-General Rasmussen devoted his remarks to the NATO-Russia relationship, which he characterized as the Alliance's most important, yet "burdened by misperceptions, mistrust, and diverging political agendas."[62] Rasmussen found the Kremlin willing to reset relations with the Atlantic Alliance, just as with Washington. In meetings in December 2009 and June 2010, the NATO-Russia Council revived many cooperative activities that had lapsed after the Russia-Georgia war.[63] At the Lisbon Summit, NATO and Russian leaders agreed to expand their partnership and to resume cooperation in theater missile defense. In April 2011, NATO-Russia Council foreign ministers produced an Action Plan on Terrorism, and in June a Russian submarine took part in a NATO exercise.[64] Practical cooperation and activities at both working and senior levels continued through 2011 and 2012, seemingly irrespective of difficulties in bilateral political relationships between Moscow and various allies.

Russia's willingness to restore relations, cooperation, and practical activities with NATO did not reflect a change of heart in Moscow's view of the Alliance. In a major article in mid-2010 on Euro-Atlantic security, Russian foreign minister Lavrov made clear that Russia's preference for creating "equal security" for all in Europe had been (and generally remained) the OSCE.[65] However, Lavrov complained, Russia's Western partners had reduced the OSCE to "supervision of the humanitarian dimension 'east of Vienna,' " thus leaving only forums such as the NATO-Russia Council where hard security questions could be discussed. Lavrov deplored the new Strategic Concept for "globalizing the policy of NATO-centrism," including the "projection of military force to any region in the world." Lavrov asserted that Russia's new military doctrine did not see NATO per se as a threat but perceived danger in some possible future evolutions of the Alliance.

Writing almost a year later, Konstantin Kosachev, chairman of the Duma's Foreign Affairs Committee, echoed Lavrov's criticism of NATO's failure to perceive how its own attitudes and actions affect the rest of the world.[66] Kosachev examines the number of places and issues where Russian and NATO interests and activities collide or intersect and makes the argument that "if Russia cannot join NATO, then the Alliance and Russia need to be integrated . . . into something common that could be made to work." Lavrov's and Kosachev's arguments are typical of those from the more moderate, Western-leaning foreign policy and political elites in Russia and do not reflect a meeting of the minds with NATO leaders and supporters. On the contrary, Russian leaders clearly maintain their criticisms of the Western approach to Europe's security architecture but express willingness for cooperation if, when, and how it suits them. Russian leaders also understood that their Western counterparts clearly made their most important decisions about security and conducted their most important hard security business within NATO. Thus many Russian leaders clearly saw the NATO-Russia Council as a more productive forum for security dialogue with the West than the OSCE, not because NATO was preferable but because it was the only real game in town.

NATO leaders tried to convince their Russian counterparts that the Alliance posed no threat to Russia as they continued along the course last adjusted and approved in Lisbon in late 2010. Although the relationship with Moscow was important for the Allies, it was one among many issues that demanded attention of an Alliance with far-flung deployments and global concerns. Among the most important questions to be addressed following the adoption of a new Strategic Concept and other decisions made at Lisbon were (1) the pace of ISAF's withdrawal and the post-2014 relationship with Afghanistan; (2) NATO's overall force posture, including the mix of nuclear and conventional forces, in a new strategic environment; and (3) how to ensure sufficient military capabilities to meet NATO's stated goals, with many European Allies experiencing continuing economic hardship. The Alliance worked through 2011 and 2012 to craft decisions for these questions, to be adopted at a summit in Chicago in May 2012. These deliberations were set against the backdrop of the victory of a new Socialist Party president in France on May 6, who promised during his campaign to get French troops out of Afghanistan by the end of the year, and the heat of battle for the Republican nomination in the US presidential campaign, replete with debates over Libya, Syria, and Russia.

Notwithstanding the political cacophony, the Chicago Summit produced several solid, noteworthy results. The overall Summit Declaration contained no real surprises and, as was usually the case, presented a grab bag of current NATO positions on the full range of regional and topical issues with which the Alliance was engaged.[67] The allied heads of state and government issued a separate

Declaration on Afghanistan after a special meeting with President Hamid Karzai, which confirmed the intention of the Alliance to complete transfer of responsibility for security to Afghan forces by the end of 2014 and noted Karzai's announcement earlier that month that 75 percent of Afghanistan's population would soon be living in areas protected by these local forces.[68] The declaration also welcomed the conclusion of bilateral agreements between several Allies and the Afghan government. Though expressing continuing support for Afghanistan, it was clear from the declaration that the Alliance was on the way out.

The "Deterrence and Defence Posture Review," adopted at Chicago in response to a requirement set out by NATO's heads of state at Lisbon, was also arguably of considerable interest, even though without any real surprises.[69] The posture review provided a balanced restatement of NATO's nuclear weapons policies, which concluded that "the Alliance's nuclear force posture currently meets the criteria for an effective deterrence and defense posture." The Alliance expressed its commitment to nonproliferation and possible reductions in nuclear weapons but emphasized NATO's "commitment to remain a nuclear Alliance as long as nuclear weapons exist." The NATO statement needs to be understood against the background of the 2010 US nuclear posture review, the 2010 US-Russian New START agreement, and the new 2010 Russian military doctrine, in which Moscow explicitly made its nuclear deterrent the ultimate guarantee of its security against conventional attack.[70] In particular, in ratifying New START, the Senate required the Obama administration to pursue negotiations with Russia over tactical nuclear weapons, a subject also addressed in the 2010 Strategic Concept.[71] The Defense Posture Review thus attempts to balance between the desire of some allies (including some Americans) to reduce the number of tactical nuclear weapons deployed in Europe with Washington's desire to preserve leverage in any possible future tactical and strategic nuclear negotiations with Moscow.

As it turned out, Russia was not particularly interested in negotiating further strategic or tactical nuclear reductions, in part because these weapons served as deterrence against other foes, and in part because of another subject in the Defense Posture Review—missile defense. The Chicago Summit Declaration announced the Alliance's achievement of an "interim BMD [ballistic missile defense] capability," and the Defense Posture Review called the proliferation of ballistic missiles "an increasing threat" to Allies' security and declared that "missile defense will become an integral part of the Alliance's overall defense posture." In both statements, the Alliance's leaders insisted that a NATO ballistic missile defense capability was not directed against Russia and called for missile defense cooperation with Moscow. Although Russian experts participated in computer-assisted theater missile defense exercises with their NATO counterparts in 2012, subsequent events indicated that assurances such as those issued by NATO at the highest levels in Chicago would not be sufficient to allay Moscow's fears once relations began to sour.

NATO's greatest concern before and after the Chicago Summit arguably was not anything to do with Russia but the sufficiency of the Alliance's conventional military capabilities. The Alliance's performance in Afghanistan and Libya only fueled the perennial debates and laments within the Alliance over burden sharing and the need for increased defense spending. Little had changed in response to Secretary of Defense Gates's June 2011 complaint that despite 2 million troops in uniform, not counting the United States, NATO struggled to keep 40,000 in the field.[72] In a separate declaration at Chicago, NATO's leaders turned to the idea of "smart defense," first advanced by Secretary-General Rasmussen in February 2012, as a method of providing greater military capabilities during a time of continuing economic austerity.[73] The idea behind smart defense was for allies to work together to prioritize their national defense capabilities in line with NATO priorities, to cooperate with other allies in production to obtain economies of scale, and to specialize in capabilities useful to the Alliance.[74] Because the same countries were involved in both exercises, the Chicago NATO declarations explicitly link the smart defense initiative with the EU's Pooling and Sharing Initiative.

The problem, as Gates pointed out, was that the Alliance faced a continuing shortage of both resources and will. Analyzing the results of the Chicago Summit, a group of longtime NATO supporters concluded that "NATO faces more than just a simple, short-term budget squeeze; the Alliance is confronted with a secular trend that will have a serious impact on NATO Europe's ability to deploy and sustain power over long distances."[75] During the run-up and at the Summit in Chicago, NATO officials announced a number of projects to increase Alliance capabilities, such as an Alliance Ground Surveillance System, in which thirteen Allies would acquire drones capable of providing real-time battlefield intelligence.[76] The Alliance also announced arrangements to continue the air-policing mission over the three Baltic Sea states, none of which had its own air assets for such an operation. Notwithstanding efforts at a more rational setting of priorities and division of labor, the fact remained that the Allies with the largest defense establishments—Britain, Germany, France, Italy, Spain, the Netherlands, and Poland—in late 2012 all faced prospective significant cuts in their military budgets.[77] No amount of increases or efficiencies from NATO's twenty other members (excluding the United States) could be expected to make up for devastating cuts by the Alliance's larger members. In the assessment of those same (well-disposed) analysts, "at best, the United States can hope that NATO Europe, including France, the United Kingdom, Italy, and Spain, can maintain a militarily credible Mediterranean capacity, with the understanding of the limits of that capability."[78]

## A EUROPEAN SECURITY AND DEFENCE POLICY
## WITHOUT FUNDING, AN EASTERN PARTNERSHIP
## WITHOUT A EUROPEAN PERSPECTIVE

Although there were differences in economic performance among the countries of the EU, Europe as a whole had recovered far more slowly and unevenly
than North America from the global economic crisis. This basic feature of
the post-2008 global economy is important not only (as we have seen above)
because it resulted in an acceleration of Germany's preponderant economic
and consequent political influence within the EU and on the continent as a
whole. Continuing economic adversity in the EU and especially in the euro
zone substantially weakened Europe's security and defense capabilities, irrespective of whether one was speaking of the European Security and Defence
Policy or the European pillar of NATO. By the time the economic troubles had
dragged on for five years and the EU faced a new challenge from Russia at the
end of 2013, even favorably inclined analysts were speaking not only of an economic crisis but also of a political crisis that might threaten the very foundations
of the European Union.[79]

The structural flaws of the EU's Economic and Monetary Union certainly
contributed to the continent's economic woes as the crisis spread from North
America, but European policies made it much worse.[80] The European Central
Bank in 2008 injected almost 100 billion into the euro zone to restore liquidity,
but it was prevented by the EU Treaty from providing a bailout to a failing euro
zone national economy, such as Greece in 2009–2010. As the largest and health-
iest economy in the EU, Germany's voice carried the most weight, and German
chancellor Angela Merkel favored routing rescue packages through the International Monetary Fund (with the usual conditionality) and policies of fiscal
austerity. For various reasons, including recovery of influence lost by President
Jacques Chirac due to the fight he picked over Iraq in 2003, French president
Nicolas Sarkozy stuck closely to Chancellor Merkel's policy line. After the 2010
Conservative–Liberal Democrat victory in the United Kingdom, that country
was also a strong voice for austerity as the approach to reducing the debt and
deficit resulting from the crisis.

The result was that from 2009 to 2013, the EU lurched from crisis to crisis
with bailouts and rescue packages in Greece, Ireland, Portugal, and Cyprus;
and with serious economic difficulties threatening deeper troubles in Spain and
Italy. EU summits during this period saw leaders repeatedly agreeing on rescue
packages and emergency measures. The EU members amended the EU Treaty
to grant the European Central Bank greater powers in rescuing euro zone members, adopted the European Stability Mechanism as an early backstop against

financial failures, and negotiated an intergovernmental "fiscal compact" that would provide greater control over the fiscal policies of individual EU states via a balanced budget provision. Even with all this activity, the euro zone was preserved arguably as much by the activism of the European Central Bank's new president, the Italian Mario Draghi, who announced that the bank would do "whatever it takes" to preserve the euro.[81]

The politics of the EU's response to the ongoing economic crisis were complex. Chancellor Merkel quickly became *primus inter pares*, because Germany would supply the bulk of the funds required for the various bailouts. Merkel favored a closer political union, perhaps akin to a European federation. Sarkozy appeared to go along with Merkel, who supported him for reelection against the eventual winner in the 2012 French presidential vote, François Hollande. The latter was a critic of both austerity and the fiscal compact, favoring more "pro-growth" expansionary policies. UK prime minister Cameron, though an advocate of austerity, was critical of the fiscal compact and anything that smacked of a closer political union. At the same time, the EU Council and the European Parliament, both endowed with new powers by the Lisbon Treaty, fought an institutional turf battle over which might be the venue for crafting and adopting the fiscal compact. Although the council's victory reflected the reluctance of a number of EU states to concede even more sovereignty to Brussels, the increase in the visibility and authority of the European Parliament helped strengthen the rise in many countries of populist parties of the left and right, and also antiausterity, Eurosceptic, and disaffected political forces.

By the time she won reelection in 2013, Chancellor Merkel had emerged as the clear leader of Europe, although she still had many rivals and critics. Irrespective of the pros and cons of its economic policies at any particular time, Europe's continuing preoccupation after 2008 with financial and economic emergencies, and with EU institutional reforms to help respond to these, had at least two crucial political consequences. First, the crisis produced popular discontent and upheaval in a number of important European countries, which may yet call into question the nature and perhaps the very existence of the EU itself. Political developments in Hungary and the United Kingdom since 2010 come immediately to mind as examples of such phenomena. Second, the EU's common foreign and defense policies essentially ran on automatic pilot during much of this time, with economic austerity policies starving and eroding military capabilities, and the attention of senior political leaders focused more on economic and institutional issues than on crucial international issues and foreign relationships.

The EU's frequent high-level distraction from defense and security issues during the worst part of its lengthy economic crisis provoked serious questioning from the other side of the Atlantic of Europe's commitment to its own defense, far beyond the glib cliché that "Americans are from Mars, and Europeans are from Venus."[82] More seriously, one Defense Department strategist wrote in 2012 that "the real issue is no longer the nature of security relations between the United States and Europe, but whether Europe has much interest in maintaining a serious defense capacity."[83] Many British experts were in agreement, with one remarking that "the real issue is that other [besides the United Kingdom] European countries are not doing enough in spite of being urged from both sides of Brussels—by the European Union and the North Atlantic Treaty Organization."[84] European defense budgets kept shrinking, and even those European states that in the past maintained robust militaries began not only to shrink their forces but to divest themselves of entire categories of military capabilities.[85] As Operation Unified Protector finished up in Libya and ISAF wound down in Afghanistan, there were no signs that any European nation, in particular those with significant military capacities, had any plans to do anything in the context of either NATO or the Common Security and Defence Policy (CSDP) other than to reduce their defense expenditures and military capacities.

The CSDP also suffered from a general lack of activism, especially during the depths of the economic crisis, and from divergent views of the EU's major powers on what that policy should be. The German abstention on UN Security Council Resolution 1973 on the intervention in Libya came as an unpleasant and worrying surprise to both Berlin's NATO Allies and EU partners.[86] Germany's unfortunate experience in Kunduz, Afghanistan, in 2009 was thought by many to have reinforced a popular aversion to kinetic military interventions, a tendency reflected by Bundestag sentiment on the UN Libya vote. Germany thus remained a restraining force on EU expeditionary ventures, and Britain's participation in the CSDP did not succeed in convincing European partners to increase their military capabilities, while British leadership in effect restrained the use of CSDP, given London's Atlanticist preferences.[87] Both the United Kingdom and France were instrumental in the decision to use NATO as the basis for the coalition action in Libya, making the operation "Paris-London Plus, rather than Berlin Plus."[88]

France produced the biggest and most surprising changes in the European security landscape. President Sarkozy had already reversed forty years of Gaullist policy by bringing France back into NATO's military structures. Paris certainly showed itself to be an energetic, activist participant in NATO during the operation in Libya. In campaigning against Sarkozy, Hollande promised to withdraw French troops from Afghanistan and to make other changes in defense policy. However, after assuming office, Hollande basically maintained continuity in French foreign and security policies, while adopting a far less frenetic style than his predecessor.[89] Hollande commissioned a new white paper on defense and national security, issued in 2013, only the fourth in French history, yet only five years after Sarkozy's 2008 study.[90] The stated rationale for the new study was a need to take into account changes in the strategic environment resulting from the Arab Spring. It was reported that Hollande had already decided on the exercise during the campaign, both to have a road map for reducing defense expenditures as well as to reverse Sarkozy's decision to pay less attention to the Maghreb and Sahel. The 2013 white paper makes clear that France is a regional power, with a primary concern for North Africa. The French-led intervention in Mali in 2013 provided clear evidence that Paris had not abandoned CSDP. However, France's ambitions would be less far-reaching, its cooperation with Washington would be more forthcoming, and its capabilities—like those of all major European powers—would be considerably reduced.

Although the European Union has sought since 2004 to maintain a common approach to the countries in its immediate region—Eastern Europe, the Middle East, and the Mediterranean—through the European Neighborhood Policy, the Eastern Partnership (EP) initiative launched in the aftermath of the 2008 Russia-Georgia war effectively made the former Soviet countries to the EU's east a distinct policy issue. In addition, and perhaps more crucial, the EP separated EU relations with the six Western former Soviet states—Belarus, Ukraine, Moldova, Armenia, Azerbaijan, and Georgia—from EU-Russia relations. There was a widespread belief in European and North American diplomatic and political circles that the most ardent advocates of the EP, such as Sweden's Carl Bildt and Poland's Radek Sikorski, hoped that the initiative would serve as much to diminish Moscow's influence over these states as to bring them closer to Europe.[91] There is not sufficient evidence to conclude that the EU as a whole intended the EP to be a vehicle for geopolitical competition with Moscow for influence. Nonetheless, the EP did work against any possible tendencies within the EU bureaucracy to treat Russia and the six "Eastern Partners" as part of a single, larger region. Given Russia's consistent, ongoing expressions of deep interest in developments in this area and these states, such an approach was a clear recipe for confrontation and collision.

The EP rapidly developed into a classic EU program—large, complex, bureaucratic, with an increasing momentum of its own. The EP may have been most notable for what it did *not* do—offer any of the EU neighbors involved the prospect of membership. Although, "in principle, every European country has the possibility of joining the EU," by 2010 domestic politics in many established EU member states, anti-immigrant sentiment, and so-called enlargement fatigue all made it clear that the deck was stacked against any aspiring new members. The EP offered the six neighbors three major benefits: closer political association with the EU; selective social and economic integration; and mobility, in other words, freer travel in EU countries. The heart of the EP was individual bilateral negotiations with each of the six partners, although there were also multilateral thematic "platforms" designed to encourage reform on a regional basis.[92] Finally, there were key thematic "flagship initiatives," such as an integrated border management program, a small and medium-sized enterprise initiative, a regional energy markets and energy efficiency program, and a flagship initiative to promote good environmental governance.

By 2010, the EU had launched negotiations on an association agreement (AA) with five of the six, Belarus being the outlier.[93] The AAs might also include provisions for a Deep and Comprehensive Free Trade Area (DCFTA), which would provide increased access to the EU's common economic space. Negotiations on AAs proceeded exceedingly well with Moldova and—surprisingly, given the accession of the Yanukovych government in the spring of 2010—Ukraine. Moldova also pushed hard on the issue of visa-free travel to the EU and made enough headway on its action plan with the EU to achieve an agreement by 2014.[94] Moldova, Ukraine, and Georgia pushed hardest to use the EP as a means of pursuing European integration. Armenia was interested but was more dependent in economic and security affairs on Russia. Azerbaijan also was interested in some aspects of the initiative, but the EU's insistence on making progress on human rights kept Baku from serious engagement in the initiative. Following widespread condemnation of Lukashenko and subsequent international sanctions after the 2010 elections in Belarus, the EU sought ways to encourage change in the country, but it was not able to engage seriously in the framework of the EP.

Meanwhile, relations between Brussels and Moscow were spotty. Both Putin and Medvedev failed in their efforts to gain entry to Europe through the back door, via a special bilateral relationship with German chancellor Merkel. Russia-EU relations were managed by periodic summits, at which discussions became increasing testy, especially after Putin's return to the presidency, with regular ministerial and working level contacts to manage an array of specific issues.[95] EU-Russia trade continued to be enormous, with the EU as an aggregate remaining Russia's single largest trading partner. Russians traveled to Europe for business and pleasure at levels unimagined during the Cold War, and an agreement on visa-free travel was consistently on the top of Moscow's list on the bilateral agenda with Brussels. Much to Putin's frustration, there was little progress on this issue, and Brussels remained displeased over Moscow's unwillingness to respond to antimonopoly concerns reflected in the EU's Third Energy Package.[96] Overall, there continued to be a great deal of activity in the EU-Russia relationship, but little of this activity resulted in significant improvement in relations or notable achievements.

In the meantime, Putin accelerated his Eurasian integration projects. Russia pushed for the nascent customs union with Kazakhstan and Belarus to become a "single economic space," introducing protectionist measures such as increased tariffs and import barriers, that prompted EU complaints and dominated negotiations on a new agreement to replace the 1994 Partnership and Cooperation Agreement.[97] By late 2011, Russia, Belarus, and Kazakhstan had formally announced plans for the transformation of the Customs Union and the Eurasian Economic Community into a full-fledged Eurasian Economic Union by 2015.[98] The three leaders announced Kyrgyzstan's intention to join the Customs Union, transition to the Single Economic Space, and creation of the Eurasian Economic Commission, which began work in January 2012.[99] The declaration notes that membership in the Eurasian Economic Union is open to other states that share its goals and principles and expresses a desire for good relations with "other international integration entities, including the European Union." Although no specific candidates for membership were identified, Ukraine was clearly a key target in this integration program.[100]

As EU preparations intensified during 2013 for the Vilnius Eastern Partnership Summit, the competition between the EU and Putin's Eurasian integration project in Ukraine, Georgia, and Moldova became more and more zero-sum. Russian authorities used economic pressure to slow negotiations with the EU, imposing at various times embargoes on the import of Moldovan fruits and vegetables, meat, and wines into Russia. With Ukraine, Moscow played the energy card, driving difficult bargains on natural gas prices and pushing projects to bypass Ukraine for natural gas deliveries to the West.[101] In midsummer, Moscow also slowed down the transit of goods across the Ukraine-Russia border, and Putin warned of possible trade difficulties if Ukraine signed the deal with the EU.[102] In at least one case, the Russian pressure worked. With Armenia moving steadily toward completion of an AA with the EU, President Serzh Sargsyan suddenly traveled to Moscow in early September, met with Putin, and announced that Armenia would pursue Eurasian integration.[103] Despite pressure from Moscow, Kyiv continued its promising negotiations with Brussels on an AA. The single major obstacle to an agreement seemed to be the continued incarceration of former prime minister Iulia Timoshenko, despite mounting EU pressure on Yanukovych to free her. If that happened, most participants and observers expected that the AA would be signed at Vilnius.

Just days before the Vilnius Summit was due to begin, Yanukovych met unexpectedly with Putin in Moscow and then stunned his own country and the EU with the announcement that he was suspending negotiations on the AA with the EU.[104] Russia apparently offered Ukraine up to $15 billion in loans and credits, as much or more than Kyiv was attempting to obtain from the International Monetary Fund. At the Vilnius Summit a week later, Georgia and Moldova each initialed AA and DCFTA texts with the EU, despite continuing criticism and pressure from Russia.[105] EU representatives formally took note in the statement of Ukraine's decision to suspend temporarily work on the AA and DCFTA but took an unusual step by adding: "They also take note of the unprecedented public support for Ukraine's political association and economic integration with the EU."[106] The appearance of masses of pro-EU demonstrators in Kyiv's central square on the last day of November to protest Yanukovych's decision was an illustration of (but probably not a response to) this assertion.

As it turned out, the Russian pressure on Ukraine, the EU determination to go forward with the Ukraine AA and DCFTA, and the response of the Ukrainian public to their government's decision to postpone continuing with EU integration started a sequence of events leading to regime change and war in Ukraine, Russian seizure and annexation of Crimea, and a confrontation between Russia and the West that shows few signs of ending at this time. The crisis was particularly unexpected because it came over the EU's expansion into the territory of the former Soviet Union and Russia's immediate western neighborhood. The 2008 war with Georgia definitively showed Russia's attitude toward further NATO expansion into that region. However, until the November 2013 confrontation over Ukraine, many Western officials and experts continued to believe that Moscow's view of the extension of EU structures and influence into the near abroad would not be so hostile. This view turned out to be clearly mistaken.

In hindsight, the obvious questions arise: could Moscow's hostile, threatened reaction have been anticipated; and could anything have been done to avert it? To the first, the reply is almost assuredly "Yes, but." In May 2011, President Medvedev asserted that "if Ukraine were to take the road of European integration, it would be more difficult for the country to integrate with the Single Economic Space and the Customs Union. You cannot at the same time sit on two chairs."[107] Senior Russian officials, including Medvedev and Putin, made many such statements between 2011 and 2013, but for various reasons their Western interlocutors were not listening or did not hear. First, one set of EU officials was talking to Russia about Russia; another set of officials talked with the EP states about their relations with the EU. Second, Moscow had objected in similar terms to NATO and EU expansion in the past, but then had done nothing to follow up such complaints. Past experience and bureaucratization of the negotiation processes both tended to lead to the same conclusion—irrespective of its grumbling, Moscow would not act, and the EP was not part of the agenda with Russia anyway.

Unfortunately, the Kremlin wanted precisely what EU leaders were least likely and least willing to give: a decisive say over the political, economic, and security orientation of its neighbors. In the end, the preferences of the leaders and voting publics in Ukraine, Moldova, and Georgia did not seem relevant to Putin, Medvedev, or their colleagues. To be sure, Russia had (and has) legitimate interests in all three of those states and in all the other post-Soviet states that border on it. However, it does not seem either reasonable or necessary to equate accommodating real Russian interests with dictating a country's geopolitical orientation. The EU's behavior in developing the Eastern Partnership thus may not have been adequately sensitive to Russian concerns and interests. However, by making the issue a zero-sum game between the EP and the Eurasian Economic Union, Moscow made it much more difficult for these concerns and interests to be addressed or satisfied. Avoiding or resolving the confrontation over Ukraine that developed at the end of 2013 required understanding, flexibility, and imagination from both sides. Unfortunately, there seemed to be little of any of these necessary qualities from either side.

## 11. CONFRONTATION IN UKRAINE

### War in Europe Again

Even though Vladimir Putin garnered 64 percent of the popular vote in the March 2012 presidential election, he did not appear to feel secure in his position as he assumed the presidency for the third time in May 2012. The Russian government and the ruling party, United Russia, went to great lengths to mobilize popular support for Putin during the campaign in the first two months of 2012. Administrative resources probably padded the vote for him, but there was still plenty of genuine support for Putin, especially from one-industry, company towns such as Nizhnii Tagil. These towns were separated from Russia's more cosmopolitan urban centers, and workers credited Putin with keeping their plants going and thus preserving their livelihoods. Putin's opposition was weak and divided, and there was little doubt from the very start of the campaign that he would win; the only real question was his margin of victory.[1]

The source and location of the much of the opposition was of justified concern to Putin, however. Although he won a clear majority in the country as a whole, his support faltered in the wealthiest, most developed, most cosmopolitan urban centers.[2] For example, Putin received less than a majority or a bare majority in several of Russia's most developed European cities, including only 47 percent in Moscow, his poorest showing anywhere in the country. The opposition to Putin was strongest in these wealthy, developed, highly educated, technologically advanced urban areas. In essence, the new urban middle and professional classes, which had developed in Russia since 2000 in large part due to the era of unprecedented economic prosperity presided over by Putin, turned out to be the president's severest critics.

Putin's actions after his victory suggest that he perceived his domestic opponents and his critics abroad as simply two facets of one overall threat to his reelection and continuation in power. Although Putin accommodated the opposition somewhat during the campaign with concessions on political participation and election of officials, such as governors, he maintained that foreign actors, in particular the United States, were behind these opponents.[3] After his victory, Putin appeared to give his critics one last chance, and in April he appealed to the Russian population for unity now that the election had been decided. He responded to continued opposition protests on inauguration day with decisive, violent police repression.[4] In June, Aleksandr Bastrykin, a longtime Putin crony and the head of the Investigative Commission, orchestrated police raids of the homes of a number of prominent opposition leaders, allegedly seeking information about the Inauguration Day protests. Criminal cases were lodged against a number of protest participants and some opposition leaders, including a corruption charge unrelated to the May protests filed against the prominent regime critic Aleksey Navalny.

The show trial during the summer of 2012 of the three Pussy Riot band members arrested for an anti-Putin protest in the central Moscow Cathedral of the Savior was used by Putin and his colleagues to deepen their populist, nationalist anti-West campaign.[5] By condemning the trio for blasphemy in an action that might well have been prosecuted on a lesser charge, such as a particularly vulgar case of disturbing the peace, the Kremlin's action dovetailed with ongoing regime condemnation of Western support for homosexuality, same-sex marriage, and other alleged cultural deviations from traditional Christian morality. Such charges resonated with large, socially conservative, traditionalist, blue-collar and rural segments of Russian society. Western institutions such as the European Union were already on record as opposing discrimination on the basis of sexual preference, a controversial and often unpopular position in many traditional Eastern European societies. Russian television also ran "documentaries" purporting to prove Western support for critics and opponents of Putin, and the Kremlin was increasingly able to convince significant segments of its domestic audience that the West aspired to undermine traditional values and to replace the regime in Russia.

The cultural campaign allegedly in defense of traditional Christian values against Western decadence was only part of an overall policy approach from mid-2012 onward, suggesting that Putin was more afraid of the dangers to Russia's domestic political stability (and his own hold on power) posed by opening Russian civil society to contact with and influence from the West than he was fearful of the possible economic consequences of limiting access to Western intellectual inquiry and innovation. The increasing restrictions placed on non-governmental organizations (NGOs), the requirement of any institution receiving foreign funds to register as a "foreign agent," the passage of a new, tougher law on treason, and the harassment and—at times—persecution of independent thinkers taken all together projected the image of a country gradually turning itself into a fortress, armed against foreign penetration and influence. To the extent possible, Putin tried to portray these measures as similar to those taken by other countries to protect their own values and systems. For example, he attempted to equate Russia's foreign agents law with US legislation requiring lobbyists hired by foreign governments to register and divulge that employer–client relationship. When all was said and done, Putin's aim was clearly to eliminate foreign influences on Russia's domestic political situation, even at the price of foregoing some of the benefits of freer intellectual, commercial, and personal contacts between Russian citizens and the external world, especially the West.

As he was clamping down on signs of independence in Russian civil society, Putin also launched steady criticism of the post–World War II, post–Cold War international order created and still largely dominated by the major Western powers, in particular the United States. Putin's disillusionment with the West was already far advanced before he returned to the presidency. In the last of a series of articles he wrote during the campaign, he accused NATO of exporting "missile and bomb democracy" and complained that "the Americans have become obsessed with the idea of becoming absolutely invulnerable. This utopian concept is unfeasible both technologically and geopolitically, but it is the root of the problem. By definition, absolute invulnerability for one country would in theory require absolute vulnerability for all others. This is something that cannot be accepted."[6]

Putin professed readiness to cooperate with European and North American partners, but he complained that they would not meet Russia halfway. In early 2012, he still explicitly referred to Russia as "an inalienable and organic part of Greater Europe and European civilization. Our citizens think of themselves as Europeans."[7] He was clearly frustrated by Europe's failure to reciprocate his desire for a "common economic and human space from the Atlantic to the Pacific Ocean." Given the apparent unwillingness of Europe to integrate Russia, he insisted on his own Eurasian integration project, which he explained to a foreign audience in late 2012 explicitly using the EU as a "reference model."[8] He particularly complained where he thought Russia was not being treated as an equal by Europe, such as the EU's forcing of the third energy package on Russian firms and the failure to grant Russian citizens visa-free travel to EU countries. Turning to the United States, he particularly complained of actions and programs such as missile defense that harmed Russia's interests and eroded

Russian security. He warned that "mutual understanding [is not] strengthened by regular US attempts to engage in 'political engineering,' including in regions that are traditionally important to us and during Russian elections."[9]

Putin asserted that the world was moving from the immediate post–Cold War unipolar order dominated by the United States to a multipolar global system with power and influence transferring to new actors. The Russian Foreign Ministry's 2013 Foreign Policy Concept (which reportedly closely reflected Putin's thinking) asserted that

> international relations are in the process of transition, the essence of which is the creation of a polycentric system of international relations. . . . The ability of the West to dominate world economy and politics continues to diminish. The global power and development potential is now more dispersed and is shifting to the East, primarily to the Asia-Pacific region. The emergence of new global economic and political actors with Western countries trying to preserve their traditional positions enhances global competition, which is manifested in growing instability in international relations.[10]

This document identified the countries belonging to the Commonwealth of Independent States as the regional priority for Russian diplomacy, and it included a thinly veiled reference to American interventionism as one of the chief threats:

> Another risk to world peace and stability is presented by attempts to manage crises through unilateral sanctions and other coercive measures, including armed aggression, outside the framework of the UN Security Council. There are instances of blatant neglect of fundamental principles of international law, such as the non-use of force, and of the prerogatives of the UN Security Council when arbitrary interpretation of its resolutions is allowed.[11]

Putin was prepared for cooperation and, perhaps, integration—only on his own terms. When criticized by foreigners for failings in Russia's domestic governance or observance of international standards, he responded aggressively with charges of his own. For example, asked in autumn 2013 about Russia's failings in democracy, he noted that twice the United States had chosen a president with a minority of the popular vote, which he called "a flaw at the very heart of American democracy."[12] In the end, Putin was not willing to pursue cooperation or integration at the risk of losing his grip on political power at home. In addition to attacks on Russian NGOs and political activists allegedly receiving support from abroad, shortly after his inauguration he launched a campaign for repatriation ("de-offshorization" was the term he used) of Russian capital held or invested abroad.[13] He reorganized the Ria Novosti news service into Russia Today, under the acerbic Dmitri Kiselev—the better to respond to Russia's foreign critics by portraying Russia as a defender of traditional, conservative Christian values.

Putin also sought to demonstrate what he saw as Russia's proper role as a great power and leader among nations through grandiose international projects, in particular hosting high-profile international sports events. The Universiade games held in Kazan in the summer of 2013 provided an opportunity to show off the Upper Volga capital of Tatarstan—impressively restored, developed, and modernized with the assistance of local oil money.[14] To win the 2018 World Cup for Russia, Putin personally visited and lobbied the 2010 Executive Committee meeting of the Fédération Internationale de Football Association. However, the grandest and most immediate spectacle was the 2014 Winter Olympiad, to be held in Sochi, after Putin similarly made a personal visit to the International Olympic Committee's 2007 meeting in Guatemala City to win the games for that semitropical Black Sea resort. He enlisted his friends, cronies, and Russian oligarchs to make massive investments in infrastructure in Sochi and designated his most trusted troubleshooter, old Saint Petersburg colleague and deputy premier, Dmitri Kozak, to manage preparations for the games.[15] Both the Russian and international press were filled with charges of excessive spending, shady contracts, corruption, delays, and other abuses. Some of Putin's critics almost seemed to wish for failure; in the end, despite fears that warm weather and inadequate infrastructure might produce a disaster, the Sochi games came off splendidly for Russia, providing both a good show and many medals for the host country.[16]

The criticism of uncontrolled spending and waste at Sochi had particular resonance given Russia's economic situation at the time. When Putin returned to the presidency and then Russia joined the World Trade Organization later in 2012, the Russian economy was outperforming most of the European economies, many of which were deeply affected by the ongoing euro zone crisis. However, as Putin himself admitted in 2012, some 50 percent of Russia's budget revenues came from oil and natural gas sales, and the economy was greatly in need of diversification. Major studies by Russian think tanks run by leading social and economic experts, such as former minister of finance Aleksei Kudrin or former Medvedev adviser Igor Yurgens, suggested that Russia's apparent prosperity and stability could deteriorate in the relatively near term due to the underlying structural weaknesses of the domestic economy and the social implications of that weakness.[17] Economic growth was gradually beginning to slow, and only improvements in investment and productivity promised a sustainable reversal of this trend. To offer a mild oversimplification of the situation, the regime faced a basic choice between reform and decay.

As long as oil prices remained relatively stable, Putin seemed prepared to risk slow economic decline in preference to the chance of political instability that might be a result of significant economic reform. Instead, the Kremlin might look to the Eurasian integration project and diversification of Russia's external trade partners, in particular deepening ties with China, as alternatives to seemingly risky domestic change. In this set of calculations, one factor that stood out was the crucial role to be played by Ukraine in the Kremlin's economic policy plans. Russian officials, including Putin himself, repeatedly made clear in private and in public Ukraine's importance for the Russian economy, the Customs Union, and the prospective Eurasian Economic Union.[18] In a discussion with Romano Prodi at the 2013 Valdai Club meeting in September 2013, Putin gave a lengthy explanation of Russia's economic interests that he saw hanging in the balance as Ukraine faced the choice between the EU and the Eurasian Economic Union.[19] Although Putin's concerns were politely stated, and included lip service to Ukraine's right of free choice, the message was clear—this is our neighborhood, and we will protect it.

## THE LIMITS OF COOPERATION: THE ROAD TO DAMASCUS

As Barack Obama won reelection and laid out priorities for his second term, the problem of Syria was among those that loomed largest on his agenda. Indeed, though the president and the appropriate senior administration officials would have attested to the importance of relations with Moscow and Kyiv, in reality Russia, Ukraine, and even European security did not seem to be anywhere near the top of the list. President Obama and Secretary of State Hillary Clinton had proclaimed a pivot (later, rebalancing) to Asia in the overall context of addressing the rise of China. The United States had left Iraq more abruptly and completely than it desired at the end of 2011, but America still remained deeply involved in the Middle East, both with the ongoing fallout of the Arab Spring and the nuclear negotiations with Iran. American and NATO troops remained in harm's way in Afghanistan, and managing a successful exit and handover to the Afghan government by the end of 2014 remained a crucial goal.

Russia was important to President Obama and his administration largely in an instrumental sense rather than for the bilateral relationship itself. With US national security adviser Thomas Donilon's visit to Moscow in April 2013, Obama tried to get Putin interested in negotiating further cuts in strategic arms. For many reasons, Moscow was not biting. Aside from arms reductions, the new administration really needed Russian cooperation for two things: (1) to push the nuclear negotiations with Iran; and (2) to address the deepening revolt and chaos in Syria. Although Moscow might share interests on these two issues that would incline it toward cooperation with Washington, there were few other political or personal reasons for Putin to seek a closer relationship with US president Obama. Obama's signature on the Magnitsky Act, and ongoing US human rights criticism of Russia, were taken by Putin and his Kremlin colleagues as attempts to weaken or change the regime in Russia.[20] One need only inspect the collection of photos of the two leaders at the June 2013 Group of Eight (G-8) Summit in Northern Ireland to understand that the relationship between the two leaders was, at best, not particularly warm.[21] When Russia granted asylum to fleeing US intelligence employee Edward Snowden, who turned up in Moscow's Sheremetevo Airport in late June 2013, there was not enough content in the bilateral relationship to keep a planned September Putin-Obama meeting in Moscow on the books.[22] Although Putin generally maintained a professional neutrality in his public references to Obama and other counterparts, Obama's characterization of Putin slouching like a "bored kid" at international meetings did nothing to improve relations, as Obama called for a "pause" in United States–Russia ties for reassessment.[23]

Despite cancellation of the summit, within weeks Putin would be pulling Obama's chestnuts out of the fire in the ongoing war in Syria. The apparent use of chemical weapons by Syrian government forces near Damascus in August 2013 in which large numbers of civilians were killed seemed a direct challenge to Obama's December 2012 warning that President Assad would be "held accountable" if he used such weapons.[24] The August attack brought to a head debates within a deeply divided US administration over the use of force and direct American involvement in Syria. Having decided earlier in 2013, after long deliberation, to provide arms to selected rebel forces, President Obama chose to place the issue before the US Congress. The White House then suffered an egregious setback when UK prime minister Cameron lost a vote in the British Parliament on potential military intervention in Syria.[25] As the United States seemed to prepare for unilateral military action, Putin and Obama exchanged barbs at the Group of Twenty Summit in Saint Petersburg over intervention in Syria. Swayed by the challenges of potential unilateral action and mounting criticism in Congress, the Obama administration suddenly accepted a Russian proposal to force Assad to account for and give up his chemical weapons.[26]

US secretary of state John Kerry and Russian foreign minister Sergei Lavrov worked out a deal in Geneva by which Syria would accede to the Chemical Weapons Convention and permit the Organization for the Prohibition of Chemical Weapons to remove and destroy its chemical arms.[27] Under apparent Russian pressure and persuasion, Assad admitted he possessed such weapons and agreed to cooperate in eliminating them. The deal was a triumph for Putin, and a relief for the Obama administration, which faced no guarantee of success either in a military intervention or in an encounter with Congress. Putin took advantage of the occasion to plug his point of view on the pages of the *New York*

*Times*, which published an op-ed piece by the Russian President on September 12, 2013.[28] Putin's arguments in favor of the primacy of the United Nations and against the use of military force were nothing new, but the vehicle for bringing them to Western publics was out of the ordinary. Although he praised President Obama for his wisdom in joining Russia to avoid war, Putin could not resist getting at least one dig. Noting Obama's reference to American exceptionalism in his address to the American people, Putin added: "It is extremely dangerous to encourage people to see themselves as exceptional, whatever the motivation. There are big countries and small countries, rich and poor, those with long democratic traditions and those still finding their way to democracy. Their policies differ, too. We are all different, but when we ask for the Lord's blessings, we must not forget that God created us equal."[29]

The agreement on Syria's chemical weapons, like Russia's continuing support for the five plus one negotiations with Iran on that country's nuclear program, was an issue-specific transactional arrangement rather than a sign of relations improving on a broader spectrum. In particular, cooperation on the joint framework of the Organization for the Prohibition of Chemical Weapons and the United Nations to remove and dispose of Syria's chemical arms did not bring Moscow and Washington appreciably closer on what to do about Assad or whether any Syrian rebel groups merited support. As far as the Kremlin was concerned, US or NATO intervention in Syria was just as likely to produce a result like that in Libya, where some two years after Western intervention the country had descended into chaos and civil war and the US ambassador had been killed by terrorists in the very city he had first helped to save in the spring of 2011. Stripped of the references to civilian hardships and casualties (which many Putin critics deemed to be crocodile tears), the Russian argument on a pragmatic level was that Western intervention had been consistently destabilizing, creating insecurity, causing local actors to arm and resist to protect themselves. In this view, foreign intervention, especially with the military, was more likely than not to make things worse rather than better. In the Middle East, Moscow remained a fundamentally conservative, status quo power.

# WHERE THE EU ENDS:
# CONFRONTATION IN UKRAINE

Speaking in the summer of 2014, a senior politician from an EU country that had been instrumental in devising the Eastern Partnership asserted that he and his EU colleagues had known, especially since 2008, of Russia's adamant opposition to Ukrainian membership in NATO, but they had little idea or warning that Moscow would also display such hostility to Kyiv's closer association with the EU.[30] A decade earlier, at the time of the Orange Revolution, there might have been some basis in fact for believing that Moscow held substantially different views with respect to NATO enlargement and EU expansion. By 2013 there could be little doubt, given direct evidence such as Putin's September exchange with Prodi at the Valdai Club, that the Kremlin also perceived EU penetration into the near abroad as a direct threat to Russian interests. EU officials continued with the process of deeper association at the heart of the Eastern Partnership despite explicit Russian objections and warnings, often characterizing such objections as unwarranted and unjustified, and apparently assuming that in the end Moscow would accommodate itself to the expansion of EU influence, as it had done in the past with previous NATO and EU enlargements.

In addition, the attention of the most senior EU political leaders remained fixed on the euro zone crisis, populist criticism of "excessive" European integration, and the economic and political future of the Union itself. Except for a banking crisis in Cyprus, which eventually required an EU–International Monetary Fund bailout and significant costs imposed on depositors as part of the settlement, the euro zone experienced a relatively tranquil year after the decisive intervention of European Central Bank president Marion Draghi in 2012.[31] However, the European Council still focused much of its attention in 2013 on economic issues such as stubborn, very high youth unemployment, sluggish to no growth in much of the Union, and implementing the so-called fiscal compact in the hope of achieving more binding rules for budget and fiscal policies across Europe. The midsummer Snowden revelations of extensive clandestine US intelligence gathering in Europe prompted widespread consternation and indignation in Europe and strained relations between Washington and many of its Allies, in particular Berlin, with reports that the National Security Agency had eavesdropped on Chancellor Angela Merkel's personal cell phone.[32]

Furthermore, the European Union was divided as well as distracted. Chancellor Merkel's personal prestige and authority were enhanced by her reelection to a third term in September 2013, but German preeminence in EU affairs was deeply resented by a number of EU states, in particular those on the southern periphery in the greatest economic difficulty.[33] The Paris–Berlin axis within the EU remained little more than an historical facade, as France labored under continued economic malaise and greatly increased strength shown by the right-wing National Front. The United Kingdom, especially after Cameron's objection to the fiscal compact, remained apart and even uncertain about staying in the EU. Scotland's September 2014 referendum on independence would distract the United Kingdom even further. Poland, which had come through the global economic crisis better than many of its EU partners, was in no hurry to adopt the euro but was increasingly frustrated at its exclusion from euro zone policy deliberations. Overall, this was not an environment conducive to crafting a decisive, unified, consistent foreign policy on any subject, let alone relations with Russia and Ukraine.

Against this backdrop, the EU negotiations with Ukraine on an Association Agreement (AA) and a Deep and Comprehensive Free Trade Area (DCFTA) were as much a bureaucratic as a foreign policy exercise. The AA talks began in 2007 and the DCFTA discussions started in 2008, both while Orange Revolution leaders Viktor Yushchenko and Iulia Timoshenko were still in office.[34] When Viktor Yanukovych defeated Timoshenko and replaced Yushchenko as president in 2010, many foreign observers were surprised that he continued to press ahead toward a closer association with the EU despite the almost universal image of him as highly pro-Russian. At the same time, from the inception of the Customs Union in 2010, Putin put steady pressure on Yanukovych to join. Seeking to play the EU and Russia off against one another to his own political advantage, Yanukovych finally signed up as an observer in the Customs Union in the summer of 2013. Meanwhile, Ukraine initialed an AA and DCFTA with the EU in 2012, and as the Vilnius Eastern Partnership Summit approached, the greatest obstacle to signing these agreements seemed to be Yanukovych's continuing reluctance, despite growing pressure from Brussels and other EU capitals, to release Iulia Timoshenko, imprisoned since 2011 on charges of corruption.

Matters came to a head in the summer and fall of 2013. Both Russia and the EU presented the issue as a zero-sum choice. EU officials told Yanukovych that membership in the Customs Union would be incompatible with an AA and DCFTA, an assertion repeated by Štefan Füle, the EU's commissioner for enlargement, in a September 2013 speech, along with a blunt warning to Moscow not to interfere with the "sovereign choices" of the countries negotiating with the EU.[35] Ten days later, in front of Western officials and experts, Putin replied bluntly: "We are . . . warning in advance and saying: we understand all this, it's your choice, go ahead if you want to, but keep in mind that we will somehow have to protect our market and introduce protective measures. We are saying this openly and in advance, so that afterwards you will not accuse us of interfering with anyone or questioning another country's sovereign right to decide in favor of the EU."[36]

Beginning in July 2013, Moscow had already started to apply economic pressure on Kyiv, imposing import bans on a number of Ukrainian products and causing great slowdowns for traffic at crossing points on the Ukraine/Russia border. Also at risk was the favorable price for Russian natural gas that Ukraine could receive in return for signing up with the Customs Union.[37] In spite of all the Russian pressure, it seemed to be Yanukovych's intent, and Ukraine's choice, to sign the AA and DCFTA at Vilnius in November.

By late 2013, Brussels and Moscow were on a collision course in Kyiv, a situation of which both seemed aware and yet unconcerned. Once Yanukovych made his surprise decision on the eve of the Vilnius gathering to postpone completion of the AA and DCFTA, Washington happily joined the pileup. In retrospect, it is difficult to understand how American, European, and Russian political leaders and diplomats failed to see the crisis coming.[38] Ukraine suffered particularly deep and lasting economic reverses from the global crisis of 2008–9, with the collapse of global commodity prices (including steel) adding to the trouble. Kyiv desperately needed external financing; the 2010 extension of the Black Sea Fleet basing agreement was reportedly a condition for obtaining a large Russian loan.[39] In 2011, Ukraine lost a large loan package from the International Monetary Fund after failing to satisfy the attached conditionality. By mid-2013, Ukraine was again in deep economic and financial trouble and seeking a bailout to avoid default in 2014. When, in mid-November, the IMF brushed off Kyiv's bid for a standby arrangement, and Yanukovych could not get a loan package from the EU, he apparently he felt he had no other choice than to accept a bailout outlined by Putin earlier in the month.

The Ukrainian president's announcement on November 21, 2013, that work on the AA and DCFTA would be suspended shocked European leaders and the Ukrainian public. At the Eastern Partnership Summit in Vilnius, the assembled European heads of state and government had one more go at Yanukovych, stressing the long-term benefits of the AA and DCFTA, and even reportedly offering to drop their demand that Timoshenko be freed.[40] Yanukovych may well have understood the long-term benefits, but his European interlocutors apparently failed to comprehend the scale of his immediate financial needs and the political peril of running for reelection in 2015 as president of a bankrupt state. Putin understood money, making public a $15 billion Russian-funded rescue package for Ukraine in December, but the Russian president completely failed to understand the Ukrainian public. Although the Ukrainian body politic may have been split relatively evenly between the EU and the Customs Union, the support for and hope in European integration was both broad and deep, touching and mobilizing at least half of Ukraine's population, especially the young, energetic, and politically active. As the country had first demonstrated during the Orange Revolution, Ukraine had an active and growing independent civil society, which in November 2013 rallied to protest Yanukovych's decision to put the EU on hold.

The story of the popular demonstrations on Kyiv's Maidan Nezalezhnosti (Independence Square, or just the Maidan), which grew into a revolt that eventually caused Yanukovych to flee the capital and the country, has been told many times and does not need to be retold here.[41] Although there are still great controversies and bitter disputes over many of the particulars of this history, a few generally undisputed aspects stand out. The EU and the United States generally supported the demonstrators and the opponents of Yanukovych, and Russia clearly sided with the Ukrainian president. Moscow portrays Yanukovych's ouster as a coup engineered by outside actors, whereas the United States and the EU generally view the Maidan and the events leading to Yanukovych's flight as an indigenous popular revolt. This disagreement reflects a growing disparity between the views of Moscow and the West on the origins and proper role of civil society and social movements in general, and in Russia's near abroad in particular.[42] Russia, the EU, and the United States found it very difficult to agree on anything or to cooperate in addressing the crisis in Ukraine. Eventually, though, on February 21, 2014, the foreign ministers of Germany, France, and Poland, along with a Russian representative as an observer, managed to broker an agreement between Yanukovych and the leaders of the main opposition parties to hold early presidential elections in December 2014. However, this agreement was shouted down when presented to demonstrators on the Maidan; Yanukovych fled overnight under circumstances that remain murky; and by midday February 22, Ukraine had a provisional government elected by the two-thirds of the Rada deputies who remained at their posts.

Putin watched the final days of the Sochi Olympiad as he received the news from Kyiv, which indubitably lessened his enjoyment of the closing ceremonies and the medal count posted by Russian athletes. What he saw in Ukraine's capital on the morning of February 22 was not what his representative had reported the previous evening to be the deal between the EU foreign ministers and the Ukrainian opposition leaders. As soon became clear, Putin was utterly disgusted with his EU and other Western colleagues. By Putin's own account, we know that he and colleagues in Russia's security forces assisted Yanukovych in his flight from Kyiv and then from Ukraine.[43] Moscow also moved with remarkable speed to infiltrate Russian special forces in unmarked uniforms into Crimea (*zelenye chelovechki*, or little green men), to surround Ukrainian military installations in Crimea with Russia naval infantry forces stationed on the peninsula under an agreement with Kyiv, and to organize a referendum, in which the population in Crimea was reported to vote overwhelmingly in favor of leaving Ukraine and joining Russia.[44] On March 18, Putin signed a treaty making Crimea and Sevastopol parts of the Russian Federation; on March 20, the State Duma ratified the treaty with only one dissenting vote. This was the first time since World War II that any European state had taken and annexed territory from another European state through the use of force.

The EU (and the United States) responded, first to the seizure of Crimea and then to the conflict in Eastern Ukraine, with a gradually increasing set of sanctions.[45] Brussels was clearly not buying Moscow's charges that its European partners had failed to implement the February 21 deal in Ukraine, or that an externally engineered right-wing coup was placing Russian citizens and Russian speakers in Ukraine in danger. By March 3, Germany, France, Italy, and the United Kingdom agreed with the United States, Canada, and Japan to halt preparations for the upcoming G-8 Summit in Sochi, and that for the time being the G-8 should once again become the G-7. The EU Council imposed travel bans and asset freezes on specific individuals identified as sharing responsibility for the crisis, suspended bilateral talks with Russia on visas and a new EU-Russia agreement, canceled the EU-Russia Summit, and began preparation of further-reaching economic and trade sanctions. Following Moscow's failure to follow through on steps agreed in high-level talks on the conflict and the MH17 tragedy (the tragic shooting down of an Air Malaysia plane in July 2014), the EU and the United States adopted far more stringent individual, economic, and trade sanctions against Russia.[46] The late July EU measures were particularly serious; they restricted Russia's public and private access to European long-term capital markets, a serious blow for many Russian state-owned and private firms in need of financing. As of this writing, the EU has strengthened these economic sanctions several times, with the latest extension coming in mid-2017.

## CONFLICT IN UKRAINE: THE OSCE RETURNS

Putin's speech to the Russian legislature on March 18 was a defiant denunciation of the post–Cold War international order in Europe set out in the Helsinki Final Act and in the post–Cold War extension of that order in the Copenhagen Document and Charter of Paris.[47] Putin called the events of February 21–22 in Ukraine a coup carried out by "neo-Nazis, fascists, Russophobes, and anti-Semites," and he claimed there was no legitimate authority in that country. He justified Russia's annexation of Crimea as defense of Russian speakers and compatriots there, adding that the peninsula was transferred illegally to Ukraine in 1954 under a totalitarian regime. He denied that Russia was violating international law, pointing to the recent referendum in Crimea and to US statements in 2009 justifying Kosovo's declaration of independence and international recognition. Putin explicitly rejected arguments by the United States and others that Kosovo was a special case, asserting that instead it was typical of Western behavior:

> Our Western partners, led by the United States of America, prefer not to be guided by international law in their practical policies, but by the rule of the gun. They have come to believe in their exclusivity and exceptionalism, that they can decide the

destinies of the world, that only they can ever be right. They act as they please: here and there, they use force against sovereign states, building coalitions based on the principle "If you are not with us, you are against us." To make this aggression look legitimate, they force the necessary resolutions from international organisations, and if for some reason this does not work, they simply ignore the UN Security Council and the UN overall.[48]

Putin charged that contemporary events in Ukraine continued a pattern of Western aggression and support for regime change seen in the 1999 NATO war with Serbia and the color revolutions throughout the post-Soviet space. Putin protested that Russia wanted only peace and cooperation with its international partners, but would defend itself, its citizens, and Russians everywhere. He noted that some "Western politicians" were already talking of punishing Russia for its actions, by imposing sanctions and the like. Putin retorted defiantly "we will respond to them accordingly."

Ominously for Ukraine, in that same speech Putin indicated possible designs also on the country's southeast: "After the revolution, the Bolsheviks, for a number of reasons—may God judge them—added large sections of the historical South of Russia to the Republic of Ukraine. This was done with no consideration for the ethnic makeup of the population, and today these areas form the southeast of Ukraine."[49] Showing that this remark was more than just a casual historical allusion, in his annual marathon call-in press conference in April 2014, Putin repeated that in tsarist times, Luhansk, Kharkov, Donetsk, Kherson, Mikolayiv, and Odesa—in total, almost a third of the country—were not part of Ukraine.[50] And, indeed, even while Russia was still digesting Crimea, protests against the new government in Kyiv broke out across Ukraine's Russophone south and east, most of them clearly with Moscow's sympathy, if not support. Putin revived the term Novorossiia ("New Russia"), first applied to this broad region when it was joined to Russia by Empress Catherine the Great. Despite sizable demonstrations against the new government in Kyiv in a number of southern and eastern Ukrainian cities (most notably, Odesa in early May), sustained separatist movements and revolts took root only in the two easternmost provinces, Donetsk and Luhansk, the heart of the so-called Donbas, with ethnic Russians making up 38 to 39 percent of the population.[51]

Russian and Western perceptions of what was going on in Ukraine at this time were diametrically opposite. Moscow focused on the extreme right-wing groups and individuals involved in the protest against Yanukovych, such as the right-wing parliamentary party Svoboda, the armed militants Pravy Sektor (Right Sector), who were at the heart of the street battles with Yanukovych's security forces, and various participants in the Maidan demonstrations who supported controversial World War II–era figures such as Stepan Bandera, who fought with the Nazis against the Soviets. The Kremlin pointed with special indignation at the abortive attempt of the Ukrainian Rada to repeal Yanukovych's 2012 language law, which permitted localities to recognize a second official language (in almost all cases this was Russian) in addition to Ukrainian. Putin and his colleagues adhered consistently to the line that the new authorities in Ukraine were neofascist nationalist Russophobes bent on repressing Ukraine's sizable ethnic Russian and Russian-speaking population.

Western supporters of the new government in Kyiv saw the events from November 2013 through the end of February 2014 as a genuine popular revolution against a corrupt, authoritarian president and regime. American and EU political leaders and experts focused on the so-called Euromaidan, those numerous participants in the demonstrations in Kyiv and elsewhere who genuinely supported a policy of European integration for Ukraine and who were fed up with the corruption, incompetence, duplicity, and antidemocratic practices of Yanukovych and his government. Western observers pointed to the use of force by Yanukovych's security organs and unofficial thugs, the so-called *titushki* used to beat up and terrorize antigovernment demonstrators, while they played down the presence and importance of far-right, neofascist, violent elements in the anti-Yanukovych forces. When all is examined, said, and done, the fact remains that the West—the EU and United States—liked the result, and the Russians did not. Each side emphasized those aspects of the protest movement that tended to support its own view, though neither appeared to seek a balanced or detached approach to events in Ukraine.

Given that the standoff in Ukraine was between Russia on one hand, and the EU, NATO, and the United States on the other hand, the Organization for Security and Cooperation in Europe (OSCE) turned out to be the sole regional forum in which all the participants and interested parties in the conflict could meet and engage substantively with one another. Ukraine held the Chair of the OSCE when the Maidan demonstrations broke out, and the OSCE Ministerial Council meeting in Kyiv in December 2013 took place within a moderate walking distance of the heart of the protests. The results of Ukraine's chairmanship were modest, but no worse than in recent years. Pursuant to a decision in Dublin, Ukraine launched the "Helsinki +40" process, a new exercise in discussing the OSCE's role and purpose.[52] The Ukrainians set progress on protracted conflicts as a priority, and they were able to negotiate ministerial statements on both the Moldova-Transdniestria and the Nagorno-Karabakh conflicts. The hosts also pointed out that for the first time in years, an OSCE ministerial meeting adopted a consensus decision in the third, human dimension basket.[53] The Kyiv Ministerial Council also held a separate NGO event, as was the OSCE custom, but the real NGO meeting was going on in Ukrainian society in downtown Kyiv.

Switzerland took over the OSCE Chair in 2014 with the expectation that one of their most difficult tasks might be preparing Serbia's relatively thin foreign ministry for the 2015 Chairmanship.[54] However, the Swiss had no more than started to make the Chairmanship's usual rounds when the emerging crisis in Ukraine brought calls for OSCE intervention. At Ukraine's request, with strong support from the United States, in March 2014 the OSCE agreed to establish a Special Monitoring Mission (SMM) in Ukraine, aimed at "reducing tensions and fostering peace."[55] The observers were to be deployed around the whole country; up to 500 were authorized, with about 250 in place toward the end of the year. Although Ukraine, Russia, the EU, Canada, and the United States disagreed over whether Crimea should be covered as part of Ukraine, the OSCE participating states otherwise all found it in their interest to establish an avowedly neutral monitoring presence in the country, given the extreme divergence of their national reporting and analysis of events in Ukraine. The SMM has provided almost daily reports on fighting, unusual movements, and other incidents, as well as several longer thematic reports on the effects of the conflict.[56] SMM observers were the first outsiders on the scene and provided much of the initial reporting on the tragic shooting-down of an Air Malaysia flight (MH17) in July. In the wake of steady expansion of the conflict in Donetsk and Luhansk and the MH17 tragedy, the OSCE accepted Russian foreign minister Lavrov's earlier invitation to deploy observers at two Russian checkpoints on the Russian/Ukrainian border near Donetsk.[57] Sixteen OSCE observers (later up to twenty-two) were duly deployed to border installations near Gukovo and Donetsk and began reporting on cross-border movements. Serious debate raged over how much transparency and confidence their presence added because the Russian authorities sought to restrict their movement to the immediate area of the checkpoints, on a border stretching hundreds of kilometers across easily passable, largely unmonitored territory.[58]

The OSCE was quickly drawn into mediation of the conflict in Ukraine. In mid-April, US secretary of state Kerry, Russian foreign minister Lavrov, EU high representative Ashton, and Ukrainian acting foreign minister Deshchytsia agreed in Geneva on a package that included an end to rebel violence and seizure of government buildings, decentralization reforms by the Ukrainian government, and a sizable role for the OSCE in managing deescalation of the conflict.[59] On this, as on many subsequent occasions, the agreement reached by diplomats outside the country had little effect on local actors and the spiral of violence on the ground in the region. In May, Swiss president and chairman-in-office Burkhalter appointed the well-known Swiss diplomat Heidi Tagliavini as the OSCE Chair's representative in the Trilateral Contact Group (TCG), along with Russian ambassador to Ukraine Zurabov and former Ukrainian president Leonid Kuchma. The TCG became the basic forum for negotiating with representatives of the rebel Donetsk and Lugansk entities, and as such was the chief vehicle for conflict resolution.

After the election of the businessman (some would say oligarch) and former foreign minister Petro Poroshenko as president in late May, talks about a possible solution in Ukraine became more serious, but the violence continued to escalate. Poroshenko met with French president François Hollande, Russian president Putin, and German chancellor Merkel at a high-level observance in France of the seventieth anniversary of D-Day, launching what immediately was called the Normandy Process, replacing the Kerry-Lavrov Geneva Format. Poroshenko announced a "peace plan" but also sought to press the rebels in Donetsk and Luhansk into submission with a military offensive. The MH17 tragedy brought a wave of international sympathy and support for Ukraine, and Kyiv's forces made steady progress in reclaiming territory from the rebels well into August. Moscow then stepped in. In addition to earlier reinforcement of the rebel leadership with veterans from other protracted conflicts around the former Soviet space, the Kremlin sent a massive aid convoy of dozens of trucks, and—most important—Russian troops to supplement the rebels' military units. Overextended Ukrainian fighters suffered sudden and grievous reverses, including a disastrous encirclement at Ilovaisk.[60] Meanwhile, Putin and Poroshenko met in Minsk on August 26, launching peace talks in the TCG format that resulted in agreement on September 5 on a cease-fire and "peace deal."[61] The Putin-Poroshenko agreement provided for a cease-fire to be monitored by the OSCE (specific terms were agreed on in a September 19 memorandum), allowing humanitarian aid, disavowal of reprisals, decentralization of authority, and local elections in the affected areas. In addition to the three members of the TCG, the Minsk Protocol and memorandum were also signed by Donetsk and Luhansk leaders Zakharchenko and Plotnitskii, thus acknowledging their presence but separating their signatures from the others just enough to show that they were not really members of the TCG.

With the Minsk Agreement, events in and around Eastern Ukraine settled into a depressing and familiar pattern. Kyiv and the rebels each accused the other of failing to live up to the deal, Donetsk and Luhansk because Ukraine did not adopt sufficiently forthcoming legislation on devolution of authority, and Ukraine because the rebels preempted Kyiv's plans by holding local elections on their own, not in accordance with Ukrainian legislation, as specified in the Minsk Protocol. Western countries charged (and Moscow denied) that Russia maintained substantial military forces on the Ukrainian border. Sporadic shelling and fighting continued despite the cease-fire agreement and OSCE monitoring. Negotiations continued at various levels in the TCG and Normandy formats; Washington seemed content to let Chancellor Merkel take the lead and ducked inquiries about the Geneva Format. The process came together in

Minsk in February 2015. After a marathon session involving Putin, Poroshenko, Merkel, and Hollande, the TCG participants signed a Minsk II Agreement, yet another cease-fire and monitoring arrangement, with an updated division of territory and provisions looking ahead to local elections, control of the border by Ukraine by the end of the year, and an eventual political settlement.[62] The fate of Minsk II was cast into doubt almost immediately by a rebel encirclement and offensive against Ukrainian forces in Debaltseve, not far from Donetsk. Throughout the rest of 2015 (and through 2016 into 2017) recriminations over alleged nonimplementation and speculation about the failure of Minsk II continued unabated.

For Poroshenko, who spent a considerable part of his youth in or near Transdniestria, and who worked on the Transdniestrian issue while serving as Yushchenko's national security adviser in 2005, the separatist movements in Eastern Ukraine may well have seemed like "déjà vu all over again." The Kremlin ensured just enough military force was available to prevent a military victory by Kyiv. The rebel demands for decentralization and local authority sounded reasonable on their face, but they always seemed to go just beyond what Kyiv was prepared to offer. In addition, Poroshenko and those like him in Kyiv who seemed prepared to negotiate were constrained by growing popular hostility toward Russia in much of the country and a sizable bloc in the Rada that continued to favor pursuit of a military solution. As with the separatist entities in Moldova and Georgia, Moscow's interest seemed to extend beyond simple support for the rebels to an aspiration to use the conflict as a means of exercising political influence or control over the metropolitan state, that is, Georgia, Moldova, or in this case, Ukraine proper.[63] One might reasonably argue that in many respects the Kremlin—after the initial fighting stabilized—did not see any particular need or advantage in quick resolution of the conflict, which served as a tool for continuing pressure on Kyiv. Even though the economic sanctions could be shown to be hurting the Russian economy, Russia's influence in and relationship with Ukraine seemed to be more important for Moscow than economic ties with the EU.[64] Meanwhile, the West insisted on restoration of Ukraine's territorial integrity and an end to Russian support for the rebels in Donetsk and Luhansk. With such diametrically opposed aims, there seemed to be little prospect for international agreement on and settlement of the Ukraine conflict.

The crisis in Ukraine gave the OSCE a real boost, not because the organization had changed in any significant way but owing to the dramatic transformation of the security environment in Europe. By mid-2014, Europe had essentially once again become divided into two separate, mutually antagonistic camps. The Western camp was much larger in 2014 than it had been in 1989, whereas the number of states in Russia's corner was much smaller. The two groups in 2014 did not deploy large conventional and strategic military forces against one another, although there are signs now appearing that—given enough time—the landmark arms reduction and control agreements of the late 1980s and early 1990s may unravel. There has appeared, however, a clear dividing line in Europe, and an ongoing struggle over which side Ukraine, Moldova, and Georgia will end up on. As of mid-2017, many of the diplomatic engagements in this battle were being fought in the framework of the OSCE, where the United States, NATO, the EU, and Russia engage as equals—now as much protagonists or antagonists as partners. As one old-time OSCE hand wrote, "the OSCE has reconfirmed its reputation as an international security organization 'of last resort' in the wake of the crisis that erupted in Ukraine."[65] With the EU and NATO acting as active participants in the struggle by imposing sanctions on Russia, the OSCE was the only international actor perceived as neutral by all and capable of both providing a forum for diplomatic and political exchanges and of deploying civilian and military field missions. Europe may have returned to an East/West divide vaguely reminiscent of pre-1989 days, and Russia may have disavowed key fundamental provisions of the Helsinki principles, but the OSCE has retained the extensive institutional capabilities built up in the two and a half decades since the Paris Summit.

All this does not necessarily make the OSCE any more capable, particularly in its ability to solve problems such as the conflict in Ukraine. However, developments since early 2014 do make the organization much more important as the regional venue and framework in which East/West disputes like that over Ukraine can be addressed. Many OSCE states acknowledged the organization's good fortune in having Switzerland, a neutral, wealthy, experienced state, in the Chair when the crisis erupted in 2014.[66] The renewed importance of the OSCE for European security in the immediate future was widely cited as the reason behind Germany's decision to seek and accept the Chair for 2016, and Austria for 2017.

## NATO: PURPOSE REDISCOVERED

For NATO, the Russian annexation of Crimea was all at once a shock, a wake-up call, and—in some senses—an indirect stroke of good fortune for the Alliance. The lengthy concluding statement of the Chicago Summit reflected a truly impressive list of important activities, valuable cooperation, and ongoing and developing relationships around the globe. However, the vast majority of these activities and relationships were at the working level (however senior) and relatively low profile. It was generally NATO's deficiencies, disagreements, or unsuccessful endeavors that garnered headlines, such as the lack of some key military capacities of European Allies revealed in the campaign against Libya, or the ongoing difficulties with pacification and nation building in Afghanistan. Yet NATO meetings such as the one in Chicago display effective cooperation of dozens of countries around the globe on hundreds of worthwhile military and civil-military projects, such as the way that use of NATO standards facilitated coalition operations in the First Gulf War. Perhaps NATO's greatest paradox and one of the greatest frustrations of NATO officials was the disparity between the overall performance of the Alliance, generally one of the most success- ful international organizations in contemporary history, and the tendency of observers and critics of the Alliance consistently to see the glass as half empty.

NATO after Chicago remained especially challenged by the fact that many European publics generally did not perceive serious, immediate military threats to Europe and were unconvinced of the need for increased defense spend- ing. The Alliance's estimates for military spending for 2013 showed only four countries meeting the announced goal of 2.0 percent of gross domestic prod- uct (GDP), and only two or three with absolute increases in military spending by any measure.[67] Speaking a year after Chicago, outgoing US ambassador to NATO Ivo Daalder lamented that the United States was providing 75 percent of the Alliance's military spending, and warned that such a situation could not go on indefinitely:

> Unfortunately, NATO's capabilities—or, more precisely, European capabilities—are dwindling. And they are dwindling for one simple reason: European investment in defense has been on a prolonged period of decline. To fund the cost of operations, European defense ministries have slashed investment in new equipment, even as the overall effort devoted to defense has gone down in most European countries. . . . Let me be clear, if spending cuts continue along their present trajectory, I am not con- fident that ten—or even five—years from now, NATO will be able to replicate its success in Libya.[68]

Daalder admitted that the problem of burden sharing was not new, pointing out that since 2000 the overall European contribution to NATO military expendi- tures had declined by one-third. The danger that the Alliance would become simply an American instrument with European window dressing was clearly greater than ever.

The period after Chicago also showed possibly significant changes in direction of America's two most important Allies. The United Kingdom had long been the most reliable go-to military partner in NATO for the United States, and along with France the UK possessed one of the two most significant military forces in Europe. However, Parliament's refusal to endorse Cameron's attempt to join a proposed US campaign in Syria was a distinct shock felt well beyond London and Washington. Military expenditures were not a top priority for the post-2010 coalition government in the United Kingdom, and the British military suffered a series of declining budgets, with commensurate reductions in capabilities.[69] As of mid-2015, long-range British military planning called for further reductions from current levels in land, sea, and air forces, with uncertain but clearly negative effects on the ability of the United Kingdom to participate in and support operations requiring projection of power.[70] Meanwhile, France played an increasingly active role in European security operations in general and in NATO in particular. Despite reductions and rationalizations in defense spending planned or projected as the result of the 2013 white paper, there was considerable continuity between the Hollande administration and the activist, NATO-oriented security policies of his predecessor.[71] France intervened energetically in Libya, Mali, and Iraq (against the Islamic States) but in a national rather than EU capacity, which led some European analysts to worry about Paris's commitment to the EU's Common Security and Defence Policy (CSDP).[72] Pointing to their intervention in the Sahel and cooperation with the United States against the so-called Islamic State, some senior French military officers asserted that Paris was now "the most activist, most engaged European ally."[73]

Whether Paris or London is Washington's most active or capable military partner is less significant than whether Europe is or will remain a unified, serious military power. The decline in European military spending by the time of the Chicago Summit had already caused knowledgeable analysts to question whether European Allies would in the near future possess military capabilities capable of anything more than projection of power into the Mediterranean.[74] Although such an evaluation might be too alarmist, the situation on the European side of the Atlantic Alliance was distinctly disquieting. Germany had clearly assumed political leadership in Europe, including with respect to security-related issues such as the imposition and retention of sanctions on Russia in response to the annexation of Crimea and war in Eastern Ukraine. Yet important elements in Berlin's political elites and German society still had an ambivalent attitude toward the application of military force, leaving a question mark regarding the ability of NATO to achieve consensus for future military operations. Continued evisceration of Britain's defense capabilities would cut muscle and bone, and not just fat, from the Alliance's ability to augment US capabilities for projecting power. Finally, whereas France's return to full military participation in the Alliance was welcome, the reduction of French participation in EU operations could call into question the existence of a real CSDP. None of these trends by itself constituted an immediate threat to the Alliance's continued existence or operations, but they did not bode well for Europe's long-term security future, whether taken singly or all together.

Fortunately for NATO, but unfortunately for European security and stability, the relationship with Russia went bad, providing a renewed raison d'être for the Alliance. After the rupture caused by Russia's war with Georgia, the NATO-Russia relationship was reactivated during the same period that the Obama administration was rebuilding Washington's bilateral relations with Moscow. By 2012, NATO deputy secretary-general Alexander Vershbow was able to celebrate fifteen years of NATO-Russia cooperation with an address to Russia's Diplomatic Academy containing a paean to cooperative operations and exercises on antiterrorism, theater missile defense, Somali piracy, and Afghanistan.[75] The main cloud on the horizon for the relationship in 2012 seemed to be missile defense, which Vershbow spent considerable effort to explain as not a threat to Russia but as a possible cooperative venture that protected both Russia and NATO Allies against ballistic missile proliferation.

As the crisis in Ukraine began to deepen in the final weeks of 2013, Russia and a number of NATO Allies were engaged in active cooperation in helping to implement UN Security Council Resolution 2118 on the elimination of chemical weapons from Syria.[76] At the same time, the Alliance as a whole was basically sympathetic to the protestors on the Maidan, hardly a surprise given the large number of Allies that were also EU members and were supportive of Ukrainian aspirations to build a closer relationship with Brussels.[77] Individual Allies followed events in Ukraine closely through the winter, but NATO as a whole next became involved after Russia seized Crimea and Poland formally requested Alliance consultations on the crisis under Article IV of the Washington Treaty.[78] The NATO ministers denounced Russia's annexation of Crimea, and in response on April 1, 2014, NATO announced its decision to suspend "all practical civilian and military cooperation" between NATO and Russia.[79] NATO held out the possibility of continued political dialogue with Moscow at the ambassadorial or higher levels but asserted that Moscow's violation of international law made it impossible to continue business as usual.[80] NATO ministers added that they would review the Alliance's relations with Russia in June, increased cooperation with and support for Ukraine, and announced they were reviewing possible steps that could be taken, such as stepping up air patrols, to address concerns of East European Allies about their security.

Russia's annexation of Crimea and support for the rebellions in Donetsk and Lugansk raised two immediate, serious questions for NATO. First, Moscow's intentions had to be evaluated to determine the extent of the military threat posed by these actions. Second, the Alliance needed to determine what capabilities it possessed and which of these capabilities it might need in order to come to the aid of those Eastern European NATO members to whose defense it had a legal, treaty obligation. After the quick seizure of Crimea and the outbreak of protests and resistance to the new Kyiv government in multiple locations across Ukraine's East and South, it was not at all clear in the spring of 2014 how far into Ukraine Putin might try to send Russian forces. Also, Putin couched his explanation for the Crimean action in terms of defending Russian citizens, co-ethnics, speakers, and "compatriots" (*sootechestvenniki*). There were substantial numbers of people corresponding to these categories in Ukraine, Moldova, Kazakhstan, Latvia, and Estonia. The passage of time and events may have lent a bit more weight to the arguments of those who maintain that Putin's aims in Ukraine were and are relatively limited. Nonetheless, in mid-2014 it was difficult to blithely dismiss warnings such as that from the Supreme Allied Commander Europe, General Philip Breedlove, that Moldova might be next at risk from destabilization given unrest in Odesa and Russian troops stationed in the Transdniestrian enclave.[81] Not only the NATO Allies Estonia and Latvia, each with ethnic Russian minorities of some 25 percent of its population, but also the non-NATO neighbors of Russia, such as Finland and Sweden, were extremely worried about Moscow's intentions at the time.[82]

On the second question, the three Baltic Allies would clearly be at the greatest risk if Moscow's intent really was to reunite ethnic Russian minorities in bordering states with Russia proper. Russian seizure of an Estonian intelligence officer in a murky operation on the Estonia-Russia border in September 2014 did little to quiet fears inflamed by political debate and speculation through much of the summer.[83] The Eastern European NATO Allies that were traditionally suspicious of Russia, in particular Poland and Romania, also produced particularly strong denunciations of Moscow's actions and speculation about its intentions vis-à-vis Eastern Europe. Given the fact that up to the outbreak of the Ukraine crisis NATO had been constructing a cooperative relationship with Moscow, there was precious little Alliance military infrastructure in Russia's immediate neighborhood beyond the national military assets of those Allies themselves. The Estonian, Latvian, and Lithuanian militaries were clearly no match for the Russian armed forces should Moscow decide to use its full power on any of these three. Because NATO's credibility was at stake in its ability to defend any member of the Alliance and Russian intentions toward the Baltic Sea republics were not at all clear in the immediate aftermath of the outbreak of war in Ukraine, it would have been surprising only if the Alliance had not decided to increase its military presence there and to discuss further measures in Eastern Europe, and the Baltic republics in particular.

The discussions of reinforcing NATO's capabilities in Eastern Europe and the debate over whether and how to assist Ukraine against Russia are two quite distinct issues, although they are frequently taken up as separate agenda items by the same officials at the same meetings and are often conflated for various purposes by other actors and observers. Ukraine, despite the Bucharest Summit pledge, is neither a NATO member nor a participant in a Membership Action Plan. Furthermore, when Yanukovych reversed course and returned Kyiv to a policy of nonalignment, the language about eventual Ukrainian membership disappeared from most routine Alliance statements about Ukraine. Nonetheless, NATO remained committed to its "distinctive partnership" with Ukraine established in 1997 and clearly saw support for Ukraine's independence and territorial integrity, as well as condemnation of Russia's violation of the Helsinki-based European security order, as keys to its own security. Thus, on April 1, 2014, the NATO ministers made explicit that "an independent, sovereign and stable Ukraine, firmly committed to democracy and the rule of law, is key to Euro-Atlantic security. Allies firmly support Ukraine's sovereignty and territorial integrity."[84] At subsequent gatherings, the NATO Allies have indicated their willingness and intent to assist Ukraine in its defense in a number of specific ways, but short of the provision of lethal military assistance.

The NATO Summit in Wales on September 4–5, 2014, was a turning point in the history of the Alliance and European security in a number of respects. First and foremost, both the short statement of purpose in the Wales Declaration on the Transatlantic Bond and the longer, more traditional Wales Summit Declaration recognized and reflected the fundamental change in the Euro-Atlantic security context.[85] The Wales Transatlantic Bond Declaration recalls the London Summit of 1990 and its vision of a "Europe whole, free, and at peace," now challenged by crises to NATO's east and south, including "violence and extremism" in North Africa and the Middle East. However, both the short and the long statement refer first of all to "the challenges posed by Russia and their strategic implications." Later, in the longer statement, the heads of state stipulate that a partnership with Russia "based upon respect for international law" would be of value but noted that conditions for a cooperative relationship with Russia "do not currently exist." The language is carefully balanced; Russia is a "challenge," and not a "threat," but the prospect of integrating Russia into a Europe "whole and free" is no longer a realistic possibility after a quarter century of trying.

Although the Wales declarations continue the Alliance's commitments developed after 1990 to crisis management and collective security, the statements clearly return to collective defense as NATO's primary purpose. Given the danger posed by Russia's actions, the Allied heads of state agreed on a NATO Readiness Action Plan, including a program of military measures to ensure the defense of those members of the Alliance perceived at greatest risk. The Wales decision specifically called for maintaining a "continuous air, land, and maritime presence and meaningful military activity in the eastern part of the Alliance," on a rotational basis. The NATO Response Force was to be upgraded in order to be able to react more quickly and decisively to emergencies. A Very High Readiness Joint Task Force was to be established, aimed at the ability to deploy within a few days, in particular on NATO's peripheries. Rotational command presences would be set up on the territory of some Allies to enhance interoperability. In addition, an enhanced program of exercises was to be developed, both for reassurance and visible presence, but also for interoperability. The decisions made at Wales did not abrogate NATO's 1997 commitment in the Founding Act not to station "substantial combat forces" on the territory of new members, but they were clearly headed in the direction of growing the Alliance's military infrastructure in Eastern Europe.

The Wales Declaration also states flatly: "We agree to reverse the trend of declining defense budgets," and it agreed that NATO defense ministers would check up regularly on the implementation of this pledge. All the Allies agreed to reverse any defense cuts and to move toward the standard of 2 percent of GDP devoted to defense spending within a decade. Those Allies that allocated less than 20 percent of their defense budget on new equipment also agreed to increase this portion of their expenditures within a decade. Finally, all the Allies agreed to ensure that all of their military forces meet NATO standards and can operate together effectively with other Alliance forces. These commitments with respect to defense budgets and capabilities were cast in especially resolute terms. However, given NATO's track record over the previous decade of failing to meet budgetary targets, only time and results would tell whether Wales truly marked a turning point on this issue.

The Wales Summit also implicitly but nonetheless unmistakably marked the boundaries of NATO's territorial reach. The Wales Declaration contains the ritual mention of Article X of the Washington Treaty and the Alliance's "open door" policy. However, this reference to enlargement, along with praise for Georgia's efforts and a brief nod to the Bucharest Summit is set out in paragraph 92, after a discussion of almost every other NATO concern and priority, hardly a ringing testament to the importance the Alliance attached to adding new members. A number of observers, in particular European experts, commented with sadness and frustration that the Alliance seemed to have reached its geographical limits.[86] Yet few of these same experts and critics found much fault with NATO's strategic choice, in effect to draw another line across Europe and defend that part already on its side of the line.

NATO at Wales did not abandon all the other activities and responsibilities it had added during the twenty-four years since the London Summit. The Wales Summit Declaration runs 113 paragraphs and makes clear that NATO is still an institution with global ambitions and global reach. Nevertheless, Wales appears to be a tectonic shift in the orientation and basic policies of the Alliance. Irrespective of whether Russia is called a threat or a challenge, the Alliance's collective perception of the global and regional security context had shifted dramatically, making collective defense of existing Alliance members once again clearly the top priority. The dream of integrating Russia into European institutions is also clearly gone, although the drafters of the Wales statements were apparently not able to abandon all the integrationist rhetoric that had dominated regular NATO statements during the past two decades. In this sense, the Wales Summit marks the end of one era in European political and security affairs and the beginning of a new era whose direction and content have yet to be defined.

## RUSSIA'S RESPONSE: PUTIN AT VALDAI

Russian leaders turned Groucho Marx on his head with their response to EU sanctions and the NATO statements and decisions coming out of Wales, in effect asserting that they did not want to be members of a club that would not have them anyway. The Russian Foreign Ministry had an immediate reaction, which condemned both the Wales decisions and NATO itself as relics of the past and tools of American policy:

> The results of the NATO summit in Wales (4–5 September) are hardly surprising. The alliance established in the Cold War era as a military and political bloc cannot change its genetic code by definition. Its strategic course on interfering in the affairs of foreign states did not emerge yesterday or today. It logically flows from NATO's search for its role and place in the global security system under the conditions of the absence of a coalition military confrontation. The results of the summit have graphically demonstrated that NATO whose policy is dictated by the United States and hawks in some European capitals has been striving for military domination in Europe in violation of the agreements on the importance of a system of equitable and indivisible security for the Euro-Atlantic region, that have been reaffirmed numerously at all levels. The efforts of the international community to counter the real threats and challenges of our time, such as terrorism, the proliferation of weapons of mass destruction, drug trafficking, piracy, and natural and man-made disasters are being sacrificed in this process.[87]

The Russian Foreign Ministry and most other Russian representatives cast Russia as the aggrieved victim in the Ukrainian crisis, forced into responding to Western actions that threatened some of Russia's most sensitive interests in its oldest, closest, and most important neighborhood.

One important Russian thinker agreed that the situation produced by the events of 2014, in particular the Ukraine crisis and the NATO Wales Summit, constituted a historical turning point—President Vladimir Putin. Speaking to foreign and Russian experts at the annual meeting of the Valdai Club on October 24, 2014, Putin delivered a blast against the post–Cold War Euro-Atlantic political order that was worthy of the session's title: "The World Order: New Rules or a Game without Rules."[88] Putin complained that, unlike the victors after World War II, the United States had constructed the post–Cold War international order for its sole benefit. The Cold War did not end with a peace treaty or other written agreements, so the Cold War "victors" proceeded to shape the world order to fit their own interests. Putin explained that

> the United States, having declared itself the winner of the Cold War, saw no need for this. Instead of establishing a new balance of power, essential for maintaining order and stability, they took steps that threw the system into sharp and deep imbalance. . . . Pardon the analogy, but this is the way nouveaux riches behave when they suddenly end up with a great fortune, in this case, in the shape of world leadership and domination. Instead of managing their wealth wisely, for their own benefit too of course, I think they have committed many follies.[89]

Putin warned that a unipolar system, no matter which country dominated, inevitably produced instability and insecurity. Citing the examples of Iraq, Afghanistan, Libya, Egypt, and elsewhere, Putin argued that in its unilateral pursuit of solutions the United States had actually made many situations worse—less stable, more violent, less secure. US military interventions, abandonment of existing arms control regimes, such as the 2002 renunciation of the Anti–Ballistic Missile Treaty, and the avoidance of multilateral bodies like the UN Security Council in favor of unilateral solutions, all—according to Putin—lead other countries to arm themselves and thus seek to ensure their own security while making conflict more likely.

On Ukraine, Putin denied that Russia had raised political objections to Kyiv's prospective association with the EU, instead claiming that Moscow expressed concerns about the economic implications of the agreement "in an entirely civilized manner." He asserted that the EU "simply told us: This is none of your business, point, end of discussion." From there, events proceeded to a coup against the legitimate government, chaos, and civil war—by implication, no fault of Moscow because Putin blamed "those who constantly throw together new color revolutions,"

Putin explicitly denied that Russia wished to establish some sort of empire or to encroach on the sovereignty of its neighbors, calling such accusations "groundless." He asserted the need to construct a new world order based on rules of interaction similar to those devised after World War II and Helsinki in the 1970s. Putin claimed that Russia had made its choice and had an "integration-oriented, positive, peaceful agenda." That choice was with the Eurasian Economic Union, the Shanghai Cooperation Association, the BRICS (Brazil, Russia, India, China, and South Africa—the world's largest fast-growing economies), and other partners, all mentioned specifically in the speech, but not—apparently—with the West.

Putin's lengthy diatribe against the post–Cold War order and his facile responses to the questions and challenges from some of the Westerners in his audience are fascinating in many respects, but for the purposes of this narrative, two major points stand out. First, Putin clearly rejects integration of Russia with the West, whether it be NATO, the EU, perhaps the OSCE, or any other Western-dominated structures. His references to the Eurasian Economic Union, the Shanghai Cooperation Organization, and the BRICS suggest that he is looking to a separate but equal integration system as a counterpart to the political and security structures such as NATO and the EU that grew up in Europe after 1990. Second, Putin seems to dismiss most of the post–Cold War settlement, based on documents such as the Charter of Paris, the Copenhagen Document, the Treaty on Conventional Armed Forces in Europe, and the 1992 Helsinki Document. His references to the post–World War II settlement, which produced a bipolar world, and to the Helsinki Final Act (but without mention of human rights) point to a view of a new world order in which Europe might well be divided into rival camps, but within which Russia would have a recognized, respected, and influential place. So much for a Europe whole and free.

## EUROPE'S THREE CRISES: UKRAINE/RUSSIA, SYRIA, AND THE EUROPEAN IDEAL

As the conflict in Eastern Ukraine dragged on throughout 2015 and 2016 and into 2017, Moscow remained critical in principle of the post–Cold War European security architecture and the United States–dominated world order, but Russian positions and actions in practice softened in a number of areas in the face of Western pressure and the course of events, in particular economic developments. Economic sanctions imposed on Russia by the European Union and the United States after the annexation of Crimea in March 2014 and the shoot-down of the Malaysian civilian airliner over rebel-held territory in the Donbas eventually began to bite. The post-MH17 restrictions on Russian access to foreign capital markets had particularly serious potential implications for Russia's long-term economic growth.⁹⁰ Although many of the EU and US measures were targeted specifically at individuals close to Putin or closely identified with Russian policies and actions in Ukraine, the effects of Western sanctions on the average Russian were compounded by Putin's defiant response, for example, in banning the import and sale of many agricultural or food products from EU and other Western nations, such as cheeses, fish, or meats.

Whatever the impact of economic measures taken by the United States, EU, and other Western nations against Russia in the wake of the Crimea annexation and war in the Donbas, an unexpected and precipitous drop in the world price of oil in 2014 arguably had an equal or greater effect on Russia's macroeconomic performance.⁹¹ During the second half of 2014, the world price of oil dropped by at least half, from more than $100 per barrel to under $50, resulting in a dramatic decrease in the Russian government's expected revenues, a ballooning deficit, and tremendous pressure on the value of the ruble in world exchange markets. Russia's central bank at first attempted to sustain the value of the ruble through injections from the country's hard currency reserves; but by the late autumn of 2014, this course was becoming increasingly unsustainable. Central bank and Economic Ministry officials managed to stabilize the ruble in early 2015, but by that time the currency had lost well over 50 percent of its value against the dollar and euro.

The cumulative effects on the Russian economy were severe, and the country slid into recession. GDP moved into negative growth in the second half of 2014 and fell by more than 3 percent in 2015. World Bank and IMF analysts projected a continued modest decline in GDP in Russia in 2016, with a return to modest positive growth (about 1 percent) in 2017. Despite an apparent return to recovery and limited growth by the end of 2016, even the most dedicated supporters of administration policy found it difficult to be optimistic.⁹² The substantial depreciation of the ruble produced a surge in inflation, especially for imported products. Skillful macroeconomic management and the government's resort to a strategy of import substitution, particularly in the agricultural sector, helped to lower inflation, although some official efforts to remove imported EU food products from Russian stores went to ludicrous extremes.⁹³ Although Russia retained substantial economic resources and Russians demonstrated considerable resilience, during 2015 real incomes in Russia declined for the first time in more than a decade, and continued declines were reported into 2016.⁹⁴

Although the competent core of economic technocrats remaining in the Russian government arguably kept Russia's economy from getting much worse under the dual pressure of Western sanctions and protracted low oil prices, Putin and the *siloviki* closest to him resorted more to appeals to Russian nationalism and condemnation of Western actions to explain the country's economic woes to its population. The charge that the United States, NATO, and the EU had sponsored and supported a right-wing coup in Kyiv against Ukraine's legitimate government became an automatic part of the official Russian narrative explaining the deterioration of Russia's relations with its Western partners and the security situation in Europe. At times some Russian officials even charged that the United States and its Allies had colluded in manipulating world oil supplies and prices in order to weaken Russia.[95]

Putin's continuing high ratings in public opinion polls seemed to demonstrate the success of this strategy in mobilizing and maintaining support for the incumbent administration and minimizing internal opposition and unrest. However, the Russian government remained extremely sensitive to possible signs of popular discontent, demonstrated for example in its rapid and perhaps disproportionate response to the emergence in the autumn of 2015 of an ongoing protest by independent truckers against a proposed new road use tax.[96] Moscow remained relentless in its use of the "foreign agents law" to restrict or suppress NGOs that manifested even slight degrees of independence or criticism of the government. Some authorities exhibited growing concern over the influence of the Internet in facilitating and promoting social and political protest, as shown in a widely read article by Public Prosecutor Aleksandr Bastrykin in April 2016 advocating regulation of the Internet in Russia similar to that already employed in China.[97]

The problem facing Putin and his colleagues in the Kremlin was that nationalism and repression were at best temporary solutions, even though they might work for an indeterminate time in suppressing opposition and maintaining public support for, or at least toleration of, Russia's socioeconomic status quo and government policies. However, most economists—even many of those working in or supporting the Putin administration—agreed that the basic problems with Russia's economy were to a considerable extent structural and could be fixed only by significant economic and political changes, and not by appeals to patriotism, forbearance, and sacrifice.[98] The high degree of government dependence on hydrocarbons for operating revenues was only part of the problem. Since Putin came to power in 2000, the role of the state in the country's economy has expanded significantly, with state-owned enterprises dominating many of the most significant sectors of the economy, and the government resistant to high-level proposals for privatization. Indeed, many Russian citizens remained dependent on the state for their livelihood, with the Russian Federation government bureaucracy equal in numbers to the Soviet bureaucracy (in a country with less than half the Soviet population), with many others working for state-owned firms, and finally, with a substantial number receiving government pensions.

Although both external and domestic observers found it hard to agree on how to evaluate Russia's international position and domestic situation, Moscow gradually began to respond to its growing difficulties at home and abroad in more moderate tones and with more moderate policies than those exhibited by Putin at Valdai in late 2014. The Kremlin did not retreat from the line that the West was responsible for events in Ukraine through its support for an illegal coup, and that the United States–led European and global order had been unjustly imposed on a weakened Russia by a triumphalist United States and NATO Alliance flushed with their sense of perceived victory in the Cold War. Nonetheless, Moscow engaged more constructively in the Contact Group on Ukraine, lowered its pressure in Eastern Ukraine to a war of attrition, and maintained its public dedication to implementation of the first and second Minsk Accords.[99] Western sanctions against Russia over the conflict in Ukraine remained in effect through 2017, in particular because of the efforts and influence of Chancellor Angela Merkel over her EU colleagues. However, as the fighting in the Donbas stabilized at relatively lower levels through 2015 into 2016, international attention diverted somewhat from a focus on Russian actions to include growing concern with Ukraine's difficulties with adopting key domestic reforms and regenerating its devastated economy, epitomized by the fall of the Yatseniuk government in early 2016.

The OSCE continued to be the sole European security institution able to work collectively and cooperatively in the disputed regions between Russia and the West, such as Ukraine. The OSCE continued to head the Contact Group engaged with negotiating a settlement to the conflict in Eastern Ukraine, with senior Austrian diplomat Martin Sajdik replacing Switzerland's Heidi Tagliavini in mid-2015.[100] The OSCE Monitoring Mission remained the sole mechanism in which Russia and its Western partners could cooperate on the ground in the conflict zone in Ukraine, and the sole official source of impartial information on events and developments in that area.[101] The tense and grudging agreement between Russia and the major Western participating states over the OSCE's role in Ukraine epitomized the dilemma of the OSCE. Most of the participating states agreed that the OSCE remains a potentially valuable neutral platform for cooperative activities and discussions, but the continuing, deeply entrenched lack of consensus among the major participating states has blocked the OSCE from any real substantive breakthroughs or achievements.

The continuing deep disagreements between Russia and the major Western powers, especially the United States, were also starkly displayed in the results (or lack thereof) of the December 2015 Belgrade Ministerial Council.[102] The concluding document of the Ministerial is filled with national statements and reports from OSCE institutions and officials on various issues. However, there are few agreed-on consensus statements or decisions, with the leading item being a statement urging the parties to the Moldova-Transdniestria conflict to resume the "five plus two" political settlement negotiations.[103] The sole decision adopted by the meeting was on the time and place of the next Ministerial Council in Hamburg in December 2016. The United States added an interpretative statement to this decision, in which it lamented the inability of the OSCE to reach agreement on many important issues, and singled out the Russian Federation as particularly responsible:

> As we look toward next year, we must express our deep disappointment that because of the apparent unwillingness of a few participating States to join consensus on many draft decisions consistent with OSCE principles and commitments, this year's Ministerial meeting has produced few consequential and valuable decisions.
>
> This is principally a symptom of the ongoing security crisis in the OSCE area precipitated by the ongoing occupation of and attempted annexation of Crimea by the Russian Federation and its abrogation of numerous OSCE commitments and violation of international law.
>
> The crisis in European security fomented by Russia has been reflected in our work here in Belgrade. We thank the Chairmanship for its good faith efforts to mitigate this reality.[104]

The United States went on to express doubt about Russia's willingness to adhere to commitments adopted under the Helsinki Final Act and the Charter of Paris. Conversely, Russian foreign minister Lavrov lamented the lack of a consensus on key issues, especially the absence of accord on any political-military questions, and explained this by Western attempts to "politicize" these questions by tying them all artificially with the conflict in Ukraine. Lavrov emphatically endorsed the OSCE for its "comprehensive approach to security" and adherence to the principle of consensus, but he called for a review and reform of its approach to the human dimension and the activities of the individual institutions.[105] Although there remained general agreement on the need for a pan-European security institution such as the OSCE, there continued to be scant evidence of agreement on what the mandate, scope, and proper activities of such an organization should be.

Against the backdrop of continuing discord over the situation in Ukraine, events in Syria in 2015–16 produced both a crisis for Europe's economic and security order and possible openings for joint efforts in pursuit of common aims against common foes. Russia's cooperation with the United States in 2013 to remove from Syria the chemical weapons stores held by the Assad government was a welcome and unusual success, but it did not halt the country's continuing slide into war and disintegration. Beginning in 2014 the Islamic State (variously referred to as ISIL, ISIS, or Daeesh) made dramatic territorial advances in both Iraq and Syria. Facing attacks by the Islamic State, a coalition of anti-Assad opposition forces supported by the West, opposition groups affiliated with al-Qaeda, and Syrian Kurdish forces attacked in Syria, and by the summer of 2015 the hold of the Assad government on power was clearly eroding. The international community was deeply fractured over whom to support in the conflict, with Russia, the United States, the EU and NATO, Iran, Turkey, Saudi Arabia, and the Gulf Arab states each backing different combatants or combinations of combatants.

In September 2015, Putin traveled to New York to attend and to speak at the seventieth UN General Assembly. Although his presentation contained many by that time customary denunciations of Western and US "arrogance" and unilateralism, portions of his address reflected a more pragmatic, cooperative tone.[106] For example, Putin blamed the West's continuing Cold War mentality and NATO enlargement as the reasons for the conflict in Europe. However, the centerpiece of the address was the portion on international terrorism and the Middle East. Here Putin first took to task unnamed countries for creating the current chaos in the region through their reflexive, unthinking support for the Arab Spring. Putin asked rhetorically:

> What was the actual outcome? Instead of bringing about reforms, aggressive intervention rashly destroyed government institutions and the local way of life. Instead of democracy and progress, there is now violence, poverty, social disasters and total disregard for human rights, including even the right to life.
>
> I'm urged to ask those who created this situation: do you at least realize now what you've done? But I'm afraid that this question will remain unanswered, because they have never abandoned their policy, which is based on arrogance, exceptionalism and impunity.[107]

Moving beyond this denunciation of Western responsibility for the mess in the Middle East, Putin turned practical. Pointing to almost universal opposition to international terrorism, the Russian president proposed the formation of an international coalition similar to that against Hitler to combat those "who sow evil and hatred of mankind." Putin announced that, in its role as Security Council president that month, Russia intended to call a meeting to discuss coordination of the efforts of those who oppose the "Islamic state and other terrorist groups." He proclaimed his hope that "the international community will be able to develop a comprehensive strategy of political stabilization, as well as social and economic recovery in the Middle East."[108]

In particular, Putin noted that in Russia's view only the Assad government and the Syrian Kurds were actually engaged in fighting the real terrorists, the Islamic State in Syria. As the Russian president was speaking to the United Nations, Russia's armed forces were preparing to put his words into practice with a military intervention in Syria.[109] Moscow surprised many Western observers and analysts with its ability to project military power effectively beyond the territory of the former Soviet Union. Although Russian officials explained that the intervention was mounted to fight the Islamic State, the targets of a large number of Russia's air attacks soon convinced many observers that Moscow's real purpose was to shore up and stabilize the Assad government by weakening its nearest opponents, often segments of the "moderate Syrian opposition" supported by Washington.[110] Tension over Russia's operations in Syria reached a peak in November 2015, when Turkish planes shot down a Russian Sukhoi fighter-bomber after a brief violation of Turkish airspace.

However, pragmatic East–West cooperation emerged gradually on the margins of and in conjunction with the Russian intervention in Syria. US secretary of state Kerry and Russian foreign minister Lavrov worked closely together within a UN framework to bring an agreed-on group of belligerents and interested parties together in Geneva for peace talks, with Kerry visiting Sochi and Moscow to discuss coordination of efforts in Syria.[111] Perhaps more notable, operational imperatives pushed the gradual restoration of US-Russian military-to-military contacts, almost entirely abrogated by Washington in the wake of Russia's annexation of Crimea. In a process that began with isolated phone calls and lower-level bilateral meetings, Russian and American military officials increasingly shared information and reached operational agreements in order to deconflict their military operations in Syria.[112] These contacts and cooperation did not eliminate most of the deep substantive disagreements between the United States and its Allies, on one hand, and Russia, on the other hand, over Syria or other contentious European security issues, in particular Ukraine. However, experience in Syria appeared to show both a willingness and an ability on Moscow's part to engage in pragmatic dialogue and transactional cooperation with its major Western antagonists when Russia officials perceived this to be in their interest.

As Putin's 2015 UN General Assembly address demonstrated, Russia had not abandoned its fierce opposition to NATO, in particular its criticism of NATO's enlargement to the East as a major threat to Russian security. To make the point clear, on December 31, 2015, Putin signed an updated version of Russia's National Security Strategy that explicitly singled out actions of the United States and NATO as a threat to Russia's security: "The buildup of the military potential of the North Atlantic Treaty Organization (NATO) and the endowment of it with global functions pursued in violation of the norms of international law, the galvanization of the bloc countries' military activity, the further expansion of the alliance, and the location of its military infrastructure closer to Russian borders are creating a threat to national security."[113]

The Russian strategy complains that the world is being made more dangerous and the use of force and resultant instability becoming more common as the United States and its Allies attempt to preserve their dominance of a unipolar world order and resist transition to a multipolar order. The document codifies and reaffirms in written policy Moscow's complaints of recent years against Washington and its major Allies, including their resort to regime change and intrastate conflicts—that is, the color revolutions—as a means of advancing their interests.

Against this backdrop, the task of restoring NATO-Russia contacts, suspended after the seizure and annexation of Crimea, and rebuilding NATO-Russia relations promised to be exceedingly slow and difficult. Relations between NATO Allies and Russia remained contentious following the Wales Summit. During 2015 the Allies, in particular the United States, conducted rotational deployments and an increased number of exercises in NATO's eastern member states, especially the three Baltic nations. For its part, Russia increased both the number and size of its planned and unplanned military exercises, including a number in the Western Military District and Southern Military District.[114] Aggressive behavior of Russian military aircraft and naval vessels also created tension with the NATO Allies, especially activities in the Baltic Sea and Black Sea. NATO military leaders, up through and in particular the NATO supreme commander, General Breedlove, repeatedly complained about Russian behavior and expressed concern about Russian military activities in Ukraine and likely threats to nearby NATO countries.[115]

Both because and in spite of these constant tensions, Russia and NATO leaders eventually agreed to renew contacts within the framework of the NATO-Russia Council, which met for the first time in almost two years on April 20, 2016.[116] Both NATO and Russia found it useful to exchange views (or complaints) on the situation in Ukraine, transparency and risk reduction in military activities (given the increasing number of near collisions), and post-NATO Afghanistan and international terrorism. The meeting ran considerably longer than any of the participants expected, indicating there was plenty to discuss, even though both sides announced emphatically that their positions on the issues discussed remained far apart.[117] NATO secretary-general Jens Stoltenberg stressed the need to keep channels of communication open but held out little hope of significant rapprochement or agreement in the near future. Russian statements continued to blast the Alliance's "destructive" course of containing rather than cooperating with Russia but did not rule out further contacts or cooperation on the basis of equality.

Indeed, for NATO containment or deterrence of Russia was increasingly the focus of discussion and preparations for the July 2016 Summit in Warsaw, particularly among the Alliance's newer, easternmost members. During 2015–16, the United States fleshed out and sought expanded funding for the European Reassurance Initiative, which had been first announced in June 2014 in the wake of

Russia's seizure of Crimea and the outbreak of war in Eastern Ukraine.[118] Work within the Alliance centered on responding to the threat posed by Russian military action against and intimidation of its neighbors by following up on key decisions from the Wales Summit, in particular implementing the Readiness Action Plan, developing an enhanced NATO Response Force, and forming the Very High Readiness Joint Task Force.[119] Preparations for the 2016 Warsaw Summit centered especially on demands from Eastern European Allies and discussions of possible US and NATO deployments of large numbers of combat forces and equipment in the Baltic states, Poland, Romania, and Bulgaria.

The NATO Summit in Warsaw on July 8–9, 2016, reaffirmed and strengthened the Alliance's return to collective defense seen at Wales in September 2014.[120] The heads of state refrained from explicitly labeling Russia a threat to European security, as the Alliance had done with respect to the USSR during the Cold War. Alliance leaders condemned Russia's aggressive actions and use of military force against its neighbors as a source of regional instability and a threat to the long-standing goal of a "Europe whole, free, and at peace."[121] However, the heads of state declined to burn all their bridges with Russia, noting that "we continue to aspire to a constructive relationship with Russia, when Russia's actions make that possible."[122] The most notable decision made at Warsaw was a long-anticipated "sustainable and rotational" deployment of four battalions (from the United States, United Kingdom, Canada, and Germany) in Estonia, Latvia, Lithuania, and Poland, with a multinational division headquarters in Poland. At Warsaw, the Allies also agreed to continue assistance and retain forces in Afghanistan after 2016, to support the EU antismuggling mission off the coast of Libya, to increase efforts against cyber threats, and to support further defense and security reform in Ukraine.

Following the summit, the Allies held a meeting of the NATO-Russia Council at the ambassadorial level on July 13, at which NATO representatives explained decisions taken at Warsaw and discussed issues including Ukraine, Afghanistan, and reduction of risk from incidents in the Baltic region.[123] Despite the apparent accord on risk reduction, the meeting did little to bridge the underlying gap between Moscow and the Alliance, with Secretary-General Stoltenberg praising the discussions as "frank and open" whereas Russian ambassador Grushko called the Alliance's decisions at Warsaw a return to the outdated approach of the Cold War.[124] Although the Warsaw Summit may not have marked a complete return to Cold War–style enmity between the Alliance and Russia, the divide across Eastern Europe was nonetheless clear and deep, with little basis to expect or hope that more cooperative relations might return anytime soon. Indeed, by the end of 2017, NATO troops—including US forces—were once more to be deployed directly across a border from Russian armed forces as a deterrent against attack from the East, thus re-creating to a somewhat lesser degree a military standoff that had been absent from Europe for more than two decades.

As NATO deliberated on how to counter the threat from Russia, another, perhaps even greater threat to the post–Cold War European political and security order was developing out of events in Syria and northern Africa. The continuing lack of real economic recovery after 2008–9 and the effects of the euro zone crisis had already increased the electoral appeal of left- and right-wing populist, nativist, and Eurosceptic political parties, not only in smaller and peripheral EU member states but also in pillars of the Union such as France, Germany, the Netherlands, and the United Kingdom. From the beginning the war in Syria had provoked flows of refugees, but the stream of people fleeing the fighting increased dramatically in 2015, partially due to the spread of the Islamic State. More crucially, a drastically increased number of these refugees began to find their way across the Mediterranean, through Greece, the Balkans, or Italy, into the heart of Europe. Chancellor Merkel's admirable initial humanitarian response to this flow of victims of the war in Syria appeared to exacerbate both the magnitude of the refugee flows and the hostile popular response in the majority of the EU's member states, in particular those on the major migration routes.[125] At the height of the crisis, popular passions were running so high that the EU states suspended operation of the Schengen agreement and reinstituted passport and identity controls on many of the EU's internal borders.

Spectacular terrorist attacks by radical jihadists producing mass casualties in Paris in November 2015 and in Brussels in March 2016 exacerbated populist opposition to refugees and migrants from the Middle East and North Africa. Even though the statistical chances of falling victim to a violent terrorist incident in Europe remained extremely low, the high-profile, well-publicized nature of the attacks and the apparent inability of European police and internal security forces to cooperate effectively in curtailing the movement and running down the terrorists all contributed to popular fears and xenophobic, nativist reactions in many European states. Irrespective of whether any firm connection could be established between the surge in refugees from the Middle East and North Africa and the frequency of terrorist incidents, right-wing, anti-immigrant, populist forces made political hay out of the crisis.

EU leaders eventually found a combination of actions that gradually facilitated the abatement of the crisis. The EU's border force, Frontex, was beefed up, NATO was enlisted to help patrol migration routes across the Mediterranean, pressure was placed on many states to accept their share of refugees, and—crucially—agreement was reached with Turkey to provide refuge for most of those fleeing Syria in return for expedited negotiations on open chapters of Turkey's application for membership. Domestic security measures in a number of states were intensified, and travel within the Schengen area continued to be subject to additional scrutiny and regulation. Resistance from many European Union member states to acceptance of Middle Eastern refugees remained high in 2017; for example, Hungary planned a referendum of dubious legality on the EU refugee quotas mandated on member states. There also is no guarantee that another crisis might not arise somewhere else and produce new waves of desperate migrants fleeing to a safe, rich haven in Europe.

The most serious effect of the Syrian refugee crisis of 2015–16, however, may well prove to be the manner in which it built upon earlier crises to call into question the ideal of European integration itself. The free movement of people from the beginning has been one of the major attractions and benefits of the European ideal, and even the temporary retreat of 2015–16 left many observers questioning whether the EU could successfully withstand the twin challenges of mass migration and terrorism. Populist, anti-EU parties in the Netherlands in April 2016 succeeded in forcing a referendum in which voters rejected the Association Agreement with Ukraine. During 2016, anti-EU parties did well in polls throughout other countries in the heart of the EU, such as Germany and Austria, where a successor to Jorg Haider nearly won the presidency.

Arguably, the greatest threat to a united Europe arose in the United Kingdom, which historically had debated since 1945 whether it was truly a part of Europe. Flushed with confidence from his party's unexpected success in the April 2015 elections, Tory prime minister David Cameron followed up on his promise to Eurosceptics in his own party by demanding renegotiation of some of the terms of the United Kingdom's EU membership, and he scheduled a popular vote on the issue in June 2016. At the time, Cameron's electoral strength seemed sufficient to take a package of minor concessions from Brussels before the British voting public and put the issue to rest within his party (and the country) for the foreseeable future. Instead, the European refugee crisis strengthened anti-immigrant and anti-EU forces within the United Kingdom and brought a solid victory for the "Brexit" advocates in the June 23 referendum, which only months before had seemed a relatively farfetched eventuality. The prospect of the United Kingdom's departure from the EU gave renewed life to advocates of Scottish independence, who seemed to have been conclusively defeated in a September 2014 referendum, and raised questions about the future of Northern Ireland, which along with Scotland voted strongly to remain in the EU. Thus the refugee and euro crises led not only to the prospective departure from the EU of one of its largest economies and most powerful security actors but also posed real questions about the possible disintegration of the United Kingdom itself.

The victory of Brexit advocates encouraged Eurosceptic parties in many other EU countries as well. Nonetheless, many European officials still express confidence that the EU will "muddle through" despite the multiple shocks and multiple crises the continent and the Union have undergone over the past few years. The collapse of the European Union would, of course, place a dramatic punctuation mark at the end of the post–Cold War era in Europe. However, even if the European Union survives more or less in its present form (as this author suspects), the bloom is clearly off the rose, and popular faith in the powers of European integration to promote reform, increase prosperity, and ensure peace has significantly diminished, if not vanished entirely. There is still much to like about life in Europe, but there are significant internal economic, social, and political problems and disputes that will likely keep Europe looking inward, rather than outward, for a considerable time in the future. In turn, this suggests a decreasing likelihood that Europe will be a united, ambitious, or determined security actor, especially in the absence of American participation and leadership. Europe may continue along its present course in foreign and security policy for some time simply due to inertia, but the socioeconomic and political context and factors that produced the present course have changed or vanished. New and emerging conditions are already pushing Europe in new directions, and this process is likely to accelerate as the generation that fought the Cold War gradually retires, leaving a younger set of leaders who no longer remember, if they ever knew, why the post–Cold War order was constructed the way it was.

## THE UNEXPECTED CHALLENGE: "TRUMP AND AMERICA FIRST"

The one key element of the Euro-Atlantic security order that did not vary and was not called into question from 1989 through 2014 was the determination of the United States to remain physically present and directly involved in European security—and, in particular, its dedication to the Atlantic Alliance as the primary guarantor of security in Europe. From George H. W. Bush to Barack Obama, both Republican and Democratic presidents and administrations adhered to a remarkably consistent, unwavering view of the centrality of the transatlantic bargain and a militarily and politically strong NATO to the security and prosperity of the United States. To be sure, over the quarter century after the fall of the Berlin Wall, significant changes in American views evolved regarding the purposes NATO served, where and how NATO should be employed, and how NATO should relate to other actors—both nation-states and institutions. Nonetheless, Washington remained firm in the conviction that support for and participation in NATO constituted the cornerstone of America's European and global security strategy.

The presidential election campaign of 2015–16 and the unexpected victory of Republican nominee Donald Trump threatened to bring an end to the extended bipartisan consensus over this key element of US defense and security policy. As part of the "America First" doctrine that characterized his campaign's approach to international affairs, candidate Trump called NATO "obsolete," asserted repeatedly that as president he would be able to "get along" with Putin and Russia, and assailed America's European Allies for not paying their fair share of the costs of their defense.[126] During the course of his campaign, Trump also welcomed the United Kingdom's vote to leave the European Union, denounced and derided German chancellor Angela Merkel for her position on accepting refugees from the Syrian conflict, and spoke positively about right-wing populist figures in Europe, even as he denounced immigration and uneven trade deals at home. The growing evidence of Russian involvement in the US political campaign, with the hacking and release of massive numbers of emails first from the Democratic National Committee and then from Democratic campaign chair John Podesta, combined with Trump's repeated favorable references to Putin and Russia as a potential antiterrorist partner, created tremendous anxiety in large segments of the political and economic elites on both sides of the Atlantic. In the wake of the Brexit vote, the prospect of a populist victory in the United States seemed too unsettling for many Allies to contemplate with equanimity.

After Trump's unanticipated victory, neither political leaders nor observers on either side of the Atlantic knew what to expect. On one hand, a remarkably (and unexpectedly) positive meeting with outgoing President Obama and the argument from many quarters that Trump would need to rely in his administration on experienced Republican colleagues provided some relief to those shocked by the prospect of a Trump presidency. On the other hand, Trump's apparent impulsiveness and unpredictability often caused consternation. For example, Trump set off massive fear and speculation of a collision between the United States and China by accepting a telephone call from Taiwan's leader, an action explained in part by a desire to "shake up" the leadership in Beijing.[127] Although some of Trump's more extreme campaign promises — such as building a wall along the southern US border and getting Mexico to pay for it — appeared increasingly less likely to be carried out, it seemed clear by the time of Trump's inauguration that massive changes could be expected in many of America's domestic and foreign policies and overall direction. The incoming president made that clear in his inaugural address:

> For many decades, we've enriched foreign industry at the expense of American industry; subsidized the armies of other countries while allowing for the very sad depletion of our military. We've defended other nation's borders while refusing to defend our own; and spent trillions of dollars overseas while America's infrastructure has fallen

into disrepair and decay. We've made other countries rich while the wealth, strength, and confidence of our country have disappeared over the horizon.[128]

No matter what the specific actions and policies of a Trump administration might eventually turn out to be, it was clear that US Allies and partners could no longer presume the unwavering approach from Washington of the past quarter century. As the new president promised, "From this moment on, it's going to be America First."[129]

Trump's actions with respect to European security during the first months of his presidency were not wholly consistent, and their long-term implications — and indeed, the president's intentions—are not entirely clear. Both US vice president Michael Pence and secretary of defense James Mattis explicitly reconfirmed the US commitment to NATO in the early weeks of the administration. Then, at a joint press conference in April 2017 with NATO secretary general Jens Stoltenberg, Trump announced that he no longer considered NATO obsolete.[130] However, at his first NATO summit in Brussels just over a month later, Trump failed to express his support for Article V of the Washington Treaty, a traditional pledge by American presidents that had reportedly been included by speechwriters in his prepared text. Instead, Trump berated the Allies for not pulling their weight by meeting established and agreed-on targets for defense spending. The administration's pledge to support Article V came only a month and a half later, after much anguished criticism on both sides of the Atlantic, during an early July visit to Poland on the way to the Group of Twenty summit in Germany.[131] By the late summer of 2017, the US commitment to NATO under the new administration had finally been reaffirmed, but in a halting and forced manner that did not necessarily instill great confidence in all of America's Allies and partners.

It is not the intent or purpose of this narrative to describe or analyze the implications of the wide range of controversial actions and changes effected by the Trump administration. Indeed, such an endeavor would likely demand multiple, weighty, analytical volumes. Insofar as European security and security institutions are concerned, as of mid-2017, one may conclude mainly that the Trump presidency constitutes the latest in a series of major shocks to the post–Cold War European security order that began with the Russian invasion of Ukraine and annexation of Crimea. Whether the Trump administration is successful in pursuing and attaining its stated goals or not, the very fact of a populist, "America First," neo-isolationist, neomercantilist president in Washington challenges the most fundamental assumptions and structures of the post–Cold War European security architecture. The narrative and analysis in this volume affirms that the American decision made in 1990–91 to remain in Europe was arguably the key decision in forming the post-1989 security order. If Washington now decides, under Trump's presidency, to withdraw wholly or partially from Europe, both European and global security orders will enter uncharted waters.

Perhaps the pressure of unexpected events and the inclinations of experienced Republican internationalists will keep Washington engaged in European security affairs. However, European leaders German chancellor Angela Merkel and European Commission president Jean-Claude Juncker have already begun to discuss openly what should be done by European institutions and the Europeans themselves to replace American involvement and leadership. Such discussions may result in the fraying and loosening of transatlantic ties, no matter what the United States ends up doing. The EU might grow closer and stronger as a result; or, conversely, the ascendance of populism in the United States might encourage others to break away from the European Union, leading to realignments within Europe. Convincing speculation along many such lines is possible and cannot be easily refuted.

What does seem clear and beyond doubt is that Trump's 2016 victory has opened up the real possibility of a Europe and European security without the United States, an eventuality that before the election would have been dismissed as so unlikely as to render discussion unnecessary. For seventy years, European leaders have counted on solidarity and support from Washington; but this state of affairs can no longer be presumed. Trump's election has shaken the long-standing status quo and opened up the possibility of drastically different alternatives. Both Americans and Europeans will have to make a conscious choice on whether the transatlantic bargain and the American presence in Europe and NATO will continue. Do the United States and the nations of Europe still share enough interests and values to join their forces and commit to a common defense? Is the American public still willing to bear the costs and burden of participating in Europe's defense? And do European publics still desire such American participation and support, including the obligations this involves? The answers to these questions no longer seem obvious, if they ever were. To build a new, post-Ukraine European security order, leaders and publics on both sides of the Atlantic will need to contemplate and answer these questions anew.

## 12. THE FUTURE OF EUROPEAN SECURITY

## The Past as Present

The paradox and ultimate irony of the European security architecture constructed over the past twenty-five years is that this security order not only failed
to prevent the outbreak of war between two of Europe's largest states but may
have contributed to the buildup to and outbreak of this conflict. Both NATO
and the European Union since the mid-1990s maintained a policy of extending their geographic scope within a cooperative European security architecture
composed of overlapping, interlocking institutions. NATO and the EU implicitly and explicitly excluded the possibility of membership for Russia, although
both organizations repeatedly expressed the aspiration and intention of building friendly, cooperative relationships with Russia. Such an approach may have
been workable in theory at the beginning of the post–Cold War era when neither NATO nor the EU subsumed much more than about half of Europe. The
theoretical flaws in this construct began to be exposed, however, when NATO
and EU territory expanded and Russia's geographic space shrank to a point that
one could foresee all of the countries in Europe within NATO and the EU—
with only Russia left out on the "other side." No matter how much the two
Brussels-based institutions might proclaim their friendship with Russia, in such
a situation it would be extremely difficult to prevent Moscow from developing a
perception of isolation and insecurity.

Of course, "the system" in Europe in and of itself did not bring about the war in Ukraine; the EU, Russian, American, and Ukrainian leaders all made mistakes, at times pursuing stubborn and unwise courses of action. However, the logic of the structure and development of Europe's security architecture, in particular after the 2008 Russia-Georgia war, pushed inexorably toward a zero-sum relationship between NATO and the EU on one side and Russia on the other, with increasing competition and the potential for conflict when one side felt its position or interests were being threatened. By the second decade of the twenty-first century, the processes of European integration had been institutionalized and bureaucratized to such an extent that both EU and NATO actions and Russian responses to them appeared to be operating largely on automatic pilot. In the face of such routinization, necessary qualities such as imagination, innovation, and flexibility rarely appeared from any side. Thus EU officials seemed unable to envision any way that Ukraine could cooperate with both the EU and the Eurasian Economic Union, epitomized by the September 2013 warning from Stefan Fule, the EU's commissioner for enlargement, that the EU would respond and defend its Eastern partners against pressure to choose the Customs Union.[1] Faced with what was explicitly described as an either/or choice in the largest of its immediate European neighbors, it is no surprise that the Kremlin acted to attempt to sway that decision in its direction.

The fact of this attempt, like many other actions taken and policies pursued by Moscow in its near abroad, was neither surprising nor ipso facto evil, authoritarian, or undemocratic. The problem was not so much that Russia defended its interests in its immediate neighborhood but *how* it did so. Since the breakup of the Soviet Union, Kremlin leaders harbored the notion that Russia had a special relationship and special rights in the countries that had been Soviet republics. (Some Russian officials excluded the three Baltic Sea states from this category, but other Russians did not.) Gorbachev voluntarily withdrew Soviet forces from the Warsaw Pact states, and post-Soviet Russian leaders mostly have seemed to accept the independence and full sovereignty of Bulgaria, Romania, Hungary, Slovakia, the Czech Republic, and Poland. However, Gorbachev sought to keep the Soviet republics under Moscow's authority, and Yeltsin originally envisioned the Commonwealth of Independent States (CIS) as a means of retaining control of these republics for Moscow, ending the Soviet state mainly as a means of getting rid of his rival Gorbachev.

Russian leaders after 1992 perceived a special right to follow, intervene, and—if necessary—control developments in the former Soviet republics. One can see evidence of this attitude toward the near abroad just as much in Yeltsin and some of his most democratic associates as one can in Putin and his *silovik* subordinates. Russian intervention in conflicts in Nagorno-Karabakh, Abkhazia, South Ossetia, Transdniestria, and Tajikistan; Russia's offer to provide border control and security in much of the CIS; and Russia's collection and assumption of control of the USSR's nuclear weapons and strategic delivery systems in cooperation with the United States all attested to Moscow's perception of its special and privileged position among the states of the former Soviet Union.[2]

Again, the problem was not so much the fact of Russian involvement in other former Soviet republics but the manner of that involvement. Large empires such as the USSR do not disintegrate peacefully in a day (or even a year, or a generation), and there were many aspects of the Soviet dissolution with which Moscow could be particularly helpful, given the greater resources, experienced cadres, and infrastructure it possessed in comparison with many of the other newly independent states. In many cases, Moscow chose to use coercion and pressure, such as cutting off energy supplies, to convince local authorities in the other post-Soviet states to follow its policy line. The distinction between carrots and sticks in Russian actions was not always clear. Russian officials frequently cited provision of natural gas to former Soviet republics at well below market prices during the 1990s as a way to help these new states through a difficult transition period. However, Moscow also allowed gas debts to accumulate in these states, and then traded this debt for ownership shares in many key local enterprises, a practice that often seemed self-aggrandizing and predatory. Similarly, Russian forces in separatist entities could be seen as protection for national or ethnic minorities, such as the Ossetians, that had been subjected to persecution by the majority population of the metropolitan state. Yet Russian negotiators were not above propping up the separatists or manipulating the conflict to achieve their aims, such as Yeltsin's use of the Abkhazia settlement to induce Shevardnadze to bring Georgia into the CIS. Some Russians believe that Moscow let slip opportunities to gain goodwill and influence by not doing more to help countries such as Moldova, Georgia, Armenia, and Azerbaijan to resolve their internal conflicts. Irrespective of historical might have beens, the fact of Russian influence in the former Soviet states was indisputable, inevitable, and in and of itself neither good nor evil.

The politics and conflicts in the former Soviet states took on greater importance and influence in the European security context and security architecture at the end of the 1990s and in the early 2000s, as NATO and the EU moved closer to the former Soviet borders and began to be more deeply and regularly involved in the affairs of these states. Some of the leaders and members of the political elites in these states saw in the increased EU and NATO presence an opportunity to balance against Russian influence. For those hostile to Moscow for one reason or another, whether legitimately or unfoundedly, it was a chance to get the Russians out. The Charter of Paris provision that all states were free to choose their own security orientation did not turn out to be a problem for Russia in the first NATO expansion when the new members were former Warsaw Pact members. However, the Adapted Conventional Forces in Europe Treaty ended up in effect hostage to resolution of conflicts inside Georgia and Moldova, in which rights and wrongs were not completely clear. Nonetheless, the ratification of this treaty rapidly became contingent upon resolution of Chisinau's and Tbilisi's grievances against Moscow. Whatever the justice of these complaints, this appears to be a clear case of the tail wagging the dog.

Once the Central and Eastern European states with the greatest fears and resentment of Russia became members of both NATO and the EU, it became much more difficult (although certainly not impossible) for either of those organizations to pursue policies friendly with or favorable to Moscow. Tallinn, Riga, Vilnius, Warsaw, and Bucharest all had good reason in relatively recent historical experience to be mistrustful of Moscow, but in international politics it is often difficult to separate reasonable suspicion and caution from geopolitical ambition and personal political aggrandizement. The NATO-Russia Founding Act and the EU-Russia Agreement of 1997 emerged from a very different context and different attitudes toward Russia than the Eastern Partnership, which reflects a considerably more suspicious and competitive attitude toward Moscow.

There was nothing inevitable about this progression from a policy aimed at integrating Russia into a common Euro-Atlantic political and security community "from Vancouver to Vladivostok" to the present situation, in which Europe is divided between a larger NATO and EU arrayed against a hostile, resentful Russia. Almost each particular step in the process appeared to make good sense in and of itself. The 1990–91 Western decision to retain and reform NATO had the immediate positive result of keeping the United States actively and operationally involved in European security. In turn, this US involvement was crucial in managing the peaceful dissolution of the Soviet Union and in responding to Yugoslavia's violent breakup. The decision to take NATO out of area in the Balkans in the early 1990s did not foretell the effects of the genocide in Rwanda, intervention to protect ethnic Albanians in Kosovo, or the September 11 attacks on the United States, which eventually took NATO along with America into Afghanistan. Policymakers throughout Europe and North America looked at each of these crises or challenges, took stock of the institutions and resources available, and responded in ways they considered effective and constructive.

Some critics, such as those who opposed NATO enlargement in the mid-1990s, maintain that in formulating more short-term, tactical responses to security problems, North American and European leaders demonstrated a lack of strategic vision and sacrificed major strategic goals in order to attain tactical objectives. There are at least a couple of responses to such critiques. First, in general, political leaders always face the need to resolve the immediate problem at hand, irrespective of how well they understand the larger strategic considerations. Many times their answer is, in effect, "We will solve the tactical need now, and take care of strategy later"—which is understandable, except the latter part often never happens. Second, with respect to Europe in the 1990s and 2000s, US, NATO, and EU leaders had a strategic vision and made a key, strategic decision that enlargement of NATO and the EU could provide stability, prosperity, and security to Central Europe, which these leaders judged to be the most important challenge facing the Euro-Atlantic community. Those who made this choice rejected two competing strategic visions. The first was that of Gorbachev, many other Russians, and some in the West, who argued that both the Warsaw Pact and NATO should end with the Cold War, and the Conference on Security and Cooperation in Europe (CSCE) should form the basis for a new values-based security order throughout all of Europe. The second vision was advanced by many leaders in Europe and North America, including high Pentagon officials, and might be called a "Russia-first" approach, arguing that top priority should be given to promotion of political, economic, and security reform in Russia because it was the largest and most important entity to emerge out of the Soviet camp. If Russia reformed successfully, this argument went, the rest of Eastern Europe would follow along.

In this volume I have chronicled when and how this strategic choice (or, some might argue, series of strategic choices) was made and what followed as the results of this choice. In many respects, the decision to enlarge NATO and the EU has been a great success. The nations of the former Warsaw Pact and the three Baltic states all have basically open, pluralist political systems, market economies, and active, diverse civil societies. These states have mostly achieved considerable prosperity, particularly in comparison with their economic levels and standards of living in 1989. They are at peace with one another, do not fear attack from neighbors within their community, and are relatively free from threats from outside the region. One might argue that observers who worried about how these nations would make the transition from Soviet rule as the Berlin Wall came down in 1989 would generally be pleased.

The greatest failing of the West's strategic choice after the end of the Cold War is, of course, the exclusion, isolation, and hostility of contemporary Russia. The early Western advocates of NATO enlargement argued that one could have it all: enlarge the Alliance, thereby assist Central Europe in its transition, and still build a cooperative relationship with a friendly, democratic Russia. Successful conclusion of the NATO-Russia Founding Act and the self-deception that Yeltsin's continuation in power meant that Russia was still democratizing seemed for a time to support this contention. Some observers argue that NATO's 1999 attack on Serbia, and not NATO enlargement, was the most important event in souring NATO-Russia relations. Yet those who argue this line then have trouble explaining Putin's rapprochement with NATO, acceptance of the second NATO enlargement (including the Baltic states), and cooperative work for a decade within the NATO-Russia Council.

The NATO-Russia relationship always had the potential for difficulty and has deteriorated for a number of reasons, none of which made such a turn of events inevitable. First, enlarging an Alliance that for much of its previous existence had been an anti-Russia body without including Russia was a recipe for making Moscow suspicious and offended. Second, making decisions in this Alliance that affected general European security, such as war and peace, especially after countries known to be traditionally anti-Russian became members, ran the risk of prompting Russian disagreement and hostility. Finally, adding offensive, expeditionary capabilities to the Alliance's military capacities and employing these capabilities in theaters increasingly distant from NATO territory made it hard to avoid arousing insecurity and suspicion, particularly among Russian military leaders. No single one of these aspects of NATO's evolution since 1990 made it inevitable that the relationship with Moscow would become hostile, but taken all together they made it much more difficult to construct and maintain friendly, cooperative relations with Russia.

The story that Bush and Baker promised Gorbachev in February 1990—that NATO would not enlarge after German unification, and that the Americans subsequently broke that promise intentionally and maliciously for their own geopolitical advantage—is essentially a fairly recent Russian narrative constructed as much to justify as to explain current anti–United States and anti-NATO policies. As we have seen, no written promise was given, although an oral promise was apparently understood on both sides. However, the territory under discussion at that time was Germany's east, and there is little evidence that any of the participants even dreamed at that time that someday NATO would be on Russia's doorstep. Further, the Russian narrative does not explain the desire as early as 1990–91 of Central and Eastern European leaders to join NATO because they did not trust Moscow to continue along its course of democratic reform. The fact remains that the proponents of NATO (and EU) enlargement have found enthusiastic partners in Central and Eastern Europe, not dupes or unwilling victims of American geopolitical ambitions.

The failure of Russia's integration into Euro-Atlantic security institutions is also inextricably tied up with the history of its domestic transition from Soviet political institutions and the planned Soviet economy. In addition to any other attributes, the Organization for Security and Cooperation in Europe (OSCE), NATO, and the EU were and are all heavily, if not primarily, based upon values. To be sure, the transformation of the CSCE at the end of the Cold War included landmark arms control agreements such as the Conventional Forces in Europe (CFE) Treaty, but the heart of the CSCE/OSCE, at least for the

Western participating states, remained the fundamental freedoms and human rights enshrined in the Charter of Paris and Copenhagen Document. Both NATO and the EU made adoption of democratic institutions and market principles key criteria in the enlargement processes begun in the 1990s. Although Western states—both old and new members of the EU and NATO—did not always fully live up to their own principles, these principles nevertheless remained a basic, indispensable part of the Western approach to security and international affairs.

Russia under Gorbachev, Yeltsin, and Putin formally accepted the values placed by the West at the heart of Europe's post–Cold War transformation. After 1990, Moscow signed and accepted a string of documents and international agreements containing obligations to hold free elections, observe human rights, due process, and the rule of law, and to accept international scrutiny and inquiries about whether it conducted both its internal affairs and its relations with other states in accordance with these standards. Russia made an outward transition from domestic Soviet institutions to a competitive, pluralist political system and an open market economy. Despite all this, Russia did not fully embrace and assimilate these values, at least in the manner and to the degree anticipated by Western interlocutors who first greeted and supported Russian reform efforts emerging in the late 1980s and early 1990s.

There are many reasons for the apparent failure of democratic reform in Russia and the reversion to moderately authoritarian rule under Putin, most of which involve the choices and actions of Russians themselves and not the involvement of foreigners. There are certainly celebrated cases of foreign, in particular Western, errors of both commission and omission, such as relying too much on Yeltsin personally rather than building institutions, exaggerating the degree of democracy in the 1990s and the amount of authoritarianism in the 2000s, and acceptance of the vulture privatizations in the 1990s that led to the emergence of ultra-rich oligarchs and extreme inequality. The notion that Yeltsin objected less than Putin and his colleagues to some US, NATO, EU, or Western policies largely because Yeltsin was more democratic is an illusion that remains hard to shake. Russia today is much wealthier and freer than it was during the late Soviet period, but it is nowhere near as free as its leaders may claim nor as unfree and oppressed as its severest Western critics allege.

One of the most important ways in which values separate Russia and the West is that even after twenty-five years of closer contact and interaction since the Cold War, many Russians still find it hard to believe that a large proportion of Western citizens, elites, and political leaders actually take seriously what they say about values. Russians looking at the EU tend to concentrate on its wealth and generally high standards of living. Yet one of the enduring strengths of the EU has been the fact that it is—among other things—a community in which basic norms of political, economic, and social behavior are accepted and respected, which has been a key to producing that wealth. Although both NATO and the United States have at times compromised their standards for the sake of political expediency (from Nicaragua under Somoza to Portugal under Salazar), the North Atlantic community was and remains dedicated to pluralism, the rule of law, and respect for basic norms of international behavior. US, NATO, and EU criticisms and denunciations of Soviet behavior and domestic practices during the Cold War were not simply exercises in geopolitical competition; they reflected a real belief in and dedication to principles such as freedom of association, expression, conscience, and movement and a desire to live in polities that observed them.

Since the end of the Cold War, Russian leaders and Russian elites have taken on the appearance but not the essence of open Western societies. Materialism, and not dialectical materialism, now rules in a Russian society made wealthy by both market economics and a hydrocarbon boom. Russian leaders and officials apparently have difficulty understanding and believing the importance that Western leaders and societies attach to human rights standards and practices in countries other than their own. They fail to comprehend how their treatment of their own citizens can be perceived as offensive by Western societies, and thus assume that Western criticisms must be based on ulterior political or economic motives.[3] This disconnect is far more acute in the globalized, post–Cold War world, in which Russians' access to global markets and freedom to travel make them participants in a larger community that may demand respect for norms in return for this access. In similar fashion, Russians often appear not to understand why the manner in which they conduct relations with their neighbors should be of concern to distant European or North American countries, especially when these countries often have a history of mistreating their own neighbors. In a time when relations were less tense and the European and American presence was more distant, this disparity over how closely and consistently norms should be observed and enforced was not so important. With the EU and the United States on Ukraine's doorstep, and Moscow's actions under constant scrutiny, such differences assume much greater immediacy and are much more likely to become a cause for dispute or conflict.

As Europe celebrated the twenty-fifth anniversaries of the Charter of Paris and reunification of Germany the continent seemed in some senses to have come full circle. In 1990 Europe was just beginning to end the long division between the Warsaw Pact and NATO; in 2016 Europe was once again divided between Russia and the West, only with the line of separation less clear and further to the east. The United States remains in Europe politically and physically, with NATO as the chief instrument for American participation and leadership in European security affairs. US foreign and security policy priorities have been shifting and continue to shift as the global center of political-economic gravity moves toward East Asia. However, the United States and the EU in aggregate remain the world's two largest economic powers and possess much of the world's military might, if not political authority. Washington's continued presence in NATO serves to connect it to Europe and to provide the means to return to European affairs in times of emergency, no matter how much global concerns and responsibilities may divert its attention.

The reemergence of Russia as a possible threat will demand a continuing US commitment to and focus on Europe, at least in the near future. However, other crises, such as the rise of the so-called Islamic State and continuing instability in the Middle East, also demand US attention, resources, and leadership, and Washington will indubitably seek greater contributions from Allies and partners in Europe. By mid-2015, critics were already commenting that President Barack Obama had outsourced his Ukraine policy to Germany; by mid-2017, President Donald Trump had bluntly and explicitly told the European Allies to pay more for their own defense. The fact is that Europe has both the security structures and the potential resources to meet such challenges should European countries make the political decision to do so. NATO after Wales (and Warsaw) has placed renewed emphasis on its original mission of territorial defense and recently has taken serious steps to provide for the military defense of its newer, easternmost members. What is less clear is whether the Alliance will solve the perennial issue of burden sharing, especially with a far less understanding and supportive administration in Washington. The Wales decisions on defense spending are clear, ambitious, adequate for most probable contingencies, but not assured of attainment. Renewed or new economic travails could derail even the best intentions of most European Allies, especially if economic troubles and the refugee crisis lead to further election victories for populist, Eurosceptic parties. No international organization is stronger than the political and economic health of its individual members. Seen in this light, NATO's success depends most of all on the recovery and health of Europe's economies, a less than certain future indeed.

Some pundits and policymakers have labeled the renewed division of Europe into opposing camps as a "New Cold War." Although the current antagonisms between Russia and the West run deep indeed, the current situation in Europe differs from the prolonged NATO-Soviet standoff in a number of crucial respects. First, there is no ideological competition between Russia and the West. Although Putin and his cronies may claim to promote different values from the contemporary, decadent West, the Kremlin is not offering any comprehensive, internally cohesive ideology in opposition to its rivals. Second, Russia is not as rich and powerful in comparison to today's EU and NATO as the Soviet Union was when weighed against its contemporary rivals. The Russian nuclear arsenal is still formidable, but US and European conventional military capabilities in the aggregate significantly exceed those available to Moscow and constitute a considerable deterrent against Russian adventurism. Third, today's global strategic context is strikingly different, with the economic, political, and military rise of Asia, in particular China. None of this should be taken to mean that today's confrontation over Ukraine is automatically less dangerous than the Cold War's bipolar world. Rather, it is important to recognize that today's situation is different in important respects, and glib analogies to Europe between 1945 and 1989 may lead to mistaken diagnoses and ineffective strategic responses.

The European Union is also mostly a success story over the past twenty-five years, but aspects of the EU's economy, politics, and Common Security and Defence Policy raise questions about the future. First, the euro crisis continues, with Greece lurching through yet another economic crisis in early 2017. Despite changes and improvements after 2012, the existence of a common currency without a common fiscal or political union continues to bedevil the EU. The EU may not fail over this issue, but this institutional deficiency will continue to cause problems, in particular in times of economic difficulty. Second, the EU itself continues to be under attack from right-wing, populist, and Eurosceptic parties. Leaders of these parties cause difficulties in most of the EU states in which they get elected, and perhaps even broader disarray when they are chosen as deputies to the European Parliament. These parties have gained additional support as a consequence of the 2015–16 Syrian refugee crisis. However, it is in Britain and France where their success is most threatening to the EU as a whole. The UK vote in June 2016 to leave the EU has both revived doubts about the UK's internal cohesion and given renewed energy and hope to anti-EU forces. Emmanuel Macron's unexpected victory over Marine Le Pen and the Front Nationale allayed some of the most alarmist fears that France might also vote to leave and that the EU itself could break up. However, the danger posed by challenges from populist right-wing parties has not passed, and the continuing strength and stability of the EU cannot be presumed without reservation.

Third, and highlighted by the Ukraine crisis, the EU's apparent achievement of its Common Security and Defence Policy has come with all sorts of unexpected and not necessarily healthy side effects. Agreement on the Berlin-Plus arrangement and then the return of France to full participation in NATO military structures ended the long tug of war between Washington and Paris (and the two sides of Brussels) over whether NATO or the EU should provide for European security. However, in the process, particularly after adoption of the Lisbon Treaty, EU security structures have become so closely coordinated with the Atlantic Alliance as to become almost indistinguishable from NATO. Provisions in the Lisbon Treaty for EU coordination with NATO affected the terms of the Association Agreements offered to Ukraine, Moldova, and

Georgia, a fact that may well have played a part in Moscow's apprehension with respect to these pacts.[4]

In fact, it is most ironic that now that the long-running rivalry between NATO and the EU has been clearly resolved, the EU may not be able to marshal the military resources to support an independent Common Security and Defence Policy, at the very moment that a Washington beset by concerns about the Islamic State and the South China Sea might really desire Europe to take over a greater portion of the security burden it its own region. The largest European countries all seem to have been downsizing their militaries, although many argue that they have been becoming more efficient, thereby reducing expenditures without sacrificing power. Berlin is now clearly the leader of Europe, but it is not at all obvious whether and to what extent that leadership extends to military security affairs. Short- and long-term UK plans for military cuts will be of extreme concern for both NATO and the EU, even after Brexit. Finally, even though most EU countries remain relatively wealthy, and therefore able to afford a larger defense burden if necessary, there is no evidence that voters in any of these major European states are inclined to welcome increased military spending. A Pew global survey taken in the late spring of 2015 showed that a majority of voters in most European countries do not approve of taking military action in support of Ukraine against Russia.[5] Presumably, this sentiment would change should the attack be against their own countries, but how far beyond their own borders the will to fight may extend is not clear.

The OSCE has returned to a position of relative prominence in European security affairs, but this is a sign of failure rather than success of the overall European security order. OSCE Headquarters in Vienna and many of the organization's structures have become the neutral ground where the competing protagonists in Europe can square off while they attempt to work out the practical differences between them. In recent years, especially after the war with Georgia, Russian officials for a time appeared to favor the NATO-Russia Council over the OSCE as a forum for dialogue and cooperation with their Western counterparts, presumably because they knew that the real decisions about European security were being made in NATO. Since the post-Crimea rupture in relations, Evert and Mons have gradually been reopening to the Russians, but it is the OSCE where they are an equal partner, with both a voice *and* a veto. To the extent that Moscow and its Western interlocutors can agree on anything, the OSCE possesses well-developed institutional structures capable of fielding potentially effective implementation operations, such as the Special Monitoring Mission in Ukraine.

From August to November 2015 the OSCE celebrated the fortieth anniversary of the Final Act and the twenty-fifth of the Charter of Paris. At this writing, it is not clear how many of the OSCE's participating states would accept all of the provisions of either of these landmark documents. When it comes to human rights, fundamental freedoms, and democratization, the post-Maidan revival of the OSCE has had little noticeable effect. Moscow and some of its like-minded partners "east of Vienna" visibly maintain their doubts about the election observation activities of the OSCE's Office for Democratic Institutions and Human Rights, freedom of the media, and other human rights issues pushed by Western states.

Meanwhile, another major achievement of the Helsinki Process may be in jeopardy: the conventional arms control regime established through the CFE Treaty and the confidence- and security-building measures contained in the Vienna Document (VDOC) series. Both Russia and the Western states-parties have in effect abandoned the CFE regime, although all sides from time to time issue statements about the need for some sort of conventional arms control in Europe. For some time after Moscow announced suspension of its participation in CFE transparency and verification activities in 2007, the provisions of the VDOC appeared to be sufficient to ensure transparency and confidence about conventional threats. However, the last VDOC update was in 2011, attempts have been made since the crisis in Ukraine and Turkey's downing of a Russian military aircraft to limit overflights under the Open Skies Agreement, and conventional weapons systems have undergone constant revision and improvement, generally without corresponding updates or improvements in transparency and confidence-building regimes. Europe does not seem likely to return to a Cold War–style conventional arms race, but there are new and different categories of arms and ways in which their proliferation could threaten European security, especially if Moscow and its major Western partners are unable to agree on common approaches to such issues.

Europe is not back where it started at the end of the Cold War, but it is not in that optimistic place that all of its states hoped it would be as November 10, 1989, dawned. Some things have improved. NATO, the EU, and the OSCE are all much stronger, more capable institutions, with demonstrated capacities to marshal resources, to deploy these to the field, and to address and resolve complex problems. Some things have gotten worse, even after they got better. Most of the Central and Eastern European states have successfully integrated into European political and security structures, but integration failed with Russia. Although Russia has undergone extensive internal changes, some of these very much for the better, for most observers the process of domestic reform in Russia has also failed. One clear lesson of the optimistic interventions of the 1990s may well be that Russia's internal development and reform, when all is said and done, depends on the Russians themselves. External efforts to direct or hasten such changes or reforms may help, but there is a roughly equal chance they may not, or even be counterproductive.

Europe is at the end of one era and the beginning of another. The Euro-Atlantic security architecture that was constructed immediately after the end of the Cold War has run its course and will need to be reformed, rebuilt, or perhaps even replaced. It may make sense to preserve some or all of the major components—the OSCE, EU, and NATO—because they possess useful capabilities and still enjoy the adherence and support of many of their members. However, it may make just as much sense to change these institutions or to invent new ones. There turned out to be no place for Russia in the post–Cold War Euro-Atlantic security architecture, although it took a quarter of a century to demonstrate that fact conclusively. The states of Europe and North America will need imagination, patience, and perseverance to construct a new regional security order, this time with a place for the Russia we have rather than the Russia we wish we had.

In the end, security institutions and a security order establish norms and standards for behavior that provide for the security of all the states that make up that order. Otherwise, the institutions and the order fail. The post–Cold War European order served for twenty-five years; in the end, perhaps not the best record, but still not a bad one. The task now is not to affix blame for the failure of that order but to learn from it, so that we may do better the next time.

# NOTES

## INTRODUCTION

1. Francis Fukuyama, "The End of History and the Last Man," *The National Interest*, Summer 1989, later published in book form in 1992. Secretary of State James Baker and his predecessor, George Shultz, frequently used the phrases "a Europe whole and free, from Vancouver to Vladivostok" as a shorthand statement of the United States' vision of a post–Cold War world. For one example, see Baker's Aspen Institute speech on the margins of the first ministerial council meeting of the CSCE: James A. Baker III, "The Euro-Atlantic Architecture: From West to East," speech to the Aspen Institute, Berlin, June 18, 1991, *US Department of State Dispatch*, June 24, 1991, 439–43.

2. As quoted by James M. Goldgeier and Michael McFaul, *Power and Purpose: US Policy Toward Russia after the Cold War* (Washington: Brookings Institution Press, 2003), 141.

3. For a good description of such currents in post–Soviet Russian thought, in particular, see Fiona Hill and Clifford G. Gaddy, *Mr. Putin: Operative in the Kremlin*, 2nd edition (Washington: Brookings Institution Press, 2015), 38–75.

4. Baker III, "Euro-Atlantic Architecture."

## 1. FROM A EUROPE DIVIDED TO A EUROPE WHOLE AND FREE

1. Secretary of State James Baker and his predecessor, George Shultz, frequently used the phrases "a Europe whole and free, from Vancouver to Vladivostok" as a shorthand statement of the United States' vision of a post–Cold War world. See note 1 in the Introduction.

2. For the best account and analysis of German politics and German-Soviet relations during the Cold War, see Angela E. Stent, *Russia and Germany Reborn: Unification, the Soviet Collapse, and the New Europe* (Princeton, N.J.: Princeton University Press, 1999).

3. There are numerous accounts of the decline and collapse of the Soviet Union. I rely most heavily for many of the accounts and much of the analysis in this volume on Jack F. Matlock Jr., *Autopsy on an Empire: The American Ambassador's Account of the Collapse of the Soviet Union* (New York: Random House 1995); Yegor Gaidar, *Collapse of an Empire: Lessons for Modern Russia*, trans.. Antonina W. Bouis (Washington, D.C.: Brookings Institution Press, 2007), orig. pub. as *Gibel' imperii: Uroki dlia sovremennoi Rossii* (Moscow, 2006); and Martin Malia, *The Soviet Tragedy: A History of Socialism in Russia, 1917–1991* (New York: Free Press, 1994).

4. For an example of how such issues have played in contemporary Russia, see Dmitri Trenin, *Post-Imperium: A Eurasian Story* (Washington, D.C.: Carnegie Endowment for International Peace, 2011).

5. Quoted at www.nato.int/history.

6. Ibid.; see also NATO, *NATO Handbook,* various iterations, now available online as *What Is NATO?* www.nato.int/nato-welcome/index.html; also see Stanley R. Sloan, *NATO, the European Union, and the Atlantic Community: The Transatlantic Bargain Challenged,* 2nd ed. (New York: Rowman & Littlefield, 2005), for one of the best histories of NATO from its beginnings into the twenty-first century.

7. The sources for this paragraph are www.nato.int/history; and Sloan, *NATO,* 13–40.

8. See Stent, *Russia and Germany Reborn,* 10–17; and Vladislav V. Zubok, *A Failed Empire: The Soviet Union in the Cold War from Stalin to Gorbachev* (Chapel Hill, N.C.: University of North Carolina Press, 2007), esp. 93–122.

9. See NATO, "Report of the Council on the Future Tasks of the Alliance (Harmel Report)," 1967, www.nato.int/cps/en/natohq/topics_67927.htm?selectedLocale=en.

10. Sloan, *NATO,* 47–69; NATO, "A Short History of NATO," www.nato.int/cps/en/natohq/topics_85928.htm.

11. For the most comprehensive treatment of the European Union from its beginnings to the present, see Desmond Dinan, *Ever Closer Union: An Introduction to European Integration,* 3rd ed. (Boulder, Colo: Lynne Rienner, 2005). A fourth edition of Dinan's work was issued by the same publisher in 2010. However, by that time my research for the earlier (i.e., pre-2003) chapters of this work was well advanced. Therefore, I have kept the page references from *Ever Closer Union* in the footnotes to the third edition because the contents of the narrative and judgments did not change appreciably. For more recent developments in the EU, I have generally drawn from

Dinan's most recent, shorter history: Desmond Dinan, *Europe Recast: A History of the European Union*, 2nd ed. (Boulder, Colo.: Lynne Rienner, 2014). An enormous amount of historical and contemporary information is also available on the EU official website, in all the EU languages, at www.europa.eu.

12. The Hague Congress produced the Council of Europe, which was formally established in 1949 and chose Strasbourg as its headquarters city. In turn, in 1950 the Council of Europe adopted the European Convention on Human Rights (or, more precisely, the Convention for the Protection of Human Rights and Fundamental Freedoms); and in 1959 it established the European Court of Human Rights to ensure observance of commitments undertaken under the convention. The Council of Europe, the European Convention on Human Rights, and the European Court of Human Rights have all survived and thrived up to the present day. The European Convention was in great part inspired by the 1948 adoption in the UN of the Universal Declaration of Human Rights, and it represents a statement of the common values that leaders such as Churchill deemed should inspire and guide a united Europe. The Council of Europe and European Convention in this sense were also a response expressed in terms of ideology and values to the Cold War challenges posed to European values by Soviet ideology. However, the Hague Congress and the Consultative Assembly of the newly established Council of Europe were unable to agree on or set up mechanisms or institutions that would be capable of translating these statements of value into practical political, economic, and social cooperation.

13. See the famous remark made in 2002 by former French president Valéry Giscard d'Estaing, "Turkey is not a European country." As quoted by the BBC, http://news.bbc. co.uk/2/hi/europe/2420697.stm.

14. For a detailed history of the origins of the CSCE, see John J. Maresca, *To Helsinki: The Conference on Security and Cooperation in Europe 1973–1975*, Duke Press Policy Study (Durham, N.C.: Duke University Press, 1985); also see also James E. Goodby, *Europe Undivided: The New Logic of Peace in US-Russian Relations* (Washington, D.C.: US Institute of Peace Press, 1998), esp. 37–64. Both Maresca and Goodby were key participants in negotiations for the Helsinki Final Act. For a comprehensive history of the first fifteen years of the CSCE, see William Korey, *The Promises We Keep: Human Rights, the Helsinki Process, and American Foreign Policy* (New York: St. Martin's Press, 1993). The OSCE website also contains key documents from the entire history of the CSCE/OSCE: www.osce.org.

15. The joint legislative-executive branch Commission on Security and Cooperation in Europe still exists. See its website at www.csce.gov.

16. Of the numerous excellent treatments of Russo-German relations during the twentieth century, and other excellent treatments of the subject contained in larger studies of the Cold War, I rely here and elsewhere in this volume especially on Stent, *Russia and Germany Reborn*.

17. For an excellent history and analysis of Soviet politics and motives during this period, see Vladislav Zubok and Constantine Pleshakov, *Inside the Kremlin's Cold War: From Stalin to Khrushchev* (Cambridge, Mass.: Harvard University Press, 1996), esp. 110–73; also see Zubok's longer history of the Cold War: Zubok, *Failed Empire*, esp. 94–163.

18. Stent, *Russia and Germany Reborn*; Zubok, *Failed Empire*, 265–335.

19. For this argument, see, in particular, Trenin, *Post-Imperium*.

20. For the argument that economic weaknesses and irrationalities were key to the demise of the USSR, in particular the role of oil prices, see Gaidar, *Collapse of an Empire*.

21. Andrei Amalrik, *Will the Soviet Union Survive Until 1984?* (New York: Harper & Row, 1970; paperback, Harper Colophon, 1981). Amalrik actually believed that the USSR might collapse sooner, but he chose 1984 because he was persuaded that the allusion to Orwell might attract more readers.

22. This argument has been made especially by supporters of US Department of Defense policies under secretaries of defense Caspar Weinberger and Dick Cheney, and many of their colleagues, such as undersecretary and then deputy secretary Paul Wolfowitz, undersecretary Douglas Feith, and director of the Office of Net Assessments Andrew Marshall.

23. For a reflection of this point of view in the analysis and comments of one of the most important American officials engaged in US-Soviet relations during this period, see two lengthy works by Reagan's senior director in the National Security Council for Soviet affairs and then ambassador to the USSR: Jack F. Matlock Jr., *Reagan and Gorbachev: How the Cold War Ended* (New York: Random House, 2004); and Matlock, *Autopsy on an Empire*.

24. For this argument, see especially Gaidar, *Collapse of an Empire*.

25. The conversation allegedly took place in Pitsunda, although some memoirs have Gorbachev making similar remarks in other places. See Raisa Gorbacheva, *Ya Nadeius'* (Moscow: Kniga, 1991), 13. Also see Archie Brown, *The Gorbachev Factor* (Oxford: Oxford University Press, 1996), 336n152; Anatoliy Cherniaev, *Shest' let s Gorbachevym*, Izdatel'skaia gruppa progress (Moscow: Kultura, 1993); and Eduard Shevardnadze, *Moi Vybor: V zashchitu demokratii i svobody* (Moscow: Novosti, 1991), 23–26.

26. Even Bush and his closest colleagues eventually appeared to come around to such a position; see President Bush's final State of the Union address, January 28, 1992, in Department of State Dispatch, February 3, 1992, 73, where he stated that "the Cold War didn't 'end'—it was won." Bush's National Security Council senior director for Europe, Robert Hutchings, attempted to cast this statement as an appeal to the American public not to disengage from foreign affairs: see Robert L. Hutchings, *American Diplomacy and the End of the Cold War: An Insider's Account of US Policy in Europe, 1989–1992* (Washington, D.C. and Baltimore, Md.: Woodrow Wilson Center Press and Johns Hopkins University Press, 1997), 343. Also see George H. W. Bush and Brent Scowcroft, *A World Transformed* (New York: Alfred A. Knopf, 1998).

27. For an argument along these lines by a high-level insider, see especially Matlock, *Reagan and Gorbachev*; see also Michael R. Beschloss and Strobe Talbott, *At the Highest Levels: The Inside Story of the End of the Cold War* (Boston, Mass.: Little, Brown, 1993).

28. See the recent account of the Reykjavik Summit by Ken Adelman, *Reagan at Reykjavik: Forty-Eight Hours That Ended the Cold War* (New York: Broadside Books, 2014).

29. See the OSCE, "Document of the Stockholm Conference on Confidence- and Security-Building Measures and Disarmament in Europe Convened in Accordance with the Relevant Provisions of the Concluding Document of the Madrid Meeting of the Conference on Security and Co-Operation in Europe," September 19, 1986, www.osce.org/fsc/41238?download=true.

30. On the breakthrough for on-site inspections, see the interview with Ambassador Robert L. Barry on the Association for Diplomatic Studies and Training Foreign Affairs History Project website, 65–72, www.adst.org/OH%20TOCs/Barry,%20Robert%20L.toc.pdf; and also Primakov to the author, June 2000; Oleg Grinevsky and Lynn M. Hansen, *Making Peace: Confidence and Security in a New Europe* (New York: Eloquent Books, 2009); and Michael Mandelbaum, *The Dawn of Peace in Europe* (Washington, D.C.: Twentieth Century Fund, 1996), 96–98.

31. For especially good accounts of Gorbachev's thinking and actions during this period, see Gaidar, *Collapse of an Empire*; and Matlock, *Autopsy on an Empire*.

32. I lived in the USSR from 1981 to 1983 and observed this type of behavior from Soviet citizens countless times. The experiences related to me by my American, European, and Soviet colleagues and acquaintances all replicated and reinforced my own observations.

33. For the involvement of NATO in arms control negotiations with the Soviets and the United States' consultations with its Allies, see, inter alia, the history of NATO on its website: www.nato.int/cps/en/natohq/topics_85928.htm. See also Sloan, *NATO*, esp. 41–72. On the CFE negotiations and treaty, see especially Richard A. Falkenrath, *Shaping Europe's Military Order: The Origins and Consequences of the CFE Treaty* (Cambridge, Mass.: MIT Press, 1995). Finally, as a member of the US delegation to the CSCE Follow-Up Meeting in Vienna in 1986–87, I witnessed and participated in many of the discussions on the mandate for a new conventional arms control negotiation.

34. Matlock, *Reagan and Gorbachev*; Falkenrath, *Shaping Europe's Military Order*. Also see Don Oberdorfer, *From the Cold War to a New Era: The United States and the Soviet Union 1983–1990* (New York: Poseidon Press, 1991), 211–72, passim.

35. For detailed accounts of the conventional arms negotiations, see the accounts by Matlock, *Reagan and Gorbachev*; Falkenrath, *Shaping Europe's Military Order*; Oberdorfer, *From the Cold War to a New Era*; Bush and Scowcroft, *World Transformed*; James A. Baker III, *The Politics of Diplomacy: Revolution, War, and Peace, 1989–1992* (New York: G. P. Putnam's Sons, 1995); and Hutchings, *American Diplomacy*.

36. OSCE, "Vienna Document 1990 of the Negotiations on Confidence and Security-Building Measures Convened in Accordance with the Relevant Provisions of the Concluding Document of the Vienna Meeting of the Conference on Security and Cooperation in Europe," November 17, 1990, www.osce.org/fsc/41245?download=true.

37. There are innumerable accounts of this key period, which saw the revolutions of 1989 in Eastern Europe and the collapse of the Soviet Union. One source is my own experience as chief of the European Division of the Voice of America during this time. In this position, I was responsible for daily US broadcasts to all the Warsaw Pact countries and the three Baltic states. In the course of these duties, I was able to follow daily news and developments very closely. Some of the published accounts I have

consulted for this narrative include Matlock, *Autopsy on an Empire*; Stent, *Russia and Germany Reborn*; Gale Stokes, *The Walls Came Tumbling Down: Collapse and Rebirth in Eastern Europe* (Oxford: Oxford University Press, 2011); Andrew Nagorski, *The Birth of Freedom: Shaping Lives and Societies in the New Eastern Europe* (New York: Simon & Schuster, 1993); and Serhii Plokhy, *The Last Empire: The Final Days of the Soviet Union* (New York: Basic Books, 2014).

## 2. BUILDING THE NEW WORLD ORDER, 1990–1991

1. For accounts of the meeting, see George H. W. Bush and Brent Scowcroft, *A World Transformed* (New York: Alfred A. Knopf, 1998), 162–72; James A. Baker III, *The Politics of Diplomacy: Revolution, War, and Peace, 1989–1992* (New York: G. P. Putnam's Sons, 1995), 167–71; and Jack F. Matlock Jr., *Autopsy on an Empire: The American Ambassador's Account of the Collapse of the Soviet Union* (New York: Random House 1995), 268–74. A transcript of the meeting is available; see Svetlana Savranskaya, Thomas Blanton, and Vladislav Zubok, eds., *Masterpieces of History: The Peaceful End of the Cold War in Europe, 1989* (Budapest: Central European University Press, 2010), 619–45. See also Joshua R. Itzkowitz Shifrinson, "The Malta Summit and US-Soviet Relations: Testing the Waters Amidst Stormy Seas—New Insights from American Archives," e-Dossier 40, Cold War International History Project of the Woodrow Wilson International Center for Scholars, www.wilsoncenter.org/publication/the-malt -summit-and-us-soviet-relations.

2. For this and subsequent statements from this discussion, see Savranskaya et al., *Masterpieces of History*, 619–45.

3. The states that belonged to the Warsaw Pact, meeting in Budapest in February 1991, agreed that the pact no longer existed. The Warsaw Treaty Organization was formally dissolved in Prague on July 1, 1991. For a detailed history of the negotiations, see Richard A. Falkenrath, *Shaping Europe's Military Order: The Origins and Conse-quences of the CFE Treaty* (Cambridge, Mass.: MIT Press, 1995), esp. 45–77.

4. For the provisions, see "Treaty on Conventional Armed Forces in Europe," November 19, 1990, www.osce.org/library/14087?download=true.

5. Falkenrath, *Shaping Europe's Military Order*, 181–219; Robert L. Hutchings, *American Diplomacy and the End of the Cold War: An Insider's Account of US Policy in Europe, 1989–1992* (Washington, D.C. and Baltimore, Md.: Woodrow Wilson Cen-ter Press and Johns Hopkins University Press, 1997), esp. 128–30, 327–29. During this period, I served in the State Department's Office of European Regional Security Affairs and observed or participated in a number of discussions concerning the CFE Treaty.

6. For Albanian accession, see OSCE, "Berlin Meeting of the CSCE Council, 19–20 June 1991, Summary of Conclusions," www.osce.org/mc/40234?download=true. See also William Korey, *The Promises We Keep: Human Rights, the Helsinki Process, and American Foreign Policy* (New York: St. Martin's Press, 1993), 344–46; Victor-Yves Ghebali, *L'OSCE dans l'Europe post-communiste: Vers une identite paneuropeenne de securite* (Brussels: Émile Bruylant, 1996), 106–8; during much of this period, I served as

the CSCE coordinator in the US Department of State and either observed or participated in discussions and negotiations on security affairs within the CSCE.

7. CSCE, "Vienna Document 1990 of the Negotiations on Confidence and Security-Building Measures Convened in Accordance with the Relevant Provisions of the Concluding Document of the Vienna Meeting of the Conference on Security and Cooperation in Europe," November 17, 1990, (hereafter, VDOC 1990), http://www.osce.org/fsc/41245?download=true.

8. VDOC 1990; see also Arie Bloed, *CSCE: Analyses and Documents 1975–1993* (Dordrecht: Martinus Nijhoff, 1994); Heather Hurlburt, "CSCE's Forum for Security Cooperation," in *The Challenges of Change: The Helsinki Summit of the CSCE and Its Aftermath*, ed. Arie Bloed (Dordrecht: Martinus Nijhoff, 1994), 47–66; and P. Terrence Hopmann, *Building Security in Post–Cold War Eurasia: The OSCE and US Foreign Policy* (Washington: US Institute of Peace Press, 1999).

9. The narrative in this section relies especially on Angela E. Stent, *Russia and Germany Reborn: Unification, the Soviet Collapse, and the New Europe* (Princeton, N.J.: Princeton University Press, 2000); Philip Zelikow and Condoleezza Rice, *Germany Unified and Europe Transformed: A Study in Statecraft* (Cambridge, Mass.: Harvard University Press, 1995); Bush and Scowcroft, *World Transformed*; and Baker, *Politics of Diplomacy*.

10. Savranskaya et al., *Masterpieces of History*, 640ff. For the one of the best and most detailed insiders' view of the process of German reunification from the US vantage point, see Zelikow and Rice, *Germany Unified*.

11. For varying versions of the famed pledge not to expand NATO to the east, see Stent, *Russia and Germany Reborn*; Bush and Scowcroft, *World Transformed*, 172, 239; Baker, *Politics of Diplomacy*, esp. 202–6, 251–54; Hutchings, *American Diplomacy*, 116–20; Zelikow and Rice, *Germany Unified*, 179–85; Mikhail Gorbachev, *Memoirs* (New York: Bantam, 1996); Anatolii Cherniaev, *Sovmestnyi Iskhod: Dnevnik dvukh epoch, 1972–1991* (Moscow, 2008); Pavel Palazhchenko, *My Years with Gorbachev and Shevardnadze: The Memoir of a Soviet Interpreter* (University Park: Pennsylvania State University Press, 1997); Matlock, *Autopsy on an Empire*, 382–88; and Mark Kramer, "The Myth of a No-NATO-Enlargement Pledge to Russia," *Washington Quarterly* 37, no. 2 (April 2009): 39–61. Thomas Blanton, "US Policy and the Revolutions of 1989," in *Masterpieces of History*, ed. Savranskaya et al., 49–98, esp. 95–96, contains a particularly good short review of the scholarly and memoir literature on the question. Writing in 1998, Michael MccGwire, "NATO Expansion: 'A Policy Error of Historic Importance,'" *Review of International Studies* 24 (1998): 23–42, quotes Ambassador Jack Matlock (who was present at most of the key 1989–90 meetings) to the effect that NATO would not move to the east if Gorbachev accepted a united Germany in NATO. I also have heard Ambassador Matlock make a similar claim, that an oral commitment was given, but qualified that it applied to Germany and the geopolitical situation in effect in 1990, that is, with the Warsaw Pact still in existence. Matlock also observed that in his view neither side felt the need for a written agreement because of a high degree of mutual trust between the senior officials on both sides. For some of the most recent scholarship on the subject, see Mary Elise Sarotte, "A Broken Promise?

What the West Really Told Moscow About NATO Expansion," *Foreign Affairs* 93, no. 5 (September–October 2014): 90–97; this article is adapted from an updated version of her book: Mary Elise Sarotte, *1989: The Struggle to Create Post–Cold War Europe* (Princeton, N.J.: Princeton University Press, 2014). The narrative in the original edition of Sarotte's study provides an excellent explanation of how each side came out of Baker's Moscow meetings with a different understanding of precisely what had been agreed on, and, consequently, the implications of that agreement. See Sarotte, *1989* (2009 ed.), 110–11. Kramer and Sarotte had a subsequent exchange on the issue, published in *Foreign Affairs*, November–December 2014, 208–9, http://adps.foreignaffairs. com/articles/142189/mark-kramer-mary-elise-sarotte/no-such-promise%E2%80%A9. By 2000, Georgian president Shevardnadze told a visiting former senior US official that Baker had made no promise with respect to NATO at the February 1990 Moscow meeting; communication to the author from a former US official, October 2015. Gorbachev himself, in recent writings and statements, has denied that there was any pledge made in early 1990 not to enlarge NATO to the east, pointing out that at the time agreement was reached on German reunification in early to mid-1990, the Warsaw Pact still existed and there could hardly have been a discussion about moving Warsaw Pact member states into NATO. See "Gorbatschow sieht in Nato-Ostweierung keinen Wortbruch," *Zeit Online*, November 9, 2014, www.zeit.de/politik/ausland/2014-11/nato -ostweiterung-gorbatschow. See also Mikhail Gorbachev, *The New Russia*, trans. Arch Tait (Cambridge: Polity Press, 2016), 308–9. During the time this book was being prepared for publication, increased access to archival records from 1990, especially in the United States, has ignited yet further debate among specialists and historians over whether and what kind of pledge was given to Gorbachev. See in particular Svetlana Savranskaya and Thomas Blanton, eds. *The Last Superpower Summits: Gorbachev, Reagan, and Bush: Conversations That Ended the Cold War* (Budapest: CEU Press, 2016), 565-796, and Joshua R. Itzkowitz Shifrinson, "Deal or No Deal? The End of the Cold War and the U.S. Offer to Limit NATO Expansion" *International Security* vol. 40 no. 4 (Spring 2016) 7-44. These recent archivals releases and discussions in my estimation have added greater detail to the debate over this issue, but have not substantially changed the basic lines of argument nor altered the judgments I offer in the text.

12. Once the Soviets accepted NATO jurisdiction in all of Germany, they focused on equipment and manpower limits in the CFE Treaty negotiations to try to minimize the effect and potential threat of a united Germany in NATO. See Stent, *Russia and Germany Reborn*, 139–41; Zelikow and Rice, *Germany Unified*, 174–85; and Don Oberdorfer, *From the Cold War to a New Era: The United States and the Soviet Union 1983–1990* (New York: Poseidon Press, 1991), passim.

13. Kramer, *Myth*; Matlock, *Autopsy on an Empire*, 382–85.

14. Zelikow and Rice, *Germany Unified*, 183.

15. Eduard Shevardnadze, Moi vybor: *V zashchitu demokratii i svobody* (Moscow: Novosti, 1991), translated as *The Future Belongs to Freedom*, trans. Catherine A. Fitzpatrick (New York: Free Press, 1991), 55; Mikhail Gorbachev, *Zhizn i reformi*, vol. 2 (Moscow: Novosti, 1995); Matlock, *Autopsy on an Empire*, esp. 295ff.

16. The narrative that follows is based especially on Matlock, *Autopsy on an Empire*; Yegor Gaidar, *Collapse of an Empire: Lessons for Modern Russia*, trans. Antonina W.

Bouis (Washington, D.C.: Brookings Institution Press, 2007), orig. pub. as *Gibel' imperii: Uroki dlia sovremennoi Rossii* (Moscow, 2006); Stephen Kotkin, *Armageddon Averted: The Soviet Collapse, 1920–2000* (Oxford: Oxford University Press, 2001); and Michael McFaul, *Russia's Unfinished Revolution: Political Change from Gorbachev to Putin* (Ithaca, N.Y.: Cornell University Press, 2001).

17. McFaul, *Russia's Unfinished Revolution*, 51–52ff.; Matlock, *Autopsy on an Empire*, 331–65.

18. For the role of national independence movements in the collapse of the Soviet Union, see Mark R. Beissinger, *Nationalist Mobilization and the Collapse of the Soviet State*, Cambridge Studies in Comparative Politics (Cambridge: Cambridge University Press, 2002). On the Baltic independence movements, see Matlock, *Autopsy on an Empire*, esp. 227–55. On Moldova, see Charles King, *The Moldovans* (Stanford, Calif.: Hoover Institution Press, 2000). On the Caucasus, see Thomas de Waal, *The Caucasus: An Introduction* (Oxford: Oxford University Press, 2010). On Ukraine, see Serhii Plokhy, *The Last Empire: The Final Days of the Soviet Union* (New York: Basic Books, 2014).

19. Gaidar, *Collapse of an Empire*.

20. Andrei Amalrik, *Will the Soviet Union Survive Until Nineteen Eight-Four?* (Gloucester, Mass.: Peter Smith Publishing, 1970).

21. Kotkin, *Armageddon Averted*.

22. See especially Matlock, *Autopsy on an Empire*, esp. 367ff.; and McFaul, *Russia's Unfinished Revolution*, 86–89. Also see the best biography of Yeltsin in English: Timothy J. Colton, *Yeltsin: A Life* (New York: Basic Books, 2008).

23. In my view Matlock, *Autopsy on an Empire*, esp. 421–97, provides a particularly detailed, balanced, insightful narrative and interpretation of Gorbachev's wavering and travails during this period. For other good overviews, see McFaul, *Russia's Unfinished Revolution*; and Plokhy, *Last Empire*. For the most prominent of the many firsthand accounts of this period from key Soviet participants see Shevardnadze, *Moi Vybor*; and Gorbachev, *Zhizn i reformy*.

24. See Matlock, *Autopsy on an Empire*, 578–604; and Plokhy, *Last Empire*, 73–130. Gorbachev offered a relatively quick account of the coup: Mikhail S. Gorbachev, *Avgustovskii putsch: Prichini i sledstviia* (Moscow: Novosti, 1991).

25. For example, in his January 1992 trip taking him to many of the capitals of the former Soviet states, Secretary Baker presented support for START, the CFE Treaty, and other arms control agreements as a key element in securing formal diplomatic relations with the United States and American support; senior State Department officials to the author.

26. For START, see the US Department of State, "Protocol to the Treaty Between the United States of America and the Union of Soviet Socialist Republics on the Reduction and Limitation of Strategic Offensive Arms," Lisbon Protocol, May 23, 1992, www.state.gov/documents/organization/27389.pdf. For the CFE, see "The Tashkent Agreement, Agreement on the Principles and Procedures for the Implementation of the Treaty on Conventional Armed Forces in Europe," Tashkent, May 15, 1992, http://fas.org/nuke/control/cfe/text/tashka.htm. See also Falkenrath, *Shaping Europe's Military Order*, 202–19.

27. See Thomas Parland, *The Rejection in Russia of Totalitarian Socialism and Liberal Democracy: A Study of the Russian New Right* (Helsinki: Finnish Society of Sciences and Letters, 1993). See also Fiona Hill and Clifford Gaddy, *Mr. Putin: Operative in the Kremlin*, 2nd ed. (Washington, D.C.: Brookings Institution Press, 2014), esp. chap. 3.

28. On the conflicts that arose on the Soviet periphery, see Thomas de Waal, *Black Garden: Armenia and Azerbaijan Through Peace and War* (New York: New York University Press, 2004), for Nagorno-Karabakh; Stuart Kaufman, *Modern Hatreds: The Symbolic Politics of Ethnic War* (Ithaca, N.Y.: Cornell University Press, 2001), for Abkhazia, South Ossetia, Nagorno-Karabakh, and Moldova; Charles King, *The Moldovans* (Stanford, Calif.: Hoover Institution Press, 2000), and William H. Hill, *Russia, the Near Abroad, and the West: Lessons from the Moldova-Transdniestria Conflict* (Washington, D.C. and Baltimore, Md.: Woodrow Wilson Center Press and Johns Hopkins University Press, 2012), for Moldova-Transdniestria.

29. Elizabeth Pond, *The Rebirth of Europe* (Washington, D.C.: Brookings Institution Press, 2000), 45–50ff.; see also Desmond Dinan, *Ever Closer Union: An Introduction to European Integration*, 3rd ed. (Boulder, Colo.: Lynne Rienner, 2005), 118–28.

30. Stanley R. Sloan, *NATO, the European Union, and the Atlantic Community: The Transatlantic Bargain Challenged*, 2nd ed. (New York: Rowman & Littlefield, 2005), 22–37.

31. Dinan, *Ever Closer Union*, 584–87.

32. This narrative is drawn especially from Dinan, *Ever Closer Union*; and Pond, *Rebirth of Europe*. A historical narrative and the documents cited are available on the EU's website, www.europa,eu.

33. European Union, "Transatlantic Declaration on EC-US Relations, 1990," http://eeas.europa.eu/us/docs/trans_declaration_90_en.pdf.

34. For the following discussion, see especially Hutchings, *American Diplomacy*, 272ff.; also see Dinan, *Ever Closer Union*, 615–18; and Bush and Scowcroft, *World Transformed*, 296–300.

35. Bush and Scowcroft, *World Transformed*, 267–68.

36. See, e.g., Hutchings, *American Diplomacy*, 275.

37. Ibid., 276–77.

38. Pond, *Rebirth of Europe*, presents a particularly good account of the development of the European Community into the European Union; it also contains an illuminating discussion on the evolution of European thinking about NATO after 1989. Hutchings, *American Diplomacy*; Baker, *Politics of Diplomacy*; Bush and Scowcroft, *World Transformed* all address in some detail the transformation of Europe in the years immediately following the fall of the Berlin Wall.

39. Baker, *Politics of Diplomacy*, 250–59, and especially Hutchings, *American Diplomacy*, 278–300, discuss the debate over NATO and the CSCE and the German attitude. For the White House view on the CSCE and where it fit in European security, see especially Bush and Scowcroft, *World Transformed*, 266–69.

40. Hutchings, *American Diplomacy*, 274–78; Bush and Scowcroft, *World Transformed*, 265–68; Baker, *Politics of Diplomacy*, 258–59.

41. For example, see various quotations from Gorbachev in Savranskaya et al., *Masterpieces of History*. For samples of more contemporary Russian attitudes toward NATO, see a collection of articles from CSCE participants and experts from various countries in Samuel F. Wells, ed., *The Helsinki Process and the Future of Europe* (Washington, D.C.: Woodrow Wilson Center Press, 1991).

42. OSCE, "Concluding Document of the Vienna Meeting 1986 of Representatives of the Participating States of the Conference on Security and Co-operation in Europe, Held on the Basis of the Provisions of the Final Act Relating to the Follow-Up to the Conference, Vienna 1989," www.osce.org/mc/40881?download=true. See also Korey, *Promises We Keep*, esp. 233–76; Vojtech Mastny, *The Helsinki Process and the Reintegration of Europe: Analysis and Documentation* (New York: New York University Press, 1992); P. Terrence Hopmann, *Building Security in Post–Cold War Eurasia: The OSCE and US Foreign Policy*, Peaceworks 31 (Washington, D.C.: US Institute of Peace Pres, 1999); and Ghebali, *L'OSCE dans l'Europe*.

43. The Paris Human Dimension Meeting ended without adopting a concluding document, a clear sign of deep disagreements among the participating states. For a description of the discussion and tenor of the meeting, see the transcript of a US CSCE Commission Hearing, July 18, 1989, available at www.csce.gov; also, the author's interviews with US participants Rudolf Perina, Paula Dobriansky, and Michael Halzel.

44. See the transcript of the Malta summit in Savranskaya et al., *Masterpieces of History*, 619–46. Also, the author's interviews with Max Kampelman and John Evans. Also see the interview with John Evans, on the Association for Diplomatic Studies and Training Foreign Affairs History Project website, 118–20, www.adst.org/OH%20TOCs /Evans,%20John%20M.toc.pdf.

45. See OSCE, "Document of the Copenhagen Meeting of the Conference on the Human Dimension of the CSCE, 29 June 1990" and "Charter of Paris for a New Europe, 19 November 1990," both available at www.osce.org.

46. OSCE, "Charter of Paris," 13.

47. Ibid.

48. For this and the following, see OSCE, "Document of the Copenhagen Meeting."

49. Hutchings, *American Diplomacy*, 284–85.

50. Scowcroft and Bush, *World Transformed*, 265–68; Michael R. Beschloss and Strobe Talbott, *At the Highest Levels: The Inside Story of the End of the Cold War* (Boston, Mass.: Little, Brown, 1993), 191.

51. Hutchings, *American Diplomacy*, 284–85.

52. OSCE, "Charter of Paris," 21–22; Korey, *Promises We Keep*, 419ff.; the author's interviews with John Evans and Robert Frowick.

53. Considerable portions of this narrative are based on my experience and observations as the US Department of State's coordinator for CSCE affairs, a position I held in 1991 and 1992; also the author's interviews with John Evans, Robert Frowick, and John Maresca.

54. See James A. Baker III, "The Euro-Atlantic Architecture: From West to East," Aspen Institute speech, Berlin, June 18, 1991.

55. This narrative is based on extensive interviews and discussions with CSCE participants and US officials: John Evans, Max Kampelman, Robert Zoellick, and John Maresca. See also Hutchings, *American Diplomacy*, 300ff.; and Baker, *Politics of Diplomacy*, 526–27.

56. Baker, *Politics of Diplomacy*, 527; Hutchings, *American Diplomacy*, 298.

57. My judgments and conclusions here are informed by numerous conversations with senior US executive and legislative branch officials from 1990 to 1992, in particular, when I was serving as coordinator for CSCE Affairs at the US Department of State.

58. Baker, "The Euro-Atlantic Architecture:"

59. As stated in this chapter, Gorbachev explicitly mentioned the CSCE as an alternative to the bloc-to-bloc structure in Europe at Malta in December 1989, and he returned periodically to the idea in 1990 and 1991.

60. See especially Bush and Scowcroft, *World Transformed*, 190–210, 265–70; also see Hutchings, *American Diplomacy*, 123, 281–82; Baker, *Politics of Diplomacy*, 43–45, 92–96, 258–59; the author's interview with Craig Dunkerley, at the time political counselor at the US Mission to NATO; and the ADST interview with Craig Dunkerley, 42–49, http://adst.org/wp-content/uploads/2012/09/Dunkerley-Craig.pdf.

61. For example, Hutchings, *American Diplomacy*, 153–57, 274–94. See also David S. Yost, *NATO Transformed: The Alliance's New Roles in International Security* (Washington, D.C.: US Institute of Peace Press, 1998), 72–90, for a good discussion of the changes in NATO immediately after the end of the Cold War; for the views of US participants in the process, see especially Bush and Scowcroft, *World Transformed*, 279–90; and Baker, *Politics of Diplomacy*, 250–55.

62. Bush and Scowcroft, *World Transformed*, 41–43.

63. "Bush Statement to NATO, December 4, 1989," in *American Foreign Policy: Current Documents: 1989* (Washington, D.C.: US Department of State, 1990), document 125, p. 297.

64. Baker, "A New Europe and a New Atlanticism," speech at Berlin Press Club, December 12, 1989, in *American Foreign Policy: Current Documents: 1989*, document 126, pp. 299–305.

65. Bush and Scowcroft, *World Transformed*, 264–69; Zelikow and Rice, *Germany Unified*, esp. 149–97.

66. Hutchings, *American Diplomacy*, 155–56.

67. Bush and Scowcroft, *World Transformed*, 262ff.

68. Ibid., 268; Hutchings, *American Diplomacy*, 128–29.

69. NATO, "Final Communiqué of the North Atlantic Council Meeting, Turnberry, UK, June 7–8, 1990," www.nato.int/cps/en/natohq/official_texts_23696.htm?selectedLocale=en.

70. NATO, "Declaration on a Transformed North Atlantic Alliance. Issued by the Heads of State and Government Participating in the Meeting of the North Atlantic Council ('The London Declaration')," July 5–6, 1990, www.nato.int/cps/en/natohq/official_texts_23693.htm?selectedLocale=en.

71. Bush and Scowcroft, *World Transformed*, 292–93.

72. Hutchings, *American Diplomacy*, 136.

73. NATO, "The Alliance's New Strategic Concept. Agreed by the Heads of State and Government Participating in the Meeting of the North Atlantic Council," Rome, November 8, 1991, www.nato.int/cps/en/natolive/official_texts_23847.htm?.

74. For more detail on the NACC, see below in this chapter.

75. Pond, *Rebirth of Europe*, 56–60ff.

76. NATO, "Declaration on Peace and Cooperation Issued by the Heads of State and Government Participating in the Meeting of the North Atlantic Council ('The Rome Declaration')," Rome, November 8, 1991, paragraph 6, www.nato.int/cps/en /natolive/official_texts_23846.htm?mode=pressrelease. On this debate, see Hutchings, *American Diplomacy*, 275–81.

77. NATO, "Declaration on Peace," paragraph 14.

78. A 1991 cartoon depicted two groups of young boys dressed in traditional costumes of NATO and Warsaw Pact countries, with the Western boys telling the Eastern boys, "You can't all be on our side. Somebody has to be the bad guy."

79. See Hutchings, *American Diplomacy*, 290–92, for a particularly insightful and revealing discussion of the NACC.

80. According to Hutchings, President Bush first used this explicit term in a September 11, 1990, address to a joint session of Congress immediately after a meeting in Helsinki with Gorbachev, where they discussed a joint plan of action in response to Saddam Hussein's invasion of Kuwait; Hutchings, *American Diplomacy*, 146–47. However, it appears from discussion throughout Hutchings's narrative that President Bush was intensely aware from the beginning of his term of the fundamental changes taking place in the world. Beginning with his five major policy speeches from April to June 1989, Bush actively wrestled with the strategic questions of how to transform the world from the forty-year Cold War order into something different; Hutchings, *American Diplomacy*, 38–47.

## 3. BUILDING THE NEW INSTITUTIONS

1. See especially Jack F. Matlock Jr., *Autopsy on an Empire: The American Ambassador's Account of the Collapse of the Soviet Union* (New York: Random House 1995), 611–12 and ff.; also see Yegor Gaidar, *Collapse of an Empire: Lessons for Modern Russia*, trans. Antonina W. Bouis (Washington, D.C.: Brookings Institution Press, 2007), orig. pub. as *Gibel' imperii: Uroki dlia sovremennoi Rossii* (Moscow, 2006), 226–49; and Robert L. Hutchings, *American Diplomacy and the End of the Cold War: An Insider's Account of US Policy in Europe, 1989–1992* (Washington, D.C. and Baltimore, Md.: Woodrow Wilson Center Press and Johns Hopkins University Press, 1997), 332–36.

2. Serhii Plokhy, *The Last Empire: The Final Days of the Soviet Union* (New York: Basic Books, 2014), 176–77, 280–81. See also Mark Kramer, *The Transfer of Crimea from Soviet Russia to Soviet Ukraine 1954*, Cold War International History Project e-Dossier 47, www.wilsoncenter.org/publication/why-did-russia-give-away -crimea-sixty-years-ago.

3. The best account in English of the Armenia-Azerbaijan war over Nagorno-Karabakh is by Thomas de Waal, *Black Garden: Armenia and Azerbaijan Through Peace and War* (New York: New York University Press, 2003); an excellent shorter account is by Stuart Kaufman, *Modern Hatreds* (Ithaca, N.Y.: Cornell University Press, 2001), 49–83. See also Christoph Zuercher, *The Post-Soviet Wars: Rebellion, Ethnic Conflict, and Nationhood in the Caucasus* (New York: New York University Press, 2009), 152–85.

4. Conversations of the author with US ambassador John Maresca; in my position at the time as coordinator for CSCE Affairs in the State Department, I followed these events from Washington and was tasked with providing guidance and support.

5. CSCE, "CSCE Advance Team to Nagorno-Karabakh: Final Report," Moscow, May 13, 1992. This report contains a detailed deployment plan for observer teams to monitor a cease-fire and, it was hoped at the time, eventual implementation of a peace treaty. The OSCE website is relatively thin on background for the so-called Minsk Process, but also contains information in the sections on the personal representative of the chairman-in-office for the conflict dealt with by the OSCE Minsk Conference, http://www.osce.org/cio/andrzej-kasprzyk. See also de Waal, *Black Garden*, 229–31. As CSCE coordinator in the Department of State in 1992, I was deeply involved in the formation of the Minsk Conference, and some of this narrative is drawn from my notes and conversations at the time. For a more detailed discussion of the institutional implications of the OSCE's response to the growing war over Nagorno-Karabakh, see below in this chapter.

6. See OSCE Minsk Conference. See also de Waal, *Black Garden*; and Thomas de Waal, *The Caucasus: An Introduction* (New York: Oxford University Press, 2010), 98–130; and Kaufman, *Modern Hatreds*.

7. See Kaufman, *Modern Hatreds*, 85–127; de Waal, *Caucasus*, 131–66; and Zuercher, *Post-Soviet Wars*, 115–51.

8. Kaufman, *Modern Hatreds*; de Waal, *Caucasus*.

9. De Waal, *Caucasus*, 164.

10. On Moldovan and Romanian identities, and the political battles of this period, see Charles King, The *Moldovans: Romania, Russia, and the Politics of Culture* (Stanford, Calif.: Hoover Institution Press, 2000); William H. Hill, *Russia, the Near Abroad, and the West: Lessons from the Moldova-Transdniestria Conflict* (Washington. D.C. and Baltimore, Md.: Woodrow Wilson Center Press and Johns Hopkins University Press, 2012); and Kaufman, *Modern Hatreds*, 129–63.

11. "Transdniestria" has been used as the term for this region by the OSCE since a mission was established in Moldova in 1993. Romanian speakers refer to the region as Transnistria; and its Russian-language name is Pridniestrov'e. I have chosen to follow the OSCE's usage throughout.

12. For the history of the conflict, see Hill, *Russia*; King, *Moldovans*; and Kaufman, *Modern Hatreds*.

13. See Kramer, *Transfer of Crimea*; and Plokhy, *Last Empire*, 176–77.

14. Plokhy, *Last Empire*, 280–81; Matlock, *Autopsy on an Empire*, 633–36, 699–702.

15. For background on the OSCE-brokered Crimea autonomy agreement, see the OSCE website: www.osce.org/ukraine.

16. See Anatol Lieven, *Chechnya: Tombstone of Russian Power* (New Haven, Conn.: Yale University Press, 1999); and Zuercher, *Post-Soviet Wars*, 70–114.

17. This is one of the major arguments of my earlier work on Moldova and the Transdniestrian conflict; see Hill, *Russia*.

18. On the causes and events leading to the breakup of Yugoslavia, see John R. Lampe, *Yugoslavia as History: Twice There Was a Country*, 2nd ed. (Cambridge: Cambridge University Press, 2000); Warren Zimmermann, *Origins of a Catastrophe: Yugoslavia and Its Destroyers—America's Last Ambassador Tells What Happened and Why* (New York: Random House, 1996); and Laura Silber and Allan Little, *Yugoslavia: Death of a Nation* (New York: Penguin USA, 1995).

19. Zimmermann, *Origins of a Catastrophe*, 133–40. Zimmermann attended Baker's meetings and reported on them to Washington and is thus the most authoritative source on the secretary's effort to avert war in June 1991.

20. As deputy head of the United States' CSCE delegation and CSCE coordinator in the Department of State at the time, I attended and at times participated directly in many of the discussions and meetings devoted to these issues; this summary of events is based in part upon my recollections and notes from that time.

21. For a discussion of the events in the former Yugoslavia and the European response, see Zimmermann, *Origins of a Catastrophe*; Silber and Little, *Yugoslavia*; Susan Woodward, *Balkan Tragedy: Chaos and Dissolution After the Cold War* (Washington. D.C.: Brookings Institution Press, 1995); Steven Burg and Paul Shoup, *The War in Bosnia-Herzegovina: Ethnic Conflict and International Intervention* (Armonk, N.Y.: M. E. Sharpe, 1999); and Misha Glenny, *The Fall of Yugoslavia* (New York: Penguin Books, 1996).

22. Zimmermann, *Origins of a Catastrophe*, 172–203.

23. For an insider's account of these events, in addition to the studies of the Yugoslav wars cited above, see David Owen, *Balkan Odyssey* (San Diego, Calif.: Harcourt Brace, 1995).

24. Burg and Shoup, *War in Bosnia-Herzegovina*, 145–46; Owen, *Balkan Odyssey*, 274–88.

25. Burg and Shoup, *War in Bosnia-Herzegovina*, 322ff.; for the events that led to the Dayton Agreement, see also David Halberstam, *War in a Time of Peace: Bush, Clinton, and the Generals* (New York: Scribner, 2001), 308–51; and Richard Holbrooke, *To End a War* (New York: Random House, 1998), esp. 79–198.

26. See the interview with Ambassador Craig Dunkerley on the Association for Diplomatic Studies and Training Foreign Affairs History Project website, www.adst.org /OH%20TOCs/Barry,%20Robert%20L.toc.pdf; and Holbrooke, *To End a War*, 290–91.

27. For the most authoritative account of involving Russia, see William J. Perry and Ashton B. Carter, *Preventive Defense: A New Security Strategy for America* (Washington, D.C.: Brookings Institution Press, 1999), 33–46. Perry's role in persuading Grachev to involve Russia in IFOR was crucial, given the skepticism of the Russian government about the endeavor, according to Perry's note taker in his key conversations with the Russian defense minister; communication to the author, July 2015. See also Holbrooke, *To End a War*, 258–59; James M. Goldgeier and Michael McFaul, *Power and Purpose:*

*US Policy Toward Russia After the Cold War* (Washington, D.C.: Brookings Institution Press, 2003), 199–200; and the author's interview with a senior US CSCE delegation and State Department official, May 2002.

28. NATO, "NATO's Operations: 1949 to the Present," NATO Allied Command Operations, available at www.aco.nato.int.

29. William H. Taft IV, "European Security: Lessons Learned from the Gulf War," *NATO Review* 31, no. 3 (June 1991): 21, www.nato.int/docu/review/1991/9103-2.htm.

30. NATO, "The Alliance's New Strategic Concept (1991)," www.nato.int/cps/natohq /official_texts_23846.7.htm.

31. On the divisions between the NATO Allies, see, for example, Michael Mandelbaum, *The Dawn of Peace in Europe* (Washington, D.C.: Twentieth Century Fund, 1996), 29–33.

32. NATO, "Final Communiqué of the Ministerial Meeting of the North Atlantic Council," Oslo, June 4, 1992, www.nato.int/cps/en/natohq/official_texts_23983.htm.

33. Ibid.

34. NATO, "Ministerial Communique," May 27, 1992, www.nato.int/cps/en/natohq /official_texts_23987.htm.

35. NATO, "Statement on NATO Maritime Operations," July 10, 1992, www.nato .int/cps/en/natohq/official_texts_23908.htm. STANAVFORMED was organized as the successor to the Naval On-Call Force for the Mediterranean on April 30, 1992; see "NATO's On-Call Force for the Mediterranean is Replaced," www.nato.int/cps/en /natohq/news_23937.htm?selectedLocale=en.

36. See the official texts for NATO meetings from late 1991 on for such ongoing statements of concern; available at www.nato.int.

37. Burg and Shoup, *War in Bosnia-Herzegovina*, 91–92ff.

38. US Deputy Secretary of State Lawrence Eagleburger to the author, April 1992; Joyce P. Kaufman, *NATO and the Former Yugoslavia: Crisis, Conflict, and the Atlantic Alliance* (New York: Rowman & Littlefield, 2002), 82–83; Burg and Shoup, *War in Bosnia-Herzegovina*, 92–96.

39. NATO, "Statement on Former Yugoslavia," December 17, 1992, www.nato.int /cps/en/natohq/official_texts_23974.htm.

40. See Kaufman, *NATO and the Former Yugoslavia*, 101; and NATO, "Ministerial Communiqué: Ministerial Meeting of the North Atlantic Council," June 10, 1993, www.nato.int/cps/en/natohq/official_texts_24151.htm. Also, for the announcement that NATO would conduct air strikes against any forces violating UNSCR 836 on the safe zones, see NATO, "Press Statement by the Secretary General Following the Special Meeting of the North Atlantic Council," August 2, 1993, www.nato.int/cps/en/natohq /official_texts_24147.htm.

41. Burg and Shoup, *War in Bosnia-Herzegovina*, 150, 286. In my position from 1992 to 1994 as director for research and analysis for Eastern Europe at the State Department, I had ample opportunity to witness US and Allied frustration at the repeated refusal of the UN to authorize attacks in defense of the six safe areas.

42. Although most observers, analysts, and news reporters presumed that the February 1994 Sarajevo market massacre was the work of Serb forces, responsibility for the attack has never been conclusively proved. I know from my own experience as chief of

research and analysis for Eastern Europe at the Department of State at the time that the ambiguities in the physical and circumstantial evidence prevented identification of the attackers. See also Burg and Shoup, *War in Bosnia-Herzegovina,* 145–46.

43. NATO, "Decisions Taken at the Meeting of the North Atlantic Council in Permanent Session 1," February 9, 1994, www.nato.int/cps/en/natohq/official_texts_24465 .htm.

44. Kaufman, *NATO and the Former Yugoslavia,* 109.

45. Burg and Shoup, *War in Bosnia-Herzegovina,* 337, 360; Silber and Little, *Yugoslavia,* 346, 352.

46. Holbrooke, *To End a War,* 57–59.

47. The narrative in this paragraph draws from, among others, Kaufman, *NATO and the Former Yugoslavia*; Geoffrey Lee Williams and Berkley Jared Jones, *NATO and the Transatlantic Alliance in the 21st Century: The Twenty Year Crisis* (New York: Palgrave Macmillan, 2001); Burg and Shoup, *War in Bosnia-Herzegovina*; and Halberstam, *War in a Time of Peace.*

48. Kaufman, *NATO and the Former Yugoslavia,* 112ff.

49. For these events, and Dayton, see Kaufman, *NATO and the Former Yugoslavia,* 120–21; Holbrooke, *To End a War,* 63–93ff.; Halberstam, *War in a Time of Peace,* 293–308; and Burg and Shoup, *War in Bosnia-Herzegovina,* 319–49.

50. See NATO, "Statement on Bosnia-Herzegovina," December 5, 1995, www.nato. int/cps/en/natohq/official_texts_24719.htm; and NATO, "Final Communiqué: Ministerial Meeting of the North Atlantic Council Held at NATO Headquarters, Brussels," December 5, 1995, www.nato.int/cps/en/natohq/official_texts_24718.htm.

51. NATO, "Final Communiqué."

52. See Remi Landry, *The European Community Monitor Mission (ECMM) in Former Yugoslavia: Lessons Learned for OAU Civilian Missions,* ACCORD Occasional Paper 5/99 (Durban: African Centre for the Constructive Resolution of Disputes, 1999).

53. Desmond Dinan, *Ever Closer Union: An Introduction to European Integration,* 3rd ed. (Boulder, Colo.: Lynne Rienner, 2005), 587ff.; Elizabeth Pond, *The Rebirth of Europe* (Washington, D.C.: Brookings Institution Press, 2000), 44–50; Sven Biscop, "The UK and European Defence: Leading or Leaving?" *International Affairs* 88, no. 6 (2012): 1297–1313, at 1299.

54. The text of the Maastricht Treaty is available on the EU website: www.europa .eu; see also Dinan, *Ever Closer Union,* 587.

55. NATO, "NATO Rome Summit Statement, November 1991"; Dinan, *Ever Closer Union,* 587ff.; see also European External Action Service, "About CSDO: The Western European Union," available at www.eeas.europa.eu.

56. Dinan, *Ever Closer Union,* 124–25; Pond, *Rebirth of Europe,* 47.

57. Pond, *Rebirth of Europe,* 50–55.

58. European External Action Service, "About CSDO."

59. David S. Yost, *NATO Transformed: The Alliance's New Roles in International Security* (Washington, D.C.: US Institute of Peace Press, 1998), 199ff.; Pond, *Rebirth of Europe,* 8off.; Charles Barry, "Combined Joint Task Forces in Theory and Practice," in *NATO's Transformation: The Changing Shape of the Atlantic Alliance,* ed. Philip H. Gordon (New York: Rowman & Littlefield, 2001), 203–19.

60. Holbrooke, *To End a War*, 318–25.

61. OSCE, "Charter of Paris for a New Europe," November 19, 1990, available at www.osce.org; see also the VDOC 90 mechanism for inquiring about unusual military activities, often referred to as the UMA mechanism.

62. See CSCE, "Vienna Document 1990 of the Negotiations on Confidence and Security-Building Measures Convened in Accordance with the Relevant Provisions of the Concluding Document of the Vienna Meeting of the Conference on Security and Cooperation in Europe," November 17, 1990, http://www.osce.org/fsc /41245?download=true; CSCE, "Document of the Copenhagen Meeting of the Conference on the Human Dimension of the CSCE," June 29, 1990, available at www.osce .org; William Korey, *The Promises We Keep: Human Rights, the Helsinki Process, and American Foreign Policy* (New York: St. Martin's Press, 1993), 407–12; and Victor-Yves Ghebali, *L'OSCE dans l'Europe post-communiste: Vers une identite paneuropeenne de securite* (Brussels: Émile Bruylant, 1996), 230, 454–57.

63. I can attest to this from my own experience as the United States CSCE coordinator in 1991–92.

64. CSCE, "Berlin Meeting of the CSCE Council, 19–20 June 1991, Summary of Conclusions," Annex 2: Mechanism for Consultation and Co-operation with Regard to Emergency Situations, www.osce.org/mc/40234?download=true.

65. CSCE, "Document of the Moscow Meeting of the Conference on the Human Dimension of the CSCE," Moscow, 1991, part I, paragraphs 1–16.

66. I have already cited my own experience as part of the US CSCE delegation in Geneva at this time; see also the CSCE journals for the VDOC negotiations; and Gajus Scheltema, "OSCE Peacekeeping Operations," in *The Challenges of Change: The Helsinki Summit of the CSCE and Its Aftermath*, ed. Arie Bloed (Boston, Mass.: Martinus Nijhoff, 1994), 23–45.

67. CSCE, "CSCE Prague MC Document," paragraph 6, www.osce.org/mc/40270? download=true.

68. See Zimmermann, *Origins of a Catastrophe*.

69. De Waal, *Black Garden*, 159–83.

70. Kaufman, *Modern Hatreds*, 112–14.

71. CSCE, "CSCE Prague MC Document," section VI, paragraph 22.

72. Ibid., section IV, paragraph 16.

73. See chapter 2; and OSCE, "Participating States," www.osce.org/participating -states.

74. CSCE, "CSCE Prague MC Document," annex.

75. For example, see James Goldgeier, *Not Whether but When: The U.S. Decision to Enlarge NATO* (Washington, D.C.: Brookings Institution, 1999), 17–19; Hutchings, *American Diplomacy*, 283–87; and J. L. Black, *Russia Faces NATO Expansion: Bearing Gifts or Bearing Arms?* (New York: Rowman & Littlefield, 2000), 6–10. I have heard claims more or less to this effect from a variety of senior Russian diplomats and government officials, including two deputy foreign ministers (interviewed in July 1999 and March 2007) and former prime minister Yevgeniy Primakov (August 2000).

76. CSCE, "CSCE Prague MC Document," section I, paragraph 3.

77. Some of this narrative is based on my personal experience and involvement in the process; see also de Waal, *Black Garden*; John J. Maresca, "The International Community and the Conflict over Nagorno-Karabakh, in *Opportunities Missed, Opportunities Seized: Preventive Diplomacy in the Post–Cold War World*, ed. Bruce Jentleson, Report of the Carnegie Commission on Preventing Deadly Conflict (New York: Rowman & Littlefield, 2000).

78. CSCE, "CSCE Advance Team."

79. Author's personal experience as CSCE coordinator; also de Waal, *Black Garden*, 225–68; Maresca, "International Community."

80. The formal title of the mission was "The OSCE Missions of Long Duration to Kosovo, Sandjak, and Vojvodina," with each locality considered a separate destination. In fact, though, the deployment was authorized in a single decision and in the end was one mission, with several parts. See CSCE journals for the summer of 1992, available at www.osce.org; also drawn from the author's experience as CSCE coordinator; and see Ghebali, *L'OSCE dans l'Europe*, 391–401.

81. *CSCE Journal*, August 14, 1992, available at www.osce.org.

82. Because of Greek objections that the name might indicate a possible claim on territory in northern Greece, most international documents, including those of the OSCE and EU, to this day refer to the country as the former Yugoslav Republic of Macedonia, or FYROM. For the sake of convenience and literary style, I use the two interchangeably.

83. *CSCE Journal*, August 14, 1992; OSCE, *Survey of OSCE Field Operations* (Vienna: OSCE, 2013), www.osce.org/cpc/74783?download=true.

84. OSCE, *Survey of OSCE Field Operations*.

85. Ibid.; OSCE journals, 1992–93; CSCE, "Adam Rotfeld Preliminary Reports," CSCE Communication No. 281, September 16, 1992, No. 281/Add. 1, November 5, 1992, No. 281/Add. 2, December 11, 1992, No. 281/Add. 3, February 2, 1993. Conversation of the author with Minister Adam Rotfeld, November 2005. See also "Journal No. 2 of the Fifteenth Meeting of the Committee of Senior Officials," Prague, August 14, 1992, agenda item 5, www.osce.org/documents/osce/1992/08/15846_en.pdf. On establishing the mission, see www.osce.org/moldova.

86. OSCE, *Survey of OSCE Field Operations*; the war between Georgia and Abkhazia was still getting under way and continued for some time. Thus the OSCE Mission to Georgia initially concentrated on negotiations with South Ossetia. The cease-fire with Abkhazia did not come until 1994, and a UN mandate was adopted for monitoring the Russian Federation peacekeeping operation there; see de Waal, *Caucasus*, 139–64; and Kaufman, *Modern Hatreds*, 110–23.

87. "Mandate of the OSCE Mission to Estonia," *OSCE Journal*, December 13, 1992; OSCE, *Survey of OSCE Field Operations*.

88. OSCE, *Survey of OSCE Field Operations*, 63.

89. Ibid., 59.

90. See NATO, "Report of the Copenhagen Round Table on United Nations Sanctions in the Case of the Former Yugoslavia," Copenhagen, June 24–25, 1996, www.nato.int/ifor/un/u960924a.htm.

91. Ibid.; also see CSCE, *CSCE Annual Report 1993* (Vienna: CSCE, 1993), available at www.osce.org.

92. CSCE, "CSCE Prague MC Document," section IV, paragraph 7.

93. CSCE, "CSCE Helsinki Document 1992: The Challenges of Change," www .osce.org/mc/39530?download=true.

94. OSCE, "Stockholm Ministerial Council Document, Section I: Regional Issues," paragraphs 1–199ff., www.osce.org/mc/40342?download=true.

95. CSCE, "CSCE Helsinki Document 1992," section IV, paragraph 2.

96. Ibid.; Heather Hurlbut, "CSCE's Forum for Security Cooperation: Creating an Arms Control Negotiation for Post-Arms Control Europe," in *Challenges of Change*, ed. Bloed, 47–66.

97. CSCE, "CSCE Helsinki Document 1992," section III.

98. Ibid., section III, paragraphs 17–56.

99. Ibid., section II.

100. Walter Kemp, *Quiet Diplomacy in Action: The OSCE High Commissioner on National Minorities* (Vienna: Organization for Security and Cooperation in Europe, 2001), http://www.osce.org/hcnm/78633; the author's experience as CSCE coordinator.

101. CSCE, "CSCE Helsinki Document 1992," section II, paragraph 2.

102. OSCE, "Stockholm Ministerial Council Document," paragraph 3, p. 12.

103. CSCE, "CSCE Helsinki Document 1992," section VII, in particular paragraphs 21–32.

104. Author's CSCE experience; see also Hutchings, *American Diplomacy*, 283–87; and Korey, *Promises We Keep*, passim.

105. Gerard J. Tanja, "Peaceful Settlement of Disputes within the Framework of the CSCE: A Legal Novelty in a Political-Diplomatic Environment," in*Challenges of Change*, ed. Bloed, 67–94; OSCE, "Valetta Document," available at www.osce.org; Hutchings, *American Diplomacy*, 296–97.

106. Tanja, "Peaceful Settlement"; CSCE, "CSCE Helsinki Document 1992," section III, paragraphs 57–62.

107. OSCE, "Stockholm Ministerial Council Document," "Decision on Peaceful Settlement of Disputes"; the author's experience as CSCE coordinator.

108. Hutchings, *American Diplomacy*, 312–18; the author's experience as CSCE coordinator.

109. Members of the US delegation to the CSCE Helsinki Summit to the author, various times during the late spring and early summer of 1992. The rumor was widespread among CSCE delegations in Helsinki.

110. Members of the US CSCE delegation to the author, December 1992; a senior former Russian official to the author, December 2016.

111. OSCE, "Stockholm Ministerial Council Document," 19–20.

112. Both the Helsinki Summit Document (subtitled "The Challenges of Change") and the Stockholm Ministerial Council Document contain provisions specifying the scope of authority and duties of the CSCE secretary-general.

113. See "Secretaries General," available at www.osce.org.

114. CSCE, "Rome Document," section VII, paragraphs 1–9, available at http://www.osce.org/mc/40401?download=true.

115. Ibid., paragraph 7.1.

116. CSCE, "Budapest Summit Document," section I, paragraph 17, available at http://www.osce.org/mc/39554?download=true.

117. Ibid., section I, paragraph 1.

118. Ibid., section I.

119. CSCE, "Budapest Summit Document," section I, paragraphs 4–13.

120. On the conflicting and competing views for the role of the OSCE and the nature of the European security architecture, see especially Elisa Niemtzov, "The OSCE's Security Model: Conceptual Confusion and Competing Visions," *Helsinki Monitor* 7, no. 3 (1996): 41–51; Michael Mihalka, "Building Consensus: The Security Model in Light of Previous Security Arrangements in Europe," *Helsinki Monitor* 7, no. 3 (1996): 20–29; and Marjanne de Kwaasteniet, "The Security Model Discussion and Its Importance for the Evolution of the European Security Architecture," *Helsinki Monitor* 7, no. 3 (1996): 30–40.

121. For a good survey of the range of views on the proper role of the OSCE and its relationship with other European security institutions, see Edward A. Killham, *NATO and OSCE: Partners of Rivals?* NATO Research Fellowship Final Report (Brussels: NATO, 1999), 40–41; and John Borawski, "The Budapest Summit Meeting," *Helsinki Monitor*, no. 1 (1995): 5–8.

122. My instructions as CSCE coordinator were generally to resist the development of a significant, UN-like bureaucracy in the CSCE. Subsequent US policy on the issue seems to have changed little over the following two decades.

## 4. NATO AND THE EU MOVE EAST

1. Yegor Gaidar, *Collapse of an Empire: Lessons for Modern Russia*, trans. Antonina W. Bouis (Washington, D.C.: Brookings Institution Press, 2007), orig. pub. as *Gibel' imperii: Uroki dlia sovremennoi Rossii* (Moscow, 2006), 250–52; see also the interviews with Chubais and Yeltsin in *Conversations on Russia: Reform from Yeltsin to Putin*, ed. Padma Desai (New York: Oxford University Press, 2006); and Strobe Talbott, *The Russia Hand: A Memoir of Presidential Diplomacy* (New York: Random House, 2002), esp. 106–7, where Talbott discusses his remark that in Russia there needed to be "less shock and more therapy."

2. For lengthy descriptions of bilateral contacts and work with Kozyrev, Gaidar, Chernomyrdin, and Primakov, see Talbott, *Russia Hand*; Bill Clinton, *My Life* (New York: Alfred A. Knopf, 2004); and Warren Christopher, *Chances of a Lifetime: A Memoir* (New York: Simon & Schuster, 2001).

3. For lengthy discussions of right-wing parties and movements in post-Soviet Russia, see Fiona Hill and Clifford Gaddy, *Mr. Putin: Operative in the Kremlin*, 2nd ed. (Washington, D.C.: Brookings Institution Press, 2015), esp. chap. 3; Thomas Parland, *The Rejection in Russia of Totalitarian Socialism and Liberal Democracy: A Study of*

*the Russian New Right* (Helsinki, Finland: Finnish Society of Sciences and Letters, 1993); and Michael McFaul, *Russia's Unfinished Revolution: Political Change from Gorbachev to Putin* (Ithaca, N.Y.: Cornell University Press, 2001). Talbott, *Russia Hand*, 110ff., describes the consternation in the West about the results of the December 1993 parliamentary elections, especially the large vote for Zhirinovskii.

4. Andrei Kozyrev, speech at the Stockholm CSCE Ministerial Council meeting, December 1992. Kozyrev referred to this speech as "shock diplomacy," as he attempted to prevent his Western interlocutors from being lulled into inaction by the presumption that democracy and reform had prevailed in Russia. Senior former Russian official to the author, December 2016.

5. For good accounts of the September–October 1993 confrontation in Moscow, see McFaul, *Russia's Unfinished Revolution*; and Timothy J. Colton, *Yeltsin: A Life* (New York: Basic Books, 2008). Also see the CNN archives for footage of the live coverage.

6. McFaul, *Russia's Unfinished Revolution*, 207–27; Colton, *Yeltsin*, 321–44.

7. "CFE Flank Agreement, Annex in Final Document of First Review Conference on the Treaty on Conventional Armed Forces in Europe," Vienna, May 1996 available at http://www.osce.org/library/14099?download=true; Talbott, *Russia Hand*, esp. 233–34, 266–68.

8. See the archived materials on the Gore-Chernomyrdin Commission, available on the US Department of State website, www.state.gov.

9. For international evaluation of the 1996 Russian Presidential elections, see "OSCE International Observer Mission: Election of the President of the Russian Federation: 16th June 1996 and 3rd July 1996: Presidential Election, June 16 and July 3, 1996: Report on the Election," http://www.osce.org/odihr/elections/russia/16288?download=true; see also the statements of the OSCE Election Observation Mission after the first round of voting, http://www.osce.org/odihr/elections/russia/16281?download=true; and second round of voting, http://www.osce.org/odihr/elections/russia/16282. The election was seen by many Russians as unduly influenced by a small group of oligarchs and foreign governments and consultants acting in support of Yeltsin, a view that I heard repeatedly in conversations with Russian officials in the late 1990s and 2000s. For contemporary coverage tending to lend support to such views, see, for example, a *Time* cover story in July 1996, in which four American consultants were featured as allegedly helping to "save" Yeltsin's campaign, Michael Kramer, "Rescuing Boris: The Secret Story of How American Advisers Helped Yeltsin Win," *Time*, July 15, 1996. Russian reactions and a rebuttal to the *Time* piece were provided by Alessandra Stanley, "Moscow Journal: The Americans Who Saved Yeltsin (or Did They?)," *New York Times*, July 9, 1996, http://www .nytimes.com/1996/07/09/world/moscow-journal-the-americans-who-saved-yeltsin -or-did-they.html. Years after the fact, the idiosyncratic expatriate news site *The Exile* published interviews with several members of the 1996 OSCE Election Observation Mission that alleged considerable favoritism for the Yeltsin campaign; see Mark Ames and Alexander Zaichik, "Who Killed the OSCE? Ex-OSCE Mission Chief Reveals 'Pressure' to Whitewash '96 Election," *The Exile Online*, 2007, republished December 9, 2011, http://exiledonline.com/how-the-west-helped-invent-russias-election-fraud -osce-whistleblower-exposes-1996-whitewash/. Contemporary Western analysis of the

election concluded that it was not completely free or fair, although the result was more to the liking of the West than the alternative Zyuganov victory; see, for example, Graham T. Allison and Matthew Lantz. "Assessing Russia's Democratic Presidential Election," on the Harvard University Belfer Center website, http://belfercenter.ksg .harvard.edu/publication/2362/assessing_russias_democratic_presidential_election.html.

10. See Kramer, "Rescuing Boris."

11. On the reported insider trading conducted by US advisers to help set up a securities market in Russia, see David McClintick, "How Harvard Lost Russia," *Institutional Investor,* February 26, 2006, http://www.institutionalinvestor.com/Article/1020662/How -Harvard-lost-Russia.html?ArticleId=1020662#/.Vy4m6mzmqZ8. For a more general study and condemnation of alleged corruption and self-serving behavior in assistance programs for Eastern Europe and the former Soviet Union, see Janine R. Wedel, *Collision or Collusion: The Strange Case of Western Aid to Eastern Europe: 1989–1998* (New York: St. Martins Press, 1998).

12. See John M. Shields and William C. Potter, eds., *Dismantling the Cold War: US and NIS Perspectives on the Nunn-Lugar Cooperative Threat Reduction Program* (Cambridge, Mass.: MIT Press, 1997); David Hoffman, *The Dead Hand: The Untold Story of the Cold War Arms Race and Its Dangerous Legacy* (New York: Doubleday, 2010); and esp. William J. Perry and Ashton B. Carter, *Preventive Defense: A New Security Strategy for America* (Washington, D.C.: Brookings Institution Press, 1999), pp. 71ff.

13. For the text of the Budapest Memorandum, see "Budapest Memorandums on Security Assurances, 1994" published December 5, 1994, http://www.cfr.org/nonproliferation -arms-control-and-disarmament/budapest-memorandums-security-assurances-1994 /p32484; Ambassador Steven Pifer (who helped negotiate the Memorandum) to the author, March 2014.

14. For the basics on the provisions and history of START II, see "Treaty Between the United States of America and the Union of Soviet Socialist Republics on Strategic Offensive Reductions (1993)," Nuclear Threat Initiative, http://www.nti.org/learn /treaties-and-regimes/treaty-between-united-states-america-and-union-soviet-socialist-republics-strategic-offensive-reductions-start-ii/. For further information on the provisions, negotiating history, ratification, and implementation, see "Strategic Arms Reduction Treaty (START II)," Federation of American Scientists, http://fas.org/nuke /control/start2/.

15. Talbott, *Russia Hand,* passim; in the mid-1990s, I worked on nonproliferation, arms transfers, and other international security issues, including US cooperation with Russia on these issues, for the undersecretary of state for international security affairs. In the course of this work, I gained a good understanding of US positions and priorities during that period.

16. There was extensive support for Milošević and his colleagues among Saint Petersburg and Moscow political and security elites during the mid-1990s; Russian diplomats and Transdniestrian separatist officials to the author, April 2001.

17. See my description of the various conflicts on the post-Soviet periphery in chapter 3. In addition to the works by King, Kaufman, de Waal, and Hill cited in the notes to chapter 3, also see an excellent collection of essays by Russian and Western experts

on these conflicts: Alexei Arbatov, Abram Chayes, Antonia Handler Chayes, and Lara Olson, eds., *Managing Conflict in the Former Soviet Union: Russian and American Perspectives* (Cambridge, Mass.: MIT Press, 1997). The great virtue of this collection is that the essays generally capture the complexity of the conflicts they describe rather than the more one-dimensional, polemical accounts that have more recently come to dominate works published in the West on many aspects of these disputes.

18. Angela E. Stent, *The Limits of Partnership: US–Russian Relations in the Twenty-First Century* (Princeton, NJ: Princeton University Press, 2014), 17–34; James Goldgeier and Michael McFaul, *Power and Purpose: US Policy toward Russia after the Cold War* (Washington: Brookings Institution Press, 2003), esp. 41–58; Talbott, *Russia Hand*, esp. 37–90.

19. For colorful descriptions and excellent insights into life in Russia during the 1990s, see David E. Hoffman, *The Oligarchs: Wealth and Power in the New Russia* (New York: PublicAffairs, 2001); Christia Freeland, *Sale of the Century: Russia's Wild Ride from Communism to Capitalism* (New York: Crown Business, 2000); Alfred Kokh, *The Selling of the Soviet Empire: Politics & Economics of Russia's Privatization—Revelations of the Principal Insider* (New York: SPI Books, 1998); and Paul Klebnikov, *Godfather of the Kremlin: The Decline of Russia in the Age of Gangster Capitalism* (New York: Harvest Books, 2001). See also Colton, *Yeltsin*.

20. On Chechnya, see Anatol Lieven, *Chechnya: Tombstone of Russian Power* (New Haven, Conn.: Yale University Press, 1999); Christoph Zuercher, *The Post-Soviet Wars: Rebellion, Ethnic Conflict, and Nationhood in the Caucasus* (New York: New York University Press, 2009), 70–114; and Sergei Markedonov, *Turbulentnaia Evraziia: Mezhetnicheskie, Grazhdanskie Konflikty, Ksenofobiia v Novykh Nezavisimykh Gosudarstvakh Postsovetskogo Prostranstva* (Moscow, 2010).

21. See Arkady Babchenko, *Alkhan Yurt*, published in English as *One Soldier's War* (New York: Grove Press, 2009).

22. See Lieven, *Chechnya*; and Zuercher, *Post-Soviet Wars*, on the Khasavvurt agreement; see also Arie Bloed, "OSCE and Conflict in Chechnya," *Helsinki Monitor* 7, no. 3 (1996): 82–87. General Lebed visited Washington in the early autumn of 1996, while still serving as Yeltsin's national security adviser, and his views and account of how the cease-fire in Chechnya was achieved were widely reported at the time.

23. Goldgeier and McFaul, *Power and Purpose*, 138–44, esp. 141.

24. Treaty on Conventional Armed Forces in Europe, available at www.osce.org.

25. "CFE Flank Agreement"; while working for the undersecretary of state for international security affairs in 1996–97, I was assigned responsibility for helping to attain ratification of this agreement by the US Senate and other states-parties.

26. Goldgeier and McFaul, *Power and Purpose*, 208. CFE was considered an arcane arms control issue by most Western journalists at the time, but the Russians considered adaptation of the original treaty an important part of the package enabling them to accept NATO enlargement. See especially the interview with Ambassador Craig Dunkerley, who managed the CFE adaptation negotiations for the United States out of the State Department in Washington, on the Association for Diplomatic Studies and Training Foreign Affairs History Project website, http://adst.org/wp-content

/uploads/2012/09/Dunkerley-Craig.pdf. During my assignment to the undersecretary of state for international security affairs, I participated in fashioning the first draft of the adapted treaty.

27. For background and discussion of the conflicts and issues mentioned in this paragraph, in addition to the works already cited on the conflicts of the post-Soviet periphery, see Fiona Hill and Pamela Jewett, *Back in the USSR: Russia's Intervention in the Internal Affairs of the Former Soviet Republics and the Implications for United States Policy toward Russia* (Cambridge, Mass.: Harvard University Kennedy School, Strengthening Democratic Institutions Project, 1994); and William Odom and Robert Dujarric, *Commonwealth or Empire? Russia, Central Asia, and the Caucasus* (Washington, D.C.: Hudson Institute, 1995).

28. See chapter 2.

29. Most of the leading treatments of NATO enlargement agree on this; see James M. Goldgeier, *Not Whether but When: The US Decision to Enlarge NATO* (Washington, D.C.: Brookings Institution Press, 1999); Goldgeier and McFaul, *Power and Purpose*, esp. 183–210; Angela E. Stent, *Russia and Germany Reborn: Unification, the Soviet Collapse, and the New Europe* (Princeton, N.J.: Princeton University Press, 2000); Ronald D. Asmus, *Opening NATO's Door: How the Alliance Remade Itself for a New Era* (New York: Columbia University Press, 2002); and Elizabeth Pond, *The Rebirth of Europe* (Washington, D.C.: Brookings Institution Press, 2000), 65–71.

30. Goldgeier, *Not Whether but When*, 18.

31. Asmus, *Opening NATO's Door*, 17.

32. Robert L. Hutchings, *American Diplomacy and the End of the Cold War: An Insider's Account of US Policy in Europe, 1989–1992* (Washington, D.C. and Baltimore, Md.: Woodrow Wilson Center Press and Johns Hopkins University Press, 1997), 291–92.

33. Goldgeier, *Not Whether but When*, 9, 20–22, 24.

34. Ibid., 30ff.; Asmus, *Opening NATO's Door*, 21–24.

35. Goldgeier, *Not Whether but When*, 33–34; Asmus, *Opening NATO's Door*, xxix–xxx.

36. Ronald D. Asmus, Richard L. Kugler, and F. Stephen Larrabee, "Building a New NATO," *Foreign Affairs* 72, no. 4 (July–August 1993): 28–40.

37. Ibid., 28.

38. Ibid., 29.

39. Ibid, 36–37.

40. Talbott, *Russia Hand*, 37–40. Talbott makes the argument throughout the book that Clinton was in essence his own Russia desk officer throughout his administration; such was the importance he placed on Washington's relations with its former chief adversary.

41. Goldgeier, *Not Whether but When*, 25–28.

42. Ibid.

43. Ibid., 36.

44. Perry and Carter, *Preventive Defense*, 23–25, Goldgeier, *Not Whether but When*, 27–29.

45. Goldgeier, *Not Whether but When*, 24ff.

46. Ibid., 182n60.

47. Ibid., 32–34; Pond, *Rebirth of Europe*, 65ff; Asmus, *Opening NATO's Door*, 24, asserts that Havel's and Walesa's pleadings had a strong effect on Clinton.

48. Pond, *Rebirth of Europe*, 67; Talbott, *Russia Hand*, 95–96.

49. Talbott, *Russia Hand*, 96–100.

50. Goldgeier, *Not Whether but When*, 39–40; Talbott, *Russia Hand*, 101–2.

51. Talbott, *Russia Hand*, 111; Clinton, *My Life*, 513.

52. David S. Yost, *NATO Transformed: The Alliance's New Roles in International Security* (Washington, D.C.: US Institute of Peace Press, 1998), 97–98; NATO, "Partnership for Peace: Framework Document"; NATO, "Partnership for Peace: Invitation Document"; NATO, "Declaration of the Heads of State and Government Participating in the Meeting of the North Atlantic Council ('The Brussels Summit Declaration')," January 11, 1994, available at www.nato.int/cps/en/natohq/official_texts.

53. NATO, "Partnership for Peace: Invitation Document."

54. Ibid.

55. See, for example, Yost, *NATO Transformed*, 97–100.

56. On the military-to-military relationship with Russia at this time, see, Perry and Carter, *Preventive Defense*, 23–28.

57. Talbott, *Russia Hand*, 101.

58. See James Goldgeier's recent commentary on the Yeltsin-Christopher October 1993 meeting, "Promises Made, Promises Broken? What Yeltsin Was Told About NATO in 1993 and Why It Matters" War on the Rocks, July 12, 2016, http://warontherocks .com/2016/07/promises-made-promises-broken-what-yeltsin-was-told-about-nato-in -1993-and-why-it-matters/; the Memorandum of Conversation, recently declassified, was contained in the Department of State cable SECTO 17027, 250704Z OCT 93, http://cdn.warontherocks.com/wp-content/uploads/2016/07/Christopher-Yeltsin-1993 -MemCon.pdf.

59. Talbott, *Russia Hand*, 100–102. It is not clear to what extent Russian inter-locutors bought the US sales pitch for PfP. One former US official who served in both the State and Defense departments commented: "PfP was presented to Yeltsin and Kozyrev as the alternative to NATO expansion, and to the Poles and others as their means of expedited membership—and on the same day! Moscow knew we were lying before we had reported the demarche." Communication to author, July 2015.

60. For example, see Andrei Kozyrev, "The New Russia and the Atlantic Alliance," *NATO Review*, no. 1 (February 1993), in which he recalls his speech to the Stockholm CSCE Ministerial in December 1992 and reiterates the warning.

61. Talbott, *Russia Hand*, 101–3.

62. Perry and Carter, *Preventive Defense*, 28–29.

63. Clinton, *My Life*, 513.

64. Background on the EFTA and EEA can be found on the organization's website, www.efta.int. See also Desmond Dinan, *Ever Closer Union: An Introduction to European Integration*, 3rd ed. (Boulder, Colo.: Lynne Rienner, 2005), 61–62 and ff.; Pond, *Rebirth of Europe*, 87–88.

65. See European Union, "Enlargement," https://europa.eu/european-union/topics /enlargement_en. Also see Dinan, *Ever Closer Union*, 136ff.

66. Until the EU-Turkey deal on Syrian refugees in the winter of 2016, it appeared to many that Turkey might never get into the EU. For examples of changing estimates on the Turkey-EU relationship and prospects for membership, see, Henri J. Barkey and Omer Taspinar, "Turkey on Europe's Verge," Brookings Institution, February 7, 2006, http://www.brookings.edu/~/media/research/files/articles/2006/2/07europe-barkey /taspinar20060207.pdf; and Omer Taspinar, Steven A. Cook, and Henri J. Barkey, "Turkey After the June 12 Elections: Challenges and Opportunities," Carnegie Europe, Brussels, June 15, 2011, http://carnegieeurope.eu/events/?fa=3299. Skeptics and cynics will recall French president Valéry Giscard d'Estaing's blunt statement that "Turkey . . . is not a European country," reported, inter alia, in *The Guardian*, November 9, 2002, http://www.theguardian.com/world/2002/nov/09/turkey.eu.

67. Pond, *Rebirth of Europe*, 88.

68. Ibid., 87–91. A widely circulated German paper in 1994 and subsequent discussion in Germany even floated the idea of an "inner core" in the EU, which would proceed faster with deepening the Union than states in the outer circle and periphery. The inference of German leadership within the EU inherent in the paper and discussion were especially worrisome and exasperating for the French.

69. See esp. Stent, *Russia and Germany Reborn*, chaps. 7 and 8.

70. Pond, *Rebirth of Europe*, 95–102; Asmus, *Opening NATO's Door*, 12.

71. George H. W. Bush and Brent Scowcroft, *A World Transformed* (New York: Alfred A. Knopf, 1998), 192–93; Hutchings, *American Diplomacy*, 96–112, 151–52.

72. Pond, *Rebirth of Europe*, 51–52; Dinan, *Ever Closer Union*, 116–17.

73. Yost, *NATO Transformed*, 117; Jonathan Eyal, "NATO's Enlargement: Anatomy of a Decision," *International Affairs* 73 (October 1997): 695–719, at 709.

74. Pond, *Rebirth of Europe*, 45, 51–52.

75. Dinan, *Ever Closer Union*, 137; see also EFTA, "European Economic Area (EEA) / Relations with the EU," www.efta.int/eea.

76. Dinan, *Ever Closer Union*, 136–38; Pond, *Rebirth of Europe*, 92–95.

77. Dinan, *Ever Closer Union*, 147–48.

78. European Union, "Conditions for Membership," https://ec.europa.eu/neighbour hood-enlargement/policy/conditions-membership_en.

79. See the discussion by Pond, *Rebirth of Europe*, chap. 6, esp. 136–37.

80. European Union, "Enlargement."

81. Ibid.

82. Arie Bloed, "OSCE Chronicle: CSCE/OSCE Summit Meeting in Budapest Ended in 'Failure,' " *Helsinki Monitor*, no. 1 (1995): 66–67.

83. See esp. Talbott, *Russia Hand*, 138–41; and also see Goldgeier, *Not Whether but When*, 87–88; and Goldgeier and McFaul, *Power and Purpose*, 190–91, on the Budapest Summit.

84. Talbott, *Russia Hand*, 140–41.

85. For developments in the former Yugoslavia, see Laura Silber and Allan Little, *Yugoslavia: Death of a Nation* (New York: Penguin USA, 1995); Susan Woodward,

*Balkan Tragedy: Chaos and Dissolution After the Cold War* (Washington, D.C.: Brookings Institution Press, 1995); Steven Burg and Paul Shoup, *The War in Bosnia-Herzegovina: Ethnic Conflict and International Intervention* (Armonk, N.Y.: M. E. Sharpe, 1999); David Halberstam, *War in a Time of Peace: Bush, Clinton, and the Generals* (New York: Scribner, 2001); and Richard Holbrooke, *To End a War* (New York: Random House, 1998).

86. On Chechnya, See Lieven, *Chechnya*; and Zuercher, *Post-Soviet Wars*, 70–114.

87. For this paragraph, see OSCE, "The Secretary General's Annual Report 1995 on OSCE Activities," and OSCE, "The Chairman's Summary of the 1995 Budapest Ministerial Council," both available at www.osce.org.

88. John Borawski, "The Budapest Summit Meeting," *Helsinki Monitor*, no. 1 (1995): 5.

89. See OSCE, *The Security Model Discussion 1995–1996: Report of the Chairman-in-Office to the Lisbon Summit* (Lisbon: OSCE, 1996) (hereafter, *Lisbon Summit Document*), available at www.osce.org; for the actual document, see http://www.osce.org /mc/39539?download=true.

90. Ibid., 4.

91. For example, see the report from the Stockholm International Peace Research Institute, "Final Report of the Independent Working Group on 'a Future Security Agenda for Europe,'" distributed by the Swiss Chair to OSCE delegations on October 11, 1996.

92. *Lisbon Summit Document*, 12.

93. Ibid., 10.

94. See Elisa Niemtzow, "The OSCE's Security Model: Conceptual Confusion and Competing Visions," *Helsinki Monitor*, no. 3 (1996): 42–45; and Heather Hurlburt, "Russia, the OSCE, and European Security Architecture," *Helsinki Monitor*, no. 2 (1995): 5–20.

95. Niemtzow, "OSCE's Security Model," 44.

96. Ibid., 45.

97. *Lisbon Summit Document*, 11. For NATO's position, see Pol De Witte, "The Past, Present, and Future of OSCE–NATO Relations," in *The Future of the OSCE in the Perspective of the Enlargements of NATO and the EU*, PSIO Occasional Paper 1/2004, ed. Victor-Yves Ghebali, Daniel Warner, and Barbara Gimelli (Geneva: Program for the Study of International Organizations, 2004), 53–58.

98. Thomas de Waal, *Black Garden: Armenia and Azerbaijan Through Peace and War* (New York: New York University Press, 2003); *OSCE Annual Reports*, 1994–1996, available at www.osce.org; *Helsinki Monitor*, no. 1 (1996). In 1995, the chair also created the post of CiO special representative for Nagorno-Karabakh, a position filled since 1997 by Polish diplomat Andrzej Kasprczyk,

99. OSCE, *Survey of OSCE Field Operations* (Vienna: OSCE, 2013), 53–54, http:// www.osce.org/cpc/74783?download=true.

100. See chapter 3; also see *OSCE Annual Reports*, 1993–96.

101. OSCE, *Survey of OSCE Field Operations*, 61–64; *CSCE Annual Report*, 1993, available at www.osce.org.

102. Talbott, *Russia Hand*, 63; Richard A. Falkenrath, *Shaping Europe's Military Order: The Origins and Consequences of the CFE Treaty* (Cambridge, Mass.: MIT Press, 1995), 186–90; Goldgeier and McFaul, *Power and Purpose*, 171–75; Victor-Yves Ghebali, *L'OSCE dans l'Europe post-communiste: Vers une identite paneuropeenne de securite* (Brussels: Émile Bruylant, 1996), 330–44.

103. For example, see Michael Mihalka, "A Marriage of Convenience: The OSCE and Russia in Nagorno-Karabakh and Chechnya," *Helsinki Monitor*, no. 2 (1996): 13–28; see also Lieven, *Chechnya*.

104. OSCE, *Survey of OSCE Field Operations*, 66; *OSCE Annual Report*, 1995; Ghebali, *L'OSCE dans l'Europe*, 31–323. Ghebali explicitly connects Russia's acceptance of the mission to Chechnya with its hope to promote the OSCE's status and thus avert the growing push for NATO expansion.

105. OSCE, *Survey*, 66.

106. Mihalka, "Marriage of Convenience."

107. Zuercher, *Post-Soviet Wars*, 84.

108. Indeed, the United States was sufficiently concerned about maintaining European support for implementation of Dayton's security provisions that it initialed the agreement on November 21, 1995, in Dayton, but arranged for the formal signing of the treaty in Paris on December 14, 1995.

109. The Dayton Accords, literally the "General Framework Agreement for Peace in Bosnia and Herzegovina," can be found online, inter alia, at www.state.gov/p/eur/rls /or/dayton/. The eleven annexes to the agreement spell out in detail the conditions and modalities for implementation. See also Holbrooke, *To End a War*. For details on the OSCE Mission to Bosnia-Herzegovina and Dayton's implementation, see Ghebali, *L'OSCE dans l'Europe*, 567–81; *OSCE Annual Report*, 1996, 8–10; *Survey of OSCE Missions*, 11–12; and Arie Bloed, "The OSCE and the Bosnian Peace Arrangement," *Helsinki Monitor*, no. 1 (1996): 73–75.

110. Dunkerley interview, on the Association for Diplomatic Studies and Training Foreign Affairs History Project website; "Can you imagine Akashi being entrusted with implementation of Dayton?" expostulated one senior American official.

111. *OSCE Annual Report*, 1996; OSCE, *Survey of OSCE Field Missions*, 8; Bloed, "OSCE and the Bosnian Peace Arrangement," 73–74; Ghebali, *L'OSCE dans l'Europe*, 567ff.

112. *OSCE Annual Report*, 1996, 9; Bloed, "OSCE and the Bosnian Peace Arrangement," 73–74.

113. *OSCE Annual Report*, 1996, 9; Arie Bloed, "OSCE Approves the Outcome of Bosnian Elections," *Helsinki Monitor*, no. 4 (1996): 86–87; Ghebali, *L'OSCE dans l'Europe*, 573–79.

114. Conversations by the author with OSCE officials, Vienna, 1997–98; for a typical criticism of the OSCE's conduct and evaluation of the elections, see Diane Paul, "Human Rights and the Elections in Bosnia," *Helsinki Monitor*, no. 4 (1996): 5–18.

115. Bloed, "OSCE and the Bosnian Peace Arrangement," 78–79.

116. Ibid. Also see *OSCE Annual Report*, 1996, 10–11; this report specifically mentions the HNCM, ODIHR, the Council of Europe, the ECMM, the UNHCR, the EU Special Envoy for Regional Issues, the ICRC, and UNTAES (UN Transitional Authority for Eastern Slavonia).

117. "US Rejects Russian Attacks on OSCE," *RFE/RL*, December 5, 2005, http://www.rferl.org/content/article/1063530.html.

118. *OSCE Annual Report*, 1996, 16.

119. ODIHR EOM, "Final Statement of the OSCE/ODIHR Election Observation Mission, Second Round," July 5, 1996, http://www.osce.org/odihr/elections/russia/16282?download=true. See also OSCE/ODIHR, "International Observer Mission, Election of President of the Russian Federation, 16th June 1996 and 3rd July 1996: Report on the Election," http://www.osce.org/odihr/elections/russia/16288?download=true. For the subsequent controversy over the OSCE's evaluation of the 1996 Russian presidential election, see the text above.

120. "CFE Treaty, Article V for the Flank Limits: Treaty on Conventional Armed Forces in Europe," November 19, 1990, http://www.osce.org/library/14087?download=true.

121. Stockholm International Peace Research Institute, *SIPRI Yearbook* (Stockholm: Stockholm International Peace Research Institute, 1995), 247.

122. For the text and terms of the so-called Flank Agreement, see "Final Document of the First Conference to Review the Operation of the Treaty on Conventional Armed Forces in Europe and the Concluding Act of the Negotiation on Personnel Strength, Vienna, 15–31 May 1996, Annex A: Document Agreed among the States Parties to the Treaty on Conventional Armed Forces in Europe of November 19, 1990," http://www.osce.org/library/14099?download=true.

123. Ibid., paragraph 19.

124. Ibid., paragraph 4.

125. *Lisbon Summit Document*.

126. Ibid., appendix, 27–30.

127. This assertion is based on my observations and work on CFE issues while assigned to the undersecretary of state for international security affairs in the mid-1990s.

128. Yost, *NATO Transformed*, esp. 97–100; Goldgeier, *Not Whether but When*, 24–42; Perry and Carter, *Preventive Defense*, 23–24, 58–60 and ff.

129. See, for example, Asmus, *Opening NATO's Door*, 69–72.

130. Ibid., 69.

131. NATO, "Partnership for Peace Programme," http://www.nato.int/cps/en/natolive/topics_50349.htm.

132. Asmus, *Opening NATO's Door*, 67–68; Talbott, *Russia Hand*, 115.

133. See "Summary of Conclusions," www.nato.int/cps/en/natohq/official_texts_24454.htm?selected. . . .

134. See Talbott, *Russia Hand*, 142–68; Asmus, *Opening NATO's Door*, 95–133; Goldgeier, *Not Whether but When*, 88–100; and Perry and Carter, *Preventive Defense*, 54–61. For the decision on the Enlargement Study, see NATO, "Final Communiqués Issued at the Ministerial Meeting of the North Atlantic Council at NATO Headquarters, Brussels, 01 December 1994," www.nato.int/cps/en/natohq/official_texts_24430.htm?selected . . .

135. Of the many accounts on the subject, in my view the two best narratives of the US-Russia dialogue are Asmus, *Opening NATO's Door*, 101–33; and Talbott, *Russia Hand*, 151–65.

136. Asmus, *Opening NATO's Door*, 116–17; Talbott, *Russia Hand*, 161–62.

137. Holbrooke, *To End a War*, esp. 133–98; Asmus, *Opening NATO's Door*, 127–32; Talbott, *Russia Hand*, 178–88; Perry and Carter, *Preventive Defense*, 41–46.

138. See esp. Perry and Carter, *Preventive Defense*.

139. NATO, "Final Communiqué Issued at the Ministerial Meeting of the North Atlantic Council at NATO Headquarters," Brussels, December 1, 1994, www.nato.int/cps /en/natohq/official_texts_24430.htm?selected. See also Asmus, *Opening NATO's Door*, 101–4, for the political reasons behind and the political benefits of the NATO Enlargement Study.

140. NATO, *Study on NATO Enlargement* (Brussels: NATO, 1995), www.nato.int /cps/en/natolive/official_texts_24733.htm?selectedLocal=en.

141. Ibid., paragraph 3.

142. Ibid., esp. paragraphs 23–28.

143. Goldgeier, *Not Whether but When*, 80–106, passim. See also the account by one of the most enthusiastic supporters of NATO Enlargement in the US Congress, Gerald B. Solomon, *The NATO Enlargement Debate, 1990–1997: Blessings of Liberty* (Westport, Conn.: Praeger, 1998). Asmus, *Opening NATO's Door*; and Talbott, *Russia Hand*, also mention domestic pressures throughout their narratives.

144. Eyal, "NATO's Enlargement," 705–6; see also Asmus, *Opening NATO's Door*, 132; and Talbott, *Russia Hand*, 151–58.

145. Eyal, "NATO's Enlargement," 703–4.

146. Ibid.

147. Ibid., 706; Asmus, *Opening NATO's Door*, 128–29.

148. Goldgeier, *Not Whether but When*, 117–20; Asmus, *Opening NATO's Door*, 221–28.

149. NATO, "Opening Statement by the Secretary General to the Press Conference," www.nato.int/docu/speech/1997/s970708e.htm. See also Asmus, *Opening NATO's Door*, 238–48.

150. See Asmus, *Opening NATO's Door*, esp. 198–210; and Talbott, *Russia Hand*, 193–95, 222–42.

151. This account of the negotiation of the NATO-Russia Founding Act is drawn especially from Goldgeier, *Not Whether but When*; Goldgeier and McFaul, *Power and Purpose*; Asmus, *Opening NATO's Door*; Talbott, *Russia Hand*; and my own personal observations while working for the undersecretary of state for international security affairs.

152. The most succinct account of these negotiations is by Goldgeier and McFaul, *Power and Purpose*, 206–10.

153. NATO, "Founding Act on Mutual Relations, Cooperation and Security between NATO and the Russian Federation," May 27, 1997, 14, http://www.nato.int/cps/en /natohq/official_texts_25468.htm?selectedLocale=en.

154. References in this paragraph are drawn from ibid.

## 5. WAR OVER KOSOVO

1. Michael McFaul makes the argument that proper analysis and categorization of the vote totals in the legislative and presidential elections in Russia during the 1990s demonstrate a consistent narrow majority or near majority of the electorate in general agreement over an overall course that might be characterized as "democratic reform." See Michael McFaul, *Russia's Unfinished Revolution: Political Change from Gorbachev to Putin* (Ithaca, N.Y.: Cornell University Press, 2001). Whatever the merits of this line of analysis, the practical effect of the elections in the lower chamber of the legislature was anything but supportive of Yeltsin's reform program, and he was in political trouble from at least 1995 on, if not from the December 1993 legislative elections.

2. The Duma actually voted at least once in 1997 by the necessary two-thirds margin to remove Yeltsin, but it was not able to muster the necessary votes in the upper chamber, the Council of the Federation. Proponents of impeachment were later restrained by fear that an unsuccessful attempt might prompt early parliamentary elections, required under the Russian Constitution if the legislature fails three times in one session at voting impeachment.

3. Angela E. Stent, *The Limits of Partnership: US–Russian Relations in the Twenty-First Century* (Princeton, N.J.: Princeton University Press, 2014), 45–48; Timothy J. Colton, *Yeltsin: A Life* (New York: Basic Books, 2008), 419–29; James Goldgeier and Michael McFaul, *Power and Purpose: US Policy toward Russia after the Cold War* (Washington, D.C.: Brookings Institution Press, 2003); Karen Dawisha, *Putin's Kleptocracy: Who Owns Russia?* (New York: Simon & Schuster, 2014), 188–90; Celestine Bohlen, "Yeltsin Gambles Again and Comes Out Ahead," *New York Times*, March 23, 1999, http://www.nytimes.com/1999/05/23/weekinreview/may-16-22-yeltsin-gambles-again-and-comes-out-ahead.html.

4. David E. Hoffman, *The Oligarchs: Wealth and Power in the New Russia* (New York: PublicAffairs, 2001); Chrystia Freeland, *Sale of the Century: Russia's Wild Ride from Communism to Capitalism* (New York: Crown Business, 2000).

5. See David McClintick, "How Harvard Lost Russia," *Institutional Investor*, February 27, 2006, www.institutionalinvestor.com/article/b15onqqs1wz84o/how-harvard-lost-russia; and Janine R. Wedel, *Collision and Collusion: The Strange Case of Western Aid to Eastern Europe, 1989–1998* (New York: Palgrave Macmillan, 1998).

6. Hoffman, *Oligarchs*; Goldgeier and McFaul, *Power and Purpose*, 211–46; Freeland, *Sale of the Century*; Strobe Talbott, *The Russia Hand: A Memoir of Presidential Diplomacy* (New York: Random House, 2002), 274–93.

7. Goldgeier and McFaul, *Power and Purpose*, 211–46; Barry Ickes and Clifford G. Gaddy, "The Virtual Economy and Economic Recovery in Russia," May 1, 2001, www.brookings.edu/research/articles/2001/05/russia-gaddy.

8. Colton, *Yeltsin*, 409–16; Goldgeier and McFaul, *Power and Purpose*, 211–46.

9. In fact, the Duma passed a resolution by a substantial majority banning the most prominent economic reformers under Yeltsin—including Chernomyrdin, Chubais, Nemtsov, and Gaidar—from holding any high government positions. The Duma also continued to pursue the impeachment of Yeltsin, but it was unable to get enough votes to ensure victory so kept the action in reserve.

10. Yeltsin emerged from the hospital where he was being treated for pneumonia in December 1998 only long enough to replace his son-in-law, Valentin Yumashev, as national security adviser, and then returned to the hospital. Against this backdrop, it was hard to take seriously the Kremlin press announcements that the president was working, active, and involved. See Bohlen, "Yeltsin Gambles Again"; and Colton, *Yeltsin*, 419–22.

11. Fiona Hill and Clifford Gaddy, *Mr. Putin: Operative in the Kremlin*, 2nd ed. (Washington, D.C.: Brookings Institution Press, 2015), 8–10; Angus Roxburgh, *The Strongman: Vladimir Putin and the Struggle for Russia* (New York: I. B. Tauris, 2012), 20–21; Stent, *Limits of Partnership*, 50–54; Dawisha, *Putin's Kleptocracy*, 188–98. It was widely rumored and reported that Yeltsin and Putin reached some sort of understanding about the former president's security after Putin took office; but no "smoking gun"—that is, fully believable documentary evidence—has ever been produced to support such reports.

12. For this account, see Bill Clinton, *My Life* (New York: Alfred A. Knopf, 2004), esp. 869–70, 882; Talbott, *Russia Hand*, 361–64; Goldgeier and McFaul, *Power and Purpose*, 264–75.

13. Talbott, *Russia Hand*, passim.

14. Clinton, *My Life*, esp. 850ff.; Talbott, *Russia Hand*, 350–69; Goldgeier and McFaul, *Power and Purpose*, 267–74.

15. Members of the Speaker's Advisory Group on Russia, US House of Representatives, 106th Congress, Hon. Christopher Cox, Chairman, *Russia's Road to Corruption: How the Clinton Administration Exported Government Instead of Free Enterprise and Failed the Russian People* (Washington, D.C.: US Government Printing Office, 2000).

16. Desmond Dinan, *Ever Closer Union: An Introduction to European Integration*, 3rd ed. (Boulder, Colo.: Lynne Rienner, 2005), 148ff.

17. Ibid., 148–49.

18. Ibid., 150.

19. Elizabeth Pond, *The Rebirth of Europe* (Washington, D.C.: Brookings Institution Press, 2000), 97–98; Dinan, *Ever Closer Union*, 504–6.

20. "Constructive abstention" could be applied in most cases, whereas decisions could be made by a qualified majority on operational or implementation measures deriving from common strategies of basic EU policy decisions already taken. See http://europa.eu/legislation_summaries/institutional_affairs/treaties/amsterdam_treaty/a19000_en.htm.

21. Pond, *Rebirth of Europe*, 87; Dinan, *Ever Closer Union*, 134; Stanley R. Sloan, *NATO, the European Union, and the Atlantic Community: The Transatlantic Bargain Challenged*, 2nd ed. (New York: Rowman & Littlefield, 2005), 18.

22. Sloan, *NATO*, 187–88; David S. Yost, *NATO Transformed: The Alliance's New Roles in International Security* (Washington, D.C.: US Institute of Peace Press, 1998), 199–205.

23. European Union, "Common Foreign and Security Policy: Summaries of EU Legislation," http://europa.eu/legislation_summaries/institutional_affairs/treaties/amsterdam_treaty/a19000_en.htm; see also Sloan, *NATO*, 190; Dinan, *Ever Closer Union*, 593–94; Pond, *Rebirth of Europe*, 80–81, 198.

24. Sloan, NATO, 191–92.

25. "Joint Declaration Issued at the British-French Summit," Saint-Malo, France, December 3–4, 1998, https://www.consilium.europa.eu/uedocs/cmsUpload/French -British%20Summit%20Declaration,%20Saint-Malo,%201998%20-%20EN.pdf.

26. Ibid.

27. Sven Biscop, "The UK and European Defence: Leading or Leaving?" International Affairs 88, no. 6 (2012): 1297–1313, at 1301.

28. Jolyon Howorth, "Britain, France, and the European Defense Initiative," Survival 42, no. 2 (Summer 2000): 33.

29. Biscop, "UK and European Defence"; Howorth, "Britain, France." François Heisbourg, "Europe's Strategic Ambitions: The Limits of Ambiguity," Survival 42, no. 2 (Summer 2000): 5–15, enumerates many of the operational capabilities that were lacking for a real intervention in Kosovo; Gilles Andreani, "Why Institutions Matter," Survival 42, no. 2 (Summer 2000): 81–95, makes similar points in discussing the institutional shortcomings of the EU in addressing real security operations.

30. Biscop, "UK and European Defence," 1301.

31. Sloan, NATO, 190.

32. Sloan, NATO, 191–92, cites interviews with Clinton administration officials; I encountered this US reasoning constantly while working on various assignments involving European security, the OSCE, and NATO during the 1990s at the State Department.

33. Sloan, NATO, 192; for a more detailed discussion of the Washington Summit, the new Strategic Concept adopted, and declarations on the European Security and Defence Policy, see below in this chapter.

34. Andreani, "Why Institutions Matter," 81.

35. European Union, "Shaping of a Common Security and Defence Policy," July 8, 2016, http://eeas.europa.eu/csdp/about-csdp/military_headline_goals/index_en.htm. See also Sloan, NATO, 192–93; David Yost, "The NATO Capabilities Gap and the European Union," Survival 42, no. 4 (Winter 2000–2001): 114–17; Andreani, "Why Institutions Matter"; Heisbourg, "Europe's Strategic Ambitions"; Biscop, "UK and European Defence."

36. See chapter 2.

37. Sloan, NATO, 153; I heard this argument frequently while working on European security affairs for the undersecretary of state for international security affairs.

38. NATO, "Basic Document of the Euro-Atlantic Partnership Council," www.nato .int/cps/en/natohq/official_texts_25471.htm?selected.

39. Ibid. See also Yost, NATO Transformed, 158–61; and Sloan, NATO, 153–55.

40. Yost, NATO Transformed, 215–16; Joyce P. Kaufman, NATO and the Former Yugoslavia: Crisis, Conflict, and the Atlantic Alliance (New York: Rowman & Littlefield, 2002), 141–42.

41. See, for example, Yost, "NATO Capabilities Gap," 98ff.

42. NATO, "An Alliance for the 21st Century: Washington Summit Communiqué Issued by the Heads of State and Government Participating in the Meeting of the North Atlantic Council in Washington, D.C. on 24th April 1999," paragraph 11, www .nato.int/cps/en/natohq/official_texts_27440.htm?selected.

43. NATO, "Madrid Declaration on Euro-Atlantic Security and Cooperation Issued by the Heads of State and Government at the Meeting of the North Atlantic Council," July 8, 1997, www.nato.int/cps/en/natohq/official_texts_25460.htm?selectedLocale=en.

44. NATO, "Membership Action Plan (MAP) Approved by the Heads of State and Government Participating in the Meeting of the North Atlantic Council, Issued on 24 April 1999," www.nato.int/cop/en/natohq/official_texts_27444.htm?selected. See also NATO, "Alliance for the 21st Century," paragraph 7.

45. NATO, "Alliance for the 21st Century," paragraph 7.

46. See chapter 2.

47. NATO, "The Alliance's Strategic Concept Approved by the Heads of State and Government Participating in the Meeting of the North Atlantic Council in Washington, D.C.," April 24, 1999, www.nato.int/cps/en/natohq/official_texts_27433.htm.

48. See NATO, "Strategic Concepts," www.nato.int/cps/en/natohq/topics_56626.htm.

49. See chapter 2; for the text, see http://www.nato.int/cps/en/natohq/official_texts_23847.htm?selected.

50. Ibid., paragraph 20/IV.

51. NATO, "The Alliance's Strategic Concept," April 24, 1999, paragraph 10, www.nato.int/cps/en/natohq/official_texts_27433.htm.

52. Ibid., paragraph 25.

53. OSCE, "Chairman's Summary, 2nd Day of the Sixth Meeting of the Ministerial Council, MC(6) Journal No. 2," agenda item 10; OSCE, *Survey of OSCE Field Operations* (Vienna: OSCE, 2013), 66–67, www.osce.org/cpc/74783?download=true; Natalie Mychajlyszyn, "The OSCE in Crimea," *Helsinki Monitor*, no. 4 (1998): 30–43; OSCE, "Address by the Chairman-in-Office of the OSCE to the Permanent Council of the OSCE," October 16, 1997.

54. OSCE, "Address by the Chairman-in-Office"; OSCE, "Chairman's Summary"; OSCE, *Survey of OSCE Field Operations*, 55–58, 66–67; Arie Bloed, "OSCE Involvement in Albania," *Helsinki Monitor*, no. 1 (1998): 40–41, 66–67; Marjanne de Kwaasteniet, "Alba: A Lost Opportunity for the OSCE?" *Helsinki Monitor*, no. 1 (1998): 15–22; Arie Bloed, "Drama in Kosovo," *Helsinki Monitor*, no. 1 (1999): 48–50.

55. OSCE, "The Charter for European Security" is contained in the "OSCE Istanbul Document 1999," 1–45.

56. See chapter 3. On the character of the negotiations and Russia's role, see especially Lars-Erik Lundin, "The Charter for European Security from a European Union (EU) Perspective," *Helsinki Monitor*, no. 1 (2000): 20–21.

57. John Borawski, "Towards an OSCE Charter: A Question of Identity," *Helsinki Monitor*, no. 4 (1998): 5–8.

58. OSCE, "Charter for European Security," paragraph 2. On the provisions and significance of this "Charter," see Lundin, "Charter," 11–21; and Victor-Yves Ghebali, "A More Capable and Balanced Alliance: The OSCE's Istanbul Charter for European Security," *NATO Review*, no. 1 (Spring–Summer 2000), www.nato.int/docu/review/2000/More-capable-balanced-allian.

59. OSCE, "Charter for European Security," paragraphs 4–5.

60. Ibid., paragraph 7.

61. OSCE, "Operational Document: Platform for Cooperative Security, Charter for European Security," 43–45; also Lundin, "Charter," 13–15.

62. For examaple, see the analysis of the Charter by Ghebali, "More Capable and Balanced Alliance"; and Pol De Witte, "The Past, Present, and Future of OSCE–NATO Relations," in *The Future of the OSCE in the Perspective of the Enlargements of NATO and the EU*, PSIO Occasional Paper 1/2004, ed. Victor-Yves Ghebali, Daniel Warner, and Barbara Gimelli (Geneva: Program for the Study of International Organizations, 2004), 66–68.

63. Lundin, "Charter," 20.

64. OSCE, "Vienna Document 1999 of the Negotiations on Confidence- and Security-Building Measures," www.osce.org/fsc/41276?download=true.

65. For basic information on the CFE Treaty and Adapted CFE Treaty, see US Department of State, "Fact Sheet: Treaty on Conventional Armed Forces in Europe (CFE): Key Facts about the Current Treaty and Agreement on Adaptation," 2009, http://2001-2009.state.gov/documents/organization/99850.pdf; considerable portions of this narrative and analysis are based on my experience while working on CFE Treaty adaptation for the Department of State and during my subsequent service for the OSCE. See also Jeffrey D. McCausland, "European/Eurasian Security and the Treaty on Conventional Armed Forces in Europe (CFE)," conference paper for Carnegie Council's Program on US Global Engagement: A Two-Year Retrospective, June 2011; also Craig Dunkerley, interview, 83ff., http://adst.org/wp-content/uploads/2012/09/Dunkerley-Craig.pdf; Anne Witkowsky, Sherman Garnett, and Jeffrey McCausland, "Salvaging the Conventional Armed Forces in Europe Treaty Regime: Options for Washington," Brookings Arms Control Paper 2, May 2010; Zdzislaw Lachowski, *The Adapted CFE Treaty and the Admission of the Baltic States to NATO* (Stockholm: Stockholm International Peace Research Institute, 2002); Kees Homan, "The Adapted CFE Treaty: A Building Block for Cooperative Security in Europe," *Helsinki Monitor*, no. 2 (2000): 52–57.

66. The text of the Adapted CFE Treaty was included in the "OSCE Istanbul Document": OSCE, "Agreement on Adaptation of the Treaty on Conventional Armed Forces in Europe—OSCE Istanbul Document 1999," 119–252. For a contemporary description of the important changes in the CFE regime, see Homan, "Adapted CFE Treaty."

67. OSCE, "Agreement on the Principles and Procedures for Implementing the Treaty on the Conventional Armed Forces in Europe," Tashkent, May 15, 1992.

68. See the GUAM website at http://guam-organization.org/en; I was working for the undersecretary of state for international security affairs on CFE adaptation when the GUAM group first appeared in the negotiations in Vienna. The group subsequently changed both its membership and its basic purpose several times.

69. Dunkerley interview, 101, 103ff.

70. Adapted CFE Final Act, Istanbul Document 1999.

71. Adapted CFE Final Act, Istanbul Summit Declaration.

72. Dunkerley interview, 106. According to both Moldovan and Russian negotiators, Moscow's agreement was not nailed down until the morning of the signing,

when Moldovan president Lucinschi, in an end run around the Russian delegation, approached an ailing Yeltsin and obtained his personal assent on the spot to the Moldovans' preferred date. Even years later, Russian diplomats expressed resentment over the maneuver. Russian and Moldovan OSCE representatives to the author, 2001 and 2003.

73. ACFE Final Act.

74. For general background on Kosovo, see Noel Malcolm, *Kosovo: A Short History* (New York: Macmillan, 1998); John R. Lampe, *Yugoslavia as History: Twice There Was a Country*, 2nd ed. (Cambridge: Cambridge University Press, 2000), esp. 363–415; and Tim Judah, *Kosovo: What Everyone Needs to Know* (Oxford: Oxford University Press, 2008).

75. Richard Holbrooke, *To End a War* (New York: Random House, 1998), 234, 346.

76. For basic descriptions of the events in Kosovo and beyond, see Ivo H. Daalder and Michael E. O'Hanlon, *Winning Ugly: NATO's War to Save Kosovo* (Washington, D.C.: Brookings Institution Press, 2001); Lampe, *Yugoslavia as History*; Kaufman, *NATO and the Former Yugoslavia*, 137–204; David L. Phillips, *Liberating Kosovo: Coercive Diplomacy and US Intervention* (Cambridge, Mass.: MIT Press, 2012), esp. 65–114; Florian Bieber and Zidas Daskalovski, eds., *Understanding the War in Kosovo* (London: Frank Cass, 2003); and Wesley Clark, *Waging Modern War* (New York: PublicAffairs, 2011).

77. NATO, "Statement on Kosovo Issued at the Meeting of the North Atlantic Council in Defense Ministers Session," June 11, 1998, www.nato.int/cps/en/natohq/official_texts_25969.htm?selectedLocale=en.

78. Arie Bloed, "The OSCE and the Kosovo Crisis," *Helsinki Monitor*, no. 3 (1998): 79–80.

79. Daalder and O'Hanlon, *Winning Ugly*, 45; Kaufman, *NATO and the Former Yugoslavia*, 163.

80. OSCE, *Survey of OSCE Field Operations*, 55; also Arie Bloed, "The OSCE Faces the Greatest Challenge in Its History: The Kosovo Mission," *Helsinki Monitor*, no. 4 (1998): 63–64; Kaufman, *NATO and the Former Yugoslavia*, 163–64.

81. Daalder and O'Hanlon, *Winning Ugly*; Kaufman, *NATO and the Former Yugoslavia*, 171. See also Clark, *Waging Modern War*, on the negotiations and run-up to war. Some Russians have long memories. See Foreign Minister Sergei Lavrov's denunciation of Walker's actions in a long article on European security affairs, the OSCE, and NATO: Sergei Lavrov, "The Euro-Atlantic Region: Equal Security for All," *Russia in Global Affairs* 10, no. 2 (April–June 2010), http://eng.globalaffairs.ru/number/The_Euro-Atlantic_Region:_Equal_Security_for_All-14888.

82. See note 81.

83. Clinton, *My Life*, 848–51; Madeleine Albright, *Madame Secretary: A Memoir* (New York: HarperCollins, 2003).

84. Albright, *Madame Secretary*, 381–410.

85. Clinton, *My Life*, 850; Evgenii Primakov, *Gody v bol'shoi politike* (Moscow: Izdatel'stvo Sovershenno Sekretno, 1999), 357–58.

86. For this discussion, I use especially Clark, *Waging Modern War*; and Daalder and O'Hanlon, *Winning Ugly*.

87. UN Security Council Resolution 1244 (1999), http://daccess-dds-ny.un.org/doc/UNDOC/GEN/N99/172/89/PDF/N9917289.pdf?OpenElement.

88. Kaufman, NATO and the Former Yugoslavia, 199–201. For detailed descriptions of the negotiations on the terms of the peacekeeping mission and the dramatic events during its deployment, I have relied especially on Talbott, Russia Hand, 328–49; and Clark, Waging Modern War, 345–403. See also Daalder and O'Hanlon, Winning Ugly, 219–20.

89. Clark, Waging Modern War, 297, 307.

90. Talbott, Russia Hand, 348–49; Clark, Waging Modern War, 390–98. British pop singer James Blunt (his stage name; his original surname is spelled Blount) was serving at the time in the UK armed forces under the command of General Jackson and related the story of receiving an order from General Clark to take Pristina Airport, only to have it countermanded by General Jackson. See "Singer James Blunt Prevented World War III," BBC-TV, November 14, 2010, www.bbc.com/news/uk-politics-11753050.

91. Talbott, Russia Hand; also see Oleg Levitin, "Inside Moscow's Kosovo Muddle," Survival 42, no. 1 (Spring 2000): 130–40.

92. Talbott's account of Yeltsin's physical condition and distracted mental state in one encounter at the Cologne G-8 is particularly striking; see Talbott, Russia Hand, 350–51.

93. These reactions were not always high level and/or planned. For example, when I arrived in Moldova in June 1999, Russian and Transdniestrian representatives who had been working for years with the OSCE Mission to Moldova refused for a time to meet with OSCE mission members from NATO countries, making an occasional exception only for a Polish military officer in the mission. Their explanation was that Poland had not been a NATO member long enough to be responsible for what the Alliance had done in the Balkans.

94. Levitin, "Inside Moscow's Kosovo Muddle," 130.

95. For one argument to this effect, see Michael MccGwire, "Why Did We Bomb Belgrade?" International Affairs 76, no. 1 (2000): 1–23. I have heard this argument subsequently from Russian officials and academics at all levels literally hundreds of times. For a discussion of the effects of the war over Kosovo on the views of the Russian military, see Oksana Antonenko, "Russia, NATO and European Security after Kosovo," Survival 41, no. 4 (Winter 1999–2000): 124–44.

96. For one argument along these lines, see Margot Light, Stephen White, and John Lowenhardt, "A Wider Europe: the View from Moscow and Kyiv," International Affairs 76, no. 1 (2000): 77–88.

97. Boris Nikolayevich Yeltsin, Midnight Diaries (New York: PublicAffairs, 2000), 259–60.

98. Igor Ivanov, quoted by Stent, Limits of Partnership, 43.

99. Tat'iana Parkhalina, "Nekotorye rezul'taty politiki rossii v khode kosovskogo krizisa. Chto dal'she?" in Miroporiadok posle balkanskogo krizisa: Novye real'nosti meniaiushchegosia mira—Materialy Konferentsii, Moskva, 1–2 noiabria 1999 goda, ed. Anatoliy Kulik (Moscow: Izd. "Dobrosovet," 2000), 118.

100. For example, see Stent, Limits of Partnership, 42–45.

101. James Steinberg, quoted by Goldgeier and McFaul, *Power and Purpose*, 251. Steinberg's remark recalls Kozyrev's complaint at one point in a discussion with Talbott over Bosnia that not only did the Americans tell Russia what to do, but that it was in Russia's interest to do so.

## 6. NEW MILLENNIUM, NEW THREATS

1. This account is based on interviews with NATO allied embassy diplomats in Moscow at the time, my own experience working with Russia in Moldova and the OSCE, and Angela E. Stent, *The Limits of Partnership: US–Russian Relations in the Twenty-First Century* (Princeton, N.J.: Princeton University Press, 2014); Fiona Hill and Clifford Gaddy, *Mr. Putin: Operative in the Kremlin*, 2nd ed. (Washington, D.C.: Brookings Institution Press, 2015); Strobe Talbott, *The Russia Hand: A Memoir of Presidential Diplomacy* (New York: Random House, 2002); Angus Roxburgh, *The Strongman: Vladimir Putin and the Struggle for Russia* (New York: I. B. Tauris, 2012); Richard Sakwa, *Putin Redux: Power and Contradiction in Contemporary Russia* (New York: Routledge, 2014); Vladimir Putin, *First Person: An Astonishingly Frank Self-Portrait by Russia's President Vladimir Putin* (New York: PublicAffairs, 2000); and Timothy J. Colton, *Yeltsin: A Life* (New York: Basic Books, 2008).

2. I will not attempt here to render judgment pro or con on charges that the bombings were actually the work of the FSB as part of a plot to whip up popular fears and thus support for Putin. See especially John B. Dunlop, *The Moscow Bombings of September 1999: Examinations of Russian Terrorist Attacks at the Onset of Vladimir Putin's Rule*, 2nd ed., Soviet and Post-Soviet Politics and Society, Vol. 110 (Stuttgart: Ibidem-Verlag, 2014); and Alexander Litvinenko and Yuri Felshtinsky, *Blowing Up Russia: The Secret Plot to Bring Back KGB Power* (New York: Encounter Books, 2007). For a Russian historical perspective on the Second Chechen War and the apartment bombings in Russia, see the television documentary on Putin in honor of the fifteenth anniversary of his election in 2000: RTV, *Prezident*, April 26, 2015, http://russia.tv/video/show/brand_id/59329/episode_id/1193264/video_id/1165983/viewtype/picture.

3. For the second war in Chechnya, see Christoph Zuercher, *The Post-Soviet Wars: Rebellion, Ethnic Conflict, and Nationhood in the Caucasus* (New York: New York University Press, 2007); and Thomas de Waal, *The Caucasus: An Introduction* (New York: Oxford University Press, 2010). For what the conflict looked like to a Russian soldier, see Arkady Babchenko, *Alkhan Yurt*, published in English as *One Soldier's War* (New York: Grove Press, 2009).

4. Vladimir Putin, "Being Strong: Why Russia Needs to Rebuild Its Military," *Foreign Affairs*, February 2012, http://foreignpolicy.com/2012/02/21/being-strong/.

5. For a detailed account and analysis of the *Kursk* incident, see Robert Brannon, *Russian Civil-Military Relations* (Farnham, UK: Ashgate, 2008).

6. See esp. Roxburgh, *Strongman*, 47–57ff.

7. See Hill and Gaddy, *Mr. Putin*, 12–17. I had the opportunity in 1999 and 2000, in discussions with many Russian officials and businessmen, to hear generally positive remarks to the effect that Putin would restore order (*vvesti poriadok*) to a Russia that had descended into chaos and many feared was decaying or disintegrating.

8. Russian Ambassador to the author, autumn 2000–summer 2001.

9. Roxburgh, *Strongman*, 27.

10. Ibid., 28–30.

11. Ibid., 91–94.

12. Talbott, *Russia Hand*, 367–69.

13. See esp. Talbott, *Russian Hand*, chap. 15, 390–94; also see Roxburgh, *Strongman*, 30, 66–72; Hill and Gaddy, *Mr. Putin*, 296–99; and Stent, *Limits of Partnership*, 46–47.

14. Talbott, *Russia Hand*, 368, Roxburgh, *Strongman*, 115, Hill, *Russia*, 39.

15. Talbot, *Russia Hand*, chap. 15, gives an excellent narrative and explanation of the Clinton's administration's discussions with the Russians during 2000 on missile defense and the Russian position and response. See also Roxburgh, *Strongman*, 42, 200–204.

16. Talbott, *Russia Hand*, chap. 15.

17. Roxburgh, *Strongman*, 30–31.

18. Stent, *Limits of Partnership*, 67–69. On Bush's first meeting with Putin and subsequent cooperation on Afghanistan, see George W. Bush, *Decision Points* (New York: Crown, 2010), 195–97; on Putin's personality, see 431–34.

19. Stent, *Limits of Partnership*, 69–70. Shortly after the Second Chechen War began, a Russian ambassador remarked to me that "we are fighting the same people that you are," as he described some of the foreign Islamic fighters whom Russian intelligence had discovered in the North Caucasus; conversation with the author, September 1999.

20. Stent, *Limits of Partnership*, 70; State Department official to the author, February 2002.

21. See esp. Stent, *Limits of Partnership*, 68–71; Roxburgh, *Strongman*, 42–43ff.; and James Goldgeier and Michael McFaul, *Power and Purpose: US Policy toward Russia after the Cold War* (Washington, D.C.: Brookings Institution Press, 2003), 316–29.

22. For example, see "Sergei Ivanov Accuses West of Double Standard on Chechnya," *Eurasia Daily Monitor* 8, no. 24 (February 2, 2002), www.jamestown.org/single/?tx_ttnews%5Btt_news%5D=23893&tx_ttnews%5BbackPid%5D=216&no_cache=1#.VYWsfKxRHIU.

23. The author has personally heard this line from a number of Russian ministers, deputy ministers, and a former prime minister. See also Stent, *Limits of Partnership*, 70.

24. See below in the text for a discussion of the two OSCE field operations in the early 2000s. Some Western diplomats also understood at the time that Russia perceived Western actions in the near abroad as a challenge to Russian interests and influence. For example, George W. Bush's announcement of the 2001 Georgia Train and Equip Program was perceived by many in both Washington and Moscow as a geopolitical response to Putin's threat to send Russian forces into Georgia's Pankisi Gorge to "clean out" Chechen fighters using it as a safe haven; former US diplomat to the author, October 2015.

25. Putin on Russian television, March 2003, as seen by the author.

26. Condoleezza Rice, "Promoting the National Interests," *Foreign Affairs* 70, no. 1 (January–February 2000): 45–62.

27. For an example of such "neoconservative" thinking, see esp. Cheney-Wolfowitz 1992 Defense Planning Guidance, which advocated a strategy aimed at preventing the emergence of another rival to the United States in the post–Cold War international order: Patrick E. Tyler, "US Strategy Plan Calls for Insuring No Rivals Develop: A One-Superpower World: Pentagon's Document Outlines Ways to Thwart Challenges to Primacy of America," *New York Times*, March 8, 1992, http://work.colum.edu/~amiller/wolfowitz1992.htm.

28. For a discussion by Vice President Dick Cheney on how the September 11, 2001, terrorist attacks had "changed everything," see NBC-TV, *Meet the Press*, transcript for September 14, 2003, www.nbcnews.com/id/3080244/ns/meet_the_press/t/transcript-sept/#.VYWxVqxRHIU.

29. See the *New York Times* archive on the anthrax attacks, September–December 2001, http://topics.nytimes.com/top/reference/timestopics/subjects/a/anthrax/index.html; and Bob Woodward, *Bush at War* (New York: Simon & Schuster, 2002), esp. 248–49.

30. See "Interview with Condoleezza Rice," CNN Late Edition with Wolf Blitzer, September 8, 2002, www.cnn.com/TRANSCRIPTS/0209/08/le.00.html.

31. George W. Bush, "State of the Union Address," January 29, 2002, http://georgewbush-whitehouse.archives.gov/news/releases/2002/01/20020129-11.html.

32. See note 27 above. The Defense Planning Guidance was classified but has subsequently been declassified and released to the public. Also see Patrick G. Tyler, "US Strategy Plan Calls for Insuring No Rivals Develop," *New York Times*, March 8, 1992.

33. See, for example, James Mann, *Rise of the Vulcans: The History of George W. Bush's War Cabinet* (New York: Penguin Books, 2004), esp. 234ff. Also see Woodward, *Bush at War*, passim.

34. See chapter 7; and George W. Bush, "Second Inaugural Address," January 20, 2005, www.npr.org/templates/story/story.php?storyId=4460172; and White House, *The National Security Strategy*, March 2006 (Washington: White House, 2006), http://georgewbush-whitehouse.archives.gov/nsc/nss/2006/.

35. For background on European Monetary Union and its introduction from 1999 to 2002, see Desmond Dinan, *Ever Closer Union: An Introduction to European Integration*, 3rd ed. (Boulder, Colo.: Lynne Rienner, 2005), 481–515; and Giorgio La Malfa, "The Orphaned Euro," *Survival* 44, no. 1 (Spring 2002): 81–92.

36. Dinan, *Ever Closer Union*, 511–12; La Malfa, "Orphaned Euro," 87.

37. Dinan, *Ever Closer Union*, 171–72.

38. Ibid., 172–74.

39. European Union, "The History of the European Union: 1999," http://europa.eu/about-eu/eu-history/1990-1999/1999/index_en.htm.

40. Stanley R. Sloan, *NATO, the European Union, and the Atlantic Community: The Transatlantic Bargain Challenged*, 2nd ed. (New York: Rowman & Littlefield, 2005), 193–94.

41. Ibid., 195.

42. Ibid.; European Union, "Shaping of a Common Security and Defence Policy," July 8, 2016, http://eeas.europa.eu/csdp/about-csdp/berlin/index_en.htm.

43. Quoted by Sloan, *NATO*, 195.

44. Ibid., 199; Sinem Akgul Acikmese and Dimitrios Triantaphyllou, "The NATO-EU-Turkey Trilogy: The Impact of the Cyprus Conundrum," *Southeast European and Black Sea Studies* 12, no. 4 (December 2012): 555–73.

45. See the text at www.nato.int/cps/en/natohq/official_texts_19544.htm?selected Locale=en; also see Sloan, *NATO*, 199; and http://eeas.europa.eu/csdp/about-csdp /berlin/index_en.htm.

46. The text is available at www.consilium.europa.eu/uedocs/cmsUpload/78414%20 -%20EU-NATO%20Consultation,%20Planning%20and%20Operations.pdf.

47. See European Union, "Shaping of a Common Security and Defence Policy"; European Union, "A Secure Europe in a Better World: European Security Strategy," December 12, 2003, www.consilium.europa.eu/uedocs/cmsUpload/78367.pdf. I will discuss the European Security Strategy in more detail later in the chapter.

48. See Dinan, *Ever Closer Union*, 150–55; and http://ec.europa.eu/enlargement /policy/from-6-to-28-members/index_en.htm.

49. Dinan, *Ever Closer Union*, 154–55; and http://europa.eu/about-eu/eu-history /2000-2009/index_en.htm. The admission of Cyprus is a particularly interesting and instructive example of the weaknesses of EU enlargement policy. The island country's application for membership had long been stalled by the complex of Greek-Turkish disputes. During the accession negotiations, many in the EU hoped that the process might be used as leverage to ease tensions between Athens and Ankara, bring Turkey closer to the EU, and push the two sides on Cyprus toward resolution of their decades-old conflict. Instead, the EU ended up with the Greek half of the island rejecting a UN-brokered settlement already accepted by the Turkish side only days before formally joining the Union. Greece and Cyprus, as full EU members, then had a veto over all aspects of Turkey's negotiations with the EU for membership.

50. There are many sources of information on the OSCE's field operations. Each mission has its own section on the master OSCE website: www.osce.org. The best collection of basic information, without analysis or descriptive narrative, is OSCE, *Survey of OSCE Field Operations* (Vienna: OSCE, 2013), www.osce.org/cpc/74783?download=true. At their most numerous, nineteen OSCE missions were actively deployed and working in the field.

51. Victor-Yves Ghebali, "The OSCE's Long-Term Missions: A Creative Tool Under Challenge," *Helsinki Monitor*, no. 3 (2004): 202–19, at 211–13.

52. OSCE, *Survey of OSCE Field Operations*, 65. The head of the group was Ambassador Hans-Georg Wieck, who had considerable experience representing Germany in the USSR; Wieck to the author, 1999–2001.

53. OSCE, *Survey of OSCE Field Operations*, 85.

54. Former OSCE head of mission to the author, October 2015.

55. For the details of the Chechnya Assistance Group, see OSCE, *Survey of OSCE Field Operations*, 66–67. See also Ghebali, "OSCE's Long-Term Missions," 202–19,

esp. 212–13; and Jutta Stefan-Bastl, "The Austrian OSCE Chairmanship: Assessment and Outlook," *Helsinki Monitor*, no. 4 (2001): 257–71, esp. 263–64.

56. Stefan-Bastl, "Austrian OSCE Chairmanship," 263.

57. Ghebali, "OSCE's Long-Term Missions," 212–13.

58. OSCE, *Survey of OSCE Field Operations*, 16–17.

59. Stefan-Bastl, "Austrian OSCE Chairmanship," 260–61.

60. Ibid., 260; OSCE, *Survey of OSCE Field Operations*, 14–15.

61. Russian Federation delegation member to the author, October 2000.

62. Ghebali, "OSCE's Long-Term Missions."

63. Robert Frowick to the author, May 2002; OSCE, *OSCE Annual Report 2001* (Vienna: OSCE, 2001), 31–32; www.osce.org/skopje; Ghebali, "OSCE's Long-Term Missions," 213–14.

64. Chivis, "The Making of Macedonia," *Survival*, no. 2 (2008); Robert Frowick to the author, May 2002.

65. Stefan-Bastl, "Austrian OSCE Chairmanship," 264; Minsk Group negotiators to the author, May 2001.

66. For example, see OSCE, *Survey of OSCE Field Operations*, 44ff.

67. William H. Hill, "Making Istanbul a Reality: Moldova, Russia, and Withdrawal from Transdniestria," *Helsinki Monitor* 13, no. 2 (2002): 129–45; Victor-Yves Ghebali, "The Bucharest Meeting of the Ministerial Council," *Helsinki Monitor*, no. 2 (2002): 165.

68. OSCE, *Survey of OSCE Field Operations*, 79–80; www.osce.org/georgia; de Waal, *Caucasus*, 190; Hill, *Russia*, 39.

69. Stefan-Bastl, "Austrian OSCE Chairmanship," 269.

70. Ibid.; Ghebali, "Bucharest Ministerial."

71. Stefan-Bastl, "Austrian OSCE Chairmanship," 269–70.

72. Ghebali, "Bucharest Ministerial," 159–61.

73. OSCE, "Decision on Combating Terrorism and the Bucharest Plan of Action for Combating Terrorism, Ninth Meeting of the Ministerial Council," Bucharest, December 3–4, 2001, 7–13, www.osce.org/mc/40515?download=true.

74. Ibid.; Ghebali, "Bucharest Ministerial," 164–65.

75. OSCE, "OSCE Charter on Preventing and Combating Terrorism, Tenth Meeting of the Ministerial Council," Porto, December 6–7, 2002, 9–11, www.osce.org/mc/40521?download=true.

76. Andrei Zagorskii, "The OSCE in the Context of the Forthcoming EU and NATO Extensions," *Helsinki Monitor*, no. 3 (2002): 221–32.

77. Sergey Karaganov, "Russia, Europe, and New Challenges," *Russia in Global Affairs*, March 24, 2003, 2.

78. Vyacheslav Nikonov, "OSCE and Russia: Old Bridges, New Divisions," *Helsinki Monitor*, no. 1 (2003): 24; Nikonov, "Back to the Concert," *Russia in Global Affairs*, November 16, 2002.

79. Nikonov, "OSCE and Russia," 24.

80. Zagorskii, "OSCE in the Context," 231. The idea was first floated by Ambassador Wolfgang Ischinger in 2000; see OSCE, *OSCE Yearbook*, 2000 (Vienna: OSCE, 2000).

81. For the difficulties and disagreements encountered during the conduct of the war and the deployment of the Kosovo Force, see Ivo H. Daalder and Michael E. O'Hanlon, *Winning Ugly: NATO's War to Save Kosovo* (Washington. D.C.: Brookings Institution Press, 2001); and Wesley Clark, *Waging Modern War* (New York: PublicAffairs, 2011).

82. Sloan, *NATO*, 109–14.

83. Ibid., 108; see NATO, "An Alliance for the 21st Century," Washington Summit Communiqué, April 24, 1999, paragraph 11, www.nato.int/cps/en/natohq/official_texts _27440.htm?selectedLocale=en.

84. For this discussion, see Sloan, *NATO*, 111ff.; also see Robert Kagan, *Of Paradise and Power: America and Europe in the New World Order* (New York: Vintage, 2004); Ivo H. Daalder, "The End of Atlanticism," *Survival* 45, no. 2 (Summer 2003): 147–65; Philip H. Gordon, "Bridging the Atlantic Divide," *Foreign Affairs* 82, no. 1 (January–February 2003): 74–83; James Thomson, "US Interests and the Fate of the Alliance," *Survival* 45, no. 4 (Winter 2003–4): 207–20; Angela Stent and Lilia Shevtsova, "America, Russia, and Europe: A Realignment?" *Survival* 44, no. 4 (Winter 2002–3): 121–34; Jolyon Howorth, "France, Britain, and the Euro-Atlantic Crisis," *Survival* 45, no. 4 (Winter 2003–4): 173–91. Julia Smith, "Introduction: The Future of the European Union and the Transatlantic Relationship," *International Affairs* 79, no. 5 (2003): 943–49, introduces an entire issue on the subject in the title, including considerable discussion of the divergence of US and European views on threats, security, and the role of NATO.

85. Hans Binnendijk and Richard Kugler, "Transforming European Forces," *Survival* 44, no. 3 (Autumn 2002): 124; the authors of this article were instrumental in the development of Secretary of Defense Donald Rumsfeld's proposal for a NATO response force, to be composed largely of European assets; see Sloan, *NATO*, 125n38.

86. NATO, "Prague Summit Declaration, Issued by the Heads of State and Government Participating in the Meeting of the North Atlantic Council in Prague," Czech Republic, November 21, 2002, www.nato.int/cps/en/natohq/official_texts_19552.htm? selectedLocale=en; Sloan, *NATO*, 113.

87. NATO, "NATO Response Force," January 16, 2017, www.nato.int/cps/en /natohq/topics_49755.htm?selectedLocale=en#.

88. NATO, "Prague Summit Declaration."

89. United Nations Security Council, Resolution 1386 (2001), www.nato.int/isaf /topics/mandate/unscr/resolution_1386.pdf; on the International Security Assistance Force, see Sloan, *NATO*, 115; also see www.nato.int/cps/en/natohq/topics_8189.htm? selectedLocale=en.

90. Howorth, "France, Britain," 83–87; for an inside account of UK-US discussions on Iraq during 2002, see the memoir of the British ambassador, Christopher Meyer, *DC Confidential: The Controversial Memoirs of Britain's Ambassador to the US at the Time of 9/11 and the Iraq War* (London: Weidenfeld & Nicolson, 2005), 222–62.

91. See George W. Bush, *Decision Points* (New York: Crown, 2010), 244–47ff.; Condoleezza Rice, *No Higher Honor: A Memoir of My Years in Washington* (New York:

Crown, 2011), 183–89ff; Donald Rumsfeld, *Known and Unknown: A Memoir* (New York: Sentinel, 2011), 440–42; and Dick Cheney, with Liz Cheney, *In My Time: A Personal and Political Memoir* (New York: Threshhold Editions, 2011), 397–99.

92. Howorth, "France, Britain," 183.

93. This argument is made particularly well by Daalder, "End of Atlanticism." See also James Thomson, "US Interests and the Fate of the Alliance," *Survival* 45, no. 4 (Winter 2003–4): 207–20.

94. Stent, *Limits of Partnership*, 75–78; senior Russian diplomat and official to the author; Stent and Shevtsova, "America, Russia, and Europe," 121–24.

95. Stent, *Limits of Partnership*, 76, quoting memo from Richard Haass.

96. Stent, *Limits of Partnership*; Daalder, "End of Atlanticism," 149–50.

97. Information on the Permanent Joint Council sessions and their agendas is available at www.nato.int; a good basic review of growing Russia-NATO discussions and cooperation can be found at www.nato.int/nato_static/assets/pdf/pdf_2012_nio/20120705_0919-12-Fiche-Info-NATO-Russia_rus-RU.pdf.

98. Roxburgh, *Strongman*, 86. The four-part 2012 BBC-TV series *Putin, Russia, and the West*, which Roxburgh produced, has invaluable candid interviews with high-level officials from Russia and key Western countries on this and later key events in Russia–West relations from 2000 to 2011.

99. NATO, "NATO-Russia Relations: A New Quality—Declaration by Heads of State and Government of NATO Member States and the Russian Federation," May 28, 2002, www.nato.int/cps/en/natohq/official_texts_19572.htm?selectedLocale=en.

100. As quoted by Roxburgh, *Strongman*, 87.

101. See ibid., 88–91, for interviews and comments shedding light on skeptical attitudes within the Bush National Security Council.

102. See chapter 5. Also see Timothy Edmonds, "NATO and Its New Members," *Survival* 45, no. 3 (Autumn 2003): 145–66, esp. 155.

103. Stent, *Limits of Partnership*, 75–78; Roxburgh, *Strongman*, 87–94. Also see Terry Terriff, Stuart Croft, Elke Keahmann, Mark Webber, and Jolyon Howorth, "One In, All In? NATO's Next Enlargement," *International Affairs* 78, no. 4 (2002): 713–29.

104. NATO, "Prague Summit Declaration."

105. Roxburgh, *Strongman*, 94; Terriff et al., "One In," 717.

106. As quoted by Terriff et al., "One In," 717–18.

107. For example, see Daalder, "End of Atlanticism," 149–50; and Edmonds, "NATO," 145; also, conversations of US officials with the author. Even those American experts who advocated taking Russian views into consideration viewed NATO enlargement as a policy that could contribute to democratic reform not only in Central and Eastern Europe but also in Russia; see Mark Kramer, "NATO, the Baltic States, and Russia: A Framework for Sustainable Enlargement," *International Affairs* 78, no. 4 (2002): 731–56.

108. In particular, see Roxburgh's account of the lineup in Washington emerging from his interviews, *Strongman*, 88–89.

109. Daalder, "End of Atlanticism," pp. 149–150.

## 7. COLORS OF REVOLUTION, RIVALRY, AND DISCORD

1. US Department of State, "The National Security Strategy of the United States, Washington, September 2002," iii, www.state.gov/documents/organization/63562.pdf. Also see Bush's January 2002 State of the Union Address: White House, "The President's State of the Union Address," US Capitol, Washington, January 29, 2002, http://georgewbush-whitehouse.archives.gov/news/releases/2002/01/20020129-11.html.

2. George W. Bush, "Second Inaugural Address," January 20, 2005, www.npr.org/templates/story/story.php?storyId=4460172.

3. Ibid.

4. US Department of State, "The National Security Strategy of the United States of America, March 2006," iii, www.comw.org/qdr/fulltext/nss2006.pdf.

5. For a wrap-up retrospective, see Sophie Lambroscini, "Russia: Nord-Ost Hostage Crisis Brings Chechen War to Moscow's Doorstep," RFE/RL, October 22, 2003, www.rferl.org/content/article/1104744.html. For a more detailed study of the incident, see John B. Dunlop, *The 2002 Dubrovka and 2004 Beslan Hostage Crises: A Critique of Russian Counter-Terrorism* (Stuttgart: Ibidem-Verlag, 2006).

6. Dunlop, *2002 Dubrovka and 2004 Beslan Hostage Crises*; also see Steven Lee Myers, "Hostage Drama in Moscow: Russia Responds; Putin Vows Hunt for Terror Cells Around the World," *New York Times*, October 29, 2002, www.nytimes.com/2002/10/29/world/hostage-drama-moscow-russia-responds-putin-vows-hunt-for-terror-cells-around.html.

7. Angus Roxburgh, *The Strongman: Vladimir Putin and the Struggle for Russia* (New York: I. B. Tauris, 2012), 86–87; for accounts of Zakaev's travels and activities in North American and Europe and Russia's efforts to extradite him, see http://articles.chicagotribune.com/keyword/akhmed-zakayev. See also Ilyas Akhmadov and Nicholas Daniloff, *Chechnya's Secret Wartime Diplomacy* (New York: Palgrave Macmillan, 2013).

8. Fiona Hill and Clifford Gaddy, *Mr. Putin: Operative in the Kremlin*, 2nd ed. (Washington, D.C.: Brookings Institution Press, 2015), 301–2; Russian ambassador, senior State Department official to the author, September 1999–January 2002.

9. Both Hill and Gaddy and Roxburgh make this argument in greater detail, describing and demonstrating how Putin's suspicions and resentments accumulated and his conclusions changed; see Hill and Gaddy, *Mr. Putin*; and Roxburgh, *Strongman*.

10. Putin's speech to the nation, September 4, 2004; the Kremlin's English-language version can be found at http://archive.kremlin.ru/eng/speeches/2004/09/04/1958_type82912_76332.shtml.

11. For this paragraph, see especially the detailed accounts of the Khodorkovskii case given by Steven Lee Myers, *The New Tsar: The Rise and Reign of Vladimir Putin* (New York: Alfred A. Knopf, 2015), 223–42; Hill and Gaddy, *Mr. Putin*; David E. Hoffman, *The Oligarchs: Wealth and Power in the New Russia* (New York: PublicAffairs, 2001); and Peter Baker and Susan Glasser, *Kremlin Rising: Vladimir Putin's Russia and the End of Revolution* (New York: Simon & Schuster, 2005). Also from many personal conversations of the author with Russian officials.

12. Andrew Wilson, *Virtual Politics: Faking Democracy in the Post-Soviet World* (New Haven, Conn.: Yale University Press, 2005); Lucan A. Way and Steven Levitsky, *Competitive Authoritarianism: Hybrid Regimes after the Cold War*, Problems of International Politics (New York: Cambridge University Press, 2010). On the term "sovereign democracy," see "Transcript of a Speech by Deputy Head of the Administration of the President of the Russian Federation Vladislav Surkov to United Russia Activists," February 7, 2006. For commentary on the concept, see, for example, Ivan Krastev, "Sovereign Democracy Russian Style," *Open Democracy*, November 16, 2006, www.opendemocracy .net/globalization-institutions_government/sovereign_democracy_4104.jsp; see also Andrei Okara, "Sovereign Democracy: A New Russian Idea or a PR Project?" *Russia in Global Affairs* 5, no. 3 (July–September 2007).

13. For this overview of the Russian economy during the 2000s, I relied especially on various articles and briefings during the decade by Clifford Gaddy, Barry Ickes, Richard Ericson, and Anders Åslund. The majority of these are online, retrievable under the authors' names.

14. Hill and Gaddy, *Mr. Putin*, 317.

15. See chapter 6.

16. For the Helsinki "headline goal," see chapter 6.

17. Paul Cornish and Geoffrey Edwards, "The Strategic Culture of the European Union: A Progress Report," *International Affairs* 81, no. 4 (2005), 802–3.

18. Ibid., 804.

19. Ibid., 805; see also Barry R. Posen, "European Union Security and Defense Policy: Response to Unipolarity?" *Security Studies* 15, no. 2 (April–June 2006): 181–82; and Michael Merlingen, *EU Security Policy: What It Is, How It Works, Why It Matters* (Boulder, Colo.: Lynne Rienner, 2012), 79.

20. Cornish and Edwards, "Strategic Culture," quoting Council of the European Union, "Capability Improvement Chart II/2004," Brussels, November 17, 2004.

21. See European Defense Agency (EDA) at https://europa.eu/european-union /about-eu/agencies/eda_en; Cornish and Edwards, "Strategic Culture," 805; for the Council action establishing the EDA, see http://europa.eu/about-eu/agencies/regulatory _agencies_bodies/security_agencies/eda/index_en.htm; http://eur-lex.europa.eu/legal -content/en/TXT/PDF/?uri=CELEX:32004E0551&from=en.

22. See European External Action Service at https://europa.eu/european-union /about-eu/institutions-bodies/eeas_en; Cornish and Edwards, "Strategic Culture," 805–6.

23. Cornish and Edwards, "Strategic Culture," 811; Merlingen, *EU Security Policy*, 204–5.

24. Merlingen, *EU Security Policy*, 205.

25. European Union, "European Defense: NATO/EU Consultation, Planning, and Operations, European Council," December 2003, www.consilium.europa.eu/uedocs /cmsUpload/78414%20-%20EU-NATO%20Consultation,%20Planning%20and%20 Operations.pdf.

26. For a particularly good, succinct description of the national positions of the major EU powers on ESDP during this period, see Posen, "European Union Security," 166–73.

27. Merlingen, *EU Security Policy*, 129. For basic information on ESDP missions, see also http://eeas.europa.eu/csdp/missions-and-operations/index_en.htm.

28. Merlingen, *EU Security Policy*, 133–34. Also see Cornish and Edwards, "Strategic Culture," 807.

29. Merlingen, *EU Security Policy*, 131.

30. See http://eeas.europa.eu/csdp/missions-and-operations/index_en.htm; Cornish and Edwards, "Strategic Culture," 807; and Merlingen, *EU Security Policy*, 132ff.

31. See, for example, the March 2004 EU declaration on combating terrorism, www.consilium.europa.eu/uedocs/cmsUpload/DECL-25.3.pdf.

32. For a good example of such dissenting opinions, see Mette Eilstrup Sangiovanni, "Why a Common Security and Defense Policy Is Bad for Europe," *Survival* 45, no. 3 (Autumn 2003): 193–206.

33. European Union, *A Secure Europe in a Better World: European Security Strategy* (Brussels: European Union, 2003), www.consilium.europa.eu/uedocs/cmsUpload /78367.pdf. See also the European External Action Service website, www.eeas.europa .eu/csdp/about-csdp/european-security-strategy/. For a discussion of the security strategy, see, Steven Everts and Daniel Keohane, "The European Convention and EU Foreign Policy: Learning from Failure," *Survival* 45, no 3 (Autumn 2003): 167–86; and Cornish and Edwards, "Strategic Culture," 809–14.

34. European Union, *A Secure Europe*, 5.

35. Ibid., 6.

36. Ibid., 9.

37. For a discussion of the origins and content of the ENP, see Karen E. Smith, "The Outsiders: The European Neighborhood Policy," *International Affairs* 81, no. 5 (2005): 757–73. See also "European Neighborhood Policy (ENP)," http://eeas.europa. eu/enp/index_en.htm.

38. See European Union, "Communication from the Commission to the Council and the European Parliament: Wider Europe—Neighborhood: A New Framework for Relations with Our Eastern and Southern Neighbors, Brussels, 11.2.2003, COM (2003) 104 final," 3–4, http://eeas.europa.eu/enp/documents/strategy-papers/index _en.htm.

39. Ibid., 4.

40. Romano Prodi, "A Wider Europe: A Proximity Policy as the Key to Stability," speech to the sixth ECSA-World Conference, Brussels, December 5–6, 2002, SPEECH/02/619, 3, as quoted by Smith, "Outsiders," 763.

41. See European Union, "European Neighborhood Policy (ENP),"http://eeas. europa.eu/enp/about-us/index_en.htm; and Smith, "Outsiders," 760.

42. European Union, "Communication from the Commission: European Neighborhood Policy—Strategy Paper, Brussels, 12.5.2004, COM(2004) 373 final," 4, http://eeas .europa.eu/enp/documents/strategy-papers/index_en.htm; http://eeas.europa.eu/russia /common_spaces/index_en.htm.

43. Smith, "Outsiders," 765ff.; European Union, "Communication from the Commission"; European Union, "European Neighborhood Policy (ENP): How Does It Work?"http://eeas.europa.eu/enp/how-it-works/index_en.htm.

44. Clelia Rontoyanni, "So Far, So Good? Russia and the ESDP," *International Affairs* 78, no. 4 (2002): 813–30; see also Merlingen, *EU Security Policy*, 226–28.

45. See, for example, Vladimir Lukin, "The Russian Bridge over the Atlantic," *Russia in Global Affairs*, November 16, 2002.

46. Merlingen, *EU Security Policy*, 227.

47. See European Union, "European External Action Service: Russia–Kaliningrad," http://eeas.europa.eu/russia/kaliningrad_en.htm.

48. For example, see Merlingen, *EU Security Policy*, 224. During my tenure as head of the OSCE Mission to Moldova, I observed this process personally. I was closely acquainted with and worked closely with the EU representatives for Moldova and the South Caucasus appointed in 2003 and 2005. I was also frequently invited to sit in on EU meetings and heard the tone of debate change with events and the addition of new members.

49. NATO, "Prague Summit Declaration, Issued by the Heads of State and Government Participating in the Meeting of the North Atlantic Council in Prague, Czech Republic," November 21, 2002, paragraph 4, www.nato.int/cps/en/natohq/official_texts _19552.htm?selected . . .

50. On the Prague decisions, see chapter 6. For typical commentary and debate on NATO's growing global role, see, Steven Larrabbee and Francois Heisbourg, "How Global a Role Can and Should NATO Pursue?" *NATO Review*, 2003 (Interpreting Prague), www.nato.int/docu/review/2003/Interpreting-Prague/global-rol . . .

51. For a typical and good discussion at that time of the effects of the Iraq war on the transatlantic relationship, see William Drozdiak, "The North Atlantic Drift," *Foreign Affairs* 84, no. 1 (January–February 2005): 88–98.

52. Henry Kissinger and Lawrence Summers (co-chairs), and Charles Kupchan (project director), "Renewing the Atlantic Partnership," Report of an Independent Task Force Sponsored by the Council on Foreign Relations, Washington, 2004, 1.

53. See the discussion in chapter 6 on the 2000 Condoleezza Rice *Foreign Affairs* article and the initial approach of the Bush administration.

54. Drozdiak, "North Atlantic Drift," 88.

55. For a timeline and description of NATO's involvement in Afghanistan, see www.nato.int/cps/en/natohq/topics_8189.htm.

56. For the history of the NATO Mission "Resolute Support" in Afghanistan, see the NATO website for the mission, https://www.rs.nato.int/about-us/history.aspx; see also Joseph J. Collins, *Understanding War in Afghanistan* (Washington, D.C.: National Defense University Press, 2011), esp. 63–70.

57. Collins, *Understanding War*, 72–73, asserts that various Taliban factions spent 2002–5 in rebuilding their strength and by 2005 were engaged in coordinated operations against the Karzai government. Collins dates the rise in US and ISAF casualties from 2004.

58. Ryan C. Hendrickson, "NATO's Secretaries General: Organizational Leadership in Shaping Alliance Strategy," in *NATO in Search of a Vision*, ed. Gulnur Aybet and Rebecca R. Moore (Washington, D.C.: Georgetown University Press, 2010), 69.

59. See NATO, "NATO and Afghanistan," www.nato.int/cps/en/natohq/topics_8189 .htm.

60. Ibid.

61. Hendrickson, "NATO's Secretaries General," 69–70.

62. For the NATO action, see NATO, "Statement on Iraq, Issued by the Heads of State and Government Participating in the Meeting of the North Atlantic Council in Istanbul," June 28, 2004, www.nato.int/cps/en/natohq/official_texts_21025.htm? selectedLocale=en; for the UN Security Council resolution, see www.un.org/depts /unmovic/new/documents/resolutions/s-res-1546.pdf.

63. For a timeline and basic history of NATO's involvement in Iraq, see NATO, "NATO's Assistance to Iraq," www.nato.int/cps/en/natohq/topics_51978.htm.

64. NATO, "The Istanbul Declaration: Our Security in a New Era, Issued by the Heads of State and Government Participating in the Meeting of the North Atlantic Council in Istanbul," June 28, 2004," www.nato.int/cps/en/natohq/official_texts_21026 .htm?selectedLocale=en.

65. NATO, "The Euro-Atlantic Partnership: Refocusing and Renewal," June 23, 2004, www.nato.int/cps/en/natohq/official_texts_21015.htm?selectedLocale=en.

66. NATO, "Report on the Partnership Action Plan against Terrorism," June 23, 2004, www.nato.int/cps/en/natohq/official_texts_21016.htm?selectedLocale=en.

67. See NATO, "Istanbul Summit Communiqué, Issued by the Heads of State and Government Participating in the Meeting of the North Atlantic Council," June 28, 2004, www.nato.int/cps/en/natohq/official_texts_21023.htm?selectedLocale=en. See also Robert F. Simmons Jr., "Ten Years of the Euro-Atlantic Partnership Council: A Personal Reflection," *NATO Review*, 2004 (Partnerships Old and New), www.nato.int/docu /review/2007/Partnerships_Old_New/10_years_NATO_Atlantic_council/EN/index.htm.

68. See NATO, "A More Ambitious and Expanded Framework for the Mediterranean Dialogue," June 28, 2004, www.nato.int/cps/en/natohq/official_texts_59357 .htm?selectedLocale=en. See also Nicola de Santis, "Opening to the Mediterranean and the Broader Middle East," *NATO Review*, 2004 (Interpreting Istanbul), www.nato .int/docu/review/2004/Interpreting-Istanbul/Opening-Mediterranean-Middle-East/EN /index.htm.

69. See NATO, "Istanbul Cooperation Initiative,: June 28. 2004, www.nato.int/cps /en/natohq/official_texts_21017.htm?selectedLocale=en; and de Santis, "Opening to the Mediterranean."

70. Gulnur Aybet, "Towards a New Transatlantic Consensus," *NATO Review*, 2004 (Interpreting Istanbul), www.nato.int/docu/review/2004/Interpreting-Istanbul/New -transatlantic-consensus/EN/index.htm.

71. For a discussion of the effects on NATO of the addition of these new members from Central and Eastern Europe, see, Roger E. Kanet, "The 'New' Members and Future Enlargement," in *NATO in Search of a Vision*, ed. Gulnur Aybet and Rebecca R. Moore (Washington, D.C.: Georgetown University Press, 2010), 153–74.

72. James L. Jones, "Transforming NATO's Military Structures," *NATO Review*, 2004 (Taking NATO's Partnerships Forward), www.nato.int/docu/review/2004/partnership -forward/Transform . . .

73. For a quick review of NATO operations, see Adam Kobieracki, "NATO's Evolving Operations," *NATO Review*, 2004 (Before Istanbul), www.nato.int/docu

/review/2004/Before-Istanbul/NATO-evolvi . . .; see also James Pardew and Christopher Bennett, "NATO's Evolving Operations," *NATO Review*, 2006 (Operations Old and New), www.nato.int/docu/review/2006/Operation-Old-New/evolving_operations /EN/index.htm.

74. For an excellent example of the kind of detailed study and sophisticated expert and policy analysis devoted to the subject during the mid-2000s, see Michele A. Flournoy and Julianne Smith, *European Defense Integration: Bridging the Gap between Strategy and Capabilities* (Washington, D.C.: Center for Strategic and International Studies, 2005), available at www.csis.org.

75. NATO, "Comprehensive Political Guidance, Endorsed by NATO Heads of State and Government," November 29, 2006, paragraph 11, www.nato.int/cps/en/natohq /official_texts_56425.htm?selected . . .

76. Ibid., paragraph 16.

77. Jaap de Hoop Scheffer, "Reflections on the Riga Summit," *NATO Review*, 2006 (Road to Riga), www.nato.int/docu/review/2006/Road_Riga/reflections_Riga . . .

78. NATO, "Riga Summit Declaration, Issued by the Heads of State and Government Participating in the Meeting of the North Atlantic Council in Riga," November 29, 2006, paragraph 2, www.nato.int/cps/en/natohq/official_texts_37920.htm?selected . . .

79. De Hoop Scheffer, "Reflections."

80. Pierre Lallouche, "Where's NATO Headed?" *NATO Review*, 2006 (Road to Riga), www.nato.int/docu/review/2006/Road_Riga/where_is_headed/E . . .

81. John R. Schmidt, "Last Alliance Standing? NATO After 9/11," *Washington Quarterly* 30, no. 1 (Winter 2006–7): 105.

82. For an enumeration, timeline, and description of NATO-Russia activities, see NATO, "NATO's Relations with Russia," www.nato.int/nato_static/assets/pdf/pdf_2012 _nio/20120705_0919-12-Fiche-Info-NATO-Russia_rus-RU.pdf. See also Andrei Kelin, "NATO-Russia Cooperation to Counterterrorism," *NATO Review*, 2005 (Combating Terrorism), www.nato.int/docu/review/2005/Comating_Terrorism/NATO-R . . .

83. Kelin, "NATO-Russia Cooperation"; NATO, "NATO-Russia Action Plan on Terrorism," December 9, 2004, www.nato.int/cps/en/natohq/official_texts_21003.htm? selected . . .

84. NATO, "Statement: Meeting of the NATO-Russia Council at the Level of Ministers of Defense," June 9, 2005, www.nato.int/cps/en/natohq/official_texts_21728 .htm?selectedLocale=en.

85. It is not my purpose in this narrative to go into a detailed discussion of either the scientific and technical arguments surrounding missile defense or the details of US bilateral negotiations with the Russians. Both Angela E. Stent, *The Limits of Partnership: US–Russian Relations in the Twenty-First Century* (Princeton, N.J.: Princeton University Press, 2014), 150–58 and elsewhere, and Roxburgh, *Strongman*, esp. 200–207, have excellent synopses of the political discussions between Russia and the West on the subject, and how disagreement on the issue affected relations.

86. NATO, "Riga Summit Declaration," paragraph 25.

87. NATO, "NATO's Relations with Russia," 3.

88. Lallouche, "Where's NATO Headed?"

89. For example, in my own personal experience working as the head of the OSCE Mission to Moldova, in 1999 the Finnish EU presidency attempted to interest its EU colleagues to undertake greater involvement and activity in Moldova, in particular in resolving the Transdniestrian conflict. EU leaders at the Helsinki EU Summit were simply not interested. However, some four to five years later, during the 2003 Dutch and 2004 Bulgarian OSCE chairmanships, I was bombarded with constant EU inquiries, requests, and visits—a drastic contrast with 1999.

90. De Hoop Scheffer to the author, January 2003. For a more comprehensive statement of the Dutch priorities, see Jaap de Hoop Scheffer, "Address of the Dutch Chairman-in-Office to the OSCE Permanent Council (13 January 2003)," *Helsinki Monitor*, no. 1 (2003): 7–10.

91. For a detailed account and analysis of the negotiation and process of conflict resolution in Moldova during 2003, see William H. Hill, *Russia, the Near Abroad, and the West: Lessons from the Moldova-Transdniestria Conflict* (Washington, D.C. and Baltimore, Md.: Woodrow Wilson Center Press and Johns Hopkins University Press, 2012).

92. Ibid. Also, senior Moldovan diplomat to the author, October 2008.

93. For an excellent short account of the Rose Revolution, see Thomas de Waal, *The Caucasus: An Introduction* (New York: Oxford University Press, 2010), 190–94. Like many of my colleagues in various countries in the CIS, I watched film of the dramatic events from the Georgian parliament broadcast over Russian television and can attest to the visceral excitement prompted by the events. For a good contemporaneous review of the Rose Revolution's events, see International Crisis Group, *Georgia: What Now?* ICG Europe 151 (Brussels: International Crisis Group, 2003).

94. For the border-monitoring operation, see www.osce.org/georgia-closed; and OSCE, *Survey of OSCE Field Operations* (Vienna: OSCE, 2013), 79–82, www.osce .org/cpc/74783?download=true.

95. Hill, *Russia*, 39; de Waal, *Caucasus*, 190.

96. De Waal, *Caucasus*, 195; Russian MFA official to the author, June 2004.

97. De Waal, *Caucasus*, 201–3 and ff.

98. Ibid., 203–5; Stent, *Limits of Partnership*, 109–10.

99. For the Maastricht meeting, see the OSCE website: www.osce.org/node/58689; see also Victor-Yves Ghebali, "The 11th Meeting of the OSCE Ministerial Council: Political Deadlock and Institutional Change," *Helsinki Monitor*, no. 1 (2004): 1–12. For the Kozak Memorandum, see Hill, *Russia*; the text is on 207–20.

100. For a detailed discussion of OSCE peacekeeping and the Dutch/OSCE proposal for Moldova in 2003, see Hill, *Russia*, 93–97, and ff. For a contemporaneous discussion of OSCE peacekeeping in general, see Branislav Milinkovic, "OSCE Peacekeeping: Still Waiting to Perform!" *Helsinki Monitor*, no. 3 (2004): 193–201.

101. See Hill, *Russia*, 40–41.

102. For the gist of the Western criticisms, see the chairman's perception statement at Maastricht, www.osce.org/node/58689; and Ghebali, "11th Meeting," 3–4.

103. OSCE/ODIHR and Council of Europe, "Russian Federation Presidential Election, 14 March 2004, International Election Observation Mission," Statement

of Preliminary Findings and Conclusions, 1, www.osce.org/odihr/elections/russia /25533?download=true.

104. Quoted by Thomas Ambrosio, *Authoritarian Backlash: Russian Resistance to Democratization in the Former Soviet Union* (Burlington, Vt.: Ashgate, 2009), 56.

105. Stent, *Limits of Partnership*, 140–47; Russian ambassador and deputy minister to the author, December 2005 and March 2006.

106. There are innumerable accounts of the Orange Revolution. The narrative here draws from, among others, Andrew Wilson, *Ukraine's Orange Revolution* (New Haven, Conn.: Yale University Press, 2005); Anders Åslund and Michael McFaul, eds., *Revolution in Orange: The Origins of Ukraine's Democratic Breakthrough* (Washington, D.C.: Carnegie Endowment for International Peace, 2006); and Stent, *Limits of Partnership*, 112–16.

107. OSCE, "Statement of Preliminary Findings and Conclusions, International Election Observation Mission, Presidential Election (Second Round)," Ukraine, November 21, 2004, www.osce.org/odihr/elections/ukraine/16565?download=true.

108. Stent, *Limits of Partnership*, 115–16; I personally heard similar allegations from Russian representatives in the OSCE, Ukraine, and Moldova during the course of 2005–2006. I also witnessed the Ukrainian OSCE representative handing out orange buttons in December 2004.

109. Stent, *Limits of Partnership*, 116.

110. Ibid., 116–18; also see OSCE, "Kyrgyz Republic Parliamentary Elections, 27 February & 13 March 2005, OSCE/ODIHR Election Observation Mission, Final Report" at http://www.osce.org/odihr/elections/kyrgyzstan/14835?download=true; and International Crisis Group, "Kyrgyzstan Report," 2005, at https://www.crisisgroup.org /europe-central-asia/central-asia/kyrgyzstan/kyrgyzstan-after-revolution.

111. Fiona Hill and Kevin Jones, "Fear of Democracy or Revolution: The Reaction to Andijon," *Washington Quarterly* 29, no. 3 (Summer 2006): 111–25.

112. For a discussion of the policy trade-offs and the debate within the US administration over the response, see Stent, *Limits of Partnership*, 118–22.

113. See Roxburgh, *Strongman*, 145–47; Stent, *Limits of Partnership*, 86–87; and Sarah E. Mendelson and Theodore P. Gerber, "Soviet Nostalgia: Impediment to Russian Democratization," *Washington Quarterly* 29, no. 1 (Winter 2005–2006): 83–96.

114. Victor-Yves Ghebali, "The 2005 Ljubljana Ministerial Council Meeting," *Helsinki Monitor*, no. 1 (2006): 4–18. For various documents and decisions, see www.osce .org/node/58822.

115. See Arie Bloed, "CIS Presidents Attack the Functioning of the OSCE," *Helsinki Monitor*, no. 3 (2004): 220–22.

116. See Arie Bloed, "CIS Countries Continue to Push for a Reform of the OSCE," *Helsinki Monitor*, no. 4 (2004): 299–302; and Vladimir Socor, "Commentary: OSCE Pressured by Russian-Led 'Reform' Campaign," *Eurasia Daily Monitor* 1, no. 93 (September 26, 2004), www.jamestown.org/single/?tx_ttnews[tt_news]=26910&no_ca . . .

117. Victor-Yves Ghebali, "The Russian Factor in OSCE Crisis: A Fair Examination," *Helsinki Monitor*, no. 3 (2005): 184–87.

118. Vladimir Chizhov, "The Thirtieth Anniversary of the Helsinki Final Act and the Problems of the OSCE," *Helsinki Monitor*, no. 3 (2005): 177.

119. Andrei Zagorski, "Make the OSCE Institutions Less Dependent on Politics, Not More," *Helsinki Monitor*, no. 3 (2005): 211.

120. OSCE, "Common Purpose: Towards a More Effective OSCE—Final Report and Recommendations of the Panel of Eminent Persons on Strengthening the Effectiveness of the OSCE," June 27, 2005, www.osce.org/cio/15805?download=true. For description and analysis of the Eminent Persons Report and the debate over OSCE reform at the time, see Arie Bloed, "Debates on the 'Reform' of the OSCE Speeded Up with the Report of the Panel of Eminent Persons," *Helsinki Monitor*, no. 3 (2005): 243–44; and Arie Bloed, "OSCE Reform Requires Bold Decisions," *Helsinki Monitor*, no. 4 (2005): 332–35. For commentary on and explanation of the work of the panel, see the remarks of one of its members: Wolfgang Zellner, "Interview with Ambassador Wilhelm Hoynck, Former Secretary General of the OSCE," *Helsinki Monitor: Security and Human Rights*, no. 4 (2007): 271–74. Speaking more than two years after issuance of the report, Hoynck acknowledges that the weaknesses in the OSCE also may be attributed considerably to the preference "by key Euro-Atlantic players" for other venues to address bilateral and multilateral political issues.

121. Hans Haekkerup, "Russia, the OSCE, and Post–Cold War European Security," *Cambridge Review of International Affairs* 18, no. 3 (October 2005): 371.

122. Victor-Yves Ghebali, "Growing Pains at the OSCE: The Rise and Fall of Russia's Pan-European Expectations," *Cambridge Review of International Affairs* 18, no. 3 (October 2005): 387–88.

123. Wolfgang Zellner, "Russia and the OSCE: From High Hopes to Disillusionment," *Cambridge Review of International Affairs* 18, no. 3 (October 2005): 398.

## 8. RUSSIA LEAVES THE WEST

1. For a good descriptive narrative of the process that produced the draft EU constitution, see Desmond Dinan, *Europe Recast: A History of European Union* (Boulder, Colo.: Lynne Rienner, 2014), 270–75; see also Finn Laursen, ed., *The Rise and Fall of the EU's Constitutional Treaty* (Leiden: Brill, 2008).

2. EU heads of state considerably jumped the gun by agreeing to appoint High Representative Javier Solana as EU foreign minister as soon as the treaty was ratified. Alas, Solana never got the title, although he acted as de facto foreign minister for years. See http://europa.eu/about-eu/eu-history/2000-2009/2004/index_en.htm.

3. Dinan, *Europe Recast*, 307–8. On reasons for the rejection and how the EU proceeded afterward, also see Steven Philip Kramer, "The End of French Europe?" *Foreign Affairs* 85, no. 4 (July–August 2006): 126–38; Richard Whitman, "No and After: Options for Europe," *International Affairs* 81, no. 4 (2005): 673–87; and Robin Niblett, "Europe Inside Out," *Washington Quarterly* 29, no. 1 (Winter 2005–6): 41–59.

4. Kramer, End of French Europe?" 131–34.

5. Whitman, "No and After," 683.

6. See esp. Dinan, *Europe Recast*, 308–10.

7. Ibid., 310–12; also see http://ec.europa.eu/archives/lisbon_treaty/glance/index_en.htm.

8. For the full text of the Treaty of Lisbon, see http://ec.europa.eu/archives/lisbon_treaty/full_text/index_en.htm. Also see Paul Craig, *The Lisbon Treaty: Law, Politics, and Treaty Reform* (Oxford: Oxford University Press, 2013); and David Phinnemore, *The Treaty of Lisbon: Origins and Negotiation* (Basingstoke, UK: Palgrave Macmillan, 2013).

9. Dinan, *Europe Recast*, 305–6; and see http://europa.eu/about-eu/eu-history /2000-2009/index_en.htm.

10. See, for example, Gideon Rachman, "The End of Enlargement," *Washington Quarterly* 29, no. 3 (Summer 2006): 51–56.

11. Ibid., 54.

12. Niblett, "Europe Inside Out," 48–49.

13. See Pew Global Surveys, 2002–2006, "GMFUS Transatlantic Trends" for 2002–2006 at http://trends.gmfus.org/archives/; and Philip H. Gordon, "The End of the Bush Revolution," *Foreign Affairs* 85, no. 4 (July–August 2006): 79–80.

14. See chapter 7.

15. David Espo, "Cheney Visits Lithuania, Touts Democracy," *Washington Post*, May 3, 2006, www.washingtonpost.com/wp-dyn/content/article/2006/05/03/AR2006050301365 .html.

16. Anatol Lieven, "Putin Versus Cheney," *New York Times*, May 11, 2006, www.nytimes .com/2006/05/11/opinion/11iht-edlieven.html.

17. "Vice President Cheney to Travel to Lithuania, Kazakhstan, Croatia," April 19, 2006, http://iipdigital.usembassy.gov/st/english/article/2006/04/200604191237181cjsam ohto.1986353.html#axzz3W4nozXHy.

18. For a description and analysis of the BTC project by some of its most ardent advocates, see S. Frederick Starr and Svante Cornell, eds., "The Baku-Tbilisi-Ceyhan Pipeline: Oil Window to the West," Central Asia Caucasus Institute, Silk Road Studies Program, 2005. For background information on the pipeline from one of the companies in the consortium, see www.bp.com/en_az/caspian/operationsprojects /pipelines/BTC.html. For a discussion of possible shipment of natural gas, see www .naturalgaseurope.com/baku-tbilisi-ceyhans-gas-pipeline. Some observers and officials who worked in the region have commented on how the perceived geopolitical advantages of the project shifted over time in internal government discussions. At first the initiative was seen as benefiting Turkey to compensate for losses suffered as the result of sanctions against Iraq. Subsequently, advocates stressed that the pipeline would help isolate Iran by preventing the flow of Caspian energy south to the Persian Gulf. Finally, as Moscow was perceived a growing danger, the anti-Russian features of the project came to the fore.

19. For cases of such policy analysis, see, Keith C. Smith, *Russia and European Energy Security: Divide and Dominate* (Washington, D.C.: Center for Strategic and International Studies, 2008); and Keith C. Smith, *Managing the Challenge of Russian Energy Policies: Recommendations for US and EU Leadership* (Washington, D.C.: Center for Strategic and International Studies, 2010).

20. See American Enterprise Institute, "NATO and European Energy Security," March 28, 2008, www.aei.org/publication/nato-and-european-energy-security/.

21. This section adopts the title used by the well-known Russian analyst Dmitrii Trenin in his 2006 *Foreign Affairs* article of the same name. Some experts may question whether post–Cold War Russia was ever really part of the "West," particularly if this term is used to describe the web of security and political institutions based in Brussels and heavily influenced by Washington. Irrespective of Russia's actual position or degree of inclusion in the West, I believe that Trenin uses the title to characterize a dramatic change in attitude and direction in Russia's leadership about this time. I agree with much of his analysis and thus borrow his title to emphasize this agreement.

22. Angus Roxburgh, *The Strongman: Vladimir Putin and the Struggle for Russia* (New York: I. B. Tauris, 2012), 146–47.

23. Angela E. Stent, *The Limits of Partnership: US–Russian Relations in the Twenty-First Century* (Princeton, N.J.: Princeton University Press, 2014), 144–47.

24. Vladimir Putin, "Annual Address to the Federal Assembly," May 10, 2006, http://archive.kremlin.ru/eng/speeches/2006/05/10/1823_type70029type82912_105566.shtml.

25. See "Transcript of a Speech by Deputy Head of the Administration of the President of the Russian Federation Vladislav Surkov to United Russia Activists," February 7, 2006, in which Surkov publicly coined the phrase "sovereign democracy." Many Western experts and analysts profess to find Surkov's formulations turgid, unclear, self-serving, and not really serious political philosophy. Irrespective of the merits of these criticisms, it is clear that Surkov was speaking for Putin and making a serious announcement of Russia's determination to follow its own path of political development. For various Western treatments of the term, see Stent, *Limits of Partnership*, 141–42; Fiona Hill and Clifford Gaddy, *Mr. Putin: Operative in the Kremlin*, 2nd ed. (Washington, D.C.: Brookings Institution Press, 2015), 68; and Roxburgh, *Strongman*, 144–45.

26. Putin, "Annual Address to the Federal Assembly, May 10, 2006," op. cit. See also Nick Paton Walsh and Ewen MacAskill, "Putin Lashes Out at 'Wolf-Like' America," *The Guardian*, May 11, 2006, www.theguardian.com/world/2006/may/11/russia.usa.

27. For a good description and analysis of the political context of the "comrade wolf" riposte, see Stent, *The Limits of Partnership*, 138–41; also Roxburgh, *Strongman*, 159–61.

28. For a brief, authoritative account of the January 2006 natural gas crisis, see Jim Nichol, Steve Woehrel, and Bernard Gelb, "Russia's Cut-Off of Natural Gas to Ukraine: Context and Implications," CRS Report for Congress, Congressional Research Service, February 15, 2006, www.au.af.mil/au/awc/awcgate/crs/rs22378.pdf; also see Roxburgh, *Strongman*, 154–56.

29. For example, Moscow cut off natural gas deliveries to Lithuania in 1993 to press Vilnius to be more forthcoming on a number of bilateral issues. Russian gas deliveries were cut off to Moldova in February 2000, while I was living in Chisinau, over issues related to the Transdniestrian conflict settlement process. For the European reaction in 2006, see Andrew E. Kramer, "Russia Cuts Off Gas to Ukraine in Cost Dispute," *New York Times*, January 2, 2006, www.nytimes.com/2006/01/02/international/europe/02russia.html?pagewanted=all; and Tom Parfitt, "Russia Turns Off Supplies

to Ukraine in Payment Row, and EU Feels the Chill," *The Guardian*, January 2, 2006, www.theguardian.com/world/2006/jan/02/russia.ukraine. On European concerns, see Nichol, Woehrel, and Gelb, "Russia's Cut-Off," 4–5.

30. For a Georgian account of the background and details of the dispute, see Mamuka Tsereteli, "Banned in Russia: The Politics of Georgian Wine," *Central Asia-Caucasus Analyst*, April 19, 2006, www.cacianalyst.org/publications/analytical-articles /item/10801-analytical-articles-caci-analyst-2006-4-19-art-10801.html. I was a resident of Chisinau at this time and derive the information in this paragraph from discussions with Georgian, Moldovan, and Ukrainian officials.

31. Nichol, Woehrel, and Gelb, "Russia's Cut-Off," 5–6.

32. Vladimir A. Orlov and Miriam Fugfogosh, "The G-8 Strelna Summit and Russia's National Power," *Washington Quarterly* 29, no. 3 (Summer 2006): 35–48. See also Stent, *Limits of Partnership*, 143–44.

33. Stent, *Limits of Partnership*, 145–46. In his recollection of senior-level United States–Russia meetings at this time and later interviews with participants, Roxburgh paints a picture of an American position that had already hardened considerably by this time, with considerable frustration on the Russian side. See Roxburgh, *Strongman*, 158–64.

34. See Roxburgh, *Strongman*, 162–67.

35. Ibid., 173–81; Stent, *Limits of Partnership*, 145–46.

36. Roxburgh, *Strongman*, 178; the value judgment is mine.

37. Dmitri Trenin, "Russia Leaves the West," *Foreign Affairs* 85, no. 4 (July–August 2006): 87.

38. Stent, *Limits of Partnership*, 147 and ff.

39. Roxburgh, *Strongman*, 196–97.

40. Senior OSCE official to the author, March 2007.

41. Vladimir Putin, "Speech and Following Discussion at the Munich Conference on Security Policy," February 10, 2007, http://archive.kremlin.ru/eng/speeches/2007/02 /10/0138_type82912type82914type82917type84779_118123.shtml. For a discussion and analysis, see esp. Roxburgh, *Strongman*, 196–200; Stent, *Limits of Partnership*, 147–48; and Hill and Gaddy, *Mr. Putin*, 316.

42. Stent, *Limits of Partnership*, 148.

43. Alexander Rahr, "Germany and Russia: A Special Relationship," *Washington Quarterly* 30, no. 2 (Spring 2007): 137–45.

44. Hill and Gaddy, *Mr. Putin*, 317.

45. Roxburgh provides a particularly interesting insider's account of the political theater involved in the succession process; see Roxburgh, *Strongman*, 208–15.

46. One leading Russian political analyst described Zubkov to me as "the one man Putin trusts to watch his back," and thus one Putin could trust not to be tempted to misuse the constitutional position of the prime minister as next in line to the presidency. Zubkov and his son-in-law, Anatoliy Serdiukov (minister of defense at this time), had also been instrumental in the prosecution of Khodorkovskii and thus had Putin's confidence in controlling potentially ambitious members of the elite during the transition period.

47. See "Extraordinary Conference of the States Parties to the CFE Treaty," Vienna, June 12–15, 2007, www.osce.org/fsc/60370; see also Ministry of Foreign Affairs of the Russian Federation, "Press Release: Convening an Extraordinary Conference to Discuss CFE Treaty," May 28, 2007, www.mid.ru/brp_4.nsf/e78a48070f128a7b4325699900 5bcbb3/2e0b88fe13533efbc32572ea00419155; and NATO, "NATO Response to Russian Announcement of Intent to Suspend Obligations under the CFE Treaty," June 16, 2007, www.nato.int/docu/pr/2007/p07-085e.html.

48. "Statement by Russia's Ministry of Foreign Affairs Regarding Suspension by Russian Federation of Treaty on Conventional Armed Forces in Europe (CFE Treaty)," December 12, 2007, www.mid.ru/brp_4.nsf/e78a48070f128a7b43256999005bcbb3 /10da6dd509e4d164c32573af004cc4be?OpenDocument.

49. The literature on missile defense is immense. This study does not attempt to deal with the technical and scientific aspects of the debate, except where such questions are directly reflected in the political policy debate over the subject. For two decent short treatments of how the issue played out in US-Russian relations and European security affairs, see Stent, *Limits of Partnership*, 153–58; and Roxburgh, *Strongman*, 200–207. For a good brief discussion of how the issue appeared at the time to the senior-level political leadership, see a piece by former undersecretary of defense Walter B. Slocombe, "Europe, Russia, and Missile Defense" *Survival* 50, no. 2 (April–May 2008): 19–24. For a representative example of informed Russian commentary on the subject, see Aleksei Arbatov and Vladimir Dvorkin, eds., *Missile Defense: Confrontation and Cooperation* (Moscow: Carnegie Moscow Center, 2013). For a brief recapitulation of NATO policy and activity with respect to missile defense, see NATO, "Ballistic Missile Defense," www.nato.int/cps/en/natolive/topics_49635.htm.

50. Stent, *Limits of Partnership*, 154. I heard the same thing from a senior officer on the Russian General Staff in a meeting in Moscow in May 2008.

51. Stent, *Limits of Partnership*, 155.

52. Roxburgh, *Strongman*, 200–201, based on an anonymous senior Russian official.

53. Roxburgh, *Strongman*, 202–3. The four-part BBC television series *Putin, Russia, and the West*, produced by Roxburgh and aired in early 2012 during the presidential election campaign in Russia, contains interviews with a number of senior Russian and American officials who took part or were principals in the meetings described in this narrative. These interviews provide not only valuable firsthand information on what happened but also unparalleled insight into the thinking of both sides.

54. Many of the same sources relating this story are cited by both Stent, *Limits of Partnership*, 157–58; and Roxburgh, *Strongman*, 204–7.

55. As quoted by Stent, *Limits of Partnership*, 157.

56. Even the strongest supporters of the OSCE admitted that the organization was in crisis during this period. One need only peruse the *Annual Reports* for the OSCE for 2006–2008 to see how few important activities (let alone accomplishments) of real substance the organization conducted. For a representative sampling of reports of crisis or lack of success from pro-OSCE officials and authors, see Marc Perrin de Brichambaut, "The OSCE and the 21st Century," *Helsinki Monitor: Security and Human Rights*, no. 3 (2007): 180–91; Andre W. M. Gerrits, "Russia and the OSCE: A Story of High Expectation, Strong Disillusionment and Obstinate Confrontation,"

*Security and Human Rights*, no. 2 (2008): 107–9; and Nina Suomalainen, "Observations on an OSCE Chairmanship: Intentions, Challenges and Outcomes," *Security and Human Rights*, no. 1 (2009): 19–24.

57. Victor-Yves Ghebali, "The 2007 Madrid Ministerial Council Meeting: A Mixed Bag of Non-Decisions and a Discrete Set of Measures," *Security and Human Rights*, no. 1 (2008): 82.

58. Tim Judah, "Kosovo's Moment of Truth," *Survival* 47, no. 4 (Winter 2005–6): 73–84; International Crisis Group, *Kosovo: Toward Final Status*, Europe Report 161 (Brussels: International Crisis Group, 2005), www.crisisgroup.org/~/media/Files/europe /161_kosovo_toward_final_status.pdf.

59. Kai Eide, "A Comprehensive Review of the Situation in Kosovo," 4, as transmitted by the Office of the UN Secretary-General to the UN Security Council, October 7, 2005, www.unosek.org/docref/KaiEidereport.pdf. See also International Crisis Group, *Kosovo: The Challenge of Transition*, Europe Report 170 (Brussels: International Crisis Group, 2006), 1–3, www.crisisgroup.org/~/media/Files/europe/170 _kosovo___the_challenge_of_transition.

60. Martti Ahtisaari, "Report of the Special Envoy of the Secretary-General on Kosovo's Future Status," March 26, 2007, www.unosek.org/docref/report-english.pdf. See also Oksana Antonenko, "Russia and the Deadlock over Kosovo," *Survival* 49, no. 3 (Autumn 2007): 91–106; and International Crisis Group, *Kosovo: No Good Alternatives to the Ahtisaari Plan*, Europe Report 182 (Brussels: International Crisis Group, 2007), www.crisisgroup.org/~/media/Files/europe/182_kosovo_no_good_alternatives _to_the_ahtisaari_plan.pdf. The latter report from the International Crisis Group contains perhaps the best succinct narrative of the history leading up to the split over the Ahtisaari Plan.

61. Ahtisaari, "Report of the Special Envoy," 1. On the Ahtisaari negotiations, see Marc Weller, "The Vienna Negotiations on the Final Status of Kosovo," *International Affairs* 84, no. 4 (2008): 659–81.

62. For one of the best expressions of this widespread point of view in the West, see Charles A. Kupchan, "Independence for Kosovo: Yielding to Balkan Reality," *Foreign Affairs* 84, no. 6 (November–December 2005): 14–20. For a representative, well-expressed statement of the official US position, see "Undersecretary of State R. Nicholas Burns, Remarks at the Council on Foreign Relations," Washington, April 16, 2007, http://2001-2009.state.gov/p/us/rm/2007/84038.htm.

63. For the Russian position on Kosovo, see Stent, *Limits of Partnership*, 159–62; Roxburgh, *Strongman*, 220–22; and Antonenko, "Russia and the Deadlock." See also Foreign Minister Lavrov's annual surveys on Russian foreign policy, January 2007 and January 2008, available at www.mid.ru. I had numerous conversations, particularly in 2006–2007, with Russian diplomats and other officials in Moldova, Ukraine, Moscow, and the OSCE on Western and Russian policy with respect to Kosovo, and to what extent Kosovo would serve as a precedent for other conflicts.

64. The tendency to see Kosovo as a precedent was widespread and predated release of the Ahtisaari Plan. For example, see Aleksandr Aksenenok, "Samoopredelenia: Mezhdu pravom i politikoi," *Rossiia v global'noi politike*, no. 5 (September–October 2006), available at www.globalaffairs.ru.

65. Russian ambassador to the United Nations Vitaliy Churkin, as quoted by Antonenko, "Russia and the Deadlock," 97–98. I was told the same thing repeatedly by officials from Transdniestria, Abkhazia, and South Ossetia. For a contemporary discussion of possible precedents for entities in the Balkans and the former Soviet Union by a Western expert, see Rick Fawn, "The Kosovo—and Montenegro—Effect," *International Affairs* 84, no. 2 (2008): 269–94.

66. Condoleezza Rice, *No Higher Honor: A Memoir of My Years in Washington* (New York: Crown, 2011), 579.

67. See chapter 5. The text of UN Security Council Resolution 1244 can be found at http://daccess-dds-ny.un.org/doc/UNDOC/GEN/N99/172/89/PDF/N9917289.pdf? OpenElement.

68. For a detailed statement of the American position and reasoning, see "Teleconference Briefing on Kosovo, Nicholas Burns, Undersecretary for Political Affairs," Washington, February 18, 2008, http://2001-2009.state.gov/p/us/rm/2008/100976.htm. For postindependence assumption of responsibilities on behalf of the international community by the EU and NATO, see Elizabeth Pond, "The EU's Test in Kosovo," *Washington Quarterly* 31, no. 4 (Autumn 2008): 97–112; also see Oisin Tansey and Dominik Zaum, "Muddling Through in Kosovo," *Survival* 51, no. 1 (February–March 2009): 13–20. For background on the United Nations Mission in Kosovo before and after 2008 and other information on United Nations involvement in Kosovo, including the basic UN decisions and documents, see www.un.org/en/peacekeeping/missions /unmik/background.shtml.

69. "Zaiavlenie MID Rossii po Kosovu," February 17, 2008, www.mid.ru/brp_4.nsf /newsline/69E1940601A4968BC32573F20053D7F7.

70. "Putin Calls Kosovo Independence 'Terrible Precedent,' " *Sydney Morning Herald*, February 23, 2008, www.smh.com.au/news/world/putin-calls-kosovo-independence -terrible-precedent/2008/02/23/1203467431503.html.

71. Vladimir Soloviev, "Slushaniia vyslushali vpolukha: Abkhazii, Iuzhnoi Osetii i Pridnestrov'iu dali poigrat' v Kosovo," *Kommersant*, March 14, 2008, www.kommersant .ru/doc/866773; Transdniestrian Supreme Soviet and Foreign Ministry officials to the author, July 2008.

72. OSCE Mission to Georgia personnel, UN military observers from Abkhazia, and Western and Russian negotiators from the 1990s and 2000s have all generally described the situation that they experienced in these terms. OSCE, UN, Russian press, and local press reports over the years before 2008 all frequently describe such incidents. For good background and analyses of the conflicts in Georgia, see Thomas de Waal, *The Caucasus: An Introduction* (New York: Oxford University Press, 2010); Christoph Zuercher, *The Post-Soviet Wars: Rebellion, Ethnic Conflict, and Nationhood in the Caucasus* (New York: New York University Press, 2007); Sergei Markedonov, *Tubulentnaia Evraziia* (Moscow 2010); and Stuart Kaufman, *Modern Hatreds: The Symbolic Politics of Ethnic War* (Ithaca, N.Y.: Cornell University Press, 2001). The final report of the EU-mandated Independent International Fact-Finding Mission on the Conflict in Georgia, headed by the Swiss diplomat Heidi Tagliavini, who had extensive experience in the region and the former Soviet area (hereafter, the *Tagliavini Report*) contains a wealth of background material on the history, population, and politics of the

region collected from various experts. The report's conclusions, which are discussed in the text, are found in volume 1 of the report, issued in late 2009. Volume 2 of the report is much larger and has much of the background material. I worked closely in various capacities for more than a decade with several special representatives of the UN secretary-general and heads of the OSCE Mission to Georgia. These contacts and conversations inform a number of my judgments offered in this narrative.

73. For background on the UN Observer Mission in Georgia, see https://peacekeeping .un.org/mission/past/unomig/. See also Dov Lynch, *Russian Peacekeeping Strategies in the CIS: The Cases of Moldova, Georgia and Tajikistan* (London: Macmillan and Royal Institute of International Affairs, 2000).

74. On the OSCE Mission, see OSCE, *Survey of OSCE Field Operations* (Vienna: OSCE, 2013), 78–83, available at www.osce.org/cpc/74783?download=true.

75. See http://eeas.europa.eu/background/eu-special-representatives/index_en.htm. The decision document creating the post is at www.consilium.europa.eu/uedocs/ cmsUpload/L169-8.7.2003.pdf.

76. Lyndon Allin, "The Passportization of Abkhazia and South Ossetia," unpublished paper, Georgetown University, May 2007; see also *Tagliavini Report*, vol. 2, 147–77.

77. De Waal, *Caucasus*, 194; to construct the narrative of events in Georgia from 2004 through 2008, I used de Waal, *Caucasus*, 190–216; Stent, *Limits of Partnership*, 163–76; *Tagliavini Report*, vol. 2, esp. 185–227; Roxburgh, *Strongman*, 229–52; International Crisis Group, *Russia vs. Georgia: The Fallout*, Europe Report 195 (Brussels: International Crisis Group, 2008); and previous reports from the International Crisis Group. The account of the lead-up and the conflict is from Ronald D. Asmus, *A Little War That Shook the World: Georgia, Russia, and the Future of the West* (New York: Palgrave Macmillan, 2010), which clearly benefited from extensive conversation with President Saakashvili. However, in my estimation, Asmus accepted far too uncritically that which he was told by senior Georgian leadership without questioning or referring to other sources. But his volume is still invaluable as a reflection of the Georgian point of view and a source of information gleaned from contacts in Tbilisi.

78. De Waal, *Caucasus*, 204–6.

79. For background on Georgia-NATO relations, see www.nato.int/cps/en/natolive /topics_38988.htm.

80. For data on the Georgian armed forces and their deployments on international missions, see the Ministry of Defense website at www.mod.gov.ge/index.php?page =samshvidobo-misia.

81. Frits Arne Petersen, Hans Binnendijk, Charles Barry, and Peter Lehman Nielsen, "Implementing NATO's Comprehensive Approach to Complex Operations," in *NATO in Search of a Vision*, ed. Gulnur Aybet and Rebecca R. Moore (Washington, D.C.: Georgetown University Press, 2010), 75–98; also see Gulnur Aybet and Rebecca R. Moore "Conclusion: Looking Forward" in ibid., 244.

82. For a representative example of the contradictions in the NATO-Russia relationship, see the "Chairman's Statement: Meeting of the NATO-Russia Council at the Level of Heads of State and Government Held in Bucharest," April 4, 2008, www.nato .int/cps/en/natohq/official_texts_8962.htm?selectedLocale=en.

83. "The Alliance's Statement on the Russian Federation's 'Suspension' of Its CFE Obligations," December 12, 2007, www.nato.int/cps/en/natohq/news_15500.htm? selectedLocale=en; NATO reaffirmed this position on the eve of the Bucharest Summit, see "Statement by the North Atlantic Council on the Treaty on Conventional Armed Forces in Europe (CFE)," March 28, 2008, www.nato.int/cps/en/natohq/official _texts_8439.htm?selectedLocale=en.

84. Senior US and Russian diplomats to the author, January–March 2008.

85. See NATO, "Bucharest Summit Declaration, Issued by the Heads of State and Government Participating in the Meeting of the North Atlantic Council in Bucharest," April 3, 2008, paragraph 2, www.nato.int/cps/en/natohq/official_texts_8443.htm? selectedLocale=en.

86. Yushchenko, Timoshenko, and Yatseniuk letter, described in "Ukraine Asks to Join NATO Membership Action Plan," January 16, 2008, www.unian.info/world/89447 -ukraine-asks-to-join-nato-membership-action-plan.html.

87. As quoted by Roxburgh, *Strongman*, 221.

88. Saakashvili and National Security Council director Damon Wilson, as quoted by ibid., 222.

89. Merkel made the German position (a cross-party position) public in two speeches before Bucharest in an effort to avoid confrontation with Washington by openly staking out Berlin's stand in a manner making it difficult to impossible to retreat. One former US official claims that neither President Bush nor Secretary Rice was fully informed of Merkel's actions and Germany's stance, causing the United States considerable surprise at the resistance encountered at Bucharest. Former US official to the author, July 2015.

90. Stent, *Limits of Partnership*, 163–68; Roxburgh, *Strongman*, 222–29; and Asmus, *Little War*, 117–40, contain interviews with almost all the major participants in the Bucharest Summit, and taken together they provide an excellent basis for reconstructing and evaluating the events and results.

91. Asmus, *Little War*, 133.

92. NATO, "Bucharest Summit Declaration," paragraph 23. On Merkel's role, see Roxburgh, *Strongman*, 228–29; Stent, *Limits of Partnership*, 167; and Asmus, *Little War*, 137.

93. NATO, "ISAF's Strategic Vision: Declaration by the Heads of State and Government of the Nations Contributing to the UN-Mandated NATO-Led International Security Assistance Force (ISAF) in Afghanistan," April 3, 2008, www.nato.int/cps/en /natohq/official_texts_8444.htm?selectedLocale=en.

94. Michael F. Harsch and Johannes Varwick, "NATO and the UN," *Survival* 51, no. 2 (April–May 2009): 5–12. The text of the declaration remains restricted on the NATO website, but the content is amply described in this and other articles. For the secretary-general's views on the direction of NATO's transformation, see Jaap de Hoop Scheffer, "Bucharest: A Milestone in NATO's Transformation," *NATO Review*, 2008, www.nato.int/docu/Review/2008/03/ART3/EN/index.htm.

95. All citations in the next two paragraphs are from Vladimir Putin, "Zaiavleniia dlia pressy i otvety na voprosy zhurnalistov po itogam zasedaniia Soveta Rossiia– NATO," April 4, 2008, www.kremlin.ru/transcripts/24903.

96. Detailed materials from the Sochi Summit from the US side are collected together with materials from the Bucharest Summit on the archived White House site at http://georgewbush-whitehouse.archives.gov/infocus/nato/. These include presidential press conferences, statements by National Security Adviser Hadley, the Strategic Declaration, and assorted fact sheets and backgrounders. See also Peter Baker, "No Pact, but Bush, Putin Leave a Map," *Washington Post*, April 7, 2008, www.washingtonpost .com/wp-dyn/content/story/2008/04/07/ST2008040700729.html. See also Stent, *Limits of Partnership*, 162–63. For another inside account of the Bucharest and Sochi summits, see Rice, *No Higher Honor*, 675–79.

97. "US-Russia Strategic Framework Declaration," Sochi, April 6, 2008, http:// georgewbush-whitehouse.archives.gov/news/releases/2008/04/20080406-4.html; in Russian, "Deklaratsiia o strategicheskikh ramkakh rossiisko-amerikanskikh otnoshenii" Sochi, 6 Aprelia 2008 goda," www.mid.ru/bro_4.nsf/newsline/99850024F4730E16C3257424 . . .

98. Stent, *Limits of Partnership*, 168; Rice, *No Higher Honor*, 675–76; BBC, *Putin, Russia, and the West*, part III.

99. Stent, *Limits of Partnership*, 163.

100. Stent, *The Limits of Partnership*, 168–69.

101. Roxburgh, *Strongman*, 232; Stent, *Limits of Partnership*, 168; BBC, *Putin, Russia, and the West*, part III; de Waal, *Caucasus*, 196; senior State Department and Defense Department officials to the author, August 2008.

102. De Waal, *Caucasus*, 207–8.

103. Rice, *No Higher Honor*, 685–86; Roxburgh, *Strongman*, 232–33. The security situations in and around both Abkhazia and South Ossetia in the first half of 2008 were extremely complex and unstable. In addition to the incidents mentioned, there were also extensive shooting incidents in the Kodori Gorge, one of which, involving not only artillery but also air power that only Russia possessed, prompting a talking point President Bush used with Putin (sadly, he had no backup to respond to Putin's lengthy retort). Also, a Russian missile fell somewhere near Ossetia. The proximate cause of Saakashvili's actions in August 2008 was Ossetian pressure on the Georgian-controlled and -inhabited villages inside the boundaries of South Ossetia; unanswered Ossetian assertion of control over these villages would have been a political disaster for Saakashvili.

104. Stent, *Limits of Partnership*, 170; Roxburgh, *Strongman*, 234–40; BBC, *Putin, Russia, and the West*, part III; Rice, *No Higher Honor*, 685–86 and ff.

105. Stent, *Limits of Partnership*, 169–70; Rice, *No Higher Honor*, 685–86; BBC, *Putin, Russia, and the West*, part III; Roxburgh, *Strongman*, 238–40.

106. De Waal, *Caucasus*, 209–10.

107. The literature on the Russo-Georgia war is too vast to list completely or recapitulate in any detail in this volume. I have relied first of all on volume 1 of the *Tagliavini Report*, as well as press accounts from Russia, Georgia, Western Europe, and the United States. De Waal, *Caucasus*, 211–16, also has a good short account of the war. Roxburgh, *Strongman*, 241–49; Stent, *Limits of Partnership*, 171–74; and Asmus, *Little War*, 165–214, all contain a wealth of inside information from extensive interviews with senior Western and Russian participants in the events of July and August 2008.

A number of these interviews can be viewed on the BBC TV program *Putin, Russia, and the West*, part III. I have also benefited from conversations with OSCE Mission members who were present in Tbilisi and Tskhinvali during the war and their views and reconstruction of events.

108. On Russian military performance in Georgia, see Rod Thornton, *Military Modernization and the Russian Ground Forces*, Strategic Studies Institute Monograph (Carlisle, Penn.: US Army War College, 2011), www.strategicstudiesinstitute.army.mil/pdffiles/PUB1071.pdf.

109. See esp. Roxburgh, *Strongman*, 247–49. Many sources confirm Lavrov's demand to Rice during the war that Saakashvilki "must go," but the Kremlin apparently decided not to attempt to make that happen unilaterally. Similarly, ibid., 248, refers to Medvedev's indirect statement that more radical military options were considered beyond degrading or destroying Georgia's military capacity. Such an internal discussion would not be unusual in any government having made a decision to go to war, but the fact remains that Russian military objectives as they played out in real life were clearly limited and not aimed at long-term occupation of significant territory in Georgia proper outside South Ossetia and Abkhazia.

110. Andrew E. Kramer, and Ellen Barry, "Russia, in Accord with Georgians, Sets Withdrawal," *New York Times*, August 12, 2008, www.nytimes.com/2008/08/13/world/europe/13georgia.html; also see Andrew E. Kramer, "Peace Plan Offers Russia a Rationale to Advance," *New York Times*, August 13, 2008, www.nytimes.com/2008/08/14/world/europe/14document.html. Roxburgh, *Strongman*, 246–51, benefits from interviews with key senior Russian and French sources.

111. The Six-Point Peace Plan can be found with a number of additions and clarifications, depending on who was explaining the plan. For example, see the explanations provided in the joint press conference of presidents Medvedev and Sarkozy in Moscow on August 12: "Zaiavleniia dlia pressy i otvety na voprosy zhurnalistov po itogam peregovorov Prezidenta Rossii D. A. Medvedeva s Prezidentom Frantsii Nikola Sarkozi" Moskva, Kreml', 12 avgusta 2008 goda, www.mid.ru/brp_4.nsf/newsline/C5661B8428F33B7AC32574A4001D7A4D. The agreement was circulated in French by French embassies: www.ambafrance-us.org/IMG/pdf/accord6points.pdf; The French text, with a letter of transmittal with clarifications from Sarkozy to Saakashvili, was posted on the Georgian government website: www.smr.gov.ge/docs/doc111.pdf.

112. See de Waal, *Caucasus*, 215.

113. "Zaiavlenie Prezidenta Rossiiskoi Federatsii D.A. Medvedeva, 26 Avgusta 2008 goda," www.mid.ru/brp_4.nsf/newsline/5A25D3A9082FB6E7C32574B1003DAF8D.

114. "Interview Given by Dmitry Medvedev to Television Channel One, Rossiia, NTV," August 31, 2008, Sochi, http://archive.kremlin.ru/eng/speeches/2008/08/31/1850_type82912type82916_206003.shtml; the Russian-language version can be found at www.kremlin.ru/events/president/transcripts/1276.

115. Asmus, *Little War*, 187–99 and ff., has a particularly good account of diplomacy during and after the war based on numerous inside sources.

116. See the interview with National Security Adviser Steve Hadley, on BBC, *Putin, Russia, and the West*, part III, in which Hadley describes the principals' meeting at which the subject was discussed. See also Asmus, *Little War*, 187–88 and ff.; and Stent, *Limits of Partnership*, 173–74.

117. See United Nations, "Georgia: UNOMIG — Background," https://peacekeeping .un.org/mission/past/unomig/background.html.

118. OSCE, *OSCE Survey of Field Operations*, 70.

119. See European Union, "EU Council Joint Action 2008/736/CFSP on the European Union Monitoring Mission in Georgia, EUMM Georgia," http://eur-lex.europa.eu /LexUriServ/LexUriServ.do?uri=OJ:L:2008:248:0026:0031:EN:PDF.

120. See the EUMM Georgia website, www.eumm.eu/en/about_eumm/facts_and _figures.

121. See "Talks on Russia-Georgia War Seen as 'Constructive' " RFE/RL, November 20, 2008, www.rferl.org/content/Geneva_Talks_On_RussiaGeorgia_War_Seen_As _Constructive/1351138.html; and International Crisis Group, *Georgia-Russia: Still Insecure and Dangerous*, Europe Briefing 53 (Brussels: International Crisis Group, 2009), 12.

122. For an excellent discussion of the harmful effects of the decision on Kosovo on Russia-Georgia relations and European security, see Alexander Cooley and Lincoln A. Mitchell, "No Way to Treat Our Friends: Recasting Recent US-Georgia Relations," *Washington Quarterly* 32, no. 1 (January 2009): 27–41.

## 9. THE RESET

1. According to one Western official involved in the Meseberg Initiative, Russian officials likely heard or understood much more than Merkel actually promised, interpreting the German chancellor's proposal as offering increased cooperation or perhaps something akin to an EU-Russia "security council" in which Moscow would have not only a voice but a veto. Senior OSCE official to the author, October 2015.

2. In Libya, for example, the United States did the heavy initial bombardment, which cleared out the air defenses and allowed the Europeans to conduct their operations. In terms of munitions expended, the majority was American, a fact not widely publicized by the Pentagon. Former Department of Defense official to the author, July 2015.

3. The literature on the global financial and economic crisis is immense and growing steadily. For a useful review and quick guide to some of the most serious studies to date, see Phillip Swagel, "Financial Crisis Reading List," *New York Times*, July 15, 2013, http://economix.blogs.nytimes.com/2013/07/15/financial-crisis-reading-list-2/?_r=0. My favorites among the many books published on the crisis include those by Joseph Stiglitz, *Freefall: America, Free Markets, and the Sinking of the World Economy* (New York: W. W. Norton, 2010); Alan S. Blinder, *After the Music Stopped: The Financial Crisis, the Response, and the Work Ahead* (New York: Penguin, 2013); and Andrew Ross Sorkin, *Too Big to Fail: Inside the Battle to Save Wall Street* (New York: Penguin, 2009).

4. For a contemporary assessment of the extent and potential geopolitical effects of the crisis, see Roger C. Altman, "The Great Crash, 2008: A Geopolitical Setback for the West," *Foreign Affairs* 88, no. 1 (January–February 2009): 2–14.

5. For a general discussion of the effects of the global economic crisis in Europe and the EU's response, see Desmond Dinan, *Europe Recast: A History of the European Union* (Boulder, Colo.: Lynne Rienner, 2014), 328–49. The EU and EC websites have basic factual and chronological information at http://ec.europa.eu/economy_finance/crisis/2008-10_en.htm, and http://europa.eu/about-eu/eu-history/2000-2009/index_en.htm. For a more detailed analysis, see, Carlo Bastasin, *Saving Europe: How National Politics Nearly Destroyed the Euro* (Washington, D.C.: Brookings Institution Press, 2012); and Costas Lapavitsas, *Crisis in the Eurozone* (London: Verso, 2012). For a contemporary assessment of the effects of the financial crisis on the economies of the various member states in the euro zone and on the euro as a whole, see Erik Jones, "The Euro and the Financial Crisis," *Survival* 51, no. 1 (April–May 2009): 41–54. On Germany's role, see William E. Paterson, "The Reluctant Hegemon? Germany Moves Center Stage in the European Union," *JCMS: Journal of Common Market Studies* 49, supplement (2011): 57–75.

6. On Russia before, during, and after the global crisis, see Anders Åslund, Sergei Guriev, and Andrew C. Kuchins, eds., *Russia After the Global Economic Crisis* (Washington, D.C.: Peterson Institute for International Economics, Center for Strategic and International Studies, and New Economic School, 2010), esp. 9–16 on precrisis conditions. See also Richard E. Ericson, "The Russian Economy in 2008: Testing the 'Market Economy,'" *Post-Soviet Affairs* 25, no. 3 (2009): 209–31. One of the best short studies of the Russian economy and the effects of the global crisis is by Clifford G. Gaddy and Barry W. Ickes, "Russia After the Global Financial Crisis," *Eurasian Geography and Economics* 51, no. 3 (2010): 281–311.

7. On the government response to the crisis, see Ericson, "Russian Economy," 223–25; and Sergei Guriev and Aleh Tsyvinski, "Challenges Facing the Russian Economy after the Crisis," in *Russia After the Global Economic Crisis*, ed. Åslund, Guriev, and Kuchins, 9–38, at 20–28.

8. See Marshall I. Goldman, *Petrostate: Putin, Power, and the New Russia* (New York: Oxford University Press, 2008), 166–68, and passim; and Igor Danchenko and Clifford G. Gaddy, "The Mystery of Vladimir Putin's Dissertation," Brookings Institution, March 30, 2006, www.brookings.edu/~/media/events/2006/3/30putin%20dissertation/putin%20dissertation%20event%20remarks%20with%20slides.pdf.

9. Ericson, "Russian Economy," 221; Angus Roxburgh, *The Strongman: Vladimir Putin and the Struggle for Russia* (New York: I. B. Tauris, 2012), 272–73.

10. Guriev and Tsyvinski, "Challenges," 20–21; Sergei Guriev, as quoted by Roxburgh, *Strongman*, 274.

11. Ericson, "Russian Economy," 221–22; Gaddy and Ickes, "Russia," 307–8; Guriev and Tsyvinski, "Challenges," 28–30; Roxburgh, *Strongman*, 279–80.

12. Dmitry Medvedev, *Rossiia vpered*, www.kremlin.ru/events/president/news/5413.

13. Roxburgh, *Strongman*, 280–83.

14. Ibid., 282–95, presents an intriguing discussion of Medvedev's efforts to attract foreign investment, the systemic nature of corruption in Russia, and the obstacles this poses to efforts to convince foreigners to bring their money to Russia.

15. Ibid., 274.

16. Ibid., 276–77.

17. Russian diplomat to the author, November 2008. Former secretary of the Treasury Henry Paulson related in his memoirs that Putin approached China in mid-2008 with a plan to dump Fannie Mae and Freddie Mac bonds in an attempt to cause the enterprises to fail. According to Paulson, the Chinese declined; Henry Paulson, *On the Brink: Inside the Race to Stop the Collapse of the Global Financial System* (New York: Grand Central, 2010). See Krishna Guha, "Paulson Claims Russia Tried to Foment Fannie-Freddie Crisis," *Financial Times*, January 29, 2010, www.ft.com/intl/cms/s/0 /ffd950c4-0d0a-11df-a2dc-00144feabdc0.html#axzz3Y8iCoiyZ. The two stories are not necessarily mutually exclusive, presuming that Moscow failed to sell off its holdings in the two corporations before the government takeover in September 2008.

18. Roxburgh, *Strongman*, 278–79.

19. Andrew Kramer, "Russia Cuts Off Gas Deliveries to Ukraine," *New York Times*, January 1, 2009, www.nytimes.com/2009/01/02/world/europe/02gazprom.html?_r=0. See also Angela E. Stent, *The Limits of Partnership: US–Russian Relations in the Twenty-First Century* (Princeton, N.J.: Princeton University Press, 2014), 196–97; and Simon Pirani, Jonathan Stern, and Katja Yafimava, *The Russo-Ukrainian Gas Dispute of January 2009: A Comprehensive Assessment* (Oxford: Oxford Institute for Energy Studies, 2009), NG 27. For extremely useful background on the role of energy in Ukrainian economics and politics, see Edward Chow and Jonathan Elkind, "Where East Meets West: European Gas and Ukrainian Reality," *Washington Quarterly* 32, no. 1 (January 2009): 77–92.

20. Stent, *Limits of Partnership*, 196–97.

21. See Chow and Elkind, "Where East Meets West," 86–91. In numerous discussions with Russian government officials and energy executives over more than a decade, most of these interlocutors have stressed to the author Russia's right and desire to sell gas at a profit and Ukraine's unreliable behavior, with remarkably little overt cognizance of how Moscow's behavior appeared to most of its Western interlocutors. For an insider's view of the mind-set of Putin and his colleagues in the Kremlin on this score, see Roxburgh, *Strongman*, 255–59.

22. Stent, *Limits of Partnership*, 185–86.

23. Dmitri Trenin, "Russia Reborn: Reimagining Moscow's Foreign Policy," *Foreign Affairs* 88, no. 6 (November–December 2009): 72–73; see also Fiona Hill and Clifford Gaddy, *Mr. Putin: Operative in the Kremlin*, 2nd ed. (Washington, D.C.: Brookings Institution Press, 2015), 320, 323–24.

24. Trenin, "Russia Reborn," 68; also Dmitri Trenin, *Post-Imperium: A Eurasian Story* (Washington, D.C.: Carnegie Endowment for International Peace, 2011), 154–55. Putin eventually changed course again, in part because of Obama's reset policies, and Russia joined the World Trade Organization in 2012. However, by that time Putin's modified and new integration projects across the post-Soviet space were well under way.

25. Hill and Gaddy, *Mr. Putin*, 248.

26. Trenin, "Russia Reborn," 64; Fedor Lukyanov, "Rethinking Security in 'Greater Europe,'" *Russia in Global Affairs*, September 5, 2009, http://eng.globalaffairs.ru/number /n_13589.

27. Trenin, *Post-Imperium*, 154.

28. For brief descriptions of the integration programs, see Trenin, *Post-Imperium*, 153–58. The website of the Eurasian Economic Union also contains a useful and interesting timeline of integration efforts among the former Soviet states dating back to a 1994 proposal by Kazakhstan's president Nazarbaev, www.eaeunion.org/?lang =en#about-history.

29. Trenin, *Post-Imperium*, 156, attributes Putin's turn to the Customs Union and away from the World Trade Organization after the global economic crisis in part to the influence of advisers such as Sergei Glazev, who saw protection for the Russian economy by integrating with its neighbors. See also Andrey Suzdaltsev, "Politics Ahead of the Economy," *Russia in Global Affairs*, 2010, no. 1 (January–March), http://eng .globalaffairs.ru/number/n_14783.

30. For background on the CSTO and the Collective Security Treaty, see the website at www.odkb.gov.ru/start/index_aengl.htm.

31. Stent, *Limits of Partnership*, 155.

32. For background on the SCO, see its official website at http://en.sco-russia.ru /about_sco/20140905/1013180761.html. See also Trenin, *Post-Imperium*, 170–71; Alexander Cooley, *Great Games, Local Rules: The New Power Contest in Central Asia* (New York: Oxford University Press, 2012), 75–96.

33. For an interesting discussion of the Medvedev presidency, the hopes it raised in some segments of Russian society and the effect of Medvedev's departure from the Kremlin on those same parts of society, all based on considerable inside information, see Roxburgh, *Strongman*, 296–315.

34. On the error in translation, see "Sergei Lavrov i Hillari Klinton zagruzili povestku dnia," *Kommersant*, March 7, 2009, www.kommersant.ru/doc/1131090; also see Glenn Kessler, "Clinton 'Resets' Russia Ties—and Language," *Washington Post*, March 7, 2009, www.washingtonpost.com/wp-dyn/content/article/2009/03/06/AR2009030600428 .html. For an excellent overview and analysis of the Obama reset policy and its results, see Stent, *Limits of Partnership*, 211–34.

35. John Vinocur, "Central and Eastern European Countries Issue Rare Warning for US on Russian Policy," *New York Times*, July 20, 2009, www.nytimes.com/2009/07/21 /world/europe/21iht-politicus.html?_r=o. See also Stent, *Limits of Partnership*, 226–27.

36. For a brief description of the new START talks and treaty, see Stent, *Limits of Partnership*, 222–25. For the text of the treaty and related protocols, see the State Department website at www.state.gov/t/avc/newstart/c44126.htm.

37. Stent, *Limits of Partnership*, 223–24.

38. For a discussion of the missile defense issue in the first Obama administration, see ibid., 225–27.

39. Hillary Clinton, "America's Pacific Century," *Foreign Policy*, October 11, 2011, http://foreignpolicy.com/2011/10/11/americas-pacific-century/.

40. For a discussion of the Medvedev European security treaty proposal, see Stent, *Limits of Partnership*, 238–41. Also see Ulrich Kuhn, "Medvedev's Proposals for a New European Security Order: A Starting Point of the End of the Story?" *Connections: The Quarterly Journal* 9, no. 2 (Spring 2010): 1–16; Jeffrey Mankoff, "Reforming the Euro-Atlantic Security Architecture: An Opportunity for US Leadership," *Washington Quarterly* 33, no. 2 (April 2010): 65–83; Adam Daniel Rotfeld, "Does Europe Need a New Security Architecture?" *Finnish Institute of International Affairs and MFA*, March 2009, 1–21; Bobo Lo, "Medvedev and the New European Security Architecture," Centre for European Reform, July 2009, www.cer.org.uk; Marcel H. van Herpen, "Medvedev's Proposal for a Pan-European Security Plan: Its Six Hidden Objectives and How the West Should Respond," October 2008, Cicero Working Paper WP 08–03, available at www.cicerofoundation.org; Richard J. Krikus, "Medvedev's Plan: Giving Russia a Voice but Not a Veto in a New European Security System," Strategic Studies Institute, Carlisle, Penn., December 2009, www.StrategicStudiesInstitute.army.mil; and Andrew Monaghan, ed., *The Indivisibility of Security: Russia and Euro-Atlantic Security* (Rome: Research Division of NATO Defense College, 2009).

41. Hill and Gaddy, *Mr. Putin*, 483–84n86.

42. Dmitri Medvedev, "Vystuplenia na vstreche s predstaviteliami politicheskikh, parlamentskikh i obshchestvennikh krugov Germanii," 5 Iiunia 2008 goda, Berlin, www.kremlin.ru/events/president/transcripts/320/.

43. Dmitri Medvedev, "Vystuplenie na konferentsii po voprosam mirovoi politiki," 8 Oktiabria 2008 goda, Evian, www.kremlin.ru/events/president/transcripts/1659.

44. "The Foreign Policy Concept of the Russian Federation, 12 July 2008," http://archive.kremlin.ru/eng/text/docs/2008/07/204750.shtml. Also see "Vystuplenie Prezidenta Rossiiskoi Federatsii D. A. Medvedeva na soveshchanii poslov i postoiannikh predstavitelei za rubezhom, Moskva, Ministerstvo Inostrannikh Del, 15 Iiulia 2008 goda," www.mid.ru/brp_4.nsf/newsline/3A2F0D08C2EAD75BC3257487004AF080.

45. Marcel de Haas, "Medvedev's Alternative European Security Architecture," *Security and Human Rights*, no. 1 (2010): 46. Rogozin was probably not the best choice to sell the proposal because his credibility was reportedly extremely low among many NATO delegations.

46. Ibid., 46; for an overall description of the EU response, see Bjorn Fagerberg, "Chapter 2: The EU and the Debate on Euro-Atlantic Security," in *Indivisibility of Security*, ed. Monaghan, 26–36; see also "Main Results of the EU-Russia Summit," http://eu-un.europa.eu/articles/en/article_8307_en.htm.

47. Sergei Lavrov, "Russian Initiative Regarding a Treaty on European Security" (from a December 4, 2008, luncheon discussion by Russian foreign minister Sergei Lavrov), MC.DEL/44/08, December 5, 2008. See also Dov Lynch, "Chapter 1: The Corfu Process," in *Indivisibility of Security*, ed. Monaghan, 15–25.

48. Discussion on the future of security in Europe at the OSCE Ministerial working lunch on December 4, 2008, MC.DEL/92/08, December 15, 2008. See also Wolfgang Zellner, "From Corfu to Astana: The Way to the 2010 OSCE Summit," *Security and Human Rights*, no. 3 (2010): 233–34.

49. Ibid., 234.

50. Senior OSCE officials to the author, autumn 2009; see also Zellner, "From Corfu to Astana," 234.

51. Dmitri Medvedev, "Vystuplenie v Universitete Khelsinki i otvety na voprosy auditorii" 20 aprelia 2009 goda," www.kremlin.ru/events/president/transcripts/3805.

52. Igor Yurgens, Alexander Dynkin, and Vladimir Baranovsky, eds., *The Architecture of Euro-Atlantic Security* (Moscow: Institute of Contemporary Development, 2009), www.insor-russia.ru/files/euro_atlantic.pdf.

53. Ibid., 8.

54. "Proekt Dogovora o evropeiskoi bezopasnosti, 29 noiabria 2009 goda," November 30, 2009, http://news.kremlin.ru/news.6152; English-language version at http://eng .kremlin.ru/text/docs/2009/11/223072.shtml.

55. Stent, *Limits of Partnership*, 238–39.

56. All references to and excerpts from the treaty are from "Proekt Dogovora o evropeiskoi bezopasnosti, 29 noiabria 2009 goda," http://news.kremlin.ru/news.6152.

57. For example, see Pal Dunay, "Revisiting and Eventually Adjusting, Though Certainly Not Revising, the European Security Architecture," *Security and Human Rights*, no. 1 (2010): 23–29.

58. Mankoff, "Reforming the Euro-Atlantic Security Architecture," 68–69.

59. See chapter 1; also see Kuhn, "Medvedev's Proposals," 10–11.

60. Rotfeld, *Does Europe Need a New Security Architecture?* 2–3.

61. For example, see Ronald Asmus, "Russia's 'Sphere' in Europe," *Washington Post*, December 26, 2009.

62. See chapters 3, 4, and 5; also see Kuhn, "Medvedev's Proposals," 10–12.

63. Senior US, Russian, and OSCE officials to the author, various dates, 2009–2012.

64. As quoted by Stent, *Limits of Partnership*, 239. For a general discussion of the US response, see Donald N. Jensen, "Chapter 3: The US Reconsiders Transatlantic Security," in *Indivisibility of Security*, ed. Monaghan, 37–44.

65. Kuhn, "Medvedev's Proposals," 12–13; see also Zellner, "From Corfu to Astana," 234–35.

66. "Ministerial Declaration on the OSCE Corfu Process: Reconfirm-Review-Reinvigorate Security and Cooperation from Vancouver to Vladivostok," MC.DOC /1/09, Athens, December 2, 2009, www.osce.org/cio/40689?download=true.

67. See Lavrov, "Russian Initiative."

68. "Vystuplenie Ministra inostrannikh del Rossii S. V. Lavrova na otkrytii Ezhegodnoi konferentsii OBSE po obzoru problem v oblasti bezopasnosti, Vena, 23 iiunia 2009 goda," www.mid.ru/brp_4.nsf/newsline/ADED9C34EE795D2BC32575DE003 DECD1.

69. See Tom Z. Collins, "CFE Treaty Talks Stall," *Arms Control Today*, August 30, 2011, www.armscontrol.org/print/4997.

70. For background on the debate over the Kazakh Chairmanship and the decision in Madrid, see Victor-Yves Ghebali, "The 2007 Madrid Ministerial Council Meeting: A Mixed Bag of Non-Decisions and a Discrete Set of Measures," *Helsinki Monitor*, no. 4 (2007): 91–92; and Eric Marotte, "Kazakhstan's OSCE Chairmanship: A Halfway State of Affairs," *Security and Human Rights*, no. 3 (2010): 176–88.

71. See "Address of H.E. Dr. Marat Tazhin, Minister of Foreign Affairs of the Republic of Kazakhstan, at the OSCE Ministerial Meeting," MC.DEL/38/07, Madrid, November 29, 2007, www.osce.org/mc/29336?download=true.

72. Dr. Pal Dunay, resident faculty member at the Geneva Centre for Security Policy and director of the International Training Course in Security Policy, in an address to a Corfu Process meeting on October 19, 2009, as quoted in OSCE, *OSCE Annual Report 2009*, (Vienna: OSCE, 2009), 13.

73. "Vystuplenie Ministra inostrannikh del Rossii S. V. Lavrova na otkrytii Ezhegodnoi konferentsii OBSE po obzoru problem v oblasti bezopasnosti, Vena, 23 iiunia 2009 goda," www.mid.ru/brp_4.nsf/newsline/ADED9C34EE795D2BC32575DE003DECD1.

74. Quoted by Kuhn, "Medvedev's Proposals," 13.

75. Zellner, "From Corfu to Astana," 236. See also Martha Brill Olcott, "Kyrgyzstan: Perspectives and Implications for the Region," in *20/20 OSCE and Central Asia: Past Visions, Future Perspectives*, OSECE Talks (Vienna: OSCE, 2010), www.osce.org/cio/73709?download=true.

76. Zellner, "From Corfu to Astana," 233; see also OSCE, *OSCE Annual Report 2010* (Vienna: OSCE, 2010), 14–18; Winsome Packer, "OSCE 2010 Informal Ministerial: Kazakhstan Persistence Earns a Summit in Astana" November 1, 2010, at www.csce.gov/index.cfm?FuseAction=ContentRecords.ViewDetail&ContentRecord_id=479&Region_id=112&Issue_id=0&ContentType=G&ContentRecordType=G.

77. OSCE, *OSCE Annual Report 2010*, 14; Kuhn, "Medvedev's Proposals," 13–14; Zellner, "From Corfu to Astana," 236–37; Isabelle Francois, *Whither the Medvedev Initiative on European Security?* (Washington, D.C.: National Defense University Press, 2011).

78. For description and analysis of the Astana summit and the Kazakh OSCE Chairmanship, see Walter Kemp, "The Astana Summit: A Triumph of Common Sense," *Security and Human Rights*, no. 4 (2010): 259–68. Kemp tries to emphasize the positive aspects of the summit; for a less positive commentary, see Matthias van Lohuizen, "Kazakhstan as the OSCE Chairman-in-Office 2010: Success or Failure for the Organization?" *Security and Human Rights*, no. 4 (2010): 269–78. For human rights criticism of the Kazakh Chairmanship, see Evgeniy Zhovtis, "The Summit Is Over, What's Next?" *Security and Human Rights*, no. 4 (2010): 255–57.

79. For the text of the summit declaration, see "Astana Commemorative Declaration: Towards a Security Community," SUM.DOC/1/10/Corr. 1, December 3, 2010, www.osce.org/cio/74985?download=true.

80. Dmitri Medvedev, "Vystuplenie na plenarnom zasedanii glav gosudarstv i predstavitel'stv stran-uchastnits OBSE, 1 dekabria 2010 goda, Astana," www.osce.org/ru/cio/73897?download=true.

81. On the provisions and ratification of the Lisbon Treaty, see Dinan, *Europe Recast*, 310–16. For a contemporary American view of the significance and potential in changes introduced by the Lisbon Treaty, see Anthony Luzzatto Gardner and Stuart E. Eizenstat, "New Treaty, New Influence? Europe's Chance to Punch Its Weight," *Foreign Affairs* 89, no. 2 (March–April 2010): 104–19.

82. For a short description of the security-related provisions of the Lisbon Treaty, see the EU / European External Affairs Service website at http://eeas.europa.eu/csdp/about-csdp/lisbon/index_en.htm. For a discussion of the significance and effects of the security and defense related provisions of the Lisbon Treaty, see, Anand Menon, "European Defence Policy from Lisbon to Libya," *Survival* 53, no. 3 (June–July 2011): 75–90.

83. Treaty on the European Union, Article 42.7, https://europa.eu/european-union/law/treaties_en.

84. Ibid., Article 43.1.

85. Dinan, *Europe Recast*, 312–13; see also Tony Barber, "The Appointments of Herman Van Rompuy and Catherine Ashton," *Journal of Common Market Studies* 48, supplement (September 2010): 55–67.

86. Michael Merlingen, *EU Security Policy: What It Is, How It Works, Why It Matters* (Boulder, Colo.: Lynne Rienner, 2012), 136–39. For a comprehensive list and links to descriptions of all past and present CSDP missions of the EU, see http://eeas.europa.eu/csdp/missions-and-operations/index_en.htm.

87. Merlingen, *EU Security Policy*, 141–43.

88. Pierre-Henri d'Argenson, "The Future of European Defense Policy," *Survival* 51, no. 1 (October–November 2009): 143–44.

89. Merlingen, *EU Security Policy*, 163–69.

90. On this point, see especially Regina Karp, "The New German Foreign Policy Consensus," *Washington Quarterly*, 29, no. 1 (Winter 2005–6): 61–82; also see Timo Noetzel and Benjamin Schreer, "All the Way? The Evolution of German Military Power," *International Affairs* 84, no. 2 (2008): 211–21.

91. For the French white paper, see *Defense et Securite Nationale: Le Livre Blanc*, Odile Jacob / La Documentation Française, June 2008, www.ladocumentationfrancaise.fr/var/storage/rapports-publics/084000341.pdf. On the return to NATO's military structures, see Jeremy Ghez and F. Stephen Larrabee, "France and NATO," *Survival* 51, no. 2 (April–May 2009): 77–90; and Gisela Muller-Brandeck-Bocquet, "France's New NATO Policy: Leveraging a Realignment of the Alliance?" *Strategic Studies Quarterly* (Winter 2009): 95–107.

92. D'Argenson, "Future," 148.

93. " 'La securite, notre mission commune' par Angela Merkel et Nicolas Sarkozy," *Le Monde*, March 2, 2009, www.lemonde.fr/idees/article/2009/02/03/la-securite-notre-miss . . .

94. Dinan, *Europe Recast*, 328–49, contains an excellent account of the development of the euro zone crisis and Germany's role in addressing it.

95. "Communication from the Commission to the European Parliament and the Council: Eastern Partnership," Brussels, December 3, 2009, COM(2008) 823 final; the actual communication has been restricted by the EU, but the Commission working document which was attached is available at http://eeas.europa.eu/archives/docs/eastern/docs/seco8_2974_en.pdf.

96. Benita Ferraro-Waldner, "Eastern Partnership: An Ambitious Project for 21st-Century European Foreign Policy," February 20, 2009, http://eeas.europa.eu/eastern/docs/eastern_partnership_article_bfw_en.pdf.

97. Dinan, *Europe Recast*, 316–27; senior EU officials to the author, February 2010.

98. Lavrov, as quoted by Valentina Pop, "EU Expanding Its 'Sphere of Influence,' Russia Says," *EU Observer* (Brussels), March 21, 2009, https://euobserver.com /foreign/27827. See also "The World from Berlin: The EU's Eastern 'Sphere of Influence,'" *Der Spiegel*, May 6, 2009, www.spiegel.de/international/europe/the-world-from -berlin-the-eu-s-eastern-sphere-of-influence-a-623163.html.

99. For basic background on EU-Russia relations, with links to key documents and descriptions, see http://eeas.europa.eu/russia/about/index_en.htm.

100. For the text of the memorandum, see www.russianmission.eu/sites/default /files/user/files/2010-06-05-meseberg-memorandum.pdf. For an account by a participant in the Moldova-Transdniestria negotiations, see Philip Remler, "Negotiation Gone Bad: Russia, Germany, and Crossed Communications," Carnegie Europe, August 21, 2013, http://carnegieeurope.eu/publications/?fa=52712. See also Bart Scheffers, "Tempering Expectations: EU Involvement with the Transdniestrian Conflict," *Security and Human Rights*, no. 4 (2010): 298–99.

101. One of the key participants in the Meseberg affair and the Moldova-Transdniestria negotiations emphasizes, on the contrary, the key roles of local factors and individual actors in the initiative's lack of success: "Meseberg itself was interesting in that it was so poorly prepared, but remember that it was with Medvedev, and one of Merkel's motivations was specifically to bolster him, as he was viewed as more liberal than Putin. And while the Meseberg initiative was playing out, Medvedev was also working hard on summiteering on Karabakh with Ilham Aliyev and Serzhik Sargsyan, supporting the 'Madrid Principles' and abandoning long-held Russian aims of a predominantly Russian PKF. Russia would have gained prestige out of brokering a Karabakh solution along those lines, but not privileged interest or a *droit de regard* over Azeri (or even Armenian) relations with the West. Also, it's hard to see a link between Meseberg and the renewal of the 5+2. Yes, the Germans provided funds for conferences, but the negotiation was entirely by the OSCE, and the tectonic shift that enabled the process was the new unity of all Russian factions on the desire to get rid of Smirnov, who as a result looked around for goodwill wherever he could find it. In order to meet with Smirnov, Filat had to contradict the strong opposition of [Foreign Minister Iurie] Leanca, who wielded great influence over the German position through [Merkel adviser Christophe] Heusgen." Senior OSCE official to the author, October 2015.

102. Stephen Castle, "NATO Hires a Coke Executive to Retool Its Brand," *New York Times*, July 16, 2008, www.nytimes.com/2008/07/16/world/europe/16nato.html.

103. For one well-written, thoughtful example of such commentary, see Rajan Menon, "NATO RIP: NATO Is Obsolete; the Atlantic World Is Anything But," *The American Interest* 4, no. 2 (November 2008), www.the-american-interest.com/2008/11/01/nato-r-i-p/.

104. For a compendium of basic background and information about NATO and ISAF in Afghanistan, see "NATO and Afghanistan," www.nato.int/cps/en/natohq/topics_8189. htm?. Also see Joseph J. Collins, *Understanding War in Afghanistan* (Washington, D.C.: National Defense University Press, 2011), esp. 77–88; Bob Woodward, *Obama's Wars* (New York: Simon & Schuster, 2010); and Alexander Mattelaer, "How Afghanistan Has Strengthened NATO," *Survival* 53, no. 6 (December 2011–January 2012): 127–40.

105. Collins, *Understanding War*, 76–77.

106. On the surge, see ibid., 81–86.

107. On the Comprehensive Approach, see Friis Arne Petersen, Hans Binnendijk, Charles Barry, and Peter Lehman Nielsen, "Implementing NATO's Comprehensive Approach to Complex Operations," in *NATO in Search of a Vision*, ed. Gulnur Aybet and Rebecca R. Moore (Washington, D.C.: Georgetown University Press, 2010), chap. 4, 75–98. See also Antonio Ortiz, "Neither Fox Nor Hedgehog: NATO's Comprehensive Approach and the OSCE's Concept of Security," *Security and Human Rights*, no. 4 (2008): 284–97. Ortiz (286–88) notes the similarity and relationship of NATO's Comprehensive Approach to the United States–conceived Effects-Based Approach to Operations, which had become part of NATO's military doctrine by the mid-2000s.

108. Robert M. Gates, "The Security and Defense Agenda (Future of NATO)," speech delivered by the secretary of defense, Brussels, June 10, 2011, www.defense.gov /speeches/speech.aspx?speechid=1581.

109. See "Strasbourg/Kehl Summit Declaration Issued by the Heads of State and Government Participating in the Meeting of the North Atlantic Council in Strasbourg /Kehl," April 4, 2009, paragraph 5, www.nato.int/cps/en/natohq/news_52837.htm? selectedLocale=en. For a description and analysis of the reasons behind the French return to full participation in NATO, see Ghez and Larrabee, "France and NATO"; and Gisela Muller-Brandeck-Bocquet, "France's New NATO Policy: Leveraging a Realignment of the Alliance?" *Strategic Studies Quarterly*, Winter 2009, 95–107.

110. Muller-Brandeck-Bocquet, "France's New NATO Policy," 98.

111. Ibid., 98–100.

112. Menon, "NATO RIP."

113. Mattelaer, "How Afghanistan Has Strengthened NATO," esp. 136; Mats Berdal and David Ucko, "NATO at 60," *Survival* 51, no. 2 (April–May 2009): 55–76. Mattelaer's analysis is reminiscent of the comments on NATO's usefulness in the first Gulf War by then–US ambassador to NATO Will Taft; see chapter 3.

114. As quoted by Berdal and Ucko, "NATO at 60," 57.

115. Zbigniew Brzezinski, "An Agenda for NATO: Toward a Global Security Web," *Foreign Affairs* 88, no. 5 (September–October 2009): 2–20.

116. Charles A. Kupchan, "NATO's Final Frontier: Why Russia Should Join the Atlantic Alliance," *Foreign Affairs* 89, no. 3 (May–June 2010): 100–112.

117. See, for example, David Yost and Lionel Ponsard, "Is It Time to Update NATO's Strategic Concept?" *NATO Review*, Autumn 2005.

118. Ronald D. Asmus and Ambassador Richard C. Holbrooke, *Re-Inventing NATO*, Riga Papers (Riga: German Marshall Fund of the United States, 2006), http://trends.gmfus .org/doc/A4_Holbrooke_c.pdf.

119. Ronald D. Asmus, "New Purposes, New Plumbing," *The American Interest*, November 1, 2008, www.the-american-interest.com/2008/11/01/new-purposes-new-plumbing/.

120. Gulnur Aybet, "The NATO Strategic Concept Revisited: Grand Strategy and Emerging Issues," in *NATO in Search of a Vision*, ed. Aybet and Moore, chap. 2, 35–50, esp. 41–42.

121. NATO, "Summit Declaration on Afghanistan Issued by the Heads of State and Government Participating in the Meeting of the North Atlantic Council in Strasbourg /Kehl," April 4, 2009, www.nato.int/cps/en/natohq/news_52836.htm?selectedLocale =en.

122. NATO, "Strasbourg/Kehl Summit Declaration Issued by the Heads of State and Government Participating in the Meeting of the North Atlantic Council in Strasbourg /Kehl," April 4, 2009, www.nato.int/cps/en/natohq/news_52837.htm?selectedLocale=en.

123. NATO, "Declaration on Alliance Security Issued by the Heads of State and Government Participating in the Meeting of the North Atlantic Council in Strasbourg /Kehl," April 4, 2009, www.nato.int/cps/en/natohq/news_52838.htm?selectedLocale=en.

124. For launching of the Strategic Concept, see "NATO Launches Public Debate on the Strategic Concept," July 7, 2009, www.nato.int/cps/en/natohq/news_56326.htm?. For the composition of the group of experts and their bios, see www.nato.int/strategic -concept/experts-strategic-concept.html.

125. NATO, *NATO 2020: Assured Security; Dynamic Engagement — Analysis and Recommendations of the Group of Experts on a New Strategic Concept for NATO*, May 17, 2010 (Brussels: NATO, 2010), www.nato.int/nato_static_fl2014/assets/pdf/pdf_2010_05 /20100517_100517_expertsreport.pdf.

126. Ibid., 7.

127. This and all subsequent references to *NATO 2020* are based on the text at the NATO website cited in note 125.

128. Karl-Heinz Kamp, "Towards a New Strategy for NATO," *Survival* 51, no. 4 (August–September 2009): 21–27.

129. "NATO Strategic Concept Seminar (Future of NATO): Remarks as Delivered by Secretary of Defense Robert M. Gates," National Defense University, Washington, D.C., Tuesday, February 23, 2010, www.defense.gov/speeches/speech.aspx?speechid=1423. Some theorists argue that in the contemporary global security environment the differences between static and expeditionary defense have diminished. For example, see David S. Yost, "NATO's Evolving Purposes and the Next Strategic Concept," *International Affairs* 86, no. 2 (2010): 489–522.

130. NATO, "Active Engagement, Modern Defence: Strategic Concept for the Defence and Security of the Members of the North Atlantic Treaty Organisation Adopted by Heads of State and Government in Lisbon," November 19, 2010, www .nato.int/cps/en/natohq/official_texts_68580.htm?selectedLocale=en.

131. NATO, "Lisbon Summit Declaration Issued by the Heads of State and Government Participating in the Meeting of the North Atlantic Council in Lisbon," November 20, 2010, www.nato.int/cps/en/natohq/official_texts_68828.htm?selectedLocale=en.

132. NATO, "Active Engagement, Modern Defence," preamble.

133. Stent, *Limits of Partnership*, 248–49.

134. See Ben Barry, "Libya's Lessons," *Survival* 53, no. 5 (October–November 2011): 5–14. For the US policy in response to the Libya crisis, see President Obama's March 28 speech: "Remarks by the President in Address to the Nation on Libya, National Defense University, Washington," www.whitehouse.gov/the-press-office/2011/03/28/remarks-president -address-nation-libya.

135. Anders Fogh Rasmussen, "NATO After Libya: The Atlantic Alliance in Austere Times," *Foreign Affairs* 90, no. 4 (July–August 2011): 2–6. On European capabilities, see Menon, "NATO RIP," 86–87; also see Gates, "Security and Defense Agenda."

136. Roxburgh, *Strongman*, 307–9.

## 10. THINGS FALL APART—AGAIN!

1. Samuel Huntington argues that the democratic revolts in Portugal and Spain in the mid-1970s began a wave spreading democratic governance throughout the world— to Latin America, Eastern Europe in 1989, Asia, and Africa. Huntington called this the third major period of the expansion of democracy in modern history. For twenty years after publication of this seminal, much-praised, and much-criticized work, the Middle East and the Arab world remained the great exception, apparently immune to the historical processes Huntington discerned as at work in the rest of the world. See Samuel P. Huntington, *The Third Wave: Democratization in the Late Twentieth Century* (Norman, Okla.: University of Oklahoma Press, 1993).

2. For example, see Lucan Way, "The Lessons of 1989," in a special section: "Comparing the Arab Revolts," *Journal of Democracy* 22, no. 4 (October 2011): 17–27.

3. See Evgeniy Satanovskii, "Revoliutsiia i demokratiia v islamskom mire," *Rossiia v global'noi politike*, no. 1 (January–February 2011), www.globalaffairs.ru/number /Revolyutciya-i-demokratiya-v-islamskom-mire-15101. For a good general discussion of the official Russian reaction to the Arab Spring, see Angela E. Stent, *The Limits of Partnership: US–Russian Relations in the Twenty-First Century* (Princeton, N.J.: Princeton University Press, 2014), 247–50. For a more detailed discussion by two US specialists, see Stephen Blank and Carol R. Saivetz, "Playing to Lose? Russia and the 'Arab Spring,'" *Problems of Post-Communism* 59, no. 1 (January–February 2012): 3–145.

4. See Arkadii Dubnov, "Poslednii mirazh nesmeniaemosti: Tsentral'naia Aziia v blizhnevostochnom anturazhe," *Rossiia v global'noi politike*, no. 2 (March–April 2011), www.globalaffairs.ru/number/Poslednii-mirazh-nesmenyaemosti-15184; and Mikhail Margelov, "Posle stabil'nosti: Arabskii mir i predely avtoritarnoi modernizatsii," *Rossiia v global'noi politike*, no. 2 (March–April 2011), www.globalaffairs.ru/number/Posle -stabilnosti-15176.

5. For example, see Vitalii Naumkin, "Snizu vverkh i obratno: 'Arabskaia vesna' i global'naiamezhdunarodnaiaSistema,"*Rossiiavglobal'noipolitike*,no.4(July–August2011), www.globalaffairs.ru/number/Snizu-vverkh-i-obratno-15277.

6. Stent, *Limits of Partnership*, 248. See also the discussion of Russian fears of popular demonstrations occurring elsewhere after the example of the "Arab Spring" in Blank and Saivetz, "Playing to Lose?" 10–11.

7. For an excellent discussion of the relationship between Putin and Medvedev during the latter's presidency, see Angus Roxburgh, *The Strongman: Vladimir Putin and the Struggle for Russia* (New York: I. B. Tauris, 2012), chap. 13, "Tandemology," 296–315. Although there is no account of the personal discussions between the two, Roxburgh's deft use of inside information from close advisers to both provides one of

the best descriptions available on how their relationship played out and affected government policy in Russia from 2008 to 2011.

8. Ibid., 307–9. Also see Blank and Saivetz, "Playing to Lose?" 11.

9. Gleb Bryanski, "Putin: Libya Coalition Has No Right to Kill Gaddafi," Reuters, April 26, 2011, www.reuters.com/article/2011/04/26/us-russia-putin-libya-idUSTRE73P4L920110426.

10. Ellen Barry, "Russian Finance Minister Says Political Change Is Needed," *New York Times*, February 18, 2011, www.nytimes.com/2011/02/19/world/europe/19russia.html.

11. Roxburgh, *Strongman*, 311–14.

12. Ibid., 316–17. Scenes from the United Russia convention, including portions of Putin's and Medvedev's remarks, can be viewed in the 2015 two-and-a-half-hour television documentary *Prezident*, prepared and shown by Russian State Television to commemorate the fifteenth anniversary of Putin's first election to the presidency, http://russia.tv/video/show/brand_id/59329/episode_id/1193264/video_id/1165983/viewtype/picture. Stent, *Limits of Partnership*, 316n29, cites "many observers" who have questioned whether Putin actually knew he wished to return to the presidency in 2007–8. Even if such observers are correct about what Putin knew in 2007–8, this does not change the political effects of the substance and manner of his remarks on September 24, 2011.

13. The description in Roxburgh, *Strongman*, 319–20, offers a particularly good picture of these events. On Kudrin's firing, see Michael Schwirtz, "Russian President Ousts Finance Minister, a Putin Ally, for Insubordination," *New York Times*, September 26, 2011, www.nytimes.com/2011/09/27/world/europe/dmitri-medvedev-fires-aleksei-kudrin-russian-finance-minister.html?_r=0. Video of the Medvedev/Kudrin clash was still available online as of May 28, 2015, with an RT voiceover, but the Russian language original is still audible, www.youtube.com/watch?v=gpCVLv-1mpA.

14. For a discussion of the protests and the government's response, see Stent, *Limits of Partnership*, 244–46; Roxburgh, *Strongman*, 322–28; and Fiona Hill and Clifford Gaddy, *Mr. Putin: Operative in the Kremlin*, 2nd ed. (Washington, D.C.: Brookings Institution Press, 2015), 229–37.

15. Vladimir Putin, "Russia and the Changing World," *Moskovskie novosti*, February 27, 2012, available in English translation at http://valdaiclub.com/politics/39300.html. This series of campaign articles released in various outlets over Putin's personal signature during the course of the campaign provided excellent insights into his mind-set and intentions at the time, and they have held up remarkably well as valuable sources for understanding Putin's views on the contemporary regional and global orders and Russia's place in them.

16. Stent, *Limits of Partnership*, 246; Roxburgh, *Strongman*, 339–40. The choice of McFaul to replace outgoing career Foreign Service officer John Beyrle was seen by many Kremlin officials as a deliberate challenge or insult to Putin because of McFaul's extensive background, writings, and association with democracy promotion. McFaul's decision not to await presentation of his credentials before publicly meeting with the opposition added fuel to this sentiment in the Kremlin. The Russian response was predictably exaggerated and boorish, but not surprising. Some Russian commentators, such as Sergey Markov, already inclined to criticize US policy and the Obama administration, went so far as to call McFaul's appointment a "gift" to Putin and those who wished a harder line with Washington. Russian officials to the author, May 2012.

17. Stent, *Limits of Partnership*, 246–47; Roxburgh, *Strongman*, 328–40; Hill and Gaddy, *Mr. Putin*, 236–37, 249–53; US State Department officials to the author, July 2012.

18. Stent, *Limits of Partnership*, 252–53; Roxburgh, *Strongman*, 337–40; Hill and Gaddy, *Mr. Putin*, 347–48.

19. On Russian military reform and capabilities, see, in particular, the commentaries from Ruslan Pukhov, director of the Center for Analysis of Strategies and Technology, and his colleagues over the years, available at the center's website at www .cast.ru/about/; see also Dale Herspring, "Anatoliy Serdyukov and the Russian Military: An Exercise in Confusion," *Problems of Post-Communism* 60, no. 6 (November–December 2013): 42–48; senior Russian Army commander to the author, March 2013; Bettina Renz, "Russian Military Capabilities after 20 Years of Reform," *Survival* 56, no. 3 (June–July 2014): 63–84; and the outstanding study based on open source materials by the Swedish Defense Research Agency: Jakob Hedenskog and Carolina Vendil Pallin, eds., *Russian Military Capability in a Ten-Year Perspective—2013*, FOI-R-3734-SE (Stockholm: Swedish Defense Research Agency, 2013), www.foi.se /sv/Sok/Sammanfattningssida/?rNo=FOI-R—3734—SE.

20. For Browder's own, detailed account of the Magnitsky affair, see Bill Browder, *Red Notice: A True Story of High Finance, Murder, and One Man's Fight for Justice* (New York: Simon & Schuster, 2015). Also from Browder to the author, November 2011.

21. See "Public Law 112–208, Dec. 14, 2012: Russia and Moldova Jackson-Vanik Repeal and Sergei Magnitsky Rule of Law Accountability Act of 2012," www.treasury.gov /resource-center/sanctions/Programs/Documents/pl112_208.pdf. See also Kathy Lally and Will Englund, "Russia Fumes as US Senate Passes Measure Aimed at Human Rights," *Washington Post*, December 6, 2012, www.washingtonpost.com/world/europe/us-passes -magnitsky-bill-aimed-at-russia/2012/12/06/262a5bba-3fd5-11e2-bca3-aadc9b7e29c5_story .html; Stent, *Limits of Partnership*, 252; and Roxburgh, *Strongman*, 340–42.

22. Roxburgh, *Strongman*, 341–42; Will Englund, "Russians Say They'll Name Their Magnitsky-Retaliation Law After Baby Who Died in a Hot Car in Va.," *Washington Post*, December 11, 2012, www.washingtonpost.com/blogs/worldviews/wp/2012/12/11/ magnitsky-retaliation-man-baby/.

23. Wolf Blitzer, "Romney: Russia Is Our Number One Geopolitical Foe," CNN interview, March 26, 2012, http://cnnpressroom.blogs.cnn.com/2012/03/26/romney-russia -is-our-number-one-geopolitical-foe/.

24. This narrative is based on the author's discussions with US State Department and National Security Council officials, December 2012–April 2013. See also Angela Stent, "US–Russia Relations in the Second Obama Administration," *Survival* 54, no. 6 (December 2012): 123–38.

25. Jackie Calmes, "Obama Asks Russia to Join in Reducing Nuclear Arms," *New York Times*, June 19, 2013, www.nytimes.com/2013/06/20/world/europe/obama-asks-russia-to -join-in-reducing-nuclear-arms.html. The fact that the Obama administration was preparing such a proposal was widely known well in advance.

26. Center for Analysis of Strategy and Technology analysts to the author, July 2013; Russian Military Academy of the General Staff experts and faculty to the author, October 2011 and March 2013. Russia's military doctrine, which was adopted in 2010 and slightly

revised in 2014, makes clear Russia's ultimate reliance on strategic and tactical nuclear weapons to deter conventional attacks: *Voennaia doktrina Rossiiskoi Federatsii*, available in English translation at http://carnegieendowment.org/files/2010russia_military _doctrine.pdf.

27. For a clear Russian expert's statement of the importance of missile defense, see Evgeny Buzhinsky, "What Has Changed Since Prague?" *Washington Quarterly* 36, no. 2 (Spring 2013): 137–49, esp. 142–45.

28. Statement by US National Security Council spokesperson Caitlin Hayden on US national security adviser Donilon's Travel to Russia, www.whitehouse.gov/the-press -office/2013/04/12/statement-nsc-spokesperson-caitlin-hayden-national-security-advisor -doni. Also see "Russian Security Official Flies to Washington for Talks with US National Security Adviser," *Russia Beyond the Headlines*, May 20, 2013, http://rbth .com/news/2013/05/20/patrushev_flies_to_washington_for_talks_with_us_national _security_adviso_26135.html). Also see conversations of State Department and National Security Council officials with the author, May 2013 and January 2014.

29. Senior State Department officials to the author, 2011 and 2012.

30. Walter Kemp, "The Astana Summit: A Triumph of Common Sense," *Security and Human Rights* 21, no. 4 (2010): 263.

31. On the plans of the Lithuanian Chairmanship, see Tomas Janeliunas, "The Lithuanian OSCE Chairmanship 2011: Ambitions and Results," *Security and Human Rights* 23, no. 2 (2012): 115–28. On the activities of the OSCE under the Lithuanian Chair, see OSCE, *OSCE Annual Report 2012* (Vienna: OSCE, 2012), www.osce.org /secretariat/89356?download=true.

32. OSCE, "Remarks, Secretary of State Hillary Rodham Clinton, OSCE First Plenary Session," MC.DEL/31/11, Vilnius, Lithuania, December 6, 2011, www.osce.org /mc/85930?download=true.

33. "Vystuplenie ministra inostrannykh del Rossii S. V. Lavrova na plenarnom zasedanii," SMID OBSE, December 6, 2011, www.mid.ru/brp_4.nsf/newsline/76DCA5448 B7811B44425795E003B3096.

34. Wolfgang Zellner, "Back to Reality: The 2011 Vilnius Ministerial Council Meeting," *Security and Human Rights* 23, no. 1 (2012): 7–9.

35. OSCE, "Attachment to MC.DEC/7/11/Corr.1: Interpretative Statement Under Paragraph IV.1(A)6 of the Rules of Procedure of the Organization for Security and Cooperation in Europe, Eighteenth Meeting of the Ministerial Council, 6 and 7 December, Vilnius, 2011: Decisions of the Ministerial Council," 27–28, www.osce.org/mc/88839? download=true.

36. For example, see the "Joint Statement by the Heads of Delegations of the Minsk Group Co-Chair Countries and the Foreign Ministers of Armenia and Azerbaijan at the Eighteenth Meeting of the Ministerial Council (MC.DEL/18/11 7 December 2011) in Eighteenth Meeting of the Ministerial Council, 6 and 7 December, Vilnius, 2011: Decisions of the Ministerial Council," 80–82, www.osce.org/mc/88839?download=true. Perhaps more surprising was the agreement of all the signatories to refer to the conflict as over Nagorno-Karabakh, whereas the lack of consensus in the past often necessitated language such as "the conflict handled by the Minsk Group."

37. See Philip Remler, "Negotiation Gone Bad: Russia, Germany, and Crossed Communications," Carnegie Europe, August 21, 2013, http://carnegieeurope.eu/2013/08/21/negotiation-gone-bad-russia-germany-and-crossed-communications-pub-52712

38. OSCE, *OSCE Annual Report 2011* (Vienna: OSCE, 2011), 10 passim. The five plus two includes Moldova and Transdniestria as parties to the conflict; the OSCE, Ukraine, and Russia as mediators; and the United States and EU, which were added as observers in 2005. Even as a participant, it was never clear to me who were the five, and who the two.

39. OSCE, *OSCE Annual Report 2012*, 17; also see OSCE, "Statement on the Negotiations on the Transdniestrian Settlement Process in the "5+2" Format (MC. DOC/1/12 of 7 December 2012), Nineteenth Meeting of the Ministerial Council, 6 and 7 December, Dublin, 2012: Statements and Declarations by the Ministerial Council," 3, www.osce.org/mc/110735?download=true.

40. OSCE, "Decision No. 3/12: The OSCE Helsinki +40 Process (MC.DEC/3/12 of 7 December 2012), Eighteenth Meeting of the Ministerial Council, 6 and 7 December, Vilnius, 2011: Decisions of the Ministerial Council," 17–21, www.osce.org/mc/110735?download=true.

41. For the OSCE's consensus description of where the issue of a legal personality for the organization stands, see "The Legal Framework of the OSCE," updated February 2, 2012, www.osce.org/mc/87192. For a description and discussion of the general issue, see Sonya Brander, "Making a Credible Case for a Legal Personality for the OSCE," *OSCE Magazine*, March–April 2009, 18–23, which contains a useful historical timeline of the issue.

42. For good background and a description of the current status of the issue, see a report from the Irish chair: OSCE, "Report to the Ministerial Council on Strengthening the Legal Framework of the OSCE in 2012," MC.GAL/15/12, December 7, 2012, www.osce.org/mc/97950?download=true.

43. For the latest update on the impasse, see a 2014 report from the Swiss Chair: OSCE, "Report to the Ministerial Council on Strengthening the Legal Framework of the OSCE in 2014 (MC.GAL/5/14/Corr.1 of 3 December 2014), Twenty-First Meeting of the Ministerial Council, 4 and 5 December 2014, Basel, Report to the Ministerial Council," 176–79, www.osce.org/mc/158436?download=true.

44. Senior ODIHR officials to the author, June and December 2012. Also see Arie Bloed, "Russian Elections Cause Turmoil," *Security and Human Rights* 23, no. 1 (2012): 65–66.

45. For one example of such coverage, see "OSCE Biased in Assessing Elections," *Russia Today*, October 4, 2011, http://rt.com/politics/election-democracy-observers-osce-035/.

46. For the OSCE assessments, see OSCE, "Statement of Preliminary Findings and Conclusions, International Election Observation, Russian Federation, State Duma Elections," December 4, 2011, www.osce.org/odihr/85757?download=true; OSCE, "OSCE/ODIHR Election Observation Mission, Russian Federation, Elections to the State Duma," December 4, 2011, www.osce.org/odihr/elections/86959?download=true; and OSCE, "Statement of Preliminary Findings and Conclusions, International

Election Observation, Russian Federation, Presidential Election," March 4, 2012, www .osce.org/odihr/88667?download=true. For an independent academic expert's report on the elections, see Henry Hale, "The Putin Machine Sputters: First Impressions of the 2011 Duma Election Campaign," *Russian Analytical Digest*, no. 106 (December 21, 2011): 2–6, www.css.ethz.ch/publications/pdfs/RAD-106.pdf. This entire issue of *Russian Analytical Digest* is devoted to material and analysis concerning the 2011 Duma elections.

47. OSCE, "Statement by Mr. Andrei Kelin, Permanent Representative of the Russian Federation, at the Meeting of the OSCE Permanent Council, 8 March 2012, Regarding the Outcome of the Presidential Elections in Russia, PC.DEL/203/12," March 9, 2012, www.osce.org/pc/88895?download=true.

48. OSCE, "Chairperson's Report, 2013 Annual Security Review Conference, Vienna, 19 and 20 June 2013, PC.DEL/730/13," July 29, 2013, www.osce.org/cio/104037? download=true.

49. Patrick Keller, "Germany in NATO: The Status Quo Ally," *Survival* 54, no. 3 (June–July 2012): 107. See also Timo Noetzel and Benjamin Schreer, "Does a Multi-Tier NATO Matter? The Atlantic Alliance and the Process of Strategic Change," *International Affairs* 85, no. 2 (March 2009): 211–26.

50. On Russia as a threat or a partner, see David S. Yost, "NATO's Evolving Purposes and the Next Strategic Concept," *International Affairs* 86, no. 2 (2010): 499–500.

51. "The Future of the Atlantic Alliance," speech by NATO secretary-general Jaap de Hoop Scheffer at Chatham House, London, July 20, 2009, www.nato.int/cps/en /natohq/opinions_56498.htm?selectedLocale=en.

52. Ibid. On the changing international context, see also Yost, "NATO's Evolving Purposes," 519–21.

53. See, in particular, the argument by Keller, "Germany in NATO," 99–100.

54. Yost, "NATO's Evolving Purposes," 507–17.

55. For example, see Ben Barry, "Libya's Lessons," *Survival* 53, no. 5 (October–November 2011): 5–14. Also see Douglas Barrie, "Libya's Lessons: The Air Campaign," *Survival* 54, no. 6 (December 2012–January 2013): 57–65.

56. See NATO, "Statement on Libya, Following the Working Lunch of NATO Ministers of Defence with Non-NATO Contributors to Operation Unified Protector," June 8, 2011, www.nato.int/cps/en/natohq/news_75177.htm?selectedLocale=en.

57. See NATO, "North Atlantic Council Statement on Libya, 21 Oct. 2011," Press Release (2011) 130, issued October 21, 2011, www.nato.int/cps/en/natohq/news_79800 .htm?selectedLocale=en.

58. See President Obama's speech on intervention in Libya on March 28, 2011, "Remarks by the President in Address to the Nation on Libya," National Defense University, Washington, video and transcript available at www.whitehouse.gov/photos -and-video/video/2011/03/28/president-obama-s-speech-libya#transcript.

59. See Barry, "Libya's Lessons," 61–63.

60. Andres Fogh Rasmussen, "NATO After Libya: The Atlantic Alliance in Austere Times," *Foreign Affairs* 90, no. 4 (July–August 2012): 2–6. For a discussion of such questions about the Alliance, see Barry, "Libya's Lessons," 9–12.

61. US Department of Defense, "The Security and Defense Agenda (Future of NATO)," speech by US secretary of defense Robert M. Gates, Brussels, June 10, 2011, www.defense.gov/speeches/speech.aspx?speechid=1581.

62. NATO, "NATO and Russia: A New Beginning," speech by NATO secretary-general Anders Fogh Rasmussen at the Carnegie Endowment, Brussels, September 18, 2009, www.nato.int/cps/en/natolive/opinions_57640.htm.

63. NATO, "NATO's Relations with Russia," www.nato.int/nato_static/assets/pdf /pdf_2012_nio/20120705_0919-12-Fiche-Info-NATO-Russia_rus-RU.pdf.

64. NATO, "NATO-Russia Council Action Plan on Terrorism: Executive Summary," April 15, 2011, Berlin, www.nato.int/cps/en/natohq/official_texts_72737.htm? selectedLocale=en; NATO, "NATO's Relations with Russia."

65. Sergei Lavrov, "The Euro-Atlantic Region: Equal Security for All," *Russia in Global Affairs*, no. 2 (April–June 2010) (originally written for France's *Revue Defense Nationale*), http://eng.globalaffairs.ru/number/The_Euro-Atlantic_Region:_Equal_Security _for_All-14888.

66. Konstantin Kosachev, "Three Birds with One Stone? Russia's Failed Attempt to Join NATO," *Russia in Global Affairs*, no. 1 (January–March 2011), http://eng.globalaffairs .ru/number/ Three-Birds-with-One-Stone-15146.

67. See NATO, "Chicago Summit Declaration, Issued by the Heads of State and Government Participating in the Meeting of the North Atlantic Council," Chicago, May 20, 2012, www.nato.int/cps/en/natohq/official_texts_87593.htm?selectedLocale =en.

68. NATO, "Chicago Summit Declaration on Afghanistan, Issued by the Heads of State and Government of Afghanistan and Nations Contributing to the NATO-led International Security Assistance Force (ISAF)," May 21, 2012, www.nato.int/cps/en /natohq/official_texts_87595.htm?selectedLocale=en.

69. NATO, "Deterrence and Defence Posture Review," May 20, 2012, www.nato.int /cps/en/natohq/official_texts_87597.htm?selectedLocale=en.

70. See Government of the Russian Federation, *Military Doctrine of the Russian Federation* (Moscow: Government of the Russian Federation, 2010). For background and a discussion of NATO's nuclear posture, see David S. Yost, "The US Debate on NATO Nuclear Deterrence," *International Affairs* 87, no. 6 (2011): 1401–38, esp. 1413–18. Also see Paul Belkin, "NATO's Chicago Summit," Congressional Research Service Report for Congress, R42529, May 14, 2012, 7–8.

71. Yost, "US Debate," 1414–15. Also see NATO, "Active Engagement, Modern Defence: Strategic Concept for the Defence and Security of the Members of the North Atlantic Treaty Organization, Adopted by Heads of State and Government at the NATO Summit in Lisbon," November 19–20, 2010, www.nato.int/nato_static_fl2014 /assets/pdf/pdf_publications/20120214_strategic-concept-2010-eng.pdf.

72. US Department of Defense, "Security and Defense Agenda (Future of NATO)."

73. See NATO, "Summit Declaration on Defence Capabilities: Toward NATO Forces 2020," May 20, 2012, www.nato.int/cps/en/natohq/official_texts_87594.htm? selectedLocale=en; and NATO, "Smart Defense," http://www.nato.int/cps/en/natohq /topics_84268.htm?selectedLocale=en.

74. Bastian Giegerich, "NATO's Smart Defence: Who's Buying?" *Survival* 54, no. 3 (June–July 2012): 69–77. The online version of *NATO Review* for 2012 contains six interviews describing and analyzing various aspects of the smart defense concept, www.nato.int/docu/review/2015/Themes/EN/index.htm#2012.

75. John Gordon, Stuart Johnson, F. Stephen Larrabee, and Peter A. Wilson, "NATO and the Challenge of Austerity," *Survival* 54, no. 4 (August–September 2012): 121–42, at 139.

76. Belkin, "NATO's Chicago Summit," 5–6.

77. Gordon et al., "NATO and the Challenge of Austerity," 121–38.

78. Ibid., 140.

79. See François Heisbourg, "In the Shadow of the Euro Crisis," *Survival* 54, no. 4 (August–September 2012): 25–32; and Nicolas Berggruen and Nathan Gardels, "The Next Europe: Toward a Federal Union," *Foreign Affairs* 92, no. 4 (July–August 2013): 134–42. For a good, short statement of the structural bases of the crisis, see Steven Philip Kramer, "The Return of History in Europe," *Washington Quarterly* 35, no. 4 (Fall 2012): 81–91, esp. 92–93.

80. For a clear, short economic explanation of the crisis in the EU and the euro zone, see Erik Jones, "The Eurozone's Goldilocks Solution," *Survival* 54, no. 4 (August–September 2012): 229–36. For one example of the PIIGS as a category for popular analysis, see "The PIIGS That Won't Fly: A Guide to Europe's Troubled Economies," *Economist*, May 18, 2010, www.economist.com/node/15838029. For a good, relatively brief description of the EU policy response to the global crisis, see Desmond Dinan, *Europe Recast: A History of European Union* (Boulder, Colo.: Lynne Rienner, 2014), 336–49. For more detailed narratives on and analyses of the euro zone crisis, see, David Marsh, *The Euro: The Battle for the New Global Currency*, rev. ed. (New Haven, Conn.: Yale University Press, 2011); Johan van Overtveldt, *The End of the Euro: The Uneasy Future of the European Union* (Farnham, UK: Ashgate, 2011); Carlo Bastasin, *Saving Europe: How National Politics Nearly Destroyed the Euro* (Washington, D.C.: Brookings Institution Press, 2012); and Costas Lapavistas, *Crisis in the Eurozone* (London: Verso, 2012).

81. Speech by Mario Draghi, president of the European Central Bank, at the Global Investment Conference, London, July 26, 2012, as quoted by Dinan, *Europe Recast*, 346.

82. Robert Kagan, *Of Paradise and Power: America and Europe in the New World Order* (New York: Vintage, 2004), coined this phrase at the height of the transatlantic debate over intervention in Iraq.

83. Kramer, "Return of History," 84.

84. Sven Biscop, "The UK and European Defence: Leading or Leaving?" *International Affairs* 88, no. 6 (2012): 1297–1313, at 1298.

85. Gordon et al., "NATO and the Challenge of Austerity"; Bastian Giegerich and Alexander Nicoli, "The Struggle for Value in European Defence," *Survival* 54, no. 1 (January–February 2012): 53–82.

86. Sarah Brockmeier, "Germany and the Intervention in Libya," *Survival* 55, no. 6 (December 2013–January 2014): 63–90, esp. 64–70.

87. Biscop, "UK and European Defence," 1297–99.

88. Ibid., 1311.

89. Bruno Tertrais, "Leading on the Cheap? French Security Policy in Austerity," *Washington Quarterly* 36, no. 3 (Summer 2013): 47–61.

90. French Ministry of Defense, *French White Paper: Defense and National Security, 2013*, with a preface by the President of the Republic (Paris: Government of France, 2013), http://defense.gouv.fr.

91. Russian, EU, and US diplomats to the author on multiple occasions, Brussels, Vienna, Moscow, and Washington, 2010–2013. Also see Neil MacFarlane and Anand Menon, "The EU and Ukraine," *Survival* 56, no. 3 (June–July 2013): 95–101, esp. 96–97, emphasize the importance of this "near abroad" for Russia. Stent, *Limits of Partnership*, 235–36, notes the inadvertently harmful effects on conducting relations with Russia of the separation of bureaucratic responsibilities within the National Security Council of US-Russian relations from US relations with neighboring members of the Commonwealth of Independent States.

92. These multilateral thematic platforms are (1) democracy, good governance, and stability; (2) economic integration and convergence with EU sector policies; (3) energy security; and (4) contacts between people. Yearly progress reports, periodic road maps for progress on bilateral and multilateral activities, summit statements, and other documents are available on the EU's European External Action Service website at http://eeas.europa.eu/eastern/about/index_en.htm.

93. European Union, "Joint Declaration of the Eastern Partnership Summit," Warsaw, September 29–30, 2011, Council of the European Union, 14983/11, http://eeas.europa.eu/eastern/about/index_en.htm. Also see European Union, "Implementation of the European Neighborhood Policy in 2010, Report: Eastern Partnership, Joint Staff Working Paper, European Commission, Brussels, 25/05/2011, SEC(2011) 641," http://eeas.europa.eu/enp/pdf/pdf/progress2011/sec_11_641_en.pdf. The progress of each country's individual negotiation with the EU can be tracked in the EU Commission staff preparatory and tracking documents for the 2013 Vilnius Summit; see European Union, "Eastern Partnership: A Roadmap to the Autumn 2013 Summit, Joint Communication to the European Parliament, the Council, the European Economic and Social Committee and the Committee of the Regions, European Commission, Brussels, 15.5.2012, JOIN(2012) 13 Final," http://eeas.europa.eu/enp/pdf/docs/2012_enp_pack/e_pship_roadmap_en.pdf. Also available are two Joint Staff Working documents, European Union, "Eastern Partnership Roadmap 2012–2013: The Multilateral Dimension, SWD(2012) 108 Final, http://eeas.europa.eu/enp/pdf/docs/2012_enp_pack/e_pship_multilateral_en.pdf; and European Union, "Eastern Partnership Roadmap 2012–2013: The Bilateral Dimension, SWD(2012) 109 Final," http://eeas.europa.eu/enp/pdf/docs/2012_enp_pack/e_pship_bilateral_en.pdf.

94. See "Commissioner Malmstrom on visa-free travel for Moldova," Brussels, April 3, 2014, http://europa.eu/rapid/press-release_STATEMENT-14-101_en.htm.

95. For a description of EU-Russia contacts, negotiations, joint activities, and achievements from 2011 to 2013, see the EU's yearly progress reports, available on the EU's webpage on relations with Russia, http://eeas.europa.eu/russia/about/index_en.htm.

96. For a description of the legislation and administrative actions making up the third energy package, see European Commission, "Market Legislation," https://ec.europa.eu/energy/en/topics/markets-and-consumers/market-legislation.

97. See European Union, "EU-Russia Common Spaces Progress Report 2011 Dated February 2012," http://eeas.europa.eu/russia/docs/commonspaces_prog_report_2011_en.pdf.

98. Putin announced the project in October 2011; see Vladimir Putin, "Novyi integratsionnyi proekt dlia Evrazii—budushchee, kotoroe rozhdaetsia segodnia," *Izvestiia*, October 3, 2011, http://izvestia.ru/news/502761. Putin's article makes exceedingly clear the very close parallels between the projected Eurasian Economic Union and the EU. A timeline—containing the various treaties and declarations constructing the Customs Union, the Single Economic Space, and the Eurasian Economic Union—is available at www.eaeunion.org/?lang=en#about-history.

99. "Deklaratsiia ob Evraziiskoi ekonomicheskoi integratsii," December 2011, signed by Putin, Nazarbayev, and Lukashenko, www.eaeunion.org/?lang=en#about-history.

100. For a discussion by one European expert, see Hannes Adomeit, "Putin's 'Eurasian Union': Russia's Integration Project and Policies on Post-Soviet Space," Neighborhood Policy Paper 04 (July 2012), Center for International and European Studies, Kadir Has University, Istanbul, www.khas.edu.tr/cms/cies/dosyalar/files/Neighbourhood PolicyPaper%2804%29.pdf. For a typical discussion and speculation along these lines, see Arkady Moshes, "Will Ukraine Join (and Save) the Eurasian Customs Union?" *PONARS Policy Memo*, no. 247 (April 2013), www.ponarseurasia.org/memo/will-ukraine-join-and-save-eurasian-customs-union.

101. See Adomeit, "Putin's 'Eurasian Union,'" 6–7. On Moldova, see Tessa Dunlop, "Why Russia Is Putting Pressure on Moldova," BBC Europe, November 21, 2013, www.bbc.com/news/world-europe-24992076.

102. Richard Balmforth, "Ukraine Leader Ignores Putin Warning on EU Path," Reuters, August 24, 2013, www.reuters.com/article/2013/08/24/us-ukraine-russia-yanukovich-idUSBRE97N05P20130824.

103. Government of Armenia, "Joint Statement on the Results of the Visit of the President of the Republic of Armenia to the Russian Federation," Moscow, September 3, 2013, www.president.am/en/press-release/item/2013/09/03/President-Serzh-Sargsyan-and-President-Vladimir-Putin-joint-statement/.

104. David M. Herszenhorn, "Facing Russian Threat, Ukraine Halts Plans for Deals with EU," *New York Times*, November 21, 2013, www.nytimes.com/2013/11/22/world/europe/ukraine-refuses-to-free-ex-leader-raising-concerns-over-eu-talks.html.

105. European Union, "Joint Declaration of the Eastern Partnership Summit, Vilnius, 28–29 November 2013: Eastern Partnership: The Way Ahead, Council of the European Union, 17130/13," www.consilium.europa.eu/uedocs/cms_Data/docs/pressdata/EN/foraff/139765.pdf.

106. Ibid., 3.

107. President Dmitry Medvedev, at a press conference at Skol'kovo, *Ria Novosti*, May 18, 2011, http://en.rian,ru/world/20110518/164092502.html, as quoted by Adomeit, "Putin's 'Eurasian Union,'" 6.

## 11. CONFRONTATION IN UKRAINE

1. On the campaign and the opposition, see Angus Roxburgh, *The Strongman: Vladimir Putin and the Struggle for Russia* (New York: I. B. Tauris, 2012), 325–29; on the company towns (*monogorody*) and the aging industrial base's support for Putin, see Natalia Zubarevich, "Four Russias: Rethinking the Post-Soviet Map," *Open Democracy*, March 29, 2012, www.opendemocracy.net/od-russia/natalia-zubarevich/four-russias -rethinking-post-soviet-map.

2. On the distribution of support and opposition to Putin in the 2012 election, and the socioeconomic sources of his support and opposition, see Fiona Hill and Clifford Gaddy, *Mr. Putin: Operative in the Kremlin*, 2nd ed. (Washington, D.C.: Brookings Institution Press, 2015), 213–32, 235–37, 37n10, 465–66. A regional breakdown of the voting totals is available on the website of the Russian Electoral Commission, www .vybory.izbirkom.ru/region/region/izbirkom?action=show&root=1&tvd=100100031793 509&vrn=100100031793505&region=0&global=1&sub_region=0&prver=0&pronetvd =null&vibid=100100031793509&type=227.

3. For example, see Andrew Osbourne, "Vladimir Putin Accuses Hillary Clinton of Inciting Protests," *Daily Telegraph*, December 8, 2011; and Andrew Osborne, "Vladimir Putin Mocks and Dismisses Protesters," *Daily Telegraph*, December 15, 2011, http:// andrewosborn.co.uk/article/817. For a wrap-up of Putin's campaign, see Ellen Barry and Michael Schwirtz, "After Election, Putin Faces Challenges to Legitimacy," *New York Times*, March 5, 2012, www.nytimes.com/2012/03/06/world/europe/observers -detail-flaws-in-russian-election.html?_r=0.

4. On actions against protesters and opposition leaders, see Roxburgh, *Strongman*, 328–32; on the sources in Russian society of opposition to Putin and the 2012 campaign, see Hill and Gaddy, *Mr. Putin*, 231–36.

5. On the Pussy Riot trial, and the segments of Russian society to which it appealed, see Roxburgh, *Strongman*, 333–36; on this trial and the uses by Putin and the regime of nationalism, see Hill and Gaddy, *Mr. Putin*, 249–56.

6. Vladimir Putin, "Russia and the Changing World," *Moskovskie novosti*, February 27, 2012, http://valdaiclub.com/politics/39300.html.

7. Ibid.

8. Vladimir Putin meets with members of the Valdai International Discussion Club; transcript of the beginning of the meeting, October 26, 2012, http://valdaiclub. com/economy/50600.html.

9. Putin, "Russia in a Changing World."

10. "Concept of the Foreign Policy of the Russian Federation, Approved by President of the Russian Federation V. Putin on February 12, 2013," www.mid.ru/brp_4.nsf /0/76389FEC168189ED44257B2E0039B16D.

11. Ibid.

12. "Vladimir Putin Meets with Members of the Valdai International Discussion Club," transcript of the speech and the meeting, September 20, 2013 (hereafter, Putin at Valdai Club, September 20, 2013), http://valdaiclub.com/politics/62880.html.

13. For a more detailed description of the measures Putin took to shore up his domestic position, see Hill and Gaddy, *Mr. Putin*, 342–54.

14. On the Kazan Universiade, seewww.fisu.net/en/Summer-Universiades-3490.html.

15. For a discussion of the political importance Putin attached to the Sochi Olympics, see Hill and Gaddy, *Mr. Putin*, 256–59. For one of the best discussions of Sochi by a Russian author, see Sergey Markedonov, *The 2014 Sochi Olympics: A Patchwork of Challenges* (Washington, D.C.: Center for Strategic and International Studies, 2014), http://csis.org/files/publication/140113_Markedonov_2014SochiOlympics_WEB.pdf.

16. On corruption, see the report and analysis compiled by opposition leader Boris Nemtsov, available in English as "Winter Olympics in the Tropics: Corruption and Abuse in Sochi—Boris Nemtsov's Latest Investigative Report," trans. Cathy Fitzpatrick, *The Interpreter*, December 6, 2013, www.interpretermag.com/winter-olympics-in-the-sub-tropics-corruption-and-abuse-in-sochi/. Former State Department and RFE/RL analyst Paul Goble produced a weekly collection of press reports on Sochi for more than a year before the games, which is available on his blog, "Window on Eurasia," http://windowoneurasia2.blogspot.com/. The subsequent scandal around charges of Russian government-sponsored doping resulted in many medals for Russian athletes being annulled and Russia's exclusion from the 2018 winter Olympics in South Korea. These events are beyond the narrative in the text, but have certainly tarnished the initially positive apparent results of the Sochi games.

17. See World Economic Forum, *Economic Scenarios for the Russian Federation* (Geneva: World Economic Forum, 2013), with a foreword by former minister of the economy German Gref, www3.weforum.org/docs/WEF_Scenarios_RussianFederation_Report_2013.pdf. See also Institut Sovremennogo Razvitiia, *Obretenie budushchego: Strategiia 2012* (Moscow: Konspekt, 2012), available in English at www.insor-russia.ru/files/INSOR_Attaining_the_Future_final.pdf. For various examples of Kudrin's analyses and criticisms, see the website of his NGO, Komitet grazhdanskikh initsiativ, http://komitetgi.ru/analytics/.

18. Hill and Gaddy, *Mr. Putin*, 358–60, 496n57, cite conversations in 2012–13 with senior EU officials. I received similar information and claims from Russian and EU officials during those same years.

19. Putin at Valdai Club, September 20, 2013.

20. In particular, see Roxburgh, *Strongman*, esp. 351–54, for a discussion of Putin's understanding of democracy, and the general failure of Russian leaders and officials to understand Western perceptions and reactions to their continuing failures in democratic governance and observance of the rule of law.

21. See a Google collection from the G-8, www.google.com/search?q=obama+putin+photos+at+los+cabos+summit&biw=1920&bih=1066&tbm=isch&tbo=u&source=univ&sa=X&ved=0CCgQ7AlqFQoTCLOJquWshcYCFWVkjAodA1gAQQ#tbm=isch&q=obama+putin+photos+at+northern+ireland+june+2013/.

22. On the Snowden affair, see Angela E. Stent, *The Limits of Partnership: US–Russian Relations in the Twenty-First Century* (Princeton, N.J.: Princeton University Press, 2014), 269–71.

484 11. Confrontation in Ukraine

23. Steve Holland and Margaret Chadbourn, "Obama Describes Putin as 'Like a Bored Kid,' " Reuters, August 9, 2013, www.reuters.com/article/2013/08/09/us-usa-russia -obama-idUSBRE9780XS20130809.

24. "Syrian Uprising Timeline of Key Events," Associated Press, September 4, 2013, www.politico.com/story/2013/09/syria-timeline-96270.html.

25. "Obama's Syria Plans in Disarray after Britain Rejects Use of Force," *The Guardian*, August 30, 2013, www.theguardian.com/world/2013/aug/30/obama-strike-syria-britain -vote.

26. White House, "Remarks by the President in Address to the Nation on Syria," September 10, 2013, www.whitehouse.gov/the-press-office/2013/09/10/remarks-president -address-nation-syria.

27. Karen De Young, "How the United States, Russia Arrived at Deal on Syria's Chemical Weapons," *Washington Post*, September 16, 2013, www.washingtonpost.com /world/national-security/how-the-united-states-russia-arrived-at-deal-on-syrias-chemical -weapons/2013/09/15/c851cd1e-1e5b-11e3-8459-657e0c72fec8_story.html. For a Russian account of the Geneva negotiations and the deal, see "Mirovie alkhimiki: Kak Sergei Lavrov bilsia za Siriiu v Zheneve," *Kommersant*, September 14, 2013, www.kommersant .ru/doc/2279382.

28. Vladimir V. Putin, "A Plea for Caution from Russia," *New York Times*, September 12, 2013, www.nytimes.com/2013/09/12/opinion/putin-plea-for-caution-from-russia-on -syria.html?_r=0.

29. Ibid.

30. Senior EU political leader, as heard by the author, Washington, August 2014.

31. On the Cyprus banking crisis, see Desmond Dinan, *Europe Recast: A History of European Union* (Boulder, Colo.: Lynne Rienner, 2014), 347. On economic concerns and policies in the EU, see ibid., 347–49; and Rajan Menon and Eugene Rumer, *Conflict in Ukraine: The Unwinding of the Post–Cold War Order* (Cambridge, Mass.: MIT Press, 2015), 67–68.

32. "Embassy Espionage: The NSA's Secret Spy Hub in Berlin," *Spiegel Online International*, October 27, 2013, www.spiegel.de/international/germany/cover-story-how -nsa-spied-on-merkel-cell-phone-from-berlin-embassy-a-930205.html.

33. For the analysis in this paragraph, see esp. Dinan, *Europe Recast*, 347–48.

34. On Ukraine's negotiations with the EU and Russia, see Menon and Rumer, *Conflict in Ukraine*, 69–71, 76–78; Olga Shumylo-Tapiola, "Ukraine at the Crossroads: Between the EU DCFTA & Customs Union," *IFRI Russia / NIS Center, Russie.NEI Reports*, no. 11, April 2012, www.ifri.org/sites/default/files/atoms/files/rnr11shumylotap-iolaapril2012.pdf; and Steven Pifer, "Ukraine's Yanukovych Caught between Russia and the European Union," *World Politics Review*, October 23, 2013, www.worldpolitics review.com/articles/13324/ukraine-s-yanukovych-caught-between-russia-and-the -european-union.

35. Štefan Füle, European commissioner for enlargement and neighborhood policy, "Statement on the Pressure Exercised by Russia on Countries of the Eastern Partnership," September 11, 2013, http://europa.eu/rapid/press-release_SPEECH-13-687_en.htm.

36. Putin at Valdai Club, September 20, 2013.

37. Menon and Rumer, *Crisis in Ukraine*, 76–77.

38. The narrative in this paragraph is drawn especially from ibid., 60–61ff. Also see an excellent piece of background history, narrative, and analysis by the *Spiegel* staff, "Summit of Failure: How the EU Lost Russia Over Ukraine," *Spiegel Online International*, November 24, 2014, www.spiegel.de/international/europe/war-in -ukraine-a-result-of-misunderstandings-between-europe-and-russia-a-1004706.html. Another excellent account of the historical background, revolution, and conflict in Ukraine is by Richard Sakwa, *Frontline Ukraine: Crisis in the Borderlands* (New York: I. B. Tauris, 2015). Another Western account of recent events is by Andrew Wilson, *Ukraine Crisis: What It Means for the West* (New Haven, Conn.: Yale University Press, 2014).

39. Deputy Prime Minister Tyhipko to the author, April 2010.

40. *Spiegel* staff, "Summit of Failure."

41. Sakwa, *Frontline Ukraine*, chap. 4, 81–99, presents, in my view, a relatively concise, balanced account of events from November 2013 through February 2014. There is still bitter controversy and disagreement among experts, political leaders, observers, and the people involved over what actually happened in Ukraine, who is responsible for what happened, and what to call these events. Sakwa lends a bit more emphasis to the right-wing forces involved in the movement against Yanukovych. Wilson gives a bit more attention to the official and nonofficial forces acting to suppress the Maidan. Menon and Rumer provide a very quick, fairly balanced overview. It appears that disagreement over even fairly straightforward narration and description of contemporary social and political upheaval and revolutionary events by experts reflects the deep divisions over basic questions of security, values, and interests that have emerged in the Euro-Atlantic community of nations over the past decades.

42. See, for example, Russian Armed Forces chief of General Staff General Valery Gerasimov's 2013 remarks on color revolutions as a means of unconventional warfare employed by the United States and its NATO Allies to effect regime change in countries around the globe. Gerasimov, his military colleagues, and Russian civilian analysts have continued to develop this line of thought.

43. See Putin's remarks in the one-hour television special prepared for and aired on the one-year anniversary of the annexation of Crimea, "Put' na rodinu," http://politikus .ru/video/45602-film-krym-put-na-rodinu.html.

44. Sakwa, *Frontline Ukraine*, chap. 5, esp. 102–7.

45. For a timeline, description, and links to specific decisions on the EU's restrictive measures, see "EU Restrictive Measures in Response to the Crisis in Ukraine," www .consilium.europa.eu/en/policies/sanctions/ukraine-crisis/.

46. See "Adoption of Agreed Restrictive Measures in View of Russia's Role in Eastern Ukraine, 31 July 2014," www.consilium.europa.eu/en/policies/sanctions/ukraine-crisis/.

47. Vladimir Putin addressed State Duma deputies, Federation Council members, the heads of the Russian regions, and civil society representatives in the Kremlin, "Address by the President of the Russian Federation," March 18, 2014, http://en.kremlin .ru/events/president/news/20603.

48. Ibid.

49. Ibid.

50. Vladimir Putin, "Priamaia liniia, Prezident Vladimir Putin," April 17, 2014, available at www.kremlin.ru.

51. On the Donbas revolt, see Sakwa, *Frontline Ukraine*, chap. 7, esp. 149ff,. For an excellent set of articles by Russian experts and analysts on the various military and political-military aspects of the conflict in Ukraine, see Colby Howard and Ruslan Pukhov, eds., *Brothers Armed: Military Aspects of the Crisis in Ukraine* (Minneapolis, Minn.: East View Press, 2014).

52. OSCE, "OSCE: Twentieth Meeting of the Ministerial Council, 5 and 6 December 2013, Kyiv," www.osce.org/mc/kyiv?download=true. On Ukraine's 2013 priorities and the relatively minimalist expectations of Ukraine from other participating states, see Arie Bloed, "Ukraine at the Helm of the OSCE," *Security and Human Rights*, no. 4 (2012): 357–58.

53. OSCE, *OSCE Annual Report 2013*, 18, www.osce.org/odihr/119809?download=true.

54. On Swiss views of the OSCE and expectations for 2014, see "The OSCE: Fighting for Renewed Relevance," *CSS Analysis in Security Policy* (Center for Security Studies, ETH Zurich), no. 110, March 2012; and Swiss diplomats and OSCE officials to the author, February–March 2014.

55. OSCE Permanent Council, "Decision No. 1117: Deployment of an OSCE Special Monitoring Mission to Ukraine," PC.DEC/1117, March 21, 2014, www.osce.org/pc /116747?download=true.

56. Documents from and information on the SMM are available at www.osce.org /ukraine-smm.

57. OSCE Permanent Council, "Decision No. 1130, Deployment of OSCE Observers to Two Russian Checkpoints on the Russian-Ukrainian Border," PC.DEC/1130, July 24, 2014, www.osce.org/pc/121826?download=true.

58. Senior OSCE officials to the author, October 2014. Also see the interpretative statements by Ukraine, the United States, the United Kingdom, and Canada appended to the Permanent Council decision establishing the mission, protesting that it was not sufficient to provide real coverage and confidence.

59. Michael R. Gordon, "US and Russia Agree on Pact to Defuse Ukraine Crisis," *New York Times*, April 17, 2014, www.nytimes.com/2014/04/18/world/europe/ukraine -diplomacy.html?_r=0; also see "Text of Joint Diplomatic Statement on Ukraine," *New York Times*, April 17, 2014, www.nytimes.com/2014/04/18/world/europe/text-of-joint -diplomatic-statement-on-ukraine.html?ref=world.

60. On the Russian reinforcements, see Andrew E. Kramer and Michael R. Gordon, "Ukraine Reports Russian Invasion on a New Front," *New York Times*, August 27, 2014, www.nytimes.com/2014/08/28/world/europe/ukraine-russia-novoazovsk-crimea.html. Kramer's subsequent dispatches were among those by foreign reporters providing a fairly good picture of the reverses suffered by Ukraine. On Russian reinforcement of the leadership, see Andrew E. Kramer, "Separatist Cadre Hopes for a Reprise in Ukraine," *New York Times*, August 4, 2014, www.nytimes.com/2014/08/04/world/europe/separatist -pro-russian-leadership-in-eastern-ukraine-with-a-goal-of-establishing-government.html.

61. "Protokol po itogam konsul'tatsii trekhstoronnei kontaktnoi gruppy otnositel'no sovmestnikh shagov, napravlennykh na implementatsiiu mirnogo plana Prezidenta Ukrainy P. Poroshenko i initsiativ Prezidenta Rossii V. Putina," September 5, 2014. On the Minsk negotiations and deal, see Sakwa, *Frontline Ukraine*, 175–77.

62. BBC World News, "Ukraine Ceasefire: New Minsk Agreement Key Points," February 12, 2015, www.bbc.com/news/world-europe-31436513.

63. In the words of a former Western negotiator in one of these "frozen" conflicts: "[In Ukraine] the federalization proposed by Russia is an update of the 'common state' proposed by Russia in the 1990s in each of the separatist conflicts: total internal autonomy for the separatists and a central state structure that ensures a separatist right to veto the central state's policy decisions. For obvious reasons this never appealed to any of the central states in question, all of whom rejected the approach." Former head of the OSCE Mission to the author, October 2015.

64. On the effect of sanctions on Russia, see, *World Bank Quarterly Economic Report on Russia*, April 2015.

65. Arie Bloed, "OSCE Revitalized by the Ukraine Crisis," *Security and Human Rights* 25, no. 1 (2014): 145–49. On the OSCE role in the field, see, Stephanie Liechtenstein, "The OSCE Special Monitoring Mission Has Become the Eyes and Ears of the International Community on the Ground in Ukraine," *Security and Human Rights* 25, no. 1 (2014): 5–10.

66. Bloed, "OSCE Revitalized," 147.

67. NATO Public Diplomacy Division, "Financial and Economic Data Relating to NATO Defense," Communiqué PR/CP (2014) 028, February 24, 2014, available at www.nato.int. Also see Federica Cocco, "NATO Summit: Which Members Are Not Pulling Their Weight with Defence Spending?" *Daily Mirror*, September 3, 2013, www.mirror.co.uk/news/ampp3d/nato-summit-members-not-pulling-4156751. For comments on NATO in Afghanistan and Libya as well as budget issues, see Ambassador Ivo Daalder's remarks at Carnegie Europe, Brussels, June 17, 2013, http://nato.usmission.gov /sp-06172013.html.

68. Ambassador Ivo Daalder's remarks at Carnegie Europe.

69. Malcolm Chalmers, research director / director, UK Defence Policy Studies, "The Squeeze Continues: UK Defence Spending and the 2013 Budget," *RUSI (Royal United Services Institute), Analysis*, March 25 2013, www.rusi.org/analysis/commentary /ref:C51506B24A254C/#.VX20SaxRHIU. Also see Richard Norton-Taylor, "UK's Armed Forces Face New Spending Crunch," *The Guardian*, November 10, 2014, www.theguardian .com/uk-news/defence-and-security-blog/2014/nov/10/british-army-defence-budget.

70. For example, see UK Ministry of Defence, "Sustainable Development Strategy: A Sub-Strategy of the Strategy for Defence, 2011–2030," London, May 1, 2011, www .gov.uk/government/uploads/system/uploads/attachment_data/file/32729/20110527SDS trategyPUBLISHED.pdf; and UK Ministry of Defence, *Global Strategic Trends: Out to 2045*, 5th ed. (London: UK Ministry of Defence, 2014), www.gov.uk/government /uploads/system/uploads/attachment_data/file/348164/20140821_DCDC_GST_5_Web _Secured.pdf.

71. See Government of France, *French White Paper: Defense and National Security*, foreword by President François Hollande, www.rpfrance-otan.org/White-Paper -on-defence-and; Dorothee Fouchaux, "French Hard Power: Living on the Strategic Edge," American Enterprise Institute, 2014, www.aei.org/publication/french-hard -power-living-on-the-strategic-edge/; and Jolyon Noworth, "The Lisbon Treaty, CSDP, and the EU as a Security Actor," in *The EU's Foreign Policy: What Kind of Power and Diplomatic Action?* ed. Mario Telo and Frederik Pnjeart (London: Ashgate, 2013), 65–77.

72. See, Lisa Watanabe, "Keeping France in the CSDP," *Policy Perspectives* (Center for Security Studies, Zurich) 3, no. 3 (May 2015), available at www.css.ethz.ch.

73. "France Displaces Britain as Key US Military Ally," Agence France-Presse, March 19, 2015, www.defensenews.com/story/defense/international/europe/2015 . . .

74. See chapter 10; and John Gordon, Stuart Johnson, F. Stephen Larrabee, and Peter A. Wilson, "NATO and the Challenge of Austerity," *Survival* 54, no. 4 (August– September 2012): 121–42.

75. NATO, "Address by NATO Deputy Secretary General Ambassador Alexander Vershbow to the International Conference 'Russia-NATO: 15 Years on the Way to partnership' (via VTC)," September 27, 2013, www.nato.int/cps/en/natohq/opinions_90257 .htm?selectedLoca.

76. NATO, "NATO-Russia Council Statement of Support for the OPCW-UN Joint Mission," December 4, 2013, www.nato.int/cps/en/natohq/news_105470.htm?selected Locale=en.

77. For example, see the brief statement on Ukraine by NATO foreign ministers at the December 2013 Atlantic Council meeting, www.nato.int/cps/en/natohq/news _105435.htm?selectedLocale=en.

78. See the initial statement on the crisis: NATO, "North Atlantic Council Statement on the Situation in Ukraine,' March 2, 2014, www.nato.int/cps/en/natohq/official _texts_107681.htm?selectedLocale=en. The results of the consultations at Poland's request are reported in "Statement by the North Atlantic Council Following Meeting under Article 4 of the Washington Treaty," March 4, 2014, www.nato.int/cps/en /natohq/news_107716.htm?selectedLocale=en.

79. NATO, "Statement by NATO Foreign Ministers," April 1, 2014, www.nato.int /nrc-website/en/articles/20140327-announcement/index.html.

80. "Ukraine Crisis: NATO Suspends Russia Co-operation," BBC World News, April 2, 2014, www.bbc.com/news/world-europe-26838894.

81. See "NATO Warns of Russian Army Build-Up on Ukraine Border," BBC World News, March 24, 2014, www.bbc.com/news/world-europe-26704205. The point is not to argue that warnings such as Breedlove's were correct or incorrect, which is far easier to debate some fifteen months later, but that they were not necessarily unreasonable at the time. In the words of one former US and OSCE official: "Nor are they [such warnings], in fact, prima facie unreasonable now. Whether one takes the view that Putin has a fully developed strategy or that he is all tactics and works his strategy out ad hoc, it is hard to conclude that we yet know the limits of Russia's aims in Ukraine and Russia's neighborhood writ large. Russia's extension of Right to Protect

to the annexation of territory based on the presence of Russian citizens and/or historical claims is open-ended; at least, we have not seen anything that could be construed as a clear boundary for Russian actions." Retired senior US diplomat to the author, May 2016.

82. Senior Swedish and Finnish diplomats to the author, May 2014.

83. See Julian Borger, "Russians Open New Front after Estonian Official Is Captured in 'Cross-Border Raid,' " *The Guardian*, September 7, 2014, www.theguardian.com/world /2014/sep/07/russia-parades-detained-estonian-police-officer.

84. NATO, "Statement of the NATO-Ukraine Commission," April 1, 2014, www.nato .int/cps/en/natohq/news_108499.htm?selectedLocale=en.

85. NATO, "The Wales Declaration on the Transatlantic Bond," Press Release (2014) 122, September 5, 2014, www.nato.int/cps/en/natohq/official_texts_112985.htm? selectedLocale=en; NATO, "Wales Summit Declaration, Issued by the Heads of State and Government Participating in the Meeting of the North Atlantic Council in Wales," September 5, 2014, www.nato.int/cps/en/natohq/official_texts_112964.htm? selectedLocale=en.

86. See, for example, Jan Techau, "NATO's Summit Between Strategy and Tragedy," Carnegie Europe, September 4, 2014, http://carnegieeurope.eu/strategiceurope/?fa =56536.

87. Comment by the Russian Ministry of Foreign Affairs on the NATO Summit in Wales, September 5, 2014, www.mid.ru/brp_4.nsf/o/6B9C80D952095F8544257D4A00 55DF80.

88. For the Kremlin's English translation of Putin's speech and the question-and-answer session, see "Meeting of the Valdai International Discussion Club," October 24, 2014, at http://en.kremlin.ru/events/president/news/46860.

89. Ibid.

90. Evaluations of the impact of Western sanctions on the Russian economy since the spring of 2014 remain widely varied and contradictory. See, Edward Hunter Christie, "Sanctions after Crimea: Have They Worked?" *NATO Review*, 2015, www.nato.int /docu/Review/2015/Russia/sanctions-after-crimea-have-they-worked/EN/index.htm, for the argument that sanctions have exacerbated other macroeconomic difficulties for Russia. An EU Parliament report in the late summer of 2015 noted the impact of sanctions on both Russia and the EU, stating that the effects were hard to separate from other macroeconomic trends and developments: "Economic Impact on the EU of Economic Sanctions over Ukraine Conflict," Briefing, October, 2015, www.europarl.europa.eu /RegData/etudes/BRIE/2015/569020/EPRS_BRI%282015%29569020_EN.pdf. Economic analysts generally critical of the Putin regime, such as Anders Åslund, tend to focus on the problems of the Russian economy, including the effect of sanctions; see Anders Åslund, "The Current Economic State of Play in Russia," Bertelsmann Foundation, June 1, 2015, www.bfna.org/sites/default/files/publications/Anders%20Aslund%20Russia% 20Paper%20FINAL%207%2018%20%282%29.pdf. Russian economic officials and analysts, though often admitting reversals in the Russian economy in the years 2014–2016, tend either to minimize the impact of sanctions or to assert that their effects are being overcome. For a discussion of the issue, see Oleg Buklemishev, "Myths and Realities of

Sanctions in Russia," Carnegie Moscow commentary, August 13, 2015, http://carnegieen dowment.org/2015/08/13/myths-and-realities-of-sanctions-in-russia/iemn.

91. For developments in the Russian economy, the regular reports from the World Bank and the International Monetary Fund provide relatively balanced and unbiased sources of information and analysis; see the links at http://documents.worldbank.org /curated/en/docsearch/collection-title/Russian%20economic%20report, and see www .imf.org/external/country/RUS/index.htm, for regular updates on this period. A World Bank report offers a particularly succinct summary of the economic and financial crisis in the second half of 2014 and early 2015: World Bank, "Russia Economic Report: The Dawn of a New Economic Era?" no. 33, April 2015, http://documents.worldbank.org/curated /en/2015/04/24348746/dawn-new-economic-era. For a current World Bank report on the Russian economy, see World Bank, "Russia Economic Report: The Long Journey to Recovery," no. 35, April 2016, www-wds.worldbank.org/external/default/WDSContent Server/WDSP/IB/2016/04/15/090224b08429dcfe/1_0/Rendered/PDF/Russiaorconomioo journeyotoorecovery.pdf.

92. See Minister of Economy Ulyukayev's statement in March 2016 that the Russian economy was in the midst of a difficult transition to a new, more stable model: "Russian Economics Minister: 'We Are Painfully Moving toward a New Model,'" *Russia Beyond the Headlines*, March 28, 2016, http://rbth.com/business/2016/03/28/russian-economics -minister-we-are-painfully-moving-toward-a-new-model_579731. See also Deputy Prime Minister Dvorkovich's attempt to make a virtue of necessity and hardship in his assertion to CNBC in March 2016 that the low ruble rate could help Russia's economic recovery: Geoff Cutmore and Antonia Matthews, "Russia Growing, Low Ruble Will Help: Deputy PM," CNBC, March 23, 2016, www.cnbc.com/2016/03/23/russia-growing -low-ruble-will-help-deputy-pm.html.

93. One video news story widely distributed on the Internet showed Russian police removing frozen Hungarian geese from a grocery store and destroying the offending prod-uct by running over it with a bulldozer! See www.youtube.com/watch?v=iwneQT_jvDE.

94. "Real'nye dokhody rossiian padaiut," *Kommersant*, May 23, 2016, www.kommersant .ru/doc/2994775.

95. For an example of such speculation at the time of the most dramatic drop in prices, see Andrew Topf, "Did the Saudis and the US Collude in Dropping Oil Prices?" December 23, 2014, OilPrice.com, http://oilprice.com/Energy/Oil-Prices/Did-The-Saudis-And-The -US-Collude-In-Dropping-Oil-Prices.html. The author has heard similar speculation from Russian and other former Soviet diplomatic and academic colleagues.

96. On the truckers' protest, see Neil MacFarquhar, "Russian Truckers, Irate over New Tolls, Block Roads Near Moscow," *New York Times*, December 4, 2015, www.nytimes .com/2015/12/05/world/europe/russian-truckers-protest-tolls.html?_r=0; and Corey Flint-off, "In a Rare Protest, Russian Truckers Rally Against Putin's Highway Tax," *Morning Edition*, NPR, December 23, 2015, www.npr.org/sections/parallels/2015/12/23/460703160 /in-a-rare-protest-russian-truckers-rally-against-putins-highway-tax.

97. See "Pora postavit' deistvennyi zaslon informatsionnoi voine: Predsedatel' Sled-stvennogo Komiteta RF Aleksandr Bastrykin—o metodakh bor'by s ekstremizmom v Rossii," *Kommersant Vlast'*, April 18, 2016, www.kommersant.ru/doc/2961578. For use and regulation of the Internet in Russia today, see Andrei Soldatov and Irina Borogan,

*The Red Web: The Struggle between Russia's Digital Dictators and the New Online Revolutionaries* (New York: PublicAffairs, 2015).

98. See former Deputy Prime Minister and Finance Minister Aleksei Kudrin's gloomy prognosis for the Russian economy at the 2016 World Economic Forum: Sergei Smirnov, "Kudrin: Pik krizisa vperedi — Pravitel'stvo dolzhno opredelit'sia so strategiei v blizhaishie mesiatsi, zaiavil eks-ministr finantsov," *Vedomosti*, January 22, 2016, www .vedomosti.ru/economics/articles/2016/01/22/625086-kudrin-krizisa; by midyear, Kudrin had returned to the government as chairman of the council at the Center for Strategic Research and deputy head of the Economic Council in the presidential administration. See Vladislav Inozemtsev, "Kudrin's Return to the Russian Government," *Eurasia Daily Monitor* 13, no. 89 (May 6, 2016), www.jamestown.org/single/?tx_ttnews[tt_news] =45407&tx_ttnews[backPid]=7&cHash=9aa140264c9b80a4327963659ef06362#. VoCZEb6wVoQ. For other good, unofficial Russian analyses of the current economy, see former deputy chairman of the Russian Central Bank Sergei Aleksashenko, "Should Putin Be Worried about the Russian Economy?" Brookings blogpost, February 9, 2016, www.brookings.edu/blogs/up-front/posts/2016/02/09-vladimir-putin-russian -economy-aleksashenko. See also a series of 2016 articles on prospects for the Russian economy by Carnegie Moscow Center analyst Andrei Movchan, beginning with "Predicting Russia's Economic Health," http://carnegie.ru/commentary/2016/03/02 /predicting-russia-s-economic-health/iuqu.

99. See Lawrence Freedman, "Ukraine and the Art of Exhaustion, *Survival* 57, no. 5 (October–November 2015): 77–106.

100. See OSCE, "OSCE Chairperson-in-Office Dačić Appoints New Special Representative in Ukraine," Belgrade, June 22, 2015, www.osce.org/cio/165696.

101. For reports and information from the Ukraine Special Monitoring Mission, see www.osce.org/ukraine-smm/reports.

102. For the Belgrade Ministerial Council, see "Twenty-Second Meeting of the Ministerial Council," December 3–4, 2015, www.osce.org/mc/230741?download=true.

103. Ibid., 3.

104. Ibid., 19.

105. Ibid., 30–31.

106. For the English-language text of Putin's 2015 UN General Assembly address, see the Kremlin website: http://en.kremlin.ru/events/president/news/50385.

107. Ibid.

108. Ibid.

109. There has been almost daily coverage of Russia's military mission in Syria in both the Western and Russian press since September 2015, and the major Russian and Middle East–related think tanks have already issued countless pieces of analysis of the motives, operations, and implications of the action. For this narrative, I have used in particular regular comment and analysis from Michael Kofman in *War on the Rocks*, Angela Stent in *Foreign Affairs*, and Samuel Charap in *Survival*. For daily Russian reports, interviews, and videos on Russian operations in Syria, see the special section of the Ministry of Defense website at http://syria.mil.ru/.

110. US Department of Defense officials to the author, December 2015 and January 2016.

111. International press coverage of high-level United States–Russia cooperation on Syria has been extensive and continuous. See, for example, Lesley Wroughton and Dennis Dyomkin, "Russia, US Agree to Speed Up Syria Peace Effort," Reuters, March 24, 2016, www.reuters.com/article/us-russia-usa-kerry-idUSKCN0WQ0PG.

112. See "Russia and US 'Planning Military Coordination against Isis in Syria,' " Reuters, March 30, 2016, www.theguardian.com/world/2016/mar/30/russia-and-us-planning -military-coordination-against-isis-in-syria. By May 2016, American and Russian military officers and officials were using a cooperation center established by Russia with Jordan in Amman in October 2015 for information exchange and deconflicting operations. Both the US Department of Defense and the Russian Ministry of Defense websites contain information on such contacts and cooperation; see www.defense.gov and www.en.mil.ru.

113. *O strategii natsional'noi bezopasnosti Rossiiskoi federatsii*, Ukaz Prezidenta Rossiiskoi Federatsii ot 31.12. 2015, http://kremlin.ru/acts/bank/40391. An English-language translation of the document is available at www.ieee.es/Galerias/fichero/OtrasPublica ciones/Internacional/2016/Russian-National-Security-Strategy-31Dec2015.pdf.

114. Johan Norberg, "Exercising to Fight," Swedish Defense Research Academy, December 2015, available at www.foi.se.

115. See accounts of the April 2016 incident involving a Russian military jet and the US destroyer USS *Donald Cook* off the coast of Poland in April 2016: "Russian Attack Jets Buzz US Warship in Riskiest Encounter for Years," *The Guardian*, April 13, 2016, www.theguardian.com/us-news/2016/apr/13/russian-attack-planes-buzz-uss-donald -cook-baltic-sea. Moscow called the presence of US warships near Kaliningrad a provocation; see Ed Adamczyk, "Russia: US Warship in Baltic Waters a Military Provocation," UPI, April 21, 2016, www.upi.com/Top_News/World-News/2016/04/21/Russia -US-warship-in-Baltic-waters-a-military-provocation/1281461240609/. For an example of General Breedlove's views, see "Posture Statement of General Philip Breedlove, Commander, US European Command," February 25, 2016, www.eucom.mil/media-library /article/35164/u-s-european-command-posture-statement-2016.

116. See "Statement of the Secretary General on NATO-Russia Council Meeting," April 8, 2016, www.nato.int/cps/en/natohq/news_129818.htm; "NATO, Russia Council to Meet on April 20 in Brussels," Reuters, April 12, 2016, www.reuters.com/article/us -russia-nato-idUSKCN0X91IK; and " 'No Business as Usual': Issues Remain after First NATO-Russia Council Meeting since 2014," *Russia Today*, April 20, 2016, www.rt.com /news/340413-nato-russia-meeting-ukraine/.

117. See Secretary General Stoltenberg's press conference immediately after the meeting: "Doorstep Statement by Secretary General Jens Stoltenberg Following the NATO Russia Council Meeting," April 20, 2016, www.nato.int/cps/en/natohq/opinions_129999 .htm. See also "Kommentarii MID Rossii v sviazi s zasedaniem Soveta Rossiia-NATO na urovne postoiannikh predstavitelei," April 20, 2016, www.mid.ru/web/guest/kommentarii /-/asset_publisher/2MrVt3CzL5sw/content/id/2245344.

118. See White House, "Fact Sheet: The FY 2017 European Reassurance Initiative Budget Request," February 2, 2016, www.whitehouse.gov/the-press-office/2016/02/02/fact -sheet-fy2017-european-reassurance-initiative-budget-request.

119. See NATO, "Statement by NATO Defense Ministers," June 25, 2015, www.nato .int/cps/en/natohq/news_121133.htm?selectedLocale=en.

120. For the results of the Warsaw Summit, see NATO, "The Warsaw Declaration on Transatlantic Security, Issued by the Heads of State and Government Participating in the Meeting of the North Atlantic Council in Warsaw," July 8–9, 2016, www.nato.int /cps/en/natohq/official_texts_133168.htm?selectedLocale=en; and NATO, "The War-saw Summit Communiqué, Issued by the Heads of State and Government Participating in the Meeting of the North Atlantic Council in Warsaw," July 8–9, 2016, www.nato.int /cps/en/natohq/official_texts_133169.htm?selectedLocale=en.

121. NATO, "Warsaw Summit Communiqué," paragraph 5.

122. NATO, "Warsaw Declaration on Transatlantic Security," paragraph 6.

123. See NATO, "NATO Secretary General Welcomes Frank and Open Discussions in NATO-Russia Council," July 13, 2016, www.nato.int/cps/en/natohq/news_134100.htm.

124. "Zasedanie Soveta Rossiia-NATO bylo otkritym, chestnym, i poleznym," *Kom-mersant*, July 13, 2016, www.kommersant.ru/doc/3037476.

125. For a good overall summary and review of the refugee crisis of 2015–16, see the interactive compendium and collection of articles by the European Council on Foreign Relations, "European Responses to the Refugee Crisis," www.ecfr.eu/refugee_crisis. For a mid-2016 EU assessment of the crisis, see European Commission, Humanitar-ian and Civil Protection, "Refugee Crisis," April 26, 2016, http://ec.europa.eu/echo /refugee-crisis_en.

126. Trump asserted NATO's obsolescence and charged the Allies with "free-riding" many times. For a useful brief review of his statements and changing positions on NATO, see a compendium by CBS news, Shayna Freisleben, "A Guide to Trump's Past Comments About NATO," April 12, 2017, www.cbsnews.com/news/trump-nato-past-comments/.

127. For this explanation, see Anne Gearan, Philip Drucker, and Simon Denyer, "Trump's Taiwan Phone Call Was Long Planned, Say People Who Were Involved," *Washington Post*, December 4, 2016, www.washingtonpost.com/politics/trumps-taiwan -phone-call-was-weeks-in-the-planning-say-people-who-were-involved/2016/12/04 /f8be4b0c-ba4e-11e6-94ac-3d324840106c_story.html?utm_term=.71c07e128e19.

128. Remarks of President Donald J. Trump—As Prepared for Delivery: Inaugural Address, Friday, January 20, 2017, www.whitehouse.gov/inaugural-address.

129. Ibid.

130. Jenna Johnson, "Trump on NATO: 'I Said It Was Obsolete. It's No Longer Obso-lete,'" *Washington Post*, April 12, 2017, www.washingtonpost.com/news/post-politics/ wp/2017/04/12/trump-on-nato-i-said-it-was-obsolete-its-no-longer-obsolete/?utm_term =.2e32458489da.

131. On Trump's failure to endorse Article V, see Susan B. Glasser, "Trump National Security Team Blindsided by NATO Speech," *Politico*, June 5, 2017, www.politico.com /magazine/story/2017/06/05/trump-nato-speech-national-security-team-215227. For the Warsaw visit, see Abby Phillip, John Wagner, and Michael Birnbaum, "Western Values Increasingly Endangered by Terrorism and Extremism, Trump Warns Europe," *Wash-ington Post*, July 6, 2017, www.washingtonpost.com/news/post-politics/wp/2017/07/06/in -poland-trump-reaffirms-commitment-to-nato-chides-russia/?utm_term=.86a22d863bb9.

## 12. THE FUTURE OF EUROPEAN SECURITY

1. Stefan Fule, "Statement on the Pressure Exercised by Russia on Countries of the Eastern Partnership," September 11, 2013, http://europa.eu/rapid/press-release _SPEECH-13-687_en.htm; also see Richard Sakwa, *Frontline Ukraine: Crisis in the Borderlands* (New York: I. B. Tauris, 2015), 77–78.

2. In fact, Russian positions and actions may not in every instance have been formulated or directed by Yeltsin or Putin, but also reflected prevailing sentiment among Russia's military and political elites. A former US diplomat with long experience in the region recounted: "[One] should also add the caveat that Russia, especially under Yeltsin, was not a monolith whose interventions were a coordinated part of an overall strategy determined by clear leadership. I'm reminded of a meeting I was told about between Georgian and Russian military authorities—I think the Sochi meeting in September 1992—in which the Georgians protested that the Russians were reneging on the terms of a deal that Yeltsin had just made with Shevardnadze. The Russian general replied, 'Let the President sit in his office, chase girls and drink vodka. We have work to do.' This state of competing satrapies was especially visible in policy towards Chechnya." The fact remains, however, that Russia's special role and rights in the "near abroad" was an idea that has been both widespread and popular among Russia's governing elites from 1991 to the present. Former US diplomat to the author, October 2015.

3. See especially the discussion of this phenomenon by Angus Roxburgh, *The Strongman: Vladimir Putin and the Struggle for Russia* (New York: I. B. Tauris, 2012), 185–89, 351–55.

4. For a discussion of this aspect of the proposed agreement with Ukraine, see Sakwa, *Frontline Ukraine,* 74–78.

5. Pew Research Center, "NATO Publics Blame Russia for Ukrainian Crisis, but Reluctant to Provide Military Aid," June 10, 2015, www.pewglobal.org/2015/06/10/nato -publics-blame-russia-for-ukrainian-crisis-but-reluctant-to-provide-military-aid/.

# INDEX

CPSIA information can be obtained
at www.ICGtesting.com
Printed in the USA
LVHW050856030519
616446LV00002B/5